T0127643

Lecture Notes in Artificial Intelligence 11684

Subseries of Lecture Notes in Computer Science

Series Editors

Randy Goebel
University of Alberta, Edmonton, Canada
Yuzuru Tanaka
Hokkaido University, Sapporo, Japan
Wolfgang Wahlster
DFKI and Saarland University, Saarbrücken, Germany

Founding Editor

Jörg Siekmann
DFKI and Saarland University, Saarbrücken, Germany

More information about this series at http://www.springer.com/series/1244

Ngoc Thanh Nguyen · Richard Chbeir ·
Ernesto Exposito · Philippe Aniorté ·
Bogdan Trawiński (Eds.)

Computational Collective Intelligence

11th International Conference, ICCCI 2019
Hendaye, France, September 4–6, 2019
Proceedings, Part II

Springer

Editors
Ngoc Thanh Nguyen ⓘ
Ton Duc Thang University
Ho Chi Minh City, Vietnam

Wrocław University of Science
and Technology
Wrocław, Poland

Ernesto Exposito ⓘ
University of Pau and Pays de l'Adour
Pau, France

Bogdan Trawiński ⓘ
Wrocław University of Science
and Technology
Wrocław, Poland

Richard Chbeir ⓘ
University of Pau and Pays de l'Adour
Pau, France

Philippe Aniorté ⓘ
University of Pau and Pays de l'Adour
Pau, France

ISSN 0302-9743   ISSN 1611-3349   (electronic)
Lecture Notes in Artificial Intelligence
ISBN 978-3-030-28373-5   ISBN 978-3-030-28374-2   (eBook)
https://doi.org/10.1007/978-3-030-28374-2

LNCS Sublibrary: SL7 – Artificial Intelligence

This Springer imprint is published by the registered company Springer Nature Switzerland AG
The registered company address is: Gewerbestrasse 11, 6330 Cham, Switzerland

Preface

This volume contains the proceedings of the 11th International Conference on Computational Collective Intelligence (ICCCI 2019), held in Hendaye, France, September 4–6, 2019. The conference was co-organized by the French SIGAPP Chapter (ACM Special Interest Group on Applied Computing), the LIUPPA (Laboratoire d'Informatique de l'Université de Pau et des Pays de l'Adour), France, and the Wrocław University of Science and Technology, Poland. The conference was run under the patronage of the IEEE SMC Technical Committee on Computational Collective Intelligence.

Following the successes of the First ICCCI (2009) held in Wrocław, Poland, the Second ICCCI (2010) in Kaohsiung, Taiwan, the Third ICCCI (2011) in Gdynia, Poland, the 4th ICCCI (2012) in Ho Chi Minh City, Vietnam, the 5th ICCCI (2013) in Craiova, Romania, the 6th ICCCI (2014) in Seoul, South Korea, the 7th ICCCI (2015) in Madrid, Spain, the 8th ICCCI (2016) in Halkidiki, Greece, the 9th ICCCI (2017) in Nicosia, Cyprus, and the 10th ICCCI (2018) in Bristol, UK, this conference continued to provide an internationally respected forum for scientific research in the computer-based methods of collective intelligence and their applications.

Computational collective intelligence (CCI) is most often understood as a sub-field of artificial intelligence (AI) dealing with soft computing methods that facilitate group decisions or processing knowledge among autonomous units acting in distributed environments. Methodological, theoretical, and practical aspects of CCI are considered as the form of intelligence that emerges from the collaboration and competition of many individuals (artificial and/or natural). The application of multiple computational intelligence technologies such as fuzzy systems, evolutionary computation, neural systems, consensus theory, etc., can support human and other collective intelligence, and create new forms of CCI in natural and/or artificial systems. Three subfields of the application of computational intelligence technologies to support various forms of collective intelligence are of special interest but are not exclusive: the Semantic Web (as an advanced tool for increasing collective intelligence), social network analysis (as the field targeted at the emergence of new forms of CCI), and multi-agent systems (as a computational and modeling paradigm especially tailored to capture the nature of CCI emergence in populations of autonomous individuals).

The ICCCI 2019 conference featured a number of keynote talks and oral presentations, closely aligned to the theme of the conference. The conference attracted a substantial number of researchers and practitioners from all over the world, who submitted their papers for the main track and four special sessions.

The main track, covering the methodology and applications of CCI, included: knowledge engineering and Semantic Web, social networks and recommender systems, text processing and information retrieval, data mining methods and applications, computer vision techniques, decision support and control systems, as well as innovations in intelligent systems. The special sessions, covering some specific topics of particular interest, included: cooperative strategies for decision making and optimization, intelligent modeling and simulation approaches for real world systems, computational collective intelligence and natural language processing, machine learning in real-world data, distributed collective intelligence for smart manufacturing, collective intelligence for science and technology, intelligent management information systems, intelligent sustainable smart cities, new trends and challenges in education: the University 4.0, intelligent processing of multimedia in web systems, as well as big data streaming, applications and security.

We received more than 200 submissions from 41 countries all over the world. Each paper was reviewed by two to four members of the international Program Committee (PC) of either the main track or one of the special sessions. Finally, we selected 117 best papers for oral presentation and publication in two volumes of the *Lecture Notes in Artificial Intelligence* series.

We would like to express our thanks to the keynote speakers: Eneko Agirre from University of the Basque Country, Spain, Costin Bădică from University of Craiova, Romania, Piotr Jędrzejowicz from Gdynia Maritime University, Poland, and Nicolas Spyratos from Paris-Sud (Paris-Saclay) University, France, for their world-class plenary speeches.

Many people contributed toward the success of the conference. First, we would like to recognize the work of the PC co-chairs and special sessions organizers for taking good care of the organization of the reviewing process, an essential stage in ensuring the high quality of the accepted papers. The workshop and special session chairs deserve a special mention for the evaluation of the proposals and the organization and coordination of the work of seven special sessions. In addition, we would like to thank the PC members, of the main track and of the special sessions, for performing their reviewing work with diligence. We thank the local Organizing Committee chairs, publicity chair, Web chair, and technical support chair for their fantastic work before and during the conference. Finally, we cordially thank all the authors, presenters, and delegates for their valuable contribution to this successful event. The conference would not have been possible without their support.

Our special thanks are also due to Springer for publishing the proceedings and sponsoring awards, and to all the other sponsors for their kind support.

It is our pleasure to announce that the ICCCI conference series continues to have a close cooperation with the Springer journal *Transactions on Computational Collective Intelligence*, and the IEEE SMC Technical Committee on Transactions on Computational Collective Intelligence.

Finally, we hope that ICCCI 2019 contributed significantly to the academic excellence of the field and will lead to the even greater success of ICCCI events in the future.

September 2019

Ngoc Thanh Nguyen
Richard Chbeir
Ernesto Exposito
Philippe Aniorté
Bogdan Trawiński

Organization

Organizing Committee

Honorary Chairs

Mohamad Amara   President of University of Pau and Pays de l'Adour, France

Cezary Madryas   Rector of Wrocław University of Science and Technology, Poland

General Chairs

Richard Chbeir   University of Pau and Pays de l'Adour, France

Ngoc Thanh Nguyen   Wrocław University of Science and Technology, Poland

General Vice-chair

Philippe Aniorté   University of Pau and Pays de l'Adour, France

Program Chairs

Ernesto Exposito   University of Pau and Pays de l'Adour, France

Nick Bassiliades   Aristotle University of Thessaloniki, Greece

Costin Bădică   University of Craiova, Romania

Gottfried Vossen   University of Münster, Germany

Edward Szczerbicki   University of Newcastle, Australia

Organizing Chair

Khouloud Salameh   American University of Ras Al Khaimah, UAE

Steering Committee

Ngoc Thanh Nguyen   Wrocław University of Science and Technology, Poland

Shyi-Ming Chen   National Taiwan University of Science and Technology, Taiwan

Toyoaki Nishida   Kyoto University, Japan

Geun-Sik Jo   Inha University, South Korea

Kiem Hoang   University of Information Technology, VNU-HCM, Vietnam

Ryszard Kowalczyk   Swinburne University of Technology, Australia

Lakhmi C. Jain   University of South Australia, Australia

Janusz Kacprzyk	Polish Academy of Sciences, Poland
Manuel Núñez	Universidad Complutense de Madrid, Spain
Yannis Manolopolos	Aristotle University of Thessaloniki, Greece
Piotr Jędrzejowicz	Gdynia Maritime University, Poland
Dosam Hwang	Yeungnam University, South Korea

Special Session Chairs

| Bogdan Trawiński | Wrocław University of Science and Technology, Poland |
| Joe Tekli | Lebanese American University, Lebanon |

Doctoral Track Chair

| Khouloud Salameh | American University of Ras Al Khaimah, UAE |

Publicity Chairs

| Philippe Arnould | University of Pau and Pays de l'Adour, France |
| Marek Krótkiewicz | Wrocław University of Science and Technology, Poland |

Webmaster

| Elio Mansour | University of Pau and Pays de l'Adour, France |

Local Organizing Committee

Elio Mansour	University of Pau and Pays de l'Adour, France
Lara Kallab	University of Pau and Pays de l'Adour, France
Karam Bou Chaaya	University of Pau and Pays de l'Adour, France
Marcin Jodłowiec	Wrocław University of Science and Technology, Poland
Bernadetta Maleszka	Wrocław University of Science and Technology, Poland
Marcin Maleszka	Wrocław University of Science and Technology, Poland
Krystian Wojtkiewicz	Wrocław University of Science and Technology, Poland

Keynote Speakers

Eneko Agirre	University of the Basque Country, Spain
Costin Bădică	University of Craiova, Romania
Piotr Jędrzejowicz	Gdynia Maritime University, Poland
Nicolas Spyratos	Paris-Sud (Paris-Saclay) University, France

Special Session Organizers

BiSAS 2019 – Special Session on Big Data Streaming, Applications and Security

Raja Chiky	ISEP Paris, France
Farid Meziane	Salford University, UK

CCINLP 2019 – Special Session on Computational Collective Intelligence and Natural Language Processing

Ismaïl Biskri	University of Québec à Trois-Rivières, Canada
Adel Jebali	Concordia University, Canada

CIST 2019 – Special Session on Collective Intelligence for Science and Technology

Habiba Drias	Laboratory of Research in Artificial Intelligence, USTHB, Algiers, Algeria
Sadok Ben Yahia	Tallinn University of Technology, Estonia
Abdellatif El-Afia	University Mohammed V in Rabat, ENSIAS, Morocco
Nadjet Kamel	University Ferhat Abbas Setif 1, Algeria

CSDMO 2019 – Special Session on Cooperative Strategies for Decision Making and Optimization

Dariusz Barbucha	Gdynia Maritime University, Poland
Ireneusz Czarnowski	Gdynia Maritime University, Poland
Piotr Jędrzejowicz	Gdynia Maritime University, Poland

DCISM 2019 – Distributed Collective Intelligence for Smart Manufacturing

Marcin Fojcik	Western Norway University of Applied Sciences, Norway
Rafał Cupek	Silesian University of Technology, Poland
Adam Ziębiński	Silesian University of Technology, Poland
Knut Øvsthus	Western Norway University of Applied Sciences, Norway

IMIS 2019 – Special Session on Intelligent Management Information Systems

Marcin Hernes	Wrocław University of Economics, Poland
Artur Rot	Wrocław University of Economics, Poland

IMSARWS 2019 – Special Session on Intelligent Modeling and Simulation Approaches for Real World Systems

Doina Logofătu	Frankfurt University of Applied Sciences, Germany
Costin Bădică	University of Craiova, Romania
Florin Leon	Gheorghe Asachi Technical University of Iaşi, Romania

ISSC 2019 – Special Session on Intelligent Sustainable Smart Cities

Libuše Svobodová	University of Hradec Kralove, Czech Republic
Ali Selamat	Universiti Teknology Malaysia, Malaysia
Petra Marešová	University of Hradec Kralove, Czech Republic
Arkadiusz Kawa	Poznan University of Economics and Business, Poland
Bartłomiej Pierański	Poznan University of Economics and Business, Poland
Miroslava Mikušová	University of Zilina, Slovakia

MLRWD 2019 – Special Session on Machine Learning in Real-World Data

Krzysztof Kania	University of Economics in Katowice, Poland
Jan Kozak	University of Economics in Katowice, Poland
Przemysław Juszczuk	University of Economics in Katowice, Poland
Barbara Probierz	University of Economics in Katowice, Poland

UNI4.0 2019 Special Session on New Trends and Challenges in Education: The University 4.0

Ernesto Exposito	University of Pau and Pays de l'Adour, France
Philippe Aniorté	University of Pau and Pays de l'Adour, France
Laurent Gallon	University of Pau and Pays de l'Adour, France

WEBSYS 2019 – Intelligent Processing of Multimedia in Web Systems

Kazimierz Choroś	Wrocław University of Science and Technology, Poland
Maria Trocan	Institut Supérieur d'électronique de Paris, France

Program Committee

Muhammad Abulaish	South Asian University, India
Waseem Ahmad	Toi Ohomai Institute of Technology, New Zealand
Sharat Akhoury	University of Cape Town, South Africa
Jacky Akoka	Conservatoire National des Arts et Métiers, France
Ana Almeida	GECAD-ISEP-IPP, Portugal
Orcan Alpar	University of Hradec Kralove, Czech Republic
Bashar Al-Shboul	University of Jordan, Jordan
Adel Alti	University of Setif, Algeria
Vardis Dimitrios Anezakis	Democritus University of Thrace, Greece
Taha Arbaoui	University of Technology of Troyes, France
Philippe Arnoult	University of Pau and Pays de l'Adour, France
Mehmet Emin Aydin	University of the West of England, Bristol, UK
Thierry Badard	Laval University, Canada
Amelia Badica	University of Craiova, Romania
Costin Badica	University of Craiova, Romania
Dariusz Barbucha	Gdynia Maritime University, Poland
Khalid Benali	University of Lorraine, France

Morad Benyoucef	University of Ottawa, Canada
Leon Bobrowski	Białystok University of Technology, Poland
Mariusz Boryczka	University of Silesia, Poland
Urszula Boryczka	University of Silesia, Poland
Abdelhamid Bouchachia	Bournemouth University, UK
Peter Brida	University of Zilina, Slovakia
Krisztian Buza	Budapest University of Technology and Economics, Hungary
Aleksander Byrski	AGH University of Science and Technology, Poland
Jose Luis Calvo-Rolle	University of A Coruña, Spain
David Camacho	Universidad Autonoma de Madrid, Spain
Alberto Cano	Virginia Commonwealth University, USA
Frantisek Capkovic	Institute of Informatics, Slovak Academy of Sciences, Slovakia
Stefano A. Cerri	University of Montpellier, France
Richard Chbeir	University of Pau and Pays de l'Adour, France
Shyi-Ming Chen	National Taiwan University of Science and Technology, Taiwan
Raja Chiky	Institut Supérieur d'électronique de Paris, France
Sung-Bae Cho	Yonsei University, South Korea
Amine Chohra	Paris-East University, France
Kazimierz Choroś	Wrocław University of Science and Technology, Poland
Christophe Claramunt	Naval Academy Research Institute, France
Mihaela Colhon	University of Craiova, Romania
Jose Alfredo Ferreira Costa	Universidade Federal do Rio Grande do Norte, Brazil
Nadine Cullot	University of Burgundy, France
Rafał Cupek	Silesian University of Technology, Poland
Ireneusz Czarnowski	Gdynia Maritime University, Poland
Paul Davidsson	Malmo University, Sweden
Camelia Delcea	Bucharest University of Economic Studies, Romania
Tien V. Do	Budapest University of Technology and Economics, Hungary
Habiba Drias	University of Science and Technology Houari Boumedienne, Algeria
Mohamed El Yafrani	Aalborg University, Denmark
Nadia Essoussi	University of Tunis, Tunisia
Marcin Fojcik	Western Norway University of Applied Sciences, Norway
Anna Formica	IASI-CNR, Italy
Naoki Fukuta	Shizuoka University, Japan
Mohamed Gaber	Birmingham City University, UK
Laurent Gallon	University of Pau and Pays de l'Adour, France
Faiez Gargouri	University of Sfax, Tunisia
Mauro Gaspari	University of Bologna, Italy
K. M. George	Oklahoma State University, USA

Janusz Getta	University of Wollongong, Australia
Daniela Gifu	University Alexandru Ioan Cuza of Iasi, Romania
Fethullah Göçer	Galatasaray University, Turkey
Daniela Godoy	ISISTAN Research Institute, Argentina
Manuel Grana	University of Basque Country, Spain
Michael Granitzer	University of Passau, Germany
Patrizia Grifoni	IRPPS-CNR, Italy
Foteini Grivokostopoulou	University of Patras, Greece
William Grosky	University of Michigan, USA
Kenji Hatano	Doshisha University, Japan
Marcin Hernes	Wrocław University of Economics, Poland
Huu Hanh Hoang	Hue University, Vietnam
Tzung-Pei Hong	National University of Kaohsiung, Taiwan
Mong-Fong Horng	National Kaohsiung University of Applied Sciences, Taiwan
Frédéric Hubert	Laval University, Canada
Maciej Huk	Wrocław University of Science and Technology, Poland
Zbigniew Huzar	Wrocław University of Science and Technology, Poland
Dosam Hwang	Yeungnam University, South Korea
Lazaros Iliadis	Democritus University of Thrace, Greece
Mirjana Ivanovic	University of Novi Sad, Serbia
Indu Jain	Jiwaji University, India
Jarosław Jankowski	West Pomeranian University of Technology, Poland
Joanna Jędrzejowicz	University of Gdansk, Poland
Piotr Jędrzejowicz	Gdynia Maritime University, Poland
Gordan Jezic	University of Zagreb, Croatia
Geun Sik Jo	Inha University, South Korea
Kang-Hyun Jo	University of Ulsan, South Korea
Christophe Jouis	Université de la Sorbonne Nouvelle Paris 3, France
Jason Jung	Chung-Ang University, South Korea
Przemysław Juszczuk	University of Economics in Katowice, Poland
Tomasz Kajdanowicz	Wrocław University of Science and Technology, Poland
Petros Kefalas	University of Sheffield, Greece
Rafał Kern	Wrocław University of Science and Technology, Poland
Marek Kisiel-Dorohinicki	AGH University of Science and Technology, Poland
Attila Kiss	Eotvos Lorand University, Hungary
Marek Kopel	Wrocław University of Science and Technology, Poland
Leszek Koszałka	Wrocław University of Science and Technology, Poland

Leszek Kotulski	AGH University of Science and Technology, Poland
Abderrafiaa Koukam	Université de Technologie de Belfort-Montbéliard, France
Ivan Koychev	University of Sofia St. Kliment Ohridski, Bulgaria
Jan Kozak	University of Economics in Katowice, Poland
Adrianna Kozierkiewicz	Wrocław University of Science and Technology, Poland
Bartosz Krawczyk	Virginia Commonwealth University, USA
Ondrej Krejcar	University of Hradec Kralove, Czech Republic
Dalia Kriksciuniene	Vilnius University, Lithuania
Dariusz Król	Wrocław University of Science and Technology, Poland
Marek Krótkiewicz	Wrocław University of Science and Technology, Poland
Jan Kubicek	VSB - Technical University of Ostrava, Czech Republic
Elżbieta Kukla	Wrocław University of Science and Technology, Poland
Julita Kulbacka	Wrocław Medical University, Poland
Marek Kulbacki	Polish-Japanese Academy of Information Technology, Poland
Piotr Kulczycki	Polish Academy of Science, Systems Research Institute, Poland
Kazuhiro Kuwabara	Ritsumeikan University, Japan
Halina Kwaśnicka	Wrocław University of Science and Technology, Poland
Imene Lahyani	University of Sfax, Tunisia
Mark Last	Ben-Gurion University of the Negev, Israel
Anne Laurent	University of Montpellier, France
Hoai An Le Thi	University of Lorraine, France
Sylvain Lefebvre	Toyota ITC, France
Philippe Lemoisson	French Agricultural Research Centre for International Development (CIRAD), France
Florin Leon	Gheorghe Asachi Technical University of Iasi, Romania
Doina Logofatu	Frankfurt University of Applied Sciences, Germany
Edwin Lughofer	Johannes Kepler University Linz, Austria
Juraj Machaj	University of Zilina, Slovakia
Bernadetta Maleszka	Wrocław University of Science and Technology, Poland
Marcin Maleszka	Wrocław University of Science and Technology, Poland
Yannis Manolopoulos	Aristotle University of Thessaloniki, Greece
Yi Mei	Victoria University of Wellington, New Zealand
Adam Meissner	Poznań University of Technology, Poland
Héctor Menéndez	University College London, UK

Mercedes Merayo	Universidad Complutense de Madrid, Spain
Jacek Mercik	WSB University in Wrocław, Poland
Radosław Michalski	Wrocław University of Science and Technology, Poland
Peter Mikulecky	University of Hradec Kralove, Czech Republic
Miroslava Mikušová	University of Zilina, Slovakia
Jean-Luc Minel	Université Paris Ouest Nanterre La Défense, France
Javier Montero	Universidad Complutense de Madrid, Spain
Ahmed Moussa	Universite Abdelmalek Essaadi, Morocco
Manuel Munier	University of Pau and Pays de l'Adour, France
Grzegorz J. Nalepa	AGH University of Science and Technology, Poland
Laurent Nana	University of Brest, France
Fulufhelo Nelwamondo	Council for Scientific and Industrial Research, South Africa
Filippo Neri	University of Napoli Federico II, Italy
Linh Anh Nguyen	University of Warsaw, Poland
Loan T. T. Nguyen	Nguyen Tat Thanh University, Vietnam
Adam Niewiadomski	Łódź University of Technology, Poland
Adel Noureddine	University of Pau and Pays de l'Adour, France
Agnieszka Nowak-Brzezińska	University of Silesia, Poland
Alberto Núñez	Universidad Complutense de Madrid, Spain
Manuel Núñez	Universidad Complutense de Madrid, Spain
Tarkko Oksala	Aalto University, Finland
Mieczyslaw Owoc	Wrocław University of Economics, Poland
Marcin Paprzycki	Systems Research Institute, Polish Academy of Sciences, Poland
Batista Paulo	Universidade de Evora, Portugal
Marek Penhaker	VSB - Technical University of Ostrava, Czech Republic
Isidoros Perikos	University of Patras, Greece
Marcin Pietranik	Wrocław University of Science and Technology, Poland
Elias Pimenidis	University of the West of England, Bristol, UK
Nikolaos Polatidis	University of Brighton, UK
Hiram Ponce Espinosa	Universidad Panamericana, Brazil
Piotr Porwik	University of Silesia, Poland
Radu-Emil Precup	Politehnica University of Timisoara, Romania
Paulo Quaresma	Universidade de Evora, Portugal
David Ramsey	Wrocław University of Science and Technology, Poland
Mohammad Rashedur Rahman	North South University, Bangladesh
Ewa Ratajczak-Ropel	Gdynia Maritime University, Poland
Tomasz M. Rutkowski	University of Tokyo, Japan
Virgilijus Sakalauskas	Vilnius University, Lithuania

Katerina Zdravkova	University St Cyril and Methodius, Macedonia
Aleksander Zgrzywa	Wrocław University of Science and Technology, Poland
Adam Ziębiński	Silesian University of Technology, Poland

Special Session Program Committees

BiSAS 2019 – Special Session on Big Data Streaming, Applications and Security

Raja Chiky	ISEP, France
Yousra Chabchoub	ISEP, France
Zakia Kazi-Aoul	ISEP, France
Mohamed Sellami	Telecom Sud Paris, France
Aliou Boly	UCAD, Senegal
Alzennyr Da Silva	EDF, France
Elisabeth Metais	CNAM, France
Farid Meziane	University of Salford, UK
Rosanna Verde	University Campania, Italy
Jacques Demerjian	Lebanese University, Lebanon
Jacques Abou Abdou	Notre Dame University - Louaize, Lebanon
Abdellah Idrissi	Mohammed V University In Rabat, Morocco
Rokia Missaoui	Université Du Quebec En Outaouais, Canada
Sana Belguith	University of Salford, UK
Saraee Mo	University of Salford, UK
Tooska Dergahi	University of Salford, UK

CCINLP 2019 – Special Session on Computational Collective Intelligence and Natural Language Processing

Ismaïl Biskri	Université du Québec à Trois-Rivières, Canada
Mounir Zrigui	Université de Monastir, Tunisia
Anca Pascu	Université de Bretagne Occidentale, France
Éric Poirier	Université du Québec à Trois-Rivières, Canada
Fatiha Sadat	Université du Québec à Montréal, Canada
Adel Jebali	Concordia University, Canada
Eva Hajiova	Charles University, Prague, Czech Republic
Khaled Shaalan	British University, Dubai, UAE
Vladislav Kubon	Charles University, Czech Republic
Louis Rompré	Cascades, Canada
Rim Faiz	IHEC, Tunisia

CIST 2019 – Special Session on Collective Intelligence for Science and Technology

Sadok Ben Yahia	Tallinn University of Technology, Estonia
Hadda Cherroun	University of Laghouat, Algeria
Raddouane Chiheb	University Mohammed V in Rabat – ENSIAS, Morocco
Gayo Diallo	University of Bordeaux, France

Dirk Draheim	Tallinn University of Technology, Estonia
Habiba Drias	USTHB Algiers, Algeria
Abdelatif El Afia	University Mohammed V in Rabat – ENSIAS, Morocco
Maria Gini	University of Minnesota, USA
Fadratul Hafinaz	University of Sains, Malaysia
Chihab Hannachi	University of Toulouse 1, France
Said Jabbour	University of Artois, France
Imed Kacem	University of Lorraine, France
Nadjet Kamel	University Ferhat Abbas Sétif 1, Algeria
Saroj Kaushik	Indian Institute of Technology Delhi, India
Samir Kechid	USTHB Algiers, Algeria
Ilyes Khennak	USTHB Algiers, Algeria
Amira Mouakher	University of Bourgogne, France
Alexander Norta	Tallinn University of Technology, Estonia
Mourad Oussalah	Nantes University, France
Houari Sahraoui	University of Montreal, Canada
Lakhdar Sais	University of Artois, France
Djelloul Ziadi	University of Rouen, France
Djaafar Zouache	UBBA, Algeria

CSDMO 2019 – Special Session on Cooperative Strategies for Decision Making and Optimization

Dariusz Barbucha	Gdynia Maritime University, Poland
Amine Chohra	Paris East University, France
Ireneusz Czarnowski	Gdynia Maritime University, Poland
Joanna Jędrzejowicz	Gdansk University, Poland
Piotr Jędrzejowicz	Gdynia Maritime University, Poland
Edyta Kucharska	AGH University of Science and Technology, Poland
Antonio D. Masegosa	University of Deusto, Spain
Jacek Mercik	WSB University in Wroclaw, Poland
Javier Montero	Complutense University, Spain
Ewa Ratajczak-Ropel	Gdynia Maritime University, Poland
Iza Wierzbowska	Gdynia Maritime University, Poland
Mahdi Zargayouna	IFSTTAR, France

DCISM 2019 – Distributed Collective Intelligence for Smart Manufacturing

Markus Bregulla	Ingolstadt University of Applied Sciences, Germany
Rafał Cupek	Silesian University of Technology, Poland
Marcin Fojcik	Western Norway University of Applied Sciences, Poland
Jörg Franke	Friedrich-Alexander-University of Erlangen-Nürnberg, Germany
Dariusz Frejlichowski	West Pomeranian University of Technology, Poland
Damian Grzechca	Silesian University of Technology, Poland

Maciej Huk	Wroclaw University of Science and Technology, Poland
Dariusz Mrozek	Silesian University of Technology, Poland
Agnieszka Nowak-Brzezińska	University of Silesia, Poland
Krzysztof Tokarz	Silesian University of Technology, Poland
Olav Sande	Western Norway University of Applied Sciences, Norway
Knut Øvsthus	Western Norway University of Applied Sciences, Norway
Alexey Vinel	Western Norway University of Applied Sciences, Norway
Adam Ziębiński	Silesian University of Technology, Poland

IMIS 2019 – Special Session on Intelligent Management Information Systems

Eunika Mercier-Laurent	Jean Moulin Lyon 3 University, France
Małgorzata Pańkowska	University of Economics in Katowice, Poland
Mieczysław Owoc	Wrocław University of Economics, Poland
Bogdan Franczyk	University of Leipzig, Germany
Kazimierz Perechuda	Wrocław University of Economics, Poland
Jan Stępniewski	Université Paris 13, France
Helena Dudycz	Wrocław University of Economics, Poland
Jerzy Korczak	International University of Logistics and Transport in Wrocław, Poland
Andrzej Bytniewski	Wrocław University of Economics, Poland
Marcin Fojcik	Western Norway University of Applied Sciences, Norway
Monika Eisenbardt	Wrocław University of Economics, Poland
Dorota Jelonek	Czestochowa University of Technology, Poland
Paweł Weichbroth	WSB University in Gdańsk, Poland
Jadwiga Sobieska-Karpińska	The Witelon State University of Applied Sciences in Legnica, Poland
Krzysztof Hauke	Wrocław University of Economics, Poland
Daria Hołodnik	Opole University of Technology, Poland
Krzysztof Nowosielski	Wrocław University of Economics, Poland
Zdzisław Kes	Wrocław University of Economics, Poland

IMSARWS 2019 – Special Session on Intelligent Modeling and Simulation Approaches for Real World Systems

Alabbas Alhaj Ali	Frankfurt University of Applied Sciences, Germany
Costin Bădică	University of Craiova, Romania
Petru Cașcaval	Gheorghe Asachi Technical University of Iași, Romania

Gia Thuan Lam	Vietnamese-German University, Vietnam
Florin Leon	Gheorghe Asachi Technical University of Iaşi, Romania
Doina Logofătu	Frankfurt University of Applied Sciences, Germany
Fitore Muharemi	Frankfurt University of Applied Sciences, Germany
Minh Nguyen	Frankfurt University of Applied Sciences, Germany
Julian Szymański	Gdańsk University of Technology, Poland
Pawel Sitek	Kielce University of Technology, Poland
Daniel Stamate	Goldsmiths, University of London, UK

ISSC 2019 – Special Session on Intelligent Sustainable Smart Cities

Costin Bădică	University of Craiova, Romania
Peter Bracinik	University of Zilina, Slovakia
Peter Brida	University of Zilina, Czech Republic
Davor Dujak	University of Osijek, Croatia
Martina Hedvičáková	University of Hradec Kralove, Czech Republic
Marek Hoger	University of Zilina, Slovakia
Jiří Horák	Technical University of Ostrava, Czech Republic
Petra Marešová	University of Hradec Kralove, Czech Republic
Hana Mohelska	University of Hradec Kralove, Czech Republic
Arkadiusz Kawa	Poznan University of Economics and Business, Poland
Waldemar Koczkodaj	Laurentian University, Canada
Ondrej Krejcar	University of Hradec Kralove, Czech Republic
Martina Látková	University of Zilina, Slovakia
Juraj Machaj	University of Zilina, Slovakia
Miroslava Mikušová	University of Zilina, Slovakia
Dorota Bednarska-Olejniczak	Wroclaw University of Economics, Poland
Jaroslaw Olejniczak	Wroclaw University of Economics, Poland
Paweł Piątkowski	Poznan University of Technology, Poland
Bartłomiej Pierański	Poznan University of Economics and Business, Poland
Peter Poor	University of West Bohemia, Czech Republic
Petra Poulová	University of Hradec Kralove, Czech Republic
Michal Regula	University of Zilina, Slovakia
Marek Roch	University of Zilina, Slovakia
Carlos Andres Romano	Polytechnic University of Valencia, Spain
Ali Selamat	Universiti Teknologi Malaysia, Malaysia
Marcela Sokolová	University of Hradec Kralove, Czech Republic
Libuše Svobodová	University of Hradec Kralove, Czech Republic
Emese Tokarčíková	University of Zilina, Slovakia
Hana Tomášková	University of Hradec Kralove, Czech Republic
Marek Vokoun	Institute of Technology and Business in Ceske Budejovice, Czech Republic

MLRWD 2019 – Special Session on Machine Learning in Real-World Data

Franciszek Białas	University of Economics in Katowice, Poland
Grzegorz Dziczkowski	University of Economics in Katowice, Poland
Marcin Grzegorzek	University of Lübeck, Germany
Ignacy Kaliszewski	Systems Research Institute, Polish Academy of Sciences, Poland
Krzysztof Kania	University of Economics in Katowice, Poland
Jan Kozak	University of Economics in Katowice, Poland
Przemysław Juszczuk	University of Economics in Katowice, Poland
Janusz Miroforidis	Systems Research Institute, Polish Academy of Sciences, Poland
Agnieszka Nowak-Brzezińska	University of Silesia, Poland
Dmitry Podkopaev	Systems Research Institute, Polish Academy of Sciences, Poland
Małgorzata Przybyła-Kasperek	University of Economics in Katowice, Poland
Tomasz Staś	University of Economics in Katowice, Poland
Magdalena Tkacz	University of Silesia, Poland
Bogna Zacny	University of Economics in Katowice, Poland

UNI4.0 2019 – Special Session on New Trends and Challenges in Education: The University 4.0

Archundia Etelvina	BUAP, Mexico
Bouassida Ismail	ReDCAD, Tunisia
Diop Codé	Activeeon, France
Gomez-Montalvo	Jorge R. UADY, Mexico
Lamolle Myriam	Laboratoire LIASD - Université Paris 8, France
Mezghani Emna	Orange Labs, France
Noureddine Adel	UPPA, France
Perez González Héctor	UASLP, Mexico
Rodriguez Laura	UPAEP, Mexico

WEBSYS 2019 – Intelligent Processing of Multimedia in Web Systems

František Čapkovič	Academy of Sciences, Slovakia
Patricia Conde-Céspedes	Institut Supérieur d'électronique de Paris, France
Jarosław Jankowski	West Pomeranian University of Technology, Poland
Ondřej Krejcar	University of Hradec Kralove, Czech Republic
Alin Moldoveanu	Politehnica University of Bucharest, Romania
Tarkko Oksala	Helsinki University of Technology, Finland
Aleš Procházka	Institute of Chemical Technology, Czech Republic
Andrzej Siemiński	Wrocław University of Science and Technology, Poland
Aleksander Zgrzywa	Wrocław University of Science and Technology, Poland

Contents – Part II

Distributed Collective Intelligence for Smart Manufacturing

Collective Intelligence for Science and Technology

Intelligent Management Information Systems

Intelligent Sustainable Smart Cities

New Trends and Challenges in Education: The University 4.0

Intelligent Processing of Multimedia in Web Systems

Big Data Streaming, Applications and Security

Contents – Part I

Text Processing and Information Retrieval

Data Mining Methods and Applications

Computer Vision Techniques

**Intelligent Modeling and Simulation Approaches for Real
World Systems**

Innovations in Intelligent Systems

Computational Collective Intelligence
and Natural Language Processing

An Empirical Analysis of Moroccan Dialectal User-Generated Text

Ridouane Tachicart[(⊠)] and Karim Bouzoubaa[(⊠)]

Mohammadia School of Engineers, Mohammed V University in Rabat,
Rabat, Morocco
ridouane.tachicart@research.emi.ac.ma,
karim.bouzoubaa@emi.ac.ma

Abstract. With the increase of web use in Morocco today, Internet has become an important source of information. Specifically, across social media, Moroccan people use several languages in their communication leaving behind unstructured user-generated text that present several opportunities for Natural Language Processing. Among languages found in this data, Moroccan Dialectal Arabic stands with an important content and several features. In this paper, we investigate online written text generated by Moroccan users in social media with an emphasis on Moroccan Dialectal Arabic. For this purpose, we follow several steps, using some tools such as a language identification system, in order to conduct a deep study of this data. The most interesting findings that have emerged is the use of code switching, multi-script and low amount of words in Moroccan UGT text.

Keywords: User-Generated text · Social media · Arabic dialect · Corpus · Lexicon · Natural Language Processing · Moroccan Dialectal Arabic · Standard Arabic · Code-switching

1 Introduction

Social media are the collection of tools that facilitate creating virtual communities and sharing information interactively through electronic communication. Typically, basic social media services are free and are available via web-based technologies. The creation of user-generated content is the most valuable feature [1] that characterizes social media services and it is considered as the social media lifeblood. The latter consists mainly of sharing text, images or videos and ensures the possibility of adding related comments. User-generated content is the main contributor to "social media analytics" raise [2], which is a new activity that consists of collecting data from social media and analyzing it in order to make, for instance, business decisions.

Over the past few years, social media has known a widespread use in Morocco and hence became one of the major means for communication and content producing in virtual communities. As an illustration, 71% of the Moroccan Internet users are active in Social Media[1]. Social media has been influencing users that prefer today using these

---

[1] According to Hootsuite https://hootsuite.com.

© Springer Nature Switzerland AG 2019
N. T. Nguyen et al. (Eds.): ICCCI 2019, LNAI 11684, pp. 3–12, 2019.
https://doi.org/10.1007/978-3-030-28374-2_1

media rather than other web alternatives since they can easily and instantly interact with others [3]. They express themselves using Moroccan Dialectal Arabic (MDA), Modern Standard Arabic (MSA) and alternatively other European languages such as French. As a result, user-generated text (UGT) constitutes new opportunities for understanding Moroccan Dialectal Arabic used in social media platforms.

Contrary to many other countries where Twitter is the most used Social Media platform, Facebook and YouTube are the most popular social media platforms in Morocco. On one hand, 59% of social media viewed pages are a Facebook pages (with more than 15 million active users in Morocco). This means that Facebook is the most popular social media in Morocco. On the other hand, YouTube stands in the second rank with 35% of social media viewed pages according to the latest statistics[2,3]. Hence, with such important number of users, a huge amount of user-generated text is produced through social media in Morocco instantly. However, there is currently no clear idea on its content and structure and this situation constitutes one of the main challenges for its processing.

Processing MDA user-generated text is an interesting area given that it reflects the language spoken by Moroccan people in their everyday life. However, it poses several challenges due to the lack of MDA NLP tools. Hence, before considering this data as a resource or processing it through NLP tools, it should be useful to study user-generated text effect by analyzing its content. The latter may help to build a clear idea about how MDA user-generated text is written, to identify its features and to get a better understanding of its rules. To the best of our knowledge, no related work has yet been conducted.

In the aim to later ease the processing of MDA UGT, this study considers three main goals that target general UGT features namely: identifying and analyzing used scripts, identifying used languages and evaluating the UGT context (amount of used words). To reach the three goals, we start by collecting Moroccan UGT and then perform some tasks such as cleaning, filtering and language identifying. Then, we analyze the pre-processed data.

The remainder of this paper is organized as follows: Sect. 2 gives an overview of the Moroccan Dialectal Arabic. Section 3 presents related works in the field of processing Arabic dialect (AD) user-generated text. Section 4 describes followed steps to collect and filter the MDA UGT then presents some statistics. In Sect. 5, we provide a discussion about results; finally, we conclude the paper in Sect. 6 with some observations.

2 Moroccan Dialectal Arabic Overview

The Moroccan constitution recognizes MSA and Tamazight as two official Moroccan languages. However, Moroccan Dialectal Arabic, which is considered as a variant of MSA, is the most used language in Morocco according to the official census performed in 2014[4] (90% of Moroccan people use MDA).

---

[2] http://www.internetworldstats.com.

[3] http://gs.statcounter.com/social-media-stats/all/morocco.

[4] http://rgph2014.hcp.ma.

Historically, MDA raised as a result of the interaction between Arabic and Tamazight in spreading Islam period and contained a mixture of these languages until the beginning of the 20th century. After the establishment of the French and Spanish protectorate, the MDA vocabulary integrated several words from these languages as shown in Table 1. For example, the word كاسكيطة \cap\ originates from French where the origin word is \casquette\. Nevertheless, MDA is strongly influenced by Arabic according to a previous work [4] especially at the lexical level. This study showed that 81% of the Moroccan vocabulary is borrowed from the Arabic language.

Table 1. MDA words origin

MDA word	Word origin	Language origin	English translation
لامبة	lámpara	Spanish	lamp
كاسكيطة	casquette	French	cap
طوبيس	autobus	French	autobus
رويدة	rueda	Spanish	wheel

3 Related Works

Over the last few years, processing Arabic language increasingly gained attention. Furthermore, while many works have been proposed to deal with standard and normalized Arabic text, we noticed that the NLP community started recently to deal with user-generated text due to the popularity of social media and the Arabic digital expansion. In this section, we highlight the most relevant works dealing with Arabic dialectal UGT.

Sadat et al. [5] presented a framework in order to detect Arabic dialects in social media using probabilistic models. To train their system, they collected data from blogs and forums where the users are located in different Arabic countries. They considered 18 classes representing 18 Arabic dialects and manually annotated each sentence with its corresponding dialect. In the training phase, the system was trained using character n-gram Markov language model and Naïve Bayes classifiers. Evaluation results showed that the Naïve Bayes classifier outperforms Markov language model classifier with 98% of accuracy. Moreover, according to n-gram comparison, it was noticed that Naïve Bayes classifier based on character bi-gram model performs better than uni-gram and tri-gram models.

Voss et al. [6] built a classifier that can distinguish Moroccan Dialectal Arabic tweets written in Latin script from French and English tweets using unsupervised learning approach and focusing on the token level. The classifier is trained on an annotated data consisting of 40 K tweets that were collected from Twitter using several keywords. Evaluation of the classifier on a test set composed of 800 tweets showed that it significantly works better in English and French than Moroccan with respectively an accuracy of 95,5%, 95% and 76%.

Albogamy and Ramsay [7] built a light stemmer for Arabic tweets. They avoided using lexicons given that the Arabic language used in Twitter may include dialectal and new words. Their approach relies on defining all possible affixes and then writing rules in order to compose a given word. Using a sample of 390 Arabic tweets, evaluation results gave an accuracy of 74%.

In order to improve the quality of Arabic UGT machine translation, Afli et al. [8] proposed to integrate an Automatic Error Correction module as pre-processing and prior to the translation phase. To train and test the proposed module, authors used a portion of QALB corpus [9] containing 1,3 M words including dialectal words. The trained and test data were manually annotated and corrected regarding MSA rules. After that, UGT sentences and their MSA corrections were aligned at the sentence level and tokenized using the MADA morphological analyzer [10]. Authors proposed to use two different systems according to tokenization. The first system is trained on data without tokenization, where the second one is trained using MADA tokenization. Evaluation results on test data containing 66 K words showed that the second system outputs with an accuracy of 68,68% while the first one outputs with 63,18% of accuracy. Hence, authors realized that including tokenized words in the training data is crucial for increasing error detection.

Abidi and Smaili [11] performed an empirical study of the Algerian dialect used in YouTube. They started by collecting a corpus containing 17 M words from YouTube comments. The corpus contains different languages where an important amount of text is written in Latin script (LS) (about 47%). They noticed also that 82% of the collected sentences include code-switching. Furthermore, authors reported that grammar was not respected when using either Arabic or Latin script. As an example, a word may be written in different ways. For this reason, they built a lexicon that contains, for each word, its correlated words to deal with the problem of spelling inconsistency.

From the above surveyed works, UGT is the subject of several Arabic dialect researches in different NLP fields such as empirical studies, building resources, text mining and machine translation, etc. To the best of our knowledge, Moroccan UGT has not been studied in Arabic NLP. Our study seeks to take a first step towards understanding, analyzing and extracting useful knowledge related to Moroccan UGT.

4   Collecting and Filtering User-Generated MDA Text

In this section, we describe followed steps in order to build an MDA corpus that is collected from social media sources and generated from Moroccan users. As stated above, we limited the scope of UGT sources to Facebook and YouTube due to their popularity in Morocco. This is proved by their extensive use compared to other social media websites[5] as shown in Fig. 1. For example, 59% of Moroccan social media traffic come from Facebook, 34% from YouTube and 7% from other social media (Twitter, Google+ , etc.).

---

[5] http://gs.statcounter.com/social-media-stats/all/morocco.

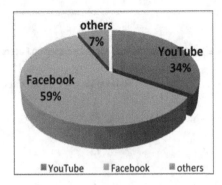

Fig. 1. Social media use in Morocco

4.1 Collecting Data

Through social media websites, users can generate texts using either the post or the comment features as indicated in the work of [12] and [13]. On one hand, post feature allows expressing an idea. On the other hand, many users can react and give their own comments to a given post through the comment feature. Therefore, comments are widely available and tend to be in general natural, more spontaneous and linguistically rich compared to posts. For this reason, we decided to focus only on collecting comments in order to build an MDA corpus that reflects the Moroccan language. Thus, we addressed the most popular Moroccan pages by harvesting user's comments that are related to a set of Facebook posts and YouTube videos using two different tools. First, after identifying the most popular Moroccan Facebook pages (using Facebook Audience Insights[6] feature - Fig. 2), we collected[7] their related comments. Since the first 20 popular pages in Facebook Audience Insights cover the majority of topics (Facebook categories), we limited comments scrapping to these pages for the period of January 2018. Secondly, to ensure that YouTube collected texts mainly concern topics posted by Moroccans (for the same period), we used YouTube Data API[8] and collected Moroccan video comments by including a list of MDA keywords. In total, raw text before cleaning and normalization was composed of 748.433 comments where Facebook comments represent almost 89% of this data. Note that, massive amount of data can be harvested using the above steps by extending either keywords list, period or number of pages. In fact, huge amount of data is suitable for several NLP application especially the machine learning applications based, statistical machine translation, etc. However, with respect to our objectives, the collected UGT is enough for the kind of our study.

4.2 Data Cleaning and Basic Normalization

The challenge we faced after achieving the previous step is the noisy data. Indeed, collected data is a mixture of several languages. MDA and MSA are written either in

---

[6] https://www.facebook.com/ads/audience-insights.

[7] Using Facebook Page Post Scraper https://github.com/minimaxir/facebook-page-post-scraper.

[8] https://developers.google.com/youtube/v3/.

Page Likes			
Facebook Pages that are likely to be relevant to your audience based on Facebook Page likes.			
Page	**Relevance** ⓘ	**Audience**	**Facebook** ⓘ▾
Avito.ma	86	1.9m	2.1m
Andaluspress - تيكة أندلس الإخبارية	72	1.8m	2m
Jumia	4	1.6m	1.6m
Maroc Telecom	65	1.5m	1.6m
أقوال كثور التاريخية	81	1.4m	1.5m
العمق المغربى	46	1.4m	1.5m
Orange	12	1.3m	1.3m
Mon Maroc	39	1.2m	1.3m

Fig. 2. Facebook Audience Insights (Page Likes feature)

Arabic or Romanized letters (Arabizi) [14], while European languages are written only in Romanized letters. Arabizi is a sort of social media script where users usually type letters alongside numbers (such as 3, 7 and 9) to represent Arabic letters that have no equivalent in Roman script such as the ق letter. The latter is represented in Arabizi by the number 9. In addition, some comments contain only special characters, emoticons or dates, etc. For this reason, it was necessary to perform a special process to convert this data into a useful corpus that can be analyzed and used for NLP purposes. Thus, we started first by removing special characters (*, $, and !) in both Arabic script and Arabizi texts. We removed also numbers and diacritics from Arabic texts. After that, we used SAFAR[9] framework [15] in order to normalize Arabic words written in Arabic script (AS). For example, the word مشغووووول is normalized to مشغول. After cleaning and performing basic normalization, data was reduced from 748.433 comments to 642.502 given that some comments do not contain words. Finally, redundant comments were deleted and only 580.751 unique sentences were retained from this step.

---

[9] http://arabic.emi.ac.ma/safar/.

4.3   Classification

Given that the resulted corpus contains several languages and it is written in both Arabic, Arabizi and Romanized letters, we separated sentences written in Arabic script and those written in Arabizi in order to separately study their content. Regarding Arabizi content, we used sequentially two language identification systems in order to determine the language of each sentence. In order to detect MDA comments, we used the Language Identification (LID) system built by authors in [16] by extending it to Arabizi. After that, we used the Stand-alone language identification system Langid.py [17] in order to distinguish between French, English and Spanish in the remaining comments. A sample of the task results is illustrated in Table 2 where sentences are grouped according to languages.

Table 2. Arabizi sentences classification

Language	Arabizi sentence	English equivalent
MDA	Allah iwaf9ak aiman falmasira dyalak al faniya ohna kantsanaw al jadid dyalak	God help you in your career. We will be waiting for your update
MDA	5alih i3abr 3la ch3or dyalo	Let him express its sentiment
English	"9amar" I really Miss you	"9amar" I really Miss you
French	non c'est pas vrai	No, that is not true
mixed	3andakom je suis dangereuse	Pay attention, I'm dangerous

Regarding Arabic script, we conducted a manual task with a group composed of 30 annotators where the goal is to label each comment as MDA, MSA or mixed. Annotators are MDA/MSA native speakers and each one was asked to read 5500 comments and accurately classify them. The manual task was preferred in place of an automatic process because on one hand, human annotations are performed almost without error rates and on the other hand, the annotated dataset can be used in future Moroccan Dialect NLP tools.

In Table 3, results of the language and code-switching identification showed that MDA is heavily used with more than 74% (33,93 + 40,86) of the collected UGT. Moreover, Arabic script and Arabizi content represent respectively almost 57% and 43%. We notice also that using foreign languages such as French, English and Spanish in the same UGT content is too low and does not exceed in total 2,1%.

Table 4 presents a set of features that characterize the content of this corpus. The shortest comment contains three words where the largest one contains 901 words. In addition, one important remark is that the majority of the collected comments (85% of the UGT) are written in short context and each comment does not exceed 13 words. Finally, comments with more than 13 words represent only 15% of the collected UGT.

Table 3. Language distribution of the UGT

Script	Language	Comments	Percentage	
Arabic	Mixed	86.522	14,81%	57,06%
	MSA	48.599	8,32%	
	MDA	198.151	33,93%	
Romanized	MDA	238.616	40,86%	42,94%
	French	6252	1,07%	
	English	2611	0,45%	
	Spanish	3291	0,56%	

Table 4. General features of the dialectal Moroccan UGT written (AS and LS).

Shortest comment (# words)	3
Largest comment (# words)	901
Weighted average (# words)	13
Comments with less than 13 words	85%
Comments with more than 100 words	1%
Comments with 13<words<100	14%

5 Discussion

Results of the performed experiments showed that Moroccan UGT displays several features that should be considered before engaging in any related NLP processing task.

- The majority of the Moroccan UGT is written using Arabic script (57%) and if we consider only the MDA, Moroccan users prefer to express their ideas using Arabic script rather than Arabizi.
- Several languages are used including MDA, MSA, French Spanish and English. Regardless the used script, MDA content represents 73% of the collected UGT and hence it is the most used language. Regarding Arabic script, code-switching phenomenon represents an important amount. In fact, users usually include in their MDA sentences some MSA words not belonging to the MDA lexicon.
- Finally, Moroccan UGT sentences are usually short given that the weighted average of the Moroccan comments is 13 words. The main cause of this phenomenon is the character limit imposed by Facebook and YouTube. This feature leads a processing difficulty when one needs to consider the word context in some NLP applications such as language identification systems. In contrast, accurate results are obtained when processing a text with short context in other NLP applications such as sentiment analysis.

This study investigates the MDA UGT regarding three features that are script, language and text context. Results of this study meet the three goals defined in Sect. 1 and lead us to better understand how to process the MDA text. Indeed, the processing of the MDA UGT requires some NLP tools in order to obtain accurate results. The problem of script and language diversity can be resolved using an MDA LID system that is currently available[10]. While an MDA morphological analyzer that takes into consideration the text context can fix the UGT context shortness.

6 Conclusion

In this paper, we analyzed the Moroccan user generated text through a corpus collected from the most used social media websites in Morocco. The collected MDA UGT was cleaned and classified then analyzed. Results of this analysis showed that Moroccan people use both Arabizi and Arabic scripts to write their comments with a slight preference for Arabic (57%). It shows also that MDA is heavily used in social media websites (74%). Finally, UGT is usually written in short context. As a future work, we plan to investigate an important amount of Moroccan UGT at the morphological level in order to pave the way to building related NLP tools.

Acknowledgements. We would like to thank the student annotators and their Professors Jamal Ezzouaine and Hakima Khamar from Mohammed V University in Rabat for their efforts on the annotation of the Moroccan user-generated text, which were necessary to classify this content according to languages.

References

1. Itani, M.: Sentiment Analysis and Resources for Informal Arabic Text on Social Media. Sheffield Hallam University, Sheffield (2018)
2. Hu, X., Liu, H.: Text analytics in social media. In: Mining Text Data, pp. 385–414. Springer, US (2012)
3. Liu, X., Wang, M., Huet, B.: Event analysis in social multimedia: a survey. Front. Comput. Sci. **10**(3), 433–446 (2016)
4. Tachicart, R., Bouzoubaa, K., Jaafar, H.: Lexical differences and similarities between Moroccan dialect and Arabic. In: 4th IEEE International Colloquium on Information Science and Technology (CIST 2016), Tangier (2016)
5. Sadat, F., Kazemi, F., Farzindar, A.: Automatic identification of Arabic language varieties and dialects in social media. In: Second Workshop on Natural Language Processing for Social Media (SocialNLP 2014), Queensland, Australia (2014)
6. Voss, C., Tratz, S., Laoudi, J., Briesch, D.: Finding romanized Arabic dialect in code-mixed tweets. In: Ninth International Conference on Language Resources and Evaluation (LREC 2014), Reykjavik, Iceland (2014)
7. Albogamy, F., Ramsay, A.: Unsupervised stemmer for Arabic tweets. In: Second Workshop on Noisy User-generated Text (WNUT 2016), Osaka, Japan (2016)
8. Afli, H., Aransa, W., Lohar, P., Way, A.: From Arabic user-generated content to machine translation: integrating automatic error correction. In: 17th International Conference on Intelligent Text Processing and Computational Linguistics (CICLING 2016), Konya, Turkey (2016)

---

[10] http://arabic.emi.ac.ma:8080/MCAP/faces/lid.xhtml;jsessionid=834e738ebfc626d2b431beac006c.

9. Zaghouani, W., et al.: Large scale arabic error annotation: guidelines and framework. In: Ninth International Conference on Language Resources and Evaluation (LREC 2014), Reykjavik, Iceland (2014)
10. Habash, N., Rambow, O., Roth, R.: Mada+tokan: a toolkit for arabic tokenization, diacritization, morphological disambiguation, POS tagging, stemming and lemmatization. In: Second International Conference on Arabic Language Resources and Tools (MEDAR 2009), Cairo, Egypt (2009)
11. Abidi, K., Smaïli, K.: An empirical study of the Algerian dialect of Social network. In: International Conference on Natural Language, Signal and Speech Processing (ICNLSP 2019), Casablanca, Morocco (2017)
12. Salloum, S.A., Al-Emran, M., Abdel Monem, A., Shaalan, K.: A survey of text mining in social media: Facebook and Twitter perspectives. Adv. Sci. Technol. Eng. syst. J. 2(1), 127–133 (2017)
13. Irfan, R., et al.: A survey on text mining in social networks. Knowl. Eng. Rev. 30(2), 157–170 (2015)
14. Bies, A., et al.: Transliteration of Arabizi into Arabic orthography: developing a parallel annotated Arabizi-Arabic script SMS/Chat corpus. In: First Workshop on Computational Approaches to Code Switching (EMNLP 2014), Doha, Qatar (2014)
15. Jaafar, Y., Bouzoubaa, K.: Arabic natural language processing from software engineering to complex pipeline. In: First International Conference on Arabic Computational Linguistics (ACLing 2015), vol. 19, no. 2 (2015)
16. Tachicart, R., Bouzoubaa, K., Aouragh, S.L., Jaafa, H.: Automatic identification of Moroccan colloquial Arabic. In: Lachkar, A., Bouzoubaa, K., Mazroui, A., Hamdani, A., Lekhouaja, A. (eds.) ICALP 2017. CCIS, vol. 782, pp. 201–214. Springer, Cham (2018). https://doi.org/10.1007/978-3-319-73500-9_15
17. Lui, M., Baldwin, T.: langid.py: an off-the-shelf language identification tool. In: 50th Annual Meeting of the Association for Computational Linguistics (ACL 2012), Jeju, Republic of Korea (2012)

Query Error Correction Algorithm Based on Fusion Sequence to Sequence Model

Jianyong Duan[1,2,3(✉)], Tianxiao Ji[1,3], Mingli Wu[1,3], and Hao Wang[1,3]

[1] College of Computer Science and Technology,
North China University of Technology, Beijing, China
duanjy@hotmail.com

[2] Beijing Urban Governance Research Center, Beijing, China

[3] Beijing Key Laboratory on Integration and Analysis of Large-scale Stream Data,
Beijing 100144, China

Abstract. The query error correction task is very important to improve user satisfaction and quality of query results. In traditional query error correction methods researchers mostly use a pipeline way to correct the error step by step. They rely heavily on manual annotation corpora. It is difficult to take into account the global effect. In this paper, we present a character-based end-to-end Sequence to Sequence (Seq2Seq) method with attention mechanism. It also incorporates the neural network language model trained on unlabeled corpora to solve the task of query correction. It can unify the modeling of different error types in query error correction and effectively overcome the shortcomings of traditional methods in query error correction tasks. Experiments show that this method can effectively capture the long-distance knowledge to correct errors, and through the Simple Recurrent Unit (SRU) it can be as good as Long Short-Term Memory (LSTM). However, there has been a significant improvement in processing time. This point is very important in query error correction tasks.

Keywords: Artificial neural networks · Information retrieval · Machine learning · Semisupervised learning · Supervised learning

1 Introduction

With the continuous development of information technology, search engines have become the main way for people to obtain information in daily life. A survey by the Pew Research Center found that 92% of users regard search engines as a good way to access information. However, there are often many spelling mistakes in the use of search engines, which seriously affect the quality of search results. The [4] shows that about 10–15% of the queries contain errors. How to deal with these mistakes is a challenging task.

Spelling error correction technology is a long-standing task. Compared with the traditional tasks of natural language processing, error correction is mainly faced with a large number of incorrect noise corpora. And query error correction

This work was supported by the National Natural Science Foundation of China (61672040) and the North China University of Technology Startup Fund.

© Springer Nature Switzerland AG 2019
N. T. Nguyen et al. (Eds.): ICCCI 2019, LNAI 11684, pp. 13–25, 2019.
https://doi.org/10.1007/978-3-030-28374-2_2

is facing a greater challenge. Firstly, in search engines, people will make mistakes more frequently because of the unfamiliar query terms. Secondly, a large number of proper nouns, names and other rare terms occur, which further increases the difficulty of analysis. Finally, query term often contains only a small amount of keywords. It is difficult to deal with query terms using grammar rules.

In the past research, English spelling errors can be divided into the following four types [5] as Table 1.

Table 1. Type of error examples.

Type of error	Before correction	After correction
Insertion	Correction	Correction
Deletion	Correction	Correction
Substitution	Correction	Correction
Transposition	Correction	Correction

Concatenation and splitting errors have also been proposed in some literature [16]. Such as "intermilan" should be "inter Milan" and "power point" should be "powerpoint". The internal errors of these individual words can be collectively referred to non-word errors. In addition to errors in single words, there are errors between words due to word misuse. As in the context of "a _ of cake", "piece" is mistakenly written as "peace". To correct these errors, traditional methods use noise channel model. Because this model is simple and efficient, most error correction methods are based on the noise channel model. In traditional machine learning methods, it is assumed that training data have the same probability distribution of features as the data to be predicted in the future. However, in practice, this assumption is most likely not true. It is likely that there is not enough data in our working areas, but there is a lot of data in other similar areas. Training data is very easy to be out of date. There is a big difference between the distribution of data obtained in a certain period before and the data obtained subsequently. In these cases, the cost of re-tagging the data and training the new model is prohibitive. Sometimes people cannot get new data.

At present, the typical methods of query error correction tasks are learning algorithms. These methods rely on a lot of manual annotation data and search engine logs. Manual annotation data is expensive and difficult to obtain. Search engine logs usually contain a large number of user privacy. There are few public data sets because the data are owned by several major search engine companies. In this work we improve the performance of query error correction by combining a large number of untagged language corpora.

2   Related Work

In the 1990s, Kernighan et al. [12] and Mays et al. [19] first proposed to use the noise channel model. Because the model is simple and efficient, it has a great impact on the development of subsequent error correction technology. Brill and Moore [2] proposed an improved method based on a noise channel model that allows for general string-to-string editing operations. The method proposed by Whitelaw et al. [26] has greatly improved the query error correction technology. Whitelaw et al. take three steps to correct the error. The first is a classification step to determine whether a word is misspelled. Then they calculate the most likely candidate set for the wrong words. Finally, it use a classifier to determine the probability of the word in candidate set.

Radlinski and Joachims [21] proposed a query chain concept. They use a stream of events that the user continually queries that use users' reorganization of the queries to learn evaluate functions. A SVM classifier that trained by manual annotation data is employed.

Zhang et al. [28] used a traditional spelling correction method to correct Web queries and re-evaluated the output through an SVM classifier. One part of the training data is obtained by automatic extraction, and the other is obtained by manual annotation. So it is a semi-supervised learning method.

Sun et al. [23] used a phrase error correction model based on users' clicked data. Li et al. [14] extended the error model by querying the similarity of words in the log.

A great deal of attention was paid to query spelling correction after Microsoft hosted the Microsoft Speller Challenge in 2011 [25]. In this competition, an annotation dataset containing 5892 query spelling corrections is also published. Many of these methods, such as the best-performing method [17] based on Hunspell's recommendations, have a significant impact on the subsequent methods [7,15]. In addition, there are some studies using large-scale search logs and clicked data [3,8].

3   Models

In this section, we introduce the language model, error correction model and some improvements made in our algorithm.

3.1   Language Model

In this paper, we need to train a language model first. Then we combine language model and error correction model for error correction.

N-gram language model is a very common model in natural language processing tasks. This method is also used in most query error correction methods. For a sentence $w_1^L = (w_1, \cdots, w_n)$ composed of L words, the probability of each word w_i depends on all words w_1^{i-1} before this word according to the conditional probability formula. Then the probability of the whole sentence is the product of the probabilities of all words. However, due to the computational complexity, it is not feasible to adopt this method directly for calculation in practice. Therefore, Markov hypothesis is generally used to assume that the probability of occurrence of each word is only related to the first n-1 words. Then the calculation can be simplified as

$$P(w_1^n) = \prod_{i=1}^{L} P(w_i|w_1^{i-1}) \approx \prod_{i=1}^{L} P(w_i|w_{i-n+1}^{i-1}) \tag{1}$$

Due to limitations of data and computational complexity, the most common model is bigram or trigram. This simplified model has achieved good results in many natural language processing tasks. But the flaw of this model is also very obvious. For example, it is unable to solve the data sparse problem, often need to adopt some smoothing algorithm. It can't capture long-distance dependencies and non-linear relationships in language models. Bengio et al. [1] proposed a neuro-probabilistic language model, which can solve the data sparse problem by representing each word as a continuous vector. On this basis, the subsequent work can deal with long-distance dependencies through recurrent neural network. Some RNN-based approaches, such as [20,27], have achieved leading level.

In order to combine the error correction model, we don't use word-based RNN, but instead take a char-based RNN. The input for each time step is one-hot representation of each character where space is also used as a valid character. Therefore our model can handle concatenation and splitting errors. First, the one-hot representation is converted to a continuous vector through the embedding layer. Then it can output the vector of which size is same as vocabulary through the multi-layer RNN. Each dimension of the vector represents the probability of output. We will fuse this probability with the results from the error correction model (described below) and we can get the output of the fusion model as input for the next step.

For the RNN model, we mainly use the basic RNN, LSTM, GRU and SRU. The basic RNN calculation is as follows,

$$h_t = \tanh(W \cdot [h_{t-1}, x_t] + b) \tag{2}$$

Although it is computationally simple, its ability to model long-distance dependencies is weak. Since we use char-based RNN, the time steps will be significantly longer than word-based RNN. So it can effectively improve this limitation through gate mechanism. LSTM is calculated as follows:

$$f_t = \sigma(W_f \cdot [h_{t-1}, x_t] + b_f) \tag{3a}$$

$$i_t = \sigma(W_i \cdot [h_{t-1}, x_t] + b_i) \tag{3b}$$

$$\tilde{C}_t = \tanh(W_C \cdot [h_{t-1}, x_t] + b_C) \tag{3c}$$

$$C_t = f_t * C_{t-1} + i_t * \tilde{C}_t \tag{3d}$$

$$o_t = \sigma(W_o \cdot [h_{t-1}, x_t] + b_o) \tag{3e}$$

$$h_t = o_t * tanh(C_t) \tag{3f}$$

h_{t-1} is the hidden state of the previous time step. x_t is the input for the current time step. $[h_{t-1}, x_t]$ is a concatenation operation. f_t determines how much information is forgotten from C_{t-1} and i_t determines how much information $\tilde{C}_t$ is updated into the cell state C_t. Finally through the current time step cell state C_t and an output gate o_t to determine the final output h_t.

Although LSTM makes RNN have the ability to solve the long-distance dependency problem, it also significantly increases the computational complexity. Since every step of the recurrent neural network relies on the previous step, it is hard to parallelize. GRU simplifies LSTM, but it does not significantly speed up. This is very detrimental for the query error correction task which needs to be completed quickly. The SRU constructs an RNN that can be computed in parallel by removing the reliance on h_{t-1}. The speed of the algorithm has been greatly improved.

SGD is a basic but efficient algorithm for optimization algorithms. It has achieved very good results in many deep learning methods for natural language processing. The main idea is also very simple. The training of neural networks can be regarded as a non-convex optimization problem,

$$\min_{\omega} \frac{1}{N} \sum_{i=1}^{N} f_i(\omega) \tag{4}$$

where f_i is the loss function at the ith data item and ω is the weight of the network.

Then each step SGD can be expressed as

$$\omega_{k+1} = \omega_k - \eta_k \nabla f(\omega k) \tag{5}$$

where η_k is the learning rate and ∇ is the gradient.

At present, there are many improved algorithms based on SGD, such as momentum SGD [24], Adam [13], Adagrad [6], RMSprop [11], etc. However, for some specific tasks, such as the language model, SGD has better generalization performance than these improved algorithms [18]. Meanwhile, Stephen Merity [20] found that an ASGD can achieve better results in a language model.

The ASGD is similar to SGD. Instead of returning the result of the last iteration, it returns an average,

$$(K - T + 1) \sum_{i=T}^{K} \omega_i \tag{6}$$

where, K is the total number of iterations, and T is a parameter that can specify the value. We employ ASGD as our language model training algorithm in this work.

3.2   Error Correction Model

Our error correction model mainly adopts the attention mechanism Seq2Seq model. The model consists of a bi-directional RNN encoder and a unidirectional RNN decoder. The encoder reads input that may contain errors and produces the final status vector as a representation. Decoder uses the encoding vector as its initial state and use the output from the previous step as input for the next step at each time step.

However, this approach uses only a single vector as a representation of the input, and it is difficult to have enough information to distinguish between similar inputs. Especially for error correction tasks, the input and output are often very similar. Unlike it's totally two different language for machine translation's input and output, there's just two-character difference between "Errorcorrecton" and "Error correction" (a letter and a space). Therefore, we adopt the - Seq2Seq model with attention mechanism adopted by many models in recent years. It is shown in the Fig. 1.

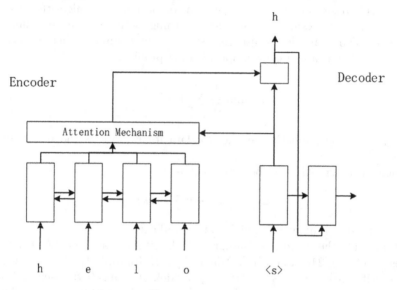

Fig. 1. Seq2Seq model with attention mechanism

The main calculation method for Attention is

$$e_i^t = v^t \tanh(W_h h_i + W_s s_t + b_{attn}) \tag{7a}$$

$$a^t = softmax(e^t) \tag{7b}$$

where h_i is the output of hidden layer of decoder, s_t is the output of encoder, b_{attn} is bias, W_h, W_s, v^t are the parameters of the model. Finally we can get attention weight a^t after softmax function.

Through the attention weight multiplied by the corresponding encoder output h_i, we can get the context vector c_t,

$$c_t = \sum_i a_i^t h_i \tag{8}$$

The context vector can be regarded as a fixed representation of the importance of each input step. After the output of the decoder is connected, the probability distribution of the output words can be obtained through a nonlinear layer.

$$P_{vocab} = softmax(W[s_t; c_t] + b) \tag{9}$$

For each step of the output, we can choose the most probable character as the next input. In the training, for the stability of numerical value, the logarithm of probability is generally adopted. It can convert maximizing the product of probability into maximizing the sum of logarithm.

In this way, the input context information can be used effectively at each step to select the next output.

3.3 Deep Fusion Correction Model

Through an end-to-end approach, Seq2Seq has achieved great success in the fields of machine translation, voice recognition, etc. However, there are some problems in query error correction. In machine translation or speech recognition, the Seq2Seq model can directly learn the language model through rich training corpora, but it is often lacking in the field of query correction. So, we improved the error correction by incorporating language models learned on a large number of unlabeled texts into the Seq2Seq model. There have been some research in machine translation and speech recognition.

Bengio [9] proposed a deep fusion method to improve the performance of machine translation. Based on this, Caglar Gulcehre et al. [22] proposed using two separate steps to train. Caglar Gulcehre et al. considered that using two separate steps to train making the Seq2Seq model cannot perceive the existence of the language model during the training phase. This is a waste of a lot of corpora in a language model. Therefore, they use a unified procedure for training, and the performance of speech recognition model is improved. However, in query error correction, this will also cause excessive use of language models to infer the next time step input, and cannot learn a valid error correction model.

Therefore, in this work, we will combine two methods to make the error correction model effectively use the knowledge of the language model, but can not overuse the language model.

The main calculation steps are as follows,

$$g_t = \sigma(W[s_t^{CM}; s_t^{LM}] + b) \tag{10a}$$

$$s_t^{DF} = [s_t^{CM}; g_t s_t^{LM}] \tag{10b}$$

$$y_t = softmax(s_t^{DF}) \tag{10c}$$

where s_t^{CM} is the hidden layer output of the error correction model, s_t^{LM} is the hidden layer output of the language model. g_t controls the effect of the language model on the final output.

The model is shown in Fig. 2.

4 Experiment

4.1 Data

In our experiments, we trained the language model using WikiText provided by Salesforce Research. Data can be publicly available online. After preprocessing of WikiText corpus, the training set contains 10592864 characters and 1961719 words. The verification set contains 1111266 characters and 204446 words, and the test set contains 1248574 characters and 229910 words.

For the error correction model, we use a large-scale query error correction corpus provided in [10]. There are about 54,772 manual annotations of real query data. About 9170 of them (16.74%) contained errors. The dataset is an order of magnitude larger than the previously query error correction dataset. According to the

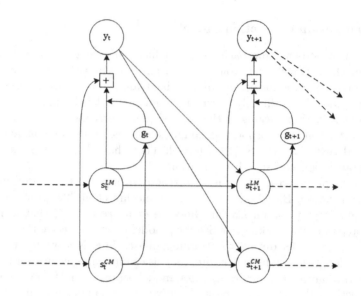

Fig. 2. Deep fusion correction model

experiment, the performance of some query correction methods on this dataset is worse than before. Because Seq2Seq error correction model requires a lot of training data, we use the Data Augmentation. We automatically generate some error correction data according to the real query data and manually marked error correction data. Generate about ten times of data by random insertion, deletion and so on. The proportion of all kinds of errors is set in accordance with the proportion of the actual data marked by the manual. As shown in the Table 2.

Table 2. The proportion of different errors.

Type	Quantity	Proportion
Deletion	3054	33.03%
Insertion	1688	18.41%
Space	2821	30.76%
Specialcharater	3229	35.21%
Substitution	1751	19.09%
Transposition	386	4.21%
Total	9170	100%

Table 3. The perplexity of language model.

Model	Perplexity	
	Valid	Test
Base RNN (2 × 32)	7.079	7.250
Base RNN (2 × 128)	4.810	4.954
Base RNN (2 × 512)	4.119	4.196
GRU (2 × 32)	6.674	6.794
GRU (2 × 128)	4.710	4.827
GRU (2 × 512)	4.105	4.195
LSTM (2 × 32)	7.073	7.260
LSTM (2 × 128)	4.990	4.115
LSTM (2 × 512)	4.158	4.269
SRU (2 × 32)	7.500	7.601
SRU (2 × 128)	5.470	5.598
SRU (2 × 512)	4.110	4.128

4.2   Experimental Setup

This experiment mainly uses pytorch. The language model is trained on Wiki-Text provided by Salesforce Research using a two-layer RNN. RNN use basic RNN, GRU, LSTM and SRU. We also test the influence of different unit. Batch size is 256; learning rate is 0.01; the number of iterations is 2000; time step is 50. We uses ASGD as the optimization algorithm.

For the error correction model, we use Seq2Seq with attention. It is a two-layers bidirectional RNN for encoder. The embedded size is 64, and the hidden size is 256. For Decoder, it is a unidirectional RNN. The maximum time step is 50, and batch size is 128. The fusion network uses a single-layer fully connected neural network and "relu" activation function. Encoder and decoder share embedding layer parameters. The optimization algorithm uses RMSprop. First, we train the language model using unlabeled corpus. Then we use the annotation data to train the error correction model. Finally, the Deep Fusion Correction Model is trained after the fusion of the language model and the error correction model.

5   Results and Analysis

The results of the language model are shown in the Table 3. Experiments show that, as the number of hidden units increases, the Perplexity gradually decreases, and the SRU structure can also obtain ideal results.

Table 4. The results of correction models.

Model	Precision	Recall	F1
Baseline Seq2Seq Model (GRU Cell)	0.601	0.592	0.596
Baseline Seq2Seq Model (LSTM Cell)	0.620	0.614	0.616
Baseline Seq2Seq Model (SRU Cell)	0.611	0.609	0.609
Seq2Seq + Bi-directional (GRU Cell)	0.655	0.646	0.650
Seq2Seq + Bi-directional (LSTM Cell)	0.680	0.662	0.670
Seq2Seq + Bi-directional (SRU Cell)	0.673	0.670	0.671
Seq2Seq + Bi-directional + Attention (GRU Cell)	0.803	0.833	0.817
Seq2Seq + Bi-directional + Attention (LSTM Cell)	0.813	0.824	0.818
Seq2Seq + Bi-directional + Attention (SRU Cell)	0.809	0.830	0.819
Seq2Seq + Bi-directional + Attention + Language Model (GRU Cell, Our DFCM)	0.877	0.864	0.870
Seq2Seq + Bi-directional + Attention + Language Model (LSTM Cell, Our DFCM)	0.889	0.874	0.881
Seq2Seq + Bi-directional + Attention + Language Model (SRU Cell, Our DFCM)	0.881	0.880	0.880

From Table 4 shown above, Bi-directional RNN can use contextual knowledge to correct errors. Attention mechanism can improve the problem of long-distance dependence in the model. Finally, there can be further improvements through learning about untagged corpus.

Moreover, on two datasets, we compared our method with two commercial search engines and Hage's re-implementation of Lueck's approach [17], who achieved the best performance within the Microsoft Speller Challenge. The results are shown in Table 5. We can see that our method has a significant improvement, but it may be slightly lower than Search engine 1's results. This is because for some new words or named entities. These errors are difficult to correct them only through its context. It requires a lot of human-built named entity libraries or user data. Our approach can also be combined with user data for better performance.

Table 5. Results on different datasets.

	Precision	Recall	F1
Microsoft Corpus [25]			
Search engine 1	0.961	0.833	0.892
Search engine 2	0.928	0.810	0.865
Lueck	0.887	0.823	0.854
Our model	0.949	0.825	0.883
Hage Corpus [10]			
Search engine 1	0.905	0.903	0.904
Search engine 2	0.833	0.833	0.833
Lueck	0.812	0.863	0.836
Our model	0.881	0.880	0.880

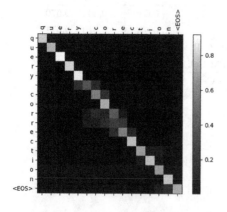

Fig. 3. The attention weights of model

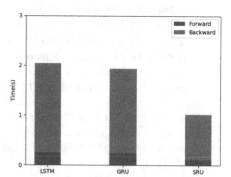

Fig. 4. The speed of different model

We can see that the performance of LSTM is largely better, but the training speed is slower. GRU is faster, but the performance is worse than LSTM. As for the SRU, it is as good as the LSTM through optimization. At the same time, it is much faster than LSTM. Speed is an important indicator for query error correction tasks. Through the Fig. 3 we can observe that the attention mechanism in most cases is based on the context of the input characters to determine the current character, but it also can capture the features of longer distances.

The Fig. 4 shows that SRU has obvious speed advantages over LSTM and GRU. So we are more inclined to use the SRU cycle unit for query error correction tasks.

6   Conclusion

In this paper, we proposed a fusion Seq2Seq model, which combines attention mechanism and a language model trained on unlabeled corpus for query error correction. It can effectively capture the long-distance features to improve error correction by attention mechanism. The performance of the error correction model is further improved by knowledge in unlabeled corpus. We can also improve the speed of the model through SRU and achieve the same performance of LSTM. Experiments show that we achieve good results in a real query corpus.

References

1. Bengio, Y., Ducharme, R., Vincent, P., Jauvin, C.: A neural probabilistic language model. J. Mach. Learn. Res. **3**(Feb), 1137–1155 (2003)
2. Brill, E., Moore, R.C.: An improved error model for noisy channel spelling correction. In: Proceedings of the 38th Annual Meeting on Association for Computational Linguistics, pp. 286–293. Association for Computational Linguistics (2000)
3. Chen, Q., Li, M., Zhou, M.: Improving query spelling correction using web search results. In: Proceedings of the 2007 Joint Conference on Empirical Methods in Natural Language Processing and Computational Natural Language Learning (EMNLP-CoNLL) (2007)
4. Cucerzan, S., Brill, E.: Spelling correction as an iterative process that exploits the collective knowledge of web users. In: Proceedings of the 2004 Conference on Empirical Methods in Natural Language Processing (2004)
5. Damerau, F.J.: A technique for computer detection and correction of spelling errors. Commun. ACM **7**(3), 171–176 (1964)
6. Duchi, J., Hazan, E., Singer, Y.: Adaptive subgradient methods for online learning and stochastic optimization. J. Mach. Learn. Res. **12**(Jul), 2121–2159 (2011)
7. Ganjisaffar, Y., et al.: qSpell: spelling correction of web search queries using ranking models and iterative correction. In: Spelling Alteration for Web Search Workshop, p. 15 (2011)
8. Gao, J., Li, X., Micol, D., Quirk, C., Sun, X.: A large scale ranker-based system for search query spelling correction. In: Proceedings of the 23rd International Conference on Computational Linguistics, pp. 358–366. Association for Computational Linguistics (2010)

9. Gulcehre, C., et al.: On using monolingual corpora in neural machine translation. arXiv preprint arXiv:1503.03535 (2015)

10. Hagen, M., Potthast, M., Gohsen, M., Rathgeber, A., Stein, B.: A large-scale query spelling correction corpus. In: Proceedings of the 40th International ACM SIGIR Conference on Research and Development in Information Retrieval, pp. 1261–1264. ACM (2017)

11. Hinton, G., Srivastava, N., Swersky, K.: Rmsprop: Divide the gradient by a running average of its recent magnitude. Neural Networks for Machine Learning, Coursera lecture 6e (2012)

12. Kernighan, M.D., Church, K.W., Gale, W.A.: A spelling correction program based on a noisy channel model. In: Proceedings of the 13th Conference on Computational Linguistics, vol. 2, pp. 205–210. Association for Computational Linguistics (1990)

13. Kingma, D.P., Ba, J.: Adam: a method for stochastic optimization. arXiv preprint arXiv:1412.6980 (2014)

14. Li, M., Zhang, Y., Zhu, M., Zhou, M.: Exploring distributional similarity based models for query spelling correction. In: Proceedings of the 21st International Conference on Computational Linguistics and the 44th Annual Meeting of the Association for Computational Linguistics, pp. 1025–1032. Association for Computational Linguistics (2006)

15. Li, Y., Duan, H., Zhai, C.: Cloudspeller: query spelling correction by using a Unified Hidden Markov model with web-scale resources. In: Proceedings of the 21st International Conference on World Wide Web, pp. 561–562. ACM (2012)

16. Li, Y., Duan, H., Zhai, C.: A generalized hidden Markov model with discriminative training for query spelling correction. In: Proceedings of the 35th international ACM SIGIR Conference on Research and Development in Information Retrieval, pp. 611–620. ACM (2012)

17. Luec, G.: A data-driven approach for correcting search quaries. In: Spelling Alteration for Web Search Workshop, p. 6 (2011)

18. Mandt, S., Hoffman, M.D., Blei, D.M.: Stochastic gradient descent as approximate Bayesian inference. arXiv preprint arXiv:1704.04289 (2017)

19. Mays, E., Damerau, F.J., Mercer, R.L.: Context based spelling correction. Inf. Process. Manag. **27**(5), 517–522 (1991)

20. Merity, S., Keskar, N.S., Socher, R.: Regularizing and optimizing LSTM language models. arXiv preprint arXiv:1708.02182 (2017)

21. Radlinski, F., Joachims, T.: Query chains: learning to rank from implicit feedback. In: Proceedings of the Eleventh ACM SIGKDD International Conference on Knowledge Discovery in Data Mining, pp. 239–248. ACM (2005)

22. Sriram, A., Jun, H., Satheesh, S., Coates, A.: Cold fusion: training Seq2Seq models together with language models. arXiv preprint arXiv:1708.06426 (2017)

23. Sun, X., Gao, J., Micol, D., Quirk, C.: Learning phrase-based spelling error models from clickthrough data. In: Proceedings of the 48th Annual Meeting of the Association for Computational Linguistics, pp. 266–274. Association for Computational Linguistics (2010)

24. Sutskever, I., Martens, J., Dahl, G., Hinton, G.: On the importance of initialization and momentum in deep learning. In: International Conference on Machine Learning, pp. 1139–1147 (2013)

25. Wang, K., Pedersen, J.: Review of MSR-Bing web scale speller challenge. In: Proceedings of the 34th International ACM SIGIR Conference on Research and Development in Information Retrieval, pp. 1339–1340. ACM (2011)

26. Whitelaw, C., Hutchinson, B., Chung, G.Y., Ellis, G.: Using the web for language independent spellchecking and autocorrection. In: Proceedings of the 2009 Conference on Empirical Methods in Natural Language Processing: Volume 2, vol. 2, pp. 890–899. Association for Computational Linguistics (2009)
27. Yang, Z., Dai, Z., Salakhutdinov, R., Cohen, W.W.: Breaking the softmax bottleneck: a high-rank RNN language model. arXiv preprint arXiv:1711.03953 (2017)
28. Zhang, Y., He, P., Xiang, W., Li, M.: Discriminative reranking for spelling correction. In: Proceedings of the 20th Pacific Asia Conference on Language, Information and Computation, pp. 64–71 (2006)

Automatic Text Summarization: A New Hybrid Model Based on Vector Space Modelling, Fuzzy Logic and Rhetorical Structure Analysis

Alaidine Ben Ayed[1,2(✉)], Ismaïl Biskri[2,3], and Jean-Guy Meunier[2,4]

[1] Department of Computer Science, Université de Québec à Montréal (UQAM),
Montreal, Canada
ben_ayed.alaidine@uqam.ca
[2] LANCI: Laboratoire d'Analyse Cognitive de l'information,
UQAM, Montreal, Canada
[3] Department of Mathematics and Computer Science, Université de Québec à
Trois-Rivières (UQTR), Trois-Rivières, Canada
[4] International Academy of Philosophy of Sciences, Brussels, Belgium

Abstract. In this paper, we present a new hybrid system for automatic text summarization. First, vector space modelling is used to compute two original metrics of coverage and fidelity. The latter metrics are combined onto a unified Fidelity-Coverage (F-C) score using fuzzy logic theory. Then, a rhetorical analysis is performed on top of sentences having the highest F-C scores in order to achieve coherence. Conducted experiments on the Timeline17 dataset show that the proposed system outperforms state of the art extractive summarization models. Also, generated abstracts generally satisfy the three criteria of a good summary, namely coverage, fidelity and coherence.

Keywords: Extractive summarization · Vector space modelling ·
Fuzzy logic · Rhetorical Structure Theory

1 Introduction

Big data is high-volume, high-velocity and/or high-variety information assets that demand innovative forms of information processing such as automatic text summarization (ATS). Indeed, ATS systems help us to efficiently process the ever-growing volume of textual information, which humans are simply incapable of handling. It creates a short, accurate, and fluent extract of a longer text document. In general, there are two broad approaches for automatic text summarization: by extraction [1,2] and abstraction [3]. The first one extracts salient sentences which contain the essence of the original text. In contrast, the latter

Supported by the Canadian Social Sciences and Humanities Research Council.

© Springer Nature Switzerland AG 2019
N. T. Nguyen et al. (Eds.): ICCCI 2019, LNAI 11684, pp. 26–34, 2019.
https://doi.org/10.1007/978-3-030-28374-2_3

one generates novel sentences by either rephrasing or using new words, instead of simply extracting the most salient sentences. Note that most of the summarization work done until today has focused on extractive summarization which is still a challenging research area. Sentence extraction depends on a bunch of statistical and/or linguistic indicators.

Extractive approaches generally compute a score that determines the importance of each sentence of the original text. Statistical models can be divided unto three broad sub-categories namely frequency, feature based and machine learning based approaches. Frequency based approaches assume that important words are more frequent than other words in a document. So, they use basic term frequency (word probability) [4,5] or inverse document frequency measures [6–8] to assign scores to each sentence of source document. Feature based approaches determine sentence relevance by the presence of different features such as the presence of title/headline Words, sentence position, sentence length, etc. [9]. Machine learning approaches learn from training data patterns of "summary sentence" and "non-summary sentence" [10–12]. On the other hand, linguistic models assume that the structure and coherence of a text can be modeled through rhetorical relations. Those models employ discourse analysis techniques that allow to establish a formal representation of the knowledge contained in the text [13,14]. Whatever the adopted approach (statistical or linguistic), automatically generated summaries should satisfy three criteria:

- Coverage: It is a measure of how much the generated summary reports the set of salient topics present in the original text.
- Fidelity: Does the summary accurately reflect the author's point of view?
- Coherence: To which extent, the generated extract is semantically meaningful?

Purely statistical models generally suffer from the absence of coherence while purely linguistic models do not guarantee coverage and fidelity. Previous models that tried to combine statistical and linguistic features did not give an idea on to which extent coverage, fidelity and coherence are met in the generated abstracts.

In this paper we present a new hybrid approach for automatic text summarization that satisfies the three criteria of a pertinent summary namely coverage, fidelity and coherence. The second section describes technical details of the proposed system. The third one describes conducted experiments and obtained results. Conclusion and future work are exposed in the fourth section.

2   HM-ATS: A New Hybrid Model for Automatic Text Summarization

2.1   System Overview

From a computational point of view, first, vector space modeling is used to propose two original metrics of coverage and fidelity. The latter ones are combined onto a unified Fidelity-Coverage (F-C) score using fuzzy logic theory. Afterwards, sentences having the highest F-C scores are extracted and are being subject to a rhetorical analysis in order to achieve coherence criterion (Fig. 1).

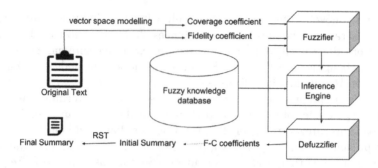

Fig. 1. Architecture of our new Hybrid Model for Automatic Text Summarization (HM-ATS).

2.2   Implementation Details

First, source text is segmented onto m sentences. Then a dictionary of all nouns is constructed and filtered in order to remove all generic nouns. Text is then represented by an $m \times z$ matrix, where m is the number of segments and z is the number of unique words. Then the conceptual space is being constructed. It will be used later on to compute two new metrics of coverage and fidelity.

Conceptual Space Construction. Each sentence S_i is represented by a column vector ζ_i. ζ_i is a vector of z components. Each component represents the *tf-idf* of a given word. Afterwards, mean concept vector τ is computed as follows:

$$\tau = \frac{1}{m}\sum_{i=1}^{m}\zeta_i \tag{1}$$

Note that each ζ_i should be normalized to get rid of redundant information. This is performed by subtracting the mean concept τ:

$$\Theta_i = \zeta_i - \tau \tag{2}$$

In the next step, the co-variance matrix is computed as follows:

$$C = \frac{1}{m}\sum_{n=1}^{m}\Theta_n\Theta_n^t = AA^t \tag{3}$$

Where $A = [\Theta_1, \ldots, \Theta_m]$. Note that C in (3) is a $z \times z$ matrix and A is a $z \times m$ matrix. Eigen concepts are the eigenvectors of the co-variance matrix. They are obtained by performing a singular value decomposition of A:

$$A = U.S.V^t \tag{4}$$

Where dimensions of matrix U, S and V are respectively $z \times z$, $z \times m$ and $m \times m$. Also, U and V are orthogonal ($UU^t = U^tU = Id_z$ and $VV^t = V^tV = Id_m$). In addition to that;

- Columns of V are eigenvectors of $A^t A$.
- Columns of U are eigenvectors AA^t.
- Squares of singular values s_k of S are eigenvalues λ_k of AA^t and $A^t A$.

Note that $m < z$. So eigenvalues λ_k of AA^t are equal to zero when $k > m$ and their associated eigenvectors are not necessary. So matrix U and S can be truncated, and, dimensions of U, S and V in (4) become respectively $z \times m$, $m \times m$ and $m \times m$. Next, conceptual space is being constructed by K eigenvectors associated to the highest K eigenvalues:

$$\Xi_K = [U_1, U_2, ..., U_K] \tag{5}$$

Each projected sentence onto the conceptual space is represented as a linear combination of K eigenconcepts:

$$\Theta_i^{proj} = \sum_k C_{\Theta_i}(k) U_k \tag{6}$$

where $C_{\Theta_i}(k) = U_k^t \Theta_i$ is a vector providing coordinates of the projected sentence in the conceptual space.

Computation of Coverage-Fidelity Scores. The goal here is to find out the closest sentences to each unitary vector of our conceptual space. Each vector ζ_i representing a given sentence S_i is normalized by subtracting the mean concept τ: $\Theta_q = \zeta_i - \tau$. Then it is projected onto our conceptual space:

$$\Theta_q^{proj} = \sum_k C_{\Theta_q}(k) U_k \tag{7}$$

Next, the distance between a given concept q and any projected sentence is defined and computed as follows:

$$d_i(\Theta_q^{proj}) = ||\Theta_q^{proj} - \Theta_i^{proj}|| \tag{8}$$

Then, Coverage-Fidelity matrix is constructed as follows: First, we fix a window length W. In the bellow example, W is set to 4. The first line corresponds to the most appropriate sentences expressing the first concept. The second line corresponds to the most appropriate sentences expressing the second concept. The first line encodes indexes of the best four sentences expressing the first most important concept. The second line encodes indexes of the best four sentences expressing the second most important concept. In each line, the order of a given sentence in a given window W depends on its distance to a given concept. For instance, the first sentence is the most appropriate sentence encoding the most important concept, the 8th sentence is the last one in a window of four sentences.

$$\text{Distance (weight)} \longrightarrow$$

$$\text{Weight of a given concept} \downarrow \begin{array}{c} 1 \\ 2 \\ 3 \\ 4 \\ 5 \end{array} \begin{pmatrix} 1 & 6 & 9 & 8 \\ 1 & 22 & 13 & 11 \\ 10 & 22 & 6 & 1 \\ 22 & 2 & 1 & 11 \\ 9 & 11 & 2 & 8 \end{pmatrix}$$

Next, the Coverage score to each sentence being projected in the conceptual space is defined as follows: it's equal to the number of times it occurs in a window of size W when taking in consideration the most important K concepts. The main intuition behind it, is that a given sentence having a height coverage sore should encode as much as possible the K most important concepts expressed in the original text.

$$C_{kw}(s) = \sum_{i=1}^{k} \alpha_i \tag{9}$$

$\alpha_i = 1$ if s occurs in the ith window. If not, it is equal to zero.

Also, the Fidelity score is defined as shown in the tenth equation. The main intuition behind it is that, a given sentence having a height fidelity score should encode the most important concepts expressed in the original text. In addition to that, it should have minimal distances $d_i(\Theta_q^{proj}) = ||\Theta_q^{proj} - \Theta_i^{proj}||$ (Eq. 8). In other words, the fidelity score encodes to which extent a given sentence s encodes a given concept. That 's why, it is weighted by its position in a given window of size W.

$$F_{kw}(s) = \sum_{i=1}^{k} \alpha_i [1 + \frac{1 - \psi_i}{w}] \tag{10}$$

$\alpha_i = 1$ if s occurs in the ith window. If not, it is equal to zero. ψ_i is the rank of s in the ith window.

Next, fuzzy logic is used to compute a unified score of coverage and fidelity (F-C score). The main idea behind that, is to extract sentences having the top F-C scores. In other words, we will identify the bet set of sentences satisfying the coverage and fidelity constraints. Then we apply a rhetorical analysis on this set of sentences in order to generate coherent abstract; this will be detailed in the next subsection.

In order to compute the F-C score for each sentence, we start by defining linguistic variables and terms. Linguistic variables are input and output variables in the form of simple words or sentences. For coverage and fidelity scores, low, medium and high are linguistic terms. Also, we define membership functions for linguistic terms as shown in Fig. 2.

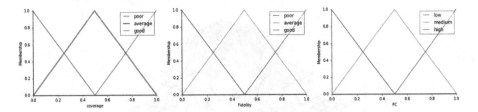

Fig. 2. Defining linguistic variables and membership functions.

Next, we build a set of rules into the knowledge base in the form of IF-THEN-ELSE structures:

- **Rule 1:** *If the coverage score is high or the fidelity score is high, then, the F-C score is high.*
- **Rule 2:** *If the fidelity score is medium, then, the F-C score is medium.*
- **Rule 3:** *If the coverage score is low and the fidelity score is also low, then, the F-C score is low.*

Next, we obtain fuzzy value of *F-C* sores. Indeed, fuzzy set operations perform evaluation of the previously defined rules. Here, the operations used for "OR" and "AND" are "Max" and "Min" respectively. Afterwards, we combine all results of evaluation to form a final fuzzy *F-C* score (Fig. 3).

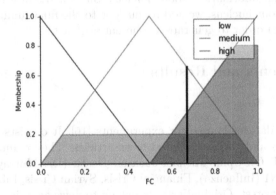

Fig. 3. Fuzzy *F-C* score.

Next, defuzzification is performed according to membership function for output variable as shown in Fig. 4. We extract sentences having the highest *F-C* scores and we apply a rhetorical analysis on top of them in order to generate a coherent abstract.

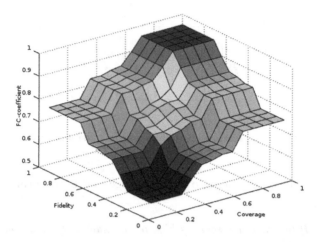

Fig. 4. Defuzzification and construction of a preliminary abstract by extraction of sentences having the highest *F-C* scores.

Rhetorical Analysis. In order to generate a coherent summary, we perform a rhetorical analysis of the original text. We use the Rhetorical Structure Theory (RST) to analyse rhetorical relations between text units. Note, here, that units of source texts are its sentences. RST [15] establishes two different types of units: nuclei and satellites, where Nuclei contains basic information and satellites contain additional information about nucleus. Since a satellite is often incomprehensible without nucleus, we add its nucleus to the final summary if it has a high *F-C* score in order to generate a coherent abstract.

3 Experiments and Results

3.1 Dataset

The Timeline17 dataset is used for experiments [16]. It consists of 17 manual-created timelines and their associated news articles. They mainly belong to 9 broad topics: BP Oil Spill, Michael Jackson Death (Dr. Murray Trial), Haiti Earthquake, H1N1 (Influenza), Financial Crisis, Syrian Crisis, Libyan War, Iraq War, Egyptian Protest. Original articles belong to news agencies, such as BBC, Guardian, CNN, Foxnews, NBCNews, etc. The contents of these news are in plain text file format and noise filtered.

3.2 Results and Discussion

In order to evaluate our proposed system for automatic text summarization, we compared it to three state of the art automatic summarizers [17–19]. We used the Recall-Oriented Understudy for Gisting Evaluation (ROUGE) metric. In Table 1, we report obtained ROUGE-1, ROUGE-2 and ROUGE-S metrics. Note that ROUGE-n (n = 1, 2) refers to the overlap of n-gram between generated and reference summaries. Also ROUGE-S refers to Skip-bigram based co-occurrence statistics, while Skip-bigram is any possible pair of words in their sentence (Here the order does not matter).

Table 1. Evaluation of the proposed system for automatic text summarization by comparing it to the Luhn, TextRank and LexRank approaches.

	ROUGE-1	ROUGE-2	ROUGE-S
Luhn	0.119	0.018	0.022
TextRank	0.206	0.042	0.047
LexRank	0.204	0.047	0.037
HM-ATS	0.241	0.061	0.058

Obtained results show that the proposed system outperforms summarizers proposed in [17–19]. Indeed, our model is able to project the text onto a lower dimensional space. The basis of this new space encodes most salient information expressed in the source document. By extracting sentences having the highest F-C scores, it guarantees that both coverage and fidelity criteria are met. Afterwords, it generates semantically coherent abstracts by adding nuclei units to the generated summaries if their associated satellites are strong candidates to be part of the final abstract.

4   Conclusion and Future Work

In this paper, we presented a new hybrid system for automatic text summarization (HM-ATS). First, vector space modelling was used to compute two new original metrics of coverage and fidelity. The latter ones were combined onto a unified Fidelity-Coverage F-C score using fuzzy logic theory. Afterwards, a rhetorical analysis was performed on top of sentences having the highest F-C scores in order to achieve coherence. Conducted experiments on the Timeline17 dataset shows that the proposed system outperforms state of the art extractive summarization models. Also, generated summaries generally satisfy the three criteria of a good summary, namely coverage, fidelity and coherence. Currently, we are applying a bunch of compression techniques [20] in order to re-phrase of the output sentences in a human-like fashion. Next, we will test our model on bigger size and multilingual corpora and we will compare its performance to more frameworks of automatic text summarization.

References

1. Mehdi A., et al.: Text summarization techniques: a brief survey. J. Comput. Lang. abs/1707.02268 (2017)
2. Andhale, N., Bewoor, L.A.: An overview of Text Summarization techniques. In: 2016 International Conference on Computing Communication Control and Automation (ICCUBEA), Pune 2016, pp. 1–7 (2016)

3. Yogan, J.K., Ong Sing, G., Halizah, B., Ngo, H.C., Puspalata, C.S.: A review on automatic text summarization approaches. J. Comput. Sci. **12**(4), 178–190 (2016)
4. Nenkova, A., Vanderwende, L., McKeown, K.: A compositional context sensitive multi-document summarizer: exploring the factors that influence summarization. In: the 29th Annual International ACM SIGIR Conference on Research and Development in Information Retrieval, Seattle, WA, USA 2006, pp. 573–580 (2006)
5. Nenkova, A., Vanderwende, L.: The impact of frequency on summarization. Microsoft Research (2005)
6. Filatova, E., Hatzivassiloglou, V.: A formal model for information selection in multi-sentence text extraction. In: The 20th International Conference on Computational Linguistics, 2004, pp. 397–403 (2004)
7. Fung, P., Ngai, G.: One story, one flow: hidden Markov story models for multilingual multidocument summarization. In: The ACM Transactions on Speech and Language Processing, 2006, pp. 1–16 (2006)
8. Galley, M.: A skip-chain conditional random field for ranking meeting utterances by importance. In: The Proceedings of the 2006 Conference on Empirical Methods in Natural Language Processing, (NLP 2006), pp. 364–372 (2006)
9. Gupta, V., Lehal, G.S.: A survey of text summarization extractive techniques. J. Emerg. Technol. Web Intell. **2**(3), 258–268 (2010)
10. Svore, K.M., Vanderwende, L., Burges, C.J.: Enhancing single-document summarization by combining RankNet and third-party sources. Microsoft Corporation (2007)
11. Burges, C., Shaked, T., Renshaw, E., Lazier, A., Deeds, M.: Learning to rank using gradient descent. In: Proceedings of the 22nd International Conference on Machine Learning, (CML 2005), ACM, pp. 89–96 (2005)
12. Hannah, M.E., Mukherjee, S.: A classification-based summarisation model for summarising text documents. Int. J. Inf. Commun. Technol. **6**, 292–308 (2014)
13. Barzilay, R., Elhadad, M.: Using lexical chains for text summarization. In: Mani, I., Maybury, M.T. (eds.) Advances in Automatic Text Summarization, pp. 111–121. The MIT Press, Cambridge (1999)
14. Kundi, F.M., Ahmad, S., Khan, A., Asghar, M.Z.: Detection and scoring of internet slangs for sentiment analysis using SentiWordNet. Life Sci. J. **11**, 66–72 (2014)
15. Mann, W.C., Thompson, S.A.: Rhetorical structure theory: toward a functional theory of text organization. Interdisc. J. Study Discourse **8**(3), 243–281 (1988)
16. Tran, G.B., Tran, T.A., Tran, N.K., Alrifai, M., Kanhabua, N.: Leverage learning to rank in an optimization framework for timeline summarization. In: TAIA workshop, SIGIR 2013 (2013)
17. Luhn, H.P.: The automatic creation of literature abstracts. IBM J. Res. Dev. **2**(2), 159–165 (1958)
18. Mihalcea, R., Tarau, P.: TextRank: bringing order into texts. In: Lin, D., Wu, D. (eds.) Proceedings of EMNLP 2004, Association for Computational Linguistics, Barcelona, Spain, Association for Computational Linguistics, Barcelona, Spain, pp. 404–411 (2004)
19. Erkan, G., Radev, D.R.: LexRank: graph-based lexical centrality as salience in text summarization. J. Artif. Intell. Res. **22**(5), 457–479 (2004)
20. Torres-Moreno, J.-M.: Automatic Text Summarization. Wiley, London (2014)

Frequent Itemsets as Descriptors
of Textual Records

Ayoub Bokhabrine, Ismaïl Biskri[(✉)], and Nadia Ghazzali

Université du Québec à Trois-Rivières, Trois-Rivières, Canada
{ayoub.bokhabrine,ismail.biskri,
nadia.ghazzali}@uqtr.ca

Abstract. The analysis of numerical data, whether structured, semi-structured, or raw, is of paramount importance in many sectors of economic, scientific, or simply social activity. the process of extraction of association rules is based on the lexical quality of the text and on the minimum support set by the user. In this paper, we propose to use frequent itemsets as descriptors and classifying them by using K-Medoids algorithm and Hierarchical cluster. We present how they can be identified and used to define a level of similarity between several segments. The experiments conducted demonstrate the potential of the proposed approach for defining similarity between segments.

Keywords: Clustering · Frequent itemsets · Descriptor · Segment · Text · K-Medoids · Ascending hierarchical cluster

1 Introduction

The digitization of documents facilitated the dissemination of information. As soon as an event occurs multiple articles are written and broadcast on different digital platforms. Several textual documents distributed on the web are composed of only a few hundred words. It is by consulting various documents that a rich description can be obtained. Different documents may address the same subject and each of these documents may contain additional information. However, the quantity of data available and their lack of structure limit our ability to capture this information, hence the need to use tools that facilitate access to information. Automatic classification is one of the strategies applied to the problem of organizing information. A classificatory process applied to textual documents, whether automated or not, organizes documents so that those who share similarities are clustered together. The resulting organization can be used to guide, for example, information retrieval, knowledge extraction, summary help, etc.

Several automatic classifiers have been published. Comparing these classifiers to determine their performance is a complex task and, above all, subjective. A classifier can perform with a particular set of data and generate noisy classes with another set. The relevance of a classification is assessed according to the homogeneity of the resulting classes. This criterion is however relative. The evaluation of a cluster is based on interveners' research objectives and their knowledge of the subject area. The quality sought for an automated classification system is to be able to target the relevant

© Springer Nature Switzerland AG 2019
N. T. Nguyen et al. (Eds.): ICCCI 2019, LNAI 11684, pp. 35–45, 2019.
https://doi.org/10.1007/978-3-030-28374-2_4

information within the targeted segments and determine how this information can be used to establish a level of similarity between these segments.

The numerical classification is based on the identification and evaluation of descriptors that differentiate one class from another. the choice of a descriptor instead of another is to take a position on the nature of the results generated. It influences the classifier's behavior because of the presence or absence of a descriptor is an index to target the class to which a document belongs.

For textual classification, the word is often used as a discriminating descriptor [11]. When several words appear at comparable frequencies in two segments then these segments are considered to be similar. However, it is common for segments to share a large number of words, even if these segments deal with different subjects. The mere presence of these words, therefore, is sparsely informative and its utility in establishing the level of similarity between segments is limited. Nevertheless, the relationship between these words and others can highlight specific peculiarities of certain segments. These relationships can be used to establish the level of similarity between segments.

2 Association Rules

Association rule mining is a technique to uncover the relationship between various items, elements, or various variables in a very large database [1]. It is also at a basic level, involves the use of machine learning models to analyze data for patterns, or co-occurrence, in a database. It identifies frequent if-then associations, which are called association rules. For example, customers who buy items X and Y also purchase item Z, in this case the association rule takes the following form: $(X, Y) \rightarrow Z$ Where the set (X, Y) is the antecedent, and Z: the consequent. Since then, the approach has been transposed to other domains, the association rules can be applied to various domains in that the concept of transaction can be defined.

Let T be a set of transactions such as: $T = \{t1, t2, t3..., tn\}$, the elements that make up the transactions $ti \in T$ are called items. An item is a datum whose nature depends on the area covered. For example, the items may correspond to descriptors extracted from a music [13], to descriptors extracted from an image [3] or simply to words extracted from a text [15]. Thus, a transaction can be defined simply as a subset of descriptors.

Let $I = \{i1, i2, i3, ..., id\}$ be a set of distinct d items, each subset that can be generated from items $ii \in T$ is called an itemsets. For a set I of size d, the number of possible itemsets is $2d$ [14]. The number of potential itemsets is exponential, depending on the size of I. The objective to be reached during the process of extracting association rules is to discover hidden relationships, there is no index to target the items to consider. Thus, the search space is equivalent to all possible itemsets. Although it is theoretically possible to create $2d$ itemsets from a set of size d, in practice several combinations appear little or just not in transactions. Therefore, these combinations can be ignored. The support is a measure that allows to target the itemsets to ignore. The support of an itemsets X represents the percentage of transactions of T that contain X. It is denoted S (X) and given by the Eq. (1.1) where n equals to the total number of transactions contained in T and $\sigma(X)$ to the support count. The support count of an itemsets X represents the number of transactions of T that contain X. It is given by the Eq. (1.2)

$$S(X) = \sigma(X)/n \tag{1.1}$$

$$\sigma(X) = |\{t_i | X \subseteq t_i, t_i \in T\}| \tag{1.2}$$

An itemsets X is considered frequent when its support is greater than or equal to a predetermined threshold. Let X and Y be two frequent itemsets such that $X \cap Y = \varnothing$, an association rule denoted $X \rightarrow Y$ expresses a co-occurrence relation between these itemsets. By convention, the first term is called the antecedent while the second is called the consequent. An association rule is considered quality according to a measure m and a previously fixed threshold. Thus, an association rule $X \rightarrow Y$ is judged of quality if $(X \rightarrow Y) \geq$ threshold.

The quantity of rules generated, their relevance and utility are highly dependent on the measures and minimum thresholds set. The evaluation of the interest measures of the association rules has been the subject of several studies [7, 9, 14]. Even if there are several variants, the extraction of association rules is usually done using the Appriori algorithm [2] or FP-Growth [8]. Other algorithms are presented in [6]. The two main difficulties in extracting association rules are memory management and the computational effort required to search for frequent itemsets. Controlling the number of items to consider is the best way to deal with these difficulties. For two decades, several studies have focused on the application of association rules for classification purposes [4, 10, 15]. The different classifiers that result from this work produce results that are able to compete with those obtained using other approaches such as decision trees [12].

Segments are considered as transactions while descriptors (Itemset, frequency of appearance of itemset, etc.). Let a set of descriptors Segments = {itemset 1, itemsets 2, itemset 3, ..., itemset l}, then a set of segments can be represented as follows:

$$Segment_1 = \{itemset_{10}, itemset_{21}, itemset_{16}, itemset_{20}, itemset_{18}\}$$
$$Segment_2 = \{itemset_{21}, itemset_{17}, itemset_{10}, itemset_{20}, itemset_{19}\}$$
$$Segment_3 = \{itemset_9, itemset_5, itemset_8, itemset_2, itemset_7\}$$

This segment set allows us to construct a binary matrix where the segments are considered as vectors and the itemsets as a descriptor, their intersection represents either the existence of the itemsets as described by 1 or in the opposite case it is considered 0.

The binary matrix is generated based on the results of the completion of the process of itemsets extraction, following that, the binary matrix is utilized as the input of the classifier. Thus, these classifiers attempt to encounter the similarity between segments and finally cluster them in separated classes.

3 Clustering Methods

Unsupervised classification or Clustering as a technique for discovering subgroups within observations is utilized broadly in applications like market segmentation wherein we attempt and discover some structure in the data. In our case we used unsupervised clustering method with textual data, our experimentation is based on two clustering methods the **Hierarchical method** and a variant of **K-means** named **K-medoids** clustering.

Dividing around Medoids, the K-medoids algorithm is a partitioning algorithm which is slightly changed from the K-means algorithm. They both try to limit the squared-error yet the K-medoids calculation is robust to noise than K-means calculation. In K-means calculation, they pick means as the centroids however in the K-medoids, data points are chosen to be the medoids. A medoid can be characterized as that object of a cluster, whose average dissimilarity to all the objects in the cluster is minimal. The distinction between K-means and K-medoids is similar to the contrast among mean and median: where mean shows the average value of all data items gathered, while median demonstrates the incentive around that which all data items are equally distributed around it. The fundamental thought of this algorithm is to initially process the K representative objects which are called as medoids [5]. After discovering the set of medoids, each object of the dataset is appointed to the nearest medoid. The Fig. 1 represent and explain the K-medoids algorithm.

Input: Dissimilarity matrix $D = \{d_{ij}\}_{m \times m}$, number of clusters k
Output: Partition $C = \{C_1, ..., C_K\}$.
1. Select the subset $k \subset \{1, ..., m\}$. Its elements are pointers to examples (prototypes)
2. **While (not** termination condition) **do**
3. Assign objects to cluster using the rule

$$C_i = \begin{cases} \arg\min d_{ij} \ if \ i \notin k \\ j \in k, \quad i = 1, ..., m \\ i \qquad otherwise \end{cases}$$

4. Update the examples, that is

$$j_r^* = \arg\min_{t: \, C_t = r} \sum_{t' : \, C_{t'} = r} d_{tt'} \ r = 1, ..., k$$

5. **End while**
6. If the index value remained unchanged after testing m objects – Stop. Otherwise return to step 2.

Fig. 1. Explanation of the K-medoids algorithm.

The Hierarchical clustering is an algorithm that cluster similar itemsets into classes. The endpoint is a set of clusters, where each cluster is distinguished from each other, and the objects within each cluster are extensively similar.

Hierarchical clustering commences by treating each itemsets as a discrete cluster. Then, it executes repeatedly the two stages: (1) recognize the two clusters that are closest together, and (2) consolidate the two most similar clusters. This lasts unless all the clusters are merged together. And the result is represented as a dendrogram graph.

4 Methodology

Our approach exploits frequent itemsets to describe documents. However, it does not require a training phase, nor a ready database as word embedding. Frequent itemsets is extracted from each of the segments and compared. The degree of similarity between two segments is a function of the number of frequent itemsets they share. The assumption behind this approach is when words co-occur frequently within sentences that make up a text, then these words are representative of that text. Thus, considering a few frequent itemsets, it is possible to identify the specific themes covered in the documents. The proposed approach has 5 steps:

- The first step is segmenting the documents to prepare them for the extraction of frequent itemsets. The documents are treated as sets of transactions where the sentences or subsections constitute the transactions, and the words are the items. The number of different words likely to appear in a set of textual documents is theoretically depending on the vocabulary size and the writing language of documents. The number of words that forms French is estimated more than 500 000 by the Quebec Office of the French Language. Considering this fact, it is possible to generate $2^{500\ 000}$ itemsets from 500 000 words, it is necessary to impose certain input text conditions to control the number of words. The diversity of a lexicon increasing with the size of a text, we must limit the input texts to a few thousand words.

- The second step is dedicated to the reduction of the number of items and therefore of the search space during the extraction of frequent itemsets. Some words deemed not very informative are removed from the transactions. A list of 502 stop words is used. Numbers and punctuation characters are also deleted. in addition, the lemmatization process is applied to unify the lexicon of the text, so the inflected forms of a word can be analyzed as a single item.

- The third step is to extract frequent itemsets. This step is performed using the Apriori algorithm. An effort is made to identify a small number of frequent itemsets. The search for frequent itemsets is done iteratively. During the first iteration, the minimum support is set to a high value. When the number of frequently itemsets is less than 10, then the minimum support is decreased by 0.1. The process stops when the number of items in the itemsets obtained is greater than a value specified by the user (e.g. number of items = 3) or the minimum support is less than 0.1.

- The fourth step is to establishes the degree of similarity between the segments. The frequent itemsets used to describe the segments are compared. The greater the number of itemsets shared by two segments, the most likely are judged similar.

- The last step consists of clustering the similarity matrix using both Hierarchical method and K-medoids clustering. The outputs of those clusters are plotted to visualize the quality of the clustering and assisting the user to analyze the results.

5   Experimentation and Discussion

In this section, we will be discussing two different experimentation writing in French language, the first experimentation is well adapted document that possesses few paragraphs, however, the second one simulates a real-world experimentation that covers a complex document.

In order to evaluate the proposed approach, we developed an application in C# capable to import documents, pre-processing them and extract itemsets using our above-mentioned methodology, then using RStudio for clustering and visualizing the results.

5.1   A Well-Adapted Experimentation

In this experimentation, we worked on a small document consists of 22 paragraphs and covered 3 various subjects where paragraphs {1 to 4} converse on sport particularly "the biography of Michael Jordan" while paragraphs {5 to 8} cover IT subject on "Microsoft company", and the last paragraphs {9 to 22} contain only music subject such as "Wolfgang Amadeus Mozart". Using this simple data as an input in our approach with their 3 different thematics that specific to each subject provides assistance in receiving the 3 expected clusters.

During our experiments, we pre-processed the document and extract the itemsets following the steps mentioned earlier in the methodology section. Thus, we measured the discriminating power of frequent itemsets. We compared the clustering produced when the descriptors are the frequent itemsets versus the clustering produced when the words are the descriptors.

Figure 2 illustrates the accuracy obtained by considering frequent itemsets using the K-medoid algorithm, herewith cluster 1 combines only the paragraphs {1 to 4} which covers sport, while cluster 2 combines the paragraphs {5 to 8} which is IT subject and the last cluster 3 combines the paragraphs {9 to 22} which is Music. These results are validated by the ascending hierarchical clustering (see Fig. 3). We acknowledge the utilization of frequent itemsets as descriptors can be used to describe more precisely the content of this document.

On the flip side Fig. 4 shows a heterogeneous clustering by considering only unique words as descriptors. We imply that various paragraphs {1, 4} "Sport" and {5, 6, 7 and 8} "IT" are combined in the same cluster 1 along with "Music". Almost the same results are confirmed by the ascending hierarchical clustering shown in Fig. 5. While using only unique words as descriptors, we notice that paragraphs dealing with subjects other than Sport are included into other paragraphs dealing with IT or Music. It should be noted when frequent itemsets are considered, the similarity classes generated converged into homogeneous clusters.

5.2   Real-World Experimentation

The purpose of this second experiment is to demonstrate the relevance of utilization of frequent itemsets as a descriptor of document, the experiment was performed on the book «La civilisation des Arabes» writing in French language. The document contains

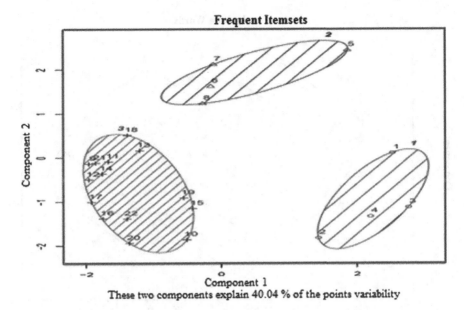

Fig. 2. K-Medoids clustering using Frequent Itemsets with K = 3.

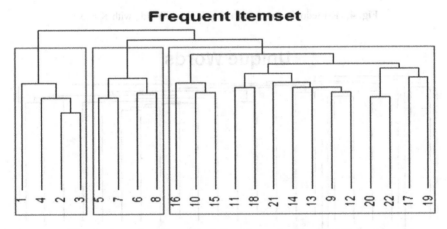

Fig. 3. Ascending hierarchical clustering using Frequent Itemsets.

6 chapters grouped into 4 parts: part 1 {chapter 1 and chapter 2} covers "L'arabie" and "Les arabes", part 2 {chapter 3} discuss "Les Arabes avant Mahomet", part 3 {chapter 4} narrate "Mahomet. Naissance de l'empire arabe", and finally part 4 {chapter 5 and chapter 6} talks about "Le Coran" and "Les conquêtes des Arabes". Using our above mention methodology, we pre-processed the document, and run various experimentations with different minimum support value ending up with satisfying result of 12% as a minimum support, the itemset extraction method gives us 43 itemsets.

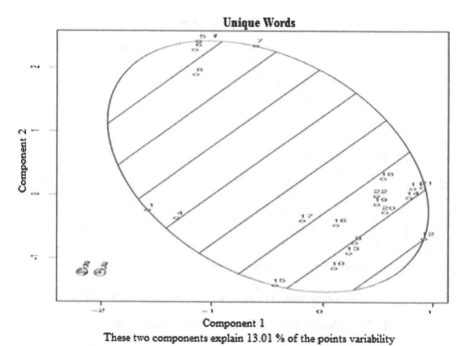

Fig. 4. K-Medoids clustering using Unique Words with K = 3.

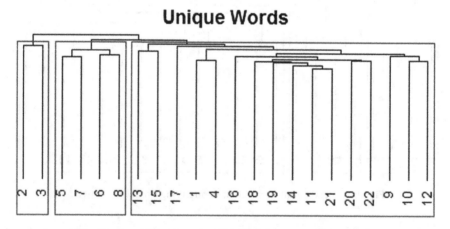

Fig. 5. Ascending hierarchical clustering using Unique Words.

The high similarity of thematic makes this document a complex experimentation, the discrimination of independent classes is not an easy process to define, even though our approach shows a huge capacity to determine homogeneous classes as shown in Fig. 6.

Frequent Itemsets

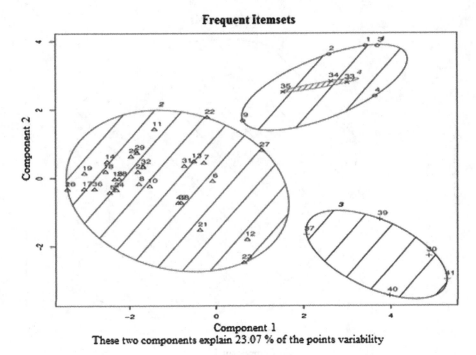

Component 1
These two components explain 23.07 % of the points variability

Fig. 6. K-Medoids clustering using Frequent Itemsets with K = 4.

Taking into consideration that our graphic representation is plotted in a two-dimension, actually the cluster 4 seems to be included into cluster 1, however, after checking our input data we figure out that segments of the cluster 4 are a specification of the big cluster 1 which both are treating the same subject just the cluster 1 is covering general topic and the cluster 4 more specified ideas in the same topic.

The Fig. 7 demonstrates the lack of clustering the data based on unique words as a descriptor, on the flip side proving the power of using frequent itemsets as a data descriptor for clustering.

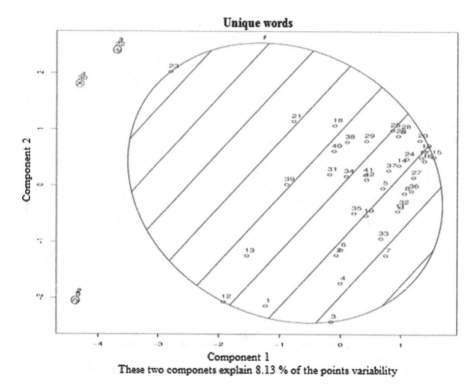

Fig. 7. K-Medoids clustering using Unique Words for relatively big document with K = 4.

6 Conclusion and Perspectives

We proposed an unsupervised approach to establishing relationships between textual records. The proposed methodology depends on the utilization of frequent itemsets. These descriptors express the co-occurrence of words within the sentences that make up a content. Frequent itemsets tend to be more discriminating than unique words. In this way, they can improve the description of a class. One of the upsides of the proposed strategy is that the outcomes delivered are easy to interpret. The experiments carried out suggest that frequent itemsets, as defined, are sufficiently informative to be used to establish coherent links between segments. Despite the good results obtained, we note that the choice of thresholds (minimum support) remains a critical and decisive step, for this, and in a perspective of improving our approach, we propose:

Develop a function using the R package «NbClust» for a dynamic choice and precise thresholds.

Utilize our extracted itemsets with various classification and/or clustering tools to figure out whether we get the same or better improvement.

• To generalize our prototype application in order to test our approach on different languages.

References

1. Agrawal, R., Imielinski T., Swami, A.: Minning association rules between sets of items in large databases. In: Proceedings of the SIGMOD Conference on Management of Data, pp 207–216 (1993)
2. Agrawal, R., Srikant, R.: Fast Algorithms for mining association rules. In: Proceedings of the 20th International Conference on Very Large Database, pp. 487–499 (1994)
3. Alghamdi, R.A., Taileb, M., Ameen, M.: A new multimodal fusion method based on association rules mining for image retrieval. In: 2014 17th IEEE Mediterranean Electrotechnical Conference (MELECON), pp. 493–499. IEEE (2014)
4. Bahri, E., Lallich, S.: Proposition d'une méthode de classification associative adaptative. 10eme journées Francophones d'Extraction et Gestion des Connaissances, EGC 2010, pp. 501–512 (2010)
5. Bin Tong, H.S., Suzuki, E.: A feature-free and parameter-light multi-task clustering framework. In: Knowledge and Information Systems, pp. 20, 17, 42 (2013)
6. Fournier-Viger, P., Lin, J.C.W., Vo, B., Chi, T.T., Zhang, J., Le, H.B.: A survey of itemsets mining. Data Mining and Knowledge Discovery, Wiley Interdisciplinary Reviews (2017)
7. Geng, L., Hamilton, H.J.: Interestingness measures for data mining: a survey. ACM Comput. Surv. (CSUR) 38(3), 9 (2006)
8. Han, J., Pei, J., Yin, Y.: Mining frequent patterns without candidate generation. In: ACM Sigmod Record, vol. 29, No. 2, pp. 1–12. ACM (2000)
9. Le Bras, Y., Meyer, P., Lenca, P., Lallich, S.: Mesure de la robustesse de règles d'association. QDC 2010 (2010)
10. Liu, B., Hsu, W., Ma, Y.: Integrating classification and association rule mining. In: Knowledge Discovery and Data Mining, pp. 80–86 (1998)
11. McCallum, A., Nigam, K.: A comparison of event models for naive bayes text classification. In: AAAI-98 Workshop on Learning for Text Categorization, vol. 752, pp. 41–48 (1998)
12. Mittal, K., Aggarwal, G., Mahajan, P.: A comparative study of association rule mining techniques and predictive mining approaches for association classification. Int. J. Adv. Res. Comput. Sci. 8(9), 365–372 (2017)
13. Rompré, L., Biskri, I., Meunier, J.-G.: Using association rules mining for retrieving genre-specific music files. In: Proceedings of FLAIRS 2017, pp. 706–711 (2017)
14. Tan, P.N., Kumar, V., Srivastava, J.: Selecting the right interestingness measure for association patterns. In: Proceedings of the Eighth ACM SIGKDD International Conference on Knowledge Discovery and Data Mining, pp. 32–41. ACM (2002)
15. Zaïane, O.R., Antonie, M.L.: Classifying text documents by associating terms with text categories. In: Australian Computer Science Communications, vol. 24, No. 2, pp. 215–222 (2002)

Contribution to a New Approach to Analyzing Arabic Words

Khaireddine Bacha(✉)

LaTICE Laboratory, University of Tunisia, Tunis, Tunisia
khairi.bacha@gmail.com

Abstract. The richness of the morphology of the Arabic language raises the problem of ambiguities at the different levels of Automatic Natural Language Processing. By addressing this problem at root level, which has not yet experienced a standard approach. In addition, the old techniques of rooting have limits that weaken the process of root extraction. In this paper, we propose a new approach to rooting based on two finite state automata.

Keywords: Stemming · The Arabic language ·
Automatic Natural Language Processing · State machine

1 Introduction

For that the computer has a day full access to texts, it must have a linguistic representation full of statements. One of the essential steps to achieve this result is the morphological analysis of the words and the identification of the grammatical category to which it belongs.

The patterns in the Arabic language, are a sort of template applied on a root to extract a derivative. They play a very important role in the process of the generation of the derived forms from a root [1, 2]. They are generally defined as a model that describes a group of words sharing certain linguistic properties. The combination of a small number of patterns with the whole of the roots would thus be sufficient to describe the majority of Arab words [3, 4]. This observation leads us to the possibility to generate, in an automatic way, almost all the Arab Lexicon on the basis of the whole of the roots and the whole patterns [5, 6].

The Arabic language has created a sense of challenge with several researchers, who have dedicated their work at its partial control, something which has given rise to the development of several approaches to its stemming. More specifically, three approaches coexist for several years now: the Manual Construction of dictionary [7], the slight stemming and morphological analysis [8, 9].

2 Context of the Work

In the context of the linguistic analysis of the Arab texts, in particular in the framework of the morphological analysis, the ancient techniques of stemming, including the slight stemming and morphological analysis have limits which weaken the process of extraction of roots.

© Springer Nature Switzerland AG 2019
N. T. Nguyen et al. (Eds.): ICCCI 2019, LNAI 11684, pp. 46–57, 2019.
https://doi.org/10.1007/978-3-030-28374-2_5

A new solution is proposed in this article. The results of these works within the framework of a morphological analyzer TELAMA "Towards Environmental Learning-Arabic-morphological Analyze" [10, 11]. This analyzer capable of a hand, to provide the different interpretations of each form analyzed. On the other hand, it will be used for the generation of educational activities for the teaching of the Arabic [12].

In the framework of this project, whose main purpose is to increase the relevance, and achieve a robust system, well structured and that takes account of the morphological characteristics of the Arabic language, an important place should be reserved to the problematic of the stemming.

3 Problem of TAL Arabic

The ambiguity is a central problem in the analysis morpho-syntactic of the Arabic. The analyzers are frequently confronted with situations of ambiguity at all levels of the analysis is at the level lexical, syntactic or semantic [13].

3.1 Model of the Word Graph in Arabic

The word graph in Arabic means a complex composition of objects. The basis of the word graph is called Minimum word, to which the addition of additional constituents considered an extension (Fig. 1). When it receives external elements, it then becomes a maximum word composed of: proclitique, Prefix, basis, suffix, enclitique [14, 15].

« Atatadhakkaronana» أتتذكّرُونَنَا	
This word expresses the phrase in French: "Is that you remember us? " The segmentation of this word gives the following constituents:	
« na» نَا │ « ona» ونَ │ « tadhakkar» تَذكّر │ « ta» تَ │ « A» أ	
Antefix :	أ interrogation conjunction
Prefix :	تَ verbal prefix of the time of the unfulfilled
Schematic body:	تَذكّر derived from the root: ذكّر according to the schema تفعّل
Suffix :	ونَ verbal suffix expressing the plural
Post Fixed :	نَا pronoun suffix noun complement

Fig. 1. Decomposition of the word graph in Arabic; "Atatadhakkaronana أتتذكّرُونَنَا" "is that you remember us ?".

3.2 Problems of Agglutination of Words

One of the major problems of Arabic comes from agglutination, because a word can mean a whole sentence. An agglutinative language in which the set of morphemes pasted together and constituting a lexical unit convey several morpho-syntactic information. Arabic shows a strong tendency to agglutination; Its analysis does not only require the verification of the membership of each word, that is to say that each graphical form can contain a concatenation of several segments which each form a lexical unit or a word. These lexical units are often translatable by the equivalent of a sentence in French. A word in Arabic can encapsulate the meaning of an entire sentence. In addressing this problem at the morphosyn-taxic level, the differentiation of the grammatical belonging of words is necessary [9].

Most Arabic verbs are composed of a root composed of three consonants, the derivatives and the bent forms of the verb being obtained by the application of certain schemes. Regular in the case of healthy verbs الأفعال الصحيحة, based on the representation "roots-schemes", and on the other hand, irregular in the case of non-healthy verbs الأفعال المعتلة and incomplete verbs الأفعال الناقصة [11].

The use patterns helps to reduce the effect sparse of the Arabic language. This implies that the level patterns can have a great potential in the construction of tools Tal for the Arabic.

4 The Work Around the Stemming

The racineurs se want first to a useful tool to the TAL, this type of analysis "simplistic", deals with the same way affixes flexionnels and dérivationnels [2]. The Algorithms stemming in Arabic The most well known are those of [17] and [20]. There has been a lot of interest for the use of patterns in the morphosyntactical analysis for the Arabic in particular for the stemming:

- The racineur of Shereen Khoja [17] is to detect the root of a lexical unit, on the one hand, it is necessary to know the pattern by which it has been derived and delete items which flexionnels were added, on the other hand compare the root extracted with a list of previously Roots designed.
- Aljlayl [18] proposes a system of using stemming the patterns and based on the algorithm of Khoja [60] for the recovery of the roots of words. The proposed algorithm begins by eliminating the suffixes, prefixes, infix a word given, then the process of extraction of the root begins by matching the positions of the letters of the word which correspond to the pattern.
- El-Beltagy [19] proposes an improved algorithm based on patterns which manages the broken plurals; this work proposes a set of rules for the detection of patterns of broken plurals and transformation to their singular forms.
- The racineur of larkey [18] is a morphological analysis relaxd. It is to try to detect the prefixes and suffixes added to the lexical unit.

They have dedicated their work at its partial control, something which has given rise to the development of several approaches to its stemming. More specifically, three approaches coexist for several years now:

- The Manual Construction of dictionary, it is impracticable for the corpus of realistic size.
- Stemming the slight is a process of abduction of prefixes and/or suffixes which generates a pseudo-root, without worrying about the infix or recognize the patterns to find the root [5].
- The morphological analysis is done on two stages. The first, is to apply a stemming lé-manages. In the second, we try to apply the correspondence between the pseudi-root, generated during the first step, and a pattern, in order to extract the root [17–20].

Previous approaches eliminate prefixes and suffixes, possibly added to words, by applying a light root, which sometimes leads to errors and ambiguities.

The problem is not so simple: in words that are not of Arab origin or that do not follow a schema (wazn): foreign words or specific words. In addition, all the algorithms realized have the same defect and also, they are impracticable. Also, some schemes can not go with certain roots. Finally, ancient rooting techniques, such as light rooting and morphological analysis, have limitations that weaken the process of root extraction. To do this, we propose another approach to rooting based on finite state automata.

5   Conversion Process to Schemes

The conversion process is carried out in two steps; First the identification of the preterminals, then the identification of the schemes.

5.1   Identification of Preterminals

Preprocessing is the step that precedes the root, it consists in making a series of modifications on the user request. Referring to previous work, the first conversion step consists in the recognition of preterminals, such as:

- Eliminate the existing punctuation in the sentence. In the case of the existence of the Chadda, the letter is doubled to the level of its location.
- Detect empty words before applying the algorithm, e.g. pronouns and prepositions, (هنا, أين, كيف, لكنكم, هاتان التي).
- Make a replacement of (آ, إ, أ) with 'ا',
- If the ي is present at the end of a word, replace it with ى,
- Also at the end of a word replaces ة by ه.

5.2   Identification of Schemes

After performing preprocessing on the graphics unit, we apply the finite state automation method. We apply our technique of rooting, the schemes are represented by automata with finite states, and the removal of the affixes is done automatically and without recourse to a predetermined list. We have designed two finite state automata (Figs. 1, 2) which represent almost all the schemes of the Arabic language.

The first represents all the verbal schemas (فاعل, فتعل, فععل, فعل), and the second one combines the most known no-minal schemas (فاعول, فاعل, فواعل, فعول, فعائل, فتعال فعل, فعوعل, فعائل, فعلال). The modification is performed on the one hand to reduce the error and ambiguity rate and on the other hand to deduce one or more possible roots from a single word.

- **Finite state automaton of verbal schemas**

The list of verbal schemas was constructed by the conjugation of the 13 basic verbal schemes with the 14 pronouns of the Arabic in 12 conjugation times. There are several tools on the Web to conjugate Arabic verbs such as the SARF system or the Arabic ACON conjugator [16]. To create our list of schemes, we opted for the software of conjugation of Arabic verbs. This choice was motivated by some advantages specific to this application, in particular the possibility of combining in 12 different times or the possibility of parameterizing some details of the conjugation, indicating for example the vowel of the character 'ع' to the present to differentiate the Verbs according to their types: 'فَعَلَ/يَفْعَلُ', 'فَعَلَ/يَفْعُلُ' or 'فَعَلَ/يَفْعِلُ'. Table 1 details the verbal schemes used, conjugation times and pronouns.

Table 1. Details of the generation of verbal schemas

The pronouns	The times	The verbal schemas	#
أنا	الماضي المعلوم	فَعَلَ يَفْعَلُ	1
نحن	المضارع المعلوم	فَعَلَ يَفْعُلُ	2
أنتَ	المضارع المجزوم	فَعَلَ يَفْعِلُ	3
أنتِ	المضارع المنصوب	فَاعَلَ	4
أنتما	المضارع المؤكد الثقيل	أَفْعَلَ	5
أنتما مؤ	الأمر	فَعَّلَ	6
أنتم	الأمر المؤكد	إنْفَعَلَ	7
أنتنّ	الماضي المجهول	تَفَعَّلَ	8
هو	المضارع المجهول	تَفَاعَلَ	9
هي	المضارع المجهول المجزوم	إسْتَفْعَلَ	10
هما	المضارع المجهول المنصوب	إفْعَلَّ	11
هما مؤ	المضارع المؤكد الثقيل المجهول	إفْعَالَّ	12
هم	-	إفْتَعَلَ	13
هن	-	-	14

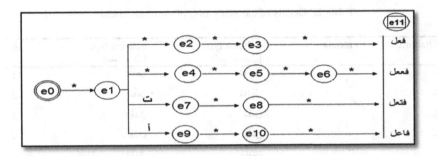

Fig. 2. Finite state automaton which represents the verbal schemas (فعل, فععل, فتعل, فاعل).

In the following, Fig. 2 shows the finite state automaton of verbal schemas (فتعل, فاعل فعل, فععل).

(e0): Initial state of the automaton, Input.

(e4): Intermediate state of the automaton.

(e11): End state of the automaton, Output.

* : Represents all possible alphabets of the Arabic language.

The finite state automaton for nominal schemes represents the set of nominal schemes most used in the Arabic language, taking into account that the nominal prefixes are recovered when the first letter is eliminated during the analysis.

- **Finite state automaton of nominal schemes**

The construction of the list of nominal schemes was also carried out in a semi-automatic manner. Table 2 details the generation of nominal schemes.

In the following, Fig. 3 shows the finite state automaton of nominal schemes (فعول فعال, فعلال, فاعال, فواعل, فعول, فعيل, فعال, فعائل, فتعال).

Note: The existence of the schema 'فعل' in both automaton does not cause problems when running the application because of the existence of the verification phase, with prefixes and suffixes nomi- And verbal reports (Fig. 4).

Table 2. Details of the generation of nominal schemes

Diacritics	Pronouns	Schema type : [اسم المفعول]	Schema type : [اسم الفاعل]	#
ـَ	أنا	مَفْعُول	فَاعِل	1
ـُ	أنتَ هو	مُفَاعَل	مُفْعِل	2
ـِ		مُفْعَل	فَعَّال	3
ـَ	هي	مُفَعَّل	فَعَّالة	4
ـُ	أنتِ	مُنْفَعَل	مِفْعَال	5
ـِ	نحن	مُتَفَعَّل	فِعِّيل	6
	أنتم	مُتَفَاعَل	مِفْعِيل	7
ة	هم	مُسْتَفْعَل	فُعَلَة	8
	هما أنتما	مُفْعَلّ	فَعِل	9
		مُفْعَالّ	مُفَعِّل	10
	هما أنتما	مُفْعَلَ	فَعِيل	11
			فَعُول	12
	أنتن هن			13

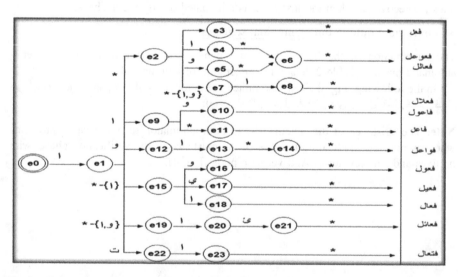

Fig. 3. Finite state automaton which represents the nominal schemes (فعوعل, فعالل, فعلال, فاعول,
فواعل, فعول, فعيل, فعال, فعائل, فتعال).

6 Evaluation

6.1 Description of the Learning Corpus

We work in parallel on the compilation of a corpus of assessment which will allow us to evaluate and compare at the same time our approach by the reports to the other. The corpus studied is composed of a set of journalistic articles published in the journal "The Diplomatic World" in its Arabic version [22]. This source has the advantage of being able to provide large quantities of texts of good quality the topics that are addressed are fairly general practitioners and treat the various themes of the news world political, economic, cultural, sports, etc. This corpus contains 1 009 articles, accumulating a total of 4 126 631 words graphs grouped under 322 156 different forms. The use of a wide variety of themes and areas covered has for objective to have a wide coverage of the words in the language [23, 24]. We used a corpus containing 7 Arab texts in UTF-8 format collected.

6.2 Comparison: Our Approach vs. The Ancient Techniques of Stemming

The evaluation of our new approach, is a crucial step. It allows you to highlight its strengths and its limits, in order to find the tracks for a possible improvement. To obtain a comparative assessment specifies of our approach, we have chosen the texts of different sizes by comparing them with three approaches coexist for several years now: the Manual Construction of dictionary, the slight stemming and morphological analysis.

In what follows, we present the results of the evaluation carried out (Table 3).

Table 3. Comparison: Our approach vs. the ancient techniques of stemming

Text	Number of words	Approaches	Number of words (Root extracted)	Number of words (Root not extracted)	Precision
Text 1	122	MDC	110	12	90.16%
		LR	115	07	94.26%
		MA	121	01	99.18%
		FSA	121	01	99.18%
Text 2	182	MDC	166	16	91.20%
		LR	171	11	93.95%
		MA	177	05	97.25%
		FSA	180	02	98.90%
Text 3	237	MDC	219	18	92.40%
		LR	223	14	94.09%
		MA	229	08	96.62%
		FSA	233	04	98.31%

(continued)

Table 3. (*continued*)

Text	Number of words	Approaches	Number of words (Root extracted)	Number of words (Root not extracted)	Precision
Text 4	251	MDC	209	42	83.26%
		LR	221	30	88.04%
		MA	239	12	95.21%
		FSA	245	06	97.60%
Text 5	302	MDC	251	51	83.11%
		LR	265	37	87.74%
		MA	269	33	89.07%
		FSA	292	10	96.68%
Text 6	393	MDC	331	62	84.22%
		LR	336	57	85.49%
		MA	357	36	90.83%
		FSA	380	13	96.96%
Text 7	454	MDC	361	93	79.51%
		LR	371	83	81.71%
		MA	406	48	89.42%
		FSA	435	19	95.81%

Note:

MDC: Manual dictionary construction:
LR: Light root
MA: Morphological analysis
FSA: Finite state automaton

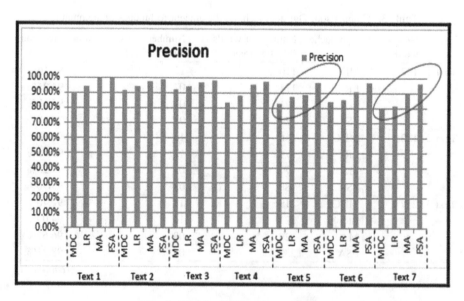

Fig. 4. Result of different approaches

The following diagram represents the variation in the number of texts (different) for the different sizes of the corpus. This allows us to have an overall view on our corpus, see its evolution by report to the technical different stemming.

Complexity of this language, in particular in the absence of vowels, the results obtained after the analysis are not exactly valid, as evidenced by the following two examples:

- When a word can be derived from several different roots, the detection of the root is even more difficult, in particular in the absence of vowels.

For example, to the Arabic word إيمان les Possible prefixes are: "∅", "ا" and "ايا" and Possible suffixes are: "∅" and "ان" without count that word may also represent a name own إيمان. The Table 4, describes the possible radicals for the word إيمان.

Table 4. Possible radicals for the إيمانmot

Stem	Prefix	Pattern	Suffix	Root	Meaning
إيمان	∅		∅	امن	Belief
يمان	ا		∅	يمن	Suitable
مان	أي		∅	مان	Will it supply
ايم	∅		∅	ايم	Two widows

- Our Stemming Algorithm is one of the algorithms which encounter problems when it comes to words containing one or several letters low (و ي ا).
- For example, for the word "أَذْهَبَ", during the execution of the application, one obtains two results: The first is the root "أذه" with the absence of the Prefix, and 'ب' as suffix, and as second results-Tat, the root "ذهب" with 'ا' as a prefix and the absence of the suffix.

Words derived:

"أَذْهَبَ"

The roots: " أذه "   "ذهب"

The primary outcome is a set of possible roots, it can extract of the unit graph. We take the example of the interrogative unit "أذهب" which has two possible roots "ذهب" and "أذه" This ambiguity makes the application low and decreases its performance (see Fig. 5).

The results of the evaluation show a gain of our approach compared to other ancient techniques of stemming. After the display of these experiments, we see that these results are closer and represent a good starting point for future research to improve our new approach to stemming of the Arabic language.

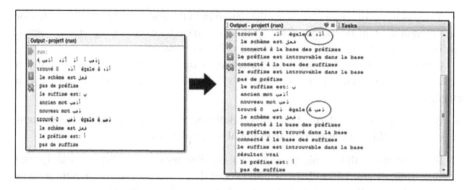

Fig. 5. Execution of the word "أذهب"

7 Conclusion and Prospects

We have tried, through this article, to present our new technique stemming of the Arabic language which is based on the finite state automata in the process of extraction of roots, in the aim to minimize the error rate and ambiguity, generally due to the removal of the affixes.

We can not without doubt say that our work is complete, where several improvements can be made. But, we hope at least that we have managed to propose a new approach for the extraction of roots based on the based on state automata, in order to minimize the error rate and of ambiguity by reports to the ancient techniques of stemming.

As perspective of this work, improvements can be made on resources carried out by increasing the size of the dictionary to cover to the maximum the Arabic language. We are currently focusing on the development and improvement of our technique stemming while trying to overcome the various problems encountered.

References

1. Rushin, S., Dhillon, S.P., Liberman, M., Foster, D.P., Maamouri, M., Ungar, L.H.: A new approach to lexical disambiguation of Arabic text. In: EMNLP 2013, pp. 725–735 (2013)
2. Attia, M.A.: Developing a robust Arabic morphological transducer using finite state technology. In: 8th Annual CLUK Research Colloquium. Manchester, UK (2015)
3. Ben Mohamed, M.: Thèse: Intégration des techniques de TAL dans l'apprentissage assisté par ordinateur pour l'enseignement de la langue arabe Sfax (2016)
4. Chen, A., Gey, F.: Building an Arabic Stemmer for Information Retrieval (2002)
5. Bacha, K., Zrigui, M.: Designing a model of Arabic derivation, for use in computer assisted teaching. In: International Conference on Knowledge Engineering and Ontology Development. KEOD, Barcelone, Espagne (2012)
6. Al-Kharashi, I., Evens, M.: Comparing words, stems, and roots as index terms in an Arabic information retrieval system (1994)

7. Bacha, K.: Machine translation system on the pair of Arabic/English. In: International Conference on Knowledge Engineering and Ontology Development. KEOD, Barcelone, Espagne (2012)
8. Beesley, K.R.: Arabic finite-state morphological analysis and generation. In COLING-96 (1996)
9. Bacha, K.: Morphological analysis in the enviroment "TELA". Procedia Comput. Sci. **62**, 191–215 (2015)
10. Bacha, K., Anis, Z.: TELA: towards environmental learning Arabic. In: The International Conference on Artificial Intelligence (ICAI 2011). WORLDCOMP 2011, Las Vegas, Nevada, USA, 6 pages (2011). http://cerc.wvu.edu/download/WORLDCOMP%2711/2011%20CD%20papers/EEE4685.pdf
11. Bacha, K., Jemni, M.: Towards a learning system based on Arabic NLP tools. Int. J. Inf. Retrieval Res. (IJIRR) **6**(4), 15 (2016)
12. Bacha, K.: Morphological analysis in the enviroment "TELA". Procedia Comput. Sci. **62**, 191–215 (2015)
13. Dichy, J.: Morphosyntactic specifiers to be associated to Arabic lexical entries - methodological and theoretical aspects. In: Proceedings of the ACIDA 2000 Conference, Monastir (Tunisia), Corpora and Natural Language Processing, pp. 55–60, 22–24 March 2000
14. Dichy, J.: On lemmatization in Arabic, a formal definition of the Arabic entries of multilingual lexical databases. In: Proceedings of the Workshop on Arabic Language Processing: Status and Prospects, Association for Computational Linguistics, 39th Annual Meeting and 10th Conference of the European Chapter, Toulouse, pp. 23–30, 6 July 2001
15. Dichy, J.: Sens des schèmes et sens des racines en arabe: le principe de figement lexical (PFL) et ses effets sur le vocabulaire d'une langue sémitique. In: Rémi-Giraud, S., Panier, L. (éd.) La polysémie ou l'empire des sens. Lexique, discours,représentations, Lyon: PUL (coll. Linguistique et sémiologie), pp. 189–211 (2003)
16. Khoja, S., Garside, R.: Stemming Arabic text. Computing Department. Lancaster University, Lancaster (1999)
17. Darwish, K., Doermann, D., Jones, R., Oard, D., Rautiainen, M.: TREC-10 experiments at Maryland: CLIR and video. In: TREC 2001. NIST, Gaithersburg (2001)
18. Larkey, L., Ballesteros, L., Margaret, E.: CONNELL, Light stemming for Arabic information retrieval
19. Larkey, L.S., Ballesteros, L., Connell, M.: Improving Stemming for Arabic Information Retrieval: Light Stemming and Cooccurrence Analysis (2002)
20. Bacha, K.: Design of a synthesizer and a semantic analyzer's multi Arabic, for use in computer assisted teaching. Int. J. Inf. Sci. Appl. (IJISA) **2**(1), 11–33 (2012)
21. Bacha, K.: Towards a model of statistical machine translation Arabic-French. In: International Conference on Advanced Learning Technologies and Education. ICALTE, Hammamet, Tunisia (2014)
22. Bacha, K.: Design and implementation of a model of segmentation environmental computer assisted learning "TELA". ICAI'Sousse, Tunisia (2014)
23. Bacha, K., Acheref, M.: Designing a model combination of Arabic, for use in computer assisted teaching. In: World Congress on Computer Applications and Information Systems, pp. 1–7 (2014)
24. Bacha, K.: Contribution to the achievement of a spellchecker for Arabic. In: 17th International Conference on Intelligent Text Processing and Computational Linguistics (CICLing), Konya, Turkey (2016)

Named Entity Extraction from Semi-structured Data Using Machine Learning Algorithms

Madina Mansurova[1]([⊠]) [iD], Vladimir Barakhnin[2,3],
Yerzhan Khibatkhanuly[1], and Ilya Pastushkov[2,3]

[1] Al-Farabi Kazakh National University, Almaty 050040, Kazakhstan
mansurova.madina@gmail.com, x.erzhan@gmail.com
[2] Institute of Computational Technologies SB RAS,
Novosibirsk, Russian Federation
[3] Novosibirsk State University, Novosibirsk, Russian Federation
bar@ict.nsc.ru, pas2shkov.ilya@gmail.com

Abstract. The modern society have been witnessed that intensive development of Internet technologies had followed to information explosion during last decades. This explosion had been expressing by an exponential growth of data volume among the low-quality information. This paper is designed to provide detailed information about some intellectual tools which are support decision taking by automatic knowledge extraction. In the first part of paper, we considered a preprocessing contains morphological analysis of texts. Then we had considered the model of text documents in the form of a hypergraph and implementation of the random walk method to extract semantically close word's pairs, in other words, pairs that often appears together. Result of calculations is matrix with word affinity coefficients corresponding to each other component of vocabulary vector. In the second part we describe training of neural network for linguistic constructions extraction. These ones include possible values of text named entities descriptors. The neural network enables to retrieve information on one preselected descriptor, for example, location, in the form of the final result of the name of geographical objects. In a general case, the neural network can retrieve information on several descriptors simultaneously.

Keywords: Entity extraction · Semi-structured data ·
Machine learning algorithms · Random walk method · Neural networks

1 Introduction

At the present, a great amount of data is being accumulated in local and global networks. Major part of this information is represented by natural language texts. Such texts are not structured, and, consequently, useful information can't be extracted and analyzed by conventional computing methods and tools. With rapidly increasing information amount, human text reading and simple substring search in large arrays of text data are obviously ineffective. The approaches for search performing on unstructured text arrays and extracting knowledge from it are becoming more and more demandable. A scientific direction of computer linguistics deals with solutions of such tasks [1].

© Springer Nature Switzerland AG 2019
N. T. Nguyen et al. (Eds.): ICCCI 2019, LNAI 11684, pp. 58–69, 2019.
https://doi.org/10.1007/978-3-030-28374-2_6

Computer linguistics include automatic extraction of structured data from non-structured or semi-structured data. Information extraction systems enable to collect data from separate parts of text and represent relevant information in form of selected relationships, knowledge bases and etc. With these systems one can put information in a semantically accurate form which grant further conclusions by using corresponding algorithms.

One of an information retrieval important branches is a named entity recognition. It means the search for named entities and their classification into predetermined categories, such as people's or organization's names, location, time value, and etc.

Solution of this subtask provide either determination the tonality of references to some company or product, or building relations between named entities, or accepting requests and answering it in natural language.

This work is a continued research of fact extraction from text documents [2]. The aim of this work is development of named entities extraction technology for news reports. To achieve this goal the following tasks were set up:

1. Carrying out a morphological analysis of texts.
2. Modeling of texts in the form of a hypergraph and the use of the random walk method for extraction of semantically closed words.
3. Creation of a neural network trained for finding the correspondence of concrete key words to descriptors.

2   Review of the Existing Methods for Information Extraction

Information extraction is not a new task in the field of a natural language processing. The main methods of information extraction are classified as follows:

Feature-based extraction methods. These methods are explained by the presence of a fixed set of features and the use of weights of features of the text elements being extracted. Thus, an extracted element, a vector of its features is built up. The most common in this class are Bayes probability classifiers [3] and hidden Markov models [4–6]. Extraction of an element comes to recognition of a certain text segment detected in its vicinity. Within the framework of this research, the method of extracting facts under study refers to this class. The peculiarity of the described in this work algorithm is the use of the random walk method for extraction of key words as well as the use of a neural network for placing facts on descriptors.

Kernel extraction methods. The essence of the method is in replacing the scalar product of vectors reflecting a characteristic representation of recognized elements with some function called the kernel [7]. This function is determined algorithmically and considers a more complex representation of recognized elements and their contexts describing the text segment structure. The disadvantage of this method is in the complexity of computing when calculating kernels as well as determination of the segment structure.

Sample matching methods. They use the samples and the rules of their comparison with the text fragments [8, 9]. The samples are meant to be a chain of limiters, where a chain is kind of pattern phases. This method is similar to the kernel method.

Ontology-based methods. In [10, 11] information is extracted using a semantic web based on ontology. The authors propose an algorithm developed on the ontological base of knowledge and carry out a frequency analysis for the results of text parsing of syntactical triples StanfordNLP [12].

Named entity recognition can be resolved by following methods:

Rule-Based Methods. The work of this method is as follows. Each token in the text is drawn into a feature set. Typical features are information about whether a token begins with a capital letter, punctuation, whether a token is a heading, organization or geographical location, to which part of speech it refers. Then a set of rules is extracted from the data in the following form: Contextual template → Action. A contextual pattern is a combination of conditions with respect to the features of a sequence of tokens. If the sequence of tokens satisfies the pattern, then this sequence is marked in accordance with the "Action" as a named entity. This method is used in specified works [13–15].

Hidden Markov Models. In this method, transition is used through a sequence of hidden states, and each state produces a token. All states are dependent on each other. Each transition from one state to another generates a data type, which can be a simple symbol or a multidimensional combination of features. Hidden Markov models were used to retrieve named entities in these works [16, 17].

Maximum Entropy Markov Models. In contrast to hidden Markov models, Markov models of maximum entropy directly form the likelihood of marking, based on states [18]. The advantage of this method is the ability to use a large set of considered features [19].

Conditional Random Fields. This method is closely related to Markov models of maximum entropy [20]. However, the restriction present in the previous method, where the probability of a certain label depends only on previous labels, has been removed. Conditional random fields take into account not only previous, but subsequent labels. Since a large range of considered tags affects the cost of training the model, it is possible to use a simplified version, considering only one adjacent label on each side. The use of this method can be found in the indicated works [21, 22].

3   The Approach to the Task of Information Extraction

To extract information, in the first stage it is necessary to extract a set of semantically (lose key) words. In this work semantically close ords (word combinations) are extracted on the basis of morphological analysis of texts and the random walk method.

3.1   Text Lemmatization

Text lemmatization consists of determination of the word form and assigning token characteristics and grammar descriptions to each form of the word.

Morphological information created for each word in the text consist of four "lines" or groups of markup:

1. The word form of a lexeme (shows a "dictionary entity" of a lexeme and determines the part of speech to which it refers).
2. A set of grammar features of a lexeme or characteristics of a word classifier.
3. A set of grammar features of a word form or word-transforming characteristics (for example, case of the noun, aspect of the verb, that is singular or plural).
4. Information about non-standard grammatical form, spelling distortion.

3.2 Random Walk Method

Let a text consisting of n documents be given:

$$D = (d_1, d_2, \cdots d_n) \tag{1}$$

In this work, we will consider separate sentences as a document. Let us introduce the following notation for a text vocabulary:

$$W = (w_1, w_2, \ldots w_n) \tag{2}$$

Simulation of the text being analyzed in the form of a hypergraph is one of the convenient and frequently used methods. Let us represent the text being analyzed in the form of a hypergraph HG(V, E), where V is a set of vertices and E is a set of hyper ribs. Here, $\bigcup_{e \in E} e = V$. In the hypergraph, vertices $v \in V$ are words of the text and hyper ribs $e \in E$ are documents of the text.

Using $HG = R^{|V| * |E|}$ we will denote the hypergraph adjacency matrix:

$$h(v, e) = \begin{cases} 1, & \text{if } v \in E \\ 0, & \text{if } v \notin E \end{cases} \tag{3}$$

Let HG(V, E, w) be a weighted hypergraph, where $w : E \to R^+$ is the hypergraph weight.

In our case, the degree of the hypergraph vertex and that of the hyper rib are determined by the following expressions:

$$d(v) = \sum_{e \in E} w(e) h(v, e) \tag{4}$$

$$\delta(e) = \sum_{v \in V} h(v, e) = e \tag{5}$$

In the task under consideration, the weight of the graph vertices, in other words – the weight of the text words, can be calculated according to the following formula based on TF-IDF method:

$$w(v_i)_{tf-idf} = \frac{tf(v_i)}{N_w} * \log \frac{N}{df(v_i)} \tag{6}$$

Where:

- tf(v_i) is the frequency of word occurrence in a document;
- N_w – the sum of all words composing the document;
- N – the number of documents in the collection of documents D;
- df(v_i) – a set of documents in D in which the words v_i occur.

Random walk is a mathematical model of the process of random changes – steps at discrete moments of time. It is supposed that the change at each step does not depend on previous steps and on time. By virtue of the analysis simplicity this model is often used on different fields. Also, this model a significant simplification of a real process. One-dimensional discrete random walk is a random process with discrete time $\{Y_n\}_{n \geq 0}$ having the form:

$$Y_n = Y_0 + \sum_{i=1}^{n} X_i \tag{7}$$

Where:

- Y_0 is the initial state;
- $X_i = \begin{cases} 1, p_i \\ -1, q_i = 1 - p_i \end{cases}, 0 < p_i < 1, i \in N$
- Y_0, X_i, i = 1, 2.. are independent random values.

One-dimensional discrete random walk is a Markov chain with whole states. Its initial distribution is given by the random value probability function X_0 and the matrix of transition probabilities has the form:

$$P = \left(p_{ij}\right)_{i,j \in Z} = \begin{pmatrix} \ddots & \ddots & \ddots \\ q_{-1} & 0 & p_{-1} \\ & q_0 & 0 & p_0 \\ & & q_1 & 0 & p_1 \\ & & & \ddots & \ddots & \ddots \end{pmatrix} \tag{8}$$

That is:

$p_{i,i+1} \equiv P(X_{n+1} = i+1 | X_n = i) = p_i,$
$p_{i,i-1} \equiv P(X_{n+1} = i-1 | X_n = i) = q_i, i \in Z,$
$p_{i,j} \equiv P(X_{n+1} = j | X_n = i) = 0, |i-j| \neq 1.$

The sequence of discrete random values $\{X_n\}_{n \geq 0}$ is called a simple Markov chain (with discrete time), if:

$$P(X_{n+1} = i_{n+1} | X_n = i_n, X_{n-1} = i_{n-1}, \ldots, X_0 = i_0) = P(X_{n+1} = i_{n+1} | X_n = i_n)$$

Thus, in the simplest case, conditional distribution of the subsequent Markov chain state depends only on the current state and does not depend on all previous states.

The range of values of random variables $\{X_n\}$ is called the space of chain states and number n is called the step number.

P(n) is called a probability matrix of transitions at n^{th} step:

$$p_{ij}(n) = P(X_{n+1} = j | X_n = i) \tag{9}$$

Vector $p = (p_1, p_2, \ldots p_n)^T$, where $p_i = P(X_0 = i)$ is Markov chain initial distribution. It is obvious that the probability matrix of transitions is stochastic, that is:

$$\sum_j P_{ij}(n) = 1, \forall n \in N \tag{10}$$

Markov chain is called homogeneous if the probability matrix of transitions does not depend on the step number, that is

$$P_{ij}(n) = P_{ij}, \forall n \in N \tag{11}$$

To range the hypergraph vertices, we will generalize the random walk process to a hypergraph. Transitions between vertices in a graph take place in the process of random walk, that is transition from the given vertex to a neighboring vertex via every step of discrete time t. We can consider vertices as a set of states $\{s_1, s_2, \ldots s_n\}$ and transitions – as a final Markov chain in these states. The transition probability is computed in the form $P(u, v) = Prob(s_{t+1} = v | s_t = u)$. This means that Markov chain at vertex v will be in time t + 1 and u – in time t. in our case, Markov chain is homogeneous, the probability of transition does not depend on time t. for each vertex $\sum_v P(u, v) = 1$.

M is homogeneous, with possibilities calculated for a single transition. For all steps, the transition matrix can be computed $P \in \mathbb{R}^{|V| \times |V|}$. Transition matrix P completely embraces transitions between vertices, which show the change of a surfing movement in a random order between vertices with such probability.

In a single graph, a random walk process is clear, it is only necessary to choose a rib ascending to the target vertex with a certain probability. Nevertheless, the hypergraph in this situation somewhat differs according to structure difference. For example, in a hypergraph there may be more than two points of the vertex for a hyper rib $\delta(e) \geq 2$.

To generalize the random walk process to a hypergraph, we model a transition between two vertices incident in regard to each other in a hyper rib in the form of walk. As a whole, the random walk process is not a one-step process but a two-step one: firstly, a random surfer chooses a hyper rib e incident to the current vertex u. Secondly, in the chosen hypergraph, the surfer chooses a target v satisfying the condition $u, v \in e$.

Random walk in a hypergraph is called generalization with a special case for random walk in a usual graph. This is the presence of only one vertex in a rib, and in a hypergraph we can choose from a set of vertices. If we determine the random walk process in a hypergraph with the help of Markov chain, here a set of vertices will make up a set of states. With every time step t the surfer changes the place on the incident hyper rib for another vertex.

Let us give a general definition of random walks in the measured hypergraph taking into account the weight of vertices with hyper ribs. In this case, the random walk process will be widened using the weight of vertices and hyper ribs. The weight of vertices is determined with the help of all incident hyper ribs, this is a vector of peculiarities:

$$\vec{v}_w = \{\omega(v_{e1}), \omega(v_{e2}), \ldots \omega(v_{d(v)})\} \tag{12}$$

That is, for each hyper rib e with vertex u the weights of vertices are different. The predicted random walk process can be described as follows: starting with vertex u the surfer chooses hyper rib e which is incident to vertex u and proportional to the hyper rib weight w(e). After that, the surfer chooses, in the same way, vertex v proportional to the vertex weight that is the considered current hyper rib.

Let us determine the incident matrix $H_w \in \mathbb{R}^{|V| \times |E|}$ in the measured hypergraph in the following way:

$$h_w(v, e) = \begin{cases} w(v_b), & \text{if } v \in e \\ 0, & \text{if } v \notin e \end{cases} \tag{13}$$

Thus, if we determine the vertex degree again:

$$\delta(v) = \sum_{e \in E} h_w(v, e) \tag{14}$$

And the hyper rib degree is:

$$d(e) = \sum_{v \in V} (v, e) = |e| \tag{15}$$

Using the above mentioned formulas, it is possible to calculate transition matrix determination:

$$P(u, v) = \sum_{e \in E} w(e) \frac{h(u, e)}{\sum_{\hat{e} \in E(u)} w(\hat{e})} \frac{h_w(v, e)}{\sum_{\hat{v} \in e} h_w(\hat{v}, e)} \tag{16}$$

Or the matrix determination:

$$P = D_v^{-1} H W_e D_{ve}^{-1} H_w^T \tag{17}$$

Here,

- D_v – a diagonal matrix of the weighted vertex degree;
- H – an incidental matrix of hypergraph vertices;
- W_e – a diagonal matrix of hyper rib weights;
- D_{ve} – a diagonal matrix of the weighted hyper rib degree;
- H_w – an incidental matrix of the measured graph.

Where the transition matrix P is stochastic and every sum of rows is equal to 1 [23].

After computing the transition matrix P, there arises the necessity to understand random walk stationary distribution π. Stationary distribution can be calculated beginning with vector $\vec{v_0} \in R^{|v| \times 1}$. These are probabilities $1/|V|$ where their sum is equal to 1. Firstly, the transition matrix P^T is computed by multiplication of a vector-column $\vec{v_0}$ by $\vec{v_0} = P^T * \vec{v}$. Thus, we will go on with iteration till vector $\vec{v}$ stops changing. Multiplication of transition matrix by the vector of probability distribution gives the next step of distribution $\vec{x} = P^T * \vec{v}$. Let x be the probability of being at vertex i. Then $x_i = \sum_j p_{ij} v_j$, v_j is the probability of untimely being of the surfer on the node j and p_{ij} is the probability of transition from j to i.

If random walk is ergodic, the vector distribution probability stops changing after n steps.

3.3   Creation and Training of a Neural Network

The next task is creation of a neural network trained to extract linguistic constructions which include the possible meanings of attributes of named entities of the texts being processed. Collecting of linguistic constructions and sets of semantically close words are beginning of a neural network training by providing descriptors candidates to use it as features.

The created neural network enable to extract information on one pre-selected descriptor, for example, location, presenting, names of geographical objects as a final result. In general case, the neural network can extract information across multiple descriptors simultaneously.

For training a neural network, a training set consisting of a feature vector was constructed. For one descriptor, a feature vector was built as follows: we took a window of five words before the entry of the element of interest in the text of the article and a window of two words after it. For each descriptor, a dictionary is formed which answers for the presence of the pointed out word in it. All the features of each descriptor are collected in one "bag of words" and a feature vector is built.

A neural network is trained by showing every input dataset and subsequent error propagation. Neural network training algorithm is based on the error back propagation method. This method is popular and widespread in machine learning, so there is its general description. The "backwards" means that calculation of the gradient proceeds backwards through the network, with the layer's gradients being calculated in reverse order. Partial computations of the gradient from one layer are reused in the computation of the gradient for the previous layer. This backwards flow of the error information allows for efficient computation of the gradient at each layer versus the naive approach of calculating the gradient of each layer separately. We use a simple neural network with two hidden layers to simplify results interpretation [24].

4 The Results of Computing Experiments

To store the data, NoSQL data base of MongoDB 3 is used. The data set includes 9723 records collected from Kazakhstani portals and Kazakhstan emergency news portals. The data are marked up as follows: class 1- locality, 0 - otherwise.

An example of a record: "main functional responsibilities maintaining state records of natural and man-made emergencies which took place on the territory of the city Almaty jointly with state and local executive bodies according to the civil protection law of Republic of Kazakhstan (RK) preparation of analytical materials on areas of activity in the field of civil protection maintenance of information reference cards maintenance and operation of information systems by the state system of civil protection control and supervision in the field of civil protection administrative practice".

At first, data pre-processing was performed to avoid markup mistakes in train and test sets. For markup, a list of localities in RK was taken and using a fuzzy search algorithm (difflib library) and a search algorithm for full match normalized words (with the help of library pymorphy2 [25]) the texts with and without names were found. The texts with names presence confirmed or declined by both algorithms were in the training and test sets with corresponding marks.

Then, using the library TensorFlow we calculated TF-IDF matrices which were used by the random walk method. At the output, we had a matrix with word proximity ratios and a dictionary that matched the vector component with the word. All the texts were encoded by the values of the obtained matrix and each was marked up as 1 or 0 depending on the presence of the locality name in the text.

The experimental data were divided in the ratio 80%–20%, 20% - for the final test. And 80% were further divided correspondingly to 70%–30%, 70% - for learning and 30% - for correct validation. Validation helps determine the retrained model.

All the experiments were carried out on a neural network with two hidden layers. The first hidden layer consists of 32 neurons, the second layer consists of 10 neurons. As an activation function for neurons of the hidden layer, we chose different variations of relu and tanh, the output layer being sigmoid. We had used the default RMSE, root mean square error as loss function.

Then, a graph of RMSE versus learning curve is presented. After the 500th era the value of loss function makes up ~ 0.17, ~ 0.22, ~ 0.87 corresponding for SGD, RMSPROP, Adam optimizers, which are an acceptable result for such a simple architecture of the network. We use RMSE because as the square root of a variance, RMSE can be interpreted as the standard deviation of the unexplained variance, and has the useful property of being in the same units as the response variable. Lower values of RMSE indicate better fit (Fig. 1). RMSE is a good measure of how accurately the model predicts the response, and it is the most important criterion for fit if the main purpose of the model is prediction. According to these results we have a neural network that predict is word sequence or word a location name or not with pretty precise accuracy with SGD optimizer. It means that with our algorithm will detect the Almaty in any news report with probability about 85%.

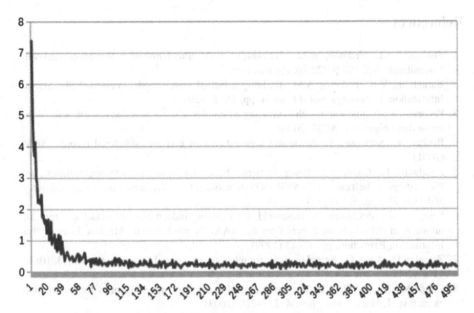

Fig. 1. RMSE loss versus learning curve

5 Conclusion

This work resulted in creation of the algorithm which allows to extract key words (word combinations) from the text corpus of uniform subject with the aim of further using the extracted key words as possible meanings of entity attributes described in the domain ontology being created assigned for organization of factual search in the widened corpus of texts of the corresponding domain. As the result we have a pipeline contains morphological parser text parts markup of speech followed by the use of the random walk method for extraction of semantically close key words (word combinations) so we can consider that task has been solved successfully. A trained neural network with a hidden layer is applied to the set of these word combinations with the aim to match a concrete word combination to a definite attribute of the entity described in the text. Thus, using a set of semantically close pairs of words, one can build an ontology, formed during the neural network operation, for a concrete document.

Acknowledgments. This work was supported in part under grant of Foundation of Ministry of Education and Science of the Republic of Kazakhstan "Development of a system for knowledge extraction from heterogeneous data sources to improve the quality of decision-making" (2018–2020) and Russian Federation RFBR grant № 18-07-01457.

References

1. Shokin, Yu.I., Fedotov, A.M., Barakhnin, V.B.: Problems of information retrieval. Novosibirsk: Sci. 196 p. (2010). (In Russian)
2. Barakhnin, V.B., Fedotov, A.M.: Building a factual search model. Vestnik NSU. Series: Information Technology, vol. 11, no. 4. pp. 16–27 (2013)
3. Pedersen, T.: A simple approach to building ensembles of naive bayesian classifiers for word sense disambiguation. ACM (2000)
4. Borkar, V., Sarawahi, S.: Automatic segmentation of text into structured records. ACM (2001)
5. Agichtein, E., Ganti, V.: Mining reference tables for automatic text segmentation. In: Proceedings of the Tenth ACM SIGKDD International Conference on Knowledge Discovery and Data Mining, Seattle, USA (2004)
6. Seymore, K., McCallum, A., Rosenfeld, R.: Learning hidden Markov model structure for information extraction. In: Papers from the AAAI-99 Workshop on Machine Learning for Information Extraction, pp. 37–42 (1999)
7. Zelenko, D., Aone, C.: Kernel methods for relation extraction. J. Mach. Learn. Res. **3**, 1083–1106 (2003)
8. Califf, M., Moony, R.J.: Bottom-up relational learning of matching rules for information extraction. J. Mach. Learn. Res. **4**, 177–210 (2003)
9. Dejean, H.: Learning rules and their exceptions. J. Mach. Learn. Res. **2**, 669–693 (2002)
10. Aung, A., Thwal, M.P.: Onthology based hotel information extraction from unstructured text. In: International Conference on Advances in Engineering and Technology (ICAET 2014), 29–30 March, Singapore (2014)
11. Anantharangachar, R., Ramani, S., Rajagopalan, S.: Ontology guided information extraction from unstructured text. Int. J. Web Semant. Technol. (IJWesT) **4**(1), 19–36 (2013)
12. Stanford CoreNLP: A Suite of Core NLP Tools. (2015). http://nlp.stanford.edu/software/corenlp.shtml
13. Atzmueller, M., Kluegl, P.: Rule-based information extraction for structured data acquisition using TextMarker. In: LWA (2008)
14. Chiticariu, L., Krishnamurthy, R., Li, Y., Raghavan, S., Reiss, F., Vaithyanathan, S.: SystemT: an algebraic approach to declarative information extraction. In: ACL (2010)
15. Kluegl, P., Atzmueller, M., Puppe, F.: TextMarker: a tool for rule-based information extraction. In: UIMA@GSCL Workshop, pp. 233–240 (2009)
16. Chopra, D., Joshi, N., Mathur, I.: Named entity recognition in Hindi using hidden Markov model. In: 2016 Second International Conference on Computational Intelligence and Communication Technology (CICT), pp. 581–586. IEEE (2016)
17. Malik, M.K., Sarwar, S.M.: Urdu named entity recognition system using hidden Markov model. Pak. J. Eng. & Appl. Sci. **21**,15–22 (2017)
18. McCallum, A., Freitag, D., Pereira, F.C.N.: Maximum entropy markov models for information extraction and segmentation. In: Icml 2000, vol. 17, pp. 591–598 (2000)
19. Ahmed, I., Sathyaraj, R.: Named entity recognition by using maximum entropy. Int. J. Database Theory Appl. **8**(2), 43–50 (2015)
20. Lafferty, J., McCallum, A., Pereira, F.C.N.: Conditional random fields: probabilistic models for segmenting and labeling sequence data (2001)
21. Lee, C., et al.: Fine-grained named entity recognition using conditional random fields for question answering. In: Ng, H.T., Leong, M.-K., Kan, M.-Y., Ji, D. (eds.) AIRS 2006. LNCS, vol. 4182, pp. 581–587. Springer, Heidelberg (2006). https://doi.org/10.1007/11880592_49

22. Chen, W., Zhang, Y., Isahara, H.: Chinese named entity recognition with conditional random fields. In: Proceedings of the Fifth SIGHAN Workshop on Chinese Language Processing, pp. 118–121 (2006)
23. Bellaachia, A., Al Dhelaan, M.: HGRANK: a hypergraph based keyphrase extraction for short documents in dynamic genre (2014)
24. Haykin, S.: Neural Networks and Learning Machines, 3rd edn. Pearson, London (2009). 936 p
25. Korobov, M.: Morphological analyzer and generator for russian and ukrainian languages. In: Khachay, M.Y., Konstantinova, N., Panchenko, A., Ignatov, D.I., Labunets, V.G. (eds.) AIST 2015. CCIS, vol. 542, pp. 320–332. Springer, Cham (2015). https://doi.org/10.1007/978-3-319-26123-2_31

Problems of Semantics of Words of the Kazakh Language in the Information Retrieval

Rakhimova Diana[1(✉)] and Shormakova Assem[2(✉)]

[1] Al-Farabi KazNU, Street Al-Farabi 71, Almaty, Kazakhstan
di.diva@mail.ru
[2] Institute of Information and Computational Technologies,
Street Pushkin 125, Almaty, Kazakhstan
shormakovaassem@gmail.com

Abstract. The theme of this research is intelligent search engines that can search and extract new information from text data in Kazakh language and education. The significance of the research topic due to the growing amount of data represented in digital form, which provide the ability to access various sources of electronic documents. The use of intelligent search engines will allow you to meet the information needs of users. In this regard, the development of information-analytical search engines that allows you to work with data in Kazakh language is relevant. The goal of this research is to develop efficient algorithms and models for intelligent search systems, based on modern technologies in the field of information retrieval and natural language processing teaching them.

Keywords: Kazakh languages · Semantics · Text · Information retrieval

1 Overview Modern Text Information Retrieval

Kazakh language belongs to the languages of agglutinative type. Agglutinative languages (from the Latin agglutinatio - gluing) are languages with a system in which agglutination is the dominant type of inflection ("gluing" of different formants (suffixes or prefixes)), each of which carries only one meaning. Kazakh language is very rich in various words forms and its semantics.

The problem of finding a document that meets certain criteria, occurs in any data warehouse that contains more than one document. It is obvious, that the solution of this problem is, somehow, confined to those which are used in the design of storage systems. One can specify two basic ways: (1) using a hierarchical model; (2) the use of hypertext models.

The use of a hierarchical multilevel model involves the categorization of information resources. To select the path to the desired document uses the description drawn up by the support of this system. Hypertext model allows to link document's links, which are located directly in the text. These two models have obvious drawbacks. As multi-level categorization, and the placement of links is performed by highly qualified specialists. And the volume treated in this document may not be very large. For this reason, suffers the relevance of the description in the array of documents. In addition,

© Springer Nature Switzerland AG 2019
N. T. Nguyen et al. (Eds.): ICCCI 2019, LNAI 11684, pp. 70–81, 2019.
https://doi.org/10.1007/978-3-030-28374-2_7

related documents, limited to any subject area, which, moreover, the user of the system has different idea than the originator of the subject. Finally, when correct document find the user of such systems, it will required to view many documents with useful information, which will only be links to other resources. These problems become, particularly, acute, when large volumes of information, high speed of updates and the high heterogeneity of users need them [1–7].

Currently, there are enough powerful information system that more or less satisfy the information needs of users [9]. However, the main disadvantages of most systems are the limitations of the analytical work with the resources and integration of resources within each system and with external systems (often not taken into account international standards and recommendations, low interoperability) [10].

There are quite a number of algorithms for intelligent processing of text documents. Each of them has their own metric by which to measure the results of clustering. Description of algorithms of cluster analysis of texts is given in [10, 11] and on the website http://www.basegroup.ru/library/analysis/clusterization/datamining/, and in this paper we propose their classification by dividing into two large groups:

- algorithms flat clustering;
- hierarchical clustering algorithms.

The first group includes algorithms that use the method of quadratic errors: the k-means algorithm (k-means), graph theory methods, methods based on the concept of density, neural network methods etc. The second group includes algorithms agglomerative hierarchical clustering (divide bottom-up) methods single and full connectivity, the clustering pair-group average and dividing algorithms (divide top-down) clustering using suffix trees.

In many leading scientific centers and commercial companies have active projects on creation of systems of semantic query processing [5–8], which are improving and developing new protocols, technologies, programming environments, agents, languages, user interfaces, methods, distributed knowledge. For example, the DBpedia project [12], aimed as extracting structured information from data generator within the project Wikipedia, named one of the most successful examples of the use of technologies in semantic processing the data of Tim Berners-Lee. Almost all well-known company IBM, Adobe or Oracle, actively use the technology of the Semantic web in their products to solve data management tasks. Microsoft invests hundreds of millions of dollars in project interactive of network resources .NET, which reflects their idea to the near future Internet. The system allows for automated exchange of network resources between separate programs, applications, databases and users.

Issues of development and creation of information retrieval systems that are able to automatically search and extract new information from semi-structured data to the scientific community, involved in various research groups [5, 10–12]. Thus, as development tools of systems, use technologies such as JSP, JavaScript, PHP, MySQL database server. With the undisputed advantages of these systems with increasing volume of processed data, there is a noticeable decrease in their performance [13].

2   Overview of the Modern Methods of Semantic Processing of Textual Resources

Currently, among the areas of information retrieval, a special place is the class of problems concerning smart search which involves: modeling representation of documents and queries; search and knowledge representation in digital form; classification (categorization) of texts; clustering; semantic knowledge extraction from texts.

Taking into account constant growth of digital data plays, an important role improving the quality of information retrieval through the use of new semantic technologies and methods.

Big data-developed various, algorithms and methods solving this problem, so as to carry out the analysis manually enable the volumes of data. Any natural language in their own complicated, unique and versatile, so extracting data from documents and textual resources is a big and time consuming job that requires preprocessing.

During the designing of the module, analytical processing of textual resources and documents were studied in different methods and models. Such as fastText, GloVe, Word2vec.

FastText is a library to the study of the attachment of words and text classifications and Laboratory of AI research at Facebook. The model is an unsupervised learning algorithm for obtaining vector representations for words. Facebook provides pre-trained models for 294 languages. This program is written in Python and C++ [22].

A popular idea of modern machine learning is the representation of word vectors. These vectors capture the hidden information about the language such as the word analogy or semantics. It is also used to improve the performance of text classifiers. In the tool fastText, one can build that dictionary vectors. fastText provides two models for calculating representations of words: skipgram and cbow ("continuous bag of words") [22].

GloVe, invented from the Global Vectors, is a model for distributed representation of words. The model is an unsupervised learning algorithm for obtaining vector representations for words. Metrics of similarity used for the estimates of nearest neighbors, creating a single scalar which quantifies the relationship between two words. This simplicity may be problematic because two words are almost always demonstrate more complex relationships, than can be captured by a single number [23].

Word2vec—tool, used for the analysis of the semantics of natural languages, which is a technology, that based on distributional semantics and vector representation of words. This tool makes it faster than using other methods to vector on huge amounts of linguistic materials.

In scientific works [24–26], there was description about the basic ideas of information retrieval. There was presented various options for finding statistic's text, which include counting the number of occurrences of words in documents and the frequency of adjacency of words, and the new model architectures for computing continuous vector representations of words from very large data sets. There was explored as vector representations of words obtained by various models on a set of syntactic and semantic language tasks. In [27] shows the use of language models as neural network to the problem of calculating the semantic similarity for the Russian language. Described the instruments, corpora and the results.

Vector representations of words trained using word2vec models because it has semantic meanings and it is useful in various tasks of NLP (natural language processing - natural language processing). In [26], detailed descriptions and explanations of the equation parameters of word2vec models, including models CBOW and skip-gram, as well as advanced optimization techniques, including hierarchical softmax and negative sampling. In the paper [28] presents the results of the word2vec algorithm for synthetic agglutinative Kazakh language. The main difficulties of the implementation of algorithm was associated with the requirement of normalization of the text.

The most difficult problem arising from the creation of intelligent systems, is to develop methods of automated knowledge extraction from documents in natural language. This problem is still, apparently, does not have any General solution, since the construction of this solution involves, in particular, sufficiently accurate modeling of cognitive human activity, and the availability of powerful tools like syntactic and semantic analysis of texts.

On the basis of the research of the developed models, mostly applied for analytical processing of textual resources the Word2Vec method. Below, represented the development of methods of the module, analytical processing and implementation based on this approach.

3 The Learning Algorithm Based on the Method of Word2Vec

Word2Vec includes a set of algorithms to calculate the vector representations of words, assuming that words used in similar contexts, i.e. are semantically close.

$$(wv * wc)(wc1 * wv)$$

- In the numerator - the proximity of words of context and target words.
- In the denominator - the proximity of all other contexts and target words [29].
- The learning algorithm In word2vec there are two main learning algorithm: CBOW(Continuous Bag of Words) is a "continuous bag of words" model architecture, which predicts the current word based on the surrounding context. CBOW predicts the word from the local context:
- inputs - one-hot representations of words dimension v;
- the hidden layer - matrix representations of the words w;
- output of the hidden layer is the average of vectors of words in context;
- the output is a rating uj for each word and taking the softmax value, which is determined by the following formula: $p(i|c1, \ldots ,cn) = \exp(uj)j' = 1Vexp(uj')$

Skip-gram works differently: it uses the current word to predict the surrounding words. Skip-gram predicts the words the context of the current word: -a word predicted by the context of the Central-now several multinomial distributions and softmax for each word context: $p(ck|i) = \exp(kck)j' = 1Vexp(uj')$.

User word2vec has the ability to switch and choose between the algorithms. Word order context does not affect the result in any of these algorithms. The calculation uses an artificial neural network. During training, the algorithm generates the optimal vector for each word using the CBOW or skip-gram.

A method of representing words as vectors, is used for clustering words and identifying their semantic proximity, i.e., shares unrelated words and connect associate that helps in the tasks of clustering and classification of texts [30].

Obtained at the output of the coordinate representation of the vectors of the words, allow one to calculate the "semantic distance" between words. As the tool word2vec, it based on the neural network training to achieve the most efficient operation. And it is necessary to use large corpora for training. It allows one to improve the quality of predictions.

In distributional semantics, words are typically represented as vectors in a multi-dimensional space of their contexts. Semantic similarity is computed as cosine similarity between the vectors of two words and can take values in the interval $[-1...1]$ (in practice often used only values above 0). A value of 0 means roughly, that there are no words of similar contexts and their values are not related to each other. A value of 1, in contrast, indicates the full identity of their contexts and hence, about the close value.

Recently, the interest in distributional semantics has increased significantly. This is mainly due to the new learning algorithms on large corpora: the so-called word embedding models (often their training uses simple artificial neural network). The result is a compressed vector for words that can be used for a variety of computer-linguistic tasks [31].

4 Implementation of the Module Analytical Processing of Text Data

For the implementation of the module analytical processing of textual resources and documents in the Kazakh language was developed a model based on word2vec. The algorithm of the model shown in Fig. 1.

Module for analytical processing of textual resources and documents for the Kazakh language consists of 3 stages:

(1) Preparation of input data
(2) model Training
(3) Work with trained model

Stage 1 Preparation of input data in turn consists of the following steps: For learning module, one need to prepare the case. The case is selected and processed according to certain rules, the set of texts used as a base for language research. They are used for statistical analysis and test statistical hypotheses, validation of linguistic rules in the language.

Search body may issue:

− all consumption of the selected word in the immediate context, on the basis of what the translator can choose a synonym if one transfer or collocations;

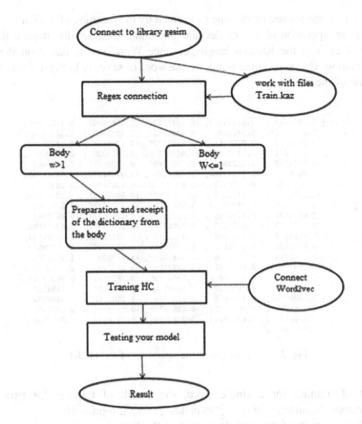

Fig. 1. The algorithm of the analytical module data processing.

- the frequency of words in a particular field of knowledge;
- words that are often next to the selected word.

Was assembled by the Kazakh monolingual corpus. For training the model, was trained monolingual Kazakh case, which is in the file train_kaz. Detailed description of the collection of monolingual housing shown in Sect. 2.3.2.

Stage 2 Learning models the
Next step in the implementation of the model is learning. To train the model, specify the following parameters:

- the dimension of the feature vectors is 100;
- the Maximum distance between the current predicted word in the sentence is 5;
- the Minimum level of learning 1;
- the Threshold cut off frequency of 4 words.

After training save the model in model_kaz.model
Stage 3. Work with the trained model.
To work with the trained model and connection Word2vec: model_kaz = Word2Vec.load("model_kaz.model").

In the result, the trained model one can search by the meaning of similar words. For more effective operation of the model and obtaining good results, require the large monolingual case in the Kazakh language, since Word2vec is based on the neural network training. One can set the input, as one word or several. In Figs. 2 and 3 shows an example of the model.

```
array([ 0.9991543 ,  0.21965139,  0.29315677,  0.10888853,  0.47598684,
        -0.28379786,  1.1473682 , -0.6190352 ,  1.0921485 , -0.3379822 ,
        -0.9026812 , -0.9696143 , -0.21033779, -1.0946484 , -0.14725323,
        -0.5968371 , -0.94785064, -0.0186517 ,  0.9273225 ,  0.02986972,
        -0.5971313 ,  1.6572342 , -0.5005268 , -0.72290874,  1.3720803 ,
         0.3576381 , -0.25446084, -0.6820295 , -0.05884275,  0.04245997,
        -1.2486485 ,  0.5666453 , -0.82413435, -0.516167 , -0.2035349 ,
        -0.65919286,  1.1125271 ,  0.79175997, -0.39865917,  0.13109162,
        -1.3794425 , -0.09773538,  1.5038078 , -0.22719735, -0.6705901 ,
        -0.01339606,  0.4934905 ,  0.36428472,  0.12966971, -0.0571641 ,
        -0.6472839 ,  0.6247625 , -0.47967348, -0.17849082,  0.06311992,
        -0.4211008 ,  0.21196847, -1.3122642 , -0.23150532,  0.47074622,
         0.63370025, -0.96714115, -0.33243644,  1.2825935 , -0.38998842,
        -0.5900854 ,  0.17189564, -0.19655013, -1.119008 , -1.2662848 ,
        -0.7881708 , -0.06033329,  0.6032156 , -0.3427293 ,  0.83609366,
        -0.6120512 , -0.12485034,  0.9940732 ,  0.58395654,  0.34109122,
        -0.35265407, -0.7005883 , -0.6270238 ,  0.5748394 ,  0.1292389 ,
         0.59908956,  0.7373656 ,  0.3227748 , -1.2803192 ,  0.6388992 ,
        -0.3058275 , -0.64198923, -0.43613726, -0.6778025 , -0.62231904,
        -1.255485  , -0.07670641,  0.7747939 ,  0.5336992 , -1.0332865 ],
      dtype=float32)
```

Fig. 2. An example of the operation of the model.

Result of training for a single word, the Result of training for two words: model_kaz.most_similar(positive = ["жылдың", "бас"], topn = 10).

The Software part of the module written in the Python programming language of version3. For feature models was connected to the library Gensim [11].

```
[('1993', 0.9606807231903076),
 ('маусымда', 0.955879271030426),
 ('ассамблеясының', 0.955683708190918),
 ('наурызда', 0.9535720944404602),
 ('сөзіне', 0.9529553651809692),
 ('қазан', 0.9526992440223694),
 ('1994', 0.9519071578979492),
 ('шырсының', 0.9517829418182373),
 ('мамырында', 0.9508242607116699),
 ('мамырда', 0.9497315287590027)] |
```

Fig. 3. Example models for the two words.

Further, for more effective work model, based the word2vec, which is based on the neural network training, it is planned to increase the volume of the housing. Since large volumes of the buildings allow one to improve search quality.

5 Develop and Implement a Method of Collecting Synonyms

5.1 Synonymy and Its Importance in Information Retrieval

One of the most important elements is influencing the results of searching information, a thesaurus of keywords, which involves expanding subject area due to synonyms and formation on this basis of a thesaurus of synonyms. In the 1970's, thesauri has been actively used for information retrieval tasks. In such thesauri words, was mapped the descriptors through which semantic relationships are established. The first modern English thesaurus was created by Peter Mark Roget (English) in 1805. It was published in 1852 and has been used to not reprints. There are also electronic dictionaries of synonyms and thesauri, English language, etc. Unfortunately, for Turkish languages, electronic language resources do not exist in the public domain, which would then be used in various applied problems of artificial intelligence. There is important to use the knowledge of synonyms to search for and to fullness the meaning of words in Kazakh language.

5.2 Development of a Thesaurus of Synonymy of the Kazakh Language

The main challenge in determination of synonyms is their lexical and morphological features, because automated version is not possible. Synonyms should be context-dependent, it is the relationship of synonyms and possible between words. In this section the authors developed a hybrid approach based on the method of Maximum entropy in the practical implementation of the semantic cube [35].

To solve this problem were used the linguistic resources of the English language, which made the implementation of the approach. Below, an example of multi-valued words in English that has different meanings in Kazakh language (Table 1).

Table 1. List of many meanings (synonyms)

Multi-valued words in English languages	Main1 in Kazakh language	Main 2 in Kazakh language	Main 3 in Kazakh language
String	Жол	Jip	ishek
Order	Ret	Jarlyk'	orden
Part	Bo'lik	Partia	dene
Small	Kishkentai	U'sak'	shagyn
Thing	Zat	Na'rse	dunie
Discover	Baikau	Ashu	tabu
Information	Ak'parat	Habar	ma'limet
Field	O'ris	Dala	alan'
Present	Tanystyru	Ko'rsetu	u'synu
Observe	Bakylau	K'arau	baik'au
Make	Jasau	K'u'ru	isteu
Go	Baru	Ketu	juru
So	Solai	Osylai	bu'lai
Call	Atau	Shak'yru	k'on'yrau shalu
Set	K'oiu	Otyrg'yzu	ornatu

This list is based on a parallel English-Kazakh corpus that identifies a particular translation of the words. Found synonyms (multi-valued words) and their adjacent words filled in the table.

A table of possible translations in the contest can be summarized as follows (Table 2):

Table 2. Translations and the frequency of words in the context

f_1	amb_word_1	freq_of_f_1
f_2	amb_word_1	freq_of_f_2
f_3	amb_word_1	freq_of_f_3
...	...	...
f_n	amb_word_n	freq_of_f_n

Here, amb_word – Multivalued words from the initial context, t - transfers, f – context of the target language, freq_of_f – frequency of occurrence of ambiguous words in context.

Using a table of frequencies while testing for the right words, it calculates the probability and selects the corresponding translation. The formula which determines the translation according to the context

$$Ps(t \lor c) = \frac{c(fi)}{\sum_{i=1}^{n} fi}$$

here (c(fi)) is the frequency of context, $\sum_{i=1}^{n} fi$ – amount needed possible factor contexts. Definition of synonyms with their equivalents, constructed a table of frequencies. The biggest argument finding probabilities of synonyms is determined by the function

$$\text{argmax. } t = \text{argmax } P(t1, t2, \ldots, tn)$$

This defines various values that are written in the semantic dimension of the cube. The cube is directly dependent on the size of the English-Kazakh parallel corpus. The semantic form of a multidimensional cube is presented in Fig. 2. The growth of the size of the case affect the quality of the right synonyms of the words, that is more than a catalogue of words and synonyms and more accurate and better will find and identify the right synonyms.

With the implementation of this approach has been used parallel English–Kazakh corpus [32] and open source online dictionary of English synonyms (Thesaurus.com) (Fig. 4).

Developed a thesaurus of synonymy, based on the algorithm of Maximum entropy and in the practical implementation of the method of semantic cube. Using this method was automated system of collection of synonyms and similar in meaning of words. Was added to the database up to 9000 entries of synonyms of Kazakh language.

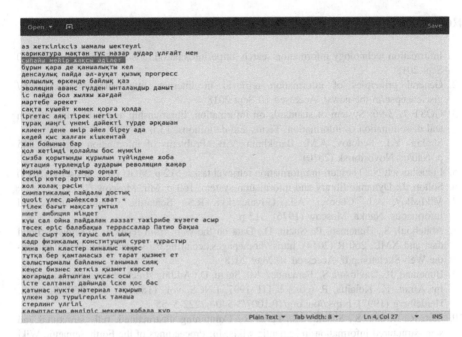

Fig. 4. Automated directory Kazakh synonyms.

6   Conclusion

The results obtained on the development of methods and models of the module analytical processing of textual resources and documents in Kazakh language:

- researched different types of methods and models for semantic analysis, that used for operation of the module analytical processing of textual resources and documents;
- collected monolingual corpora of Kazakh language to train the word2vec model;
- implemented pre-processing text data for use as input data, the selection of words that are similar in vector representation;
- the module for analytical processing of textual resources and documents in Kazakh language is implemented and based on the model word2vec;
- developed thesaurus of synonyms of Kazakh language module analytical word processing;
- developed automation replenishment system database of synonyms of Kazakh language.

The experiments show good values for the learning system analytical processing of data. In the future, increases the quality, due to the input and casing of Kazakh language, and through the creation of a marked body of Kazakh language.

Acknowledgments. This research performed and financed by the grant **Project IRN** AP05132950 "Development of an information-analytical search system of data in the Kazakh language", awarded to The Republican State Enterprise (RGP) on the right of economic management (PVC) «Institute of Information and Computational Technologies».

References

1. Information technology information search. http://inftis.narod.ru/is/is-n8.htm/. Accessed 10 Sept 2018
2. General principles of information retrieval in Internet. https://sites.google.com/site/gisciencepsu/in-the-news/. Accessed 10 Sept 2018
3. GOST 7.73-96: System of standards on information, librarianship and publishing. Search and dissemination of information. Terms and definitions, 13 p (1998)
4. Shokin, Y.I., Fedotov, A.M., Barakhnin, V.B.: Problems of information retrieval, 245 p. Nauka, Novosibirsk (2010)
5. Lukashevich N.: Thesauri in information retrieval tasks, 512 p. MGU publ., Moscow (2011)
6. Solton, J.: Dynamic library and information system, 160 p. Mir, Moscow (1979)
7. Mikhailov, A.I., Chernyi, A.I., Gilyarevskyi, R.S.: Scientific Communications and Informatics. Nauka, Moscow (1976). 312 p
8. Abiteboul, S., Buneman, P., Suciu, D.: Data on the web: from relations to semistructured data and XML, 260 R (2014). https://homepages.dcc.ufmg.br/~ laender/material/Data-on-the-Web-Skeleton.pdf. Accessed 10 May 2018
9. Buneman, P., Davidson, S., Fernandez, M., Suciu, D.: Adding structure to unstructured data. In: Afrati, F., Kolaitis, P. (eds.) ICDT 1997. LNCS, vol. 1186, pp. 336–350. Springer, Heidelberg (1997). https://doi.org/10.1007/3-540-62222-5_55
10. Sint, R., Stroka, S., Schaffert S., Ferstl R.: Combining unstructured, fully structured and semi-structured information in semantic wikis. In: Proceedings of the Forth Semantic Wiki Workshop, Heraklion, Crete, Greece, pp. 56–60 (2009)
11. Masterman, M.: Semantic message detection for machine translation, using an interlingua. In: Proceedings of International Conference on Machine Translation, pp. 438–475 (1961)
12. Schrader, Y.A.: Quantitative characteristics of semantic data. STI.Ser.2, pp. 35–39 (1963)
13. ISO 25964–1:2011 Information and documentation – Thesauri and interoperability with other vocabularies. Thesauri for information retrieval, Part 1, 119 p (2011)
14. ISO 25964-2:2013 Information and documentation – Thesauri and interoperability with other vocabularies. Interoperability with other vocabularies. Part 2, 150 p (2013)
15. Tukeev, W.A., Turgunova, A.: Morphological analysis of the Kazakh language on the basis of a complete system of endings. In: Proceedings of International Conference on computational and cognitive linguistics (TEL-2016), Kazan, Republic of Tatarstan, pp. 225–231 (2016)
16. Wang, J., Guo Y.: Scrapy-based crawling and user-behavior characteristics analysis on taobao. In: 2012 International Conference on Cyber-Enabled Distributed Computing and Knowledge Discovery, pp. 44–52. IEEE (2012)
17. Myers, D., McGuffee, J.W.: Choosing scrapy. J. Comput. Sci. Coll. **31**(1), 83–89 (2015)
18. Drakshayani, B., Prasad, E.V.: Semantic based model for text document clustering with idioms. Int. J. Data Eng. (IJDE) **4**(1), 1–13 (2013)
19. Verma, R., Vuppuluri, V.: A new approach for idiom identification using meanings and the web. In: Proceedings of Recent Advances in Natural Language Processing, Hissar, Bulgaria, pp. 681–687 (2015)
20. Kenesbayev, S.K.: Phraseological dictionary of the Kazakh language, p. 711. Nauka, Alma-ATA (1977)
21. Vinogradov, V.V.: The main types of phraseological units in the Russian language. Selected works. Lexicology and lexicography, Moscow, 135 p (1977)
22. Fasttext. https://fasttext.cc/. Accessed 10 Sept 2018
23. GloVe. https://nlp.stanford.edu/projects/glove/: 12.09.2018

24. Manning, C.D., Raghavan, P., Schütze, H.: Introduction to Information Retrieval. Cambridge University Press, New York (2008)
25. Mikolov, T., Chen, K., Corrado, G., Dean, J.: Efficient estimation of word representations in vector space, 210 p. https://arxiv.org/pdf/1301.3781.pdf. Accessed 10 July 2018
26. Xin R.: word2vec parameter learning explained. https://arxiv.org/pdf/1411.2738.pdf. Accessed 10 July 2018
27. Kutuzov, A., Andreev, I.: Texts in that meaning out: neural language models in semantic similarity tasks for English. https://arxiv.org/ftp/arxiv/papers/1504/1504.08183.pdf. Accessed 20 Apr 2018
28. Kalimoldayev, M.N., Koibagarov, K.Ch., Alexandr, A., Pak, S., Zharmagambetov, A.: The application of the connectionist method of semantic similarity for Kazakh language. In: Twelve International Conference on Electronics Computer and Computation (ICECCO), pp. 1–3 (2015)
29. Word2Vec. https://ru.wikipedia.org/wiki/Word2vec. Accessed 15 Sept 2018
30. Algorithm of Word2vec. https://ru.megaindex.com/support/faq/word2vec. Accessed 15 Sept 2018
31. Webvectors. https://rusvectores.org/ru/about/. Accessed 15 Sept 2018
32. The Thesaurus. https://ru.wikipedia.org/. Accessed 15 Sept 2018
33. Balabaev Schwa: Kazakh tln synonymer szdg, 236 p. Mektep, Almaty (1975)
34. The Principle of Maximum Entropy. https://ru.wikipedia.org/wiki/. Accessed 07 Oct 2018
35. Rakhimova, D., Amirova, D., Karibayeva, A.: Problems of lexical polysemy for the Kazakh language. In: Mater. 3rd International scientific Confeence on "Informatics and applied mathematics" dedicated to Prof. The 80th anniversary of Professor R.G. Biyasheva and the 70th anniversary of Professor Aidarkhanova M.B., Almaty, vol. 2, pp. 18–28 (2018)
36. Translator. https://translate.google.kz/?hl=ru&tab=wT. Accessed 10 Mar 2019

Machine Learning in Real-World Data

Image Preprocessing Techniques
for Facial Expression Recognition
with Canny and Kirsch Edge Detectors

Kennedy Chengeta and Serestina Viriri[✉]

School of Mathematics, Statistics and Computer Science,
Westville University of KwaZulu-Natal, Durban, South Africa
{216073421,viriris}@ukzn.ac.za

Abstract. With facial expressions, humans can interconnect and relay
information and feelings between one another. Recognizing emotions
involves the four key stages namely facial expression recognition, preprocessing, feature extraction and classification. The facial images have
more information than necessary; the images' background noise can also
impact automated expression recognition. To resolve unnecessary information and background noise, filtering and edge detection algorithms
were used during the preprocessing phase. The edge detectors were used
in facial expression recognition to highlight frequent facial components,
locating sharp discontinuities and filtering less important data. Key edge
detectors including Sobel, Prewitt, Differences of Gaussian, Laplacian of
Gaussian, Roberts, Kirsch and Canny Edge detector were used for preprocessing of facial expression images. Viola Jones facial detection algorithm and local feature extraction algorithms, local directional patterns
as well as k-nearest neighbor algorithms are used for image detection,
feature extraction and classification respectively. The best results were
based on the Cohn-Kanade database (CK+) with local directional patterns, canny edge detector and k-nearest neighbor.

Keywords: Cohn-Kanade database (CK+) ·
Local Directional Patterns (LDP) · Local Binary Patterns (LBP) ·
Canny edge detection

1   Introduction

Automated facial expression recognition applications are being widely used in
transport, crowd control, marketing, manufacturing, aviation, medicine and hospitals [6]. Major facial expression used are namely disgust, sad, anger, neutral,
happy, contempt and surprise [5]. Facial expression recognition processes involve
facial detection, image preprocessing, feature extraction and classification. The
Viola Jones algorithm facial detection technique is used for image detection.
Image preprocessing techniques involve various techniques including edge detection, image normalization. Feature extraction involves extracting images into

© Springer Nature Switzerland AG 2019
N. T. Nguyen et al. (Eds.): ICCCI 2019, LNAI 11684, pp. 85–96, 2019.
https://doi.org/10.1007/978-3-030-28374-2_8

a histogram. The extraction algorithms are either holistic or localized. Holistic algorithms cover the whole facial image whereas the localized algorithms breakdown a facial image into components. In the case of local feature extraction, different facial components namely nose, mouth, ear, cheek and eyes are extracted as separate components and aggregated into a single aggregate histogram. Algorithms like local binary patterns, local directional patterns and their variants as well as SURF and SIFT are prominent [5]. Features are extracted using key algorithms like local Gabor binary patterns which is a LBP variant with Gabor filtering [5,6,18]. The LBP is a feature extraction algorithm successfully used to extract features from 2D images [6,18]. The facial expression images were then modeled as a histogram sequence which is an aggregate of local facial regions [5]. Facial expression images feature vectors were modelled as an aggregated histogram which was achieved by combining the histogram pieces. Feature selection was enhanced by the PCA algorithm and edge detection.

Because of the need to remove the noise and unwanted components whilst maintaining the status quo, edge detection is used as a critical component in facial expression identification. First order and second order differential edge detection algorithms including Sobel, Prewitt, Laplacian of Gaussian (LOG), Roberts and Canny, Kirsch and Differences of Gaussian are compared in terms of accuracy and performance. The local binary pattern algorithm is used as the local based feature extraction algorithm. The experiments used the extended Cohn-Kanade (CK+) database and the JAFFE dataset. The images contained noise, which also generates sudden transitions of pixel values. Facial expression preprocessing involves normalization of the facial image and image alignment in the form of rotation, scaling or translation of the image. The edge detection processes use binary to preserve the edge data in either black or white. This paper introduces a study and design of the system of facial expression recognition based on edge detection algorithms applied with localized feature extraction algorithms, for image recognition. Classification in facial expression detection is based on a major machine learning supervised algorithm called k-nearest neighbor [6].

In the paper, Sects. 2 and 3 review the previous edge detection and facial recognition literature of FER, Sect. 4 shows the proposed implementation method for feature extraction and edge detection and analyses the results and finally the conclusions are presented.

2 Related Works: Edge Detection in Facial Expression Preprocessing

Edge detection is a fundamental piece of facial expression identification and computer vision. Wide applications have been witnessed in industry, manufacturing, physics, medical and engineering sectors [3]. It is used in network optimization by tracking flow of data in a network and extracting specific data packets or features of interest. The larger the mask width, the less the sensitivity and the more the edge accuracy [4,7,15]. Edge detection is based on the argument that if neighbouring pixels in same vicinity are not similar then there is an edge either in vertical or horizontal format [3,4,8]. An edge is defined as a grouping of pixels that are related to form a margin that distinguishes 2 different regions that are disjoint [14,16]. The operators are based on specific convolution masks which do discrete approximations [3,4].

Edge detection finds presence of edges or pronounced lines on facial expression images [3,7] to eliminate noisy data and unwanted features or textures [7]. Disconnected edges were identified using main edge detectors like Prewitt and Sobel operators. To identify connected edges, various algorithms like Canny edge detector have been used as described by Susan and Canny-Deriche [7,18]. A comparison among four edge detectors: Robert, Sobel, Laplace and Canny has been done on several trials [7]. Success in edge detection in image processing has been seen in previous studies [12,20]. Several edge detectors can be applied to face images recognition preprocessing. The edge detectors are either one order or two order derivatives [8]. They are also used to measure deltas in the image brightness. Facial expressions are recognized based on the mouth feature using Susan edge detector [7]. The Canny edge detector blurs the image hence thinning the edges [3]. Through edge detection, the pixels or data is reduced but the image structure is retained for analysis [3,4,8]. The edge is the basic feature for a facial picture. One order and 2 order derivatives are used to describe these edges [7,14,16]. The study reviews at the commonly used edge detectors, Sobel (first order derivatives), Laplacian (2nd order derivative) based edge detector and others like kirsch and canny edge detectors and compares them in terms of accuracy.

Edge Detection Using Derivatives. Edge detection uses derivatives calculus to describe the continuous functions for 2D image edges. The points on the edge can be found by detecting the local maxima and minima based on the first derivative [3,7]. The edge detection algorithms are also used to detect the zero crossing based on the second derivative [3,4,15]. The key steps in edge detection include noise reduction through smoothing and edge enhancements where key edges are highlighted [3,8]. Edge localization also looks at possibility of edges maxima from previous filters. The edge detection algorithms include first derivatives and second derivative based algorithms using convolution masks [15].

Sobel Edge Detector. The Sobel-Feldman operator uses 2 masks to detect vertical and horizontal edge gradients [3,4,8,15]. It is an algorithm based on the first derivative calculated separately on both the X and Y axes [3] and the Detector is defined as $\sqrt{G_x^2 + G_y^2}$ with gradient $arctan(G_x/G_y)$ for an image denoted by A and where

$$G_x = \begin{bmatrix} -1 & 0 & +1 \\ -2 & 0 & +2 \\ -1 & 0 & +1 \end{bmatrix} A \quad G_y = \begin{bmatrix} -1 & 0 & +1 \\ -2 & 0 & +2 \\ -1 & 0 & +1 \end{bmatrix} A \quad (1)$$

The kernel is approximated on the Gaussian first derivative as shown in Eq. (1). The operator is based on a three by three kernel convolved on the original image in both axes (X and Y axes). The Prewitt edge detector is also a 3 by 3 kernel convoluted based on the initial derivatives of Gx and Gy where the 2 take the values shown based on the two matrices in Eq. (2)

$$G_x = \begin{bmatrix} +1 & +0 & -1 \\ +1 & +0 & -1 \\ +1 & 0 & -1 \end{bmatrix} A \quad G_y = \begin{bmatrix} +1 & +1 & -1 \\ +0 & +0 & +0 \\ -1 & -1 & -1 \end{bmatrix} A \tag{2}$$

Roberts Edge Detector. The Roberts Edge Detector uses a 2 by 2 matrix to find changes in both the horizontal and vertical directions based on an approximation model to the first derivative [4,8,15]. Only edge points are marked and edge orientation information is not considered [4]. There are two forms of the detector with the second one preferred due to computational efficiency. The Roberts edge detector is approximated as $|G|$ or $\sqrt{G^2_x + G^2_y}$ where

$$\frac{\delta f}{\delta x} = f(x, y) - f(x + 1, y + 1) \quad and \quad \frac{\delta f}{\delta y} = f(x + 1, y) - f(x, y + 1) \tag{3}$$

Canny Edge Detector. Robustness in first order edge detectors has not been proven to be sound [3]. The first order derivatives also suffer from high noise sensitivity and need to have a threshold [3]. Second order derivatives are then used to detect edges at its zero crossing which has been found to be more accurate and sound with less noise sensitivity [8]. The Gradient of Gaussian Canny edge detector takes gray scale images as input to produce an image showing positions of intensity discontinuity or edges. The edge detector does a Gaussian convolution for image smoothening and noise removal [3,4]. The first derivative is applied to point out positions with high spatial frequency on the first derivative. The algorithms achieved good detection by reducing probability of marking false edge points, good localization and reduced response on the edges [3].

1. The Gaussian filter is used to smoothen the image to eliminate noise and other unwanted details or texture.

$$g(x, y) = G_\sigma(x, y).f(x, y) \quad where \quad G_\sigma = \frac{1}{\sqrt{2\pi\sigma^2}} exp\left(-\frac{x^2 + y^2}{2\sigma^2}\right) \tag{4}$$

2. Calculate the gradient of $g(x, y)$ based on these gradient operators (Roberts, Sobel, Prewitt, Laplacian or Kirsch)

$$M(x, y) = \sqrt{g_x^2(x, y) + g_y^2(x, y)} \quad and \quad \theta(x, y) = tan^{-1}[g_y(x, y)/g_x(x, y)] \tag{5}$$

3. Threshold M based on $M_T(x, y) = M(x, y)$ if M(x,y) > T where T is the selected value where the given edge elements are maintained and noise is suppressed.
4. Edge segments are linked to become continuous edges in T_2.

Canny algorithm steps involves preprocessing done by convolution of the images with a 5×5 Gaussian mask, finding the edge strength with for instance a sobel operator in both axes (X, Y) and key four important directions are chosen and suppressed [3].

Laplacian Operator. Laplacian operator is a second order edge detection derivative mask. The edges are either positive or negative Laplacian operators [3]. It is more easier to implement and has a single mask [3,4,8,15]. The Laplacian operator is given as

$$\theta^2 = \theta x \theta = \begin{bmatrix} \frac{\delta}{\delta v} & \frac{\delta}{\delta w} \end{bmatrix} \cdot \begin{bmatrix} \frac{\delta}{\delta v} & \frac{\delta}{\delta w} \end{bmatrix} = \frac{\delta^2}{\delta v^2} + \frac{\delta^2}{\delta w^2} \tag{6}$$

$$\theta^2 f = \left(\begin{bmatrix} \frac{\delta}{\delta v} & \frac{\delta}{\delta w} \end{bmatrix} \begin{bmatrix} \frac{\delta}{\delta v} & \frac{\delta}{\delta w} \end{bmatrix} \right) I = \frac{\delta^2 I}{\delta v^2} + \frac{\delta^2 I}{\delta w^2} \tag{7}$$

Discrete approximation will give below for $\theta^2 f$

$$\theta^2 f = -4f(i,j) + f(i,j+1) + f(i,j-1) + f(i+1,j) + f(i-1,j) \tag{8}$$

The Laplacian operator matrix is represented as follows.

$$L_o = \begin{bmatrix} 0 & -1 & +0 \\ -1 & +4 & -1 \\ 0 & -1 & +0 \end{bmatrix} A \qquad L(diagonals) = \begin{bmatrix} -1 & -1 & -1 \\ -1 & +8 & -1 \\ -1 & -1 & -1 \end{bmatrix} A \tag{9}$$

The Laplacian-of-Gaussian (LOG) (Marr-Hildreth) edge detector does smoothing before a Gaussian filter is applied. The LoG kernel is precalculated and one convolution only is required on the facial image [8] and given $G(x,y)$ being denoted as $e^{-frac{x^2+y^2}{2\alpha^2}}$ it can be proved that

$$\theta^2[f(x,y) * G(x,y))] = \theta^2 G(x,y).f(x,y) \tag{10}$$

$$\theta^2 G(x,y) = (\frac{r^2 - \sigma^2}{\sigma^2})e^{-r^2/2\sigma^2}, (r^2 = x^2 + y^2) \tag{11}$$

$$\theta^2 G \approx G(x,y;\sigma_1) - G(x,y;\sigma_2) \tag{12}$$

The Laplacian of Gaussian can be approximated by the difference between two Gaussian functions. This is the difference of Gaussians or DoG kernel. Laplace operation use only one template, so the amount of calculation is small. Laplace algorithm is sensitive to the noise in the image. Sobel edge detection operator is used to better edge effect at the same time, and could smoothen noise, reduce the sensitivity to noise [3,8]. The Robert edge detection operator is the most simple. It is the difference of adjacent pixels detection using two diagonal directions of the image gradient magnitude [4]. Detecting horizontal and vertical edges is good, but in the tilt direction of the edge detection, accuracy its relatively poor and more sensitive to noise. Its advantages are being simple and fast [15]. The outline for detection of eyes and mouth parts are directly related to the accuracy of face recognition, which requires the operator to have good anti-noise ability [3].

Kirsch Compass Mask. The Kirsch compass mask uses a mask which is base-lined on the requirements or specification [10, 15]. The operator takes in one kernel mask which it rotates clockwise by 45° increments given the 8 directions [2, 8, 21]. Local Directional Patterns use kirsch masks. This differs from Robinson algorithm which uses a standardized mask (Fig. 1).

$$\begin{bmatrix} -3 & -3 & 5 \\ -3 & 0 & 5 \\ -3 & -3 & 5 \end{bmatrix} \begin{bmatrix} -3 & 5 & 5 \\ -3 & 0 & 5 \\ -3 & -3 & -3 \end{bmatrix} \begin{bmatrix} 5 & 5 & 5 \\ -3 & 0 & -3 \\ -3 & -3 & -3 \end{bmatrix} \begin{bmatrix} 5 & 5 & -3 \\ 5 & 0 & -3 \\ -3 & -3 & -3 \end{bmatrix} \begin{bmatrix} 5 & -3 & -3 \\ 5 & 0 & -3 \\ 5 & -3 & -3 \end{bmatrix} \begin{bmatrix} -3 & -3 & -3 \\ 5 & 0 & -3 \\ 5 & 5 & -3 \end{bmatrix} \begin{bmatrix} -3 & -3 & -3 \\ -3 & 0 & -3 \\ 5 & 5 & 5 \end{bmatrix} \begin{bmatrix} -3 & -3 & -3 \\ -3 & 0 & 5 \\ -3 & 5 & 5 \end{bmatrix}$$

Fig. 1. Local Directional Patterns based Kirsch Mask

3   Local Based Facial Expression Feature Extraction

Facial expression analysis influences wide areas in human computer interaction [10]. Local binary patterns and their 2D and 3D variants have been used in this field. Holistic and local based feature extractors have also been used successfully. PCA feature extractors are prominent holistic algorithms. Local binary patterns, Gabor filters and Gabor wavelets and local directional patterns have been used as expression feature extractors [2, 5, 17]. Local binary patterns are based on facial images being split into local sub regions and use gray level images to enable for invariance [2]. The facial region's components like eyes and forehead are used as sub regions. The challenges of facial occlusion and rigidness are faced though grey scale image conversion [2, 9, 13]. The features extracted are used to form a histogram for classification with machine learning algorithms like support vector machines or random forest [2, 9, 13]. The basic local binary pattern non center pixels use the central pixel as the threshold value taking binary values [2, 9, 13]. Uniform local binary patterns have uniform bitwise transition and 256 textural patterns with radius r and neighbors n. This is represented in the equation below as

$$LBP_{(n,r)} = \sum_{n-1}^{n=0} s(p_n - p_c)2^n. \tag{13}$$

The gray level has 2^n-bin unique codes and the value p_c is the center grayscale value, p_n is the neighbour gray scale value.

Local Directional Patterns. LDP includes a compass mask based on the Kirsch algorithm or edge detector [2,11,21]. The compass mask allows for extraction of facial data and encodes it with the prominent directional indexes [2,21]. The Kirsch compass masks undergo convolution based on the original image to identify the edges. The algorithm is a non linear edge detector which returns the highest edges in specific directions [2,21]. The Kirsch operator's edge size is deduced with all directions considered as the maximum magnitude and this is shown in the local directional pattern kirsch convolutionary equation with the associated example M_0:

$$LDP_x(\sigma) = \sum_K \sum_L f(LDP_q(o,u),\sigma). \qquad (14)$$

(with $r=0$ $r=0$ above the summations)

4 Facial Expression Implementation

The implementation involved analyzing the extended CK+ and JAFFE databases. The Viola Jones Open CV implementation was used for detection. The images were preprocessed with histogram equalization and edge detection. The key edge detectors include Sobel, Prewitt, Roberts, Laplacian of Gaussian, Difference Of Gaussian, Laplacian and the Canny edge detector. These were used to remove unwanted noise. The images were then feature extracted using local binary and directional patterns. The supervised learning algorithm used is k-nearest neighbor. The expressions included fear, anger, happy, sad, neutral, contempt and surprise. Training of the models was done using the k-nearest neighbor classifier. The following section details the algorithm, datasets and implementation.

The study executed several experiments to get the accuracy of the feature vectors from the local directional and binary pattern algorithms. The data was from the JAFFE dataset and the CK+ facial dataset. Different feature extraction tests were executed namely basic LBP and local directional patterns. The images were measured by different edge detection algorithms like Canny, Sobel, Prewitt and Kirsch. For preprocessing, the images were also enhanced by different filters for image equalization. The machine learning classifier k-nearest neighbour was used for the classification and feature selection. The algorithm used is shown in Algorithm 1. The study analyzed images from the CK+ dataset and the JAFFE dataset.

Preprocessing and Feature Selection. Preprocessing was achieved using the Principal Component Analysis algorithm. With this, the number of parameters was streamlined to include only relevant and important parameters only [17]. The principal component architecture or PCA was used to eliminate unwanted dimensions of feature vectors post feature extraction. Gabor linear filters were used in the static domain and are similar to a Gaussian kernel with modulations based on a sinusoidal wave [17,19].

Data: Download and detect facial image datasets
Result: Selected facial expressions
while *For every selected image I in the CK+ or JAFFE dataset* do
| 1. Split training and test images;
| 2. Process each facial image from the dataset by:
| 3. Detecting the local face components with Viola Jones and OpenCV
| python
| 4. Preprocess with histogram equalization and normalization
| 5 Edge detectors are executed to eliminate unwanted edges
| 6. Apply Gabor Filters and extract the LBP and LDP features;
| 7. Apply the classification on each with k nearest neighbor classifier
| End For'
end

Algorithm 1: LBP and LDP algorithms to analyse images [17]

Datasets. The study used python and anaconda to implement the feature extraction and classification of the facial images. The images were turned into base sizes based 680 to 480 dimensions. The LDP and LBP algorithm used k-nearest neighbor classifier. The study used a MEAN stack framework powered by micro services executed on an python, Node.js and REST Framework. The study chose the JAFFE and CK+ dataset for implementation [19]. For static image analysis, the study used the CK+ dataset and JAFFE set dataset. The images include different facial expressions reflecting mixed facial emotions. The given emotions included fear, sadness, happiness/joy, disgust and neutral. The facial JAFFE dataset was classified based on Japanese faces. It was chosen due to its diversity with images from the Asian community. The CK+ dataset was selected because of interracial mix in the images and young age groups. It was composed of 100 faces of American, Asian and Latin origin [21] and 123 participants. Other races accounted for six percent of the images [19]. The study considered the expressions to include anger, happiness, sadness, disgust, fear and surprise [21].

Classification. Successful facial expression has been achieved using support vector machines, k nearest neighbors, neural networks, random forest and decision trees. The study uses k-nearest neighbor [11,13] for classification and kirsch based local directional pattern gives the edge detection advantage to remove unwanted features and reduce the error rater [?]. The k-nearest neighbor, a lazy algorithm, allows for keeping all training data and the classification is based on the entire dataset. The algorithm is very accurate on multi-class issues and with high speed. The PCA or principal component analysis algorithm is used to resize the number of images. The study used the k-nearest neighbor [11] with nearest neighbor, given x_q, and k nearest discreet neighbors and having k nearest neighbors is defined as kNN in equation below [1,21].

$$kNN = f(x_q)\frac{\sum_{i=1}^{k} f(x_i)}{k} \quad \sum_{i}^{k} 1/(i+1) = 1 + \frac{1}{2} + ... + \frac{1}{4} + .. + \frac{1}{k} \quad (15)$$

4.1 Experiment and Results

The classification results of the CK+ database based on the edge detection algorithms and k nearest neighbor as well as the local binary pattern feature extractor is shown in the following table with different accuracies based on each edge detector. The JAFFE and CK+ datasets were used with 210 and 400 images respectively. Preprocessing was done with histogram equalization and the various edge detectors. Static image analysis experimental results on CK+ Dataset is shown in the following Table 1.

Table 1. Classification results

	k-Nearest Neighbour and LBP Variants (CK+)							
	Sobel	Kirsch	LoG	Canny	Laplace	Prewitt		
r, n = 16, 2	0.954	0.972	0.961	0.979	0.971	0.978	400 images	CK+
r, n = 8, 2	0.947	0.969	0.959	0.970	0.968	0.975	400 images	CK+
r, n = 8, 2	0.955	0.957	0.962	0.972	0.972	0.969	400 images	CK+
ELBP	0.963	0.969	0.966	0.976	0.968	0.975	400 images	CK+
CS-LBP	0.960	0.950	0.970	0.974	0.965	0.969	400 images	CK+
RLBP	0.915	0.972	0.961	0.969	0.962	0.978	400 images	CK+
	k-Nearest Neighbor and LBP Variants (JAFFE Dataset)							
	Sobel	Kirsch	LoG	Canny	Laplace	Prewitt		
r, n = 16, 2	0.964	0.958	0.955	0.973	0.959	0.963	210 images	JAFFE
r, n = 8,2	0.957	0.969	0.953	0.976	0.961	0.961	210 images	JAFFE
r, n = 8,2	0.945	0.961	0.949	0.966	0.964	0.969	210 images	JAFFE
ELBP	0.961	0.963	0.968	0.975	0.958	0.958	210 images	JAFFE
CS-LBP	0.961	0.961	0.964	0.971	0.956	0.971	210 images	JAFFE
RLBP	0.953	0.970	0.950	0.973	0.969	0.965	210 images	JAFFE
ELBP	0.943	0.969	0.957	0.979	0.974	0.973	210 images	JAFFE

Best results were observed when the Central Symmetric LBP algorithm was paired with the Canny Edge Detector and classified with the k nearest neighbor. The kirsch algorithm performed well but its accuracy was less than the canny edge detector.

Table 2. kNN, LDP on CK+ 400 images

	Sobel	Robinson	LoG	Canny	Kirsch	Prewitt
k = 2	0.964	0.972	0.941	0.982	0.951	0.958
k = 3	0.949	0.965	0.979	0.978	0.948	0.965
k = 4	0.975	0.963	0.962	0.977	0.962	0.959

The local directional pattern algorithm was also applied to an image set of 400 with k nearest neighbour classifier for CK+ dataset as well as various edge detectors and the results are shown in the following table. Static image analysis experimental results on CK+ and JAFFE Dataset are shown in the Tables 2 and 3.

Table 3. kNN and LDP on JAFFE 213 images

	Sobel	Robinson	LoG	Canny	Kirsch	Prewitt
k = 2	0.943	0.954	0.959	0.970	0.699	0.948
k = 3	0.921	0.932	0.945	0.976	0.960	0.934
k = 4	0.911	0.893	0.905	0.977	0.955	0.956

Static image analysis experimental results on CK+ Dataset. The same experiments were also executed using the JAFFE dataset. The Canny edge detector improved results for the CS-LBP and ELBP variants. The CS-LBP had an accuracy of 97% for k = 2 on the k-nearest neighbor, JAFFE dataset, 98.2 for the LDP and 97.9% for the ELBP variant as shown in Table 1. The following 2 graphs show accuracy trends for both CK+ and JAFFE datasets with Canny and Kirsch detectors.

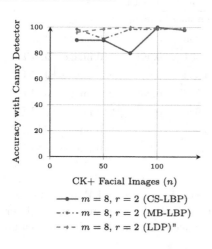

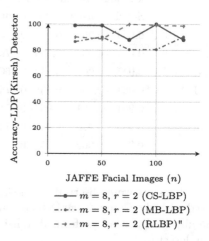

4.2 Confusion Matrix for the Canny Edge Detector and Local Binary Pattern

The confusion matrices for the Canny Edge Detector and Local Binary Pattern showed a success of between 97% and 98% when Gabor Filtered on the CK+ and JAFFE database. The following confusion matrix gives detail of the precision recall accuracy for the CK+ dataset which included 400 images. For classification, k-nearest neighbor was used. The CK+ dataset had 400 images analyzed over the 6 expression types namely anger, disgust, fear, happy, sadness and neutral. For the CK+ dataset, the sadness expression type showed modal frequency in the confusion matrix and for the JAFFE datasets, the anger expression type was the highest and the confusion matrix is represented as follows (Figs. 2 and 3).

	Predicted								Predicted					
Actual		Angry	Sad	Happy	Disgust	Neutral	Surprise			Angry	Sad	Happy	Disgust	Neutral	Surprise
	Angry	61	1	2	2	2	3		Angry	74	1	2	4	2	3
	Sad	0	36	0	1	2	1		Sad	3	86	2	4	2	1
	Happy	2	2	21	2	1	0		Happy	2	2	48	2	1	0
	Disgust	1	0	2	12	1	0		Disgust	3	4	1	41	1	0
	Neutral	2	1	0	0	19	0		Neutral	2	1	2	2	71	0
	Surprise	1	0	3	1	0	31		Surprise	3	0	2	1	0	27

Fig. 2. JAFFE Dataset   **Fig. 3.** Extended CK+ Dataset

4.3 Conclusions

Edge detection plays a very important role in preprocessing of facial expressions. This paper discussed various edge detectors as well as the strengths of each. Key algorithms include Canny, Sobel, Kirsch and Laplacian. The Sobel operator brings simplicity but is impacted by noise. The Canny edge detector allows for image smoothening to reduce noise levels, improve the signal to noise ratio. The facial expression accuracy was higher on using the Canny method over the Kirsch algorithm. The kirsch algorithm is the foundation of local directional pattern and the histogram computational time was reduced by 40% since specific edges were selected. Both the Canny and Kirsch algorithms saw execution times reduced because they enable feature selection by removing redundant information.

References

1. Aggarwal, C.C.: Data Mining. Springer, Cham (2015). https://doi.org/10.1007/978-3-319-14142-8
2. Aung, M.S., et al.: The automatic detection of chronic pain-related expression: requirements, challenges and the multimodal EmoPain dataset. IEEE Trans. Affect. Comput. **7**(4), 435–451 (2015)
3. Canny, J.: A computational approach to edge detection. IEEE Trans. Pattern Anal. Mach. Intell. **8**(6), 679–698 (1986)
4. Nadernejad, E., Sharifzadeh, S.: Edge detection techniques: evaluations and comparisons. Appl. Sci. **2**(31), 1507–1520 (2008)
5. Fasel, B., Luettin, J.: Automatic facial expression analysis: a survey. Pattern Recogn. **36**(1), 259–275 (2003)
6. Huang, X., Zhao, G., Pietikäinen, M., Zheng, W.: Dynamic facial expression recognition using boosted component-based spatiotemporal features and multi-classifier fusion. In: Blanc-Talon, J., Bone, D., Philips, W., Popescu, D., Scheunders, P. (eds.) ACIVS 2010. LNCS, vol. 6475, pp. 312–322. Springer, Heidelberg (2010). https://doi.org/10.1007/978-3-642-17691-3_29

7. Karande, K.J., Talbar, S.N.: Canny edge detection for face recognition. In: Independent Component Analysis of Edge Information for Face Recognition. SpringerBriefs in Applied Sciences and Technology, pp. 21–33. Springer, India (2014). https://doi.org/10.1007/978-81-322-1512-7_2

8. Lakshmi, S., Sankaranarayanan, D.V.: A study of edge detection techniques for segmentation computing approaches. IJCA "Computer Aided Soft Computing Techniques for Imaging and Biomedical Applications" CASCT, pp. 35–40 (2010)

9. Lemaire, P., Ben Amor, B., Ardabilian, M., Chen, L., Daoudi, M.: Fully automatic 3D facial expression recognition using a region-based approach. In: Proceedings of the 2011 Joint ACM Workshop on Human Gesture and Behavior Understanding, New York, USA, pp. 53–58. ACM (2011)

10. Kaur, M., Vashisht, R.: Comparative study of facial expression recognition techniques. J. Comput. Appl. **13**(1), 43–50 (2011)

11. Nurzynska, K., Smolka, B.: Smiling and neutral facial display recognition with the local binary patterns operator. J. Med. Imaging Health Inform. **5**(6), 1374–1382 (2015)

12. Othman, Z., et al.: Comparison of Canny and Sobel edge detection in MRI images. Comput. Sci. Biomech. 133–136 (2009)

13. Padgett, C., Cottrell, G.W.: Representing face images for emotion classification. In: Advances in neural information processing systems, pp. 894–900 (1997)

14. Papageorgiou, C.P., Oren, M., Poggio, T.A.: General framework for object detection. In: Sixth International Conference on Computer Vision (IEEE Cat. No. 98CH36271). IEEE (1998)

15. Acharjya, P.P., Das, R., Ghoshal, D.: Study and comparison of different edge detectors for image segmentation. J. Comput. Sci. Technol. Graph. Vis. 12(13) 2012. Version 1.0

16. Rani, S., et al.: Pre filtering techniques for face recognition based on edge detection algorithm. J. Eng. Technol. 13–218 (2017)

17. RaviKumar, Y., RaviKumar, C.: An improved LBP to extract nonuniform patterns with Gabor filter to increase face similarity. In: CCIP 2016, pp. 1–5 (2016)

18. Sanin, A., et al.: Spatio-temporal covariance descriptors for action and gesture recognition. In: 2013 IEEE Workshop on Applications of Computer Vision (WACV)

19. Spizhevoy, A.S.: Robust dynamic facial expressions recognition using Lbp-Top descriptors and Bag-of-Words classification model. Pattern Recogn. Image Anal. **26**(1), 216–220 (2016)

20. Saini, V., Garg, R.: A comparative analysis on edge detection techniques used in image processing. IOSR J. Electron. Commun. Eng. (IOSRJECE), 56–59 (2012). ISSN: 2278-2834

21. Viola, P., Jones, M.J.: Robust real-time face detection. Int. J. Comput. Vis. **57**(2), 137–154 (2004)

22. Gao, W., Yang, L., Zhang, X., Liu, H.: An improved Sobel edge detection. IEEE 978-1-4244-5540-9/10/$26.00 (2010)

23. Yang, M.H., Kriegman, D.J., Ahuja, N.: Detecting faces in images: a survey. IEEE Trans. Pattern Anal. Mach. Intell. **24**(1), 34–58 (2002)

24. Shah, Z.H., Kaushik, V.: Performance analysis of canny edge detection for illumination invariant facial expression recognition. In: 2015 International Conference on Industrial Instrumentation and Control (ICIC), IEEE (2015)

Violent Vocabulary Extraction Methodology: Application to the Radicalism Detection on Social Media

Amal Rekik[1,2(✉)], Salma Jamoussi[1,2],
and Abdelmajid Ben Hamadou[1,2]

[1] Multimedia InfoRmation Systems and Advanced Computing
Laboratory MIRACL, University of Sfax, Sfax, Tunisia
rekik.amal91@gmail.com, jamoussi@gmail.com,
abdelmajid.benhamadou@isimsf.rnu.tn
[2] Digital Research Center of Sfax DRCS, 3021 Sfax, Tunisia

Abstract. Nowadays, social networks have become powerful mediums of communication providing information, learning and entertainment. Unfortunately, these platforms can be sorely manipulated by vicious users sharing malicious contents. Therefore, the process of mining and analyzing such published suspicious content is a considerably challenging task that serves to fight against the online radicalization. For this purpose, we propose, in this paper, a new methodology for extracting and analyzing violent vocabulary shared on social networks with the exploration a set of natural language processing and data mining techniques. Our method relies mainly on extracting a set of profiles judged by a domain expert as extremist and non-extremist' users. Then, we focus on their shared textual content in order to detect malicious vocabulary published within the radical context as well as their violence' degrees. Finally, in order to evaluate the performance of our method, we resort to an expert who verifies the final list of the extracted vocabulary annotated by our method. Thus, the given results show its effectiveness as well as its efficiency.

Keywords: Violent vocabulary · Vocabulary extraction · Terrorist user · Radicalism detection · Social network analysis

1 Introduction

Today, the religious radicalization becomes one of the most furious peril threatening the public security around the whole world. Indeed, the term radicalization is implied as a process through which individuals evolve towards extremism by either practicing, promoting or defending violence to achieve their goals. For this purpose, this trend should be seen in light especially with the emergency of the enormous impact of social networks which ensure the swift development of online radicalization. In fact, radical organizations rely heavily on social networks to promote extremism and share suspicious content which can be either open and transparent or under cover and coded. As a result, social networks have become a gateway for extremists and a starting point of radicalization playing the role of facilitators and amplifiers within the community. On

© Springer Nature Switzerland AG 2019
N. T. Nguyen et al. (Eds.): ICCCI 2019, LNAI 11684, pp. 97–109, 2019.
https://doi.org/10.1007/978-3-030-28374-2_9

the other hand, extremists on these networks are frequently exploring a terribly evil, violent and vindictive vocabulary in order to propagate their vicious ideas. Therefore, the process of mining and analyzing such published suspicious content on social networks is a considerably challenging task that raises several requirements to be addressed and serves to fight against the online radicalization. So, faced to this dangerous phenomenon, the prevention of the online radicalization has become a very indispensable action that frustrates recruitment and avoids transitions from excitement of emotions and ideological influence to the active participation by force and violence.

In this context, we propose in this paper a new methodology for violent vocabulary extraction in order to detect radicalism on social networks. Our method relies first on a set of social networks collected profiles annotated by a domain expert as extremist and non-extremist' users. Then, we focus precisely on their textual content in order to extract the vocabulary specific to both radical and non-radical contexts. This analyzed content is generally shared in the Arabic language which raise additional requirements to be respected in the context of data analyzes field. Finally, by using a set of natural language processing and data mining techniques, our methodology attempts to extract a fierce vocabulary weighted by their violence's degree. In fact, exploring our methodology to analyze malicious shared content and extract violent vocabulary specific to radical discourses leads to discover various extremists' profiles and thus detect radicalism on social networks.

The reminder of this paper is planned as follows: the next section is devoted for the related work. In Sect. 3, we go into details of our proposed methodology for the violent vocabulary extraction from social networks. Section 4 reports some statistics of the collected vocabulary and the experiments results relying on the expert observations. We end up with the conclusion and the future work in Sect. 5.

2   Related Work

The vocabulary extraction and the social network analysis are two of the most important tasks that interest researchers in the data mining field. In this context, several studies have been proposed in the literature [1–5]. So, this section surveys previous work in the vocabulary extraction field.

In [6], the author proposes a new principle for vocabulary selection dedicated for the theme detection task. This method is based mainly on the preposition that each theme is defined by its own vocabulary. Moreover, the author assumes that if the vocabulary selection method is the same as the word frequency method, some non-important frequent word will be selected to form the vocabulary. While, other non-frequent and relevant words will not be preserved. For this purpose, the proposed method consists first on evaluating the frequency measure for all the words of the theme's learning, for each given theme. Then, the author keeps only the words with the highest values. In this case, he obtains a vocabulary for each treated theme. Next, he performs the union of these obtained vocabularies by using the same size of each theme's vocabulary or using different sizes in order to form the final vocabulary.

In [7], authors employ the SVM applying the Random forest technique in order to select the vocabulary. In fact, the Random forest is a classification method that provides feature importance. The decision tree forest algorithm performs learning on multiple decision trees trained on slightly k different subsets of data. The k predictions of the variable of interest are stored for each original observation. Then, the prediction of the random forest is deducted as a simple majority vote through the Ensemble learning algorithm. Thus, important features are selected to form the final vocabulary.

In [8], author proposed an unsupervised algorithm to select task-specific Chinese words from a large general vocabulary. The proposed method is based on measuring the correlation of two adjacent character strings by calculating their mutual information (MI) [9]. Authors segmented the training data into word sequences based on a general vocabulary. Each word can be segmented into two adjacent character strings. Next, they computed the MI of each word by choosing the segmentation that provided a minimum MI value. If the MI of a word is greater than a predefined threshold, they consider that it matches the target task. Thus, this word belongs to the extracted vocabulary.

In [10], authors assume that the vocabulary used by each individual is a combination of two vocabularies which are: A topic-independent lecture vocabulary, that contains vocabulary common to spontaneous speech, and a topic dependent vocabulary. So, authors proposed a novel method for vocabulary selection to automatically adapt automatic speech recognition This method proceeds with the topic-independent lecture vocabulary, that consists of stop words and common words used in spontaneous lecture speech. Moreover, they select a topic-specific vocabulary for each lecture utilizing materials that are available before the lecture begins, like lecture slides. Using these documents, the proposed method collects automatically a large corpus of related documents from the World-Wide-Web. Finally, an active recognition vocabulary is selected using a feature-based word ranking computed using this corpus.

So, during this stage, we have arrived to deliver the weaknesses of the studied approaches. In fact, some methods do not occur in the language we are dealing with which is Arabic. Other methods neglect the semantic context during the extraction of vocabulary. Thus, all these methods are not designed exactly for our goals since we are mainly interested on the dangerous vocabulary extraction which is a highly sensitive field.

3   Proposed Methodology

Online religious radicalization on social networks is a malicious stir which is generally practiced by Arabic extremists. Thus, we are mainly interested in our methodology by the Arabic language analyzes in order to extract the violent vocabulary shared by radical communities. Meanwhile, analyzing Arabic language contents raises several requirements to be addressed and assists to make of our methodology a scoop in the data mining field. In addition, extracting such dangerous vocabulary serves to discover several extremists' users and thus extract radicalism on social networks. Our methodology contains mainly three major stages: (1) The suspicious data collection step from two social media sites which are Twitter and YouTube. (2) The frequent n-grams and itemsets extraction from the collected contents as well as their violence' degrees. These two primal steps are accomplished for both radical and non-radical communities. (3) The violent vocabulary extraction. Figure 1 represents the overall process of our methodology.

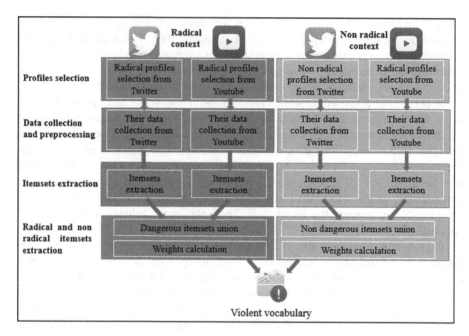

Fig. 1. The overall process of our proposed methodology

3.1   Data Collection and Preprocessing

The data collection step consists mainly on extracting textual content shared by both radical and non-radical communities on Twitter and YouTube. For this purpose, we start initially by collecting a set of extremists and non-extremist users from these two social media sites. To do so, we explore our data collection methodology proposed in [11]. This later consists first on preparing an incremented list of dangerous keywords which are judged by a domain expert such as Islamic state, Sharia, Jihad… Then, it excerpts Twitter users who talk about these suspicious keyword as well as the impli-cated users in terrorists' attacks. Nevertheless, the strategy adopted to collect data from YouTube consists on keeping users that are reactive towards videos of extremism and thus have a clear attitude to the radicalism. Then, the collected profiles are annotated by a domain expert in order to distinguish between radical and non-radical users. So, exploring this methodology, we conserve two communities in order to analyze their textual content: (1) the radical community containing extremist users and (2) the non-radical communities holding non-extremist users.

After this step, we proceed the data collection stage. So, we extract all the published textual data of each Twitter user belonging to each community. On the other hand, for every YouTube user of each community, we keep all his comments toward malicious videos as well as the titles and descriptions of his liked and shared videos.

Originally, the data extracted from these social media is reached by open sources obtained from the content generated by different users. Meanwhile, the results of the data mining method depend heavily on the quality of the data. For this reason, the preprocessing of the collected data is very crucial to achieve a performant data analyzes step. Therefore, during this stage, we perform the preprocessing of the collected data. To do so, we clean first all characters that are not in Arabic Language. Then we remove diacritics, punctuation marks, numbers and stop words from the Arabic textual data. Hence, we obtain two final datasets appropriated for radical and non-radical textual content which are prepared to be analyzed.

3.2 N-Grams and Itemsets Mining

After the data collection stage, we move to the extraction of the frequent n-grams and itemsets from the two collected preprocessed datasets. In fact, radical organizations as well as their used vocabulary differ from one social network to another. For this purpose, this step consists on analyzing the data of each community collected from Twitter and Youtube separately and then merge the obtained results. So, initially, we have separated each data shared by the radical community on Twitter and Youtube in n-grams with n <= 3. Similarly, we have represented each data shared by the non-radical community in n-grams with n <= 3. In fact, an n-gram is defined as a subsequence of n words constructed from a given sequence respecting the order. Some examples of these used n-grams are represented as follows:

Unigram (n=1): Example: "دولة (state)"," يوم (day)", …
Bigram (n=2): Example: "دولة إسلام (Islam state)"; "متحف باردو (Bardo museum)", …
Trigram (n=3): Example: "الإمارات العربية المتحدة" (United Arab Emirates), …

After the representation of the textual content shared by both radical and non-radical communities, we proceed the frequent n-grams and itemsets extraction step. Actually, an itemset is an association of n-grams occurring together in the collected data ignoring the order. Each n-gram has a support which is defined as its frequency in the collected dataset. Likewise, each itemset possesses a support corresponding to the frequency of simultaneous appearance of n-grams contained in the data set and which can be calculated as follow:

$$Support(itemset\ I) = \frac{NumberDataContaining(I)}{TotalNumberOfData}$$

Where NumberDataContaining(I) refers to the number of data composing the itemset I, and TotalNumberOfData is the size of the overall dataset.

Each n-gram or itemset is considered as frequent if its support is greater than or equal to a predefined threshold. Indeed, the frequent n-grams and itemsets extraction from data play one of the most essential role since it tries to find interesting patterns from databases, and thus constitutes the core stage of our methodology.

At this step, our approach explores the A-priori algorithm in order to extract the frequent n-grams and itemsets. In fact, the A-priori algorithm is a data mining algorithm designed in the field of learning association rules. It is used to recognize properties that come up frequently in the analyzed data.

In the dataset appropriated to the radical community, there are x elements corresponding to the tweets extracted from radical organizations on Twitter and Youtube also known as transactions. Each element is described by a set of attributes $A = \{a_i\}$ where each a_i corresponds to an item or an itemset.

So, we have extracted all the n-grams and itemsets and then calculated their supports to prune those which are non-frequent. Next, we keep as frequent n-grams and itemsets the union of the obtained frequent n-grams and itemsets from Twitter and Youtube. The final support of each obtained n-grams or itemsets is calculated as follow:

If the n-gram or the itemset is acquired from Twitter and not obtained from Youtube, then:

$$Support(itemset\ I) = Support(I)_{Twitter}$$

If the n-gram or the itemset is acquired from Youtube and not obtained from Twitter, then:

$$Support(itemset\ I) = Support(I)_{Youtube}$$

If the n-gram or the itemset is acquired from both Twitter and Youtube, then:

$$Support(itemset\ I) = \frac{Support(I)_{Twitter} + support(I)_{Youtube}}{2}$$

Where $Support(I)_{Twitter}$ is the support of the itemset I extracted from Twitter, and $Support(I)_{Youtube}$ is the support of the itemset I extracted from Youtube. After the computation of the support of each n-gram and itemset, we notice that these obtained supports are closed and scattered. Thus, it is difficile to distinguish between them. Accordingly, we have ranked the obtained frequent n-grams and itemsets in descending order of their supports. Afterwards, we assign for each item and itemset a weight referring to its importance in the dataset. This weight can be calculated as follow:

$$Weight(Itemset\ I) = \frac{(N+1) - Rank(I)}{(N+1)}$$

Where N is the number of the extracted frequent n-grams or itemsets and Rank is the order of the n-gram or itemset according to its support. For example, the following transaction contains 3 n-grams (1 unigram and 2 bigrams) and 2 itemset having the pursuant supports. On that account, their weights will be as follow (Table 1):

These previous steps are carried out similarly for the dataset appropriated to the non-radical community. So, we obtain likewise for each n-gram and itemset extracted from the non-radical content, their assigned weight. For instance, the following transaction contains 3 n-grams (unigrams) and 3 itemsets extracted from the non-radical context and having the pursuant supports. Hence, their weights will be presented in Table 2:

Table 1. Example of radical itemsets, their supports and their weights

Itemsets and their English translation	Supports	Weight Radical
{باقية تتمدد, قتل} {Residual stretch,kill}	0,4	0,83
{جيش إسلام} {Army of Islam}	0,35	0,66
{قصف، مجاهد} {Shell, mujahid}	0,3	0,5
{جيش عزة, قتل} {Army of Azza, kill}	0,22	0,33
{دولة} {Country}	0,1	0,16

Table 2. Example of non-radical itemsets, their supports and their weights

Itemsets and their English translation	Supports	Weight NonRadical
{خير} {benevolent}	0,5	0,86
{دولة} {Country}	0,3	0,71
{سوريا،سلام} {Syria, peace}	0,25	0,57
{سعادة} {happiness}	0,2	0,43
{مكافحة،إرهاب} {Counter, terrorism}	0,15	0,29
{عالم،حب} {world, love}	0,11	0,14

Hence, we have obtained at this stage two types of n-grams and itemset: (1) a set of n-grams and itemsets designing the radical context and (2) a set of n-grams and itemsets designing the non-radical context.

3.3 Violent Vocabulary Extraction

After the frequent n-grams and itemsets extraction step, we proceed the dangerous vocabulary mining task. At this stage, we aim to explore the obtained frequent n-grams and itemsets of both radical and non-radical contexts in order to extract the violent vocabulary employed by the extremists. Several frequent n-grams and itemsets are used by both radical and non-radical organizations. Thus, we cannot categorize these common n-grams/itemsets as radical or non-radical. For this purpose, we assign for each one a violence degree referring to its degree of danger. The danger degree is calculated as follow:

$$ViolenceDegree(Itemset\ I) = weight(I)_{Radical} - weight(I)_{NonRadical}$$

Where $weight(I)_{Radical}$ is the weight of the n-grams and itemset I extracted from the radical context and $weight(I)_{NonRadical}$ is the weight of the n-grams and itemset I in the non-radical context.

For example, following the two previous examples represented in Tables 1 and 2, we obtain the following final vocabulary presented in Table 3 and composing by the set of n-grams and itemsets accompanied by their violence' degrees as well as their annotation:

Table 3. Example of itemsets composing the final vocabulary

Itemsets and their English translation	Weight Radical	Weight NonRadical	Violence Degree	Class
{باقية تتمدد, قتل} {Residual stretch,kill}	0,83	0	0,83	Radical
{جيش إسلام} {Army of Islam}	0,66	0	0,66	Radical
{قصف، مجاهد} {Shell, mujahid}	0,5	0	0,5	Radical
{جيش عزة, قتل} {Army of Azza, kill}	0,33	0	0,33	Non-Radical
{دولة} {Country}	0,16	0,71	-0,55	Non-Radical
{خير} {benevolent}	0	0,86	-0,86	Non-Radical
{سوريا، سلام} {Syria, peace}	0	0,57	-0,57	Non-Radical
{سعادة} {happiness}	0	0,43	-0,43	Non-Radical
{مكافحة، إرهاب} {Counter, terrorism}	0	0,29	-0,29	Non-Radical
{عالم،حب} {world, love}	0	0,14	-0,14	Non-Radical

We can note from the previous table that n-grams and itemsets having positive degree of danger are annotated as radicals. Yet, those which have negative degree are considered as non-radicals. As a result, we obtain the violent vocabulary of radical users on social networks. This vocabulary can be explored later in order to detect extremists' users spreading on social networks.

4   Evaluation

Each data mining methodology should inevitably be evaluated in order to verify its performance in reaching the targeted aim. That's why, we present in this section, the used experiments to evaluate the performance of our methodology to collect the radical vocabulary shared by extremists on social networks. Thus, we have used different library and APIs on the RStudio platform that require a set of development tools to automate their main tasks so that we perform our dangerous vocabulary collection methodology. Furthermore, we have referred to a domain expert in order to evaluate the annotation of the collected dangerous vocabulary. Moreover, in order to validate our expert's annotation, we have resort to a sociologist which plays the role of a second expert for the aim of estimating the inter-annotation agreement between these two experts. So, the rest of the paper will introduce a set of statistics describing our analyzed data as well as our extracted vocabulary and results.

4.1   Implementation Details

In order to perform the required steps and collect violent vocabulary from social networks, we have explored several packages on the RStudio platform. These libraries are described as follow:

Twitter API: In order to target suspicious data from Twitter, we have used the package rtweet on the Rstudio platform. This library provides a simple interface to the Twitter web API. It provides most functionality of the API, with a bias towards API calls that are very useful in data analysis. This limits namely that it doesn't allow extracting historic data since it gives access to only 3200 posts per user [12].

Youtube API: In order to collect data from users' channels on YouTube, we have used the Tuber package on RStudio framework. In fact, the Tuber package [13] provides access to the YouTube API via R. It permits searching for videos having a particular content, getting their statistics and consulting their comments. This package is not only efficient in terms of results but also simple in its manipulation. However, different limitations are encountered using the Youtube API. This later provides only the 50 recent activities of each user. Moreover, for each channel, it returns maximum 50 subscriptions and for each video, 100 comments.

arabicStemR: Since the Arabic text preprocessing raises several issues to be addressed, we have used for this task the arabicStemR package [14] on R Studio framework. This library allows to preprocess Arabic texts for text analysis. It provides several functionalities as removing numbers, cleaning Latin characters, remove punctuation, remove prefixes and remove suffixes.

arules: In order to extract the frequent n-grams and itemsets of radical and non-radical communities on social networks, we have used the arules package [15] for mining association rules and frequent itemsets on R. Studio platform Indeed, this library provides the infrastructure for representing, manipulating and analyzing transaction data and patterns which are the frequent itemsets and the association rules.

4.2   Evaluation and Results

Following the different step described in our methodology, we have collected 8301 n-grams and itemsets annotated as radical and non-radical. Hence, we will report a static that describe our collected data and our extracted vocabulary. The following sectors contain these statistics. The first sector of the Fig. 2 represents the static about the proportion of radical and non-radical analyzed profiles. However, the second sector of the Fig. 2 represents the static about the proportion of radical and non-radical analyzed data. Figure 3 represents the static about the proportion of radical and non-radical extracted vocabulary.

Statistics that will be present in the previous sectors can be explained by the failure of sharing data from radical communities. This is due to their malicious intent in disguising. For this purpose, although the analyzed radical users are more than those who are non-radical, the collected radical data are few comparing with those which are non-radical. In fact, our extracted vocabulary is composing of several n-grams and

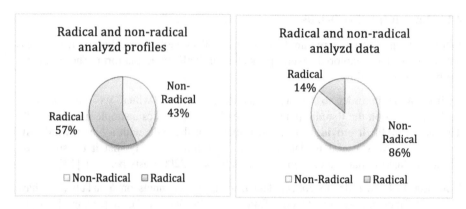

Fig. 2. Statistics about the analyzed profiles and their collected textuel data

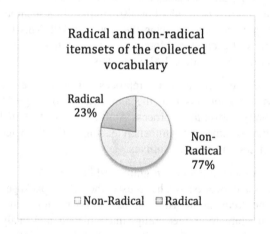

Fig. 3. Statistics about the itemsets composing the extracted vocabulary

itemsets having different sizes. Tables 4 and 5 represent statistics about the obtained n-grams and itemsets size composing the final vocabulary respectively.

Table 4. Statistics about the n-grams composing the extracted vocabulary

n-grams size	Number of n-grams
Unigram	3441
Bigram	47
Trigram	2

In addition, in order to evaluate the effectiveness of the vocabulary annotation provided by our method, we have resort to a domain expert who verifies for each collected n-grams and itemsets whether it is really a radical or non-radical element or

Table 5. Statistics about the itemsets composing the extracted vocabulary

Itemsets size	Number of obtained itemset
9-itemset	1
8-itemset	15
7-itemset	89
6-itemset	285
5-itemset	567
4-itemset	802
3-itemset	1057
2-itemset	1995
1-itemset (n-grams)	3490

not. In fact, the evaluation of our method aims mainly at analyzing its effectiveness and making a judgment that is articulated around a range of criteria. Thus, we can appreciate the quality of our proposed method, according to four of the most important general criteria, which are: recall, precision, F-measure and accuracy. The results given through the expert annotation are represented in Table 6.

Table 6. Results of our proposed methodology

Evaluation measures	Value
Accuracy	0.945
Recall	0.976
Precision	0.951
F-measure	0.96

The obtained results demonstrate the performance of our proposed algorithm, in terms of accuracy, recall, precision and F-measure. Thus, we can confirm that our methodology is highly effective in extracting violent vocabulary shared by radical communities on social networks.

At this stage, we refer to two other sociologists in order to estimate the inter-annotation agreement between them and our expert. This agreement rate is dependent on the number of information having the same annotation by these experts on a test corpus composing of 1000 itemsets composing the extracted vocabulary. To do so, we have explored the Cohen's kappa coefficient (κ) [16]. This later can be calculated as follow:

$$k = \frac{P_0 - P_c}{1 - P_c}$$

Where Po is the proportion of observed agreements and Pc is the proportion of agreements expected by chance.

So, we obtain 0.756 as a Cohen's Kappa coefficient between these two sociologists and our expert. Thus, according to [17], the intra-agreement between these two experts is rather strong. These results show the effectiveness of our methodology in the extraction of violent vocabulary shared by radical communities on social networks. Moreover, our method can be adapted to work for different language since we have explored the n-grams models. This can be considered as an important benefit of our methodology.

5 Conclusion

To crown all, we presented, in this paper, a new methodology for violent vocabulary extraction from social networks. Our methodology is based mainly on collecting a set of extremists and non-extremist users. Then, we focused on their textual content and extracted the frequent n-grams and itemsets appropriated to each community. Finally, we selected the violent vocabulary from the obtained results. The experts' evaluation prompt that our methodology can extract efficiently the radical vocabulary frequently shared by extremists. In the future, we plan to explore our methodology in order to detect dangerous users spreading on social networks. Moreover, we aim to explore our methodology in order to pick up the psyching out of users and extract terrorist communities on social network. In brief, our methodology serves to fight against the violence and the online radicalization.

Acknowledgements. This publication was made possible by NPRP grant #9-175-1-033 from the Qatar National Research Fund (a member of Qatar Foundation). The statements made herein are solely the responsibility of the authors.

References

1. Serrat, O.: Social network analysis. In: Serrat, O. (ed.) Serrat, O. Knowledge solutions, pp. 39–43. Springer, Singapore (2017). https://doi.org/10.1007/978-981-10-0983-9_9
2. Kumar, N., Srinathan, K.: Automatic keyphrase extraction from scientific documents using N-gram filtration technique. In: Proceedings of the Eighth ACM Symposium on Document Engineering, pp. 199–208 (2008)
3. Bednár, P.: Vocabulary matching for information extraction language. In: IEEE 15th International Symposium on Applied Machine Intelligence and Informatics (SAMI), pp. 149–152 (2017)
4. Rekik, A., Jamoussi, S.: Deep learning for hot topic extraction from social streams. In: Abraham, A., Haqiq, A., Alimi, A.M., Mezzour, G., Rokbani, N., Muda, A.K. (eds.) HIS 2016. AISC, vol. 552, pp. 186–197. Springer, Cham (2017). https://doi.org/10.1007/978-3-319-52941-7_19
5. McCormick, T.H., Lee, H., Cesare, N., Shojaie, A., Spiro, E.S.: Using Twitter for demographic and social science research: tools for data collection and processing. Sociol. Methods Res. 46(3), 390–421 (2017)
6. Brun, A.: Détection de thème et adaptation des modèles de langage pour la reconnaissance automatique de la parole. Ph.D. Nancy 1 (2003)

7. Breiman, L.: Random forests. Mach. Learn. **45**(1), 5–32 (2001)
8. Zhang, Y., Zhang, P., Li, T., Yan, Y.: An unsupervised vocabulary selection technique for Chinese automatic speech recognition. In: Spoken Language Technology Workshop (SLT), pp. 420–425 (2016)
9. Battiti, R.: Using mutual information for selecting features in supervised neural net learning. IEEE Trans. Neural Netw. **5**(4), 537–550 (1994)
10. Maergner, P., Waibel, A., Lane, I.: Unsupervised vocabulary selection for real-time speech recognition of lectures. In: IEEE International Conference on Acoustics, Speech and Signal Processing (ICASSP), pp. 4417–4420 (2012)
11. Abid, A., Ameur, H., Mbarek, A., et al.: An extraction and unification methodology for social networks data: an application to public security. In: Proceedings of the 19th International Conference on Information Integration and Web-based Applications and Services, pp. 176–180 (2017)
12. Gentry, J.: Package 'twitteR'. http://cran.r-project.org/web/packages/twitteR/index.html. Accessed 29 Aug 2016
13. Sood, G.: Package 'tuber'. http://cran.r-project.org/web/packages/tuber/index.html. Accessed 28 May 2017
14. Nielsen, R.: Package 'arabicStemmeR'. http://cran.r-project.org/web/packages/arabicStemmeR/index.html. Accessed 7 Feb 2017
15. Hahsler, M., et al.: Package 'arules'. http://cran.r-project.org/web/packages/arules/index.html. Accessed 7 Feb 2018
16. Sim, J., Wright, C.C.: The kappa statistic in reliability studies: use, interpretation, and sample size requirements. Phys. Ther. **85**(3), 257–268 (2005)
17. Landis, J.R., Koch, G.G.: The measurement of observer agreement for categorical data. Biometrics, pp. 159–174 (1977)

Tuser^2: A New Method for Twitter and Youtube Matching Profiles

Atika Mbarek[1,2(✉)], Salma Jamoussi[1,2],
and Abdelmajid Ben Hamadou[1,2]

[1] Multimedia InfoRmation Systems and Advanced Computing Laboratory
MIRACL, Sfax, Tunisia
Mbarek.atika91@gmail.com,
salma.jammoussi@isims.usf.tn,
Abdelmajid.benhamadou@isimsf.rnu.tn
[2] Digital Research Center of Sfax DRCS, 3021 Sfax, Tunisia

Abstract. Matching user profiles is an efficient way to map users across social networks and communicate an accurate portrait of a user. This study can be applied in different application domains such as recommendation, privacy, cyber-security, etc. In this paper, we address the problem of matching profiles in two popular social networks: YouTube and Twitter. First, we identify users by their shared publicly information and private information implicitly extracted from their published contents. Based on this information, we propose a method that matches profiles in both social networks using different features extraction. Then, we propose an algorithm we call Tuser^2 that returns for a targeted profile in Twitter its matched profiles in YouTube and vice versa based on public and inferred attributes comparison. Our preliminary results show that profiles in YouTube and Twitter can be matched with high accuracy. Therefore, exploiting both publicly shared attributes and inferred ones can improve the reliability of the results.

Keywords: Matching profiles · Social networks · Twitter · Youtube

1 Introduction

Nowadays, it is impossible to deny the fact that social networks become a force for societal change. In fact, this pace of change is accelerating throughout the world. As more people from all ages begin to log in to this growing phenomenon, a recent statistic [1] shows that in January 2018, approximately 2 billion internet users are using social networks, which means that billions of tweets, Facebook posts and Instagram pictures are posted every day.

Inevitably, Social networks have access to the most personal information of its users like their friends, interests, likes, etc. leading to help businesses in targeting their advertisements. However in reality, users are not required to prove that their identities in social networks match their real-life identity. Thus identifying users through their personal profiles in one social network is neither guaranteed nor sufficient in gathering real information about one user. Indeed, one of the greatest things that characterize

© Springer Nature Switzerland AG 2019
N. T. Nguyen et al. (Eds.): ICCCI 2019, LNAI 11684, pp. 110–121, 2019.
https://doi.org/10.1007/978-3-030-28374-2_10

social networks is that users can create several accounts on various sites due. This helps so far to create a linkage between users and enrich the user's information. In this context, matching profiles is an efficient way to map users in social networks and communicate an accurate portrait of a user.

The main issue we are focusing on in this paper is matching profiles that belong to the same user in two social networks. In fact, this study can be applied in different application domains such as recommendation, privacy, cyber-security, etc. In order to clearly motivate this work, we demonstrate it with a real word example. For instance, in a job offer mission, to deal effectively with the threat of selecting the right employee for the right job, recruiting companies need different sources of data about candidates to select them. Unfortunately, as social networks become a force that cannot be ignored today, people exploit it in spreading their activities and interests. Apparently, most users are now able to hide their identities for security reasons. As a result, it becomes difficult to identify one user profile to be recruited in a job in only one site. Meanwhile, users can create several accounts on multiple sites such as Facebook, Twitter, You-Tube, etc. This makes users provide links to their profiles in different social networks. These linking accounts help some systems and enterprises to gather more information about users and so allow them to decide which profile deserves to be recruited for a job offer.

This work targets the problem of matching profiles across two social networks. We made three contributions that can be summarized as follow: (i) We extract features from the user's profile including public attributes and user's generated contents (UGCs).Then, we formulate the matching process as the similarity measurement on two users; (ii) We introduce a supervised machine learning model to match users in two social networks. We use several classifiers to measure the features similarity; (iii) We propose an algorithm we call Tuser² (Twitter user <-> youTube user), that determines the matched profile of a targeted user in twitter and vice versa based on their attributes similarity.

2 Related Work

Authors in [2–13] addressed the problem of matching profiles in its globality by providing a suitable matching framework for considering all the profile's attributes. They demonstrate the performance of their method by giving particular attention to some attributes and assigning each attribute a similarity measure.

Authors in [3] proposed an approach that aims to discover a semantic equivalence between contacts described in online profiles, through a metric which computes a weighted semantic similarity between their individual attributes. Contacts found to be semantically equivalent to persons that are already represented within the user's personal information model are linked together. Additionally, in some studies [4–6] the graph matching methods are used to link accounts from different social networks. Furthermore, a study in [6] proposed a framework for analyzing privacy and anonymity in two social networks Flickr and Twitter and developed a generic re-identification algorithm for anonymized social networks. Bartunov, Sergey, et al. proposed a new approach for user profile matching based on Conditional Random Fields that extensively combines usage of profile attributes and social linkage [4].

More recently, Wang et al. in [7] used only usernames to identify users across different social networks. In fact, they consider that the other attributes are hard to collect for researchers. In this respect, a similar work [8] had a discussion about social identity linkage on Chinese users based on usernames. Indeed, authors propose a kind of language mapping method that can translate different type of Chinese words of a given username into their corresponding Pinyin words. In [15], Zafarani et al. employs a MOBUIS method that links accounts across social networks based on usernames. However, performing the matching by considering only the username similarity is not always sufficient for some cases. In particular, when the problem of fake profiles is addressed, these methods are not applicable because generally these profiles do not reveal their real names. Although the results are promising, their work suffers from lack of attributes since it is limited to only publicly shared attributes and does not consider implicit attributes.

Having the same aim, we attempt in our work to overcome the limitations of previous studies. We further explore both publicly shared and private attributes.

3 Proposed Method

As previously mentioned, the conceptual problem addressed in this paper is matching profiles that belong to the same user in social networks. To deal with this issue, we investigate two main steps. First, we try to gather as much information as possible about users from twitter and YouTube. Some features are explicitly extracted from the user's profile, while others are implicitly inferred through some data mining methods and tools that will be clearly described in the following subsections. Then, the extracted features will be used to compute the similarity between two users. In order to do so, we define similarity metrics to make decision whether two profiles belong to the same user or not. Second, we propose an algorithm we call Tuser^2 that returns for a targeted user in one social networks his/her correspondent user in the other social network and vice versa.

Clearly, to improve the performance of the matching profiles process, we do not consider all the attributes for the initial search. Instead, based on the name attribute, our algorithm starts by searching for candidate profiles that belong to a targeted user. Indeed, our aim is to increase the recall value since the found candidate profiles will strongly have the same name. Then, we perform the similarity metrics between all attributes to return the final matched profiles with a high precision. An overview of the matching profiles process is shown in Fig. 1.

3.1 Features Extraction

A rich user profile is very important for providing a high quality match profiling. However, public attributes given explicitly by the user are not enough to give information of high quality. Therefore, it's necessary to infer additional information from publicly available information to build a complete profile.

In order to extract data from twitter and YouTube, we have used two Packages namely twitterR [16] and Tuber [17] on RStudio framework. These packages are

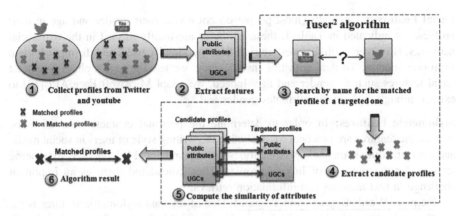

Fig. 1. Overview of the matching profiles process

simple to manipulate because they provide access to the YouTube and Twitter APIs via R and allow to benefit from several features such as tweets and videos published by the users. Actually, we mainly focus on four types of features:

Personal Features: It refers to name, country, createdProfileDate and shared tweets/videos attributes which are explicitly extracted from user's profile. As shown in Table 1, the name, shared tweets/videos and createdProfileDate are available in the two social networks while the country is missed in some profiles.

Table 1. Availability of features.

Attribute	Twitter	Youtube
Name	100%	100%
Picture	70%	70%
CreatedProfileDate	100%	100%
Country	50%	50%
Shared tweets/videos	100%	100%
Gender	0%	0%
Age	0%	0%
Langue	77%	77%

Timeline Features: Based on UGCs, we extract other attributes related to time. In particular, shared tweets and videos contain temporal information that indicates the real time of user's posting. Such temporal information is relevant for user identification. For example, some users like to post their content at night, while other users share their posts at morning. On the other hand, there are also users who are very active in the weekend unlike other users who share posts frequently in ordinary days. Through this time indication, we collect three types of information: the posting time in which the user is very active: either at night, morning, afternoon or all the day; the days of the week: either in the weekend, an ordinary day or during the whole week; and the season in which the user is very active: either in winter, spring, summer, autumn or during the whole year.

Facial Features: Generally, most people do not reveal their gender and age in their profiles. As indicated in Table 1, these attributes are totally missed in the two social networks. However, such features are significant to identify users and distinguish them from one another. To deal with this insufficiency, we use the user's photo to extract facial features such as gender and age. Indeed, we adopt Microsoft Face API [12] to extract through a photo the attributes gender and age.

Stylometric Features: In order to determine the personal characteristics of users, stylometric features are practical for analyzing the writing style of users in social media and understanding someone's personality. Some researchers [14] have used stylometric features for the purpose of linking profiles. They considered them as an important challenge in text analysis and information retrieval.

Frequent-Words/Bigrams and Trigrams: One of relevant stylometric features is the mostly used words, bigrams and trigrams. Consequently, the most frequent words will benefit to know what the best user interest is. For example, if the user is interested in sports, normally, he uses words such as football, tennis, etc.

Writing Style: In this type of features, we aim at extracting the user's written language because it constitutes a crucial class of linguistic varieties that merits consideration. Generally, it is difficult for a user to change written language from one site to another except for rare cases. Thus, we perform this attribute for our matching task. As this attribute is missed in some profiles, we used rosetteApi [18] tool which returns through shared content the most used language.

Htags: Another way to analyze the writing style of users is to employ htags. Generally htags are mostly used as keywords to highlight some topics or events. They are sometimes the most important "words" in a post. Therefore, adding htags feature may significantly improve the user identification.

3.2 Normalization Step

After extracting the features, we conduct a necessary step, which is the process of normalization. Our aim here is to convert noisy text into a normalized one. In fact, due to the nature of shared content, text may contain noisy words such as Unicode characters, useless stop-words, URL, etc. Therefore, to make content look clearer and improve the text analysis, we make a dictionary for the useless stop words and create a code that eliminate all noisy words from the original text.

Formally, each profile in each social network is presented as a vector which integrates all the used attributes. Thus, we define a profile P in a social network j as a vector P_j of n attributes $\{A_1, A_2, ..., A_n\}$ which $j \in [T, Y]$.

$$P_j(A_1, A_2 ... A_n) \tag{1}$$

3.3 Similarity Attributes

In order to compare two profiles in two social networks, we need to compare their attributes. We consider that the more similar the values of attributes of two profiles, the greater the chance to be matched. Thus, we define similarity metrics between attributes values. For each attribute we assign a similarity measure.

Name Similarity: We consider that two usernames with high similarity are very likely to belong to the same user. Therefore, to compare two usernames, we used rosetteApi which returns for two given names the probability that they can match.

Photo Similarity: As mentioned earlier, we extracted from the photo of the user the attributes: gender and age. For the gender attribute we have only two possible values either male or female. Then, the gender similarity is represented as below.

$$Sim_{Gender}(P_T, P_Y) \begin{cases} 1 \ \textit{if } P_T \textit{ and } P_Y \textit{ have the same gender}; \\ 0 \ \textit{otherwise} \end{cases} \tag{2}$$

In order to compute the age similarity we used the difference between two age values that belong to two profiles from twitter and YouTube P_T, and P_Y. We consider that the lower the difference of ages, the higher the probability of being the same person. This similarity is computed as below:

$$Sim_{Age}(P_T, P_Y) = |Age_T - Age_Y| \tag{3}$$

Country Similarity: We created a dictionary which contains all countries with their capitals and cities, because there are some users who give the name of their country (e.g. France), and others give the name of the city where they live (e.g. Lyon). So, two users are likely to be the same if they belong to the same country.

$$Sim_{Country}(P_T, P_Y) \begin{cases} 1 \ \textit{if } P_T \textit{ and } P_Y \textit{ have the same country}; \\ 0 \ \textit{otherwise} \end{cases} \tag{4}$$

Language Similarity: After extracting the attribute language from the published contend of the user, we can easily compute the language similarity.

$$Sim_{Language}(P_T, P_Y) \begin{cases} 1 \ \textit{if } P_T \textit{ and } P_Y \textit{ use the same Language}; \\ 0 \ \textit{otherwise} \end{cases} \tag{5}$$

Timeline Similarity: We have 9 measurements to compute the posting time attribute; the frequency of posting at night, at morning, in afternoon, in winters, in summer, in autumn, in spring, in the weekend and in an ordinary day. This frequency is computed in the same way, e.g. the frequency of posting at night is computed by the sum of posts shared at night divided by the total number of posts. The similarity of timeline can be represented as the difference between two frequency of posting time that belong to two profiles.

$$Sim_{Timeline}(P_T, P_Y) = |Freq(Timeline)_T - Freq(Timeline)_Y| \qquad (6)$$

Frequent-Words/Bigrams/Trigrams/Htags Similarity: Frequent words, Bigrams, Trigrams and Htags similarities are computed in the same way. For example, to compute the bigrams similarity between two user profiles P_T and P_Y, we first extract the common bigrams mostly used by the two users and divide them on the minimum of the two initial bigrams.

$$Sim_{Bigrams}(P_T, P_Y) = CommonBigrams(P_T, P_Y)/MinBigrams(P_T, P_Y) \qquad (7)$$

To compute the similarity attributes between two profiles, we do not consider each profile as a vector apart and then compute their similarities. Instead, we construct a new vector of similarities that computes the similarity between two profiles P_T and P_Y. This vector integrates all attributes similarity (Sim_{Name}, Sim_{Age}...Sim_{Htags}) and is classified in matched or non matched if it's the same profile. Formally, let $S_{PT,PY}$ the new constructed vector:

$$S_{PT,PY}(Sim_{Name}, Sim_{Age}, \ldots Sim_{Htags}) \qquad (8)$$

3.4   Tuser^2 Algorithm

In this subsection, we propose an algorithm called Tuser^2 that links a targeted profile in YouTube by its correspondent in twitter and vice versa. Our algorithm will match profiles in an iterative way, which means that the corresponding profile is not found in the first step. Instead, we start by searching for a set of candidate profiles that are likely to match, and then these candidates are used to discover new ones. In the first step, we use a search method based on the importance of the attributes to find the first candidate matching.

Search Method: Actually, not all attributes have the same importance. In other words, some attributes are relevant and carries more information. Thus, giving more importance to some attributes allows find which attributes contribute the most to the matching task. In this context, there are basically two methods for feature selection that we focused on; namely wrapper method and filter method [10, −11]. We applied the feature selection methods to select relevant attributes. As a result, we obtained the name as the most important attribute with a percentage higher than 50%. We show how giving more importance to name attribute improves the accuracy of the matching in our algorithm.

The Algorithm: As the name is the most important attribute, so given a targeted profile in YouTube, the algorithm starts by searching for twitter users with the same name or a close name using all combinations of the words that make up the name. This step is done through the function ExtractCandidates() which takes as input the targeted profile and returns profiles with similar names. For example, for a YouTube user name "xxx yyy zzz", the algorithm extract twitter users having in their names the words xxx, yyy, zzz, xxx yyy, yyy zzz, xxx zzz, xxx yyy zzz. A set of candidate profiles C will be extracted. Based on these candidates, the algorithm extracts new candidates according to the similarity of all attributes A. In this step, the algorithm computes the similarity between the targeted profile in YouTube P_Y and each candidate matched profile in twitter P_t basing on their attributes. For each pair (P_Y, P_t) we create a vector of similarities $Vsim(P_Y, P_t)$ and for each vector we compute its importance of similarities through the function ComputeScore(). This function is in the form of a similarity score between 0 and 1which takes as input $Vsim(P_Y, P_t)$ and returns the mean of all the similarities contained in this vector. Its goal is to put a selection criterion to choose only the most similar profiles to the targeted profile. This function is calculated as follows:

$$\sum\nolimits_{a\in A} Sim_a / \sum\nolimits_{a\in A} a \qquad (9)$$

We define a threshold Th to determine if two profiles are similar. The algorithm chooses only candidate profiles having a similarity score higher than the threshold. We obtained this threshold from the experiments that we did to measure how consistent users are in providing the same value for an attribute across two social networks. Finally the algorithm returns the final matching profile of the targeted one.

Algorithm: Tuser^2(P_Y, A)

1. initialize set of candidate matching profiles C = Ø
2. initialize set of matched profiles M = Ø
3. C= ExtractCandidates (P_Y)
4. **for** every profile Pt a ϵ C do
5. $Vsim(P_Y, P_t)$ = Ø
6.   **for** every attribute a ϵ A do
7.   insert sim (P_Y, P_t) into $Vsim(P_Y, P_t)$
8.   si=ComputeScore($Vsim(P_Y, P_t)$)
9.   **if** (si >= Th) **then**
10.   insert P_t into M
11. **Return** M

---

4   Experimental Results

4.1   Data Collection

In order to conduct our experiments, we collected profiles from two social networks: Twitter and YouTube. Fortunately, several accounts in YouTube put their twitter link on their profiles. This information allows mapping users on twitter and YouTube. Actually, our methodology for collecting data is based on a keyword search strategy. This method focuses on searching profiles related to predefined keywords. So, we prepare a set of keywords related to different domains such as health, music, sport, etc. to target users from different domains. We start by extracting YouTube profiles based on the predefined keywords and searching for their correspondents in twitter. We also extract profiles from the two social networks that do not seem to be matched. We then got 2000 couples from YouTube and Twitter. Excluding profiles related to media or pages, we finally got 1200 couples: 400 as matching profiles and 800 as non-matching profiles. An overview of the statistics of the dataset used in this paper is shown in Table 2.

Table 2. Dataset statistics.

Attribute	Twitter	Youtube	Twitter/Youtube
Accounts number	600	600	1200
Male number	379	379	758
Female number	221	221	442
Matched profiles number	–	–	400
Non matched profiles number	–	–	800

4.2   Evaluation of the Matching Method

In order to evaluate the effectiveness of our matching method, we need to compare it with prior methods. However, such comparisons are not easy because profile descriptions are different and not all works use the same attributes. So to show the effectiveness of our method in another way, we conduct three types of experiments. First, we use solely usernames for the matching process, then we use solely UGCs and finally we test our method with all the features. To do so, we use our dataset to train five classifiers: Bayes Naïve, SVM, Decision tree, KNN and Boosting. We use 10-fold cross validation to train and evaluate the classifiers. We compare the accuracy of classifiers using only user names, UGCs with the accuracy when we use all the features. Then, we take three measurements for our evaluation: precision, recall and F-Measure. The best results are underlined and bold.

Performance of Matching Using Solely Usernames
Table 3 shows the results when we use solely usernames. As shown in Table 3, we can get high recall that reaches 94.3% with Boosting classifier. We observe that Boosting and J48 Decision Tree perform better than the other classifiers.

Table 3. Profile matching performance using solely usernames.

Classification techniques	Precision (%)	Recall (%)	F-Measure (%)
J48 Decision Tree	94.4	94.2	94.0
Naïve Bayes	92.7	92.7	92.6
LibSVM	94.3	94.0	93.9
KNN	92.9	92.9	92.8
Boosting	**94.5**	**94.3**	**94.1**

Performance of Matching Using Solely UGCs

Table 4 shows the results when we use solely UGCs including timeline and stylometric features. We observe that the use of UGCs performs worse with all the classifiers. The best reached F-Measure is 81% obtained by Boosting classifier. This indicates that using only UGCs is not always sufficient because some users are not active in social media and don't share many contents with public.

Table 4. Profile matching performance using solely UGCs.

Classification techniques	Precision (%)	Recall (%)	F-Measure (%)
J48 Decision Tree	86.1	83.3	81.6
Naïve Bayes	86.6	83.4	81.6
LibSVM	85.9	82.1	79.8
KNN	84.2	82.8	81.3
Boosting	**86.8**	**83.5**	**81.7**

Performance of Matching Using all Features

As shown in the Table 5, results are not significantly different among these classification techniques. Our method reaches a F-Measure value of around 97% with J48 Decision Tree while the minimum achievable Measure is 93%. Compared to previous experiments, there is a significant difference between using all features and using solely part of features. In fact, our method achieves the best F-Measure with all classifiers. As the 3 classifiers J48 Decision Tree Learning, KNN and Boosting gave better results, we adopt them to evaluate our algorithm.

Table 5. Profile matching performance using all the features.

Classification techniques	Precision (%)	Recall (%)	F-Measure (%)
J48 Decision Tree	96.7	96.7	96.6
Naïve Bayes	96.5	96.4	96.4
LibSVM	93.8	93.3	93.1
KNN	95.1	95.1	95.1
Boosting	**96.7**	**96.7**	**96.6**

4.3   Tuser^2 Evaluation

Now, we investigate the reliability of Tuser^2 algorithm with the three selected classifiers that gave good results in the previous tests. For the evaluation, we randomly select 30 Twitter profiles that are not used for training set. Clearly, after a series of evaluation of our matching method, we found that the best value of Th is 0.3. Therefore, we adopt this value to find the matched profiles of the test set.

The returned results are significant and so are the three classifiers. As shown in Table 6, our algorithm achieves 90% precision in average. In fact, the algorithm found that the first returned candidate profiles that are matched using only the name are not the same final profiles that are matched using all the attributes. This proves the effectiveness of the use of all attributes for ginving the real matched profiles.

Table 6. Algorithm performance for three classification techniques.

Classification techniques	Precision (%)	Recall (%)	F-Measure (%)
J48 Decision Tree	89	75	78
KNN	**90**	65	72
Boosting	89	**75**	**78**

However, in practice some twitter users may not have a youtube profile or vice versa. Ideally, the algorithm should return zero profiles in this case. Thus, to test the reliability of our algorithm in this case, we take the dataset used for the evaluation, e.g. for a targeted twitter profile, we remove the youtube matching accounts from the candidate set. Our matching method returns false matching profiles for 80%. This proves the reliability of our algorithm in the absence of matching profile in the other social network. Furthermore, another very important area of use for our algorithm is to match profiles in the same social network. In other words, some users create more than one account in a social network, so extracting the matched profiles in twitter of a targeted user in YouTube can help us to find accounts that belong to the same user in twitter. This shows the efficiency of $Tuser^2$ algorithm to achieve two goals at the same time.

5 Conclusion and Perspectives

In this work, we addressed the problem of matching profiles in two social networks: YouTube and twitter. Our method uses public and private attributes to identify users. Further, we have proposed the $Tuser^2$ algorithm to find the matched profile of a targeted user in two social networks. The experiments demonstrate the robustness of our methods by achieving high accuracy of matching.

Our future directions of this work are to collect more information about users to target them in different domains. Furthermore, researches didn't consider the problem of matching profiles that belong to malicious users. So, we also plan to analyze anonymous profiles to identify which profiles belong to fake users.

Acknowledgements. This publication was made possible by NPRP grant #9-175-1-033 from the Qatar National Research Fund (a member of Qatar Foundation). The statements made herein are solely the responsibility of the authors.

References

1. https://www.statista.com/statistics/272014/global-social-networks-ranked-by-number-of-users/
2. Raad, E., Chbeir, R., Dipanda,A.: User profile matching in social networks. In: 2010 13th International Conference on Network-Based Information Systems (NBiS). IEEE (2010)
3. Cortis, K., et al.: Discovering semantic equivalence of people behind online profiles. In: Proceedings of the Resource Discovery (RED) Workshop, ser. ESWC (2012)
4. Bartunov, S., et al.: Joint link-attribute user identity resolution in online social networks. In: Proceedings of the 6th International Conference on Knowledge Discovery and Data Mining, Workshop on Social Network Mining and Analysis. ACM (2012)
5. Narayanan, A., Shmatikov, V.: Robust de-anonymization of large sparse datasets. In: IEEE Symposium on Security and Privacy, SP 2008. IEEE (2008)
6. Narayanan, A., Shmatikov, V.: De-anonymizing social networks. arXiv preprint arXiv:0903. 3276 (2009)
7. Wang, Y., et al.: Identifying users across different sites using usernames. Proc. Comput. Sci. **80**, 376–385 (2016)
8. Li, Y., et al.: Connecting Chinese users across social media sites (2015)
9. Halimi, A., Ayday, E.: Profile matching across unstructured online social networks: threats and countermeasures. arXiv preprint arXiv:1711.01815(2017)
10. Dy, J.G., Brodley, C.E.: Feature selection for unsupervised learning. J. Mach. Learn. Res. **5** (Aug), 845–889 (2004)
11. Talavera, L.: Feature selection and incremental learning of probabilistic concept hierarchies. In: Proceedings of the Seventeenth International Conference on Machine Learning (2000)
12. Maheshwari, K., et al.: Facial recognition enabled smart door using microsoft face API. arXiv preprint arXiv:1706.00498 (2017)
13. Li, Y., et al.: Matching user accounts based on user generated content across social networks. Future Gener. Comput. Syst. **83**, 104–115 (2018)
14. Vosoughi, S., Zhou, H., Roy, D.: Digital stylometry: linking profiles across social networks. In: Liu, T.Y., Scollon, C., Zhu, W. (eds.) Social Informatics. LNCS, vol. 9471, pp. 164–177. Springer, Cham (2015). https://doi.org/10.1007/978-3-319-27433-1_12
15. Zafarani, R., Liu, H.: Connecting users across social media sites: a behavioral-modeling approach. In: Proceedings of the 19th ACM SIGKDD International Conference on Knowledge Discovery and Data Mining. ACM (2013)
16. Gentry, J.: Package 'twitteR'. http://cran.r-project.org/web/packages/twitteR/index.html. Accessed 29 Aug 2016
17. Sood, G.: Package 'tuber'. http://cran.r-project.org/web/packages/tuber/index.html. Accessed 28 May2017
18. Park, C., et al.: Package 'RosetteApi'. https://cran.rproject.org/web/packages/rosetteApi/index.html. Accessed 16 Mar 2019

Classification of the Symbolic Financial Data on the Forex Market

Jan Kozak, Przemysław Juszczuk[✉], and Krzysztof Kania

Faculty of Informatics and Communication, Department of Knowledge Engineering,
University of Economics, 1 Maja 50, 40-287 Katowice, Poland
{jan.kozak,przemyslaw.juszczuk,krzysztof.kania}@ue.katowice.pl

Abstract. A symbolic representation for any data can be used as a tool for reducing the irrelevant noise. Any methods of reducing noise are extremely useful in the field of financial data, where a good trading signal is crucial to achieving the profits for the long term trading approach. In this article, we use the concept of symbolic representation to transform the market situation described as a time series of successive price changes into the simplified representation of this situation. Every element of such symbolic representation is further treated as an attribute in the decision table. On the basis of historical data transformed in the same manner, we try to identify the market situations leading to the increase in the instrument value on the forex market.

We use a set of well-known classifiers built and trained with the use of historical data. Finally, we use these classifiers to estimate the possible efficiency of the present market situation. There is no need to exactly identify the quality of the signal. We are interested in price direction rather than the exact price of the instrument, thus we use the concept of fuzzy accuracy. Fuzzy accuracy allows us to properly classify objects belonging not only for the actual decision class but also for the neighboring decision classes.

The presented approach is verified with the use of the large set of data collected from the forex market.

Keywords: Symbolic representation · Classification · Forex market

1 Introduction

Developing a fast and efficient trading system capable to achieve profits on any market is one of the most difficult problems on the borderline of finance and computer science. Various methods related to technical analysis, fundamental analysis, and sentiment analysis, as well as the complex approaches, are used in this field. Nowadays a large percent of trading systems dedicated not only to achieve profits but also to generate liquidity on the market are connected with the idea of High-Frequency Trading [8]. Besides that, there is still plenty of room for improvement. One of the main issues with these approaches is their complexity and difficulty to follow by retail decision makers. Methods based on

© Springer Nature Switzerland AG 2019
N. T. Nguyen et al. (Eds.): ICCCI 2019, LNAI 11684, pp. 122–132, 2019.
https://doi.org/10.1007/978-3-030-28374-2_11

neural networks, no matter if data are distributed [7], without [9,17], or with missing data [26,27] are very complicated – as well as fuzzy systems [3,18]. Moreover, there is no agreement, that these approaches are effective. There is a large number of works, in which there are some doubts concerned on the case, is there a possibility to derive such an effective system on the market.

A large number of instruments and derivatives possible to invest by retail decision makers today is enormous. We can invest in bonds, assets, funds, currency pairs, cryptocurrencies and more. Among these instruments, the forex market and currency pairs seem to be especially interesting. Forex market is considered as one of the most liquid markets in the world. Large possibilities to trade even with small capital and a very high number of instruments available on the market makes it the perfect solution for both: decision makers as well as trading systems operating on various methods.

Various methods related to generating signals, achieving profits in some given time interval, as well as methods of maintaining the positions of the market were recently studied in many papers. Focusing directly on the generating signals, we can extract a few different approaches. In the first group, the vast majority of works is related to the technical analysis and methods capable to generate new signals. These methods include genetic programming [21] and evolutionary methods [22] for which a new set of rules is generated. Detailed survey about evolutionary methods in finance can be found in [2]. There is also plenty of articles related to the problem of deriving a new indicator like [25].

The simplicity of generating rules for the technical analysis seems to fit perfectly for the rule-based trading systems, where the decision is made on the basis of the simple rules. However, it is possible to use the same rule-based mechanics in the case of the fundamental analysis. Methods like text mining were used in [20]. Twitter accounts were analyzed in the [1], and in [19] systematic review for methods related to text mining can be found. While sentiment analysis is not as popular as two previous methods, however, there are some papers dedicated to this field like [11].

Above considerations are mostly related to simplifying the information acquired from the market. There are a few articles focused on extending the description of the market situation. In this article, we propose a method devoted to deriving some additional information to the decision maker. We try to acquire information about the dynamics of the instrument on the market and describe it as a symbolic representation. For that purpose, we use a string of symbols representing the different price ranges. Further, such a string of symbols is presented as an object in the decision table. Thus we transform the current market situation into the symbolic representation, which is used to classify the string into one of the decisions: buy or sell. This method is a step towards transforming the problem of generating trading signals into the classification problem, for which the classifier is learned on the basis of the historical data.

The outline of this paper is as follows. In Sect. 2 we derive details about the proposed symbolic representation and details of our methodology – especially focusing on the concept of fuzzy accuracy. Section 3 includes a description of different classification methods used in numerical experiments. Section 4 includes the results of numerical experiments and short discussion. Section 5 concludes.

2   Proposed Methodology

In this work, we focus on the forex market which is considered as the most volatile market in the world. The single instrument on the forex is the currency pair, which is the ratio of the one currency to the another. One should know, that the proposed approach could be used in any market and for any set instruments. The forex market was selected due to the high volatility of the data, which affects the difficulty of the problem. Moreover, the forex data is available to use and does not involve any preprocessing-related problems, like the missing values.

Among the most prominent examples of transforming the time-series into the symbolic representation is the Symbolic Aggregate Approximation (SAX) algorithm [15]. However, among the most important drawback, we could mention difficulties with the algorithm parameters like the alphabet size. Other methods related to the subject besides the SAX approach are ESAX [16].

Above methods are rather dedicated to simplify the data and lead towards the dimensionality reduction. In our work, we rather tread the symbolic representation as the additional indicator, which can be used to limit the impact of the noise on the data. This can be considered as the approach, in which the main goal is to reduce the non-important price fluctuations.

For all analyzed currency pairs we used the price data observed at the end of the day (end of the session). Such information is transformed into the symbolic representation according to the following formula (originally introduced in [10]):

$$d = (f(x_i, x_{i-1}), f(x_i, x_{i-2})..., f(x_i, x_{i-n})) = (f(\Delta x_{-1}), f(\Delta x_{-2}), ..., f(\Delta x_{-n})),$$
(1)

where

$$f(\Delta(x_i)) = \begin{cases} k \text{ if } (2 \cdot k + 1) \cdot s \le \Delta x_i \\ ... \\ 1 \text{ if } s \le \Delta x_i < 3 \cdot s \\ 0 \text{ if } |\Delta x_i| \le s, -1 \text{ if } -s \le \Delta x_i < -3 \cdot s \\ ... \\ -k \text{ if } -(2 \cdot k + 1) \cdot s > \Delta x_i, \end{cases}$$
(2)

where $s = \overline{\Delta x_{-1}}$, k is a symbol corresponding to the change between two successive price readings, and x_i is the value of the currency pair in time i.

Strings of symbols generated on the basis of the above equation were used to prepare the decision tables. Every symbol in the string corresponds to the conditional attribute. Thus an overall number of conditional attributes is equal to 10. For the 1-day time window (where every new reading is derived at the end of the day session) we assumed, that the overall time span of two weeks will be sufficient, to derive the valuable trading pattern. Every object is the string of symbols, where every symbol can be anything in the range $(-5, -4, ..., 5)$. The length of all strings of symbols was equal to 11, where the first 10 elements correspond to the conditional attributes in the decision table, while the last element was the decision class. In general, the string of symbols describes the single situation on the market, while the additional, eleventh symbol (the decision attribute) derives the information about the price direction.

One should know, that values for all attributes are ordered, thus the value equal to 5 is close to the value 4 and so on. This concept was used in [10], where differences between patterns in the symbolic representation were calculated on the basis of similar symbols. Due to specifics of the analyzed data, the promising situation on the market occurs not only, when the predicted value of the decision class of the string of symbols is exactly the same, as the real decision class, but also, when the object is classified to the neighboring class.

In this work, we also analyze the efficiency of the fuzzy accuracy introduced by authors in [12]. Such approach allows to estimate the efficiency of classification in the case, where there is a slight deviation between the predicted and expected decision class:

$$d(DT, D)_{fuzzy} = \frac{TP^{-n\%} + TP + TP^{+n\%}}{|D|} \tag{3}$$

where $TP^{-n\cdot\%}$ is the number of objects classified to the neighboring class (lower than the target class), and $TP^{+n\cdot\%}$ applies for the neighboring class greater than the target class. All decision classes are sorted and labeled from 1 up to N_i, where N_i is an overall number of classes for the attribute i. Neighboring classes size are defined as:

$$neighbor_{size} = n\% \cdot N_i \tag{4}$$

Example classification can be seen in Fig. 1, where a classification matrix is presented. This is presented as a reference, for the fuzzy classification concept. For the original classification measure, we are interested in the diagonal of this matrix, which means the exact classification. The fuzziness equal to 0.1 was used – which corresponds the 10%. Thus we accept the classification of objects to the actual decision class as well as the neighboring class (for both sides of the diagonal). The same approach will be used further in the numerical experiments. Dark squares in the diagonal correspond to the properly classified objects, while light grey color denotes the fuzzy accuracy.

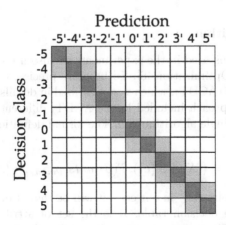

Fig. 1. Example of the fuzzy accuracy used in the experiments

3   Decision Trees and Classification

Decision trees are among the most effective and widely used tools for the classification. Variety of different methods related to the building the decision tree from scratch makes it a perfect approach for investigating the efficiency of the method proposed by authors in the previous section. In this section, we focus on the ACDT algorithm which is nowadays among the best methods related to the problem of building the decision trees. As a comparison, we selected two well-known from literature methods: CART and C4.5.

More information about the different methods for constructing the decision trees can be found in [14]. Despite the long history, the CART algorithm and C4.5 (and further – commercially used C5.0) are nowadays among the most popular methods used in the process of constructing the decision trees.

3.1   Classical Algorithms

The CART algorithm was introduced by Breiman and others in 1984 [5]. The idea behind this approach was to construct decision trees and regression trees. This method is among the most popular state-of-art algorithms used in the classification. One of its most important advantages is the capability to handle both: discrete and continuous attributes. This can be especially useful in financial data.

The second algorithm used as a comparison is proposed by Quinlan [24] C4.5 algorithm based on the earlier developed ID3 algorithm [23]. Extension of this method included classification improvements (on the basis of the split criterion) for the large sets of data. In financial data, there are often problems with missing values or with outliers. While C4.5 is capable to handle missing data. To maintain the relatively small height of the decision trees, pruning methods like pessimistic pruning or error-based pruning were introduced as well. Additionally, the C4.5 algorithm is adjusted to easily handle continuous data.

3.2   ACDT Algorithm

To diversify algorithms used in the experiments we also use the approach based on the Ant Colony Optimization [6]. To be more precise, we selected the Ant Colony Decision Tree (ACDT), which was described in details in [13]. Due to the non-deterministic approach included in the ACDT, different decision trees are generated for every single algorithm run. The formal definition of this approach is as follows:

$$ACDT = \langle (X, A \cup \{c\}), T(S), ants, p_{m,m_{L(i,j)}}(t), S \rangle \tag{5}$$

where X is set of all objects – in our case, it will be the set of strings of symbols transformed into the decision table, A is the set of attributes including the decision attribute c. These elements are used to define the decision tables. Result of the algorithm is the decision tree $T(S)$; $ants$ parameter is the information about the number of ants included in the algorithm, S is the set of all acceptable objects, while $p_{m,m_{L(i,j)}}(t)$ is the selection rule (concept of the selection rule was initially proposed in the CART algorithm).

One should know, that the main advantage of this approach is based on switching the goal function for agents-ants by the modification of the fitness function calculation. The fitness function is used to evaluate the quality of the decision tree (Eq. (7)). Among the crucial aspects of this method is the pheromone trail:

$$\tau_{m,m_L}(t+1) = (1 - \gamma) \cdot \tau_{m,m_L}(t) + Q(T), \tag{6}$$

where $Q(T)$ is a quality of the decision tree (compare with the formula (7)) and γ is the parameter representing the evaporation rate (in this approach equal to 0.1).

The pheromone trail concept is used to indicate the most rewarding fragments of the decision tree. In the presented research the evaluation of the quality of the classification for the single decision tree is given as follows:

$$Q(T) = \phi \cdot w(T) + \psi \cdot ev(T, P), \tag{7}$$

where $ev(T, P)$ is the selected method of the evaluation of the classification of the decision tree T built by the agent-ant with the use of the data set P. Value of the $ev(T, P)$ is calculated on the basis of the selected measure.

One should know, that detailed description of the above algorithms can be found in relevant papers. In this work we use the CART, C4.5 and ACDT to built the classifiers (decision trees) on the basis of data derived by the symbolic representation introduced in the previous section. Thus this method could be used as well by any method capable to handle the knowledge presented as the decision tables.

4   Experiments

In this section, described the results of the real-world data prepared on the basis of the symbolic representation described in Sect. 2. Decision tables were prepared separately for every analyzed currency pair. All datasets included the training set (1250 objects – strings of symbols) and test set (1250 objects). Please note, that in this case, the decision attribute was also in the range $\langle -5, 5 \rangle$. However, we were rather interested in the general price direction (positive or negative value of the last symbol) rather than the exact value. To summarize, for every single currency pair, the overall 2500 string of symbols transformed into the decision table was derived. Among the possible validation methods, we focused on the simple validation, where training and test sets are disjoint. This was due to the fact, that in the case of cross-validation it was the possibility, that some of the patterns on the market could be repeated. However, it is worth considering, that the patterns derived for the single currency pair should be used as a predictive tool for other instruments.

All experiments were performed with the use of four algorithms: classical implementation of the C4.5 and CART (implemented in the WEKA system [4]). The third algorithm was the ACDT approach based on the swarm intelligence [13]. We also included the Random Tree [4], which was used here as a random method.

4.1 Results of Experiments

The results of experiments were presented in Table 1, where the accuracy of the classification along with proposed by us the fuzzy accuracy is presented. The fuzziness in our approach was equal to 10%, which is equal to the maximal difference between the actual and predicted decision class by 1. In other words, the classification was valid, if the difference between the actual decision class and predicted decision class was equal or less 1. The best-achieved results were marked with the bold font.

As it can be noted, the proposed solution generated promising results in the case of transforming the symbolic representation into the decision table. The decision table used in the process of classification leads to very good results even for the classical accuracy measure. One should know, that we were rather interested in deriving the general price direction rather than exact decision class.

The best prediction (measured with the use of the classical accuracy) was achieved with the use of the ACDT algorithm. One should note, that in the case of the fuzzy accuracy this approach achieved rather weak results – often the worst from all analyzed methods. Analysis of the confusion matrix leads to the conclusion, that those wrong decisions (classification to the different decision class) were rather scattered. At the same time, for most cases, the best results were observed for the CART algorithm (the right side of the Table 1).

Table 1. Accuracy and the fuzzy accuracy for selected currency pairs – four different classification methods

	Accuracy				Fuzzy accuracy			
	CART	RT	C4.5	ACDT	CART	RT	C4.5	ACDT
AUDUSD	0.6221	0.4516	0.6221	**0.6362**	**0.9832**	0.8935	**0.9832**	0.8006
EURCHF	0.7005	0.5751	0.6875	**0.7083**	**0.9746**	0.9275	0.9703	0.8615
EURGBP	0.5910	0.3858	0.5794	**0.6009**	**0.9732**	0.8600	0.9616	0.8952
EURUSD	0.6093	0.4267	0.5741	**0.6295**	**0.9608**	0.8655	0.9496	0.9331
GBPUSD	0.5805	0.4243	0.5612	**0.6179**	**0.9608**	0.8719	0.9416	0.8327
JPYUSD	0.6101	0.4075	0.5861	**0.6122**	**0.9616**	0.8383	0.9448	0.9039
NZDJPY	0.6535	0.5100	0.6327	**0.6648**	**0.9828**	0.9132	0.9770	0.7402
NZDUSD	0.5997	0.3742	0.5765	**0.6089**	**0.9819**	0.8593	0.9724	0.8502
USDCAD	0.4880	0.3691	0.5069	**0.5210**	0.8956	0.7897	**0.9376**	0.7135
USDCHF	0.5047	0.3930	0.5062	**0.5269**	**0.9427**	0.8231	0.9376	0.8012

Table 2. Confusion matrix – EURGBP – CART algorithm

	$-5'$	$-4'$	$-3'$	$-2'$	$-1'$	$0'$	$1'$	$2'$	$3'$	$4'$	$5'$
-5	11	0	4	0	0	0	0	0	0	0	0
-4	2	0	19	1	0	0	0	0	0	0	0
-3	0	0	34	27	6	0	0	0	0	0	0
-2	0	0	22	89	59	2	0	0	0	0	0
-1	0	0	0	35	190	64	0	0	0	0	0
0	0	0	0	1	60	174	42	2	0	0	0
1	0	0	0	0	9	51	150	39	1	0	0
2	0	0	0	0	0	4	44	79	14	0	0
3	0	0	0	0	0	0	2	18	47	7	0
4	0	0	0	0	0	0	0	2	14	17	2
5	0	0	0	0	0	0	0	1	0	8	24

Table 3. Confusion matrix – EURUSD – ACDT algorithm

	$-5'$	$-4'$	$-3'$	$-2'$	$-1'$	$0'$	$1'$	$2'$	$3'$	$4'$	$5'$
-5	85	36	6	1	0	0	16	0	0	0	0
-4	26	156	39	4	0	0	1	1	0	0	0
-3	3	39	203	48	2	1	0	0	0	0	0
-2	0	3	61	165	32	0	0	0	0	0	0
-1	0	0	3	41	84	15	0	0	1	0	0
0	0	1	0	1	24	40	0	0	3	0	0
1	18	5	0	0	0	0	27	2	0	0	2
2	0	1	0	0	0	0	6	6	0	0	4
3	0	0	0	0	1	7	0	0	8	2	0
4	0	0	0	0	0	0	0	0	4	9	0
5	0	0	0	0	0	0	0	0	0	0	6

To analyze the confusion matrix in details we derived the example table with results for the CART algorithm and the EURGBP currency pair. Results can be seen in Table 2. Rows of Table 2 include the real decision class. Columns give information about the class, for which the prediction was made (these were noted by the apostrophe).

As a comparison, we also derived the confusion matrix for the ACDT algorithm and the EURUSD currency pair (see Table 3). A large number observed on the diagonal of the matrix shown, that the classification for most of the objects was also very good. However, in the middle of the matrix, we observe the situation, for which part of observations was classified into the neighboring decision class. This situation for the classical accuracy measure would be classified as the prediction error. What was surprising, there was a very small number of elements observed in the low right side of the matrix. This may be related with the strong falling trend present in the case of this currency pair and a large number of strings of symbols with the negative value of the decision class (-1, -2 and less).

Results indicated, that the exact classification was observed in the situation, where the values greater than 0 were on the diagonal of the table. For all remaining situations, the classification error was observed. One should know, that most of the wrong classifications occurred near the diagonal, which means that these were an error of classification to neighboring class. Since the symbols towards value 5 mean the graduation of the rising trend (and falling trend for the -5 value), the classification to the neighboring class does not mean the wrong decision from the point of the view of the decision maker.

5   Conclusions

In this paper, we presented the method of transforming the price chart into the symbolic representation, which assures, that the eventual noise present in the data can be reduced. Moreover, such an approach allowed for easier classification of situations occurring on the market. The idea of the symbolic language for the predictions on the forex market was initially proposed in [10]. However, in this work, we focused on using the knowledge representation based on the decision tables, which was used in the process of classification. Such an approach seems to give very promising results.

Derived decision tables were used to build the classifiers (decision trees). We focused on three algorithms: the CART, C4.5, and the ACDT algorithm and the fourth method used as a control approach – the random tree. Since there is no need for the exact classification of strings of symbols, we used the concept of fuzzy accuracy. This method allowed us to evaluate results in the case, where the real decision class and the predicted decision class differ by 1.

To estimate the usefulness of our approach we derived a set of numerical experiments. All experiments were performed on real-world data. Classification for both: the classical accuracy, as well as the fuzzy accuracy, was calculated. Some summary related to the confusion matrix was derived as well. Results indicate, that the proposed approach could be very effective especially in the case, where strong trend (falling or rising) was observed for the analyzed financial instrument.

References

1. Abid, F., Alam, M., Yasir, M., Li, C.: Sentiment analysis through recurrent variants latterly on convolutional neural network of Twitter. Future Gener. Comput. Syst. **95**, 292–308 (2019)
2. Aguilar-Rivera, R., Valenzuela-Rendón, M., Rodriguez-Ortiz, J.: Genetic algorithms and Darwinian approaches in financial applications: a survey. Expert Syst. Appl. **42**(21), 7684–7697 (2015)

3. Bahrepour, M., Akbarzadeh-T., M., Yaghoobi, M., Naghibi-S., M.: An adaptive ordered fuzzy time series with application to FOREX. Expert Syst. Appl. **38**(1), 475–485 (2011)
4. Bouckaert, R.R., et al.: WEKA Manual for Version 3-7-10 (2013)
5. Breiman, L., Friedman, J.H., Olshen, R.A., Stone, C.J.: Classification and regression trees, Belmont, C.A. (1984)
6. Dorigo, M., Stützle, T.: Ant Colony Optimization. MIT Press, Cambridge (2004)
7. Górny, A., Tkacz, M.: Using artificial neural networks for processing data gained via OpenDAP and consolidated from different databases on distributed servers. In: Szczepaniak, P.S., Kacprzyk, J., Niewiadomski, A. (eds.) AWIC 2005. LNCS (LNAI), vol. 3528, pp. 176–182. Springer, Heidelberg (2005). https://doi.org/10.1007/11495772_28
8. Harris, L.: What to do about high-frequency trading. Finan. Anal. J. **69**(2), 6–9 (2013)
9. Jingtao, Y., Chew Lim, T.: A case study on using neural networks to perform technical forecasting of forex. Neurocomputing **32**(1–4), 79–98 (2000)
10. Kania, K., Juszczuk, P., Kozak, J.: Investigating patterns in the financial data with enhanced symbolic description. In: Nguyen, N.T., Pimenidis, E., Khan, Z., Trawiński, B. (eds.) ICCCI 2018. LNCS (LNAI), vol. 11056, pp. 345–354. Springer, Cham (2018). https://doi.org/10.1007/978-3-319-98446-9_32
11. Kelly, S., Ahmad, K.: Estimating the impact of domain-specific news sentiment on financial assets. Knowl. Based Syst. **150**, 116–126 (2018)
12. Kozak, J., Juszczuk, P.: Association ACDT as a tool for discovering the financial data rules. In: IEEE International Conference on INnovations in Intelligent SysTems and Applications (2017)
13. Kozak, J.: Decision Tree and Ensemble Learning Based on Ant Colony Optimization. SCI, vol. 781. Springer, Cham (2019). https://doi.org/10.1007/978-3-319-93752-6
14. Lim, T.-S., Loh, W.-Y., Shih, Y.-S.: A comparison of prediction accuracy, complexity, and training time of thirty-three old and new classification algorithms. Mach. Learn. **3**(40), 203–228 (2000)
15. Lin, J., Keogh, E., Lonardi, S., Chiu, B.: A symbolic representation of time series, with implications for streaming algorithms. In: Proceedings of the 8th ACM SIGMOD Workshop on Research Issues in Data Mining and Knowledge Discovery, pp. 2–11 (2003)
16. Lkhagva, B., Suzuki, Y., Kawagoe, K.: Extended SAX: extension of symbolic aggregate approximation for financial time series data representation. In: DEWS (2006)
17. Mizuno, H., Kosaka, M., Yajima, H., Komoda, N.: Application of neural network to technical analysis of stock market prediction. Stud. Inf. Control **7**(3), 111–120 (1998)
18. Naranjo, R., Arroyo, J., Santos, M.: Fuzzy modeling of stock trading with fuzzy candlesticks. Expert Syst. Appl. **93**, 15–27 (2018)
19. Nassirtoussi, A.K., Aghabozorgi, S., Wah, T.Y., Ngo, D.C.L.: Text mining for market prediction: a systematic review. Expert Syst. Appl. **41**, 7653–7670 (2014)
20. Nassirtoussi, A.K., Aghabozorgi, S., Wah, T.Y., Ngo, D.C.L.: Text mining of news-headlines for FOREX market prediction: a multi-layer dimension reduction algorithm with semantics and sentiment. Expert Syst. Appl. **42**, 306–324 (2015)
21. Neely, C.J., Weller, P.A., Dittmar, R.: Is technical analysis profitable in the foreign exchange market? A genetic programming approach. J. Finan. Quant. Anal. **32**, 405–426 (1997)

22. Ozturk, M., Toroslu, I.H., Fidan, G.: Heuristic based trading system on Forex data using technical indicator rules. Appl. Soft Comput. **43**, 170–186 (2016)
23. Quinlan, J.R.: Induction of decision trees. Mach. Learn. **1**(1), 81–106 (1986)
24. Quinlan, J.R.: C4.5: Programs for Machine Learning. Morgan Kaufmann, San Francisco (1993)
25. Silagadze, Z.K.: Moving Mini-Max - a new indicator for technical analysis. Invest. Manag. Finan. Innov. **8**(3), 46–49 (2011)
26. Tkacz, M.: Artificial neural networks in incomplete data sets processing. In: Kłopotek, M.A., Wierzchoń, S.T., Trojanowski, K. (eds.) Intelligent Information Processing and Web Mining. AINSC, vol. 31, pp. 577–584. Springer, Heidelberg (2005). https://doi.org/10.1007/3-540-32392-9_70
27. Tkacz, M.A.: Artificial neural network resistance to incomplete data. In: Kłopotek, M.A., Wierzchoń, S.T., Trojanowski, K. (eds.) Intelligent Information Processing and Web Mining. AINSC, vol. 35, pp. 437–443. Springer, Heidelberg (2006). https://doi.org/10.1007/3-540-33521-8_48

Deep Learning Models for Time Series Forecasting of Indoor Temperature and Energy Consumption in a Cold Room

Nédra Mellouli[1(✉)], Mahdjouba Akerma[2], Minh Hoang[2(✉)], Denis Leducq[2], and Anthony Delahaye[2]

[1] LIASD EA4383, IUT de Montreuil, Université Paris 8,
Vincennes Saint-Denis, France
n.mellouli@iut.univ-paris8.fr
[2] Irstea, UR GPAN, Anthony, France
{minh.hoang,anthony.delahaye}@irstea.fr
http://liasd.univ-paris8.fr

Abstract. We propose to study the dynamic behavior of indoor temperature and energy consumption in a cold room during demand response periods. Demand response is a method that consists in smoothing demand over time, seeking to reduce or even stop consumption during periods of high demand in order to shift it to periods of lower demand. Such a system can therefore be tackled as the study of a time-series, where each behavioral parameter is a time-varying parameter. Four deep neural network architectures derived from the LSTM architecture were studied, adapted and compared. Their validation was carried out using experimental data collected in a cold room in order to assess their performance in predicting demand response.

Keywords: Time series · Deep learning ·
Electricity production and consumption

1 Introduction

In Europe like anywhere in the world, the balance between electricity production and consumption is a necessity. It could be maintained by using a strategy of electrical Demand to Response (DR). Involves changing the electricity consumption behaviour of end users over a period of time in response to financial incentives. It may therefore be a non-consumption of electricity (power outage) or a shift in consumption to ensure electricity demand closer to electricity supply. The refrigerated storage industry represents a substantial electrical load with a total number of 1.7 million of cold stores in Europe, accounting for 60–70 million m3 of storage volume and high energy consumption [1].

Energy efficiency in cold warehouse is becoming an important issue in terms of energy consumption [8] environmental and economic benefits [6,14]. In this context we have therefore focused our study on the large-scale use of electrical cut-off in cold warehouse in particular. A cold warehouse is a very complex

© Springer Nature Switzerland AG 2019
N. T. Nguyen et al. (Eds.): ICCCI 2019, LNAI 11684, pp. 133–144, 2019.
https://doi.org/10.1007/978-3-030-28374-2_12

system and its parameters depend on the warehouse design and outdoor weather conditions [9]. Issues related to the behaviour of the system and the possibility of an increase in product temperature during RD are current hindering the adoption of this strategy by food industry stakeholders. In order to choose the best way to implement DR, it is necessary to predict the system behaviour during and after the DR application.

Three types of modelling approaches are used in the literature for predicting system behaviour such as temperature or energy consumption: data-based approach, physics-based approach and "Gray Box" approach. Some of these approaches are reviewed in [10]. In particular, the physics-based approach is a set of equations describing the physical phenomena that occur in the system. This approach requires detailed knowledge on the characteristics of the system such as heat exchanges in the storage or the behaviour of the refrigeration machine and the influence of each element on the control of the system [11]. Due to this high complexity and when the main objective is the final result obtained at the output of the system independently of internal operation, it may be interesting to examine the use of Black Box models, the purpose being to predict the output parameters according to the inputs. The study of the dynamic behavior of such a system can therefore be approached as the study of a time series, where each behavioral parameter is a time-varying parameter.

A time series is a sequence of real-valued signals that are measured at successive time intervals. Long short-term memory (LSTM) [2], a class of recurrent neural networks (RNNs) [3], is particularly designed for sequential data. For time series prediction task LSTM has particularly shown promising results. Four deep neural network architectures derived from the LSTM architecture were studied, adapted and compared. Their validation was carried out using experimental data collected in a cold room in order to evaluate their performance in predicting demand response.

In this paper, we present our methodology which allows us to provide answers to the following issues: (1) Which deep learning models are best suited to represent our specific data? (2) From the selected models, we have sought to define and characterize the most efficient predictive models and to highlight all the parameters that induce them. (3) In addition to their relevance, we have also assessed the robustness of the selected models at the last iteration against the data quality (noise), data temporal window scaling and large scaling data. The paper is structured as follows. In the next section we present the related work, then we detail our approach. Finally we describe the datasets used to compare four deep learning architectures and we discuss their results.

2   Related Work

In this section, we compare some common methods used to analyze data that change over time. We first discuss the disadvantages of conventional time series models for predicting DR energy. Then, we particularly compare them to non-linear models that are more relevant to fit the dynamic behaviour of cold stores.

2.1 Time Series Models in Electrical Demand Response Prediction

Time series is defined as a sequence of discrete time data. It consists of indexed data points, measured typically at successive times, spaced at (often uniform) time intervals. Time series analysis comprises the different methods for analyzing such time series in order to understand the theory behind the data points, i.e. its characteristics and the statistical meaning [17]. A time series forecasting model predicts future values based on known past events (recent observations). Conventional time series prediction methods commonly use a moving average model that can be autoregressive (ARMA) [4,12], integrated autoregressive (ARIMA) [5] or vector autoregressive (VARMA) [18], in order to reduce data. However such methods must process all available data in order to extract the model parameters that best fit the new data. These methods are useless face to massive data and real-time series forecasting.

To address this problem, online time learning methods have emerged to sequentially extract representations of underlying models from time series data. Unlike traditional batch learning methods, online learning methods avoid unnecessary cost training again when processing new data. Due to their effectiveness and scalability, online learning methods, including linear model-based methods, ensemble learning and kernels, have been successfully applied to time series forecasting. Each time series forecasting model could have many forms and could be applied to many applications. For more details we can see [13,21].

2.2 Non-linear Models

When the main objective is the final result obtained at the output of a system, regardless of internal operation, it may be interesting to look at the use of non-linear models, whose purpose is solely to predict the output parameters according to the inputs. In addition, non-linear models are easily generalizable. Indeed they not require a problem reshaping or parameter's adaptation when studying a new system.

In particular, Artificial Neural Networks (ANN) could provide an alternative approach, as they are widely accepted as a very promising technology offering a new way to solve complex problems. ANNs ability in mapping complex non-linear relationships, have succeeded in solving several problems such as planning, control, analysis and design. The literature has demonstrated their superior capability over conventional methods, their main advantage being the high potential to model non-linear processes, such as utility loads or energy consumption in individual buildings. At present, although studies [22,23] have been carried out within the wide framework of demand response, no such method does appear to be applied to DR in the field of refrigeration.

In consideration of the energy importance of this field which provides a panel of significant opportunities, the use of a relevant modelling approach as shown in [16] could demonstrate (or invalidate) the use of demand response in cold stores, allowing (or not) a significant increase of electrical cut-off deployment. An

LSTM network, or "Long Short Term Memory", is a model for retaining short-term information (recent variations and current trends in data) and long-term ones (periodicity, recurring or non-recurring events). It is a deep learning model widely used for time series processing. It is popular due to its ability of learning hidden long-term sequential dependencies, which actually helps in learning the underlying representations of time series [19]. [7,24] showed the superiority of Long Short Term Memory (LSTM) in predicting electricity consumption data on one hour and one-minute time-step load data. A convolutional LSTM model was proposed based on the Fully Connected LSTM model [20], particularly for its application to predicting changes in spatial images. This model has allowed them to obtain better results than when using a simple LSTM or Fully-Connected LSTM network.

The architecture of an LSTM network therefore consists of a sequence of LSTM layers for both past and future data, which are then processed together to predict current data. To conclude, the modeling of a refrigeration system being characterized by the non linearity and the coupling of several parameters, classical physical models have difficulties predicting the dynamic behaviour of such systems, in particular during disturbances such as electrical cut-off periods. Neural network methods, due to their ability to adjust and self learning, can therefore be very promising in responding to this type of issues offering a new way to solve complex problems.

3 Our Approach

A cold room or cold store ensures that the products are kept in satisfactory conditions. This therefore requires the use of a refrigeration system, which can take the form of a regular supply of cold air, in order to keep the air and products below a setpoint temperature, generally below -18 °C. This phenomenon follows the refrigeration cycle, passing through its four main stages, namely compression, condensation, expansion and evaporation. In order to avoid significant heat leakage, it is also necessary to reduce external inputs, through optimal thermal insulation and to minimize door openings as well as human or mechanical activities.

3.1 Features of Cold Stores System

The main features of a cold room are of two categories. As a first category, we find fixed features which take into account building geometry (as building dimensions, wall thickness), building composition (as material conductivity, density and overall heat exchange coefficient), outdoor contributions (as outdoor temperature, solar flux, air renewal), cold production (as setpoint temperature, blowing temperature, blowing rate, operation of the refrigeration machine, cooling capacity) and operations on building (as loading, product conductivity, product density, human presence, lighting, ventilation, defrosting, etc). The second category includes mainly temporal features like the demand response periods

(DR) including both the demand response phase itself (switching off the cooling system) and the recovery phase of the cooling system (restoring the set temperature); The defrost periods, (Def) which occur several times a day without any decision-making power on their time occurrences. These periods correspond to a specific increasing temperature related to the defrosting period; The compressor on/off periods ($compressor$), which occur very regularly and on an ad hoc basis; The time elapsed since the last demand response period ($\delta(DR)$), allowing the model to better predict the behavior of the cold room in the moments following the demand response period, while its condition is not yet restored; And the time elapsed since the last defrost ($\delta(Def)$), also allowing better prediction of the behaviour of the cold room in the moments following defrosting, when the condition of the cold room is not yet stabilized.

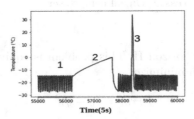

Fig. 1. Three modes: (1) Steady state, regular temperature variations according to set points (high/low); (2) Electrical demand response, temperature increases over a long period of time (30 min–3 h); (3) Defrosting, sudden temperature increase for a very short time (5–10 min)

3.2   Electrical DR Problem Formalisation with Time Series

According to the time parameters defined below we obtain a system with three modes behavior. The first mode (*cf.* Fig. 1(1)) represents the steady state where regular temperature variations according to set points (high/low) are measured. The second mode (*cf.* Fig. 1(2)) is the critical state of the system refers to electrical DR. During this mode, the temperature increases over a long period of time. This period depends mainly on the DR time interval, but typically varies between 30 min and 3 h. The third mode (*cf.* Fig. 1(3)) is the defrost state in which the temperature suddenly increases over a short period of time. The main input and output of the cold room system are summarized in Table 1.

We note by y_t and x_t time series observations representing respectively any output and input parameter in Table 1. We note by f a non-linear prediction function with $m + p$ inputs such that

$$y_{t+1} = f(y_t, y_{t-1}, ..., y_{t-m+1}, x_t, x_{t-1}, ..., x_{t-p+1}) \tag{1}$$

We consider h as a discrete period on $[1, m]$. Having a serie of observations $y_t, y_{t-1}, ..., y_{t-m+1}$ on a fixed period h we propose to estimate $\hat{y}(m, H)$ on future

Table 1. Inputs and outputs of the DR system

	Name	Description
Output	$Temp_{In}$	Indoor Temperature
	$Temp_{Air}$	Recovery Temperature of the Air
	$Temp_{Prod}$	Product Temperature
	Ep	Electric power consumed
Input	$Temp_{out}$	Outdoor Temperature
	DR	Demand Response period
	Def	Defrost Period
	$\delta(DR)$	The elapsed time since the last erasure
	$\delta(Def)$	The elapsed time since the last defrost
	$Compressor$	On/off compressor

dates m within a given horizon H. This problem is equivalent to estimate the optimal $\hat{f}$ of Eq. 1 which minimize:

$$Error = (\widehat{y} - y)^2 \qquad (2)$$

3.3 LSTM Models to Forcasting Electrical Demand Response

As it is proven in the literature, Long Short Term Memory (LSTM) is required to discover a dependence relationships between the time series data by using specialized gating and memory mechanisms. We propose to define the non-linear function f (Eq. 1) by an LSTM model. For this purpose, we aimed to compare four LSTM models according to prediction *Error* (Eq. 2): LSTM, Convolutional LSTM, Stacked LSTM, Bidirectional LSTM. As a first model we have used LSTM. After a huge number of experiments following several evaluations of the model, the parameters were selected for this model:

- 1024 units are able to store enough information. This choice was made balancing the learning time and the quality of obtained prediction
- A linear or SeLu activation function
- A cost function using the Root Mean Square Error (RMSE)

The second model is **stacked LSTM**. The developed Stacked LSTM model is a modification of the LSTM network described above, with the addition of several layers of LSTM.

For this purpose, and after experimental tests, the selected model consists of a stack of three layers of LSTM, namely: A first layer of 1024 memory units, allowing to store a large amount of information in the short and long term; A second layer of 512 memory units; A third layer, of 256 memory units. Each layer of the network is separated from the next layer by a dropout layer, allowing less overtraining and robust generalization results.

The **Bidirectional LSTM** network consists in a stack of two layers of LSTMs each with 512 memory units. This model thus created makes it possible to keep information related to both past and future data.

The **convolutional LSTM** network was chosen with the following parameters: 40 filters, corresponding to the outputs of the convolutional part of the model; A kernel size of 2 × 10, corresponding to the dimensions of the convolution window; A normalization layer, allowing to normalize the activations of the convolutional LSTM layer.

3.4 Error Estimation and Evaluation Metrics

In order to compare our different models and select the best model(s) for our study, different criteria were implemented and computed.

We consider the average $\bar{y}$ of the reference values and N the number of observations. The Fit criterion is needed to measure the distance between the reference values and the predicted values. The closer its value is to 100%, the more it indicates a correctly predicted variable. It therefore corresponds to a percentage and is defined by: $Fit(Y) = 100(1 - \frac{|\hat{Y}-Y|}{|Y-\bar{Y}|})$.

The Mean-Squared-Error (MSE), or mean square error, is the arithmetic mean of the squares of the differences between the forecasts and the actual observations. The objective of a good prediction is therefore to obtain the lowest possible mean square error. The advantage of squaring is to highlight high errors, and therefore to minimize low prediction errors. This value is therefore defined by: $MSE(Y) = \frac{1}{N}\sum_{i=1}^{N}(\hat{Y}_i - Y_i)^2$.

The root of this value, or Root-Mean-Squared-Error (RMSE), is also often used, which is simply calculated by: $RMSE(Y) = \sqrt{MSE(Y)}$.

The Mean Absolute Error (MAE), or absolute mean error, is the arithmetic mean of the differences between forecasts and actual observations. Since there is no squaring, this measure treats each difference with equal importance. The objective is of course to minimize this value, and it is defined over prediction horizon $[t + 1, t + H]$ by: $MAE(Y) = \frac{1}{N}\sum_{i=1}^{N}|\hat{Y}_i - Y_i|$.

The coefficient of variation (CV) is a little-known measure that has been proposed by [15] to evaluate the prediction of models for building energy consumption. This value is defined as a percentage, by the formula: $CV(Y) = 100\frac{RMSE(y)}{\bar{y}}$. As this value is only used in the field of energy consumption, it will therefore only be evaluated on consumption values, and not on temperatures (the latter may also be negative).

4   Experimental Results and Discussions

As mentioned above, we implemented the four LSTM architectures described in Sect. 3.3. To evaluate their performance in predicting demand response, a set of use cases were developed based on experimental data collected in cold rooms. For the cold room, we had access to large periods of measurement time with acceptable accuracy where measurements were made every five seconds. These measurements were made in a cold room that was replicated in a controlled environment to obtain data to form the models and prove their predictive power. For these purposes, we have proposed five use cases us to efficiently answer the following questions: (1) Which deep learning models are more adapted to represent our specific data? (2) Which model(s) is less sensitive to the stochastic occurrence of electrical demand response? (3) Which model(s) is more robust to the data quality, i.e. signal noise (electrical demand response) and horizon window?

4.1 Experimental Setup

We assume that the reference behaviour of a cold room is characterized by an ideal "undisturbed" operation, with no phenomenon of demand response or door opening and this over a long period of time, in order to stabilize the internal temperature. These data measurements are only used to initialize the four architectures. Then we have established five time series datasets to evaluate each LSTM architecture. These datasets are described as follows. We note by E_i a dataset time series where $i = 1..5$ elaborated for each use case i:

- The use case 1 (train: 127975, test: 60000) hypothesis is to consider a set of measurements with three electrical demand response periods, uniformly distributed over 3 days. Here we simulate the stochastic disturbance of the system with a uniform distribution of the noise signal. Hence $\delta(DR)$ is randomly decreased and DR is fixed;
- The use case 2 (train: 223545, test: 149030) hypothesis is to consider a set of measurements with two electrical demand response periods per day, uniformly distributed over 5 days. In this case we increase the frequency of occurrence of the noise in use case 1 and increase the total number of measurements. Indeed, this case allows us to study the bias of the frequency of noise occurrence as well as the amount of data;
- The case 3 (train: 490985, test: 294590) hypothesis is to consider a set of measurements over 5 days with one electrical demand response period randomly occurred per day and with a random period. It means both $\delta(DR)$ and DR are random.
- The case 4 (train: 630920, test: 420610) hypothesis is to consider the union of the three previous hypothesis. It corresponds to a generalized model of the electrical demand response problem, i.e. we have a large amount of data, more noise and more randomness.
- The case 5 (train: 214080, test: 142700) hypothesis is to consider a fixed $\delta(DR)$, a fixed DR varying between 1 and 3 hours and we increase prediction horizon H.

Each dataset E_i ($i = 1..5$) is split into 60% of data for training (Train) and 40% for validation (Test) sets.

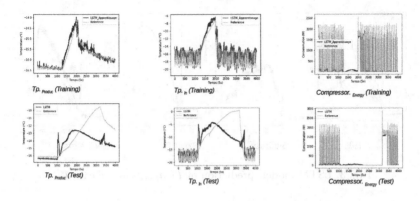

Fig. 2. LSTM data time series prediction with $E1$ datasets

Table 2. E_i Temperature $Temp_{prod}$ prediction with the four derived LSTM models

T_p	LSTM	Con LSTM	Stacked LSTM	Bidirectional LSTM
E_1	(Mae = 0.38, Fit = 35.8)	(Mae = 0.38, Fit = 60.5)	(Mae = 0.44, Fit = 42.8)	(Mae = 0.5, Fit = 41.7)
E_2	(Mae = 0.16, Fit = 29.7)	(Mae = 0,33, Fit = 14.8)	(Mae = 0.14, Fit = 30.4)	(Mae = 0.31, Fit = 24.4)
E_3	(Mae = 0,27, Fit = 48.0)	(Mae = 0.26, Fit = 46.9)	(Mae = 0.23, Fit = 50.9)	(Mae = 0.31, Fit = 52.1)
E_4	(Mae = 0.27, Fit = 58.2)	(Mae = 0.33, Fit = 55.5)	(Mae = 0.27, Fit = 61.1)	(Mae = 0.37, Fit = 48.4)
E_5	-	-	(Mae = 0.19, Fit = 69.64)	-

Table 3. E_i Ep prediction with the four derived LSTM models

$CV(Ep)$	LSTM	Con LSTM	Stacked LSTM	Bidirectional LSTM
E_1	18.9	23.5	18.9	20.3
E_2	15.7	13.7	47.1	20.08
E_3	15.1	13.8	54.42	22.6
E_4	16.2	15.9	16.1	16.1
E_5	-	-	28.5	-

4.2 Results and Discussions

As shown graphically (Figs. 2, 3, 4), we obtained significant results thanks to the use of the convolutional LSTM network using the E_1 dataset, on all variables except Ep, which could be verified graphically.

The other models derived from the LSTM model give us interesting but much less significant results than those found with the convolutional LSTM model.

However, it can be noted that the Stacked LSTM and Bidirectional LSTM models obtain fairly high performance in terms of air temperature. Yet, these results are still very modest, due to the small amount of data. In addition, it should be noted that some variables, such as $Temp_{prod}$, are insufficiently predicted by all models. These problems seem to be partly related to the sensors. A more detailed analysis will be carried out later to check the proper functioning

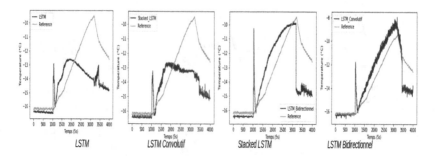

Fig. 3. LSTM models prediction of $Temp_{prod}$ in use case 1

of these different sensors. The results obtained with the dataset E_2 are less efficient for predicting temperature-related variables. In particular, we note a sudden increase in the predicted temperature as soon as the electrical cut-off is triggered, followed by an equally sudden decrease at the end of the demand response period. As far as the energy consumption is concerned, the behaviour is always reproduced as faithfully as ever. With this dataset Bidirectional and Stacked LSTM outperform the other models. We can note that Stacked and bidirectional LSTM are less sensitive the amount of data.

With the E_3 dataset, simple and Convolutional LSTM outperform the other models. They seem to be more efficient in the presence of random noises. Bidirectional and Stacked LSTM are able to predict the dynamics of time series but are sensitive to noise, especially during the starting times of both the demand response and the retakes. This is manifested by peaks of values predicted by the last two models. With the E_4 dataset we obtained similar results with LSTM and Stacked LSTM. Their predictive accuracy outperforms the other two models. It should be noted, however, that four models are trained on the union of E_1

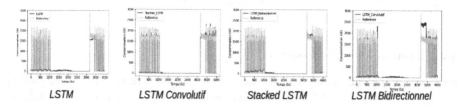

Fig. 4. LSTM models prediction of Ep in use case 1

and E_2 and they have to predict on the E_3 dataset according to the percentages of the Train and Test samples. What is interesting is that we expected the results in this use case to be similar to the previous use case (use case 3). However, learning more noise allows stacked systems to better predict noise and random data. Also they seem to be less sensible to the amount data. Finally the dataset E_5 is used as Test sample for the pre-trained Stacked LSTM. Since the horizon size of E_5 is 20 min, four times longer than the previous ones, time series data are limited. As long as the size of the E_5 horizon is four times larger than the previous ones, the data are more smoothed and less noisy. As a result, the model was able to better predict with a Gain of approximately 10%. The Ep is efficiently predicted in all use cases where the fitting is around 90% and the MAE is around 0.1. This is due to its independent state from the defrosting and electrical demand response and it has a stationary state.

5 Conclusion and Perspectives

Although the results obtained in the study of series E_1 and E_4 were quite satisfactory, the results of series E_2 and E_3 remain rather moderate, as can be seen from values given above (Tables 2, 3). Indeed, the different models, although trained and then tested on larger data sets, seem to have difficulties in generalizing prediction on test values. However, some models and their predictions are encouraging, suggesting that the use of deep learning methods could lead to better results through improvements and with the use of more data. In particular, Stacked LSTM seems to be the efficient deep learning architecture providing acceptable predictions in the context of our specific data. Indeed, the modeling of a refrigeration system being characterized by the non linearity and the coupling of several parameters, classical physical models encounter difficulties in predicting the dynamic behaviour of such systems, in particular during disturbances such as electrical demand response periods. Stacked LSTM, due to its ability to adjust and self-learn, can therefore be very promising in responding to this type of issues. To increase its efficiency, it could be interesting to use weight masks during training. Therefore, transfer learning could favour the adjustment of weights during demand response periods, and would obtain predictions closer to the reference values.

References

1. Evans, J.A., et al.: Specific energy consumption values for various refrigerated food cold stores. Energy Build. **74**, 141–151 (2014)
2. Hochreiter, S., Schmidhuber, J.: Long short-term memory. Neural Comput. **9**(8), 1735–1780 (1997)
3. LeCun, Y., Bengio, Y., Hinton, G.: Deep learning. Nature **521**(7553), 436–444 (2015)
4. Rojo-Alvarez, J.L., Martınez-Ramon, M., de Prado-Cumplido, M., et al.: Support vector method for robust ARMA system identification. IEEE Trans. Sign. Process. **52**(1), 155–164 (2004)
5. Hamilton, J.D.: Time Series Analysis. Princeton University Press, Princeton (1994)
6. Afroz, Z., Shafiullah, G.M., Urmee, T., Higgins, G.: Prediction of indoor temperature in an institutional building. Energy Procedia **142**, 1860–1866 (2017)
7. Deb, C., Zhang, F., Yang, J., Lee, S.E., Shah, K.W.: A review on time series forecasting techniques for building energy consumption. Renew. Sustain. Energy Rev. **74**, 902–924 (2017)

8. Lee, W.L., Tan, K.W., Lim, Z.Y.: A data-driven approach for benchmarking energy efficiency of warehouse buildings, School of Information Systems at Institutional Knowledge at Singapore Management University (2017)

9. Frausto, H.U., Pieters, J.G., Deltour, J.M.: Modelling greenhouse temperature by means of auto regressive models. Biosyst. Eng. **84**, 147–157 (2003)

10. Afram, A., Janabi-Sharifi, F.: Review of modeling methods for HVAC systems. Appl. Therm. Eng. **67**, 507–519 (2014)

11. Berthou, T., Stabat, P., Salvazet, R., Marchio, D.: Comparaison de modèles linéaires inverses pour la mise en place de stratégies d'effacement, p. 6. Rencontres AUGC-IBPSA, Chambéry, Savoie (2012)

12. Ohtsu, K., Peng, H., Kitagawa, G.: Time series analysis through AR modeling. Time Series Modeling for Analysis and Control. SS, pp. 7–56. Springer, Tokyo (2015). https://doi.org/10.1007/978-4-431-55303-8_2

13. Amjady, N.: Short-term hourly load forecasting using time series modeling with peak load estimation capability. IEEE Trans. Power Syst. **16**, 498–505 (2001)

14. Ziekow, H., Goebel, C., Struker, J., Jacobsen, H.A.: The potential of smart home sensors in forecasting household electricity demand (2013)

15. Amasyali, K., El-Gohary, N.: Building lighting energy consumption prediction for supporting energy data analytics. Procedia Eng. **145**, 511–517 (2016)

16. Chou, J.S., Tran, D.S.: Forecasting energy consumption time series using machine learning techniques based on usage patterns of residential householders. Energy **165**, 709–726 (2018)

17. Nataraja, C., Gorawar, M.B., Shilpa, G.N., Harsha, J.S.: Short term load forecasting using time series analysis: a case study for Karnataka, India. Int. J. Eng. Sci. Innov. Technol. **1**, 45–53 (2012)

18. Rios-Moreno, G.J., Trejo-Perea, M., Castañeda-Miranda, R., Hernández-Guzmán, V.M., Herrera-Ruiz, G.: Modelling temperature in intelligent buildings by means of autoregressive models. Autom. Constr. **16**, 713–722 (2007)

19. Kuo, P.-H., Huang, C.-J.: A high precision artificial neural networks modelfor short-term energy load forecasting. Energies **11**, 213 (2018)

20. Shi, X., Chen, Z., Wang, H., Yeung, D.-Y., Wong, W.-K., Woo, W.-C.: Convolutional LSTM network: a machine learning approach for precipitation nowcasting (LSTM Convolutif) (2015)

21. Aman, S., Frincu, M., Chelmis, C., Noor, M., Simmhan, Y., Prasanna, V.K.: Prediction models for dynamic demand response. In: IEEE International Conference on Smart Grid Communications (SmartGridComm) (2015)

22. Hu, M., Xiao, F., Wang, L.: Investigation of demand response potentials of residential air conditioners in smart grids using grey-box room thermal model. Appl. Energy **207**, 324–335 (2017)

23. Xue, X., Wang, S., Yan, C., Cui, B.: A fast chiller power demand response control strategy for buildings connected to smart grid. Appl. Energy **137**, 77–87 (2014)

24. Marino, D.L., Amarasinghe, K., Salvazet, R., Manic, M.: Building energy load forecasting using deep neural networks. In: IECON 2016 - 42nd Annual Conference of the IEEE Industrial Electronics Society (2016)

Discovery of Leaders and Cliques in the Organization Based on Social Network Analysis

Barbara Probierz[✉]

Faculty of Informatics and Communication, Chair of Knowledge Engineering,
University of Economics, Katowice, Poland
barbara.probierz@ue.katowice.pl

Abstract. This article proposes an approach related to the analysis of social networks, as well as the practical possibilities of using these networks to study the flow of e-mails between employees in an organization. The aim of the work is to analyze contacts between individual employees of a corporation, used to appoint leaders (key users) to spread information or influence people in the immediate vicinity. The proposed method has been tested on the Enron E-mail Dataset.

Keywords: Social Network Analysis · Enron E-mail dataset ·
Leaders · Cliques

1 Introduction

Each organization has its own unique communication system. With the development of modern technologies, ways of communication change. The process of globalization and universal access to the Internet is also of great importance - at one time the entire company was in the conference room and the chairman of the board could personally convey the vision - now companies have branches all over the world and also implement a coherent vision that was forwarded via e-mail to several thousand employees at the same time. The importance of this system is huge because it provides the organization with information flow, both between team members and between teams and departments. Using the communication processes, team members know what tasks they have to perform, what is the company's goal and mission.

The first element for the information flow processes is the reconstruction of the contact map within the organization in the form of a network of social connections. A thorough analysis of the contact map between individual employees of the organization allows finding places where messages are distorted, but also indicates employees - leaders from the point of view of information spreading or influencing people in the immediate vicinity. In addition, it allows the user to designate clicks, or groups of employees interacting with each other much more regularly and intensively than with other employees not belonging to a clique.

© Springer Nature Switzerland AG 2019
N. T. Nguyen et al. (Eds.): ICCCI 2019, LNAI 11684, pp. 145–154, 2019.
https://doi.org/10.1007/978-3-030-28374-2_13

The aim of this work is to create a social network based on contacts between senders and recipients of e-mails. Then during the analysis and observation of the social network, the leaders are identified and the user groups constituting the cliques are identified. The proposed method has been applied to the collection of e-mails from mailboxes obtained from the publicly available Enron Email dataset.

This article is organized as follows. Section 1 comprises an introduction to the subject of this article. Sections 2 and 3 describes Social Network and Social Network Analysis (SNA). In Sect. 4, measures of network analysis is presented. Section 5 describes Enron E-mail dataset. Section 6 presents experimental research related to the creation of a contact map illustrating the flow of information and the discovery of leaders and cliques in the organization. Finally, we conclude with general remarks on this work and a few directions for future research are pointed out.

2   Social Network

Social networks play an important role in our daily lives, they not only determine interpersonal relationships, but also appear in economic and political activities. It is therefore crucial to visualize the social structure and analyze social networks based on user-defined data. In particular, it is important to build patterns of relationships between people and groups and to study the consequences of the structure, such as the flow of information.

The important thing is that when analyzing a network, we do not focus on a specific actor, his individual characteristics, but his place in the whole structure is important. Based on simple numerical data, we can draw very interesting and useful conclusions. They may concern, for example, hidden relations between employees in the company, or they will select a natural leader of a local community.

In 1923, Jacob L. Moreno conducted the first social network research and was recognized as one of the founders of the social network analysis discipline. SNA is a branch of sociology which deals with the quantitative assessment of the individual's role in a group or community by analyzing the network of connections between individuals. Moreno's 1934 book that is titled "Who Shall Survive?" presents the first graphical representations of social networks as well as definitions of key terms that are used in an analysis of social networks and sociometric networks [8].

In the work [3] the Enron E-mail data was analyzed to find out how the structures in the organization are defined. A. Chapanond, M. S. Krishnamoorthy and B. Yener conducted an analysis that was based on the construction of an e-mail graph and investigated its both theoretical properties and the graph of spectral analysis techniques. The theoretical analysis of the graph included a number of indicators, such as the degree diagram, the average distance indicator or the coefficient of grouping in the graph, it has been shown that the preprocessing of data has a significant impact on the results, so a standard form is needed to establish the reference level of the data.

A social network is represented as a graph. According to the mathematical definition, a graph is an ordered pair:

$$G = (V, E), \tag{1}$$

where V denotes a finite set of a graph's vertices, and E denotes a finite set of all two-element subsets of set V that are called edges, which link particular vertices such that:

$$E \subseteq \{\{u, v\} : u, v \in V, u \neq v\}. \tag{2}$$

Vertices represent objects in a graph whereas edges represent the relations between these objects. Depending on whether this relation is symmetrical, a graph which is used to describe a network can be directed or undirected.

Edges in a social network represent the flow of information, interactions, social relationships or similarity. The strength of a connection depends on the attributes of the nodes (e.g. the degree of relationship) that are connected to each other and the structure of their neighborhood (e.g. the number of common neighbors) but this strength also is measured based on the frequency, reciprocity and type of interactions or information flow.

3   Social Network Analysis

In the study of data sets based on a direct examination of the relationship between entities rather than relationships between variables, an extremely important role is played by the Social Network Analysis [11]. This is primarily a specific perspective of analysis that does not focus on individual individuals or macro-structures, but examines the links between individuals or groups. By analyzing the network, we can study large-size networks and determine the specificity of their topology and evolution [2].

Social Network Analysis (SNA) is an interdisciplinary research approach that provides data analysis techniques of a relational character, in which the basic method of reality representation is the network. It is created and developed on the borderline of graph theory, matrix algebra, computer science and statistics, and used among others in economics, sociology, physics and biology [12].

Social Network Analysis has a wide range of applications. First of all, it is used in large organizations and companies as a tool supporting strategic human resource management or knowledge management in an organization. SNA supports the innovation of the company, and also serves to analyze business processes and analyze the training needs. In addition, it is used for marketing research in creating a map of the social network of clients. Analysis of social networks, however, allows primarily the management to get acquainted with the informal structure of the organization and information flow in the company.

The origins of SNA are based on an attempt to quantify social structures [10] and it incorporates insights from social science, mathematics and theoretical physics [7]. A lot of research on networks concerned the finding of correlations between the social structure of the network and its efficiency [6]. Initially, the analysis of social networks was carried out on the basis of surveys filled in by hand by participants [4], however, over time, studies conducted using the e-mail message became popular [1]. Some studies have found that research teams are more creative when they have more social capital [5]. Social networks are also associated with the discovery of a communication network. Such an approach was considered, among others Wilson and Banzhaf, as described in their paper [14].

It is assumed that with the use of SNA, the network can be analyzed at three basic levels:

- at the macro level (defining the general picture of communication in the organization, the number of relations, information flow between elements of the network);
- at the meso level (defining relations between different groups, indicating central and isolated groups in the network, indicating bottlenecks between groups);
- at the micro level (indication of elements that are network integrators, indication of leaders).

4   Measures of Social Network Analysis

Social network analysts use various measures to calculate how important each actor (node) is inside a network. Although there are various metrics, focusing on different graph notions and applying to different graph types, they are usually referred to as centralities collectively. Centrality measures attempt to quantify how much central is each actor inside the social network [9]. To do so, these measures usually examine the ties attached to an actor as well as the geodesic distances (shortest path lengths) to other actors.

The main indicators, that characterize a given social network, are degrees of vertices and the degree centrality of vertices. **Degree of a vertex** (indegree and outdegree) denotes the number of head endpoints or tail endpoints adjacent to a given node such that:

$$Deg(v) = \sum_{u=1}^{n} k_{v,u},\tag{3}$$

where k_{vu} is the edge between the vertex v and the vertex u.

In contrast, **Degree Centrality** is used to determine which nodes are crucial from the point of view of spreading information or influencing nodes located in the immediate vicinity. Most often the central vertex is defined as the vertices that have the most relations with other vertices (they have the largest number of edges). The maximum vertex height v in the G network is given by:

$$\Delta(G) = \max\left\{ Deg(v) : v \in V(G) \right\}.\tag{4}$$

Additional indicators characterizing the social network can be distinguished by indicators such as closeness centrality or betweenness centrality, as well as the average distance in the network. These measures are calculated according to the following formulas.

Closeness Centrality CC_v of vertix v:

$$CC_v = \frac{V-1}{\sum_{u \in V} d_{v,u}},$$ (5)

This CC_v index focuses on how close each node is to all other nodes in the network. Nodes with high closeness centrality are those who can reach many other nodes in few steps. The idea is that a node is more central if it can quickly interact with more of the others. CC_v is also interpreted as the ability to access information through the grapevine of network members.

Betweenness Centrality BC_v of vertix v:

$$BC_v = \frac{\sum_{w \in V} \sum_{u \neq w \in V} \frac{p_{w,v,u}}{p_{w,u}}}{(V-2)(V-1)},$$ (6)

where $p_{w,v,u}$ is the number of roads in the G graph between vertices w and u passing through v.

For each node v, BC_v is the ratio of all geodesics between pairs of nodes which run through v. It reflects how often that node lies on the geodesics between the other nodes of the network. The BC_v score of each actor can be interpreted as a measure of potential control as it quantifies just how much that actor acts as an intermediary to others. An actor which lies between many others is assumed to have a higher likelihood of being able to control information flow in the network. In essence, BC_v assumes that communication in a network occurs along the shortest possible path, the geodesic.

Average distance L (average length of all shortest paths between all pairs of connected vertices) on the network:

$$L = \frac{\sum_{v \neq u \in V} d_{v,u}}{V(V-1)},$$ (7)

where d_{vu} is the shortest path in the graph G between vertices v and u.

In graph theory, a **Clustering Coefficient** reflects the degree to which the nodes tend to cluster together. In social network analysis, it is often used to characterize the transitivity of a network. There are two versions of Clustering Coefficient: the global and the local.

The global Clustering Coefficient [12] is based on triplets of nodes to give an indication of the overall clustering in the whole network. A triplet consists of three connected nodes. A triangle therefore includes three closed triplets, one centered on each of the nodes. The global clustering coefficient is the number of closed triplets (or 3 × triangles) over the total number of triplets (both open and closed). This metric can be applied to both undirected and directed networks.

The local Clustering Coefficient [13] is an indication of the embeddedness of single nodes, and it is also used as an indication of the network transitivity. Specifically, the Clustering Coefficient of a node quantifies how close the node and its neighbors are to being a complete subgraph (clique).

The Clustering Coefficient C_v is useful in determining which nodes are critical as far as the dissemination of information or the influence exerted on immediate neighbors is concerned. Centrality is often a measure of these nodes' popularity or influence. The probability that the immediate neighbors of vertex v are also each other's immediate neighbors is described by the Clustering Coefficient C_v of vertex v such that:

$$C_v = \frac{\|\{e_{jk} : v_j, v_k \in N_i, e_{jk} \in E\}\|}{k_i(k_i - 1)}, \tag{8}$$

where k_i the number of vertices, in the neighbourhood N_i of a node i [15].

5   Enron E-Mail Dataset

Enron E-mail Dataset is a collection of data collected and prepared by the CALO project (A Cognitive Assistant that Learns and Organizes). It contains over 600 000 e-mails sent or received by 150 senior employees from Enron Corporation. The data collection was taken over by the Federal Energy Regulatory Commission during the investigation after the collapse of the company, and then it was made public. A copy of the database was purchased by Leslie Kaelbling from the Massachusetts Institute of Technology (MIT), after which it turned out that there are big problems with data integrity in the collection. As a result of work carried out by a team from SRI International, especially by Melinda Gervasio, the data were corrected and made available to other scientists for research purposes.

Each mailbox of employees Enron Corporation is stored in a separate folder and the name of the staff member. In each of these folders there are automatically created folders (for example: sent mail, all documents, deleted items) and folders created by the user. These folders include consecutively numbered e-mails.

All messages in the collection of Enron E-mail Dataset may the same construction. These are text files that contain in the following lines the details i.e.: message ID, date sent, sender's postal address, email address of the recipient, subject, message, recipient, to which a copy of the messages sent, first and last name the sender of the message, the name of the recipient of the message, the name of the folder in which the message, the name of the mailbox, which is a message and the body of the message.

6   Experiments

In order to create and analyze the map of social connections based on the Enron E-mail dataset, the studies were divided into several stages. In the first stage, analysis was carried out at the macro level, looking at the organization as a whole, thanks to which it was possible to determine the nature of the company in terms of communication and cooperation of all employees. During the conducted research on the creation and analysis of the network of links based on the Enron

E-mail dataset, all sent and received e-mails were taken into account. All e-mail addresses appearing at least once in the entire set have been objects on the network. However, the links between these objects are information about sending or receiving at least one e-mail message.

The next stage of the conducted research focused on the analysis of a group of employees being managers of Enron. Network analysis limited to a certain social group within a given enterprise is defined at the meso level. This analysis focuses on internal relations of a given group of objects, separated due to formal criteria of division, i.e. affiliation to relevant departments, seniority or position. Using this method, informal groups of employees can be identified who in a special way cooperate with each other or communicate with each other, thanks to their knowledge, or participate in the same process regarding, for example, a given project.

Additionally, the experiment focused on creating and analyzing a social network regarding the flow of e-mails between one employee and the other. The employee was selected on the basis of the knowledge and information flow criterion, and therefore was identified as the most important object in the network, because the most mail was sent from his mailbox.

All network objects are connected with each other by edges, reflecting the contact between individuals. The frequency of information flow is the number of e-mails sent. The values of the described parameters on three levels of analysis are presented in Table 1.

Table 1. The values of the parameters on three levels of analysis

Parameters	Macro level	Meso level	Micro level
Number of vertices	1 914	150	105
Number of edge	4 378	1 361	301
Frequency of information flow	462 976	15 024	5 844

The communication network at the macro level is built of objects (vertices), which include employees as well as customers and other external persons who have contacted each other via e-mail. The meso-level network consists of objects that are only employees of the Enron corporation, while the network objects at the micro level are people contacted by the analyzed employee. However, it should be remembered that the presented network concerns only the relationship of the selected object with the rest. In the case of choosing another object as the most important, the relationships in the new social network are completely different than those presented so far, and the unrelated objects in this network have connections with other objects of the new network.

During the analysis of the network, it was decided to reject from the Enron Email Dataset those folders that were created automatically by the email program. First of all, these are folders: *Inbox, Sent, Sent Items, Trash, All documents, Draft, Calendar, Contacts, Discussion Threads, Deleted Items.*

These folders appeared in all mailboxes, and users had no influence on the creation of these folders. After removing these folders, it turned out that there were no other folders in 32 boxes, and only one in 22 boxes. Therefore, all empty mailboxes and those containing only one folder were removed from the data set.

In the next step, the tree structure of the folders was flattened, leaving only the first level of folders in each box and deleting the nested folders. E-mails that were originally in nested folders were moved to folders from the first level of the tree structure. The last modification of the Enron E-mail dataset was to delete folders containing only one message.

An essential aspect of these studies is the separation of leaders (key users) and contact groups for these users. To this end, according to the network of contacts established, the nearest neighbors of this central user should be identified. After the modification of the dataset, a social network of Enron Corporation employees was created, which is presented in the Fig. 1.

Table 2. The parameters for the selected nodes of the social network

Dataset	Number of objects	Number of class	Closeness centrality	Degree centrality	Betweenness centrality
kean-s	25351	198	78	1670	544.30
dasovich-j	28234	64	85	1626	10453.18
shackleton-s	18687	12	83	1214	1190.70
jones-t	19950	10	102	1145	9345.81
taylor-m	13875	88	84	964	4288.94
stclair-c	3030	14	76	836	126.30
hain-m	3820	5	93	547	12866.37
whalley-l	3335	9	76	492	622.90
panus-s	437	5	79	478	7864.91
whalley-g	1878	24	78	425	1154.72
semperger-c	721	13	79	420	4036.68
kitchen-l	5546	60	106	416	19992.35
symes-k	10827	27	77	363	392.27
guzman-m	6054	4	73	325	4344.45
williams-w3	3440	24	71	282	3729.37
sanders-r	7329	51	98	273	1718.53
heard-m	1623	7	97	255	10506.33
skilling-j	4139	12	75	238	581.03
bailey-s	478	5	73	185	3050.67
lavorato-j	4685	33	94	154	1609.58
haedicke-m	5246	12	109	148	20563.59
salisbury-h	1632	5	64	138	41.00
sager-e	5200	14	109	115	23779.66
delainey-d	3566	8	73	63	300.75
cash-m	2969	31	102	48	13335.37

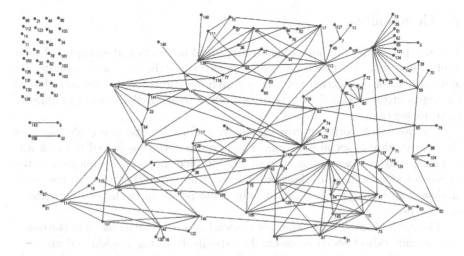

Fig. 1. Visualization of the social network for Enron E-mail dataset

Using the social network analysis package in R, the key network metrics were calculated for all individuals in the largest connected component. Parameters of selected nodes are visible in Table 2. The network nodes are all users of mailboxes from the Enron E-mail Dataset, while the edges are connections for which the frequency of interaction, i.e. the number of messages sent between individuals, was more than 10. Network nodes that are not associated with any other vertices are people who have less than the number of sent emails.

Table 3 presents key users (leaders) separated on the basis of calculated parameters of the created network. Then, the nearest neighbors were determined for designated leaders in accordance with the principles of graph theory. A person with a high Degree Centrality and low Betweenness Centrality may be the best choice for communicating information to an arm of a network. This logic extends to other parts and features of the network.

Table 3. Selected cliques for Enron Email dataset

Number of clique	Leader in clique	Nearest neighbors
Clique 1	delainey-d	whalley-g, whalley-l, skilling-j
Clique 2	kean-s	dasovich-j, hain-m, sanders-r
Clique 3	salisbury-h	guzman-m, williams-w3, symes-k, semperger-c
Clique 4	shackleton-s	jones-t, heard-m, taylor-m, panus-s
Clique 5	skilling-j	bailey-s, jones-t, taylor-m, panus-s, shackleton-s
Clique 6	stclair-c	jones-t, taylor-m, shackleton-s
Clique 7	symes-k	guzman-m, hain-m, semperger-c
Clique 8	whalley-g	kitchen-l, lavorato-j, whalley-l

7 Conclusions

The article presents methods of analyzing social networks and examples of their applications in organization and management research. The basic assumptions and specifics of conducting network research are presented, we are introducing the types of problems, data types, methods of their analysis and examples of their applications.

The presented work concerns the analysis of a collection of e-mails based on the construction of social networks. The purpose of the conducted research was to create and analyze a map of contacts between individual employees of the Enron corporation used to designate the most important people from the point of view of spreading information or influencing people in the immediate vicinity of these people.

The methods used in the analysis of social networks are included in the quantitative methods of social research. The specificity of the models and analyzes used results from the concentration on the relations between the network objects and the structures created by them.

References

1. Aral, S., Van Alstyne, M.: Network structure & information advantage (2007)
2. Barabási, A.L., Jeong, H., Néda, Z., Ravasz, E., Schubert, A., Vicsek, T.: Evolution of the social network of scientific collaborations. Physica A **311**(3), 590–614 (2002)
3. Chapanond, A., Krishnamoorthy, M.S., Yener, B.: Graph theoretic and spectral analysis of Enron email data. Comput. Math. Org. Theor. **11**(3), 265–281 (2005)
4. Cummings, J.N., Cross, R.: Structural properties of work groups and their consequences for performance. Soc. Netw. **25**, 197–210 (2003)
5. Gloor, P., et al.: Measuring social capital in creative teams through sociometric sensors. Int. J. Org. Des. Eng. **2**, 380–401 (2012)
6. Gloor, P.A.: Swarm Creativity: Competitive Advantage through Collaborative Innovation Networks. Oxford University Press, Oxford (2006)
7. Kane, G.C., Alavi, M., Labianca, G.J., Borgatti, S.: What's different about social media networks? A framework and research agenda. MIS Q. (2012)
8. Moreno, J.L.: Who Shall Survive? Foundations of Sociometry, Group Psychotherapy and Sociodrama. Beacon House, Beacon (1953, 1978)
9. Rocha, L.E., Liljeros, F., Holme, P.: Simulated epidemics in an empirical spatiotemporal network of 50,185 sexual contacts. PLoS Comput. Biol. **7**(3), e1001109 (2011)
10. Scott, J.: Social network analysis. Sociology **22**(1), 109–127 (1988)
11. Tran, M.T.T., Jeeva, A.S., Pourabedin, Z.: Social network analysis in tourism services distribution channels. Tour. Manag. Perspect. **18**, 59–67 (2016)
12. Wasserman, S., Faust, K.: Social Network Analysis: Methods and Applications, vol. 8. Cambridge University Press, Cambridge (1994)
13. Watts, D.J., Strogatz, S.H.: Collective dynamics of 'small-world' networks. Nature **393**(6684), 440 (1998)
14. Wilson, G.C., Banzhaf, W.: Discovery of email communication networks from the Enron corpus with a genetic algorithm using social network analysis (2009)
15. Zhang, P., Wang, J., Li, X., Li, M., Di, Z., Fan, Y.: Clustering coefficient and community structure of bipartite networks. Physica A **387**(27), 6869–6875 (2008)

MapReduce-Based Convolutional Neural Network for Text Categorization

Eman Ferjani[1], Adel Hidri[1], Minyar Sassi Hidri[1(✉)], and Ali Frihida[2]

[1] Deanship of Preparatory Year and Supporting Studies,
Imam Abdulrahman Bin Faisal University, Dammam, Saudi Arabia
{eferjani,abhidri,mmsassi}@iau.edu.sa
[2] National Engineering School of Tunis, Tunis El Manar University, Tunis, Tunisia
ali.frihida@enit.utm.tn

Abstract. Convolutional Neural Network (CNN) is an algorithm among deep learning. It is an effective method of solving common Natural Language Processing tasks such as text categorization. In this paper, we investigate the text categorization problem using a deep learning approach in particular CNN method. However, due to the rise of Big Data and increased complexity of tasks, the efficiency of CNNs have been severely impacted because of their extensive training time and high computational cost. To overcome these obstacles, we propose a MapReduce-based CNN by reformulating the CNN's training from a single training network to a series of parallel trained smaller networks. Each smaller network processes a sub-sample of input text.

Keywords: Distributed text representation · CNN · Word2vec · MapReduce · Text categorization

1 Introduction

CNN methods have made impressive advances in many fields such as computer vision and pattern recognition. Several works have explained these advances [15] by the ability of the convolutional model to learn a hierarchical feature representation from pixels to line, contour, shape and object. This paradigm has also been applied in text categorization, with different networks being proposed in the literature and having achieved good results.

Text categorization (or text classification) is the task of assigning predefined categories to documents according to their content. It can provide conceptual views of document collections and has important applications in topics such as parsing, semantic analysis, information extraction and Web searching [1]. It becomes a source of attraction for many researchers.

However, large scale classification systems such as Google spam filters [13], or Netflix [14] require massive amounts of computational resources because of the large training data and the huge number of parameters that need to be fine-tuned. This has been the main problem for CNNs use in real-world applications

© Springer Nature Switzerland AG 2019
N. T. Nguyen et al. (Eds.): ICCCI 2019, LNAI 11684, pp. 155–166, 2019.
https://doi.org/10.1007/978-3-030-28374-2_14

and has also severely impacted their efficiency. Besides performance, the scalability of CNNs is a big challenge as well. This work is motivated by this challenge and we hope to bring elements of a response by proposing a distributed solution for training CNNs using MapReduce paradigm [6]. In this paper, we investigate the text categorization problem using a deep learning approach in particular CNN method.

The rest of the paper is organized as follows: in Sect. 2, we describe the distributed text representation and emphasize its importance in relation to CNNs. In Sect. 3, we review state-of-the-art text classification methods using CNNs. In Sect. 4, we clarify the problem we are focusing on and how distributed computing helps to reduce execution time of training CNNs and we explain our proposed MapReduce architecture. Finally, we conclude the paper and highlight future directions in Sect. 5.

2 Distributed Representation

Learning word or character representation is a fundamental step in a deep learning model. Word or character embeddings are often used as the first data processing layer in a CNN.

In this section, we will present distributed representation in two forms: word and character embeddings.

Word embedding is a way to build a vector space model to represent words based on a *distributional hypothesis* [7]. It states that words that occur in the same context or same positions in two different documents tend to have similar meanings.

This hypothesis was earlier adapted in what we call *distributed representations of words* by back-propagating an error function through a neural network in order to learn word embeddings.

The same idea was later adapted in statistical language modeling to learn both word vectors and a probability function for word sequences. This model in particular has shown a considerable success in capturing words semantic and syntactic similarities.

In general, distributed representations presented an alternative to the *sparsity* and the *curse of dimensionality* issues by representing words in a continuous, real-valued dense space with a remarkably lower dimensionality than the size of the vocabulary.

Since the appearance of the neural probabilistic language model, many other attempts to learn word embeddings have appeared in order to reach more precision or more computational efficiency. Particularly, Word2vec [11] has shown considerable accuracy and remarkable computational efficiency due to its simple and distributed architecture.

In Word2vec, we aim to construct word embeddings in a fixed low-dimensional vector space model. This goal is achievable by building a neural network architecture that computes the probability of existence of a sequence of words based on a context window. We call context the words that exist in adjacent positions to a particular term that we want to process.

A common phenomenon for languages with large vocabularies is the unknown word issue or Out-Of-Vocabulary word (OOV) issue. Character embeddings naturally deal with it since each word is considered as no more than a composition of individual letters.

Some works employ deep learning applications on languages where text is not composed of separated words but individual characters and the semantic meaning of words map to its compositional characters (such as Chinese), in such cases building systems at the character level is a natural choice to avoid word segmentation [3].

In character embeddings, the first step is defining a list a characters. For example, alphanumeric and some special characters. Then, characters will be transferred as one-hot encoding and got a sequence for vectors. The output is a fixed-length vector per every single character. Then, a 1D CNN layers are used to learn the sequence.

3   Text Classification Using CNNs

3.1   Convolutional Neural Networks

A convolutional neural network (CNN) is a class of deep neural networks which uses a variation of multilayer perceptrons. CNNs were inspired by biological processes in that the connectivity pattern between neurons resembles the organization of the animal visual cortex. They use relatively little pre-processing compared to other classification algorithms. This means that the network learns the characteristics that in traditional algorithms were hand-engineered.

In the first layer of CNN architecture, an input sequence $\{s_1, s_2, ..., s_n\}$ of n tokens was transformed into a series of vectors $\{w_1, w_2, ..., w_n\}$ by applying the look-up table to each of its tokens.

Let $w_i \in \mathbb{R}^d$ represent the token embedding for the i th token in the sentence, where d is the dimension of the token embedding.

A sentence with n tokens, can now be represented as an embedding matrix $\mathbf{W} \in \mathbb{R}^{n \times d}$ depicts such a sentence as an input to the CNN framework.

Let $\mathbf{w}_{i:i+j}$ refer to the concatenation of vectors $\mathbf{w}_i \mathbf{w}_{i+1}, ..., \mathbf{w}_j$.

Convolution is performed on this input embedding layer. It involves a filter $k \in \mathbb{R}^{h \times d}$ which is applied to a window of h tokens to produce a new feature. For example, a feature c_i is generated using the window of tokens $w_{i:i+h-1}$ by:

$$c_i = f(w_{i:i+h-1}.k^T + b) \tag{1}$$

where $b \in \mathbb{R}$ is the bias term and f is a non-linear activation function, for example the hyperbolic tangent. The filter k is applied to all possible windows using the same weights to create the feature map.

$$c = [c_1, c_2, ..., c_{n-h+1}] \tag{2}$$

In a CNN, a number of convolutional filters, also called kernels (typically hundreds), of different widths slide over the entire embedding matrix.

Each kernel extracts a specific pattern of n-gram. A convolution layer is usually followed by a max-pooling strategy,

$$\hat{c} = max\,\{c\} \tag{3}$$

which sub samples the input typically by applying a max operation on each filter. This strategy has two primary reasons. Firstly, max pooling provides a fixed length output which is generally required for classification. Thus, regardless the size of the filters, max pooling always maps the input to a fixed dimension of outputs.

Secondly, it reduces the output's dimensionality while keeping the most salient n-gram features across the whole sentence. This is done in a translation invariant manner where each filter is now able to extract a particular feature (e.g., negations) from anywhere in the sentence and add it to the final sentence representation.

The word embeddings can be initialized randomly or pre-trained on a large unlabeled corpora. The latter option is sometimes found beneficial to performance, especially when the amount of labeled data is limited.

This combination of convolution layer followed by max pooling is often stacked to create deep CNN networks. These sequential convolutions help in improved mining of the sentence to grasp a truly abstract representation comprising rich semantic information. The kernels through deeper convolutions cover a larger part of the sentence until finally covering it fully and creating a global summarizing of the sentence features.

3.2   CNN-Based Text Classification

A number of CNN text classification methods have been proposed to incorporate semantic relations between words in text classification. These methods can be grouped into two main categories, namely; word-level methods and character-level methods.

In [9], a simple CNN for text classification operating on word level was proposed. It used three parallel convolution layers; these process a sentence using a sliding window that examines three, four, and five words at a time. The three convolutions then feed into a Maxpool across the entire sentence, which selects the most potent features in each convolution and concatenates them into a single feature vector. Finally, the selected features are fed into a dense softmax layer for classification.

A series of experiments was reported with this CNN by varying the input word vectors: the first variant consists of keeping the word vectors static and learning only the other parameters of the model. Another variant consists of learning task-specific vectors through fine-tuning. A simple modification to the architecture was introduced to allow for the use of both pre-trained and task-specific vectors by having multiple channels (see Fig. 1).

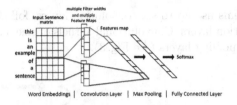

Word Embeddings | Convolution Layer | Max Pooling | Fully Connected Layer

Fig. 1. A simple CNN model with a single convolution layer followed by a max pooling layer and finally a fully connected layer

The above CNN architecture (see Fig. 1) was explored for a variety of sentence classification tasks including sentiment, subjectivity and question type classification, showing competitive results.

Due to its simplicity and strong performance in many tasks, Kim's CNN architecture is still commonly used today in many text classification tasks [12]. However, the CNN's inability to model long distance dependencies standing as the main issue.

Another word-level CNN was proposed in [8] called deep pyramid CNN (DPCNN). After converting discrete text to continuous representation, the DPCNN architecture simply alternates a convolution block and a downsampling layer over and over, leading to a deep network in which internal data size (as well as per-layer computation) shrinks in a pyramid shape. The network depth is a meta-parameter.

The first layer performs text region embedding, which generalizes commonly used word embedding to the embedding of text regions covering one or more words. It is followed by stacking of convolution blocks (two convolution layers and a shortcut) interleaved with pooling layers with stride 2 for down-sampling. The final pooling layer aggregates internal data for each document into one vector. The max pooling was used for all pooling layers (see Fig. 2).

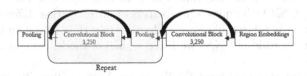

Fig. 2. The DPCNN model [8]

In [16], the authors introduced character-based CNN. They found that character includes key signal to improve model performance. They showed by experiments that text classification task does not require the knowledge about the syntactic or semantic structure of a language, since characters always constitute a necessary construct regardless of whether segmentation into words is possible.

The proposed character-based CNN also has the advantage that abnormal character combinations such as misspellings and emoticons may be naturally learned. Their systems use up to six convolution layers, followed by three fully connected classification layers. Convolutional kernels of size 3 and 7 are used, as well as simple max-pooling layers (see Fig. 3).

Fig. 3. The character based CNN model [16].

In [5], the author proposed a very deep CNN architecture (VDCNN) for text processing which operates directly at the character level and uses only small convolutions and pooling operations.

The model begins with a look-up table that generates characters embeddings. A convolutional layer of 64 convolutions of size 3 is then applied, followed by a stack of temporal "Convolutional Blocks", two design rules were applied: (i) for the same output temporal resolution, the layers have the same number of feature maps, (ii) when the temporal resolution is halved, the number of feature maps is doubled. The author showed that the performance of the described model increases with the depth (using up to 29 convolutional layers) (see Fig. 4).

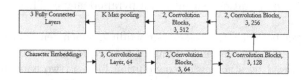

Fig. 4. The VDCNN [5].

We should note that the mentioned CNN models represent a non-exhaustive list of existing CNN techniques. Our focus is on investigating different types of CNNs in terms of input granularity and depth rather than listing all the existing methods. From word-level CNNs we listed a shallow model proposed in [9] and a deep one [8].

The same for character-level CNNs, where both shallow [9] and deep [5] models were described.

An overall analysis of the existing CNN architectures shows that the two main criteria to be considered when designing a CNN are: the granularity of input (either character or word inputs are considered) and the depth of the CNN (the number of layers).

In [10], they showed that increasing CNN depth helps the performance of character-level CNNs but not word-level CNNs. They further demonstrated that a shallow word-level CNN similar to Kim's proposed structure can outperform much deeper and more complex CNN architectures on a wide range of text classification tasks.

The listed models were tested on different datasets varying from small to large scale ones. To offer fair comparisons between models described above, we referred to experiments reported by authors in original papers, we collected results on common tested datasets for CNNs described in [5,8,16] which are: Yelp, Yahoo and Amazon datasets [16] (Table 1).

Two different evaluation metrics was used: the accuracy which represents the number of correctly identified items out of total identified items, and the error rate which represents the number of items wrongly identified out of the total identified items. The error rate have been commonly used for comparing different CNNs performances. We tried our best to select results based on the same evaluation metrics and the same datasets that can provide comparable results.

We selected best test error rate among a number of variations presented in the respective papers [5,8,9,16]. This method was applied with all models and without any model selection.

Table 1. Error rates of CNNs

Model	Yelp.p	Yelp.f	Yahoo	Ama.f	Ama.p
DPCNN [8]	2.64	30.58	23.90	34.81	3.32
Char-based CNN [16]	4.36	37.95	28.80	40.43	4.93
VDCNN [5]	4.28	35.28	26.57	37.00	4.28

In order to experiment their models, the authors used different experimental setups. Kim's CNN [9] was tested by varying the word vectors initialization (Randomly initialized, static, non-static and multichannel), the best accuracy achieved was **89.6** with the use of pre-trained word2vec vectors. The CNN described in [8], authors used large datasets on their experiments, they also varied the depth of the model (3, 7 and 15 layers) and the use or not of unsupervised embeddings.

The character-level CNN described in [5] was experimented on large datasets, the model depth varied from 9 to 47, many pooling functions was tested (Max pooling performed the best results). A similar model introduced in [16], which was experimented by varying the reprocessing step (like using a Thesaurus data augmentation technique) and changing the vocabulary used.

We noticed that all CNN models having been trained using large scale datasets, used GPU-based framework to accelerate the training time.

4 MapReduce-Based CNN Architecture

4.1 Motivation and Aim

Different CNN architectures have been proposed in the literature to solve text classification problems and have achieved quite promising results as shown in the previous section. The efficiency of CNNs is basically related to the large amounts of training data available. However, the associated computational complexity increases as the networks go deeper, which poses serious challenges in practical applications.

On the condition of the high accuracy, time-cost is a significant concern before this algorithm goes out of labs. A balance between accuracy and cost is a usual dilemma for classifier. To CNN its even more serious due to its incredible construction and calculation complexity especially for large scale systems.

Different parallel computing based methods have been proposed in recent years as common solution for big data. The two main methods are to distribute the data used for training - training set level parallelism, or to distribute the computation performed by the neural network - neural-network level parallelism. In our proposed solution we adopted the first method with MapReduce framework.

In [4], the authors provided a brief description of back-propagation's (NN learning algorithm) Map-Reduce adaptation.

In this manner back-propagation performs a batch learning phase. The authors have implemented their adapted algorithm on top of a custom multicore MapReduce framework – their aim was to prove that the "summation form" of a learning algorithm allows an easy parallelization on multicore computers.

Getting inspired by their work, we decide to use this distributed computing to design our CNN algorithm. The training phase will be transformed to a series of parallel trained smaller networks. Each smaller network processes a sub-sample of input text. Our objective is mainly about the computation cost and the scalability of CNNs when applied in Big Data context.

4.2   CNN Training's Optimization Based on MapReduce

CNN existing models have already reached a reasonable accuracy. However, the training process costs much time and our aim is to reduce the time consumption by using MapReduce programming model.

A number of research efforts have been proposed to take advantages of data distribution and parallelization to increase the speed of learning algorithms. Most of these efforts have been gears towards traditional machine learning algorithms.

In [4], they used the MapReduce paradigm to parallelize a number of algorithms including linear regression, k-means, logistic regression, naive Bayes, SVM (Support Vector Machine), ICA (Independent Component Analysis), PCA (Principal Component Analysis), Gaussian discriminant analysis, EM (Expectation Maximization) and backpropagation using ANN (Artificial Neural Networks).

In [2], they implemented a distributed CNN for handwritten digit recognition to reduce the time cost, the training process was divided and a final model is formulated by the combination of each trained model.

The computation in MapReduce model consists of two phases, i.e., a map phase and a reduce phase. In the Map phase, the input dataset (stored in a distributed system) is divided into a number of disjoint subsets which are assigned to mappers in terms of $<key, value>$ pairs. In parallel, each Mapper applies the user specified map function to each input $<key, value>$ pair and outputs a set of intermediate $<key, value>$ pairs which are written to local disks of the map computers.

The underlying system passes the locations of these intermediate pairs to the master who is responsible to notify the reducers about these locations.

In the Reduce phase, when the reducers have remotely read all intermediate pairs, they sort and group them by the intermediate keys. Each Reducer literately invokes a user-specified reduce function to process all the values for each unique key and generate a new value for each key. The resulting $<key, value>$ pairs from all of the Reducers are collected as final results which are then written to an output file.

In the MapReduce system, all the map tasks (and reduce tasks) are executed in a fully parallel way. Therefore, high-level parallelism can be achieved for data processing through the use of the MapReduce model. Convolutional Neural Networks is one deep learning algorithm that can benefit from the distributed computation offered by the MapReduce programming model. CNNs iteratively adjusts weights in the network by computing their partial gradients after each set of the training data is propagated through the network.

Thus parallelization during the CNN's training phase can be accomplished by mapping different parts of the input dataset into different machines. Each machine can then train its own CNN using its training part. The outputs of the parallel trained CNNs can then be aggregated to produce the final results which are then used to update the weights for the next iteration.

Figure 5 shows a high level overview of the procedure.

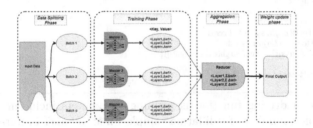

Fig. 5. MapReduce based CNN

The mappers take as input the training data $(batch, label)$ where $batch$ is a training instance and $label$ is the ground truth label for that instance, and a set of randomly initialized weights $[w_1, w_2, ..., w_n]$. The set of weights contain n weights to represent the number of hidden layers in the network so w_i corresponds to the weights for the hidden layer i.

The training data is represented as a set of pairs $(batch, label)$. Each mapper initializes the network with the given set of weights and the network is trained using the input samples. The output is a set of newly trained $WeightsUpdate$ $[\Delta w_1, \Delta w_2, ..., \Delta w_n]$ which is then fed to the reducer. After each iteration the mappers receive a set of updated weights which are processed through the network until the max number of iterations is reached. The pseudo code for the Map function is shown in Algorithm 1.

Algorithm 1 The Mapper function

Require: Set of pairs (batch,label) where batch is a training sample and label is the ground truth label for that sample.
$Weights$: list of randomly initialized weights for each hidden layer.

1: **function** MAP()
2:     Get initial Weights
3:     Initialize CNN with Weights
4:     Train the current CNN over the input batch: forward propagation, backward propagation, calculate gradient descent
5:     **for** i from 0 to $numLayers$ - 1 **do**
6:         $WeightsUpdate[i] \leftarrow$ WheightsUpdate[i]+Weights[i]
7:     **end for**
8:     **return** $WeightsUpdate$
9: **end function**

The reducer receives as input the intermediate output by the mappers and aggregates the weights produced from each of the mappers. Since the position of weights in the output of mappers are sorted according to the hidden layer they belong to, the reducer can simply aggregate weights according to their layer's index.

The aggregation computes a cumulative sum over weights and then divides by the number of training instances in the batch to form an average of weights. The final result is used to update the weights in the network and sent to the mapper for the next iteration. The pseudo code for the reduce function is shown in Algorithm 2.

Algorithm 2 The Reducer function

Require: Intermediate output by mappers which are the updated weights for each hidden layer.
$SumWeights$: list which stores the cumulative sum of $Weights$.
Ensure: Updated weights

1: **function** REDUCE()
2:     Initialize $SumWeights$ to list of zeros
3:     **for** i from 0 to $numLayers$ - 1 **do**
4:         $SumWeights[i] \leftarrow$ SumWeights[i]+Weights[i]
5:     **end for**
6:     **return** $SumWeights$
7: **end function**

The input of driving function is training parameters including number of training samples, number of validation samples, max number of iterations, max epochs, batch size, learning rate, and optimization method.

The pseudo code for the driver function is shown in Algorithm 3.

Algorithm 3 The driver function

Require: maxIterations
1: **function** DRIVER()
2:     **for** $layer$ from 0 to $numlayers - 1$ **do**
3:         Initialize $Weights[layer]$ Randomly
4:     **end for**
5:     $numIteration \leftarrow 1$
6:     **while** $numIteration <= maxIterations$ **do**
7:         Run Map() (see Algorithm 1)
8:         Run Reduce() (see Algorithm 2)
9:         Update weights of each hidden layer
10:         numIteration + +
11:     **end while**
12:     **return** $FinalWeights$
13: **end function**

4.3 Complexity Analysis

CNNs were extended from artificial neural networks. Therefore, they have similar theoretical complexity. In [4], they showed that the MapReduce adaptation of a simple neural network (with one hidden layer) has a theoretical improvement of the computational cost.

Assume the dimension of inputs is n, the number of training examples is m and the number of cores used for the algorithm execution is P. The authors analyzed the theoretical cost of a single backpropagation iteration and demonstrated that when we use a single core, the time complexity is $\mathcal{O}(mn + nc)$, this cost will be reduced to $\mathcal{O}(\frac{mn}{P} + nc \log(P))$($c$ is a factor).

5 Conclusion

In this paper, we reviewed some existing CNN models and we showed their efficiency on different datasets. However, with the rise of big data and increased complexity of tasks, the efficiency of CNNs is severely impacted, resulting in long training times and high computational cost especially in large scale datasets.

To be able to solve even greater problems of the future, learning algorithms must maintain high speed and accuracy through economical means. To that end, this paper takes advantage of the MapReduce framework to describe a parallel CNN algorithm which is an effective way to improve their speed and scalability.

This job is being implemented under Spark MapReduce. We also aim to adopt consensus training to ensure data privacy that prohibits data sharing between nodes in a cluster.

References

1. Altinel, B., Ganiz, M.C.: Semantic text classification: a survey of past and recent advances. Inf. Process. Manag. **54**, 1129–1153 (2018)
2. Basit, N., et al.: MapReduce-based deep learning with handwritten digit recognition case study. In: Big Data (2016)
3. Chen, X., Xu, L., Liu, Z., Sun, M., Luan, H.: Joint learning of character and word embeddings. In: Proceedings of the 24th International Conference on Artificial Intelligence, IJCAI 2015, pp. 1236–1242. AAAI Press (2015)
4. Chu, C.T., et al.: Map-reduce for machine learning on multicore. In: Proceedings of the 19th International Conference on Neural Information Processing Systems, NIPS 2006, pp. 281–288. MIT Press, Cambridge (2006)
5. Conneau, A., Schwenk, H., Barrault, L., Lecun, Y.: Very deep convolutional networks for natural language processing (2016)
6. Dean, J., Ghemawat, S.: MapReduce: simplified data processing on large clusters. In: Proceedings of the 6th Conference on Symposium on Operating Systems Design and Implementation - Volume 6, OSDI 2004, p. 10. USENIX Association, Berkeley (2004)
7. Harris, Z.: Distributional structure. Word **10**(23), 146–162 (1954)

8. Johnson, R., Zhang, T.: Deep pyramid convolutional neural networks for text categorization. In: Proceedings of the 55th Annual Meeting of the Association for Computational Linguistics (Volume 1: Long Papers), Vancouver, Canada, pp. 562–570. Association for Computational Linguistics, July 2017
9. Kim, Y.: Convolutional neural networks for sentence classification. In: Proceedings of the 2014 Conference on Empirical Methods in Natural Language Processing, EMNLP 2014, Doha, Qatar, A meeting of SIGDAT, A Special Interest Group of the ACL, pp. 1746–1751, 25–29 October 2014
10. Le, H.T., Cerisara, C., Denis, A.: Do convolutional networks need to be deep for text classification? In: AAAI Workshops (2018)
11. Mikolov, T., Chen, K., Corrado, G., Dean, J.: Efficient estimation of word representations in vector space. CoRR abs/1301.3781 (2013)
12. Qiu, J.X., Yoon, H., Fearn, P.A., Tourassi, G.D.: Deep learning for automated extraction of primary sites from cancer pathology reports. IEEE J. Biomed. Health Inform. **22**, 244–251 (2018)
13. Google Spam: http://www.google.com/mail/help/fightspam/spamexplained.html. Accessed 29 Jan 2019
14. Google Spam: http://www.netflixprize.com. Accessed 15 Feb 2019
15. Zeiler, M.D., Fergus, R.: Visualizing and understanding convolutional networks. CoRR abs/1311.2901 (2013)
16. Zhang, X., Zhao, J., LeCun, Y.: Character-level convolutional networks for text classification. In: Proceedings of the 28th International Conference on Neural Information Processing Systems - Volume 1, NIPS 2015, pp. 649–657. MIT Press, Cambridge (2015)

Context-Based News Headlines Analysis
Using Machine Learning Approach

Shadikur Rahman, Syeda Sumbul Hossain[✉], Saiful Islam,
Mazharul Islam Chowdhury, Fatama Binta Rafiq,
and Khalid Been Md. Badruzzaman

Daffodil International University, Dhaka, Bangladesh
{shadikur35-988,syeda.swe,saiful35-865,islam35-897,
fatama.swe}@diu.edu.bd, khalid@daffodilvarsity.edu.bd

Abstract. An increasing number of people are changing their way of thinking by reading news headlines. The interactivity and sincerity present in online news headlines are becoming influential to society. Apart from that, news websites build efficient policies to catch people's awareness and attract their clicks. In that case, it is a must to identify the sentiment polarity of the news headlines for avoiding misconception. In this paper, we analyze 3383 news headlines generated by five major global newspapers during a minimum of four consecutive months. In order to identify the sentiment polarity (or sentiment orientation) of news headlines, we use 7 machine learning algorithms and compare those results to find the better ones. Among those Bernoulli Naïve Bayes technique achieves higher accuracy than others. This study will help the public to make any decision based on news headlines by avoiding misconception against any leader or governance and will help to identify the most neutral newspaper or news blogs.

Keywords: Sentiment analysis · Machine learning ·
Semantic orientation · News headline · Text mining

1 Introduction

News headlines are the key indicator of nature of any news. By reading any headlines, readers become interested towards any news. In most cases, we do not read the whole news as we think headline is the essence of any news. There are no boundaries in spreading news among any classes or nations with the rapid growth of social media. Sometimes we are misguided by reading the headline of any news. That often results political or social impact on any nation or class. In Ecker et al. (2014), it is investigated that how headlines affected the readers' reasoning and biasing them towards misinterpretation. In that case, it is a must to identify the sentiment polarity of the news headlines for avoiding misconception.

© Springer Nature Switzerland AG 2019
N. T. Nguyen et al. (Eds.): ICCCI 2019, LNAI 11684, pp. 167–178, 2019.
https://doi.org/10.1007/978-3-030-28374-2_15

Depending on the context of news, semantic orientation would be different. Moreover, any specific news sometimes presented differently in different news blogs or newspaper. So it is essential to find the semantic orientation of any news headline. There are missing enough study to find out the semantic orientation of an news headlines based on the context of news. The impact of news on social, business and political behaviour has reported on several studies. The measurement of financial news influence in market is reported in Nardo et al. (2016). Alanyali et al. (2013) shows that market behaviour is intuitively interlinked with the financial news. How the commodity price is affected by the news presented in Feuerriegel et al. (2015).

In this study, we present the effectiveness of machine learning techniques to find the semantic orientation of any news. We use Naïve Bayes (Rish et al. 2001), Multinomial Naïve Bayes (MNB) (Rennie et al. 2003), Bernoulli Naïve Bayes (McCallum et al. 1998), logistic regression (Ho et al. 1994), Stochastic Gradient Descent (SGD) (Bottou 2010), Linear Support Vector Classifier (SVC) (Gunn et al. 1998), and Nu support vector classifier (Schölkopf et al. 2000) to find out the most appropriate semantic orientation. The result of this study will help to identify the most neutral newspaper or news blogs.

This paper is structured as follows: Related work is described at Sect. 2 that followed by Research Methodology and Result and Discussion at Sects. 3 and 4 respectively. The final Sect. 5 summarizes our contribution and furnishes the conclusion.

2   Related Work

Many works have been done on product reviews using opinion mining and sentiment analysis. It is shown in Medhat et al. (2014) that most of the sentiment analysis was done on product review data. Other than that news data, social media data and web blogs data are also used. In Pang et al. (2002), Naïve Bayes classification, maximum entropy classification, and support vector machines these tree machine learning algorithm were used to perform sentiment analysis on movie review. They compared the human generated and machine learning results. And this study shows that SVM gives the best result where as Naive Bayes gives the worst. SVM and Particle Swarm Optimization (PSO) is used in Chiong et al. (2018) for analysis financial news and shows better results than deep learning model in terms of accuracy and time. A survey (Hussein 2018) was done to identify sentiment analysis challenges relevant to different approaches and techniques. A feature-based opinion summarizing technique is presented in Hu and Liu (2004) of product reviews using data mining and natural language processing. A system Opinion Observer (Liu et al. 2005) is implemented using proposed holistic lexicon-based approach (Ding et al. 2008). A lexicon-based approach is used in Im et al. (2013) to identify the positive or negative polarity of the financial news. A large-scale sentiment analysis system is presented in this paper (Godbole et al. 2007) to indicate positive and negative opining of news and blogs by assigning score. In Maynard et al. (2012) the author performed a sentiment analysis by indicating positive, negative or neutral sentiments. They correctly identified the sentences of with an accuracy 66%. Computational linguistics is used in Lerman et al. (2008) to predict the impact of news on public perception towards political candidates. Focusing on the lexical patterns, an election prediction system (Crystal) was presented in Kim and Hovy (2007). They use SVM and get result of predicting future election with an accuracy of 81.68%. Opinion Lexicon-based algorithm and Naïve Bayes algorithm is used in Shuhidan et al. (2018) for sentiment analysis of financial news headlines of Malaysia.

In recent, deep learning is also used for sentiment analysis. Severyn and Moschitti (2015) uses deep learning approach for predicting polarities of tweets at both message level and phrase level. Micro blogging and movie reviews datasets are used in Araque et al. (2017) to measure the performance of sentiment analysis using deep learning. In Tang et al. (2015), authors provide an overview of deep learning approaches for sentiment analysis and also suggest some mitigation to address the challenges.

3   Research Methodology

In this section, we briefly describe the methodology adopted for the analysis see at Fig. 1. In order to categorize online news headlines, at first we collected news from five major news sources of online newspapers. Then we preprocessed the collected data and categorized. Then we inferred their sentiment.

3.1   Collecting News Headlines from Sources

We crawled data from five different news headlines sources: Daily Star[1], Dhaka Tribune[2], The New York Times[3], The New Age[4], and The Daily Observer[5]. All of them are world wide known online news media with millions of readers daily. For Daily star, Dhaka Tribune and The New York Times we monitored their RSS feed daily for four months. Headlines on the main page of the website were crawled. We focused only on the top news headlines. Table 1 summarizes the statistics about these five data sets.

3.2   Categorizing

After collecting data sets, we categorize the headlines based on context. For this paper, we mainly consider only 5 categories. For doing this, we categorize the headlines using the meta data of each headline's URL. Table 2 shows the categories of the news of we identified. The distribution of the number of news items for each newspaper is shown in Table 3.

---

[1] https://www.thedailystar.net/.
[2] https://www.dhakatribune.com/.
[3] https://www.nytimes.com/.
[4] www.newagebd.net/.
[5] www.observerbd.com/.

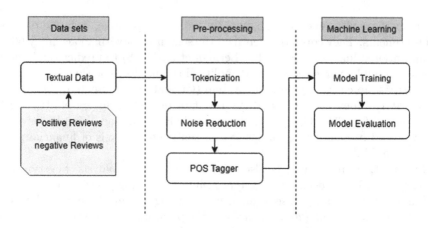

Fig. 1. Research methodology

Table 1. Statistics of data sets

News Source	Time length	Headlines	Ratio
Daily Star	Nov, 2018 to Feb, 2019	1345	49.76%
Dhaka Tribune	Nov, 2018 to Feb, 2019	681	20.13%
The New York Times	Nov, 2018 to Feb, 2019	390	11.53%
The New Age	Nov, 2018 to Feb, 2019	694	20.51%
The Daily Observer	Nov, 2018 to Feb, 2019	273	08.07%
	Total	3383	100%

Table 2. Categories of news headlines

Category	Description
Politics	News related to politics, government, political leader
Business	Focusing on market and policy news relevant to business
World	National and International news (other than above)
Health	Covering news on Health, Health care, Medical science
Sports	All games, athletics

Table 3. Distribution of news headlines based on context

Context	Daily Star	Dhaka Tribune	The New York Times	The New Age	The Daily Observer
Politics	41%	26%	09%	77%	18%
Business	39%	19%	43%	10%	24%
World	13%	19%	36%	13%	18%
Health	02%	17%	10%	-	22%
Sports	05%	18%	02%	-	18%

3.3 Preprossessing

For analyzing our data set, we preprocess all the headlines. Firstly, we decapitalized all the words of headlines, as a common feature of news headlines is capitalized words. Then we tokenized the headlines and removed the noise words considering the selected POS tag.

3.3.1 Tokenization

We segment text by splitting it by spaces and punctuation marks, and form a bag of words. However, we make sure that short forms such as "don't", "I'll", "she'd" will remain as one word.

3.3.2 Noise Reduction

The news article contains many parts of speech which are irrelevant to detect semantic orientation in our case. We consider only JJ, VB and RB Parts of Speech (POS) tag from Penn Tree bank annotation (Taylor et al. 2003).

3.4 Inferring Sentiment

We quantify the polarity of headlines in a scale of 0 (Negative) and 1 (Positive). The overall headlines is often inferred as positive or negative from the sign of the polarity score. Table 4 shows how we consider headlines polarity score.

Table 4. Polarity score of headline

Scale	Polarity	News Headline
1	Positive	House Democrats Prepare to Scrutinize DeVos's Education Department
0	Negative	Sanders Returns to NY Roots, Says He Can Defeat Trump

3.5 Training Model

For training our model, we have used 7 machine learning algorithms. Used algorithms are: Naïve Bayes (Rish et al. 2001), Multinomial Naïve Bayes (MNB) (Rennie et al. 2003), Bernoulli Naïve Bayes (McCallum et al. 1998), Logistic Regression (Ho et al. 1994), Stochastic Gradient Descent (SGD) Bottou (2010), Linear Support Vector Classifier (SVC) (Gunn et al. 1998), and Nu support vector classifier (Schölkopf et al. 2000). The data set for training model is available at[6].

---

[6] https://github.com/sadirahman/Context-based-News-Headlines-Analysis-UsingMachine-Learning-Approach.

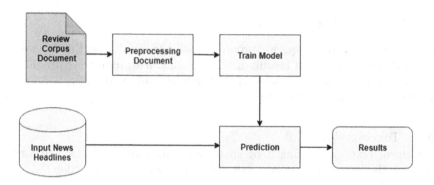

Fig. 2. Training process of models

We have trained our models with selected short review document corpus data sets. Figure 2 shows the training process of our models.

3.6 Validation

In our corpus datasets that we used to train the models, contains 10664 lines (positive-5332 and negative-5332 lines). We train our models considering 75% as training dataset and test the models with remaining 25% test dataset. Test dataset is used to provide an unbiased evaluation of a final model to fit with the training dataset (See Footnote 6). Section 4.1 shows the details the validation results.

4   Result and Discussion

In this section, we explain the classification results, the evaluation contexts and the polarity estimation of our research.

4.1   Classification Results

In order to classify the news headlines as positive or negative, we used 7 different classification algorithms. Table 5 shows the accuracy of different classifiers we used. It is tremendous to see some of the widely used algorithms fail to achieve satisfactory performance for this case. Most notably, the Naïve Bayesian, SVM and Logistic Regression classifiers achieve an average accuracy of about 77%. However, other variants of Bayesian classifiers, SVM and Logistic Regression gave accuracy of more than 77% in some cases. The Bernoulli Naïve Bayes classifier gives the best accuracy.

Table 5. Accuracy of different classifiers

Algorithm	Accuracy (%)
Naïve Bayes	80.57
Multi nomial Naïve Bayes (MNB)	76.51
Bernoulli Naïve Bayes	82.68
Logistic Regression	76.05
Stochastic Gradient Descent (SGD)	74.55
Linear Support Vector Classifier (SVC)	75.90
Nu support vector classifier	75.75

4.2   Polarity Estimation

In this section, we explain the sentiment results, the evaluation contexts and the polarity estimation of our research.

4.2.1   Polarity Consideration

We present the words polarity in Table 6. Our train model gives most informative words in trained data sets. In the first instance, model gives informative words base on our sentiment ratio score.

Table 6. Sentiment ratio

Words	Sentiment	Sentiment ratio
engrossing	positive	19.0
boring	negative	14.8
inventive	positive	13.7
refreshing	positive	12.5
stupid	negative	12.1
warm	positive	11.7
wonderful	positive	11.4
refreshingly	positive	11.4
dull	negative	11.4
realistic	positive	11.0

4.2.2   Polarity of News Headlines Against News Sources

Our research group members read these 3383 news headlines and created files for each of the news headlines which included details whether the headlines are positive or negative. This data set is then used to outcome the model for classification and also for evaluation mining task. Figure 3 shows the polarity of news headlines against different news sources.

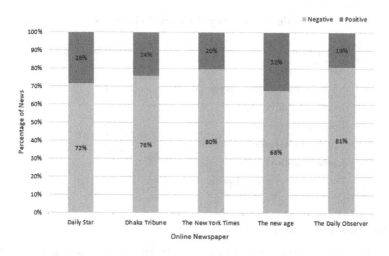

Fig. 3. Polarity of news headlines against news sources

4.2.3   Polarity of News Headlines as per News Context

In this section, we present the polarity of news headlines as per news context. Figure 4 shows the polarity of news headlines as per news context.

4.3   Precision, Recall and F-Measure for Positive and Negative Reviews Data Sets

As we found highest accuracy with Naïve Bayes classifier, so we trained our model by Naïve Bayes classifier. This time, we run random shuffle in our trained date sets (positive and negative). This classifier gives the accuracy measuring the trained data set. We collect the reference values and observed values for each label (positive or negative), then use those sets to calculate the precision, recall, and F-measure of the Naïve Bayes classifier. In Table 7, we present the resultant confusion matrix that is often used to describe the performance of a classification model on a set of test data for which the true values are known. It allows the visualization of the performance of an algorithm.

Table 7. Confusion matrix of reviews data sets

Sentiment	Precision	Recall	F-measure
Positive	0.65	0.85	0.78
Negative	0.96	0.58	0.64

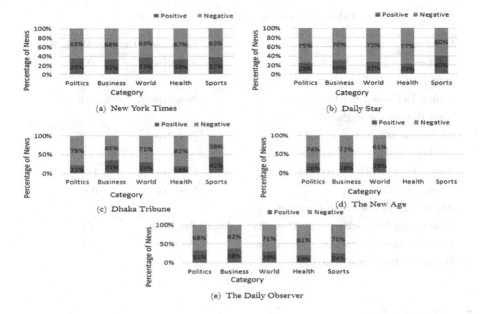

Fig. 4. Polarity of news headlines as per news context

- Every positive trained data in the data sets is correctly identified with 85% recall. This means very few false negatives in the positive class.
- As positive data while classifying is only 65% likely to be correct. So poor precision with 35% leads to false positives for the positive data set.
- Any trained data that is identified as negative is 96% likely to be correct (high precision). This means very few false positives for the negative data set.
- Hence many negative data sets are incorrectly classified. Low recall causes 42% false negatives for the negative data set.
- F-measure provides no useful information. There is no insight to be gained from having it, and we would not lose any knowledge if it was taken away.

4.4 Sentiment Polarity Considering Procedure

In this section, train model give sentiment against our news headlines. Instance model gives headline sentiment based on our confidential score. If the confidential score is −0.1 to −1.0 then it gives the result as negative sentiment and also for confidential score between 0 and 1.0 it gives the result as positive sentiment. Table 8 shows some of the confidential score of news headlines.

Table 8. Confidential score's of headlines

Headlines	Sentiment	Confidential score
Sanders Returns to NY Roots, Says He Can Defeat Trump	Negative	−0.6
Trump Delivers a Slashing Speech That Rouses the Right	Negative	−0.6
Klobuchar and Kennedy Kid Washington Elite at Gridiron	Negative	−0.6
Taskin happy with his recovery so far	Positive	1.0
Morata finally scores, Atletico keeps pace with Barcelona	Positive	0.8
Stakes high for England after Grenada washout	Negative	−1.0
House Democrats Prepare to Scrutinize DeVos's Education Department	Positive	1.0

5 Conclusion

Headlines are the influential element of any news. In this paper, we proposed a technique to identify the neutral newspaper or micro news blogs in terms of semantic orientation using machine learning approach. The objective is to find out the context based tagging of news headlines to avoid prejudicing the readers. Our work will mostly help the public to make decision based on news headlines by avoiding misconception against any leaders or governance. Moreover, this technique can also be implemented in a tool for identifying most neutral newspapers or news blogs.

In future, current work can be extended to analyze the news headings and readers' reviews in together to find out the most authenticate news on social media.

References

Ecker, U.K., Lewandowsky, S., Chang, E.P., Pillai, R.: The effects of subtle misinformation in news headlines. J. Exp. Psychol. Appl. **20**(4), 323 (2014)

Nardo, M., Petracco-Giudici, M., Naltsidis, M.: Walking down wall street with a tablet: a survey of stock market predictions using the web. J. Econ. Surv. **30**(2), 356–369 (2016)

Alanyali, M., Moat, H.S., Preis, T.: Quantifying the relationship between financial news and the stock market. Sci. Rep. **3**, 3578 (2013)

Feuerriegel, S., Heitzmann, S.F., Neumann, D.: Do investors read too much into news? How news sentiment causes price formation. In: 2015 48th Hawaii International Conference on System Sciences, pp. 4803–4812. IEEE (2015)

Rish, I., et al.: An empirical study of the Naive Bayes classifier. In: IJCAI 2001 Workshop on Empirical Methods in Artificial Intelligence, vol. 3, pp. 41–46 (2001)

Rennie, J.D., Shih, L., Teevan, J., Karger, D.R.: Tackling the poor assumptions of Naive Bayes text classifiers. In: Proceedings of the 20th International Conference on Machine Learning, ICML 2003, pp. 616–623 (2003)

McCallum, A., Nigam, K., et al.: A comparison of event models for Naive Bayes text classification. In AAAI-98 Workshop on Learning for Text Categorization, vol. 752, pp. 41–48. Citeseer (1998)

Ho, T.K., Hull, J.J., Srihari, S.N.: Decision combination in multiple classifier systems. IEEE Trans. Pattern Anal. Mach. Intell. 1, 66–75 (1994)

Bottou, L.: Large-scale machine learning with stochastic gradient descent. In: Lechevallier, Y., Saporta, G. (eds.) COMPSTAT 2010. Physica-Verlag HD (2010)

Gunn, S.R., et al.: Support vector machines for classification and regression. ISIS technical report, vol. 14, no. 1, pp. 5–16 (1998)

Schölkopf, B., Smola, A.J., Williamson, R.C., Bartlett, P.L.: New support vector algorithms. Neural Comput. 12(5), 1207–1245 (2000)

Medhat, W., Hassan, A., Korashy, H.: Sentiment analysis algorithms and applications: a survey. Ain Shams Eng. J. 5(4), 1093–1113 (2014)

Pang, B., Lee, L., Vaithyanathan, S.: Thumbs up?: Sentiment classification using machine learning techniques. In: Proceedings of the ACL-02 Conference on Empirical Methods in Natural Language Processing, vol. 10, pp. 79–86. Association for Computational Linguistics (2002)

Chiong, R., Fan, Z., Hu, Z., Adam, M.T., Lutz, B., Neumann, D.: A sentiment analysis-based machine learning approach for financial market prediction via news disclosures. In: Proceedings of the Genetic and Evolutionary Computation Conference Companion, pp. 278–279. ACM (2018)

El-Din Mohamed Hussein, D.M.: A survey on sentiment analysis challenges. J. King Saud. Univ. Eng. Sci. 30(4), 330–338 (2018)

Hu, M., Liu, B.: Mining and summarizing customer reviews. In: Proceedings of the Tenth ACM SIGKDD International Conference on Knowledge Discovery and Data Mining, pp. 168–177. ACM (2004)

Liu, B., Hu, M., Cheng, J.: Opinion observer: analyzing and comparing opinions on the web. In: Proceedings of the 14th International Conference on World Wide Web, pp. 342–351. ACM (2005)

Ding, X., Liu, B., Yu, P.S.: A holistic lexicon-based approach to opinion mining. In: Proceedings of the 2008 International Conference on Web Search and Data mining, pp. 231–240. ACM (2008)

Im, T.L., San, P.W., On, C.K., Alfred, R., Anthony, P.: Analysing market sentiment in financial news using lexical approach. In: 2013 IEEE Conference on Open Systems, ICOS, pp. 145–149. IEEE (2013)

Godbole, N., Srinivasaiah, M., Skiena, S.: Large-scale sentiment analysis for news and blogs. In: ICWSM 2007, vol. 21, pp. 219–222 (2007)

Maynard, D., Bontcheva, K., Rout, D.: Challenges in developing opinion mining tools for social media. In: Proceedings of the@ NLP can u tag# usergeneratedcontent, pp. 15–22 (2012)

Lerman, K., Gilder, A., Dredze, M., Pereira, F.: Reading the markets: forecasting public opinion of political candidates by news analysis. In: Proceedings of the 22nd International Conference on Computational Linguistics, vol. 1, pp. 473–480. Association for Computational Linguistics (2008)

Kim, S., Hovy, E.: Crystal: analyzing predictive opinions on the web. In: Proceedings of the 2007 Joint Conference on Empirical Methods in Natural Language Processing and Computational Natural Language Learning (EMNLP-CoNLL) (2007)

Shuhidan, S.M., Hamidi, S.R., Kazemian, S., Shuhidan, S.M., Ismail, M.A.: Sentiment analysis for financial news headlines using machine learning algorithm. Proceedings of the 7th International Conference on Kansei Engineering and Emotion Research 2018. AISC, vol. 739, pp. 64–72. Springer, Singapore (2018). https://doi.org/10. 1007/978-981-10-8612-0_8

Severyn, A., Moschitti, A.: Twitter sentiment analysis with deep convolutional neural networks. In: Proceedings of the 38th International ACM SIGIR Conference on Research and Development in Information Retrieval, pp. 959–962. ACM (2015)

Araque, O., Corcuera-Platas, I., Sanchez-Rada, J.F., Iglesias, C.A.: Enhancing deep learning sentiment analysis with ensemble techniques in social applications. Expert Syst. Appl. **77**, 236–246 (2017)

Tang, D., Qin, B., Liu, T.: Deep learning for sentiment analysis: successful approaches and future challenges. Wiley Interdisc. Rev. Data Min. Knowl. Discov. **5**(6), 292–303 (2015)

Taylor, A., Marcus, M., Santorini, B.: The Penn Treebank: an overview. In: Abeillé, A. (ed.) Treebanks. TLTB, vol. 20, pp. 5–22. Springer, Dordrecht (2003). https:// doi.org/10.1007/978-94-010-0201-1_1

Distributed Collective Intelligence for Smart Manufacturing

BDI Model of Connected
and Autonomous Vehicles

Inga Rüb[✉][iD] and Barbara Dunin-Kęplicz[iD]

University of Warsaw, Warsaw, Poland
{inga.rub,keplicz}@mimuw.edu.pl

Abstract. It is expected that connected and autonomous vehicles (CAVs) will become a regular mean of transportation by the year 2022. To fully leverage the potential of this new technology it is necessary to equip such cars with efficient algorithms permitting them to drive in a safe and optimal manner. Thereby we aim to design and implement tools for convenient evaluation of strategies for driving and interactions in various settings.

In this paper we present results of the first stage of our bigger research program on a simulation framework of CAVs. A search for balance between complexity and comprehensibility of the solution led us to the field of multiagent systems. Beliefs-Desires-Intentions (BDI) systems offer useful abstractions for activities of a single self-driving car and collective intelligence of such vehicles. Indeed, the BDI framework helps to combine two distinct natures of a self-driving car: its reactiveness and proactiveness. Moreover, modularity of the resulting architectures for an individual CAV and urban traffic induced by these cars makes the design intelligible and flexible. Our prototype verifies feasibility of this concept.

Keywords: BDI model · Connected and autonomous vehicles · Simulation architecture

1 Modelling CAVs

Representatives of biggest automotive manufacturers predict that connected and autonomous vehicles (CAVs) will be deployed in five years [20,27]. Self-driving cars, trucks and buses have been heralded as a solution to many problems in transportation [9,13,21]: from car accidents, through traffic jams, to insufficient number of parking slots. In order to observe the expected improvements in the nearest future, this technology needs to be carefully evaluated, for example with the use of a simulation. Hence, our ultimate goal is creating an efficient and flexible framework suitable for simulating CAVs. In particular, we intend to represent interactions and driving strategies of CAVs in a comprehensible way and thereby to allow experts in traffic engineering to understand and modify the algorithms without necessitating strong programming skills.

© Springer Nature Switzerland AG 2019
N. T. Nguyen et al. (Eds.): ICCCI 2019, LNAI 11684, pp. 181–195, 2019.
https://doi.org/10.1007/978-3-030-28374-2_16

For this purpose we model traffic induced by CAVs on a detailed, microscopic level but with no consideration for inner-workings of the technology itself. CAVs are represented as entities capable of getting from a location A to another location B along a given path that is determined a priori. They possibly differ in size or certain properties but implement the same algorithms and protocols. The vehicles should be able to exchange data with the infrastructure and all neighbours within a distance not exceeding a specified maximum while keeping their driving **safe** (i.e. preventing all collisions that are physically avoidable) and **optimal** (i.e. without unnecessary delays). Thus, the agent should head towards its destination with the maximal allowed speed and do not stop or slow down unless it is compelled to do so. When informed of unexpected situations that make the current route impassable, it needs to ask the navigation system for an alternative path. More efficient ways of improving driving involve coordinated group interactions, group decision-making and other forms of cooperation that together establish vital aspects of collective intelligence of CAVs.

In our framework, in order to explore this kind of optimizations, we focus on traffic conditions of modern urban and suburban areas: district-size territories which are densely cut by streets, jammed with cars in rush hours. The environment includes basic elements of road infrastructure (roads, traffic lights and a traffic management system) and is highly non-deterministic: presence of other traffic members and possible malfunctions of CAVs result in unexpected events that require immediate reactions. Therefore, agents behave cautiously, that is, they keep a proper distance to a car in front and take into account the limited precision of the collected data. With these restrictions there is hardly a possibility for a single CAV to improve its performance in terms of driving time. CAVs need to communicate with each other (to learn about the environment) and cooperate as well (to influence the environment). Clearly, collective intelligence is essential to optimizing the system as a whole.

To model self-organizing CAVs and their collaboration, a paradigm of multiagent systems combining goal-directed reasoning with event-driven behaviour seems to be appropriate (for a discussion see [29] and references there). Specifically, our research leads us to the classic BDI concept. While referring to beliefs, desires and intentions, this paradigm satisfies our requirements (for a discussion see [7] and references there). First, the BDI framework introduces useful abstractions for most of CAV activities, like collecting data or planning actions. Secondly, by mimicking human-like behaviour, BDI allows us to represent complex reasoning in a comprehensible way: this would allow end-users to analyze and modify decision algorithms. However, to create efficient simulation tools we need to introduce a tailor-made version of BDI notions.

In the sequel we present a BDI architecture for modelling both: a single self-driving car and a whole system of such vehicles. In Sect. 2 more aspects of BDI are discussed in the context of CAVs. Then we describe the architectures: for a single self-driving car in Sect. 3 and for the multiagent system in Sect. 4. We also consider technical aspects of implementation for a regular desktop computer on a large scale of thousands vehicles. Section 5 reviews the proposed architecture and outlines our future work.

2   The BDI Approach

Among advantages of the BDI framework, especially compelling is the ability of agents to differentiate between goals that **should** be pursued in general and obligations that **must** be fulfilled at a given moment [28]. Such categorization helps to express motivations for actions planned by an agent and allows CAVs to coordinate their behaviour in accordance with global priorities, e.g.: a vehicle cannot optimize its route at the cost of safety of other self-driving cars.

2.1   Interactions

The need for coexistence between individual CAVs implies two basic rules that govern the simulated interactions: (1) a CAV **should** try to optimize its travel time, (2) a CAV **must** help others in their attempt to drive faster only if there is no conflict of interests. A good example of interactions that rely on these rules is *vehicle platooning* [6]: while almost all of CAVs travelling as a group derive significant advantages, there is no benefit for the leader. Even though, if leading a platoon causes no losses, a CAV is required to agree whenever asked for the favour.

In other situations, like crossing an intersection with no signal controls, self-driving cars are forced to reach an agreement even though it may slow down at least some of the involved agents. Yet, it is possible to solve such conflicts of interests, e.g. by ordering inconsistent requests in accordance with timestamps or introducing more sophisticated mechanisms (like efficient scheduling [15] or negotiations [5]). Reaching a consensus applies also to planning optimal routes: to minimize congestion or travel time, agents can try to avoid traffic jams by changing their paths voluntarily [30].

The above examples prove that modelled CAVs should be able to constitute a cooperating system with no central management. To choose the right solution together, CAVs have to take a comprehensive view on the situation, specifically, they need to be aware of individual commitments and long-term goals. Hence, our model of a self-driving car embraces abstractions of **beliefs**, **desires** and **intentions**, whose meaning underwent slight changes to better suit the context of CAVs.

2.2   Beliefs

Since we assume correctness of collected data, we deal with knowledge rather than beliefs. At the same time, the access to information is limited: vehicles do not receive regular messages about distant cars or areas, nor explore them remotely. The only exception is an emergency situation, when a CAV gets alerted to a road becoming impassable. For this reason the procedures of driving are designed to run algorithms on restricted input, whereas data of a CAV include: (1) knowledge the car is endowed with at the very beginning of its travel (e.g. information about the map and kinematics), (2) regularly updated information on the environment (e.g. a phase of traffic lights, other agents within the range), (3) alerts about non-deterministic events, e.g.: a car accident or an obstacle, (4) self-awareness about the physical and mental state of itself.

2.3 Desires

Desires refer to an agent's pro-attitudes: everything that a CAV wants to achieve or maintain. We divide them into **basic** and **meta desires**. *Basic desires* are always valid and bring about short-term modifications of the physical state. Their opposite, *meta desires*, are triggered by events and make a long-term impact on the mental state.

Basic desires propel a CAV to go along the given path in a safe and optimal manner: (1) **drive fast** (do not slow down for no reason), (2) **follow the route** (do not change the path for no reason), (3) **obey the traffic rules** (do not violate the Highway Code for no reason), (4) **do not crash** (avoid any obstacles). As crucial for the agent's survival and mission, they need to be taken into account for each action of a CAV. However, the reoccurring phrase 'for no reason' signalizes that the agent may decide to pursue all its desires but the last one only to some extent. Specifically, the order of itemization reflects priorities: the wish to drive fast is the least important whereas avoiding collisions is absolutely crucial and can invalidate preceding desires. While the priorities are fixed, a particular basic desire may undergo changes dictated by a meta desire.

Meta desires make a CAV react to external stimuli in a different way: (1) **replan the route** (if anything unexpected happens), (2) **cooperate with platoons** (if there is such a possibility), (3) **coordinate traffic** (if approaching an intersection). Again, desires are ordered deliberately in a linear manner. E.g., *replan the route* should be considered before joining a group, otherwise it might be necessary to cancel the participation almost immediately. In contrast to basic desires, meta desires do not influence the agent's behaviour until certain events take place. When triggered, they result in a long-term modification of an agent: coordination of traffic influences beliefs about the environment; joining a platoon replaces basic desire *follow the route* with a desire *stay in platoon*; finally, replanning the route changes the agent's *goals*.

2.4 Goals and Intentions

In our model **goals** are defined as the vehicle's achievement (not maintenance) tasks that are consistent, valid and specified in advance. In practice, goals constitute the reference points for desire *follow the route*: they determine sequence of physical parameters that need to be obtained by the agent.

A CAV's response to a mixture of various constraints and obligations is modelled as its **intention**: commitment to an action planned along with the desires and their priorities. Here our approach diverges again from the standard model. We propose the design, where a commitment results from the practical reasoning that involves not one but all basic desires. The process is performed by the core of the agent architecture.

3   Agent Architecture

The architecture of a CAV defines modules that manage mental and physical aspects of a CAV as well as their interdependencies. Its proposed scheme is presented in Fig. 1.

3.1   Knowledge

The base of the reasoning process is the agent's knowledge. Findings about the environment and the internal state are represented as a nested hierarchy of interacting instances, which are compliant with specified schemas. The other kind of knowledge, about mechanisms of simulated world, is encoded within algorithmic procedures that allow to predict consequences of potential actions and future events.

3.2   Goals

Goals are defined at the very beginning of the vehicle's 'lifetime', but may be changed adequately to the situation by meta desires (arrow 7 in Fig. 1). A single goal determines a physical state the CAV should achieve. It dictates position, how the CAV should be oriented, and, optionally, its speed and acceleration.

Since goals describe the CAV's route, an agent needs to purse them in a fixed order. Also, the tasks are one-off: as soon as any of them is fulfilled, it becomes no longer valid. Thus, the most appropriate structure for organizing them is a **stack**: a CAV always strives to complete a target at the top. It is assumed that subsequent tasks are consistent.

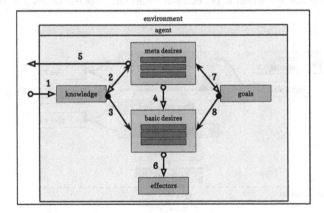

Fig. 1. The agent architecture; an arrow from A to B informs that B is directly influenced by some changes in A: if B uses A an arrowhead is filled; if B is modified by A an arrowhead is empty.

3.3   Reasoning Pipelines

Basic and meta desires should be separated. First, they generate behaviours of different nature and independently interact with other modules. Secondly, they cannot share computational resources: costly deliberation must not stop the agent from reacting to rapid changes in its immediate environment.

Basic Reasoning Pipeline. The basic-reasoning module is divided into distinct *units* of code that correspond to individual basic desires and create a plan of actions for the nearest simulation step. The plan is modified and confirmed in its final version by each unit. Since some basic desires are more important than other, the whole process is organized as a pipeline. It is performed **sequentially** and in a **fixed order** (the central controller calls units one by one): the initial plan of actions is first modified by low-priority layers and then it is redesigned and acknowledged by layers of higher priorities. That way, consecutive modifications to a planned commitment can be automatically applied (they are more important than a currently designed plan): contrary to similar subsumption architecture [4], there is no need for interfaces nor communication between the layers.

The basic-reasoning process is presented in Fig. 2. It starts with creating an *initial plan* of actions, which orders the car to move forward with its current configuration. This neutral proposal is altered in accordance with basic desires, where desires of high priority can modify or reject low-priority suggestions (e.g. a self-driving vehicle may modify its route to avoid a car crash). The resulting plan is executed by the vehicle's effectors (arrows 6 in Fig. 1). The algorithms within the pipeline are designed to be simple and minimalist so that simulated time constraints are not violated. We assume that a CAV is ready to perform basic reasoning always when it is necessary and the process takes a fixed amount of time.

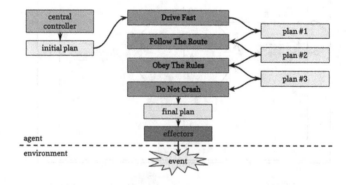

Fig. 2. The pipeline constituted by basic desires.

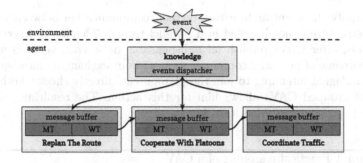

Fig. 3. The pipeline constituted by meta desires.

Meta Reasoning Pipeline. Whereas basic desires make the agent react to the environment, meta desires propel vehicles to shape the environment (arrow 5 in Fig. 1). Meta desires involve communication with other cars (e.g. when creating a platoon) and time-consuming computations (e.g. when replanning the route), results of which are not needed urgently. Initially, we designed each of them to work in a separate thread (MT) and spawn an additional worker thread (WT) if needed, not to block or slow down other modules of the system (Fig. 3). Since meta desires can impact decisions of each other (e.g: replanning the route may open opportunities to join a platoon), they exchange messages via the framework controller.

4   System Architecture

Another architecture we need to design manages the simulation of hundreds of CAVs as a whole, with consideration for limited computing resources of a desktop computer.

4.1   Single-Thread Agents

We begin with determining the potential number of threads needed for the simulation. Mainly due to separation of meta-desire units, hundreds of CAVs result in at least thousands of threads and, thereby, in significant overhead for switching the context as well as troublesome synchronization. To limit the number of threads, we decide to perform both kinds of reasoning in the same thread rather than in parallel. Then both kinds of desires are considered in a similar manner and in accordance with their linear order.

To apply this solution, algorithms performed formerly by main threads of meta desires cannot consume too much of resources. Advanced computations (e.g. finding a common path with a platoon's one) should be offloaded to a thread pool: a group of threads spawned by the program at the start. An optimal pool's size can be determined, based on the probability distribution of task requests [22].

To simplify the agent architecture further, communication between vehicles and infrastructure is not handled in a parallel thread. Thanks to determinism of protocols, after CAVs publish all indispensable data, each agent is able to find the outcome of potential communication without exchanging messages. For example, an agent intending to join the platoon can directly check whether the number of grouped CAVs allows him for this action. The resulting practical reasoning is presented as Algorithm 1.

Algorithm 1 Practical reasoning of a CAV

```
 1: procedure CREATE A PLAN
 2:     for each item D in meta desires do
 3:         M ← D.read messages from the buffer
 4:         I ← D.learn about the environment
 5:         triggered ← D.check conditions(M, I)
 6:         if triggered then
 7:             D.compute and prepare optimizations
 8:         end if
 9:         D.adjust basic desires                          ▷ optionally
10:     end for
11:     P ← empty plan                            ▷ just keep going forward
12:     for each item D in basic desires do
13:         I ← D.learn about the environment
14:         P ← D.adjust the plan(P, I)
15:     end for
16:     return P
17: end procedure
```

Algorithm 2, in turn, shows an exemplary procedure **check conditions** of a meta desire *replan the route*. The procedure, given information about the environment (I) and messages from preceding meta desires (M), decides on modifications to a vehicle route and switches between basic desires: *wander around* and *follow the route*.

4.2 Single-Thread System

The altered agent architecture is supposed to be a compromise between technology restrictions and ability to mimic the world accurately enough. Single-thread agents introduce an additional difficulty: simulated CAVs need to provide the information that is necessary for others in a synchronized way. In practice each CAV has to know at least the plan prepared by the car in front (only then it can avoid a rear-end collision). It is not straightforward how to reconcile this condition with other properties: (1) CAVs run their computations in parallel, (2) CAVs can plan actions based on 'predicted' future t_p seconds of their local environment. To explain the problem, let t_c denote time needed to communicate and get data, while t_r is time needed to reason about actions for next t_p seconds. Values of t_c and t_r depend on t_p: the more predictions to be made and the more actions to design, the greater are t_c and t_r. In the following examples, let the variables be assigned some fixed values: $t_p = 6\,\text{s}$, $t_c = 1\,\text{s}$ and $t_r = 1\,\text{s}$.

Algorithm 2 Unit replan-the-route

```
 1: procedure CHECK CONDITIONS(M, I)
 2:     if any route became passable(I) then
 3:         triggered ← true; update beliefs
 4:     end if
 5:     if WT has finished its work then
 6:         if there is no route then
 7:             triggered ← true; wander around ← true; return
 8:         end if
 9:         if should apply the new route(I, M) then
10:             save the old route as fallback and apply the new one
11:         end if
12:     end if
13:     if current goal cannot be obtained(I, M) then
14:         if no fallback route is applicable now then
15:             triggered ← true; wander around ← true; return
16:         end if
17:         apply the fallback route
18:     end if
19:     if future goals cannot be obtained(I, M) then
20:         triggered ← true; return
21:     end if
22:     follow the route ← true                           ▷ do not wander around
23: end procedure
```

Single-Agent Scenario. Given these constraints, we consider a situation, where a single vehicle drives on an empty road. It is able to deduce what the environment will look like during next 6 s. Also, for simplicity, it is informed by the simulation framework about 'unexpected events' and the intended actions are planned as if such events were truly unexpected (e.g. a CAV 'plans' to break rapidly due to a jaywalker). Consequently, after 1 s of reasoning, the resulting plan is final and valid for 5 s. The optimal strategy for a single agent (a CAV drives smoothly while the reasoning is performed as rarely as possible) is presented in Fig. 4. Intervals for which the vehicle has already designed actions are light grey. Time spent on executing plans is marked with the dark shadow, whereas periods for which there were/are no commitments are left blank. An hourglass represents the reasoning.

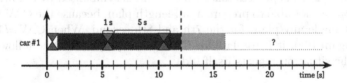

Fig. 4. After 12 s the agent realized 1/5 of the current plan and has commitments for next 4 s. (Color figure online)

Multiagent Scenario. In the multiagent scenario there are n vehicles on a one-lane road that passed the traffic lights and one that has to wait for the green light (the car m), as shown in Fig. 5. Each of them plans its actions using the

Fig. 5. A multiagent scenario on a one-lane road. (Color figure online)

same basic-reasoning. However, in this case, the single-agent strategy cannot be applied: CAVs function concurrently but they are not independent. For each $1 < i \leq n$, commitments of CAV $\#(i-1)$ are essential for decisions of CAV $\#i$ and a vehicle needs to prepare plans more frequently. Otherwise, CAVs are not able to reason in time, as illustrated in Fig. 6.

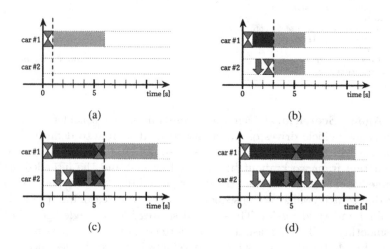

Fig. 6. The single-agent strategy in the multiagent scenario.

Like previously, CAV $\#1$ reasons during the first second (6a). Then its plan is sent to car $\#2$. This process takes time t_c and is symbolised by a down arrow (6b). CAV $\#2$ is not able to prepare a full-length plan, because the CAV in front has not yet made any plans for the 7th and 8th second. When CAV $\#1$ starts to reason again (6c), it is too late for CAV $\#2$ to prepare for the following 2 s. After 8 s, the situation repeats itself (6d).

Frequency of Reasoning. Unlike in the discussed scenario agents need to plan their actions in advance. Hence, CAVs should perform the reasoning whenever neighbours ask for information. We call this *Reasoning On Demand (ROD)* and present it in Fig. 7. After first 3 s CAV $\#2$ requests data necessary for practical reasoning. CAV $\#1$ has already defined the commitments for the next 2 s but, to provide as much data as possible, it plans additional actions for further 3 s. When the car at the back obtains the data both agents have their plans ready until the 9th second (7a). Then, another cycle begins. Due to this arrangement,

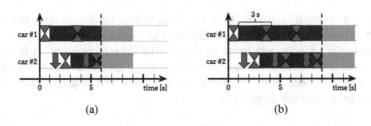

Fig. 7. CAV #1 creates plans incrementally.

the CAV in front plans actions for shorter intervals but more frequently – every 3 s (Subfig. 7b). For n vehicles in line, the period T, with which agents need to perform the reasoning equals $t_p - nt_r - (n-1)t_c$ and T must satisfy the condition $t_r < T$ (otherwise CAVs are not able to prepare their plans in time).

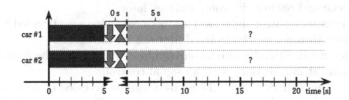

Fig. 8. *Simplified Reasoning On Demand, $T = 5$ s*

Our Solution. *Reasoning On Demand* can be reduced to *Simplified Reasoning On Demand (SROD)* presented in Fig. 8. Here, the simulation time 'freezes' while agents collect information and plan what to do for the next T seconds. After the normal time flow is restored, CAVs execute their actions. This modification semantically results in just one difference. *ROD* requires CAV #2 to prepare a plan based on commitments of CAV #1 adopted about t_c seconds ago. In the modified arrangement, when CAV #2 reasons at a certain moment t_0 it takes into account commitments of CAV #1 adopted at the same moment, at t_0. Consequently, CAV #2 is given information it should not have when reasoning, that is information about reactions to unexpected events of CAV #1. Therefore, actions taken due to an unexpected event should be labelled so that CAV #2 can pretend not to know about non-deterministic incidents of CAV #1 in advance.

Since *SROD* can be implemented as consistent with *ROD*, we apply sequential reasoning of agents that results in: simplicity (an easier way to implement, analyse and debug the program), repeatable behaviour of agents (unaltered by management of multiple threads) and fully controlled timing (if CAVs perform their tasks in parallel their threads interleave in accordance to an uncontrolled schedule). In particular, controlled value of T allows us to determine the optimal period of reasoning and its dependency on other parameters in our future research.

There is a concern, however, that the single-thread solution does not utilize multicore processors. We propose splitting the computations into parts that involve mutually independent areas of the simulation environment. It is possible thanks to signal controls that stop the traffic along a given direction, as in Fig. 5: car $\#m$, does not need any data from car $\#n$ if the red phase of traffic lights lasts for at least another T seconds.

4.3   The Final Design

The discussed concepts result in a powerful and efficient architecture for the simulation framework, presented in Fig. 9. Interactions between particular modules are marked with numbered arrows (similarly as in case of Fig. 1):

1–2. Controllers manage reasoning within a single independent area. They keep agents organized in a queue and initialize the reasoning sequentially. If a CAV awaits information from another vehicle it is pushed at the back of the queue and resumes its computations later.
3–4. Time-consuming algorithms used for meta reasoning are offloaded to a pool of worker threads, which is shared between all the agents.
5–6. Vehicles are able to influence the environment directly, e.g. by coordinating the traffic at intersections with no signal control.
  7. CAVs know their own state. These data can be accessed directly by other agents via imitated communication.
8–9. Beliefs representing the public knowledge are models and procedures common for all cars. Information available for a CAV is limited in distance.
 10. Every change in the environment is immediately expressed as data.

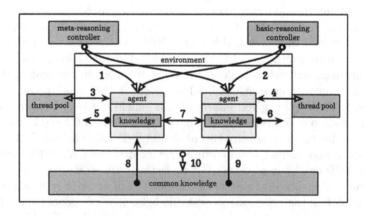

Fig. 9. The architecture of the whole system.

5 Discussion

Even though BDI has been considered in the context of CAVs, its potential has not been utilized: existing architectures are either solely reactive [12] or focus on a single kind of interactions [18]. More general solutions that combine reactiveness and proactivity, like [17, 24], or classical multiagent systems, like [8, 25], are not oriented towards specificity of CAVs and their environment. However, the proposed architecture derives inspiration from existing solutions [3, 4, 10, 11, 16, 23] and applies some of their ideas. To our best knowledge, though, no other validated models of CAVs like [2, 14, 19, 26] incorporate all of the features characteristic for our design. For instance, one of the conceptually closest designs, TouringMachines [10], embeds a complex framework controller that governs modelling, planning and reactive layers given specified situation-related rules. Our framework controller, in turn, only initializes the reasoning process and provides data to agents. Thereby, the architecture preserves transparency of how modelled CAVs make decisions and plan actions.

It is comprehensibility, indeed, that is a unique feature of our system: the simple and clear design of mechanisms that control driving strategies enables end-users to easily modify algorithms of CAV steering and the configuration. We created a prototype version of the simulation framework [1] which proves feasibility of our design. The implementation is currently being improved to allow for quantitative comparison with other existing architectures. As for now our program can be used to test various techniques that coordinate traffic at intersections and to find out how making a road impassable influences total time travelled by the CAVs. We aim to enhance the tool with an additional module for finding routes that satisfy specific requirements, investigate how agents of different attitudes are able to coexist and verify if gamification systems could be an efficient solution to traffic jams in cities.

Concerning our future work, we examine the architecture with regard for such properties as extensibility, resilience and scalability. The first property is assured by the system's modular structure, especially in case of reasoning pipelines, where manoeuvres are implemented by separate units. The same design concept guarantees the system's resilience in case of any malfunction of a desire-related unit: units are not aware of each other and if no meta procedures are executed, the basic reasoning is capable of driving the car on its own. We are still working on scalability, limited mainly due to the sequential reasoning process and microscale precision.

Currently our prototype is meant for small-scale traffic: the maximal considered area should correspond to an average district in a big city with a thousand of travelling vehicles at most. Such scale of computations already allows us to observe major traffic phenomena (e.g. creation of traffic jams, efficiency of coordinated intersections) and can be supported by a single PC. To run the simulation for a larger scale and keep all its advantages intact, we need to leverage high reasoning costs, for example by parallelizing the computations as suggested in the previous section. If, in the following stages of our research program, there is a need to increase efficiency of our framework further, the main property of the model that should be preserved at all costs is its BDI basis: these abstractions and mechanisms allowed us to simulate variety of interactions between CAVs, including paradigmatic activities like cooperation, coordination and communication, while enforcing simplicity of the system.

Acknowledgements. This work was supported by the Polish National Science Centre Grant 2015/19/B/ST6/02589.

References

1. Charlcar: prototype implementation. https://www.mimuw.edu.pl/~inga/charlcar. tgz
2. Al-Zinati, M., Zalila-Wenkstern, R.: Matisse 2.0: a large-scale multi-agent simulation system for agent-based its. In: 2015 IEEE/WIC/ACM International Conference on Web Intelligence and Intelligent Agent Technology (WI-IAT), vol. 2, pp. 328–335 (2015)
3. Behere, S., Torngren, M.: A functional architecture for autonomous driving. In: 2015 First International Workshop on Automotive Software Architecture (WASA), pp. 3–10 (2015)
4. Brooks, R.: A robust layered control system for a mobile robot. IEEE J. Robot. Autom. **2**, 14–23 (1986)
5. de Campos, G.R., Falcone, P., Sjöberg, J.: Autonomous cooperative driving: a velocity-based negotiation approach for intersection crossing. In: ITSC 2013, pp. 1456–1461 (2013)
6. Davila, A., Nombela, M.: Platooning - safe and eco-friendly mobility (2012)
7. Dunin-Kęplicz, B., Verbrugge, R.: Teamwork in Multi-Agent Systems: A Formal Approach. Wiley (2010)
8. Pollack, M.E., Israel, D., Bratman, M.: Towards an architecture for resource-bounded agents (1987)
9. Fagnant, D.J., Kockelman, K.: Preparing a nation for autonomous vehicles: opportunities, barriers and policy recommendations. Transp. Res. Part A: Policy Pract. **77**, 167–181 (2015)
10. Ferguson, I.A.: Touring machines: autonomous agents with attitudes. Computer **25**(5), 51–55 (1992)
11. Georgeff, M.P., Ingrand, F.F.: Decision-making in an embedded reasoning system. In: Proceedings of the 11th International Joint Conference on Artificial Intelligence, IJCAI 1889, vol. 2, pp. 972–978 (1989)
12. Gora, P., Rüb, I.: Traffic models for self-driving connected cars. Transp. Res. Proc. **14**, 2207–2216 (2016)
13. Gruel, W., Stanford, J.M.: Assessing the long-term effects of autonomous vehicles: a speculative approach. Transp. Res. Proc. **13**, 18–29 (2016)
14. Guériau, M., Billot, R., El Faouzi, N.E., Hassas, S., Armetta, F.: Multi-agent dynamic coupling for cooperative vehicles modeling. In: Proceedings of the Twenty-Ninth AAAI Conference on Artificial Intelligence, AAAI 2015, pp. 4276–4277. AAAI Press (2015)
15. Jin, Q., Wu, G., Boriboonsomsin, K., Barth, M.: Multi-agent intersection management for connected vehicles using an optimal scheduling approach. In: 2012 International Conference on Connected Vehicles and Expo (ICCVE), pp. 185–190 (2012)

16. Johansson, R., et al.: Functional safety and evolvable architectures for autonomy. In: Watzenig, D., Horn, M. (eds.) Automated Driving, pp. 547–560. Springer, Cham (2017). https://doi.org/10.1007/978-3-319-31895-0_25

17. Dennis, L., Fisher, M., Lincoln, N.K., Veres, S.M., Lisitsa, A.: An agent based framework for adaptive control and decision making of autonomous vehicles. IFAC Proc. Vol. **43**(10), 310–317 (2010). https://doi.org/10.3182/20100826-3-TR-4015. 00058. http://www.sciencedirect.com/science/article/pii/S1474667015323843

18. Kamali, M., Dennis, L.A., McAree, O., Fisher, M., Veres, S.M.: Formal verification of autonomous vehicle platooning. Sci. Comput. Program. **148**, 88–106 (2017)

19. Krajzewicz, D.: Traffic simulation with SUMO - simulation of urban mobility. In: Barceló, J. (ed.) Fundamentals of Traffic Simulation, vol. 145, pp. 269–293. Springer, New York (2010). https://doi.org/10.1007/978-1-4419-6142-6_7

20. Lambert, F.: BMW will launch the electric and autonomous iNext in 2021 (2016). https://electrek.co/2016/05/12/bmw-electric-autonomous-inext-2021/

21. Leary, K.: Japan is testing driverless buses to help the elderly get around (2017). https://futurism.com/japan-is-testing-driverless-buses-to-help-the-elderly-get-around/

22. Ling, Y., Mullen, T., Lin, X.: Analysis of optimal thread pool size. SIGOPS Oper. Syst. Rev. **34**(2), 42–55 (2000)

23. Lygeros, J., Godbole, D.N., Sastry, S.: A design framework for hierarchical, hybrid control. Technical report, Machines and Robotic Laboratory, University of California, Berkeley (1997)

24. Maleš, L., Ribarić, S.: A model of extended BDI agent with autonomous entities (integrating autonomous entities within BDI agent). In: 2016 IEEE 8th International Conference on Intelligent Systems (IS), pp. 205–214 (2016)

25. Müller, J., Pischel, M.: The agent architecture inteRRaP: concept and application (1993)

26. Passos, L., Rossetti, R., Kokkinogenis, Z.: Towards the next-generation traffic simulation tools: a first appraisal, pp. 1–6 (2011)

27. Sage, A., Lienert, P.: GM executive credits silicon valley for accelerating development of self-driving cars (2016). http://www.reuters.com/article/us-ford-autonomous/ford-plans-self-driving-car-for-ride-share-fleets-in-2021-idUSKCN10R1G1

28. Thangarajah, J., Harland, J., Morley, D.N., Yorke-Smith, N.: On the life-cycle of BDI agent goals. In: Proceedings of the 19th European Conference on Artificial Intelligence, ECAI 2010, Lisbon, Portugal, 16–20 August 2010, pp. 1031–1032 (2010)

29. Wooldridge, M.: An Introduction to MultiAgent Systems, 2nd edn. Wiley, Hoboken (2009)

30. Zhang, R., Rossi, F., Pavone, M.: Routing autonomous vehicles in congested transportation networks: structural properties and coordination algorithms (2016)

Soft Real-Time Systems for Low-Cost Unmanned Ground Vehicle

Adam Ziebinski[1(✉)], Rafal Cupek[1], Marek Drewniak[2], and Bartlomiej Wolny[1]

[1] Institute of Informatics, Silesian University of Technology, Gliwice, Poland
{Adam.Ziebinski,Rafal.Cupek}@polsl.pl,
bartlomiej@wolny.cc
[2] AIUT Sp. z o.o. (Ltd.), Gliwice, Poland
mdrewniak@aiut.com.pl

Abstract. Many small Unmanned Ground Vehicle today are used as IoT systems. Some of these systems are equipped with low-cost resources that are not guaranteed to perform the high quality movements that are required by an operator or an application. To improve the quality of these systems they should be equipped with real-time functions. For this type of solutions, embedded systems are often constructed as soft real-time systems that are equipped with a microcontroller without a real-time clock. The authors focus on possibilities and limitations of soft real-time systems implemented on Raspberry Pi based on measurements with usage cyclictest and ftrace tools. The prepared experiments allowed to determine which configuration of a soft real-time system gives the minimum jitter for the set period of cycle time and the stability of execution of a real-time process.

Keywords: Embedded systems · Soft real-time system on Raspberry Pi · Unmanned Ground Vehicle

1 Introduction

Internet of Things (IoT) enable to exchange the data between physical objects things like sensor, actuator, control systems, autonomous systems [1], Cyber-Physical Systems [2], and Industry 4.0 solutions [3]. Unmanned Ground Vehicle (UGV) [4] require an enormous quantity of data collecting and processing. Through IoT, the UGV shares information about the road, measurements and realized tasks. This data are exchanged with other systems for analyse and improvement algorithms for automation of driving. Some of UGV often use low-cost embedded systems that are not equipped with a real-time clock. The lack of a real-time clock is especially visible in the case of slower systems, which, in addition to supporting control functions, perform additional functions such as analysing and sharing data. In such cases, a system may not be able to handle control processes in a timely manner. As a result, a system could partially or completely lose control of the hardware when the data is wrong or the decision is made too late. Multithreading enables many pieces of code to be executed pseudo-simultaneously. A system scheduler deals with fast task switching, which gives the

© Springer Nature Switzerland AG 2019
N. T. Nguyen et al. (Eds.): ICCCI 2019, LNAI 11684, pp. 196–206, 2019.
https://doi.org/10.1007/978-3-030-28374-2_17

impression that they are being executed continuously. The real-time part of the system has the ideal pattern for executing tasks to be determined while meeting the real-time constraints. It can precisely determine a system's response time to a given event. This solution allows threats to be avoided by guaranteeing a response before a deadline. In many solutions often are used microcontrollers that are based on the Linux operating system without a real-time clock [5]. The Linux operating system works in an asynchronous mode in which a system scheduler decides when a process is executed by default. While that system lacks determinism, it can react fast enough. The default scheduler is "Completely Fair Scheduler" (CFS) [6] in which all processes are usually assigned to the process queue SCHED_OTHER. In the queue, the values of the priorities (called nice) are set for each process within the range of most favourable (−20) to least favourable (19) [7, 8]. The scheduler keeps track of all of the threads. The ready threads are selected to be executed depending on what priority they have assigned. Processes that have a lower priority are pre-empted by processes that have a higher priority. Another type of scheduling algorithm without time slicing is SCHED_FIFO, which enables the priorities to be set within the range of 1 to 99, where 99 is the highest priority. In this case, SCHED_OTHER threads have a priority of 0. In SCHED_FIFO, the threads are blocked by a higher priority process, an I/O request or a calls sched_yield() function [8]. SCHED_RR is an enhancement of SCHED_FIFO in which each thread is only allowed to run for a pre-defined time slice. The main difference from SCHED_FIFO occurs when a running thread needs time that is longer than the pre-defined time slice. In this case, it is sent to the end of the priority queue.

A non-real-time system can be expanded to have real-time functionality by modifying the Linux kernel. The RT-preempt patch includes all of the necessary modifications such as making the kernel code as pre-emptible as possible, setting the priority inheritance and supporting RT throttling [9]. The main purpose of this solution is to stabilize the behaviour of time-critical processes. A priority inheritance occurs when a lower priority process uses a shared resource (interface, storage etc.). Without this resource, the high priority process could not continue its own task in some cases. This solution gives the lower priority process the priority of the high priority process. So this process, completes its own tasks fast and releases the blocked resource after which the high priority process can continue its own tasks. An operating system should have mechanisms that provide safety when realizing real-time applications. It is expected that applications will perform its tasks and then return access to the processor for use by other threads. However, it should be remembered that incorrectly prepared code can cause the entire system to hang. An application in the SCHED_FIFO queue should have the highest priority in the system. No other process can pre-empt it in this case. This can cause all other tasks to be blocked and result in a 100% CPU load. The real-time mechanism throttling enables such situations to be avoided and limits the execution time of tasks for a defined period. The parameters of the time period and the maximal execution time (in ms per period) can be set in the files sched_rt_period_us and sched_rt_runtime_us, which are then stored in the directory /proc/sys/kernel/ [8]. The Linux kernel does not calculate the values of dynamic priority in the case of real-time tasks. The real-time scheduling policies presented above implement the static priorities. This mechanism ensures that a real-time process that has a high priority will always be executed because any lower priority process will be pre-empted.

Hard real-time systems [10] guarantee the any scheduling requirements will be fulfilled within certain limits. Soft real-time systems [11] enable issues of sharing resources and connected systems to be solve, which enables some specific criteria to be optimized for a given application. It is assumed that the quality of scheduling may become degraded but that system can continue to operate. A Linux operating system does not guarantee the performance of tasks in real time. The behaviour of soft real-time systems provides real-time scheduling policies in Linux [12], which means that the Linux kernel will run tasks at certain times, but does not promise that it will always be able to realize these conditions. Tasks are run each time the system is able to run them. Despite this fact, the real-time scheduling performance in the Linux 2.6 kernel is capable of fulfilling very stringent timing requirements.

Taking the above into consideration, it is important to verify the possibilities and limitations of soft real-time system. The speed of the correct and regular reaction of such a system is necessary in order to determine how quickly measurements and calculations can be performed. The main goal of the presented approach is to obtain information which configuration of a soft real-time system implemented on RPi gives the minimum jitter for set period of cycle time and the execution stability of a real-time process. The main contribution of the proposed approach is to verify the performance of this type of system in various use cases, depending on the use of real-time mode on RPi. The proposed approach is presented on the use case of an UGV solution based on a mobile platform that uses a Raspberry Pi controller (RPi), Raspbian operating system and a real-time application that requires a guaranteed response within strict timing constraints, what was described in the second chapter. In chapter three were presented a real-time mode on RPi. In chapter four, the authors describe the results of system performance on the basis experiments that were executed using cyclictest and ftrace tools. The conclusions are presented in last chapter.

2 The Architecture of an Autonomous Mobile Platform

The main idea of the proposed solution is to build an autonomous mobile platform (AMP) as an UGV solution that is constructed as a modular project that is based on a simple mobile platform, an engine control module, the required sensors, a Central Unit (CU) and Data Acquisition Unit (DAU) to support motion control. The motion control of an AMP is executed through an application that runs on the CU. The CU works cyclically by acquiring and interpreting the signals from the sensors that are installed on the platform, performing the calculations and setting the engine parameters. The DAU was operated using a STM32 controller and the CU was operated using a Raspberry Pi 3 model B controller. The two-way communication between the DAU and CU was realised using a SPI [13]. The DAU software supports the sensors: ultrasound, accelerometer, magnetometer, gyroscope, encoder, GPS and the ADAS module Lidar (Fig. 1). The fusion of several sensors [14] such as an accelerometer, gyroscope, magnetometer and encoders enables the CU to calculate the speed, direction of movement and travelled distance.

A FreeRTOS operating system kernel that supports the execution of multiple threads or tasks at once runs on an STM32. Each DAU program module includes functions for initializing the communication interface, writing the configuration data, reading the data into correct data structure and inserting the obtained structures into the transmit buffers. The DAU sends the data (measurements and control data) that is stored in transmits buffer to the CU. Moreover, it receives data from the CU (PWM values, configuration data) and puts it in the correct data structures for the appropriate threads.

The CU is composed of a couple of modules that work together to fulfil the autonomous platform tasks. As inter-process communication method between each CU module, used the mmap (shared memory) mechanisms that handle a specific address in the RAM memory for a file (Fig. 2). That mechanism permits one process to write to a file and many processes to read a file. Therefore, fewer processes use the same memory space, which accelerates their performance and access to current data. The main Raspberry Daemon processes read the data from the DAU by the SPI and to map it into shared memory of the RPi. As a result, the current data is shared with other processes on the RPi.

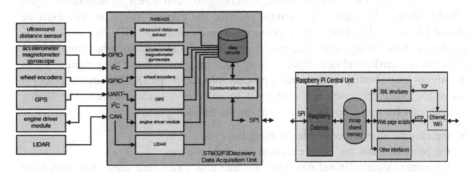

Fig. 1. The DAU architecture   **Fig. 2.** The CU architecture

The freshness of the measurements on the RPi is critical for the logic computations so this process should work in real-time. The main task of Raspberry Daemon is to process the measurements and control data for the current steering movements of the mobile platform. A Raspberry Daemon process performs these actions:

- reads the data from the DAU by the SPI,
- rewrites the obtained values into the structures in mmap,
- calculates the physical values, e.g. distance, speed, direction, position, detecting the distance to obstacles, the PWM values to set engines power,
- writes the data to the DAU by the SPI.

That solutions enable the functionality of obstacle avoidance [15], the indoor localization [16] and Emergency Brake Assist to be performed in the CU. A complete system can be equipped on embedded system [17] which enable processing in hard real-time.

3   A Real-Time Mode on Raspberry Pi

The Raspbian operating system does not support real-time functions. Additionally, a standard Linux install includes services that generate a great deal of overhead. Therefore, it is recommended all unnecessary services be removed. In order to generate the deterministic timing pulses, a RPi requires a real-time clock and a pulse generator. However, these solutions are not enough to guarantee a real-time mode. Such a system is required to support sharing resources and processing multiple threads that have unique priorities and timing.

To obtain a real-time mode on Raspbian systems a designer should compile or download a precompiled version of the kernel and replace the current system kernel [18] and the contents of the two main Linux directories (/boot and /lib) must be replaced. After that, the system has to be checked to ensure that it has active real-time capabilities. On such Raspberry Daemon system, the process of attempting to work in real-time mode and becoming a daemon process should begin. In order to obtain a real-time mode, active process scheduler to SCHED_FIFO and the required process priority must be set using the functions sched_setscheduler() and sched_getscheduler() from sched.h library. To obtain the daemon process, the current parent process must be cloned (forking). The new child process changes Session ID (SID) and works independently in the background. The parent process and all of the streams (input, output and error streams) are closed. Finally, an application is created and the program begins an infinite loop. Putting an important process into the SCHED_FIFO queue places it above the other processes and enables it to work in a cyclic manner. The timing mechanisms for cyclic applications work in the following way:

- the current time is stored after starting the cycle,
- the processes that are to be executed regularly are run,
- the current time is stored again to calculate how much time these processes have taken,
- the time to the end of a cycle is calculated,
- the process goes to a sleep mode for the duration of the remaining time and the CPU resources are made available for other threads in the system,
- the system continues executing the other processes and its own tasks,
- the cycle starts again.

This method enables the constant cycle period to be executed. The main issue with the Linux operating system is that this fixed period cycle cannot be guaranteed and the planned wake-up time of a cycle will be precisely executed. The accuracy that is obtained depends on the correct configuration of such a system. A scheduling latency is the delay between the scheduled wake-up and the actual wake-up and it should be regular and small as possible. The new architecture of the AMP enables a CU to operate more quickly based on the four cores of CPU and a DAU unit that are available, which supports taking measurements from connected sensors. As a result, the required time of a cycle cannot easily be determined.

4   System Performance Testing

A series of tests should be performed to determine how effective the installation of a real-time patch in the kernel was for the CU. The main task that should be realized in real-time is the Raspberry Daemon process that controls the movements of the AMP. All of the other tasks do not need to be performed in the real-time mode. The test cases should include measurements of the key factors that will improve the work of a system the most. For this solution, the time metrics of the wake up differences between cycles and latency of cycle period and cycle durations of Raspberry Daemon process should be verified in various conditions. The main purpose is to stabilize the behavior of the time-critical tasks. The tests were carried out for a number of measurements that were performed using cyclictest and ftrace tools. All of the tests were performed in cases with a real-time patch (RT) and without a real-time patch (nRT), using the specified cores in systems (1 or 4 cores "c", in mode for 4 cores exclusive core use "i" or auto affinity "a") that were in the idle or under stress ("s") modes. The concept of real-time software can be expressed in the following pseudo-code:

> *initialisation()*
> *planned_wake_up_time = now() + 20ms*
> *loop:*
> > *sleep_until(planned_wake_up_time)*
> > *perform_cyclic_tasks()*
> > *planned_wake_up_time += 20ms*
> > *goto loop*

The exact implementations use the system functions clock_nanosleep and clock_gettime [8]. All of the data that were logged into a specified file were obtained and calculated during the operation process. The following data were logged: the relative timestamp from an unknown startpoint (using the clock_gettime function and CLOCK_MONOTONIC system clock), the calculated wake-up latency (defined as the difference between the actual wake-up and the planned wake-up), the cycle number and go_to_sleep time. The tests were performed in several environment configuration variants and the tools that were used were:

1. The system scheduler in Raspbian Linux cores can be excluded by appending a parameters file /boot/cmdline.txt a keyword such as isolcpus = 0,2,3 to the boot-loader, which results in only core #1 being used by the system scheduler for all of the active tasks. The three cores did not have jobs assigned to them.
2. A task set is a Linux tool that is used to assign the process affinity specifically to a selected core. Together with isolating a core (excluding from usage by system), a specific process can run exclusively on one core. To run it on a selected core the user must execute #> task set -c 3 PROCESS_NAME, which will run it assigned to the fourth core.
3. The priority of a process (not nice parameter) and the scheduler queue can be set by the process itself using the function sched_setscheduler [8].

4.1   Testing Based on Cyclictest

The first method was based on the cyclictest tool measurements. This tool treats a system like a black box. It logs the delay times between the successive wake-ups (wake-up latency) of the same thread with a given priority. The deviation in the delays from the average is called "jitter". It is one of the most important measures that the application checks. The higher the deviation, the less deterministic the wake-up times are and therefore the smaller the deviation value is, the more regularly the system works.

During start-up, the cyclictest creates a defined number of threads with a given priority. During the tests, the program takes the time measurements and calculates the differences between the planned waking time and the actual waking time. This allowed the time differences that were measured to be added and the maximum, minimum and average to be calculated. The program's run parameters are the number of threads that are specified, the priority for the first thread, when the application should wake up, the number of samples and which system clock to use. Despite being a fairly simple algorithm, the program allows meaningful tests to be conducted. The cyclictest tool was started with the following parameters "cyclictest-m -t1 -p 80-n -i500-l 500000".

The system with the "RT Preempt" modification had much lower maximum delay times in each subsequent test (Fig. 3). The same was true for the difference between the typical delay time, the average delay time and the maximum delay time. It is several times larger in the system without the "RT Preempt" modification, which made the delays less predictable. That problem is more visible in for the test that was performed without a real-time patch (nRT1c and nRT4c). In this case, the delays even exceeded 500 µs in the idle mode. In the case of the test that was performed with a real-time patch, the delays were more predictable and did not exceed 100 µs even in the stress mode. So using a real-time patch enabled the Raspbian system to work more regularly.

The cyclictest tool is not perfect; it lacks synchronization between the testing threads. The threads can overlap and cause delays. The application also has imperfections that are caused by its cyclic execution. By default, the application is woken up every 1000 ms. In the meantime, if there was a wake-up process that blocks the switching of the test thread, cyclictest will return an erroneous measurement of the switching time. In addition, the tool has no mechanisms to detect blockades and therefore the results may be distorted. Due to the imperfections of the cyclictest tool, additional tools are required to perform a system analysis.

| | without real-time patch | | | | | | | | with real-time patch | | | | | | | |
| | system idle | | | | under stress | | | | system idle | | | | under stress | | | |
	min	max	diff	avg	min	max	diff	avg	min	max	diff	avg	min	max	diff	avg
RPi3 - 1 core	4	502	498	12	4	1820	1816	26	5	78	73	14	6	56	50	9
RPi3 - 4 cores	5	117	112	11	5	2442	2437	26	5	74	69	11	5	91	86	11

Fig. 3. The results of the latency measurements [µs] with using cyclictest (*diff* = *max-min*)

4.2 Testing Based on Ftrace

In order to determine the delay times more accurately, it is important to check them from the perspective of the switching mechanism ("Scheduler") using the ftrace tool. The experiments were performed based on the ftrace kernel logs that monitor the Raspberry Daemon process and log its wake-up and go-to-sleep timestamps. The ftrace is an in-built kernel tool for tracing function calls, kernel events and their timings. It allows custom text markers to be inserted into the log files, which are then available paired with an ftrace -assigned timestamp. This mechanism is assumed to be precise as it is realized at the system level. In order to determine how the real-time Raspberry Daemon process is performed, experimental measurements were executed on a RPi. The Raspbian systems was tested under various configuration conditions with and without real-time patch. The value of priority was set to 80 and the value of the cycle time period was set to 20 ms for all of the experiments performed on Raspbian system. Implemented real-time patch should guarantee deterministic value for delay and jitter (delay variation). The jitter for all delays was calculated with using the standard deviation. Additionally interquartile range (difference between Q75 and Q25) which contains 50% of measured samples was calculated for cycle duration. The result of the wake-up latency and delay for the cycle time period and cycle duration of Raspberry Daemon process are presented on Fig. 4 for all of the executed experiments.

The best results were obtained in the case of the RT4ci. The average value of the wake-up latency was 20 ms, which exactly corresponded to the value of the cycle time that had been set. The standard deviation that was obtained was 0.047 ms, which was the best in all of the experiments that had been performed. The main problem was that max delay of the wake-up latency was 4005 ms. The average value of the cycle durations of real-time Raspberry Daemon process was 1.145 ms and the standard deviation was 0.323 ms. The results for cycle durations show that sometimes the real-time process Raspberry Daemon was executed for much longer than the average value. The worst case occurred in the case of the system with a real-time path RT4ca for which the standard deviation of the wake-up delay was 25953 ms. That problems occurred due to the expropriation of a real-time process by another system process despite the 80-degree priority. That effect can be seen in the column *min* and *max* for wake-up latencies and wake-up delays, especially for real-time solutions. The experiments showed that they still occurred at a priority value of 95. The SCHED_FIFO threads could be blocked by a higher priority process, an I/O request or the calls sched_yield() function [18]. Therefore, it is important to set the right priority value for a real-time process according to the documentation for the CPU and operating systems. Because a thread that is scheduled under the SCHED_FIFO can potentially block all other threads, the value of the priority could not be set so high. Linux 2.6.25 includes methods for the run-away real-time and deadline processes [8]. A RLIMIT_RTTIME resource enables the ceiling limit to be set on the CPU time that a real-time process can consume. The two /proc files enable a certain amount of CPU time to be reserved (in microseconds) to be used for non-real-time processes. The file sched_rt_period_us specifies a scheduling period that is within the range of 1to INT_MAX (equivalent to 100% CPU bandwidth). The file sched_rt_runtime_us specifies the period of time that can be used by all of the real-time and deadline scheduled processes on the system. The period is within the range of –1 to INT_MAX-1. The value "–1" means there is no time for non-real-time processes. Typically, this value is set to 950 what means 95% of the time is for real-time processes and 5% is for non-real-time processes. This setting was unnecessary in the tested system because during the sleep function, the system had time to service every non-real-time process.

name	The time of the wake-up latencies				The time of the wake-up delay				The time of the cycle durations of Raspberry Daemon process							
	min	max	avg	std_dev	min	max	avg	std_dev	min	max	avg	std_dev	Q25	Q50	Q75	Q75-Q25
RT4ci	16.03	23.97	20.000	0.047	8.00	4005	15	32.38	0.57	23.92	1.145	0.323	0.816	1.275	1.345	0.529
nRT4cas	17.90	22.09	20.000	0.088	10.00	2163	62	72.75	0.46	19.46	0.696	0.179	0.614	0.706	0.755	0.141
nRT1cs	0.29	99.56	20.000	0.736	8.00	79649	76	895.87	0.27	99.51	0.624	0.806	0.570	0.594	0.638	0.068
nRT4ci	0.69	88.16	20.000	0.762	8.00	68191	32	869.56	0.31	88.10	0.834	0.900	0.615	0.904	0.961	0.346
RT1c	0.38	103.50	20.000	0.960	8.00	83535	40	1140.61	0.36	103.46	0.865	1.134	0.629	0.937	0.996	0.367
RT4cas	0.58	88.50	20.000	1.068	9.00	68651	56	1191.63	0.54	88.44	0.860	1.270	0.765	0.818	0.883	0.118
nRT4cis	0.31	781.56	20.000	5.497	9.00	761732	829	19871.87	0.29	781.49	0.762	5.589	0.628	0.675	0.784	0.156
RT4ca	0.59	847.26	20.000	7.098	8.00	827302	1341	25953.49	0.43	847.18	1.213	7.233	0.830	1.246	1.350	0.520
nRT1c	0.29	709.94	20.000	9.245	8.00	689959	2201	31562.53	0.26	709.90	0.835	9.378	0.531	0.782	0.815	0.284
RT1cs	0.38	1520.12	20.000	12.133	9.00	1500212	3820	61537.37	0.35	1520.07	0.813	12.224	0.665	0.688	0.732	0.067
RT4cis	0.46	1462.26	20.000	17.056	8.00	1442305	7563	72050.09	0.43	1462.20	1.200	17.246	0.788	0.853	0.914	0.126
nRT4ca	0.29	764.19	20.000	22.837	8.00	744237	13534	77734.83	0.26	764.12	1.522	23.144	0.582	0.788	0.885	0.303

Fig. 4. The results of latency [ms] that were obtained from ftrace priority was set to 80

Taking this into account, experiments were performed with set the value of –1 for the sched_rt_runtime_us. Additionally, the value of the priority was set to 25 and the value of the cycle time was set to 20 ms. For these tests, a number of measurements were performed that monitored the Raspberry Daemon process and logged its wake-up and go-to-sleep timestamps using the ftrace tool. This time, the best result for the wake-up latency was also obtained in the case of the RT4ci. The average value was 19.967 ms and the standard deviation was 0.802 ms. The average value of the cycle durations of real-time Raspberry Daemon process was 1.109 ms and the standard deviation was 0.266 ms but the max value of the cycle durations was 9.09 ms. The average value of the time of the wake-up delay was 2.843 ms but the standard deviation was 75.238 ms (Fig. 5). The worst case of real-time solution was for the RT1c which had an average value of the wake-up latency was 20.008 ms and the standard deviation was 3.635 ms. This case was tested several times but the results that were obtained were similar. The same case, but in a non-real-time mode nRT1c, obtained the third result of the wake-up latency with a standard deviation was 1.278 ms. Some of the samples showed that sometimes the process was executed for much longer than the average value. This was particularly apparent in the max of the wake-up difference column values. This is a typical result that shows that there was an expropriation by another process, which was especially visible for the non-real-time cases and which can happen in stress testing mode. The main problem was that it was also in the case of the real-time processes. The differences between the values of quartiles Q75 and Q25 of the cycle durations (for set priority 25 and 80), were slightly improved in case of RT1c and RT4ci. The values of max, avg and standard deviation of the time of the wake-up delay and the cycle durations have decreased significantly in the most cases, so the system worked more stable at the set priority of 25.

name	The time of the wake-up latencies				The time of the wake-up delay				The time of the cycle durations of Raspberry Daemon process							
	min	max	avg	std_dev	min	max	avg	std_dev	min	max	avg	std_dev	Q25	Q50	Q75	Q75-Q25
RT4ci	1.20	32.43	19.967	0.802	0.01	2954.00	2.843	75.238	0.55	9.09	1.109	0.266	0.800	1.235	1.311	0.511
RT4ca	0.70	108.43	19.962	1.162	0.01	3574.10	4.297	101.565	0.47	108.37	1.149	0.932	0.836	1.249	1.366	0.530
nRT1c	0.35	160.89	19.994	1.278	0.01	5713.85	2.629	101.425	0.26	1.61	0.682	0.143	0.525	0.762	0.787	0.262
RT4cas	0.53	108.99	19.958	1.370	0.01	4278.69	6.150	132.587	0.50	108.94	0.859	1.140	0.766	0.827	0.906	0.140
RT1cs	0.47	101.47	19.995	1.424	0.01	2177.61	1.623	48.740	0.44	79.34	0.676	0.733	0.632	0.667	0.703	0.071
nRT4ca	0.37	264.46	20.001	2.072	0.01	5596.62	2.525	98.535	0.26	2.45	0.807	0.204	0.610	0.858	0.945	0.335
nRT4ci	19.93	381.93	20.029	3.015	0.01	71.36	0.022	0.583	0.31	91.27	0.762	0.788	0.564	0.825	0.890	0.326
nRT4cis	0.40	448.69	20.014	3.595	0.01	7152.71	4.063	140.390	0.38	23.90	0.704	0.218	0.619	0.670	0.785	0.166
RT1c	0.36	444.28	20.008	3.635	0.01	1994.16	1.431	43.022	0.34	444.25	0.867	3.626	0.628	0.926	0.978	0.350
RT4cis	0.45	729.85	20.014	5.987	0.01	5420.54	6.178	148.794	0.42	729.81	0.890	5.953	0.790	0.842	0.897	0.107
nRT1cs	0.27	450.72	20.188	10.134	0.01	19640.33	29.179	620.563	0.25	4.05	0.554	0.121	0.485	0.545	0.580	0.095
nRT4cas	0.30	449.72	20.253	10.175	0.01	6981.13	3.920	135.781	0.25	121.35	0.726	1.359	0.631	0.707	0.753	0.122

Fig. 5. The results of latency [ms] that were obtained from ftrace, priority was set to 25

5 Conclusions

The authors describe methods to verify the possibilities and limitations of soft real-time systems based on cyclictest and ftrace tools. The experiments were performed based on an embedded system without a real-time clock on the use case of a UGV that uses a Raspberry Pi controller, the Raspbian operating system and a real-time application that requires a guaranteed response within strict timing constraints. The results of the experiments allowed to indicate the most effective version of the configuration of the soft real-time system, taking into account the use of the RPi CPU cores for real-time application. Additionally, they showed the impact of the priority in the soft real-time system on the execution stability of a real-time process. The best result of standard deviation was obtained for real-time mode operated on four CPU cores with one core isolated being used to work with one real-time application. The result with stress showed that although the quality of a soft real-time system is decreased, that the system will still work and execute its own tasks. The ftrace tool slightly loads the operating system so to obtain greater accuracy, other methods of measurements should be used.

Acknowledgements. This publication was supported as part of the Rector's grant in the field of scientific research and development works. Silesian University of Technology, grant no. 02/020/RGJ18/0124.

This work was supported by the Polish National Centre of Research and Development from the project "Knowledge integrating shop floor management system supporting preventive and predictive maintenance services for automotive polymorphic production framework" (grant agreement no: POIR.01.02.00-00-0307/16-00). The project is realised as Operation 1.2: "B+R sector programmes" of the Intelligent Development operational programme from 2014–2020 and is co-financed by the European Regional Development Fund.

References

1. Desai, M., Phadke, A.: Internet of Things based vehicle monitoring system. In: 2017 Fourteenth International Conference on Wireless and Optical Communications Networks (WOCN), pp. 1–3. IEEE, Mumbai (2017)

2. Lee, J., Bagheri, B., Kao, H.-A.: A cyber-physical systems architecture for industry 4.0-based manufacturing systems. Manufact. Lett. **3**, 18–23 (2015)
3. Wang, Y., Vuran, M.C., Goddard, S.: Cyber-physical systems in industrial process control. ACM SIGBED Rev. **5**, 1–2 (2008)
4. Gage, D.W.: UGV history 101: A brief history of Unmanned Ground Vehicle (UGV) development efforts. Naval command control and ocean surveillance center (1995)
5. Stój, J., Smołka, I., Maćkowski, M.: Determining the usability of embedded devices based on Raspberry Pi and programmed with CODESYS as nodes in networked control systems. In: Gaj, P., Sawicki, M., Suchacka, G., Kwiecień, A. (eds.) CN 2018. CCIS, vol. 860, pp. 193–205. Springer, Cham (2018). https://doi.org/10.1007/978-3-319-92459-5_16
6. Tabuada, P.: Event-triggered real-time scheduling of stabilizing control tasks. IEEE Trans. Autom. Control **52**, 1680–1685 (2007)
7. Linux man page: Nice. https://linux.die.net/man/1/nice
8. Linux man page: Shed. http://man7.org/linux/man-pages/man7/sched.7.html
9. Linux Foundation: Real-time. https://wiki.linuxfoundation.org/realtime/start
10. Buttazzo, G.C.: Hard Real-Time Computing Systems: Predictable Scheduling Algorithms and Applications. Springer, Boston (2011). https://doi.org/10.1007/978-1-4614-0676-1
11. Fontanelli, D., Greco, L., Palopoli, L.: Soft real-time scheduling for embedded control systems. Automatica **49**, 2330–2338 (2013)
12. Buttazzo, G.C., Bertogna, M., Yao, G.: Limited preemptive scheduling for real-time systems. a survey. IEEE Trans. Ind. Inform. **9**, 3–15 (2013)
13. Ziebinski, A., Cupek, R., Piech, A.: Distributed control architecture for the autonomous mobile platform. Presented at the Computational Methods in Sciences and Engineering, Thessaloniki, Greece (2018)
14. Szafranski, G., Czyba, R., Janusz, W., Blotnicki, W.: Altitude estimation for the UAV's applications based on sensors fusion algorithm. Presented at the International Conference on Unmanned Aircraft Systems. IEEE, May 2013
15. Ziebinski, A., Cupek, R., Nalepa, M.: Obstacle avoidance by a mobile platform using an ultrasound sensor. In: Nguyen, N.T., Papadopoulos, G.A., Jędrzejowicz, P., Trawiński, B., Vossen, G. (eds.) ICCCI 2017. LNCS (LNAI), vol. 10449, pp. 238–248. Springer, Cham (2017). https://doi.org/10.1007/978-3-319-67077-5_23
16. Grzechca, D., Wrobel, T., Bielecki, P.: Indoor location and identification of objects with video survillance system and WiFi module, September 2014
17. Kobylecki, M., Kania, D., Simos, T.E., Kalogiratou, Z., Monovasilis, T.: Double-tick realization of binary control program. Presented at the AIP Conference Proceedings (2016)
18. Frank Dürr: Raspberry Pi Going Real-time with RT Preempt. http://www.frank-durr.de/?p=203

The Cycle Time Determination for a Soft Real-Time System

Adam Ziebinski[1(✉)], Rafal Cupek[1], and Damian Grzechca[2]

[1] Institute of Informatics, Silesian University of Technology, Gliwice, Poland
{Adam.Ziebinski,Rafal.Cupek}@polsl.pl
[2] Institute of Electronics, Silesian University of Technology, Gliwice, Poland
Damian.Grzechca@polsl.pl

Abstract. Nowadays many Internet of Things solutions used embedded systems that are not equipped with real-time clock. Some of them are used in Unmanned Ground Vehicle platforms that require precise measurements and calculations to move properly and safely. Often such systems are realised as soft real-time Linux systems equipped with real-time path. To improve quality of such systems it is necessary to determine a minimum cycle of time that will allow a stable work of embedded system. In this paper, the authors focus on approaches to verify the performance of Rasbian system in various use cases to obtain a minimum jitter and duration of cycle time for real–time applications that requires a guaranteed response within strict timing constraints of UGV. Additionally, was described a simple approach to determine a minimum cycle time period for a soft real-time system implemented on Raspberry Pi3 based on the maximum confidence interval.

Keywords: Cycle time determination · Embedded systems · Rasbian system · Soft real-time systems

1 Introduction

Cyber-Physical Systems (CPS) [1] enable embedded functionality to be combined through their interactions with the physical world using the infrastructure of the Internet [2] to connect with the digital world. CPS are used in the following fields: manufacturing [3], monitoring [4], distributed [5] and local [6] control, automotive solutions [7] and transportation systems. Developers continuously strive to find new ways to control and monitor end-point devices from any place in the world using stationary and mobile devices [8]. CPS are important for the development of future technologies [9] including the Internet of Things (IoT) [10] and Industry 4.0 [11] because they increase the functionality, efficiency, reliability, adaptability and autonomy of systems. CPS are usually developed as embedded systems [12] equipped with communication functionality in order to control physical processes using feedback loops. Moreover, they are often used for safety and diagnostic purposes [13].

Automotive systems have become more and more complex due to the increasing need for mobility [14]. In addition, many different types of mobile platforms are used to transport various components in many fields. To provide the security and control of the

© Springer Nature Switzerland AG 2019
N. T. Nguyen et al. (Eds.): ICCCI 2019, LNAI 11684, pp. 207–217, 2019.
https://doi.org/10.1007/978-3-030-28374-2_18

movements of mobile platforms, they are equipped with various automotive and electronic sensors [15] and proven Advanced Driver Assistance Systems (ADAS) modules [16], e.g. radar, lidar, infrared, camera or ultrasound sensors. Numerous data acquisition devices and methods with using sensor fusion [17] are used in vehicles for autonomous driving [18]. Often, this is realized by a combination of the simple functions that are performed for a specified task [13]. For example, in order to avoid obstacles [19], a system should calculate the distance and velocity to an obstacle, recognize obstacles and determine the route.

Real physical moving devices should be made as safely as possible for their operators and everything in their surrounding. Therefore, autonomous platforms should be designed in such a way that the timings between a measurement and a reaction are minimized, at the same time they must also be as deterministic as possible [20]. The reduction of any internal latencies should be as large as possible. The repetitiveness and regularity of running specified tasks are also important. Such a system should guarantee deterministic boundaries on delay and jitter (delay variation). Such requirements are necessary when a computer or a controller supervises a physical process. These types of systems are used in all sorts of machines and robots in industrial environments as well as in drones, and autonomous vehicles [21]. Due to the basic level of security of their use, these requirements should also be used in small Unmanned Ground Vehicle (UGV). Programmable logic controllers, which are constructed with inbuilt real-time solutions, are often used in advanced mobile platforms. However, the solutions in cheaper ones often use microcontrollers that are based on the Linux operating system without a real-time clock [22]. In non-real-time system a real-time system functionality can be provided by modifying the Linux kernel with use of the RT-preempt patch.

When an operating system must interact with real physical or cyber physical systems, it should respond as fast as possible [23]. Otherwise, it allows for a possibility to use outdated data, which can cause errors in the current calculation, and as a result, the system makes the wrong decisions. When an operating system must react within expected time limits, time determinism is necessary as in real-time systems [24].

The experimental verification of the performance of such a system in various use cases, enable developers to obtain information about cycle time that could be used in final solution. Additionally it enable to shortening the cycle of work [25] a real-time systems.

In [26] authors performs several experiments on Raspberry Pi 3 (RPi) with usage cyclictest and ftrace tools in idle and stress modes with usage and without the real-time patch. The ftrace tool gives better results than the cyclictest tool. However it turned out, that the time accuracy of the ftrace tool depends on the system load and the ftrace mechanism's wake-up frequency. Nevertheless, it is possible to obtain a better level of precision of time measurements. It was assumed that the timestamps would be registered from within application on RPi prepared for Autonomous Mobile Platform (AMP). Additionally it was assumed that it would be possible to shorten the cycle time of an application for control of an AMP, based on the properties of the maximum confidence interval. The proposed solution was prepared for an UGV controlled by embedded system [26] consist of RPi3 model B and STM32 controller with connected sensors: ultrasound, accelerometer, magnetometer, gyroscope, encoder, GPS and the ADAS module Lidar.

The rest of this paper is organized as follows: in the Sect. 2, the authors describe the results of the system performance on the basis measurements wake-up and go-to-sleep timestamps of a dedicated real–time application for a Raspbian system. In Sect. 3, the authors presented the approach to determine a minimum period of cycle time for a soft real-time system to obtain a minimum jitter and duration of cycle time for real–time applications. The conclusions are presented in Sect. 4.

2 Measurements of Real-Time Determinism

Based on results of experiments with usage cyclitest and ftrace tools presented in [26] it was assumed that measurements of real-time determinism would be realised on dedicated process on the Rasbian system. For that reason, all of the calculations and timestamps (obtained from the clock_gettime) were appended to file directly from the observed process. This could have introduced some overhead but it was assumed that it was possible to obtain a better than mediocre performance of the ftrace logging. To minimise even further, the writing to the SD card overhead, the logs were written to a / tmp/path, which was mounted in the RAM using the tmpfs mechanism. In order to do this, another configuration line was inserted into the /etc/fstab file: tmpfs /tmp tmpfs defaults, noatime, nosuid 0 0.

For the purpose of these tests, a number of measurements were performed using a dedicated process on Rasbian that monitored the Raspberry Daemon process (which control the AMP) and logged its wake-up and go-to-sleep timestamps (Fig. 1). The sched_rt_runtime_us was set the value of −1, the value of the priority was set to 25 and the value of the cycle time period was set to 20 ms for all of the experiments on Raspbian system. During the experiments, several different cores of a CPU (4 or 1 cores "c", in case of 4 cores in mode auto affinity "a" or exclusive core use "i" (core isolated)) were used to execute real-time applications in operating systems that work in idle and stress modes (name of the test in stress was marked with the letter "s") with the real-time patch RT-preempt (RT) and without the real-time patch (nRT). Implemented on Raspbian system real-time patch "RT Preempt" should guarantee deterministic value for delay. The jitter was calculated with using the standard deviation. Moreover were calculated interquartile range based on difference between quartiles Q75 and Q25. It allows to calculate the time range which contain 50% of measured samples of cycle duration of Raspberry Daemon process. The result of all experiments were presented on Fig. 1 and included the wake-up latency and delay for the set of cycle time period and cycle duration of Raspberry Daemon process.

The best result for the wake-up latency was obtained in the case of the RT4ci. The results obtained from the experiments were more precise than in case with usage ftrace tool [26]. The average value was 20.000 ms and the standard deviation was 0.014 ms (compared to results obtained from ftrace tool [26] where average value was 19.967 ms and the standard deviation was 0.801 ms.) The average value of the time of the wake-up delay was 0.029 ms and the standard deviation was 0.014 ms. The average value of the cycle durations was 0.939 ms and the standard deviation was 0.171 ms but the max value of the cycle durations was 18.78 ms. The real-time RT4ca solutions obtained good results too. The average value was 20.000 ms and the standard deviation was a

name	The time of the wake-up latencies				The time of the wake-up delay				The time of the cycle durations of Raspberry Daemon process							
	min	max	avg	std_dev	min	max	avg	std_dev	min	max	avg	std_dev	Q25	Q50	Q75	Q75-Q25
RT4ci	19.95	20.06	20.000	0.014	0.01	0.07	0.029	0.014	0.63	18.78	0.939	0.171	0.876	0.936	0.997	0.121
RT4ca	19.92	20.08	20.000	0.015	0.01	0.13	0.037	0.016	0.59	9.21	0.874	0.133	0.795	0.858	0.940	0.145
RT1c	19.87	20.16	20.000	0.020	0.01	0.18	0.022	0.014	0.50	18.53	0.708	0.176	0.652	0.709	0.754	0.102
nRT4cis	19.94	420.13	20.029	3.279	0.01	34.65	0.057	0.283	0.40	54.58	0.755	0.453	0.670	0.721	0.835	0.165
RT1cs	0.45	676.14	20.047	5.413	0.01	2698.55	0.270	23.542	0.45	110.22	0.868	0.914	0.642	0.950	1.005	0.363
nRT1c	0.63	800.88	20.118	8.392	0.01	780.89	0.092	6.555	0.27	800.84	0.758	6.578	0.533	0.779	0.805	0.272
nRT4ca	0.50	986.15	20.116	9.166	0.01	966.18	0.110	8.454	0.27	986.12	0.782	8.066	0.535	0.755	0.836	0.301
nRT4ci	0.33	1472.95	20.270	15.046	0.01	1452.97	0.199	13.939	0.32	1472.92	0.920	12.064	0.597	0.897	0.932	0.335
nRT1cs	19.05	607.17	20.392	15.146	0.01	1.86	0.032	0.064	0.28	8.80	0.590	0.174	0.498	0.582	0.640	0.142
nRT4cas	19.26	596.55	20.578	18.140	0.01	27.11	0.064	0.246	0.26	47.02	0.764	0.544	0.671	0.747	0.793	0.122
RT4cas	0.35	1664.63	20.384	21.990	0.01	2612.11	0.313	23.562	0.34	830.22	1.210	6.837	0.853	1.237	1.395	0.542
RT4cis	0.51	1676.58	20.879	31.429	0.01	3358.99	2.433	72.719	0.51	1459.47	1.308	13.587	0.800	1.242	1.314	0.514

Fig. 1. The results of the latency [ms] based on a dedicated process on the AMP

little bigger and it was 0.015 ms. The average value of the time of the wake-up delay was 0.037 ms and the standard deviation was 0.016 ms. The average value of the cycle durations was 0.874 ms and the standard deviation was 0.133 ms but the max value of the cycle durations was much lower and it was 9.21 ms. The real-time solutions obtained the best results. The set of cycle time period was maintained with the standard deviation between 0.014 and 0.020 ms for the real-time solutions. In the stress mode, one core solution RT1cs obtained the best results while the four cores with exclusive core use RT4cis obtained the worst results from all cases of real-time solutions. The non-real-time solutions were in the middle of obtained experimental results.

The differences of measurements between dedicated process on the AMP (Fig. 1) and ftrace tools (presented on Fig. 5 in [26]) for RT1c, RT4ca and RT4ci were improved in all cases of the values of std_dev and in case of the values of interquartile range (quartiles Q75 and Q25) of the cycle durations. The values of max, avg and std_dev of the time of the wake-up delay have decreased significantly in the most cases, so proposed method give greater accuracy of measurements then ftrace tool. The comparison of real-time solutions were presented on Figs. 2, 3 and 4. The axis Y contains the measurement time [ms]. For more visibility and not allowing to overlap samples, the measurements results were shifted on axis Y for each case of real-time solutions (the same method was used in the case of Figs. 6, 7 and 8).

3 Determination of Cycle Time

It was assumed that would be possible to determine stable and short the cycle time of work of an application for control AMP running on Linux system in an easy way. Assuming that the measurement results were close to the normal distribution, the multiples of the standard deviation were used in order to obtain the value of the maximum confidence interval, based on the values of average and standard deviation of cycle duration of real-time application (Raspberry Daemon process). In all of the methods (including results in Sect. 2 and [26]) that were used for the measurements, the best result of standard deviation for the wake-up latency was obtained for case real

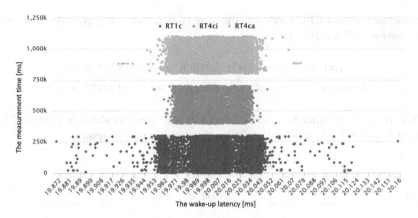

Fig. 2. The comparison of wake-up latency for the real-time cases

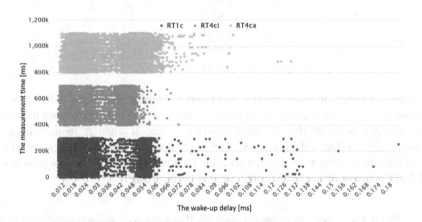

Fig. 3. The comparison of the wake-up delay for the real-time cases

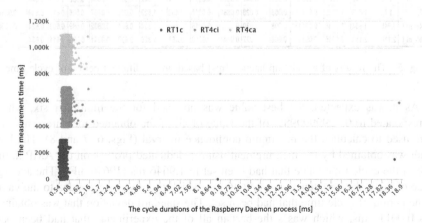

Fig. 4. The comparison of the cycle durations for the real-time cases

time operated on four CPU cores with one core isolated, so further considerations were made for case RT4ci (Fig. 1):

$$\text{Average value of cycle duration} \quad avg = 0.938826 \; [\text{ms}]$$
$$\text{Standard deviation of cycle duration} \quad std = 0.170954 \; [\text{ms}]$$

The values of maximum confidence interval (*mci*) were calculated in a range of 1 to 7 (*m_std*) (value 7 was used only to show the deterioration of results).

$$mci = avg + std \cdot m\_std$$

m_std	mci(m_std) [ms]
1	1.1098
2	1.2807
3	1.4517
4	1.6226
5	1.7936
6	1.9646
7	2.1355

Next, a number of measurements were performed that monitored the Raspberry Daemon process using the calculated values of the *mci* that were used to set the cycle time for each experiment (Fig. 5). Additionally the value of sched_rt_runtime_us were set to −1 and the value of the priority was set to 25. It was assumed that the name of the test include the number related to the set cycle time and symbol "Ft" as usage of ftrace tool ("nFt" in case of usage dedicated process on the AMP).

name	The time of the wake-up latencies				The time of the wake-up delay				The time of the cycle durations of Raspberry Daemon process							
	min	max	avg	std_dev	min	max	avg	std_dev	min	max	avg	std_dev	Q25	Q50	Q75	Q75-Q25
17936_Ft	1.75	1.842	1.7936	0.003501	0.007	0.047	0.0864	0.0017	0.444	1.342	0.633	0.0864	0.590	0.624	0.648	0.0580
17936_nFt	1.78	1.813	1.7936	0.001244	0.008	0.028	0.0887	0.0018	0.453	1.523	0.636	0.0887	0.596	0.617	0.649	0.0530
19646_nFt	1.946	1.984	1.9646	0.001171	0.008	0.030	0.0802	0.0016	0.473	1.314	0.621	0.0802	0.589	0.603	0.624	0.0350
21355_nFt	2.118	2.153	2.1355	0.001176	0.008	0.027	0.0841	0.0016	0.467	1.326	0.627	0.0841	0.593	0.611	0.634	0.0410

Fig. 5. The results of a wake-up latency [ms] based on set different period of cycle time

As it was expected, the best value was obtained for the multiplier six, which corresponded to 0.999999998% of the value of all of the obtained measurements that were used to calculate the maximum confidence interval (Figs. 6, 7 and 8). The best result was obtained by the measurement using a dedicated process on the AMP in the case of the cycle time value that had been set to 1.9646 ms (19646_nFt). The average value of the wake-up latency was 1.9646 ms, which exactly corresponded to the value of the period of cycle time that had been set. The standard deviation that was obtained was 0.00117 ms, which was s the best in all of the experiments that had been performed. The average value of the cycle duration was 0.621 ms, the standard deviation was 0.0802 ms and the max value of the cycle duration was 1.314 ms. The average value of the time of wake-up delay was 0.0802 ms and the standard deviation was 0.0016 ms. The values of quartiles Q75 and Q25 of the cycle durations were more improved in all cases in comparison to value of RT4ci (Fig. 1). The 50% of cycles were executed within a range of 0.035 ms in case of 19646_nFt. So the embedded system based on Rasbian system with running application for control AMP and cycle time value that had been set to 1.9646 ms are much more stable and had the minimum cycle duration then other solutions, even in case RT4ci (Fig. 1). The worst results were obtained for the measurements using the ftrace tool (Ft) performed with the same cycle time that was 1.7936 ms (17936_Ft) in relation to achieved result based on the dedi-cated process on the AMP (17936_nFt). So this difference in the results of measure-ments shows the impact of the system load on the ftrace mechanism's wake-up frequency.

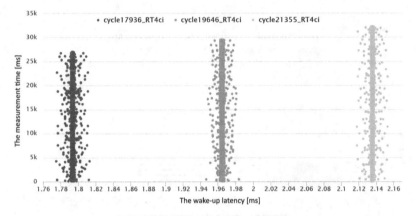

Fig. 6. The comparison of the wake-up latency based on set different period of cycle time

The proposed approach enables the determination a period of cycle time for a soft real-time system to obtain the min jitter and average duration for the stable execution of real-time applications, based on the four steps described below. Firstly, the following should be set: the CPU core to be used, which depends on the available CPU cores and the number of processes that should work in the system in the real-time mode, value −1 in sched_rt_runtime_us and the selected value of the priority, which depends on the Linux operating system. Secondly, measurements of the scheduling latency using a dedicated process on an embedded system that monitors the real-time processes and logs its wake-up and go-to-sleep timestamps should be prepared. For the data that logs the processes could also use the ftrace tool but this would produce less precise results than the dedicated process prepared for this solution. Thirdly, based on the obtained measurements results, calculation of the average and standard deviations of the wake-up latency, cycle durations of real-time application and latencies should be done. Fourthly, based on the earlier calculation, the maximum value of confidence using the multiplier six should be calculated based on average and standard deviation of cycle

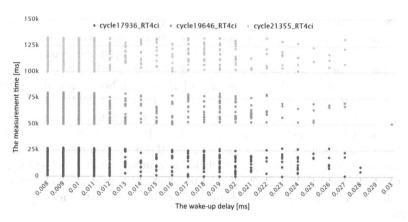

Fig. 7. The comparison of the wake-up delay based on set different period of cycle time

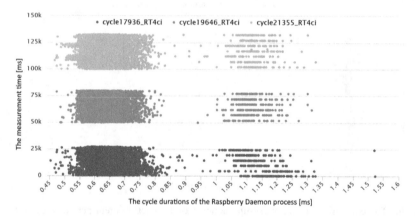

Fig. 8. The comparison of the cycle durations based on set different period of cycle time

duration. The obtained result should be used to the set period of cycle time of soft real-time system.

Based on the proposed method were prepared experiments on the Raspberry Pi 3 with a Rasbian operating system equipped on a real-time RT-preempt patch and with set parameters: period of cycle time 1.9646 ms (the value was calculated based on results obtained from earlier experiments prepared for period of cycle time set to 20 ms), sched_rt_runtime_us value −1 and priority value 25. This method allow to decrease the average cycle duration of real-time application (Raspberry Daemon process) to 0.62 ms with the minimum standard deviation that was 0.0802 ms. Additionally the conducted experiment showed that the adopted value of period of cycle time allows to work regularly for the soft real-time system implemented on Rasbian. This phenomena shows that the real-time application is not pre-empted by other threads.

4 Conclusions

The authors describe a simple method of measurements of real-time determinism based on dedicated process on Linux embedded systems without a real-time clock. During the experiments on Raspbian system, several different cores of a CPU were used to run real-time applications that work in the idle and stress modes with and without a real-time patch installed in the operating system. The obtained results were compared with results of experiments with usage cyclitest and ftrace tools presented in [26]. Experiments showed that cyclictest is a good tool that generally allows the performance of a system and its limitations to be seen. Ftrace is a much better tool for monitoring the switching mechanism. However, the best results were obtained when based on a dedicated process on the AMP. This is because the ftrace tool loads more on the operating system than a dedicated process on the AMP. Application of the presented measurement methods allows to obtain an effective version of the configuration of the soft real time system depending on the use of real-time mode and the specific processor cores. Additionally the authors describe a simple approach to determine a minimum period of cycle time for a soft real-time system, based on the maximum confidence interval for the average and standard deviation of the duration of the cycle of real-time application. The obtained minimum period of cycle time allow for real-time applications be stable executed with minimum average cycle duration and jitter. The results that were obtained experimentally confirmed the correctness of the proposed approach.

Acknowledgements. This publication was supported as part of the Rector's grant in the field of scientific research and development works. Silesian University of Technology, grant no. 02/020/RGJ18/0124.

References

1. Cyber-Physical Systems (CPS) (NSF17529) | NSF - National Science Foundation. https://www.nsf.gov/pubs/2017/nsf17529/nsf17529.htm
2. Wu, F.-J., Kao, Y.-F., Tseng, Y.-C.: From wireless sensor networks towards cyber physical systems. Pervasive Mobile Comput. **7**, 397–413 (2011). https://doi.org/10.1016/j.pmcj.2011.03.003
3. Wang, Y., Vuran, M.C., Goddard, S.: Cyber-physical systems in industrial process control. ACM SIGBED Rev. **5**, 1–2 (2008). https://doi.org/10.1145/1366283.1366295
4. Ziebinski, A., Bregulla, M., Fojcik, M., Kłak, S.: Monitoring and controlling speed for an autonomous mobile platform based on the hall sensor. In: Nguyen, N.T., Papadopoulos, G.A., Jędrzejowicz, P., Trawiński, B., Vossen, G. (eds.) ICCCI 2017. LNCS (LNAI), vol. 10449, pp. 249–259. Springer, Cham (2017). https://doi.org/10.1007/978-3-319-67077-5_24
5. Cupek, R., Huczala, L.: Passive PROFIET I/O OPC DA Server. Presented at the IEEE Conference on Emerging Technologies & Factory Automation. ETFA 2009 (2009)
6. Kobylecki, M., Kania, D.: FPGA implementation of bit controller in double-tick architecture. Presented at the AIP Conference Proceedings (2017). https://doi.org/10.1063/1.5012400
7. Li, R., Liu, C., Luo, F.: A design for automotive CAN bus monitoring system, September (2008). https://doi.org/10.1109/VPPC.2008.4677544

8. Jazdi, N.: Cyber physical systems in the context of Industry 4.0. Presented at the 2014 IEEE International Conference on Automation, Quality and Testing, Robotics, May 2014. https:// doi.org/10.1109/AQTR.2014.6857843

9. Baheti, R., Gill, H.: Cyber-physical systems. the impact of control technology. IEEE Control Syst. Soc. **12**, 161–166 (2011)

10. Buk, B., Mrozek, D., Małysiak-Mrozek, B.: Remote video verification and video surveillance on android-based mobile devices. In: Gruca, D.A., Czachórski, T., Kozielski, S. (eds.) Man-Machine Interactions 3. AISC, vol. 242, pp. 547–557. Springer, Cham (2014). https://doi.org/10.1007/978-3-319-02309-0_60

11. Shafiq, S.I., Sanin, C., Szczerbicki, E., Toro, C.: Virtual engineering object/virtual engineering process: a specialized form of cyber physical system for Industrie 4.0. Procedia Comput. Sci. **60**, 1146–1155 (2015). https://doi.org/10.1016/j.procs.2015.08.166

12. Marwedel, P.: Embedded System Design: Embedded Systems Foundations of Cyber-Physical Systems. Springer, Netherlands (2010). https://doi.org/10.1007/978-94-007-0257-8

13. Grzechca, D., Ziębiński, A., Rybka, P.: Enhanced reliability of ADAS sensors based on the observation of the power supply current and neural network application. In: Nguyen, N.T., Papadopoulos, G.A., Jędrzejowicz, P., Trawiński, B., Vossen, G. (eds.) ICCCI 2017. LNCS (LNAI), vol. 10449, pp. 215–226. Springer, Cham (2017). https://doi.org/10.1007/978-3-319-67077-5_21

14. Ji, Z., Ganchev, I., O'Droma, M., Zhao, L., Zhang, X.: A cloud-based car parking middleware for IoT-based smart cities: design and implementation. Sensors **14**, 22372–22393 (2014). https://doi.org/10.3390/s141222372

15. Fleming, W.J.: Overview of automotive sensors. IEEE Sens. J. **1**, 296–308 (2001). https:// doi.org/10.1109/7361.983469

16. Bengler, K., Dietmayer, K., Farber, B., Maurer, M., Stiller, C., Winner, H.: Three decades of driver assistance systems: review and future perspectives. IEEE Intell. Transp. Syst. Mag. **6**, 6–22 (2014). https://doi.org/10.1109/MITS.2014.2336271

17. Garcia, F., Martin, D., de la Escalera, A., Armingol, J.M.: Sensor fusion methodology for vehicle detection. IEEE Intell. Transp. Syst. Mag. **9**, 123–133 (2017). https://doi.org/10.1109/MITS.2016.2620398

18. Behere, S., Törngren, M.: A functional architecture for autonomous driving. Presented at the Proceedings of the First International Workshop on Automotive Software Architecture (2015)

19. Jia, X., Hu, Z., Guan, H.: A new multi-sensor platform for adaptive driving assistance system (ADAS). In: 2011 9th World Congress on Intelligent Control and Automation, pp. 1224–1230 (2011). https://doi.org/10.1109/WCICA.2011.5970711

20. Pułka, A., Milik, A.: Dynamic reconfiguration of threads in real-time system working on precision time regime. Presented at the 2010 International Conference on Signals and Electronic Systems (ICSES) (2010)

21. Murikipudi, A., Prakash, V., Vigneswaran, T.: Performance analysis of real time operating system with general purpose operating system for mobile robotic system. Indian J. Sci. Technol. **8**, 1–6 (2015). https://doi.org/10.17485/ijst/2015/v8i19/77017

22. Vijayakumar, N., Ramya, R.: The real time monitoring of water quality in IoT environment. In: 2015 International Conference on Innovations in Information, Embedded and Communication Systems (ICIIECS), pp. 1–5. IEEE, Coimbatore (2015). https://doi.org/10.1109/ICIIECS.2015.7193080

23. Mollison, M.S., Erickson, J.P., Anderson, J.H., Baruah, S.K., Scoredos, J.A.: Mixed-criticality real-time scheduling for multicore systems. In: 2010 10th IEEE International Conference on Computer and Information Technology, pp. 1864–1871. IEEE, Bradford (2010). https://doi.org/10.1109/CIT.2010.320

24. Bruzzone, G., Caccia, M., Bertone, A., Ravera, G.: Standard Linux for embedded real-time manufacturing control systems. In: 2006 14th Mediterranean Conference on Control and Automation, pp. 1–6. IEEE, Ancona (2006). https://doi.org/10.1109/MED.2006.328773

25. Sidzina, M., Kwiecien, A., Stoj, J.: Shortening of the automata cycle of industrial communication system nodes. In: Lee, G. (ed.) 2nd International Conference on Advances in Computer Science and Engineering, pp. 169–175, France (2013)

26. Ziebinski, A., Cupek, R., Drewniak, M., Wolny, B.: Soft real-time systems for low-cost unmanned ground vehicle. In: Nguyen, N.T., Chbeir, R., Exposito, E., Aniorte, P., Trawiński, B. (eds.): ICCCI 2019, LNAI, vol. 11684, pp. 196–206. Springer, Heidelberg (2019)

An OPC UA Machine Learning Server for Automated Guided Vehicle

Rafal Cupek[1(✉)], Łukasz Gólczyński[2], and Adam Ziebinski[1]

[1] Institute of Informatics, Silesian University of Technology, Gliwice, Poland
{rcupek,aziebinski}@polsl.pl
[2] AIUT Sp. z o.o. (Ltd.), Gliwice, Poland
lgolczynski@aiut.com

Abstract. Preparing training data sets for supervised machine learning is particularly difficult when the input information has a serial nature and the data sources are non-deterministic. This paper discusses a problem related to preparing a data set for the machine learning algorithms that are used for Automated Guided Vehicles (AGV). An OPC UA server that is dedicated for machine learning support was designed in order to comply with the communication standards and information models that are used in the new generation of manufacturing systems. The proposed approach not only utilises communication features of OPC UA technology but also its rich possibilities for information modelling. The OPC UA server that was created converts raw input data into a format that can be easily applied for the machine learning process. The presented solution is dedicated for the AGV that are used for internal logistics in flexible production systems. The authors discuss the different information models that are available for the OPC UA standard and explain the design choices that were made when preparing the server. The presented solution was verified during the development process for a new family of AGV that is being designed and produced by the AIUT Company.

Keywords: Automated Guided Vehicle · AGV · Machine learning ·
Communication middleware · OPC UA (IEC 62541) ·
Machine-to-Machine (M2M) communication

1 Introduction

Automated Guided Vehicles (AGV) have become a key enabling technology for the flexible internal logistics that is required for agile production systems. The usefulness of AGV results not only from their technical features, but also from ability to cooperate, which determine their efficient use as a part of flexible manufacturing services. Modern production systems are characterised by frequent changes that result from orders that are changed by customers, low material buffers, the agile production technologies that are performed by robotised production stands and the many variants of production technology that can be selected [1]. All of the above-mentioned factors require the production process to be supported online by highly advanced information services, which are performed during the successive steps of the production chain. This

© Springer Nature Switzerland AG 2019
N. T. Nguyen et al. (Eds.): ICCCI 2019, LNAI 11684, pp. 218–228, 2019.
https://doi.org/10.1007/978-3-030-28374-2_19

means that the production activities cannot be centrally planned, but have to be optimised locally with respect to the ongoing production tasks, available materials, production equipment and technologies. The new generation of manufacturing execution systems has to support the autonomy and distribution of decision-making processes.

In this context, internal logistics that are based on AGV have to be dynamically adjusted to frequently changing production tasks [2]. Artificial intelligence that is based on supervised machine learning can be used to optimise logistical tasks. This requires a multi-criteria optimisation that takes into an account the opposing goals that are connected with the requirements for of materials and semi-product movements. This process must be performed in a distributed, dynamic and autonomous way [3]. Moreover, AGV have to communicate with production stands, Manufacturing Execution Systems (MES) and other AGV. For this reason, the machine learning data has to be analysed within the broader context of Machine-to-Machine (M2M) communication. This requires, on the one hand, adjusting the information that is collected from the production systems into a form that is suitable for automatic processing by artificial intelligence algorithms, and, on the other hand, the results that are produced by these algorithms have to be converted into a form that can be used by the production systems [4]. One of key enabling technologies for creating communication middleware is OPC UA. OPC UA is an industrial communication standard that is widely supported not only by specific technology providers but also by a number of national level industry hubs such as the US Industrial Internet Consortium or German Industry 4.0 [5].

This work focuses on the information models for communication middleware that support the supervised machine learning process for AGV. The authors not only analyse the communication standards that are used for AGV but also the meaning of specific information parts. OPC UA forms a bridge between the raw process data that is used by the AGV and the annotated and structuralised information that is used by the machine learning algorithms. OPC UA not only enables data exchange but also enables significant components of the data vector to be selected and their appropriate conversion into the required representation formats to be ensured. The presented use case is an OPC UA server that is used to develop new artificial intelligence algorithms that are dedicated for a new family of AGV that are being designed and produced by the AIUT Company. The rest of this paper is organised as follows: the Sect. 2 presents the information modelling features that are available for the OPC UA technology. The control architecture for AGV and internal information flow is presented in Sect. 3. The Sect. 4 presents the main design choices that were made when preparing the OPC UA server. It also presents some details about the information models that were used and the OPC UA services that were utilised. The conclusions are presented in Sect. 5.

2 OPC UA Communication Middleware

OPC UA is a service-based communication middleware that not only supports the exchange of information but also provides meta information about the models that are used to organise the OPC UA's address space. It utilises WebServices to communicate with enterprise management systems and for the TCP-based communication with the control systems. In terms of security, OPC UA uses the solutions that are appropriate for a given family of protocols. The security of the information exchange is managed by a Secure Channel Service Set, which defines a long-running logical connection between an OPC UA client and server [6]. This channel maintains a Public Key Infrastructure (PKI) that is used to authenticate and encrypt the messages that are sent across the network. OPC UA is a scalable, reliable and safe middleware that can not only be used as a data connector but also as a translator for information models that can be used to match different information systems [7].

OPC UA communication follows a stateful model. The state information is maintained inside each Session, which is defined as the logical connection between the OPC UA Client and Server. Examples of state information are subscriptions, user credentials and continuation points for any operations that span multiple requests. Each Session is independent of the underlying communications protocols. Failures of these protocols do not automatically cause the Session to terminate [8]. OPC UA became the IEC 62541 standard in 2012.

OPC UA is based on an object-oriented paradigm and offers rich information modelling capabilities, which are used to present information and meta information. The automatic components of OPC UA are its Nodes and References [9]. All nodes and references are exposed as an OPC UA server's address space, which can be browsed by connected clients. There is also a reference mechanism that is also object oriented. The types of all of the references are known so that the type of relationship between the nodes can be determined. When using this mechanism, clients have the possibility to discover all of the information models that are managed by the server.

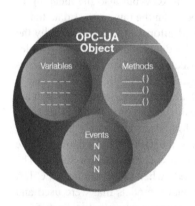

Each OPC UA node is uniquely identified by its NodeID and belongs to one of eight classes, which are indicated by their NodeClass attribute. Nodes that belong to the class Objects represent real-world objects such as system components or software items. Each instance of an OPC-UA object (Fig. 1) is defined by its type and must have a reference to its ObjectType. Objects can be used to organise other Objects and Variables. Objects can generate Event Notifications in order to inform clients about object's state change. Clients can also execute Methods available for a given object [10].

Fig. 1. OPC-UA object [9]

The physical process variables and properties are represented as instances of VariableType. Variables change their values in time and can be read, written and subscribed by the OPC Clients. Each Variable must have a reference to its VariableType. The attribute that is called DataType indicates the data type of the value that is represented by a given Variable.

Methods represent any function that can be called by a client. Methods can have properties that describe their input and output arguments. Views are used to present a subset of the Nodes in the server's Address Space. The View Node organises the Nodes and acts as the root for the Nodes that are contained in the View.

Effective communication is supported by a Data Access mechanism. Subscriptions are the information services that are performed as part of individual sessions. The number of Monitored Items for each subscription is agreed upon between the client and server. These mechanisms allow clients to access the process data directly. In this model, a client subscribes to variables with given parameters – Sampling Interval (ms) and Filter Conditions. According to the defined tracking conditions, the OPC UA server sends new information to the client only if the source information changes and the change fit the defined filters. Data transfers are optimised by grouping them within sessions for efficiency. The published request responses are not sent immediately, but are queued by the server. The responses (NotificationMessages) are sent back according to the Subscription's publishing interval. The NotificationMessages contain either Notifications of MonitoredItems (when there is an event to be reported to the client) or a KeepAlive message (a dummy message to notify the client that the server is operational). The main principles of OPC UA server organisation are presented in Fig. 2.

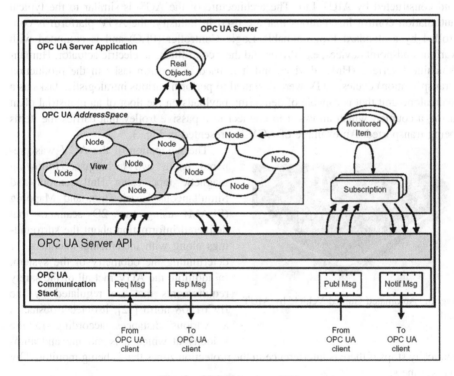

Fig. 2. OPC-UA server [11]

The OPC Historical Access (HA) provides an interface to a historical archive that can be used by various applications such as the HMI, Report Generation, Analysis etc. The data that is provided by the historical interface consists of historical records and, optionally, various calculated values such as the min, max, average etc. The HA enables a client to access the historical variable values and events. The Client can read, write or modify these data. Since OPC UA is only a communication interface, the historical data is stored in an external database. Both the Data Access and Historical Access modes follow a common memory model. Each client can freely choose the information in the server's address space and request access to the data in accordance with the requirements that they have defined. A different communication principle was adopted for the information about Events. All subscribed clients receive precisely the same messages about events (which is not the case in the common memory model). Clients do not subscribe to an event itself but select the information source, which can be any OPC UA object.

3   Automated Guided Vehicles – Architecture and Data Flow

An OPC UA machine learning server was created to support the machine learning algorithms that are used for the Automated Guided Vehicles (AGV) being designed and constructed by AIUT Ltd. The architecture of the AGV is similar to the typical automation control installations that are used in industry: the AGV platform is controlled by a standard Programmable Logic Controller (PLC) and is equipped with various end-point devices, e.g. drives and their controllers, an electric actuator, Human-Machine Interface (HMI) devices and it is used to perform tasks in the production (transportation) cycles. AGV were designed to perform various intralogistics tasks as a standalone unit that is capable of delivering payloads on the floor of an industrial plant using a coupler, which allows it to connect to a passive trolley that carries the items being transported. An example of AGV is presented in Fig. 3.

Fig. 3. Automated Guided Vehicle by AIUT Ltd.

The navigation of the AGV was prepared using two techniques: following magnetic tape using Hall sensors and Simultaneous Localisation and Mapping (SLAM) using two 2D scanners that delivered information about the surroundings along with incremental encoders for determining the odometry of the system. In addition, the AGV met all of the safety requirements that are regulated by the IEC61508 norm [12]; it detects obstacles at various distances according to the velocity at which it is moving and automatically stops if there is interference in the protection zones that is being monitored by the scanners.

The transportation tasks that are performed by AGV vary depending on the customers and their applications. Typically, the routes and execution of transportation orders are set by either an external IT system, e.g. a Manufacturing Execution System (MES) or a Warehouse Management System (WMS), or manually by technical personnel using a dedicated HMI device. Once the AGV is on the route, it executes all of the necessary actions by itself; however, remote access remains possible if the platform is within the range of the internal communication network. In the event that more AGV are moving on the same floor, a supervisory unit is required in order to control the traffic and avoid deadlocks, e.g. Fleet Control software or a master PLC.

The increasing demands of customers to monitor and diagnose industrial equipment forced AIUT Ltd. to develop a solution that grants access to all of the process data that is generated by all of the onboard devices. Such data contains all of the processing signals that are produced by the PLC controller (permissions, control signals, statuses), safety system (safety control signals, statuses), odometry (velocities and distances travelled by wheels), navigation systems (settings, statuses, location coordinates, the steps that are currently being performed and orders) and other onboard devices (energy consumption signals, control statuses and settings from the drive controllers). Although this data is stored for potential use in the event that anomalies are detected, it can also be used for other applications, e.g. predictive or preventive maintenance of onboard devices, optimisation of the transportation tasks as well as business analytics, which includes calculating the Key Performance Indicators (KPI) and Overall Equipment Efficiency (OEE).

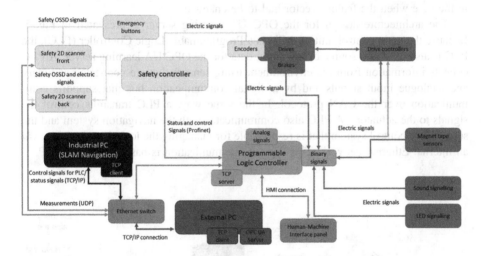

Fig. 4. General architecture and data flow for the AGV solution.

Because of the variety of processing signals that are gathered from the onboard systems and produced by the main onboard controller, storing them for future applications can play a significant role in developing and diagnosing AGV. Therefore, the existing system for communicating with external industrial IT systems was enhanced with methods that apply the concept of OPC UA that were proposed by the authors in previous chapters. The concept of a modified data flow for the AGV solution is presented in Fig. 4.

4 OPC UA Machine Learning Server for AGV

The supervised machine learning approach requires a set of learning data to be properly prepared. In most cases, this process focuses on eliminating any instances of noise, deviations that have too many null feature values, normalising values, converting symbolic attributes, selecting the feature subset, eliminating outliers etc. [13]. The most important design requirements for an OPC UA based learning server for AGV were: (i) to permit access to the information that is produced, processed and consumed by the AGV for the machine learning algorithms. The server had to provide stable connectivity that could be understood as the immutability of the data descriptors and the way that the information was presented even in the event of changes in the internal AGV data structure (for example, changes connected with the location of the information or changes in its scaling algorithms); (ii) to permit repetitive and selective access to the collected information; (iii) to permit the free selection of the input data that would be used by the machine learning algorithms. The server should support the repeatability of the machine learning process based on the collected experimental data set, permit the repeatable selection of the input vector and ensure consistent training experiments even in the case when the feature vector had to be changed.

The architecture design for the OPC UA learning server is presented in Fig. 5. Because the main control unit of AGV is a Programmable Logic Controller (PLC), the PLC is also used as a source of raw input data for the OPC UA learning server. A PLC collects information from the environment using sensors that are connected as binary and analogue input signals and by a digital communication bus that supports communication over the CAN protocol. In the same way, a PLC transmits control the signals to the actuators. A PLC also communicates with the navigation system and the supervisory control system that is responsible for managing the logistics operations *via* an internal Ethernet network. This type of communication is based on the TCP/IP.

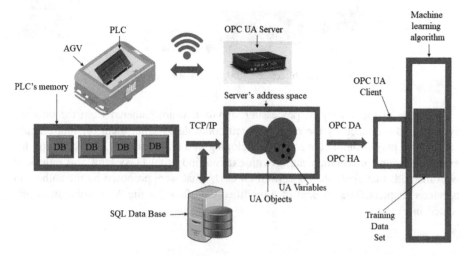

Fig. 5. Architecture of an OPC UA Machine Learning Server for AGV.

TCP/IP was also selected for the communication between the PLC and the OPC UA server. The solution was based on the cyclical transmission of TCP frames that contain selected areas of the PLC's memory. The frames were determined by specific identifiers and were divided into several types according to the data they contain, e.g. ID = 6000 contained the signals and statuses of all of the onboard devices, ID = 6001 contained the general processing signals of the whole AGV, ID = 7000 contained the odometry signals etc. The OPC UA server established the connection with the passive TCP server that was activated in the PLC and the data started to be transmitted. The cyclical transmission timers were set differently (from 100 to 2000 ms) for each frame in relation to their priority.

All of the information that was processed by the PLC was organised as Data Blocks (DBs). Each DB was a repository for a number of machine words [14]. The stored information was interpreted according to the context of the read/write operation as a single bit, a 16- or 32-bit-long machine word or as a more complex structure such as a float, double or date-time. The memory content was cyclically updated with the information that was downloaded from the sensors. The information that was prepared for the actuators was also stored in the PLC's memory and exchanged on a cyclical principle. Such a solution is typical for the majority of industrial control systems. Communication with the PLC was organised under a common memory paradigm, which creates the illusion of free multiple access for all of the devices that share the information. In fact, it should be remembered that in real-time systems, the validity of the information is limited to a specified period of time. In the case of communication *via* a common memory data exchange, the period has to be determined by the temporal validity of data. This principle also applies to the communication between the PLC and the OPC server.

Fig. 6. OPC UA objects that reflect information send by communication frames

The information exposed by the OPC UA server is available to OPC clients that are using the subscription mechanism online. According to the OPC UA Data Access communication principle, each client determines the individual period for each subscribed data item (OPC Variable), which determines how often the OPC UA server has to check at the source to determine whether any new information is available. Because the communication band is optimised, information between the server and client is only sent when there is a data change in the source. It should be remembered that the period of information exchange between the OPC UA server and the OPC UA client is independent from the period of information exchange between the PLC and OPC UA server. The selection of a period that is too short by the client will not affect the more up-to-date data, but will only increase the load on the OPC server. On the other hand, a data exchange cycle that is too long can cause the variables to be out of date. For this reason, each of the variables that are provided by the OPC server indicates the source the refreshing time that is visible to the OPC clients. The OPC UA Object Type definition for communicating with AGV is presented in Fig. 6.

In order to permit the repeatable use of the collected information, the OPC UA server stores the subsequent frames that are received from the AGV in an external database. This process is controlled by the OPC clients that can call the StartRecording and StopRecording methods on the OPC server. The Methods StartReplay and StopReplay are used to replay the information that was stored during the training sessions. The time and speed for replaying is selected using the appropriate parameters. The information is then available for the machine learning process by the selective Data Access mechanism, which is performed by the OPC UA clients and are used as data connectors for the machine learning algorithm. Because DA uses two time stamps, one for the data production and the second for the OPC server, historical data can be used repeatedly without losing their consistency. For the analysis of the information that is produced by AGV, the source timestamp is used. The server timestamp is used for connection control by client in order to ensure continuity of data flow.

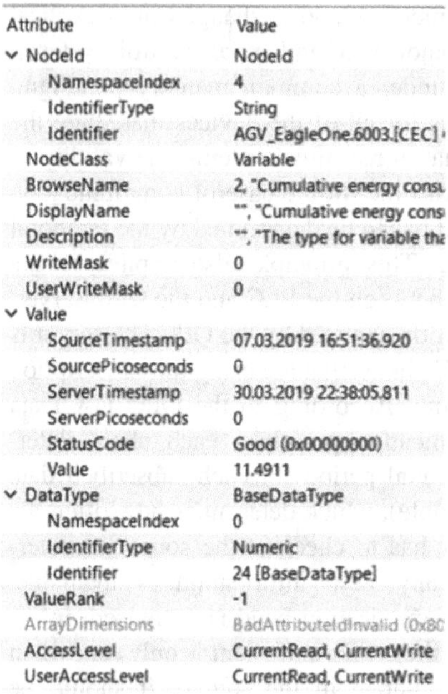

Attribute	Value
∨ NodeId	NodeId
NamespaceIndex	4
IdentifierType	String
Identifier	AGV_EagleOne.6003.[CEC]
NodeClass	Variable
BrowseName	2, "Cumulative energy const.
DisplayName	"", "Cumulative energy cons
Description	"", "The type for variable tha
WriteMask	0
UserWriteMask	0
∨ Value	
SourceTimestamp	07.03.2019 16:51:36.920
SourcePicoseconds	0
ServerTimestamp	30.03.2019 22:38:05.811
ServerPicoseconds	0
StatusCode	Good (0x00000000)
Value	11.4911
∨ DataType	BaseDataType
NamespaceIndex	0
IdentifierType	Numeric
Identifier	24 [BaseDataType]
ValueRank	-1
ArrayDimensions	BadAttributeIdInvalid (0x80
AccessLevel	CurrentRead, CurrentWrite
UserAccessLevel	CurrentRead, CurrentWrite

Fig. 7. UA Variable's attributes

The second OPC UA mechanism that is available to access the training data set is the Historical Access (HA). In this case, the OPC HA client receives selected information from the server that was collected during the required time period. The HA mechanism can be used simultaneously by several clients, each of which determines an individual time range and data content for the retrieved historical information. Compared to the DA mechanism, HA requires a much greater complexity to process data on the client side. The HA client has to store the large data sets that are received from the server. Usually, HA clients use an external database system. Regardless of the method that is used by a client for data access, both approaches permit multiple repetitions of the machine learning process and ensure the consistency of the data The information access layer of the OPC UA server is organised as a set of OPC UA objects that are connected to the data that is transmitted by an AGV as TCP frames. The information that is sent to clients in the DA or HA mode is converted according to the presentation rules that are defined in .xml files. These rules specify how to decode the raw data into specific variable formats as well as which part of the TCP frame contains the required information. The XML descriptions are prepared independent of the data collection process. Such an approach enables the iterative refinement of the training vector structure that is used in subsequent experiments. The example, a UA object that exposes the amount of electricity that was consumed by the AGV is presented (Fig. 7).

5   Conclusions

In this paper, the authors have described the architectural design and implementation details for the OPC UA learning server that was used for machine learning for Automated Guided Vehicles. The presented solution uses the communication mechanisms and data modelling capabilities that are available for the OPC UA standard. All of the operations connected with preparing the training set including collecting the data, selecting the information to be included in the feature vector, scaling the individual components and selecting the time range of the data to be used for the experiment were performed by the OPC UA server. Such an approach makes it possible to separate the machine learning process from the process of preparing the training data. The knowledge about the data structure and AGV communication mechanisms is used to prepare the training data set more efficiently compared to the approach in which the information is prepared on the side of the machine learning algorithms.

The most significant benefit of the proposed methodology is the stable and repeatable access to the information that is produced, processed and consumed by AGV. The machine learning algorithms have the ability to freely select the input feature vector and the data that is collected during the tests. This supports the repeatability of the machine learning process that is based on the collected experimental data set that can be used for training with a different composition of the input feature vector and for selected experimental observations.

Acknowledgements. (1) This work was supported by the Polish National Centre of Research and Development from the project "Knowledge integrating shop floor management system supporting preventive and predictive maintenance services for automotive polymorphic production framework" (grant agreement no: POIR.01.02.00-00-0307/16-00). The project is realised as Operation 1.2: "B+R sector programmes" of the Intelligent Development operational programme from 2014–2020 and is co-financed by the European Regional Development Fund.

(2) This publication was supported as part of the Rector's grant in the field of scientific research and development works. Silesian University of Technology, grant no. 02/020/RGJ19/0169.

References

1. Maskell, B.: The age of agile manufacturing. Supply Chain Manag. Int. J. **6**(1), 5–11 (2001.)
2. Cupek, R., Ziebinski, A., Fojcik, M.: An ontology model for communicating with an autonomous mobile platform. In: Kozielski, S., Mrozek, D., Kasprowski, P., Małysiak-Mrozek, B., Kostrzewa, D. (eds) Beyond Databases, Architectures and Structures. Towards Efficient Solutions for Data Analysis and Knowledge Representation. BDAS 2017. CCIS, vol. 716, pp. 480–493, Springer, Cham. https://doi.org/10.1007/978-3-319-58274-0_38
3. Wan, J., Yi, M., Li, D., Zhang, C., Wang, S., Zhou, K.: Mobile services for customization manufacturing systems: an example of industry 4.0. IEEE Access **4**, 8977–8986 (2016)
4. Cupek, R., Ziebinski, A., Drewniak, M., Fojcik, M.: Knowledge integration via the fusion of the data models used in automotive production systems. Enterp. Inf. Syst. 1–26 https://doi.org/10.1080/17517575.2018.1489563

5. Lin, S.W., et al.: Whitepaper zu "Architecture Allignment and Interoperability" von Platform Industrie 4.0 und Industrial Internet Consortium, pp. 1–19, December 2017. https://www. iiconsortium.org/pdf/JTG2_Whitepaper_final_20171205.pdf

6. Virta, J., Seilonen, I., Tuomi, A., Koskinen, K.: SOA-based integration for batch process management with OPC UA and ISA-88/95. In: Proceedings 15th Conference on Emerging Technologies & Factory Automation ETFA, Bilbao, Spain, September 2010

7. Imtiaz, J., Jasperneite, J.: Scalability of OPC-UA down to the chip level enables "Internet of Things". In: 2013 11th IEEE International Conference on Industrial Informatics (INDIN), pp. 500–505. IEEE, July 2013

8. Cupek, R., Folkert, K., Fojcik, M., Klopot, T., Polaków, G.: Performance evaluation of redundant OPC UA architecture for process control. Trans. Inst. Measur. Control 39(3), 334–343 (2017)

9. Lange, J., Iwanitz, F., Burke, T.J.: OPC – From Data Access to Unified Architecture, pp. 111–130. VDE Verlag, Berlin (2010)

10. Mahnke, W., Leitner, S.H., Damm, M.: OPC Unified Architecture, pp. 156–175. Springer, Berlin (2009)

11. OPC Foundation, "OPC Unified Architecture Specification Part 1: Overview and Concepts Release 1.04", 22 November 2017

12. IEC 61508: Functional safety of electrical/electronic/programmable electronic safety-related systems

13. Kotsiantis, S.B., Kanellopoulos, D., Pintelas, P.E.: Data preprocessing for supervised leaning. Int. J. Comput. Sci. 1(2), 111–117 (2006)

14. Berger, H.: Automating with SIMATIC: Controllers, Software, Programming, Data. Wiley, Somerset (2012)

Monitoring of Chronic Arthritis Patients with Wearables - A Report from the Concept Phase

Paweł Mielnik[1], Krzysztof Tokarz[2], Dariusz Mrozek[2], Piotr Czekalski[2], Marcin Fojcik[1,3(✉)], Anja Myhre Hjelle[1], and Mateusz Milik[2]

[1] Section for Rheumatology, Department for Neurology, Rheumatology and Physical Medicine, Helse Førde, Førde, Norway
{pawel.franciszek.mielnik,anja.myhre.hjelle}@helse-forde.no
[2] Institute of Informatics, Silesian University of Technology, Gliwice, Poland
{krzysztof.tokarz,dariusz.mrozek,piotr.czekalski}@polsl.pl
[3] Western Norway University of Applied Sciences, Bergen, Norway
marcin.fojcik@hvl.no

Abstract. This paper presents the concept of the IoT system for chronic arthritis patients monitoring with the usage of an inexpensive and comfortable wrist-band, avoiding expensive, medical equipment. We based on the raw data from the wristband to collect and analyze patients activity using dedicated, Android-based application to record and temporarily store data also considering its privacy and protection. We present detailed plots and linear regression analysis on circadian measurements on raw acceleration data, heart rate and a number of steps taken by a sample subject, then weekly analysis of the activity based on the aggregated accelerometer activity data. Finally, we present an IoT solution architecture for current and future studies, showing detailed information on the wristband used, including wristband's protocol analysis over Bluetooth Low Energy, application level communication via MQTT and cloud data storage.

Keywords: Patient monitoring · Internet of Things · Wristband · Chronic arthritis

1 Introduction

Nowadays we can observe growing attention for using Internet of Things (IoT) technology in area of healthcare. IoT technology can be successfully used in gathering information about physical activities, including simple activity like walking distance. It can be very valuable for example in elderly people healthcare [1]. Currently available IoT devices, especially wearables, can gather information about major life parameters as heart rate, ECG, body temperature, blood pressure and saturation. Data can be collected locally and presented only for the

© Springer Nature Switzerland AG 2019
N. T. Nguyen et al. (Eds.): ICCCI 2019, LNAI 11684, pp. 229–238, 2019.
https://doi.org/10.1007/978-3-030-28374-2_20

subject. More promising solution is to send data to the medical center for professional analysis. The mobile phone can be used as the universal sensing and communication platform. Additionally it is possible to send information about the current location of the user, body position, even falls and strokes [2]. The main drawback of utilizing the smartphone as the monitoring device is the need to carry the device with the user all the time. Continuous measurements and data transmission has also adverse effect on battery lifetime during the day and requirement of frequent charging. Biomedical parameters and activity can be collected with wristband which allows to monitor amount of physical exercise (walking, running, number of steps, distance) pulse, quality of sleep [3]. Data can be send to the medical center by smartphone or dedicated device which plays role of the network gateway. Connection between the wristband and communication device can be established using Bluetooth wireless link. In the most smart bands the Bluetooth Low Energy (BLE) protocol is used because its energy efficiency and simple implementation [4].

Chronic arthritis is a heterogeneous group of autoimmune diseases affecting mainly joints. Despite outstanding progress in the therapy they are still important case of disability and have enormous economic impact both on societies and individuals [5]. Better monitoring of patients' physical activity can in theory lead to better follow up of the patients and improve disease outcomes. Wearables seem to be an ideal candidate for this propose but clinical data is limited. The aim of our project is to develop a research tool to assess daily mobility of the patients with chronic arthritis. The propose of this manuscript is to assess usefulness of a sport watch (Xiaomi MiBand 3®) in this area. This is important issue because the band is not developed as scientific but fitness tool. We had to assess if it has acceptable accuracy and reproducibility.

2   Wristband Operating Analysis

There are some wearables dedicated for medical/research use on the market [6]. We decided however to choose, due to more optimal prize, one of available sport band, Xiaomi MiBand 3®. We believe that our chose provides many advantages. The wristband is little, comfortable in wearing, as well as waterproof with 5ATM protection level. It allows to take normal daily activities like bath or shower when the band is worn. The band uses the Bluetooth 4.2 protocol to communicate with other devices. It uses the Health Device Profile (HDP) that is a standard used in the medical devices like scales, glucometers, thermometers, pulse and blood pressure meters and others. For advanced users it allows also to check the current number of steps on built-in display. Its battery ensures operating time up to 20 days that reduces the need of frequent charging.

Unfortunately, detailed hardware and software specification was not published by the manufacturer. This apply also to the protocol which the device uses to store and exchange the data. This is the main disadvantage.

The band stores data about pulse, steps and average accelerometer activity on minute basis in quite long period. The exactly data logging period is not specified by the manufacturer. According our experience it is minimum 40 days and possibly longer. The data is saved in order: time, activity, average acceleration measurement, steps and pulse. Steps and pulse data is easy understandable, despite it is not known counting algorithm. If pulse was not measured it is logged value "255" is recorded. If a measurement attempt was unsuccessful "1" value is saved.

The meaning of saved acceleration data and activity category is not clear. The saved acceleration values correlate with general physical activity, but calculation method is not available. Some of the activity categories explanation is possible to stipulate. For example value "6" is written during charging. Values over "1002" correspond with very low physical activity, often with relatively low heart rate (HR) what can be observed in sleep. Values between "1" and "100", excluding "6", correlate inversely with physical activity insensitivity.

There is possible to obtain live, raw data from the accelerometer, as well as live pulse measurements. The frequency of the accelerometer refresh rate, we were able to acquire, was 24 Hz. Raw acceleration data are represented in numerical values in a range ±1020. In a simple experiment with longitudinal acceleration measurement from the device resting on the horizontally leveled base, we calculated that values about "255" correspond with standard gravity. It can be anticipated that maximal acceleration value is about 4G. Estimated error was ±0.0223G. All information above was deduced basing on available specification and personal experience with the device.

We collected information from both saved data and raw accelerometer activity. We used it in preliminary analysis in aim to asses if MiBand 3®. is suitable for our further research. Data was collected from one of the authors. It was therefore consider as not medical study, not requiring informed consent.

3 Literature Review

Outstanding technological development in wearables and IoT area increases interest for use it in medical research and eventually medical practice. Amount of publications in this area grows extremely fast.

Paper by Wu et al. [7] describes a health monitoring system composed of an electrocardiograph, a heart rate monitor, two thermometers measuring the body and ambient temperature as well as a three axial accelerometer. Measurements made by the device were sent to the computer via the Bluetooth protocol.

The authors of the project described in [8] assembled a system from sensors placed on the body of the monitored person. It was connected to an intermediate device, a smartphone or microcontroller, which send the measurements to the Web Service in the cloud.

In the system design presented in the next publication [9] the mobile application collected data from sensors such as motion sensor, blood pressure meter, heart rate monitor. The mobile application saved data in the local database and synchronized it with the database stored in the cloud. The project also assumed that the mobile application was capable to read the geographical location of the subject by the GPS receiver and send the location to the medical caregivers and/or to the family. Authors of the solution described in [10] monitored the physical state of the supervised person. The system reported parameters such as consumption of beverages, use of the toilet and the number of calories burned while walking based on the localization data.

In [11] authors presented the system that collected data from two types of sensors: body temperature and blood pressure. To achieve the communication certainty three redundant communication channels were proposed for data transfer and alerting the medical center – WiFi, Bluetooth, cellular phone and built-in GSM module. Authors of the next paper [12] compared nine commercially available motion tracking devices that could be used in continuously and closely monitoring individuals' activities. Such devices are not typically designed for medical application where it is needed high accuracy. However, they can provide measurements of various parameters that can help the user as well as the physician to follow up health status. Medical data are by definition sensitive and should be safeguarded before out-sourcing to the cloud environment. In [13] authors propose strong authentication and configuration controls that should be implemented at the cloud environment. Security of data transmission is achieved by using the GSM module that is password protected with encrypted communication. The data can be accessed by the medical caregivers after successful logging to the web page.

There is only few publication about use of wearables in rheumatic diseases, particularly in the chronic arthritis.

Condell et al. presented sensor equipped gloves which is able to recognize complicated fingers movement patterns [14]. Authors provided tools to detect fingers stiffness that is one of essential disease activity parameter in arthritis affecting hands.

Accelerometer based devices can be used to calculate daily physical activity as was shown in cross - sectional study on rheumatoid arthritis patients (RA) [15]. It can help to predict cardiovascular risk. Other study shows that step detector can underestimate steps count by 26% in patients with RA [16]. It can lead to fail estimation of physical activity. Such discrepancies were not observed for accelerometer data.

Different approach was presented in work by Andreu-Perez et al. [17]. Authors made acitgraphies from accelerometer placed at L5 vertebral level for 10 RA patients and 20 healthy controls. They analyzed different type of simple activity, such walking or sitting, to find characteristic pattern. Similar methods can detect abnormalities in movement pattern dependent on disease activity.

4   Results of Measurements

Data from minute based logging was collected in a period 40 days. We analyzed circadian rhythm for all parameters. Results from acceleration data are shown in the Fig. 1, from steps counting at the Fig. 2 and HR at the Fig. 3. All activity parameters correspond well with self-observed physical activity. It can be observed pause in accelerometer and steps activity dependent on sleep. No fail spontaneous activity was observed at this period. Physiological tendency to bradycardia and more regular pulse at sleeping can be also observed.

Figure 4 shows activity category as it is recorded by the device. As mentioned above values over 100 correspond with sleeping or very low physical activity. Numbers under 100 inversely correlate with insensitivity of activity both as observe by subject and by linear regression function of acceleration, HR and steps. Linear regression coefficients were: -0.16665, -0.05712, -0.02551 with $p < 0.001$ for all terms.

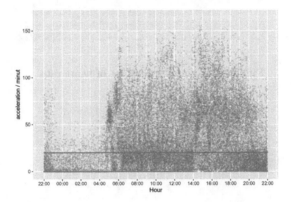

Fig. 1. Scatter-plot of circadian acceleration activity saved by the wristband.

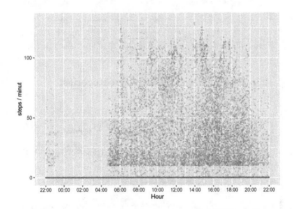

Fig. 2. Scatter-plot of circadian steps log recorded by the wristband.

Figure 5 show the data grouped by week day. It is easy to observe different pattern for different days.

We could not collect enough raw accelerometer data to conduct more advanced analyzes but acceleration signal was stable, with low noise. Pattern for different activity was easy to recognize (Figs. 6 and 7).

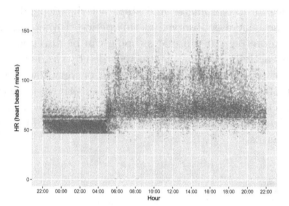

Fig. 3. Circadian scatter-plot of heart rate.

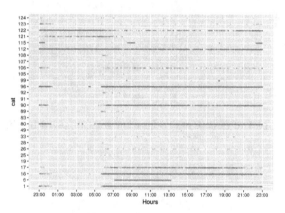

Fig. 4. Physical activity categories.

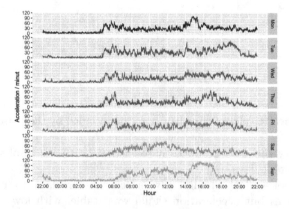

Fig. 5. Recorded accelerometer activity divided by week day

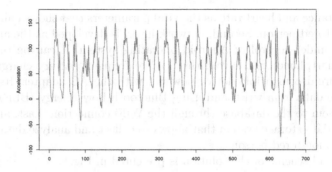

Fig. 6. Plot of raw accelerometer data from a one axis during walking.

Figure 6 was recorded while the subject was going round a table, Fig. 7 when the subject was standing and typing. X axis of the plot presents each time point data were collected. As the frequency is 24 Hz, recording period was about 29 s.

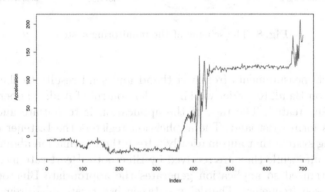

Fig. 7. Plot of raw accelerometer data from a one axis while standing.

5   Discussion

There are 3 possible scenarios for future studies:

1. The wristband standard saved data can be collected
2. Raw accelerometer data can be collected at the site, during patient visit,
3. Raw accelerometer and/or saved data can be collected.

The two first possible scenarios do not need further software or hardware development as data can be transferred directly to site based computer. For the third scenario we plan to set up a system based on previous experiences. The solution created previously was intended for monitoring elderly people. It consists of three layers corresponding to the IoT layered architecture as described in the literature [18]. The device that operates in the first, perception layer is the wristband. We used the Xiaomi MiBand 2® that is capable to measure the step-ping, walking distance and heart rate as the vital parameters that shows daily activity of the monitored person. Second, network layer, is developed as the application that works under control of Android operating system. It can be run on any Android smartphone or, to avoid the need of frequent battery charging, standalone Android compatible device powered with the AC adapter. Its function is to receive data from wristband using Bluetooth Low Energy (BLE) protocol and send them to the database through the WiFi connection. Last, application layer is the data storage system that allows to collect and analyze data gathered from many monitored persons.

The overall scheme of the solution is presented in Fig. 8.

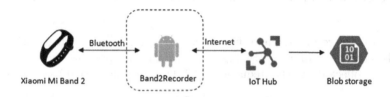

Fig. 8. The scheme of the monitoring system.

To collect measurements from wristband and send results to the database the application Band2Recorder working under control of Android operating system has been created. The task of the application is to initiate and perform the readings form wristband. The application registers the Listener objects in the operating system that automatically refresh the information about the measurement results while they are received by Bluetooth. Heart rate measurement must be initialized so application generates the appropriate Bluetooth frame with the chosen frequency. The delay between heart rate measurements influence the battery life time so it can be set by the user between 1 and 30 min. The actual number of steps is sent by the wristband automatically while the monitored person is moving, there is no need to initiate every measurement. It is enough to send only once an initial data frame to turn on receiving messages about the number of steps performed. Messages with information on the number of steps taken are sent even every few seconds if the user moves constantly.

Application sends the gathered data to the database that was implemented in the Cloud system. Communication between mobile phone and the Cloud storage is done with the Message Queue Telemetry Transport (MQTT) protocol widely used in the IoT systems. This protocol supports short data frames which are sufficient for proposed solution. A single transmitted message has always the size of 862 B.

In the proposed solution we plan to replace the MiBand 2® with the new MiBand 3® wristband. It is due to better physical parameters of the newer device, especially better water resistance. To ensure the measurement data protection the Cloud storage is planned to be replaced with dedicated server with access control managed by the local administrator. Additionally it is planned to test the possibility to run the Band2Recorder application on the stationary platform working under control of Android operating system like Odroid or similar.

6 Conclusion

Xiaomi Mi band 3® seems to be promising option for clinical studies in rheumatic diseases. The wristband is reliable, provide sufficient data and is conformable for a subject. Additional software and hardware development can be necessary to meet the researchers' need and regulatory requirements. It is especially important to satisfy privacy and data protection requirements.

References

1. Wan, J., et al.: Wearable IoT enabled real-time health monitoring system. EURASIP J. Wirel. Commun. Netw. **2018**(1), 298 (2018)
2. Dubey, D., Amritphale, A., Sawhney, A., Amritphale, N., Dubey, P., Pandey, A.: Smart phone applications as a source of information on stroke. J. Stroke **16**(2), 86 (2014)
3. Zhang, T., Lu, J., Hu, F., Hao, Q.: Bluetooth low energy for wearable sensor-based healthcare systems. In: 2014 IEEE Healthcare Innovation Conference (HIC), pp. 251–254. IEEE (2014)
4. Sawamto, J., Watanabe, K., Yajima, H., Kurosawa, M., Taniguchi, Y.: Research on hybrid information evaluation type watching technology for the improvement of QOL of the elderly. Procedia Comput. Sci. **126**, 967–975 (2018)
5. Williams, E.M., Walker, R.J., Faith, T., Egede, L.E.: The impact of arthritis and joint pain on individual healthcare expenditures: findings from the Medical Expenditure Panel Survey (MEPS) 2011. Arthritis Res. Ther. **19**(1), 38 (2017)
6. Iqbal, M.H., Aydin, A., Brunckhorst, O., Dasgupta, P., Ahmed, K.: A review of wearable technology in medicine. J. R. Soc. Med. **109**(10), 372–380 (2016)
7. Wu, S., Li, D., Wang, X., Li, S.: Examining component-based city health by implementing a fuzzy evaluation approach. Ecol. Ind. **93**, 791–803 (2018)
8. Doukas, C., Maglogiannis, I.: Managing wearable sensor data through cloud computing. In: 2011 IEEE Third International Conference on Cloud Computing Technology and Science, pp. 440–445. IEEE (2011)
9. Navya, M., Nihitha, A., Koundinya, A.K.: Cloud based applications for health monitoring systems using wearable sensors. In: 2016 International Conference on Computation System and Information Technology for Sustainable Solutions (CSITSS), pp. 370–374. IEEE (2016)
10. Park, C., Kim, J.: A location and emergency monitoring system for elder care using zigbee. In: 2011 Seventh International Conference on Mobile Ad-hoc and Sensor Networks, pp. 367–369. IEEE (2011)
11. Swaroop, K.N., Chandu, K., Gorrepotu, R., Deb, S.: A health monitoring system for vital signs using IoT. Internet Things **5**, 116–129 (2019)
12. Haghi, M., Thurow, K., Stoll, R.: Wearable devices in medical internet of things: scientific research and commercially available devices. Healthc. Inform. Res. **23**(1), 4–15 (2017)

13. El Zouka, H.A., Hosni, M.M.: Secure IoT communications for smart healthcare monitoring system. Internet Things (2019). https://doi.org/10.1016/j.iot.2019.01.003

14. Condell, J., et al.: Finger movement measurements in arthritic patients using wearable sensor enabled gloves. Int. J. Hum. Factors Model. Simul. **2**(4), 276–292 (2011)

15. Khoja, S.S., Almeida, G.J., Chester Wasko, M., Terhorst, L., Piva, S.R.: Association of light-intensity physical activity with lower cardiovascular disease risk burden in rheumatoid arthritis. Arthritis Care Res. **68**(4), 424–431 (2016)

16. Larkin, L., Nordgren, B., Purtill, H., Brand, C., Fraser, A., Kennedy, N.: Criterion validity of the activ PAL activity monitor for sedentary and physical activity patterns in people who have rheumatoid arthritis. Phys. Ther. **96**(7), 1093–1101 (2016)

17. Andreu-Perez, L., et al.: Developing fine-grained actigraphies for rheumatoid arthritis patients from a single accelerometer using machine learning. Sensors **17**(9), 2113 (2017)

18. Andrea, I., Chrysostomou, C., Hadjichristofi, G.: Internet of things: security vulnerabilities and challenges. In: 2015 IEEE Symposium on Computers and Communication (ISCC), pp. 180–187. IEEE(2015)

Quality of Service in Real-Time OPC UA Applications

Marcin Fojcik[1]([✉]), Rafal Cupek[2], Adam Ziebinski[2], Olav Sande[1],
and Martyna Katarzyna Fojcik[3]

[1] Western Norway University of Applied Sciences, Bergen, Norway
{marcin.fojcik,olav.sande}@hvl.no
[2] Silesian University of Technology, Gliwice, Poland
{rafal.cupek,adam.ziebinski}@polsl.pl
[3] Volda University College, Volda, Norway
martyna.fojcik@hivolda.no

Abstract. There are many different requirements for communications systems and therefore the types of communications systems in the modern world. There are also special requirements in automation. It is not only necessary to provide data exchange to monitor and control the processes but also to gather, store and process all of the data to optimise production as well. There are different requirements for the amount of data, for the delivery time and for the semantic relationships between the measurements. Although there are some standards, none of these is good enough as yet. One of those standards is OPC UA. Unfortunately, in many practical situations, OPC UA is also regarded as not being good enough to be used. The issues are primarily about the time parameters – the client does not always receive the information in the specified time. In this paper, the authors will present some of the limitations and give some suggestions for improving the time parameters of OPC UA systems in practical applications.

1 Introduction

Industry 4.0 is an actual trend in the automation processes. The main idea is to change and improve the communication system between all of the devices and to enable more effective operations. There are many different solutions to this problem. One of these is the OPC Unified Automation standard – IEC standard 62541. The German organisation – *Reference Architecture Model for Industrie 4.0 (RAMI 4.0) recommended OPC Unified Architecture (OPC UA) for implementing the communication layer* [1]. As a result, any product being advertised as "Industrie 4.0-enabled" must be OPC UA capable (either integrated or via a gateway) [2].

The term industry 4.0 (I4.0) describes 'the fourth industrial revolution' where the internet merges with production and products. The term 'Industrial Internet of Things – IIoT, is used for systems in which industrial assets communicate with end users over the internet. If the end user is a customer accessing industrial

N. T. Nguyen et al. (Eds.): ICCCI 2019, LNAI 11684, pp. 239–248, 2019.
https://doi.org/10.1007/978-3-030-28374-2_21

assets through the IIoT, the I4.0 principle requires factory production systems to not only process a product, the product itself communicates with the production system by giving the production instructions to the industrial assets. The production systems organise themselves, thus enabling customers' orders to be automatically converted to manufacturing instructions [3].

The idea is that future factories will be so flexible that every product can be customised without any increased cost relative to a large-scale production series. To achieve this, it is necessary to have a capable data system. The data system must be compatible with the communication system. It is important that the communication system should be efficient both for both real-time control and for sending large amounts of data [4,5]. In addition, it should store the semantic structure of the information. Nowadays, there are some solutions for communication systems such as OPC UA, DDS, MQTT and CoAP. However, none of them meets all of the requirements. They each have both strengths and weaknesses. OPC UA has communication that corresponds with addressing the memory model on the server. This model fits with the hardware and helps with the compatibility and cooperation between devices. On the other hand, OPC is not effective for quickly sending information to many clients. DDS is effective in transmission, which has many properties, does not have information about the origin of the data [6].

The most important parameter for communication systems is the quality of the transmission. One of the ways to evaluate communication is to measure some of its properties. This can be done by using Quality of Service. QoS is the description or measurement of the overall performance of a server. There are several related aspects of network communication such as throughput, transmission delay, jitter etc. This paper describes some of the parameters that can affect the real-time requirements for the whole production system.

This paper is divided into six sections. Section 2 presents the OPC protocols. Section 3 presents the industry requirements for OPC communication. Section 4 describes the experimental stand. The results of the tests are presented in Sect. 5. Section 6 includes a summary and some ideas for future research.

2   OPC UA as an Industrial Standard

The Standard OPC UA describes both the communication and the addressing model in one system. OPC UA is based on a Client/Server architecture and it uses the object-oriented data model. All available services are independent of any specific protocols (Fig. 1).

On the one hand, OPC looks very promising as the standard for automation. On the other hand, there have been many complaints that there are problems with real-time communication [8]. There are hardly any scientific publications on its success in industry real-time systems that use OPC UA. Theoretically, it should work correctly, some problems arise but in specific situations. Some of the problems with using OPC UA in industry may result from the structure of the system. The OPC UA standard only covers some industry systems. This can

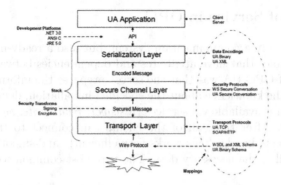

Fig. 1. Protocol stack for OPC UA [7]

cause some problems with gathering information in real time. The server is not the source of the data for the clients. The server receives the information from an underlying communication structure and the communication performance of this structure affects the overall communication performance of the overlying OPC UA communication system. The next problem is that according to the actual standards, communication between the server and the client is realised by the standard TCP/IP protocol suite, which cannot guarantee real-time transmissions of the data. For each client, the server needs a different copy of the data (MonitoredItems) and has to transmit each of the MonitoredItems separately (Fig. 2), which is not effective.

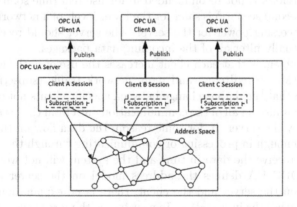

Fig. 2. Server-Client structure [7]

There are different applications and solutions for OPC UA. This results in a problem in determining the situations in which the server-client communication can work properly in real time.

3 Quality of Service in OPC

OPC UA is not only a communication system, but also a ready-made model of addressing variables that have attributes and dependencies between them. The very first idea of OPC UA was that the server prepares the information model, including all of the knowledge about the specified installation, device or process. This information is available via services (*discover, read, write, subscribe, event, call method*) [7]. After that, all of the clients can connect to the server and perform the expected tasks. This works very efficiently and smoothly as long as the server has all of the necessary data. The two most common scenarios in the industry are:

- the server should receive the data from an automation device such as a PLC or smart sensor each time the client wants it,
- the server is passive; it gathers the available data from the underlying devices and filters them as necessary.

The second scenario has some additional options. The server can listen to (observe) the ongoing communication, which can be based on the regular polling or transmitting data from the devices on any data change – event-based communication. The other possibility is to use the embedded server in the automation device and smart sensor to get rid of the underlying network.

Although the first scenario is easier to realise, it disrupts the real-time exchanges on the lower levels of a network, which causes interruptions in the network, which could result in more data packages suddenly appearing in the network. This can hinder real-time communication and can lead to some malfunctions. Therefore, is not recommended in for use real-time solutions.

While the second scenario is safer for the lower levels of a network, it requires much more processing power for the server. The server should receive, analyse, store and eventually filter all of the incoming data packages.

Another problem is that each client increases the use of both the processing on the server (MonitoredItems) and more network traffic (subscription). It is visible in Fig. 3 that the data exchange between specific clients not only depends on the server, but also on all of the communication data from the lower levels that are processed by the server. If, for some reason, the data flow on the lower level is not efficient enough in processing or communicating through the network, the server will not receive the data in time and the system will not work correctly.

Although OPC UA defines the address model on the server and communication between the server and the client, there is no explanation of how the server should gather the information. In a system with more levels, [9] the servers receive different data packages. On the higher levels of communication, the server communicates with one or more clients. On the lower levels, however, the server receives the data from sensors, PLS or networks [10].

There are some limitations to the OPC system. Firstly, the communication system between the server and the client is limited by the amount and size of the data packages. OPC UA does not define one, specific protocol. There are many possible protocols that can be used such as OPC binary, HTTP and HTTPS.

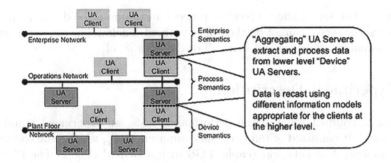

Fig. 3. Aggregation in OPC UA [7]

All of the above are based on TCP/IP, which can be used in different solutions, although none of these solutions directly deals with the real-time issue.

Each client can subscribe to its own variables (MonitoredItems) and the server should store separate copies of the same variables for different clients. This leads to increased use of both the computational power of the server and the traffic on the network.

All of the problems with the OPC UA services are caused by the delays in processing. It is obvious that each action requires time. In the next part of the paper, the authors will present some of the elements that affect the server's performance. The elements can be divided into three parts:

1. processing the incoming data (from the sources to the server)
2. processing the address model (inside the server)
3. processing the outgoing communication (from the server to the clients)

There is much current research that is investigating points 2 and 3 in an effort to improve the standard. Among others, there are new exchange types – PubSub [11], through which the server can no longer be connected directly to the client, although there is another element between them – Middleware. The server sends data to the Middleware once and the clients can read the data from the Middleware on demand. This improves both the traffic (point 3) and processing on the server (point 2) and enables the server to prepare one common MonitorItem for each subscribed value regardless of how many clients subscribe. A solution that can improve outgoing communication would be to use Time Sensitive Networking (TSN) [12], which is planned to be in the OPC roadmap in 2019 [13].

As to point 1, no action has been taken to improve the communication between the source and the server. This is not covered in the OPC UA standard and each application must solve this problem on its own. The server can poll each of the required data. This is safe for the server, but causes additional traffic on the network, which, in some situations, can lead to problems with the time parameters. The other solution that is used in the industry, listening to the data from the network, is safe for the network, but it adds an additional load for the server. The server should receive, process and update the data. In some of situations, the server cannot do these jobs without a delay. The processor on the server is unable to receive and store all of the data [8,14].

4   Experiment Description

In order to conduct some of the performance tests, an experiment stand was constructed. It consisted of ten personal computers (PC), which were connected to two independent networks (cable, 1 Gb with a switch) (Fig. 4) The PC were divided: four of them produced the data for the tests (Datasource), two PC with OPC UA Servers and four PC acted as the Clients. One of the servers (Server1) was set on an i7-8700K with six cores (12 threads)@3.7 GHz, 64 GB RAM, 2×1 GB network cards with Windows 7. The second (Server2) was set on an i5-2320 with two cores (four threads)@2.5 GHz, 8 GB RAM, 2×1 GB network cards also on Windows 7. The data sources sent the data every 50 ms through the Ethernet (with size that ranged from 50 to 1000 values depending on the tests). The Servers received the data, filtered and processed it, and finally used it to update the address model. The Clients subscribed to different amounts of data.

Only service subscriptions were used in the test; there were no read or write services. The Servers collected and processed the data and many of their internal parameters such as the processing time for the network, filtering, updating, memory use, CPU use, network use, the amount of the data for each Client and the amount of MonitoredItems. These additional values were observed as Historical Data on the Clients after the tests.

5   Experiment

In the efficiency tests that are performed in local networks there are often enough to test the average situation. Short delays can be treated as an inconvenience for end users. In automation (production), the worst-case scenarios should be tested. This is because all of the data that are transferred are important and it is not allowed to miss any of them. In a normal situation of production, there are only a few measurements/parameters that change often and quickly. However, most of the values do not change. Unfortunately, in the event of a failure, the number of changing elements increases drastically. Industry networks have to send all of the data that is required to control the production in a safe and efficient manner. In future experiments, the worst case will be tested.

5.1   Impact of Amount of Incoming Data on Servers

There were four PC that sent 100, 200 and 500 values to the Servers every 50 ms. Each of these values was subscribed (each 500 ms) to by Clients. Both Servers collected and updated the data. The idea of the test was to determine whether

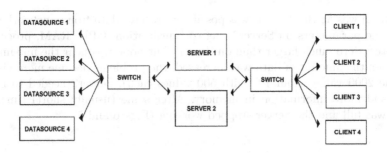

Fig. 4. The structure of the system

the Servers were capable of receiving and processing all of the data. It was not necessary to send the data to Clients. Some of the values were observed and are presented on the charts. For the 800 values (four PC with 200 values each), Server1, which had an i7, had no problems updating. Server2 had visible delays. In Fig. 5, the top chart presents the correct presentation of the sinus values from the data sources. All of the data are correct. The bottom chart presents the disruptions. The values are not presented correctly.

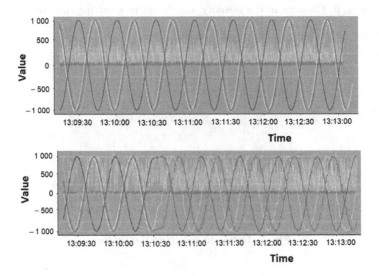

Fig. 5. Problems in correct updating

The data in the Servers were saved with a timestamp in the receiving data. It was possible to improve the situation when Server2 was not using its own timestamp but the one from the Datasource, which helped to get the correct time history for the values. Visible disruptions were caused by fact that Server2 could not receive and process the incoming data in real time. In addition to the CPU use (which was at 70–80%), it was possible to receive data from a network card. All of the parameters on Server2 (network utilisation, CPU, RAM, processing time etc.) were much larger than on Server1 but none was near the maximum.

When the amount of data was increased, the problems became more visible. For the 2000 values (four PC with 500 values each), Server2 needed to buffer more and more information in memory. After some (usually short) time, the RAM was full and the Server stopped working (Figs. 6 and 7).

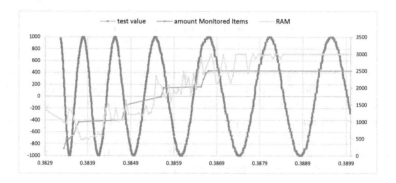

Fig. 6. Changes in the memory and delays in receiving the values

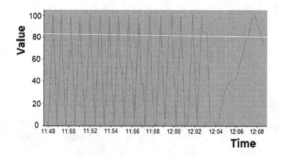

Fig. 7. Delays in receiving the values

The Datasources sent 800 values (four PC with 200 values each). During the tests, the number of Clients that were connected and had a subscription was increased. Each Client subscribed to all of the data. Figure 7 presents the situation for 20 clients. A total of 16 000 MonitoredItems were created and updated on each server.

It is visible that the server was able to receive the correct data from some of the datasources. At the same time, the servers could not receive the data from the other datasources. The top chart is for Server1. Server1 had some problems with one of the datasources. The bottom chart is for Server2. The information from Datasources 3 and 4 was unusable. However, none of the properties (RAM, CPU, network) of Server2 was near the maximum. During the observations, there was no single parameter that indicated problems on Server2. It was the combination of CPU, RAM and MonitoredItems that caused delays on the servers. The combination was different on each server (Fig. 8).

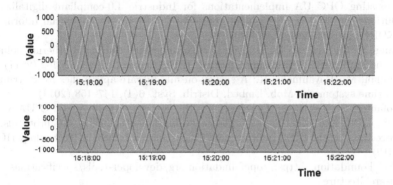

Fig. 8. Measurements from different sources

6   Conclusion

The OPC UA system has some advantages and some disadvantages. In a real-time environment, it is not possible to use OPC UA "from the box" as the standard. It is necessary to configure both the server and incoming traffic. One of the solutions could be the intelligent filtration of the network. Using an "intelligent" switch, the system can reduce the traffic and processing time on the server. However, filtration can lead to "missing" data. For the time being, OPC UA uses a mechanism that enables the client to subscribe to values at defined intervals. However, no information is available on the client application that shows how often the data should be read. If the client subscribes to the data too quickly, it uses the server unnecessarily. If the client subscribes to the data to slowly, it leads to the loss of values.

A subscription is often not an effective enough solution. PubSub looks more promising especially for servicing a large number of clients because it reduces both CPU use and the network load.

Delays that are the result of processing incoming traffic are always possible and are very difficult to avoid completely. Although there is no single parameter in the server (application on PC) that would be entirely and solely responsible for this, there are combinations of parameters. Monitoring these parameters makes it possible to determine the limitations of the server.

Future work will focus on finding ways to intelligently filter and prepare OPC servers (through additional software and connection) to deliver reliable data in real time.

References

1. OPC Foundation. https://opcconnect.opcfoundation.org/2017/06/there-is-no-industrie-4-0-without-opc-ua/
2. Usländer, T., Epple, U.: Reference model of Industrie 4.0 service architectures. at-Automatisierungstechnik **63**(10), 858–866 (2015)
3. Haskamp, H., Meyer, M., Möllmann, R., Orth, F., Colombo, A.W.: Benchmarking of existing OPC UA implementations for Industrie 4.0-compliant digitalization solutions. In: 2017 IEEE 15th International Conference on Industrial Informatics (INDIN), pp. 589–594. IEEE (2017)
4. Wang, S., Ouyang, J., Li, D., Liu, C.: An integrated industrial ethernet solution for the implementation of smart factory. IEEE Access **5**, 25455–25462 (2017)
5. Saghian, M., Ravanmehr, R.: A survey on middleware approaches for distributed real-time systems. J. Mob. Embed. Distrib. Syst. **6**(4), 147–158 (2014)
6. Profanter, S., Tekat, A., Dorofeev, K., Rickert, M., Knoll, A.: OPC UA versus ROS, DDS, and MQTT: performance evaluation of industry 4.0 protocols. In: Proceedings of the IEEE International Conference on Industrial Technology (ICIT) (2019)
7. OPC Foundation. https://opcfoundation.org/developer-tools/specifications-unified-architecture
8. Fojcik, M., Folkert, K.: Introduction to OPC UA performance. In: Kwiecień, A., Gaj, P., Stera, P. (eds.) CN 2012. CCIS, vol. 291, pp. 261–270. Springer, Heidelberg (2012). https://doi.org/10.1007/978-3-642-31217-5_28
9. ISA95. https://opcfoundation.org/markets-collaboration/isa-95/
10. Cupek, R., Fojcik, M., Sande, O.: Object oriented vertical communication in distributed industrial systems. In: Kwiecień, A., Gaj, P., Stera, P. (eds.) CN 2009. CCIS, vol. 39, pp. 72–78. Springer, Heidelberg (2009). https://doi.org/10.1007/978-3-642-02671-3_8
11. OPC Foundation. https://opcfoundation.org/developer-tools/specifications-unified-architecture/part-14-pubsub/
12. Pfrommer, J., Ebner, A., Ravikumar, S., Karunakaran, B.: Open source OPC UA PubSub over TSN for realtime industrial communication. In: 2018 IEEE 23rd International Conference on Emerging Technologies and Factory Automation (ETFA), vol. 1, pp. 1087–1090. IEEE (2018)
13. OPC Foundation. https://opcfoundation.org/about/opc-technologies/opc-ua/opcua-roadmap/
14. Fojcik, M., Sande, J.: Some problems of integrating industrial network control systems using service oriented architecture. In: Kwiecień, A., Gaj, P., Stera, P. (eds.) CN 2013. CCIS, vol. 370, pp. 210–221. Springer, Heidelberg (2013). https://doi.org/10.1007/978-3-642-38865-1_22

Some Solutions for Improving OPC UA Performance

Marcin Fojcik[1]([✉]), Olav Sande[1], Martyna Katarzyna Fojcik[2],
Are Sjåstad Bødal[1], Tor Erik Haavik[1], Kristoffer Hjartholm Kalstad[1],
Bjørnar Brask Sittlinger[1], and Torbjørn Ryland Steinholm[1]

[1] Western Norway University of Applied Sciences, Bergen, Norway
{marcin.fojcik,olav.sande}@hvl.no,
{246941,160260,160271,160262,160264}@stud.hvl.no
[2] Volda University College, Volda, Norway
martyna.fojcik@hivolda.no

Abstract. The need to exchange more data in industry is growing. Automation requires more and more data to adapt technology to industrial needs correctly. This is visible in both industry (Factory 4.0) and in the Internet of Things (IoT). All these data are produced, transferred, processed and stored for further use. An affordable communication system that permits all of the necessary operations to be performed quickly and reliably is needed. One of the proposals is OPC UA. Unfortunately, there are many situations in which OPC UA is not efficient for various reasons. One of them is the lack of real-time communication in OPC UA. Another situation that is not suited for OPC UA is the setup of the server and incoming data.

In this paper, the authors will try to present some of the limitations and propose ways in which to improve the time parameters of OPC UA systems in practical applications.

1 Introduction

Nowadays, there are new technologies and factories that can design each product to meet customer requirements without increased costs relative to a large-scale production series. Figure 1 presents a typical production facility that is organised according to ISA95 [1]. The customer orders (and pays for) a product electronically using some type of web technology. The Enterprise Resource Planning (ERP) system confirms the order, adapts the order to the capabilities of the production control system and transfers the modified order to the Manufacturing Execution System (MES). The MES converts the order into production instructions and transmits the production instructions to the Human Machine Interface (HMI) for further modifications and verifications in real-time. Ideally, the MES transmits production instructions directly to the Production Control System (PCS) without any human interaction. The PCS automatically adapts and coordinates the production assets in order to produce the ordered product.

© Springer Nature Switzerland AG 2019
N. T. Nguyen et al. (Eds.): ICCCI 2019, LNAI 11684, pp. 249–258, 2019.
https://doi.org/10.1007/978-3-030-28374-2_22

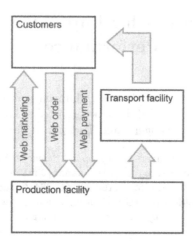

Fig. 1. General view on production method

During the production process, the product communicates interactively with the PCS, which makes the production process highly dynamic.

The communication protocol for data exchange in an I4.0-compliant plant is OPC UA (Fig. 2) [2,3]. The OPC UA (Unified Architecture), protocol is highly flexible with respect to data modelling, which is necessary in an I4.0-compliant production facility [4]. Models are dynamic with model views so that the production system elements and production assets can adapt and expose their model depending on the production context.

OPC UA can also be a protocol that is used by the production system to communicate with the customer. The production system exposes the product to the customer as a dynamic view of the complete OPC UA model, the customer modifies the OPC UA view and thereby the product features. The production system capabilities limit the possibilities of customer modifications. During production, the customer can dynamically interact with and modify this view as long as the actual production process permits it. If a product feature is pending in the manufacturing process and there is no conflict with the already manufactured features, the customer production system permits the customer to alter the product features without or with little or no impact on the costs. The production system dynamically exposes the state of the product in OPC UA view to the end customer through the constant flow of information from the production assets to the customer [5].

OPC UA has a communication that corresponds to the addressing memory model on the server. The model fits the hardware and helps with the compatibility and cooperation between devices. On the other hand, OPC UA is not effective in sending information to many clients quickly [6,7].

One important parameter on the communication system, between the server and the client, depends on the quality of the transmission of the data. This quality can be measured by certain network communication features such as throughput, transmission delay, jitter etc.

This paper describes some of the parameters and attempts to find a solution to improve them. The paper is divided into six sections. Section 2 presents the OPC UA standard. Then, Sect. 3 shows some methods for data flow that are described in the standard. Section 4 describes the experimental stand. The results from tests are presented in Sect. 5. Section 6 is a summary and ideas for future research.

2   The OPC UA Standard

The wide variety of industrial automation and communication systems presents a technological challenge. The harmonisation and exchange of data between the different components of industrial enterprises is required. All of these activities are called Factory 4.0. [8] OPC UA plays a key role in this process and is a widely recognised standard in industrial automation in terms of interoperability and data exchange from the sensor level, through control and communication systems to production management and even to the cloud. The goal of OPC UA is to achieve uniform, standardised and secure communication between suppliers, devices and automation levels. In order to achieve this, OPC UA provides both a communication model and an addressing model in one system. OPC UA is based on a Client/Server architecture and it uses an object-oriented data model. All of the available services are independent of the specific protocols. An additional advantage is the object-oriented data structure, which combines data from several sources and the relationship between the information as the semantic model of the data (Fig. 2).

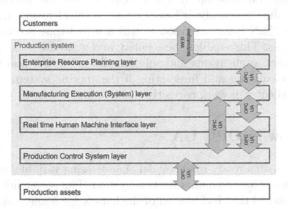

Fig. 2. Structure of production with OPC UA

The disadvantage of OPC UA is that because of the service-oriented structure, it is not easy to calculate the time requirements. In many situations, all of the advantages of OPC UA cannot balance the problems with the failure of data delivery. If a system cannot deliver the data on time, it means that the system is not useful [7]. There are some new extensions [9] in OPC UA standard such as the PubSub service (Fig. 3) or Time Sensitive Network (TSN) [10]. Both of these improve data communication between the Server and Clients. The Pub-Sub service separates the Server and the Client by using Middleware. The server sends the data to the Middleware first, after which all f the Clients can read the required data from the Middleware.

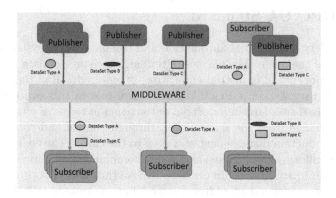

Fig. 3. PubSub structure [11, 12]

In the subscription service, each Client with the same subscription elements creates a separate copy of the elements (MonitoredItems) on the server and starts a new cyclic data transmission. In the PubSub service, the server performs all of the activities simultaneously. It has one copy of the elements, which is sent to the Middleware. TSN is an extension in which a real-time protocol is used for data transmissions. This enables the security and guarantees the data transfer. There are different applications and solutions for OPC UA and this creates a problem with calculating and forecasting if the specific system using an OPC UA server and client will work correctly.

3   Data Flow in OPC UA

OPC UA comes with a ready-made model of addressing variables and dependencies, which is more than a communication system. The server initially prepares an information model that includes all of the knowledge about a specified installation, device or process. This information will be is then available via services (discover, read, write, subscribe, event, call method). In practical applications, it is necessary to have real-time properties on the entire system. The OPC UA standard only partially covers the production process. The process of data collection by the server is very important. In the first idea of OPC UA, the client sends the requirements to the server. After this, the server should receive the data from sensors, Programmable Logic Controllers (PLC) or similar devices. In this situation, a special network is required for OPC UA transmission, which can double the costs. An alternative is that the server does not interfere with the lower level network, but only retrieves all of the data from it. Although this is safer for the lower network, it requires much more processing-power from the server because then the server should receive, analyse and eventually filter all of the incoming data packages.

The OPC UA system has some limitations and problems with OPC UA services that are mainly caused by processing delays, which change when the system parameters are frequently used. In the next part of the article, the authors will present some elements that affect server performance. In general, they can be divided into three parts:

1. processing incoming data (from the source to the server)
2. processing address model (inside the server)
3. processing outgoing communication (from the server to the clients) [12]

All of the elements above were tested in [13]. Now, it is necessary to determine whether it is possible to improve OPC UA.

4   Experiment Description

Performance tests were carried out to test the communication between these elements: Datasource, Server and Client. The first part of the tests consisted of ten Personal Computers (PC), which were connected by two independent networks (cable, 1 Gb/s, with switch).

All of the PC were divided: four of them produced the test data, two PC with OPC UA servers and four PC acting as clients. One of the servers (Server1) was set on an i7-8700K with six cores (12 threads)@3.7 GHz, 64 GB RAM, 2×1 Gb/s network cards with Windows 7. The second (Server2) was set on an i5-2320 with two cores (four threads)@2.5 GHz, 8 GB RAM, 2×1 Gb/s network cards also on Windows 7. The Datasources sent data every 50ms over Ethernet (100 values) to both servers. The servers retrieve data, filter and process it and then use it to update the address model. The clients on the other hand, subscribe all the available data (Fig. 4).

The second stand consisted of two Siemens PLCs with an embedded OPC UA server, 1 Gb/s network and up to 20 clients. The clients were based on JAVA or Python, respectively, and all of them subscribed to four analogue values each 250 ms (Fig. 5).

Only subscription was used in the test. Both the process data and internal parameters were collected by the server and then observed on the clients as Historical data after the tests. These parameters were network processing time, filtering, updating, memory usage, CPU usage, network usage, the amount of data for each client and the amount of MonitoredItems.

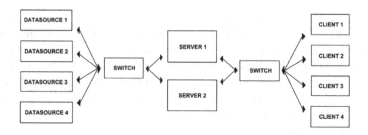

Fig. 4. Structure of the system with the PC

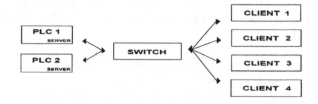

Fig. 5. Structure of the system with the PLS's

5   Experiment

The aim of the experiment was to find some solutions that can improve the effectivity of a server's performance. The experiments were conducted for applications written in different programming languages (Java, Python) and for operating systems (Windows, Siemens PLC). The idea was to determine how to detect any limitation of server processing and to use a secondary server if a limit was detected.

5.1   OPC UA Servers on Two PC

The servers (Server1 and Server2) collected the same data from the underlying network. The CPU load on both servers was almost identical (in shape), and the only difference was in the level. The "better" PC used only 10–25%, while the "worse" PC used 10–90%. Regularly (Fig. 6), the clients subscribed to the same data on both servers. It was visible that both servers had a larger CPU load.

5.2   Connecting Five Clients to OPC UA Server on the PLC

In the tests, there were five clients, each of which subscribed to four values from the server on the PLC. The server tried to process all of the requests but had a delay. For every subscription, the timestamps from the server and from the client was saved. All of the times that were measured in the Java program are presented in Fig. 7. It is visible that the clients received the data in the defined periods. A client requested a subscription every 250 ms. The server sent the subscriptions in

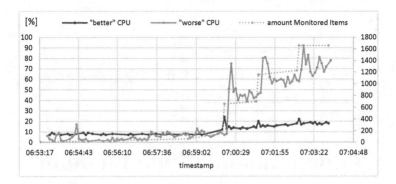

Fig. 6. CPU load on both servers

periods that were multiples of the subscription period. Simultaneously, the server tried to process the incoming data and MonitoredItems as quickly as possible. Nevertheless, the server was not able to keep the requested time.

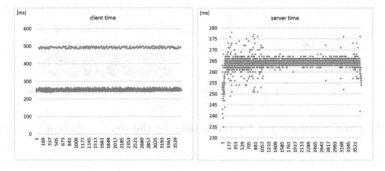

Fig. 7. Time difference for the incoming packages for a client and server on PLS – clients in the JAVA applications

The next figure (Fig. 8) presents the same results (20 clients) that were performed by the Python software.

It is quite visible that different applications had different results. The measurements from Python are more coherent and concentrated/both for server and client. The software on OPC UA Server was identical in both situations. It was not possible to calculate time parameter before the tests.

5.3   Twenty Clients with a Subscription to One OPC UA Server

It is visible that server cannot send data properly. Instead of 250 ms, the data are transmitted each 250, 500 and 750 ms. Clients have similar pattern. It was not possible to find those patterns before the tests (Fig. 9).

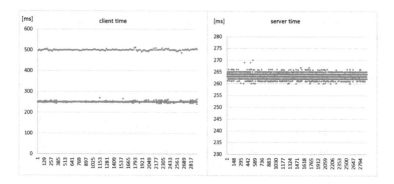

Fig. 8. Time difference for incoming packages for a client and server on PLS – clients in the Python applications

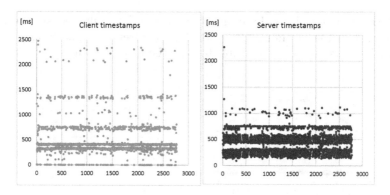

Fig. 9. Time difference between the timestamps for the server and client for 20 clients

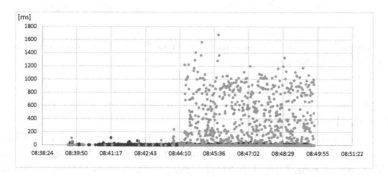

Fig. 10. Different loads on two servers

5.4   Two PLC with OPC Servers – Case of Different Loads

One of the ways to have a system work correctly is to use many servers. The results from the experiment – the time differences between the requested and obtained timestamp are visible in Fig. 10. In the beginning, there were two clients with four subscribed variables. Both servers worked correctly – the time differences were near zero. At some point, 48 more clients were connected to one of the servers, which caused an increased tine difference of up to 1000 ms on that server. All of its clients did not receive the correct data. The second server worked correctly all of the time. It was possible to monitor the server traffic and in the event of delays, to block the server to another clients.

6 Conclusion

It seems impossible to find the one parameter that can represent the load of a server. It is possible to find many parameters and their relationships. Nevertheless, a parameter set can only be used when the source code of an application is available. It is almost impossible to monitor these parameters on a PLC. The other solution looks more promising. However, it is necessary to have an additional device that can monitor the servers. If a delay is detected, the server should be blocked for any new subscriptions. All of the clients should first ask this device about the available server. Then, if the client encounters a problem, the subscription should transfer to the next server. With some of the available servers, the system can process requests (subscriptions) from many more clients than a single server.

References

1. ISA95. https://opcfoundation.org/markets-collaboration/isa-95/
2. Industrie 4.0 Communication Guideline. https://industrie40.vdma.org/documents/4214230/20743172/Leitfaden_OPC_UA_Englisch_1506415735965.pdf/a2181ec7-a325-44c0-99d2-7332480de281
3. Zezulka, F., Marcon, P., Bradac, Z., Arm, J., Benesl, T., Vesely, I.: Communication systems for industry 4.0 and the IIoT. IFAC-PapersOnLine **51**(6), 150–155 (2018)
4. Haskamp, H., Meyer, M., Möllmann, R., Orth, F., Colombo, A.W.: Benchmarking of existing OPC UA implementations for industrie 4.0-compliant digitalization solutions. In: 2017 IEEE 15th International Conference on Industrial Informatics (INDIN), pp. 589–594. IEEE (2017)
5. Industrie 4.0. https://www.plattform-i40.de/PI40/Redaktion/EN/Downloads/Publikation/criteria-industrie-40-products.pdf?__blob=publicationFile&v=5
6. Profanter, S., Tekat, A., Dorofeev, K., Rickert, M., Knoll, A.: OPC UA versus ROS, DDS, and MQTT: performance evaluation of industry 4.0 protocols. In: Proceedings of the IEEE International Conference on Industrial Technology (ICIT) (2019)
7. Fojcik, M., Folkert, K.: Introduction to OPC UA performance. In: Kwiecień, A., Gaj, P., Stera, P. (eds.) CN 2012. CCIS, vol. 291, pp. 261–270. Springer, Heidelberg (2012). https://doi.org/10.1007/978-3-642-31217-5_28
8. Usländer, T., Epple, U.: Reference model of Industrie 4.0 service architectures. at-Automatisierungstechnik **63**(10), 858–866 (2015)
9. OPC Foundation. https://opcfoundation.org/about/opc-technologies/opc-ua/opcua-roadmap/

10. Bruckner, D., et al.: OPC UA TSN-A new solution for industrial communication. In: B&R Industrial Automation, Schneider Electric, ABB Automation Products, TTTech Computertechnik, General Electric Company, Huawei Technologies, Fraunhofer IOSB-INA, Phoenix Contact Electronics, Intel Corporation, Bosch Rexroth, Cisco Systems, Hirschmann Automation and Control, Moxa, Kalycito Infotech (2018)
11. OPC Foundation. https://opcfoundation.org/developer-tools/specifications-unified-architecture
12. OPC Foundation. https://opcfoundation.org/developer-tools/specifications-unified-architecture/part-14-pubsub/
13. Fojcik, M., Cupek, R., Ziebinski, A., Sande, O., Fojcik, M.K.: Quality of service in real-time OPC UA applications. In: Nguyen, N.T., Chbeir, R., Exposito, E., Aniorte, P., Trawiński, B. (eds.) ICCCI 2019. LNAI, vol. 11684, pp. 239–248. Springer, Heidelberger (2019)

Collective Intelligence for Science and Technology

Clustering Algorithms for Query Expansion Based Information Retrieval

Ilyes Khennak(✉), Habiba Drias, Amine Kechid, and Hadjer Moulai

Laboratory for Research in Artificial Intelligence, USTHB, Algiers, Algeria
{ikhennak,hdrias,akechid,hamoulai}@usthb.dz

Abstract. Clustering is by far the most commonly used unsupervised data mining techniques for discovering interesting knowledge and patterns. It aims to group a set of data objects into clusters that are coherent internally but basically different from each other. In this work, we involve clustering algorithms in Information Retrieval (IR) to strengthen the user's original query with appropriate additional terms and return more relevant information. The overall procedure consists of the following steps: (i) use the k-medoids clustering algorithm to group terms into clusters with similar characteristics, (ii) involve k-means algorithm to calculate the centroid of query terms, (iii) select the relevant clusters to the original query and return the expansion term candidates, (iv) evaluate the expansion term candidates to the centroid and add the best ones to the original query, (v) run a search with the expanded query. We present numerical experiments based on real data from a large online health database. The results of our numerical testing demonstrate the effectiveness of the proposed method compared to prior state-of-the-art.

Keywords: Data mining · Clustering · k-means · k-medoids · Information retrieval · Query expansion

1 Introduction

Data mining techniques have received considerable interest and attention of research communities due to their ability to discover useful knowledge from large volumes of data. Some commonly used techniques in data mining are decision trees, neural networks, clustering and association rules. Clustering is a well-known unsupervised data mining technique. It attempts to group data objects into clusters so that objects within the same cluster are closer to each other than to those in other clusters. Nowadays, clustering is widely applied in several domains such as medicine [12], energy [5], agriculture [7] and commerce [20]. k-means and k-medoids algorithms are among the most well-known clustering algorithms. They are distance-based clustering methods. Owing to their simplicity, we employ k-means to improve the effectiveness of query expansion based information retrieval by retrieving the centroid of the user's query and we

© Springer Nature Switzerland AG 2019
N. T. Nguyen et al. (Eds.): ICCCI 2019, LNAI 11684, pp. 261–272, 2019.
https://doi.org/10.1007/978-3-030-28374-2_23

use k-medoids to enhance the retrieval efficiency by clustering the terms of the document set in offline mode.

The information retrieval aims to find documents that satisfy and meet the user's query, whereas Query Expansion (QE) aims to enrich the user's original query with new meaningful terms, so that the system generates more appropriate results. QE is currently considered among the most effective and promising method to enhance retrieval effectiveness of search engines and it is successfully applied in many applications, such as e-commerce [17], question answering [4] and mobile search [3].

To find the relevant additional terms, we propose to use k-medoids clustering algorithm to group the terms of the document set into clusters, involve k-means algorithm to calculate the centroid of query terms, select the relevant clusters to the query and return the expansion term candidates, evaluate the expansion term candidates to the centroid, add the best ones to the original query, and finally run a search with the expanded query to return more relevant information.

We evaluate our proposed approach using MEDLINE, a real data from a large online health database. We use Rocchio and RSJ methods, two popular query expansion approaches, as basis for comparison. The remainder of the paper is organized as follows. In Sect. 2, we present a brief review of related literature. In Sect. 3, we provide some background on query expansion and clustering. Section 4 describes the proposed k-means and k-medoids clustering algorithms for query expansion. In Sect. 5, we show the outputs of the experimental evaluation and finally, we present some concluding remarks in Sect. 6.

2   Related Work

Many previous efforts and attempts have addressed the performance issues of information retrieval systems and query expansion limits with clustering algorithms.

Chifu et al. [2] proposed a clustering method that uses word sense discrimination to re-rank the first documents retrieved in response to the initial search query and improve retrieval effectiveness. Najafabadi et al. [15] attempted to enhance the accuracy of collaborative filtering recommendations using clustering and association rules mining. The authors used clustering technique to reduce the size of data and dimensionality of the item space. A sample-based hierarchical k-means clustering algorithm for large-scale video retrieval was introduced by Liao et al. [13]. The authors used k-means algorithm to specify the correct number of clusters and to build an unbalanced cluster tree. Jun et al. [8] built a combined clustering method using dimension reduction and k-means clustering based on support vector clustering and silhouette measure in order to overcome the sparsity problem of document clustering. Carol et al. [10] proposed two approaches for efficient text document clustering. The first one is a combination between c-means algorithm with particle swarm optimization and the second one is a hybridization of k-means algorithm with particle swarm optimization. Younus et al. [19] suggested a new hybrid method that combines particle swarm optimization with k-means clustering to retrieve images accurately from large image databases similar to the query image based on the similarity between image colors and textures. Lin et al. [14] employed also the k-means algorithm for image retrieval. The authors proposed a new k-means algorithm to reduce the length of time spent on training the image database centroids and to overcome the cluster centers re-training problem. Still in the same direction, Kathuria et al. [11] implemented a new method to automatically classify web search engines queries using k-means algorithm. The authors clustered user searches based on intent in terms of the type of content specified mainly by the query. A semantic expansion using word embedding clustering and convolutional neural network is another stream of work which based on clustering algorithms [18]. In this work, a fast clustering algorithm is involved to discover the semantic cliques in embedding spaces. These semantic cliques are then used as supervision information to detect precise semantics. Bernhard [1] introduced a new method for using lexical-semantic resources in query expansion. The author first extracted lexical resources and grouped them to obtain definitions clusters, and then selected the most relevant expansion terms from the appropriate definitions clusters to expand the original query. Another relevant work is the one presented in [9]. In this study, clustering and genetic algorithm were combined with vector space model and an agglomerative algorithm to categorize medical documents.

In contrast to previous works, we propose to combine both k-means and k-medoids clustering algorithms to further improve the retrieval performance of query expansion.

3 Background

In this section, we provide some background needed for the reset of this paper. We first survey the standard modelling of query expansion. Then, we introduce the clustering algorithms.

3.1 Query Expansion

Nowadays, retrieving relevant information on the Internet has become a challenging task for users, not only for the huge amount of data available on the Web and which is growing exponentially, but also because of the quality of queries submitted by users to search engines. The users' original queries often do not describe the information needs in a satisfactory manner. This is mainly due to: (i) users express their needs with short queries. (ii) Users employ ambiguous terms to characterize their needs. (iii) Users often not sure about what they are looking for until they see the results. To overcome these drawbacks, query expansion has been introduced. It aims to enhance the retrieval effectiveness, minimize ambiguity and return more relevant results. QE consists in reformulating the user's original query by adding new related terms with similar meaning.

Given a user's initial query Q that consists of N terms $Q = \{t_1, t_2, ..., t_n\}$. In addition to the original query terms, the reformulated query includes new terms denoted as $\acute{Q} = \{\acute{t}_1, \acute{t}_2, ..., \acute{t}_m\}$. The expanded query Q_{exp} can be represented as follows:

$$Q_{exp} = Q \cup \acute{Q} = \{t_1, t_2, ..., t_n, \acute{t}_1, \acute{t}_2, ..., \acute{t}_m\} \tag{1}$$

Many query expansion techniques have been proposed to select the good expansion terms and refine the original search query. One of the successful techniques is Pseudo Relevance Feedback (PRF). This technique supposes the pseudo-relevant documents, the top-ranked documents returned for the original query, as relevant and extracts from those documents the best expansion terms. PRF starts by performing a preliminary search with the original query Q to retrieve the pseudo-relevant documents. The top-ranked documents are determined by calculating the relevance of documents to the query Q using a document-scoring function denoted by $RSV(Q, d)$. One popular document-scoring functions has been introduced within Okapi BM25 model [16] and is given by Eq. 2:

$$RSV(Q, d) = \sum_{t_i \in Q \cap d} w_i^{BM25} \tag{2}$$

Where:

w_i^{BM25}, is the weight of term t_i in document d:

$$w_i^{BM25} = \frac{tf}{k_1 \left((1 - b) + b\dfrac{dl}{avdl} \right) + tf} \log \frac{N - n_i + 0.5}{n_i + 0.5} \tag{3}$$

Where:

tf, is the frequency of the t_i in document d;

k_1, b, are constants;

dl, is the document length;

$avdl$, is the average of document length;

N, is the number of documents in the whole collection of documents;

n_i, is the number of documents in the whole collection containing t_i.

PRF then extracts the appropriate expansion terms from the pseudo-relevant documents and ranks them using a term-scoring function. Among the most successful term-scoring functions are Robertson/Sparck Jones term-ranking function (RSJ) and Rocchio weight, given respectively by Eqs. 4 and 5:

$$w_i^{RSJ} = \log \frac{(r_i + 0.5)(n - r - n_i + r_i + 0.5)}{(n_i - r_i + 0.5)(r - r_i + 0.5)} \tag{4}$$

$$w_i^{Rocchio} = \sum_{d \in R} w_i^{BM25} \tag{5}$$

Where:

n, is the number of documents in the whole collection;

r, is the number of documents judged relevant;

n_i, is the number of documents in the collection containing term t_i;

r_i, is the number of judged relevant documents containing term t_i.

R, is the set of pseudo-relevant documents.

Finally, PRF augments the original query with the top-ranked expansion terms and runs a second search with the expended query using the above document-scoring function.

3.2 Clustering

Clustering is a popular data mining technique. It attempts to partition a set of objects into subsets or clusters with similar properties. Each object is attributed to a cluster based on its attribute values and using distance measures. There are many clustering algorithms in the literature.

The k-means and k-medoids algorithms are the most well-known clustering algorithms. The k-means algorithm is the simplest one. It starts by producing an initial set of clusters, where each cluster is represented by a centroid. A centroid is the center point of the cluster. Next, k-means initiates an iterative relocation process to improve the quality of clusters by moving objects from one location to another [6].

The k-means algorithm is sensitive to outliers since an object with an extremely large value may easily corrupt the distribution of the rest of objects and negatively impact the centroids. Instead of taking the centroid of the objects in a cluster as a center point, the medoid can be used. A medoid is the most centrally located object in a cluster.

k-medoids algorithm is a refinement version of k-means. It starts by choosing an initial set of K objects as medoids and assigning the remaining non-medoids to the clusters of their closest medoids. Then, it iteratively replaces bad medoids with new medoids to improve the quality of clustering result. Given a set of N objects denoted as $X = \{x_1, x_2, ..., x_N\}$ where $x_i = \{x_{i1}, x_{i2}, ..., x_{ip}\}$ is an object represented by p attribute values. The k-medoids divides the objects in X into K ($K \leq N$) clusters denoted as $C = \{C_1, C_2, ..., C_K\}$. The clusters are described by a set of medoids denoted as $M = \{m_1, m_2, ..., m_K\}$ where each m_i is the representative element for cluster C_i. Each non-medoid x_i is attributed to its closet medoid using Eq. 6:

$$x_i \in C_k \Leftrightarrow D(x_i, m_k) = \min_{1 \leq j \leq K} D(x_i, m_j) \tag{6}$$

Where:

$D(x_i, m_k)$, is the distance measure between x_i and m_k. It computes the similarity between two objects. A small value of $D(x_i, m_k)$ means that x_i and m_k are close. One frequently used distance measure is the Euclidean distance, given by Eq. 7:

$$D(x_i, m_k) = \sqrt{\sum_{p=1}^{p} (x_{ip} - m_{kp})^2} \tag{7}$$

To evaluate the quality of current medoids, k-medoids algorithm uses the absolute-error criterion, given by Eq. 8:

$$E = \sum_{k=1}^{K} \sum_{x_i \in C_k} D(x_i, m_k) \tag{8}$$

To swap a non-mediod object x_i with a given mediod m_j, k-medoids algorithm first considers x_i as medoid instead of m_j, computes the new value of absolute-error and then calculates the total cost of swapping between the new absolute-error and the actual absolute-error, denoted as S. If the total cost is negative, then m_j is replaced by x_i, otherwise m_j is considered acceptable. The main steps of k-medoids algorithm are given in Algorithm 1.

Algorithm 1. k-medoids algorithm

1: Determine the number of clusters k;
2: Choose randomly k objects as initial cluster medoids;
3: **repeat**
4:     Attribute the non-medoids objects to their closest medoids (Equation 6);
5:     **for** each medoid object m_j **do**
6:         **for** each non-medoid object x_i **do**
7:             Calculate the total cost of swapping S;
8:             **if** S < 0 **then**
9:                 Replace the medoid m_j with the non-medoid object x_i;
10:            **end if**
11:        **end for**
12:    **end for**
13: **until** the medoids are stable

The Centroid in k-means. As indicated previously, the centroid in k-means is replaced by the medoid in k-medoids. The centroid computes the mean of all objects within a cluster as given by Eq. 9:

$$c_k = \frac{1}{|C_k|} \sum_{x_n \in C_k} x_n \tag{9}$$

Where:
   c_k, is the centroid of cluster C_k.

4   Clustering Algorithms for Query Expansion

This section describes our proposed k-means and k-medoids clustering algorithms for query expansion. The whole process includes five steps: first, we use the k-medoids algorithm to divide the terms of the document set into separated clusters. Second, we involve k-means algorithm to calculate the centroid of query terms. Third, we select the relevant clusters to the query and return the expansion term candidates. Fourth, we evaluate the expansion term candidates to the centroid and add the best ones to the original query. Fifth, we run a search with the expanded query and return more appropriate results.

Group Terms into Clusters. The aim of this step is to subdivide the set of terms in such a way that similar terms fall into the same cluster. Accordingly, we consider the terms of the whole document set denoted by $T = \{t_1, t_2, ..., t_N\}$ as objects and each term $t_i = \{w_{i1}, w_{i2}, ..., w_{ip}\}$ as an object represented by a vector of weights, where w_{ij} is the weight of t_i in document d_j calculated using Eq. 3. We use the Euclidean measure to calculate the distance between two terms. We apply and adapt k-medoids algorithm to group the terms. The k-medoids for term clustering is given by Algorithm 2:

Algorithm 2. k-medoids for term clustering

1: Determine the number of clusters k;
2: Choose randomly k terms as initial cluster medoids;
3: **repeat**
4:     Attribute the non-medoids terms to their closest medoids (Equation 6);
5:     **for** each medoid term t_j **do**
6:         **for** each non-medoid term t_i **do**
7:             Calculate the total cost of swapping S;
8:             **if** S < 0 **then**
9:                 Replace the medoid t_j with the non-medoid term t_i;
10:            **end if**
11:        **end for**
12:    **end for**
13: **until** the medoids are stable

Calculate the Centroid for the Query. The goal of this step is to find the center point that describes all the query terms. Thus, we consider the terms of the query Q as a cluster. Then, we involve the concept of centroid defined in k-means algorithm to calculate the center of these terms, denoted as C_Q, using Eq. 9.

Select the Relevant Clusters. The purpose of this step is to find for each query term its similar terms from the whole set of terms. Hence, we select for each term of the query the cluster to which it belongs. Then, we consider the returned clusters as relevant clusters, denoted by C_{rel}, and their components as expansion term candidates.

Select the Expansion Terms. The goal of this step is to find a set of terms that are similar to the centroid C_Q and close to all the terms of the original query. Therefore, we recover the expansion term candidates from the relevant clusters C_{rel} and calculate their similarities with the centroid C_Q using the Euclidean measure. The expansion term candidates are then ranked according to their distances values with the centroid C_Q and the top ranked terms are added to the original query in order to constitute the new query Q_{exp}.

Run a Second Search. The aim of this step is to return more relevant documents to the user query. Once the expansion terms are retrieved and the original query expanded, a search is run with the new query Q_{exp} using the above document-scoring function.

Algorithm 3 summarizes our proposed k-means and k-medoids clustering algorithms for query expansion.

Algorithm 3. k-means and k-medoids for query expansion

1: Divide the terms of the document set into separated clusters (Algorithm 2);
2: Initialize C_{rel};
3: **for** each query Q **do**
4:     Compute the centroid C_Q (Equation 9);
5:     **for** each query term t_Q **do**
6:         Add the cluster to which t_Q belongs to C_{rel};
7:     **end for**
8:     **for** each expansion term candidate t_C in C_{rel} **do**
9:         Compute the distance between t_C and C_Q (Equation 7);
10:        Update expansion term candidates ranking;
11:    **end for**
12:    Add the top ranked terms to the original query Q;
13:    Run a search with the new query Q_{exp} (Equation 2);
14: **end for**

---

5   Experimental Results

In this section, we discuss the experiment results. We first present the dataset and the evaluation metrics. Then, we compare our proposed approach with the existing methods.

5.1   Dataset

Our experiments are conducted over a subset of the MEDLINE database, a large online health repository. It consists of 348 566 scientific articles, 106 queries and 16140 query-document pairs upon which relevance judgments are made. The articles are taken from 270 medical journals. Each article contains title, abstract, multiple index terms known as Medical Subject Headings (MeSH), author, source and publication type.

5.2   Evaluation Metrics

In order to evaluate the performance of the proposed approach with the existing retrieval methods, we take precision at 5 documents ($P@5$) and mean average precision (MAP) as the evaluation metrics.

5.3   Results

As mentioned earlier, we use Rocchio and RSJ methods, two popular query expansion approaches, as basis for comparison.

In the first series of experiments, we compare the precision of result obtained by our proposed approach with those achieved by Rocchio and RSJ. The number of additional terms $\acute{Q}$ is varied from 2 to 14 in increments of 2. Figure 1 shows the precision values achieved by the proposed approach, Rocchio and RSJ after retrieving 5 documents ($P@5$).

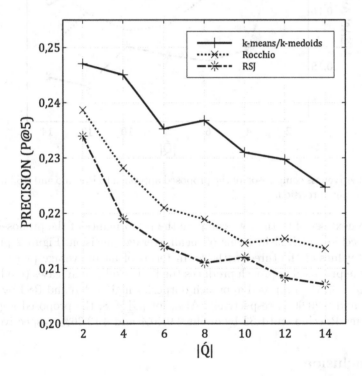

Fig. 1. Effectiveness comparison of the proposed approach to Rocchio and RSJ in terms of precision.

As can be seen from Fig. 1, we observe that the proposed approach yields the highest precision values on all the cases and reports significant enhancement over the baselines, e.g. for $|\acute{Q}| = 4$, precision improves from 0.2282 and 0.2191 to 0.2451 over Rocchio (+7.40%) and (+11.87%), respectively. Also, for $|\acute{Q}| = 8$, precision improves from 0.2189 and 0.2112 to 0.2368 over Rocchio (+8.18%) and (+12.12%), respectively.

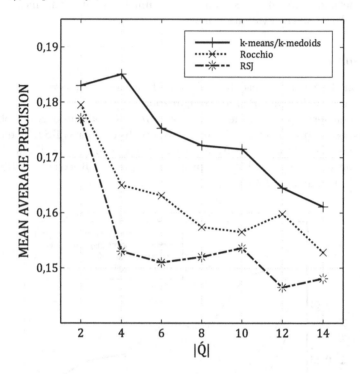

Fig. 2. Effectiveness comparison of the proposed approach to Rocchio and RSJ in terms of mean average precision.

In the next set of testing, we compare the performance of the proposed approach, Rocchio and RSJ in terms of mean average precision. Figure 2 presents the MAP values of the three methods. In terms of mean average precision, we see that the proposed approach produces the best results in all cases (see Fig. 2), e.g. for $|\acute{Q}| = 4$, the proposed approach outperforms Rocchio and RSJ by about +12.25% and +20.90%, respectively. Also, for $|\acute{Q}| = 8$, the proposed approach outperforms Rocchio and RSJ by about +9.40% and +13.36%, respectively.

6   Conclusion

In this paper, we use k-means and k-medoids clustering algorithms to select the best expansion terms for query expansion. We involve k-medoids to group the terms and k-means to compute the centroid of query terms. Then, the best expansion terms are selected from the relevant clusters with the smallest distance to the centroid and added to the original query in order to return more relevant results.

We thoroughly evaluate our approach on MEDLINE, the large online health database. The results of the numerical experiments demonstrate that the proposed k-means and k-medoids for query expansion manages to enhance the retrieval performance and produces a significant improvement over the baselines in terms of precision and mean average precision.

In the future, we will try to test and experiment the proposed approach on other existing Web datasets. Another possible research direction is to extend our study to other fields of Web search applications, such as Twitter search.

References

1. Bernhard, D.: Query expansion based on pseudo relevance feedback from definition clusters. In: Proceedings of the 23rd International Conference on Computational Linguistics: Posters, pp. 54–62. Association for Computational Linguistics (2010)
2. Chifu, A.G., Hristea, F., Mothe, J., Popescu, M.: Word sense discrimination in information retrieval: a spectral clustering-based approach. Inf. Process. Manag. **51**(2), 16–31 (2015)
3. Gao, K., Zhang, Y., Zhang, D., Lin, S.: Accurate off-line query expansion for large-scale mobile visual search. Sig. Process. **93**(8), 2305–2315 (2013)
4. Gao, L., Lu, Y., Zhang, Q., Yang, H., Hu, Y.: Query expansion for exploratory search with subtopic discovery in community question answering. In: 2016 International Joint Conference on Neural Networks (IJCNN), pp. 4715–4720. IEEE (2016)
5. Grigoras, G., Scarlatache, F.: An assessment of the renewable energy potential using a clustering based data mining method. Case study in Romania. Energy **81**, 416–429 (2015)
6. Han, J., Pei, J., Kamber, M.: Data Mining: Concepts and Techniques. Elsevier, New York (2011)
7. Hou, J., Li, L., He, J.: Detection of grapevine leafroll disease based on 11-index imagery and ant colony clustering algorithm. Precision Agric. **17**(4), 488–505 (2016)
8. Jun, S., Park, S.S., Jang, D.S.: Document clustering method using dimension reduction and support vector clustering to overcome sparseness. Expert Syst. Appl. **41**(7), 3204–3212 (2014)
9. Karaa, W.B.A., Ashour, A.S., Sassi, D.B., Roy, P., Kausar, N., Dey, N.: MEDLINE text mining: an enhancement genetic algorithm based approach for document clustering. In: Hassanien, A.-E., Grosan, C., Fahmy Tolba, M. (eds.) Applications of Intelligent Optimization in Biology and Medicine. ISRL, vol. 96, pp. 267–287. Springer, Cham (2016). https://doi.org/10.1007/978-3-319-21212-8_12
10. Karol, S., Mangat, V.: Evaluation of text document clustering approach based on particle swarm optimization. Open Comput. Sci. **3**(2), 69–90 (2013)
11. Kathuria, A., Jansen, B.J., Hafernik, C., Spink, A.: Classifying the user intent of web queries using k-means clustering. Internet Res. **20**(5), 563–581 (2010)
12. Khanmohammadi, S., Adibeig, N., Shanehbandy, S.: An improved overlapping k-means clustering method for medical applications. Expert Syst. Appl. **67**, 12–18 (2017)
13. Liao, K., Liu, G., Xiao, L., Liu, C.: A sample-based hierarchical adaptive k-means clustering method for large-scale video retrieval. Knowl. Based Syst. **49**, 123–133 (2013)

14. Lin, C.H., Chen, C.C., Lee, H.L., Liao, J.R.: Fast k-means algorithm based on a level histogram for image retrieval. Expert Syst. Appl. **41**(7), 3276–3283 (2014)
15. Najafabadi, M.K., Mahrin, M.N., Chuprat, S., Sarkan, H.M.: Improving the accuracy of collaborative filtering recommendations using clustering and association rules mining on implicit data. Comput. Hum. Behav. **67**, 113–128 (2017)
16. Robertson, S., Zaragoza, H., et al.: The probabilistic relevance framework: BM25 and beyond. Found. Trends Inf. Retrieval **3**(4), 333–389 (2009)
17. Saraiva, P.C., Cavalcanti, J.M., de Moura, E.S., Gonçalves, M.A., Torres, R.D.S.: A multimodal query expansion based on genetic programming for visually-oriented e-commerce applications. Inf. Process. Manag. **52**(5), 783–800 (2016)
18. Wang, P., Xu, B., Xu, J., Tian, G., Liu, C.L., Hao, H.: Semantic expansion using word embedding clustering and convolutional neural network for improving short text classification. Neurocomputing **174**, 806–814 (2016)
19. Younus, Z.S., et al.: Content-based image retrieval using pso and k-means clustering algorithm. Arab. J. Geosci. **8**(8), 6211–6224 (2015)
20. Zhong, X., Enke, D.: A comprehensive cluster and classification mining procedure for daily stock market return forecasting. Neurocomputing **267**, 152–168 (2017)

A Software Prototype
for Multidimensional Design of Data
Warehouses Using Ontologies

Manel Zekri[1], Sadok Ben Yahia[2(✉)], and Inès Hilali-Jaghdam[3]

[1] Faculty of Sciences of Tunis, University of Tunis El Manar,
LIPAH-LR11ES14, Tunis, Tunisia
manel.zekri@fst.utm.tn
[2] Department of Software Science,
Tallinn University of Technology, Tallinn, Estonia
sadok.ben@taltech.ee
[3] Community College, Princess Nourah Bint Abdulrahman University,
Riyadh, Saudi Arabia
imalihilali@pnu.edu.sa

Abstract. One of the key success points of a data warehousing project is
the design of the multidimensional schema. Many researches shows that
the use of ontologies in information system design is becoming more and
more promising. In this paper, we propose a method for multidimensional design of data warehouses, from an operational data source, using
ontologies. Furthermore, we introduce the concept of multidimensional
ontology as a tool for the specification of multidimensional knowledge.
In addition, we present an ontology-based method for data modeling
schema that eventually covers different phases of the data warehouse life
cycle, and takes into account the users by considering their personalized
needs as well as their knowledge of the domain.

Keywords: Data warehouse · Conceptual data model ·
Multidimensional design · Ontology

1 Introduction

Data warehouses are a powerful technology that receives a permanently very high
interest in the scientific community and a widespread deployment among decision
makers in different domains [11]. They represent one of the most important
aspects of decisional information systems and databases. Indeed, companies rely
on decision support systems based on the data warehouse approach to exploit
large volumes of information for analysis and decision support. In fact, a data
warehouse is used to store data for decision making as it is funded by extractions
of data, said data sources, and accumulated in files and operational databases
over many years. Designing a data warehouse is known as a crucial task for the
success of a decision support system [9].

© Springer Nature Switzerland AG 2019
N. T. Nguyen et al. (Eds.): ICCCI 2019, LNAI 11684, pp. 273–284, 2019.
https://doi.org/10.1007/978-3-030-28374-2_24

Several methodologies and approaches have been interested in the design of multidimensional data warehouses in the literature. The approach that we introduce in this paper, is mainly based on the pioneering works of [17,19]. These approaches can be classified into three categories. One was introduced by [5]. It is called "guided by the requirements", since it starts from end-users needs. However, not considering the sources from which the data warehouse will be powered may fail whenever the data query by users is not available. To overcome this down side, researchers have proposed to start the design of the data warehouse from data sources and this approach is referred to as "approach guided by data sources". The authors of [6,8,14,20] have based their works on this latter approach. Other researchers, such as [2,4,6,21], argued that the availability of information sources does not necessarily mean that the user is concerned by this information. To leverage from the advantages of both previous approaches, researchers offer hybrid approaches based on the data sources and the user's requirements. Among the works that adopt this approach, these following works [2,5,6,13,20] are worthy of cite. These different methodologies and approaches that have been presented to design multidimensional data warehouses are typically carried out manually by experts.

In the last years, a few research efforts have tried to automate the design of multidimensional databases. To do so, these approaches start from a detailed analysis of the data sources to determine the multidimensional concepts in a re-engineering process, aimed to identify relevant multidimensional knowledge contained in the operational data sources.

In this paper, we propose a new method, with a new design, for multidimensional design of data warehouses, from an operational data source, using ontologies. Furthermore, we introduce the concept of multidimensional ontology as a tool for the specification of multidimensional knowledge. In addition, we present a new ontology-based method for data modeling schema that eventually covers different phases of the data warehouse life cycle, and takes into account the users by considering their personalized needs as well as their knowledge of the domain.

The remainder of this paper is organized as follows: Sect. 2 sketches a brief presentation of the related work and presents the multidimensional ontology. In Sect. 3, we describe the introduced approach. Section 4 shows the results of the validation step through the rules of extraction that we have used. Finally, a conclusion is presented in Sect. 5.

2   Related Work

Designing a data warehouse is known as a crucial task for the success of a storage project [9,11]. Several approaches have been proposed and those based on data sources can be classified into two categories: (1) data source-guided approaches; and (2) mixed approaches. Approaches falling within the first category are based on data sources for the derivation of multidimensional schemas. They are also based on the data model business and take benefit from the relations between data in order to develop a multi-dimensional diagram in a structured way. This type of approach has been respectively adopted by [3,8,20]. However, these works cannot be automatized. Indeed, despite the derivation of a multidimensional schema based on the identification of the facts, they do not specify a formal criterion for the facts identification from the data model. They are satisfied by the manual identification of these facts. Moreover, such approaches do not incorporate user needs. They ensure information availability. However, this latter does not guarantee that the user will be satisfied by the data warehouse. Mixed approaches consider the data sources and user needs in order to ensure that the user finds the information of interest and that this information is available. Among the works that adopt this approach type, we can cite [2,5,6,13,16]. For operations, authors of [2,5] derived a constellation from the data sources validated by user needs. Besides, [6,13,16] derived a set of stars from user needs in order to validate the schema data sources. For the identification of facts, the first approaches consider "entities and n-ary associations with at least one numeric attribute" as a fact. [12] considers that the latter assumption generates a large number of results while majority of them does not correspond to valid facts. This applies entity and association with digital key attributes or attributes that do not match measures such as "zip code" or "phone number". To tackle such deficiencies, they propose a new hypothesis "entity or association with non-key numerical attributes". [6,16] are worthy of mention since they consider that facts are defined by user needs.

In data warehouse design, different modeling techniques are used to represent the multidimensional concepts extracted from data sources, as well as the sources themselves. It can be ER diagram, UML diagram or graphs [7], etc. Unlike ontologies, which are ready for computing, these techniques are conceptual formalizations intended to graphically represent the domain and not thought for querying and reasoning. This work is a continuation of a research [7,10] and it aims at integrating ontologies in the data warehouse design process. So, our starting point was our meta-model of data warehouse scheme [10]. A data warehouse is a collection of tables. These tables are either dimension tables or fact tables. A dimension is a perspective of analysis. A subject is measured according to multiple perspectives. These perspectives are attributes characterizing the measures of the analyzed subject. Each dimension table has one or more levels of granularity and forms a hierarchy of dimensions used to define the granularity of a dimension. In fact, the attributes of a dimension are organized using a "is finer than" relationship to restrict or increase the level of detail of the analysis. For example, (day-month-year) is a hierarchy of the frequency dimension. Each level can be generated by a set of rules of aggregation, contains a set of attributes and has a primary key. Thus, each level corresponds either to a set of explicit attributes or to rules generated attributes. Additionally, the fact tables have one or more measures and a primary key which is a composition of the foreign keys (primary key of some dimension tables). A fact consists of measures corresponding to the information of the analyzed activity. Various approaches were proposed to guide creating ontologies [4,9,20], we mainly based our multi-dimensional ontology construction process on the approach proposed in [9,20].

1. Multidimensional Concepts Here we take a more detailed look at the multidimensional concepts of our ontology. Based on our meta-model of data warehouse scheme [10], we defined the following concepts: Fact, Fact_ID, Measure, Dimension, Dimension_Id, Hierarchy, Level, and Attribute. These concepts are the elements that form a multidimensional model, in this case, the snowflake schema [9][14].
2. **Multidimensional Relationships** : We need to specify the relationships that exist between them. Each relationship is of the form Relation (X, Y), where Relation is a binary predicate, and X and Y are concepts. Both multidimensional concepts and relationships are represented in Fig. 1.

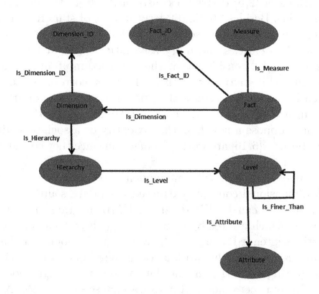

Fig. 1. Graphical representation of multidimensional ontology

While other techniques (mentioned above) for representing multidimensional knowledge are an appropriate choice for their respective approaches, they use ends when the task of designing the data warehouse is accomplished. On the other hand, the multidimensional ontology can still be useful. It can cover the various phases of the life cycle of a decisional information system, that is to say, from the requirements specification, the design of data warehouse and data marts, until the exploitation and evolution phases. This is convenient because the recent DBMSs allow storing ontologies alongside data in the same database structure [9,18]. Such database is called OBDB (ontology-based database).

Ontologies are scalable and extendable, and they showed their effectiveness for information systems and requirements specification [13]. More concretely and in the same way, as ontologies are used for clarifying the semantics of data sources, they are used to identify and manage semantic conflicts between concepts. This allows us to add as many extensions as needed to the multidimensional ontology to cover the various phases of the life cycle of a decisional information system. To demonstrate this aspect, we propose an extension that represents the operational data source conceptual schema, in this case, an ER diagram. As illustrated in Fig. 2, the extension is composed of three new concepts, which are Entity, Relationship, and Link. This way it's easier to automate the process of extracting multidimensional knowledge from the source. The heuristic used in [7,12] to determine facts and dimension fetches potential facts from associations and dimensions from relationships. Hence, the relations: Is_potential_fact, Is_valid_fact, Is_potential_dimension, and Is_valid_dimension. Using these relations to keep track of which multidimensional element corresponds to which source element may be useful in later stages, for example, ETL design.

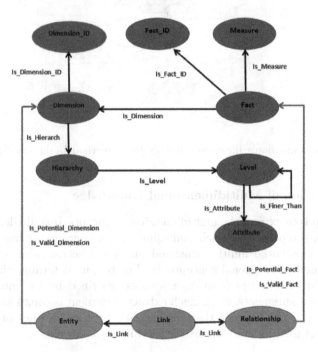

Fig. 2. Graphical representation of multidimensional ontology with extension

3 Design Approach

In this section, we present an overview of the first phase of our approach. Our approach is progressive and iterative. The assistance of the designer throughout this construction is optional. The approach can be executed autonomously, but the intervention of a designer during validation steps is advised and will result in better output. The steps are sketched by Fig. 3. The proposed approach is based on the conceptual data model of the production database. Ensuring data availability was one of our initial objectives. For this, we rely on the data sources that are represented as a conceptual data model. In our case, it is a model entity relationship model "ER" from the operational database, which will be used to derive a multidimensional diagram with the guarantee that it will be possible afterward to feed the data warehouse from a source by means of an ETL tool.

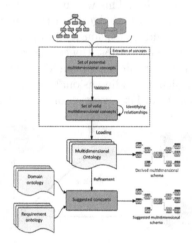

Fig. 3. Our data warehouse life cycle: ontology-based method for data modeling schema

3.1   Extraction of Multidimensional Knowledge

The first step is to extract the multidimensional concepts. It is divided into three stages that are repeated for each multidimensional concept. At first, we determine a set of potential multidimensional, using extraction rules. - Extraction of potential multidimensional concepts: In this step, we determine the potential multidimensional concepts from data sources described by ER models (facts, dimensions, measurements, etc.). Each extracted element becomes an individual (i.e. instance) of the concept that represents its role. The rules of extracting these concepts used in this step are detailed in the following.

- *Validation*: In the previous step, we obtained a set of potential multidimensional concepts (with the property "valid" = False). We move on to the validation of this set. To do so, the designer intervention is required. Upon validating a concept, its valid property will become "valid" = True.
- *Extraction of multidimensional relationships*: After identifying all valid multidimensional concepts, multidimensional relationships are determined between them. The rules of extracting these relationships used in this step are detailed in Sect. 4.

3.2   Ontology Loading

The loading of the multidimensional ontology consists in inserting the valid concepts from the previous step and the relationships between them. At the end of this stage, we obtain a populated ontology obtained by all multidimensional knowledge that we could extract from the source.

3.3   Generating a Derived Multidimensional Schema

At this stage of our approach, our multidimensional ontology is loaded with multidimensional concepts extracted from the data sources. In addition, the roles of these concepts and the relationships between them are identified. We can then generate the stars of the data warehouse.

3.4   Refinement Based on Ontologies

In this section, we will define the refinement step that is based on ontologies. In fact, the term "ontology" originates in a branch of philosophy called "metaphysics" that studies the principles of reality and aims to define the nature of beings and of the world. The ontologies were subsequently included in the field of artificial intelligence for knowledge-based systems and then adapted to the problems of information extraction. The main characteristic of ontologies, namely the development of an abstract model of the existing (conceptualization) and its formalization for use by machines. The ontology type varies according to the scope of this modeling. In the framework of our work, we will be interested in so-called "domain" ontologies [1,15]. In the following, we propose a second multidimensional schema that contains other multidimensional concepts that do not exist in the data source. This schema, which we will call "suggested multidimensional schema", proposes to introduce new concepts that we recommend to add to the derived scheme in order to improve the data warehouse. The contribution will be, for example, the addition of a new dimension to an existing fact, or even the addition of a new fact and therefore a new star. The derived multidimensional schema will be contained in the suggested multidimensional schema. To generate the suggested multidimensional scheme, we follow the following steps:

1. Choosing a domain ontology: By using ontology libraries, this first step aims at choosing a domain ontology that corresponds to our warehousing project.
2. Analyze the domain ontology: The goal of this step is to extract the multidimensional concepts from the domain ontology. We analyze the domain ontology. This will give us interesting concepts to build the conceptual model. We use the ontology and its reasoning ability to perform the task of analysis. Since ontology can capture the concepts of a domain in a formal and semantic way, each source of the data warehouse can be represented using an ontology.
3. Analyze requirements: Develop a requirement tree to obtain information on the needs of decision-makers.

4. Correspondence: In this step, we will match the concepts in the analysis step of the domain ontology and the needs analysis step, and between the derived multidimensional schema.
5. Propose the suggested multidimensional scheme: This is the final step of the approach.

Here, introduced by [19] is an algorithm to automatically identify the interesting concepts available in the global ontology representing the source. The output of this algorithm is a list of multidimensional concepts existing in the source. For each attribute (e.g. dataproperty) of the concept class under consideration, we compute the ratio "r" of the numerical attributes with respect to the total number of attributes (r = attr_num/total_attr). Concepts with a ratio above the threshold are marked as facts. The threshold is a numerical value that must be chosen arbitrarily by the designer. The numeric attributes of the fact are identified as measurements (list_num) and the non-numeric attributes (list_non_num) are identified as levels.

Then, we use an algorithm introduced by [19] to identify the dimensions of the facts obtained as a result of the preceding result. Considering all the facts of the list, we begin by identifying the list of concepts related to "fact". We rely on the cardinalities of relations with "fact" to identify the dimensions. The concepts related to "fact" by a relation 1...n, are added to the list of dimensions of this fact.

Requirements Analysis. This stage aims to obtain information on the requirements of the decision-makers. These requirements represent measures and contexts for analyzing these measures. Since decision-makers are concerned about the goals the data warehouse must fulfill, they are unaware of how to adequately describe their needs. Therefore, a requirement analysis phase for the data warehouse should begin by discovering the objectives of the decision makers. From these objectives, requirements can be more easily discovered. Indeed, the needs can be linked to multidimensional concepts, that is to say, the measures to be analyzed or the contexts of the analysis of these measures.

In the following, we focus on the modeling of warehouse requirements using ontology. The use of ontologies for the representation of requirements has several advantages such as communication, traceability, completeness and consistency [4]. It also supports detection of redundant or conflicting requirements. To model information requirements, we need to know the needs of decision makers. We propose to represent the requirements of the decision-makers using an ontology of requirements which has the form of a tree. The top of the hierarchy is the main goal of the organization. The relations are of type "is a", and they make it possible to decompose the main goal into sub-goals. The leaves are annotated by "measure" or "context". The measures are the subjects of analysis and the contexts are the dimensions.

Matching Requirements with Sources. To build the conceptual model, we precede this phase by filtering the results obtained using algorithm 1 by matching them with the requirements of the decision makers and the terms used in the domain ontology. This diversity of terms means that the same concept can be presented in different forms. Then, we proceed to a stage of matching during which we group the concepts that bear different terms but shares the same role in the decision-making information system. For this, we define a set of relations, called terminological relations, which are used to compare the terms of concepts.

- **Identity**: it is a relation between two terms that have the same syntax and semantics.
- **Synonymy**: it is a relation between two terms of different syntax expressing the same. For example, the terms remuneration and payment are synonyms.
- Equivalence: it is a relationship between two terms playing the same role. For example, the terms factory and supplier are equivalent.
- **Homonymy**: It is a relationship that expresses that the same concept can have two different meanings. For example, Quantity means "ordered quantity" or "delivered quantity".

Proposing the Suggested Multidimensional Scheme. The final step in our approach is to present a suggested multidimensional scheme. Thereafter, the designer must examine this schema and choose the elements to keep, as it is not mandatory to keep all suggested changes. For the chosen concepts, the designer must manually make the necessary modifications to the data sources to provide the data that will be used to feed these concepts. For example, one of the concepts chosen can be a new dimension that is of interest to the decision-maker. If the designer decides to keep this dimension, it is up to him to return to the source, and modify it (i.e., add one or more classes, attributes, relations) so that the new source can provide data for the new dimension.

4   Validation

In order to show the feasibility of our proposed design approach, we have developed a software prototype of CASE type (Computer Aided Software Engineering), called ODMD (Multidimensional Ontology Driven Designer).

This prototype provides assistance during the design phases of a data warehouse project. Indeed, it helps the decision makers to express their analytical needs and the designer to generate the multidimensional schema of the warehouse by following a mixed approach. ODMD offers different capabilities to achieve the goals of our automated data warehouse schema design. Figure 4 shows the functional architecture of ODMD. First, we extract the multidimensional concepts from the source ontology. Figure 5 shows the interface for entering the input information. We start by choosing the file of the source ontology and its format. Then we specify its IRI (Internationalized Resource Identifier) and give it an abbreviation in the following format: abbreviation: <IRI \#> Example: om: <http://www.w3.org/2002/07/ ontologie-multidimensionnelle\#> This makes it possible to simplify SPARQL queries, and avoid conflicts in case of redundant

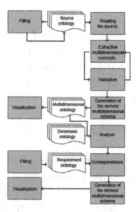

Fig. 4. Functional architecture

terms. Then, the prototype uses the Jena API [https://jena.apache.org/] and SPARQL queries to identify the concepts and relationships of the source. As an example, here is the query that makes it possible to identify the concepts of the "Entity" type:

```
PREFIX ns: <http://www.w3.org/2002/07/owl\#>
PREFIX rdf: <http://www.w3.org/1999/02/22-rdf-syntax-ns\#>
PREFIX rdfs: <http://www.w3.org/2000/01/rdf-schema\#>
PREFIX owl: <http://www.w3.org/2002/07/owl\#>
PREFIX xsd: <http://www.w3.org/2001/XMLSchema\#>
PREFIX tg:<http://www.turnguard.com/functions\#>
PREFIX om:<http://www.w3.org/2002/07/ontologie-multidimensionnelle\#>
SELECT * WHERE {?x   rdf:type   om:Entity}
```

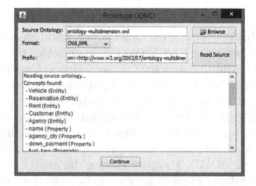

Fig. 5. ODMD interface

Then, we go on to the first step of extracting multidimensional concepts, which is the extraction of facts. The prototype presents the user with a list of potential facts, as shown in Fig. 5. The user has to choose the facts to retain as valid facts. After each concept extraction iteration, the designer is prompted with a validation interface. Figure 6 shows the graphic representation of the result schema.

Fig. 6. Example result schema

Finally, we open the multidimensional ontology with Graphviz in Protégé to visualize the results. By only selecting the concepts that are of interest to us, we get a visualization of a star. At this point, the generation of the derived multidimensional schema has been completed, and we can move to the refinement step to generate the suggested multidimensional schema. We select the domain ontology we want to use. The prototype will analyze it and extract new potential concepts. The last step is to match the terms semi-automatically as shown below:

5   Conclusion

In this paper, we focused on the design phase and showed how the use of the multidimensional ontology combined with a domain ontology and requirements ontology can be beneficial to the design process and can offer more than what the sources alone can. In our future work, we plan to implement intelligent retrieval and semantic expansion in the retrieval process as a solution for data mapping problem between data of the sources and data coming from the users. Second, we plan to deal with other semantic and modeling formalism such as XML.

References

1. Abran, A., Cuadrado, J.J., Barriocanal, E.G., Mendes, O., Alonso, S.S., Sicilia, M.Á.: Engineering the ontology for the SWEBOK: issues and techniques. In: Ontologies for Software Engineering and Software Technology, pp. 103–121 (2006)
2. Bellatreche, L., Valduriez, P., Morzy, T.: Advances in databases and information systems. Inf. Sys. Front. **20**(1), 1–6 (2018)
3. Bonifati, A., Cattaneo, F., Ceri, S., Fuggetta, A., Paraboschi, S.: Designing data marts for data warehouses. ACM Trans. Softw. Eng. Methodol. **10**(4), 452–483 (2001)

4. Borgo, S., Hitzler, P., Kutz, O. (ed.): Formal Ontology in Information Systems - Proceedings of the 10th International Conference, FOIS 2018, Cape Town, South Africa, 19–21 September 2018, volume 306 of Frontiers in Artificial Intelligence and Applications. IOS Press (2018)
5. Boussaid, O, Bentayeb, F., Maïz, N. (ed.): A publishing system based on ontologies for the virtual storage Hammamet-Tunisie, 31 May–3 June 2006
6. Cabibbo, L., Torlone, R.: A logical approach to multidimensional databases. In: Schek, H.-J., Alonso, G., Saltor, F., Ramos, I. (eds.) EDBT 1998. LNCS, vol. 1377, pp. 183–197. Springer, Heidelberg (1998). https://doi.org/10.1007/BFb0100985
7. Gallinucci, E., Golfarelli, M., Rizzi, S.: Schema profiling of document-oriented databases. Inf. Syst. **75**, 13–25 (2018)
8. Giorgini, P., Rizzi, S., Garzetti, M.: GRAnD: a goal-oriented approach to requirement analysis in data warehouses. Decis. Support Syst. **45**(1), 4–21 (2008)
9. Golfarelli, M., Maio, D., Rizzi, S.: Conceptual design of data warehouses from E/R schema. In: Thirty-First Annual Hawaii International Conference on System Sciences, Kohala Coast, Hawaii, USA, 6–9 January 1998, pp. 334–343 (1998)
10. Golfarelli, M., Rizzi, S.: A survey on temporal data warehousing. IJDWM **5**(1), 1–17 (2009)
11. Kimball, R.: The Data Warehouse Toolkit: Practical Techniques for Building Dimensional Data Warehouses. Wiley (1996)
12. Mazón, J.N., Lechtenbörger, J., Trujillo, J.: A survey on summarizability issues in multidimensional modeling. Data Knowl. Eng. **68**(12), 1452–1469 (2009)
13. Mazón, J.N., Trujillo, J.: A hybrid model driven development framework for the multidimensional modeling of data warehouses!. SIGMOD Rec. **38**(2), 12–17 (2009)
14. Moody, D.L. Kortink, M.A.R.: From enterprise models to dimensional models: a methodology for data warehouse and data mart design. In: Proceedings of the Second International Workshop on Design and Management of Data Warehouses, DMDW 2000, Stockholm, Sweden, p. 5, 5–6 June 2000
15. Ovchinnikova, E., Kühnberger, K., Thiele, M., Lehner, W.: Aspects of automatic ontology extension: adapting and regeneralizing dynamic updates. In: Proceedings of the 6th of the Second Australasian Workshop on Advances in Ontologies, vol. 72, pp. 51–60 (2006)
16. Phipps, C., Davis, K.C.: Automating data warehouse conceptual schema design and evaluation. In: Design and Management of Data Warehouses 2002, Proceedings of the 4th International Workshop DMDW 2002, Toronto, Canada, 27 May 2002, pp. 23–32 (2002)
17. O. Romero and A. Abelló
18. Soussi, A., Feki, J., Gargouri, F.: Automatic generation and validation of schemas of data marts. In: Entrepôts Tunisie, 10 Juin 2005
19. Thenmozhi, M., Vivekanandan, K.: A tool for data warehouse multidimensional schema design using ontology. Int. J. Comput. Sci. Issues (IJCSI) **10**(02), 161–168 (2013)
20. Zekri, M., Marsit, I., Abdellatif, A.: A new data warehouse approach using graph theory. In: IEEE International Conference on e-Business Engineering (ICEBE 2011), 19–21 Octobre 2011, China (2011)
21. Zekri, M., Marsit, I., Abdellatif, A.: Query history based approach for data warehouse design. In: 1st International Conference on Model & Data Engineering (MEDI 2011), 28–30 Septembre 2011, Obidos, Portugal (2011)

Exploratory Analysis of Collective Intelligence Projects Developed Within the EU-Horizon 2020 Framework

Shweta Suran[(✉)], Vishwajeet Pattanaik, Sadok Ben Yahia, and Dirk Draheim

Department of Software Science, Tallinn University of Technology, Tallinn, Estonia
{shweta,vishwajeet.pattanaik,sadok.ben,dirk.draheim}@taltech.ee

Abstract. Over recent years, Collective Intelligence (CI) and crowd-sourcing platforms have become a vital resource for learning, problem-solving, decision making and predictions. Unfortunately, the only generic model for developing CI systems (i.e., the CI Genome model) was published nearly a decade ago. Most articles that discuss this model only use examples of older CI projects, thereby raising the question 'Can the genome model comprehensively describe recent CI platforms? If not, what new genes could be proposed to improve the model'? In this article, we answer this question by conducting an analysis of 10 CI projects developed after 2015. We first analyze these projects with respect to the genome model, and then identify three new components namely: Beneficiaries, Knowledge and Social Cause, and Collaboration-based Contest; that could help us improve the genome model, thereby improving our understanding of more recent CI initiatives.

Keywords: Collective intelligence · Wisdom of crowds · Crowdsourcing · Genome model · Exploratory analysis

1 Introduction

The idea of collective intelligence (CI) or 'wisdom of crowd', has been a keen interest among researchers at least ever since the 1780 s; when Marquis de Condorcet proposed the "Jury Theorem" [6]. Since then, numerous authors, researchers and philosophers from different research areas have provided a wide range of insights into the social and biological aspects of CI. The first formal definition of CI in Information and Communications Technology (ICT) how-ever, was provided by Pierre Lévy in 1994 (i.e., after the inception of the World Wide Web). Lévy described CI as "a form of universally distributed intelligence, constantly enhanced, coordinated in real time, and resulting in the effective mobilization of skill." [7]; followed by the several others, among which the most cited definitions are the ones proposed by Glenn (in 2013 [5]) and Malone et al. (in 2015 [10]). Interestingly, both Glenn's and Malone's work were influenced by the rising interest in the Social Web, which gained popularity in the early 2000s.

© Springer Nature Switzerland AG 2019
N. T. Nguyen et al. (Eds.): ICCCI 2019, LNAI 11684, pp. 285–296, 2019.
https://doi.org/10.1007/978-3-030-28374-2_25

Since then, numerous research institutes and organizations have developed and deployed several CI platforms that have enabled coordination, collaboration and competition among individuals [7] over the Web. Some commonly discussed applications of such platforms include: prediction markets [11], crowdsourcing [13], and open innovation [4]. This interest in applications of CI has allowed for distinct research in a variety of fields such as biology [2], management [1], computer science [5] and citizen science [15]. And this has, therefore, lead to the development of distinct CI frameworks and models like the ones proposed by Luo et al. [8], Malone et al. [11], Lykourentzou et al. [9] and Nguyen et al. [12]. Most of these models are designed using insights from specific domains, and are based on domain-specific requirements; presented as completely distinct entities. Unfortunately, this abundance of knowledge has not yet lead to the development of a comprehensive generic model for CI. Among the available models, the most cited is the "the CI genome" model proposed by Malone et al. [11].

Malone's genome model describes the components of CI systems by answering the questions about "Who? Why? What? How?" [11]. Deriving from the answers of these questions, the authors propose the 'genes' of CI systems and explain that the combination of these genes (i.e., genome) is what classifies one CI system from another. Although widely accepted, the model, however, lacks granularity and needs to be developed further [11]. Furthermore, the CI platforms (Linux, Threadless, Wikipedia and InnoCentive) used to describe these genes are some of the most commonly discussed examples and were developed at least two decades ago. This implies that the comprehensiveness of the genome model could be conclusively evaluated by examining newer CI platforms using the model. And, the results of the analysis could provide us with new insights, which could help us come up with new genes (i.e., components).

With these hypotheses in mind, we conduct an exploratory analysis of 10 CI projects developed within the EU's Horizon 2020 research framework. Each of the chosen projects were developed in or after 2015 (some ongoing) and were selected based on the availability of their deliverables, technical reports and publications. To ensure the reproducibility of our research, we only selected the projects whose related documents were openly available on the Web. Furthermore, to gain a deeper understanding of the inner functioning of these platforms, we also registered and participated in each of the platforms. Finally, based on the findings of the analysis, we present a set of components that could help us improve the CI genome model. The remainder of the paper is structured as follows. In Sect. 2, we briefly describe Malone's genome model for CI. In Sect. 3, we describe the previously mentioned 10 CI platforms. Section 4 discusses the findings of the analysis and Sect. 5 concludes the paper.

2   The Collective Intelligence Genome

The genome model defines CI systems using the analogy of biological 'genes,' i.e., its building blocks. And to better explain and classify these building blocks, Malone et al. use four questions "*Who* is performing the task? *Why* are they doing it?" and *"What* is being accomplished? *How* is it being done?" [11]. The answers to these questions namely *staffing, motivation, goal* and *structure/process* are classified into different 'genes' and "the full combination of *genes* [...] can be viewed as the *genome"* [11] of any particular CI system. It is this 'genome' of each CI system that distinguishes it from other similar systems.

To better explain the genome model, we describe the components of the CI platform *Kaggle* 'Home for Data Science' using the 'genes' proposed by Malone et al. [11]. Launched only a decade ago, the *Kaggle* platform is designed to gather solutions to complex data science problems by "tapping CI of worldwide data science community" [3].

- *Who genes:* These genes answer the question "Who undertakes the activity?" [11] and are classified into two basic genes 'hierarchy' and 'crowd'. *Hierarchy* describes an individual or a group who have been assigned some tasks by the host (the organization that built the CI system or the one that raised the challenge). For instance, in *Kaggle*, an organization that hosts (i.e., provides the dataset and evaluates the solutions) the competition is the *Hierarchy*. Such organizations work in collaboration with *Kaggle*, which allows them to host competitions on the platform.
  Crowd on the other hand, describes an individual who is not assigned specific tasks (by an authoritative figure) and may choose to contribute according to their own will. In *Kaggle*, individuals or groups of participants who participate in competitions, share new datasets or provide new solutions and feedback, are all part of the *Crowd*.
- *Why genes:* These genes answer the question "Why do people take part in the activity?" [11]. These genes are classified into three basic genes, namely 'money', 'love' and 'glory'. *Money* or financial gain can be an important motivator for both individuals employed by the host and the members of the Crowd, who are willing to share new ideas and innovative solutions. *Love* or interest/passion are intrinsic motivators that can encourage an individual to contribute to the system even in the absence of financial motivators. Finally, individuals interested in earning recognition or reputation are motivated by the *Glory* gene.
  Kaggle motivates its users using all three *Why genes*. Participants who submit solutions in competitions are motivated by *money*, while others are either motivated by the 'Kaggle Rankings' in Competitions, Kernels and Discussion, i.e., *glory*; or are motivated by their *love* and interest in learning about data science and machine learning.
- *What genes:* These genes answer the question "What is being done?" [11] and are classified into two genes 'create' and 'decide'. *Create* describes activities where an individual or a group contributes to the system by generating new ideas, artefacts or solutions. *Decide* describes the activities where members of the platform evaluate others' contributions and select the best ones.
  In *Kaggle*, participants *Create* by submitting new datasets, pieces of codes and answers to questions (in discussions); and *Decide* the best topics of discussions, answers and kernels (i.e., codes) by up-voting others' contributions.

- *How genes:* These genes answer the question "How is it being done" [11]. Malone et al. classify this genes as 'collection' (independent-create activities), 'collaboration' (dependent-create activities), 'individual decisions' (independent-decide activities) and 'group decision' (dependent-decide activities). *Collection* can be described as the creation of new ideas, solutions and artefacts independently contributed by individual members of the Crowd; a sub-type of this gene is *Contest*, in which submitted contributions are evaluated and the best ones are rewarded. In contrast to the 'collection' gene, *Collaboration* occurs when members of the Crowd work together to come up with new things. Lastly, *Group decisions* and *Individual decisions* occur when members of the Crowd make some choice or decision; that can have an effect on the group as a whole, or on just the individual (respectively).
  In *Kaggle*, the *Collection* gene occurs when participants contribute to the platform in form of data-sets, kernels and questions/answers (in discussions). While, kernels submitted in *Kaggle Competitions* belong to the *Contest* gene. And, the overall aggregated knowledge (in the form of codes, suggestions and feedback) about any given dataset or challenge can be viewed as a *Collaboration*. Similarly, *Individual decisions* are represented by the individual up-votes participants give to a dataset, kernel or question/answer. Whereas, the 'Hotness' of the datasets, kernels or questions/answers (calculated based on the overall up-votes) and represents the *Group decision* of the community.

3   Exploratory Analysis

As mentioned in Sect. 1 we now attempt to evaluate the comprehensiveness of the CI genome model by examining several ongoing/recent CI projects with respect to the different 'genes' proposed by Malone et al. [11]. To this end, we decided to investigate CI and crowdsourcing projects developed within the EU's Horizon 2020 Research Framework, considering that the deliverables and technical reports of such research projects are openly accessible on the Web. We opted to investigate EU funded projects over other popular business-oriented CI projects like GoldCorp and Threadless, since business-oriented platforms are typically owned by private organizations and therefore the technical descriptions of such platforms are not available in published literature. Business-oriented platforms that are discussed in scientific articles are generally published as case-studies and focus more on the theoretical aspects of the projects and not the technical aspects.

As an additional selection criterion, we decide to choose only those projects that were launched in the last five years. And, had alteast 3000–5000 registered users. Based on the availability of the projects' documentation and access to the projects' website, we decided to examine 10 CI platforms listed in Table 1.

To gain a clear understanding of these platforms, we first examined the available reports (from the projects' website) and then registered as a participant on each of the platforms; after which we studied the different components, activities, motivations and goals of these platforms, over the duration of a month

Table 1. List of selected Collected intelligence projects

PID	Project title	Start date	End date	URL
P1	CIPTEC	May' 2015	April' 2018	ciptec.eu
P2	POWER	Dec' 2015	Nov' 2019	power-h2020.eu
P3	Crowd4Roads	Jan' 2016	Dec' 2018	c4rs.eu
P4	Open4Citizens	Jan' 2016	June' 2018	open4citizens.eu
P5	Saving Food 2.0	Jan' 2016	Dec' 2017	savingfood.eu
P6	CAPTOR	Jan' 2016	Dec' 2018	captor-project.eu
P7	COMRADES	Jan' 2016	Dec' 2018	comrades-project.eu
P8	SOCRATIC	Jan' 2016	Feb' 2018	socratic.eu
P9	ChildRescue	Jan' 2018	Dec' 2020	childrescue.eu
P10	Share4Rare	Jan' 2018	Dec' 2020	share4rare.org

(February' 2019 - March' 2019). Participating in these platforms, helped us gain a better understanding of the inner functioning of each of these projects.

Combining our finding from the related documents and based on our experiences while using the platforms, we first present a brief summary on the selected CI projects; followed by the list of different components of the platforms classified according to the genome model.

- *CIPTEC:* CIPTEC aims to bring new innovative solutions in the form of services or business models, which can help improve urban public transport (PT). The platform gathers and analyzes customer & market intelligence to understand the demand for urban PT. Based on its finding CIPTEC then uses crowdsourcing and co-creation workshops to come with innovative ideas to solve the previously identified PT challenges and issues.

  To gather innovative ideas from its users (i.e., *Crowd*), CIPTEC uses competitive crowdsourcing (i.e., *Contest*); whereas collaborative crowdsourcing (i.e., *Collaboration*) is used to review, rate and discuss the submitted ideas. Members of the CIPTEC (*Crowd*), motivated by *Love* can choose to rate and provide feedback to the submitted ideas (*Individual Decisions*). Based on the users' feedback the best ideas are selected for the co-creation workshop, where the 15 most up-voted ideas (i.e., *Group decision*) are discussed and ranked by CIPTEC's expert advisory board (i.e., *Hierarchy*). After which, the top two ideas with the highest ranking/scores are rewarded with *Money* and free entrance to public transport (for a period of time).

  In addition to its platform, the CIPTEC project also provides a free online toolkit to improve coordination in the planning of solutions and measures in urban PT. The tool can be used by citizens as well as by the transport authorities and policymakers; and allows its users to provide feedback for new implemented ideas in terms of feasibility, ability and novelty.

- *POWER:* The main goal of POWER is to spread awareness and take actions on four water challenges namely: reduction of water consumption (in Milton

Keynes, UK), water quality (in Sabadell, Spain), flood risk (in Leicester, UK) and water conservation (in Jerusalem, Israel). POWER provides a channel for interaction, idea contests and knowledge sharing among citizens, municipal authorities, research organizations and policymakers. The motive of POWER idea contests is to generate new innovative ideas for climate change (specifically problems related to floods and droughts) and to engage communities in order to solve water sustainability issues.

Members of the *Crowd* can provide contributions in the form of sustainability apps and educational/awareness-building projects. The types of users, their motivations and the idea submission-selection process of POWER is similar to the CIPTEC project. The contributors of 10 most up-voted ideas (in any given POWER competition) are invited to a conference, where the community (i.e., *Hierarchy* including municipal authorities, policy makers and research organizations) select the best contributions; and assist the contributors in developing their ideas by providing both guidance and funding. As an intrinsic motivator, the POWER platform also provides its users with a community and personal progress score that indicates their preparedness on problem awareness, know-how and readiness to act to save water.

- *Crowd4Roads:* The Crowd4Roads project combines two initiatives, i.e., trip sharing and crowd sensing; and attempts to solve two well-known sustainability issues of road transport: low occupancy rate in cars and delay in road maintenance. The project attempts to resolve these issues by combining two transport related services, namely *BlaBlaCar* (a ride-sharing service) and *SmartRoadSense* (a crowdsourced road-quality sensing tool).

  BlaBlaCar is a trusted trip sharing (i.e., carpooling) initiative that allows people travelling between pairs of cities to connect and share rides. Car owners travelling from one city to another can offer available seats in their cars, to people who would like to join the trip in exchange for fuel expenses. SmartRoadSense, on the other hand, is a crowd sensing system that exploits the accelerometers of car-mounted smartphones to collect data about road roughness; and helps policymakers in taking well-informed road maintenance decisions.

  Crowd4Roads plans on integrating the carpooling services of BlaBlaCar into its SmartRoadSense app. Doing so the platform intends to provide citizens (i.e., *Crowd*) with a platform where users can contribute information about road quality (i.e., *Collection*) and policymaker could then use this collective knowledge (i.e., *Collaboration*) to make better-informed decisions about road maintenance (i.e., *Group decision*). Finally, the *Individual decisions* of the users on the platform can be seen in their choice of using the BlaBlaCar carpooling service. The users of the Crowd4Roads project can either be motivated by their *Love* for sustainable transport or by *Glory* and geo-coins (i.e., virtual *Money*) within the system's gamification mechanism.

- *Open4Citizens:* The aim of the Open4Citizens project is to empower citizens by allowing them to work with programmers, researchers and policymakers, with the goal to make better use of the open data provided by different governing bodies and organizations; thereby helping in improving the quality of life in urban areas, specifically in Copenhagen (Denmark), Karlstad (Sweden), Rotterdam (Netherlands), Milano (Italy) and Barcelona (Spain). To achieve this aim, Open4Citizens organized multiple hackathons in each of the previously mentioned cities.

Each of these hackathon events was divided into three sub-events, namely pre-hackathon, second hackathon and post-hackathon. During the first stage (pre-hackathon) citizen groups and communities (i.e., *Crowd*) present challenges/issues which could be solved by open data (motivated by *Love*); to public officers and stakeholders (i.e., *Hierarchy*). The public authorities then take a *Group decision* and select the most important issues they would like to get solutions for through the hackathon. After this, the public authorities, together with the open-data owners, decide the specifications and framing of the dataset that would be provided to the participants of the hackathon. During the main hackathon (i.e., *Contest*) event citizens, programmers and researchers (i.e., *Crowd*) work together and co-create solutions (i.e., *Collaboration*) that are then evaluated by a panel of judges (employed by the governing bodies) and the best solutions are rewarded in cash (i.e., *Money*).

In the post-hackathon event, the solutions provided by the participants are made available on the 'OpenDataLab platform: ODL' (designed by the Open4-Citizens team). The goal of this platform is to provide citizens, students, researchers and policymakers with the consolidated knowledge and tools acquired from the hackathon events; and to raise awareness among citizens about the advantages and uses of open data, through experimental tools.

– *Saving Food 2.0:* The SavingFood project is a collective awareness platform that attempts to tackle food waste in the UK, Greece, Hungary and Belgium. The aim of the project is to raise awareness about food waste among citizens and to provide a solution by which organizations like supermarkets, restaurants and catering services can donate extra food to the people in need. The platform classifies its participants (i.e., *Crowd*) into three groups: donors, recipients and volunteers. The donors are organizations that prepare and store food in large quantities on a daily basis and would like to donate excess food items that might go to waste. The recipients are non-profit organizations like Boroume, Feedback and HFA who provide food to the vulnerable groups and people in need. Finally, the volunteers are citizens who would like to help in the social cause by transporting the food from the donors to the recipients. The collective activities of all three participant groups can be viewed as *Collaboration* as groups of participants come together and help in preventing the wastage of food.

The SavingFood project provides its participants with a Crowdsourced map that bridges the gap between donors and recipients. Both donors and recipients can mark their locations or events on the map within the platform; thereby providing a *Collection* of addresses of possible collection or drop points for excess food. Participants of the platform can also provide *Individual decisions* in the form of ratings, to each other. The system aggregates the ratings and contributions of participants to reward them with individual scores and badges, thereby motivating them not just by *Love* but also by

Glory. In addition to the badges, the system also provides the donors with a 'Food Waste Cost Calculation Tool' that motivates them to donate excess food by calculating the economic and environmental cost of the food waste.

– *CAPTOR:* The CAPTOR project aims to monitor ozone pollution levels in three European regions: Barcelonès-Vallès Oriental-Osona (Catalonia, Spain), Pianura Padana (Po Valley, Italy) and Burgenland, Steiermark and Niederösterreich (Austria). The project empowers citizens and governing bodies by providing them with real-time ozone pollution data and helps them in making well-informed decisions for behavioural and policy changes. The project also attempts to raise awareness about elevated ozone levels, and it's effects on the day-to-day life of citizens. The developers of the CAPTOR project have designed two main artefacts that support this cause. First, an ozone sensor that is developed, updated and serviced by the CAPTOR team; and second, the CAPTOR tools (AirTact and CaptorAIR) that allow citizens to visualize the ozone data on an interactive map (on the Web). Citizens who wish to host an ozone sensor at their residence can participate in the project as volunteers (i.e., *Crowd*), and are only motivated by *Love*. Once established, these ozone sensors capture the pollution data in the local vicinity and send the data to the CAPTOR repositories (i.e., *Collection*). This collected data is then aggregated and presented on the project's website (i.e., *Collaboration*). Using this knowledge citizens, communities and, non-governmental organizations (NGO)s and governing bodies (i.e., *Hierarchy*) can then propose and introduce new policies (i.e., *Group decision*) to help reduce the ozone pollution in the city. Finally, the CAPTOR team, in collaboration with researchers and NGOs, also conduct workshops where they motivate and educate citizens to take part in the project initiatives.

– *COMRADES:* The COMRADES project aims to provide an open source platform that can assist communities by helping them "reconnect, respond to, and recover from crisis situations"[1]. The project does so by providing communities with two open source services, namely CREES Services (Crisis Event Extraction Service) and Rumour veracity classifier. The services allow its users to analyze tweet and shorts messages from citizens and communities experiencing or witness any kind of crisis; by either validating the truthfulness of a given text or by determining key components (like event type and information discussed) of a crisis related tweet.

The users of the COMRADES project are categorized into three main groups: first, the communities affected by the crisis (i.e., beneficiaries); second, the reporters (i.e., *Crowd*) or the intrinsically motivated (i.e., *Love*) citizens and communities (i.e., *Crowd*) who share details of the crisis (i.e., *Collection*) on platforms like Twitter; and finally, volunteers and technical communities (i.e., *Hierarchy*) who host and use the COMRADES services to analyze and interpret incoming tweets and messages, and then provide this aggregated information (i.e., *Collaboration*) to the professional responders (i.e., *Hierarchy*) like: members of civil protection authorities, emergency services, government

---

[1] https://comrades-project.eu/.

agencies, local and international NGOs and UN agencies. These professional responders then take *collaborative* actions to assist, rescue, and support the affected.

- *SOCRATIC:* The main goal of the SOCRATIC project is to provide a collaborative space for citizens and organizations so that both can work together to identify, share and develop innovative solutions to achieve the three sustainable goals set by the United Nations[2].

  The SOCRATIC platform offers a set of tools and services that support 'Social Innovation Project Life Cycle'. The workflow for creation and selection of new ideas is exactly the same as to ones seen in the CIPTEC project. The key users of the system include individual or groups of challenge solvers (i.e., *Crowd*), challenge owners, coordinators and platform owners (i.e., *Hierarchy*), and beneficiaries. The challenge owners and platform owners raise challenges, solutions to which are proposed by challenge solvers who *compete* to achieve financial rewards. And finally, individuals and coordinators choose the best contributions.

- *ChildRescue:* The ChildRescue project aims to "effectively reduce the primary period between the moment a child is reported missing and the one when it is found"[3]. The project intends to attain three primary goals: to develop reliable scientific methodologies that can assist in missing investigation, to develop of a ChildRescue platform that is integrated to platforms of relevant government bodies and finally, to educate and familiarize citizens with the ChildRescue platform.

  The ChildRescue app classifies the process of finding missing children into four phases. During the first phase, law enforcement agencies, other governing bodies and ChildRescue administrators (i.e., *Hierarchy*) *collect* the details of missing migrant children and share it on the ChildRescue platform. The uploaded information is then examined by NGOs, caretakers and search & rescue teams (i.e., *Hierarchy* motivated by *Love*), who attempt to gather more details about the children. This aggregated information (i.e., *Collaboration*) is then viewed by members of society (i.e., *Crowd* motivated by *Love*) and by search & rescue teams who help in tracking down the whereabouts of the missing children. The details of the whereabouts of the children are then shared on the platform, after which the law enforcement agencies and other government bodies rescue the children in a safe and respectful manner.

- *Share4Rare:* The Share4Rare (S4R) platform provide a safe environment where patients, their family members and carers can share their experiences with clinicians and researchers; and can help in making other patients' lives better by contributing in ongoing research. The project is piloted towards two rare conditions: rare paediatric tumours and neuromuscular disorders; and intends to gather clinical data from 2019 to 2020.

  The project would have two types of communities: the awareness community (i.e., *Crowd*) that would constitute of patients with rare conditions and

---

[2] https://www.socratic.eu/about-us-3/.
[3] https://www.childrescue.eu/.

their carers; and the empowerment community (i.e., *Hierarchy*) which would constitute of the medical practitioners, experts and researchers. Both intrinsically (i.e., *Love*) motivated communities would share their knowledge and experiences over the platform (i.e., *Collection*); and combining this knowledge (i.e., *Collaboration*) the empowerment community would propose new research and guidelines that could help support/improve the condition of the patients.

4   Additional Components for the Genome Model

Based on our exhaustive exploratory analysis described in the previous section, we are able to classify different components of the studied CI platforms based on the genome model. However, as we expected, during our investigation we found that each of the CI platforms had some components that could not be described using 'genes' [11]. These components include: *Beneficiaries, Knowledge and Social Cause*, and *Collaboration-based Contest*, and are described as follows:

- *Beneficiaries:* As mentioned in Sect. 2 the genome model classifies the *Who* genes as *Hierarchy* and *Crowd* [11]; however, we found that each of the above described CI platforms also had a third member of the staffing namely, the *Beneficiaries*. These *Beneficiaries* could be both organizations and end-users; while, the *beneficiary* organizations use the solutions and knowledge generated by CI to develop new products and services; the end-users aim to utilize the services and knowledge production on the platform for individual benefits, including their interest to learn about innovative ideas and ongoing research. Such members of the platform, do not participate in any *create* or *decide* activities but still aim to gain from the platform in one form or another. Example of such *Beneficiaries* can be seen in *Crowd4Roads* where users interested in road quality data can simply check the same at *SmartRoad-Sense* website; whereas, in *Saving Food 2.0* its the vulnerable groups that are provided with the food; and in *CAPTOR* its the citizens who just want to keep an eye on the ozone pollution levels in their vicinity, but are not willing or cannot afford to establish a CAPTOR sensor at their place of residence.
- *Knowledge and Social Cause: Knowledge* and *Social Cause* are another set of possible 'genes' that we found in each of the CI projects. Although these motivators are similar to *Love* which is defined as intrinsic enjoyment, we realized that an individuals thirst for *Knowledge* and enthusiasm to support a *Social Cause* could be distinctly identified when compared to mere interest or passion. However, to understand the exact difference between these motivators and *Love*, we would have to investigate theories of motivation from a social science perspective.
- *Collaboration-based Contest:* Finally, we found that many of the CI platforms allowed groups of individuals to participate in *Contests* as 'teams'; thereby allowing not just collection-based contests, but also collaboration-based contests. However, as we stated earlier, the genome model suggests that only

creation activities conducted by independent members of the *Crowd* can be described using the *Contest* gene. This is a vital finding, because although literature suggests that 'collaboration-based contests' are an important part of CI [14]. However, none of the published CI frameworks and models explicitly define it as a component. Therefore, we are convinced that adding a new *How* gene that describes creation activities by dependent members of the *Crowd* viz. 'collaboration-based contests' could help improve the comprehensiveness of the genome model.

5   Conclusion

To summarize, this article attempts to validate the comprehensiveness of the genome model for CI and presents a set of components that could be included in the genome model to improve its granularity. To this end, we first provide a brief description of the genome model and then explain the different genes using the example of a crowd oriented data science platform 'Kaggle'. We then identified a set of recent or ongoing CI platforms that were developed within the EU's Horizon 2020 research framework. And, selected 10 CI projects based on the availability of the project documentation and accessibility of the project's website. We exhaustively analyzed the related documents of each of these platforms; and then, for a deeper understanding of the projects' inner functionalities, we examined the platforms as participants. Based on our findings, we compared the different components of these platforms to the 'genes' of the genome model and identified three components which could not be described using the model. We believe that this article is just a first step towards developing a novel comprehensive generic CI model. And, we hypothesize that analyzing and aggregating other CI models with the genome model could help us achieve this goal.

References

1. Boder, A.: Collective intelligence: a keystone in knowledge management. J. Knowl. Manage. **10**(1), 81–93 (2006). https://doi.org/10.1108/13673270610650120
2. Bonabeau, E., Meyer, C.: Swarm intelligence: a whole new way to think about business. Harv. Bus. Rev. **79**(5), 106–115 (2001)
3. Brackbill, D.: The network structure of collective innovation. Ph.D. dissertation, University of Pennsylvania (2017)
4. Bugshan, H.: Open innovation using web 2.0 technologies. J. Enterp. Inform. Manage. **28**(4), 595–607 (2015). https://doi.org/10.1108/JEIM-09-2014-099
5. Glenn, J.C.: Collective intelligence and an application by the millennium project. World Futures Rev. **5**(3), 235–243 (2013). https://doi.org/10.1177/1946756713497331
6. Ladha, K.K.: The condorcet jury theorem, free speech, and correlated votes. Am. J. Polit. Sci. **36**(3), 617 (1992). https://doi.org/10.2307/2111584
7. Lévy, P.: Collective Intelligence: Mankind's Emerging World in Cyberspace. Perseus Books, Cambridge (1997)

8. Luo, S., Xia, H., Yoshida, T., Wang, Z.: Toward collective intelligence of online communities: a primitive conceptual model. J. Syst. Sci. Syst. Eng. 18(2), 203–221 (2009). https://doi.org/10.1007/s11518-009-5095-0
9. Lykourentzou, I., Vergados, D.J., Kapetanios, E., Loumos, V.: Collective intelligence systems: classification and modeling. J. Emerg. Technol. Web Intell. 3(3) (2011). https://doi.org/10.4304/jetwi.3.3.217-226
10. Malone, T.W., Bernstein, M.S.: Handbook of Collective Intelligence. The MIT Press, Cambridge (2015)
11. Malone, T.W., Laubacher, R., Dellarocas, C.N.: Harnessing crowds: mapping the genome of collective intelligence. SSRN Electron. J. (2009). https://doi.org/10.2139/ssrn.1381502
12. Nguyen, V.D., Nguyen, N.T.: Intelligent collectives: theory, applications, and research challenges. Cybern. Syst. 49(5–6), 261–279 (2018). https://doi.org/10.1080/01969722.2017.1418254
13. Salminen, J.: The role of collective intelligence in crowdsourcing innovation. Ph.D. dissertation, Lappeenranta University of Technology (2015)
14. Surowiecki, J.: The Wisdom of Crowds. Anchor (2005)
15. Tinati, R., Simperl, E., Luczak-Rösch, M., Kleek, M.V., Shadbolt, N.: Collective intelligence in citizen science - a study of performers and talkers. Comput. Res. Reposit. (CoRR) (2014). https://eprints.soton.ac.uk/363608/

Framework for Self-adaptation and Decision-Making of Smart Objects

Adil Chekati[1]([⊠])⬚, Meriem Riahi[2]⬚, and Faouzi Moussa[3]⬚

[1] Faculty of Sciences of Tunis (FST), University of Tunis ElManar, Tunis, Tunisia
adil.chekati@fst.utm.tn
[2] High National School of Engineers of Tunis (ENSIT),
University of Tunis, Tunis, Tunisia
meriem.riahi@ensit.rnu.tn, meriem.riahi2013@gmail.com
[3] Faculty of Sciences of Tunis (FST), University of Tunis ElManar, Tunis, Tunisia
faouzimoussa@gmail.com

Abstract. The Internet of Things (IoT) is at the heart of all modern technological developments. In fact, the number of connected objects doubles approximately every three years and in the long term, it is very likely that there will be digital in every object in our daily lives. Nowadays, we even talk about Internet of Everything (IoE) and we consider the interactions between different objects and those between the objects and persons. However, these connected objects cannot adapt their behavior to users activities and preferences. Relative to that contest, the contribution of this work consists in allowing objects connected in an IoT environment to be smarter and personalized to the needs and state of the user and other objects around them. More precisely, the idea is to add the aspect of self-adaptation and decision-making in the existing connected objects. We propose in this paper a framework for self-adaptation and decision making of smart objects called SADM-SmratObjects. This framework is applied on a case study of crisis management.

Keywords: Smart Objects · Internet of Things · Decision Making · Self-adaptation

1 Introduction

Internet of Things (IoT) could be defined as a dynamic global network infrastructure with self configuring capabilities based on standard and interoperable communication protocols where physical and virtual 'things' have identities, physical attributes, and virtual personalities and use intelligent interfaces, and are seamlessly integrated into the information network [1]. Hence, Internet of Things is a paradigm in which computing and networking capabilities are embedded in an object [2]. Internet of Everything (IoE) emerged from IoT combining people, process, data, and things. Thereby, any object can be equipped with digital

© Springer Nature Switzerland AG 2019
N. T. Nguyen et al. (Eds.): ICCCI 2019, LNAI 11684, pp. 297–308, 2019.
https://doi.org/10.1007/978-3-030-28374-2_26

features and can be connected to other objects in the network, people and processes. The objective of IoE is to facilitate information exchange and to help decision making.

In fact, according to Gartner [3], almost 14.2 billion connected objects will be expected to be used in 2019, a number that will increase by 31% in one year. 900 billion Dollars will be spent by companies on connected devices in 2018–2019. 21 billion devices will be connected globally by 2020, and by the same year, 2 out of 5 cars in the world will have some form of wireless network connection. Therefore, the main problem persists is that these connected objects still do not know how to adapt their behaviour to our the daily activities of people, their preferences and other things around. The main reason of that is the lack of intelligence and autonomy in these objects.

It is in this stream of ideas this research is conducted to propose autonomous objects. Autonomous objects, also called smart objects, will perform tasks with the ability to interact more efficiently with their environment. So, what is a smart object?

According to WordReference, an object is "Anything that can be seen or touched and is for the most part stable or lasting in form, and is usually not alive". According to Oxford, an object is "a material thing that can be seen and touched" [4].

From thereon, a possible definition of the word object in the field of IoT could be: "Any electronic device which can be connected to the Internet and collect data, such as a sensor, or a device which perform an action on an other object, called an actuator." "A Smart Object is a physical device that can be identified throughout its life and interact with the environment and other devices". It can act in an intelligent and independent manner under certain conditions. In fact, Smart Objects have an integrated operating system and can usually include actuators, sensors or both. This allows intelligent objects to better communicate with other objects, with process and environmental data [4]. According to these properties, A smart object is every real world object that has the ability to adapt with its environment, make decision autonomously, and communicate with other objects. However, introducing this aspects in IoT system is challenging due to the heterogeneity of objects and the lack of standardizations of ensuring interaction between objects, and between users and objects.

In this paper, we propose a framework called "SADM-SmartObjects" for Self Adaptation and Decision Making of Smart Objects. The main purpose is to incorporate a kind of intelligence into real world things so that these entities can interact efficiently in real time with changes in their environment.

The remainder of paper is organized as follows: Sect. 2 reviews some related works. Section 3 details the proposed framework for self adaptation and decision making of smart objects. Section 4 shows how SADM-SmartObjects framework can be applied through a case study. Finally, Sect. 5 summarizes the proposition and outlines the prospects of this research.

2   Related Work

The view of the internet of things can be seen from two perspectives: "Internet Centric" and "Thing Centric". The Internet Centric perspective is an Internet-based architecture focusing on Internet services, communication protocols and managing the data coming from objects. In contrast, in the object-centred architecture "Thing Centric" intelligent objects occupy the center of the architecture. We summarize here the main works in these two perspectives which seems to us the most relevant.

2.1   Internet-Centric Approaches

From the internet-centric perspective, the authors in [2] present a cloud-based vision for the implementation of the Internet of Things. It is a Cloud architecture that interacts between private and public clouds, with a conceptual framework integrating ubiquitous objects and applications to take advantage of the full potential of cloud computing and ubiquitous detection. However, a very high-cost architecture in terms of resources (private clouds...) is not a simple solution accessible to everyone. The research work in [5] proposed a Cloud-centric IoT based on student healthcare monitoring framework, it consists of three phases: First one is acquiring students health data from medical devices and sensors. In the second phase, medical diagnosis system uses the medical measurements to take a decision related to student health. Finally in the third phase 3, alerts are sent to caretakers related to students health. Besides the high-cost of implementing this solution, it depends on a huge calculation rate and many parameters to be configured.

Table 1 shows a comparison between these approaches in terms of: Response time (Res.time), consideration of Real-Time aspect, flexibility in term of adopting the proposed architecture in various fields, visualization in term of possibility to monitor the architecture via a graphical user interface (GUI), and decision making (DM) precising either the decision is taken autonomously by each object or collaboratively between many objects.

Table 1. Comparison table between internet-centric approaches

	Res. time	Real-time	Flexibility	Visualization	DM
Gubbi et al. [2]	Medium	Yes	Yes	No	Collaboratively
Verma et al. [5]	Low	Yes	No	No	Collaboratively

We notice that Gubbi et al.'s approach based on combination between private and public clouds are offers better response time and is more flexible, but it is a very expensive solution. Although, the decision making is taken in collaboratively on both solutions.

2.2   Thing-Centric Approaches

Several efforts have been performed in the thing-centric perspective, that focus on modelling objects as the heart of the proposed system. The authors in [6] proposed a cognitive management framework for IoT. The framework includes three levels of functionality, where cognitive entities provide the means for self-management and learning. However, the process is long, there is a lot of exchange of flows between the different entities what can causes serious problems if one of these flows is lost. In [7] authors proposed a new semantic model for smart objects description and users request resolution using ontological techniques combined with description logics. The research work in [8] proposed an architecture integrating IoT technologies into a single platform, the architecture based on the use of the Smart Object framework encapsulate identification, sensor technologies, embedded object logic, object ad-hoc networking. The proposition in [9] introduces an algorithm for decision making in an IoT environment that takes into consideration the following: Data in motion, multi-objective, data increase and missing data. However, there is a need for introducing a storage module to save results and solutions, and a need to adding the real time aspect which will help to minimize response time. The authors in [10] presented a Multi-Agent-System based architecture for developing IoT solutions, the idea consists in using MAS features in order to provide an efficient IoT model. Although, the combination between IoT and MAS has many problems in ensuring the full beneficiation and exploitation of IoT's object capabilities as far as they are limited only with either cognitive or reactive agents.

Table 2 presents a comparison between these approaches. It shows that the approach of Kelaidonis et al. [6] is the best solution, offering autonomous decision making by smart objects with the adequate response time.

Table 2. Comparison table between thing-centric approaches

	Res. time	Real-time	Flexibility	Visualization	DM
Kelaidonis et al. [6]	Medium	Yes	Yes	Yes	Autonomous
Yachir et al. [7]	High	No	No	No	Collaboratively
Sanchez et al. [8]	High	No	Yes	No	Autonomous
Manqele et al. [9]	High	Yes	Yes	No	NaN
Sofia et al. [10]	Medium	Yes	Yes	Yes	Collaboratively

Most of these proposals relate to a separate area of application, which infects the flexibility and the ability of these architectures to be used in several application domains. Therefore, the configuration and manipulation of connected objects seems to be harder due to the absence of visualization and monitoring interface.

In the other hand, several authors have considered the modeling aspect of persons in the interaction. Like In [11] authors introduced the concept of Process of Thing "POT" to overcome restrictions on objects that appear with traditional workflow languages by integrating the aspect of Storyline, where human beings are a main component in the story. A more comprehensive modeling can be found in [12], authors introduces the aspect of agentification of objects according to conceptual perspectives using standards, and operational perspectives using commitments, user-to-thing interaction is considered one of the business norm.

To this end, as we are interested of the Thing-Centric approach in our research, and we focus on the intelligence aspects of connected objects. Thus, we propose an architecture allowing to:

- Increase the autonomy of decision-making by objects, which is significant to make objects smarter: passing from connected objects to intelligent objects.
- Use virtualization to create virtual copies of objects in the real world, in order to facilitate the management and the handling of these objects.
- Consider the aspect of Real Time, in order to allow solutions based on this proposal to be more effective.
- Develop a more flexible architecture, which could be compatible with use in different application domains.

This framework is now presented.

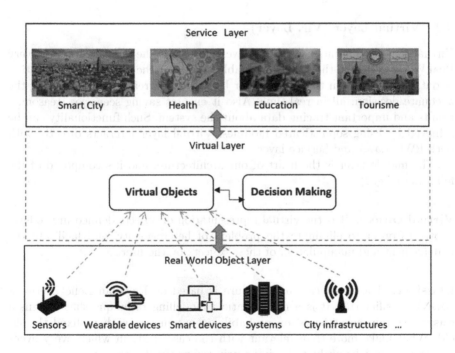

Fig. 1. Architecture of SADM-SmartObjects.

3   Framework SADM-SmartObjects

Framework SADM-SmartObjects is based on multi-layer architecture proposed for Self-Adaptation and Decision Making for Smart Objects (Fig. 1). It aims to introduce a general structure for developing Internet of Things solutions, inspired from Kelaidonis et al.'s work [6] and proposing an optimal solution for autonomous decision making.

It is made up of three layers named respectively: Real-World Object Layer (RWO Layer), Virtual Layer (Vir. Layer) and Service Layer (Srv. Layer). SADM-SmartObjects layers are detailed as follows:

3.1   Real-World Object Layer (RWO Layer)

RWO Layer represents the lower layer, or the physical layer. It gathers all real-world objects of the IoT system. Real-World Object is any physical object, device or peripheral (sensors, Actuators, etc.), associated with everyday objects or people (a table, a room, a person, etc.).

RWO Layer ensures the following functionalities: perception, communication and connection between objects. It interacts directly with Virtual layer. We consider this level as an input to our virtualization level.

3.2   Virtual Layer (Vir. Layer)

Virtual Layer represents the middle layer. it ensures the virtualization of every Real World Object in the system. It enables achieving the maximum exploitation of data delivered from the RWO Layer by analyzing, reasoning and taking the adequate decision, all in real-time. Also it ensures saving scenarios, reasoning results and important tracing data about the system. Such functionality can be achieved by using sophisticated modules. Virtual layer interacts directly with both RWO Layer and Service layer.

The middle layer is the heart of our architecture, and it's composed of the following (Fig. 2):

Virtual Object. It is the virtual representation of objects defined in the level above. In order to eliminate the problem of heterogeneity, and facilitate the management and manipulation of these objects by the user.

Classifier. The classification procedure is based on Bayesian Belief Network (BBN) classifier [13]. It is a mathematical modelling technique that assigns a class to certain event based on probabilistic parameters with prefixed threshold. What make more than relevant with the case study in which every event occurrence must be evaluated using a primary parameter measure.

The classifier precept measurements and data coming from real-world sensors and devices, and push it through a BBN in order to be classified, in real-time. Depending on the class, classifier sends these measurements either to Decision

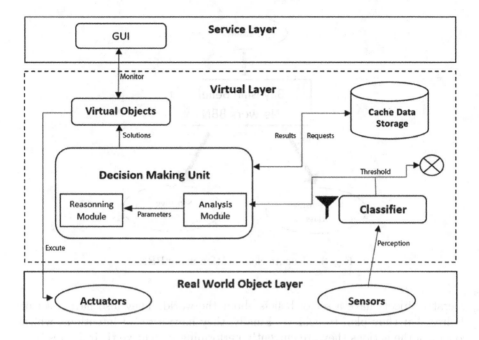

Fig. 2. The framework of SADM-SmartObjects.

Making (DM) to be treated, or just ignore them. Figure 3 depicts the classification procedure adopted for classifying an event in SADM-SmartObjects architecture.

Decision Making Unit. An IoT solution that enables making sense of all collected data is the main aim of our work, to pass from connected objects to smart objects. It means to go ahead from just collecting IoT data for later process to make decisions and take actions in real-time. Therefore, the decision making unit in our SADM framework represents the intelligent core of Virtual Layer. it is a based on two dependents modules: Analysis and Reasoning.

Analysis Module. By order, Analysis module is the first to receive measurements coming from Classifier. After parameterizing these measurements, first thing to do is to check in the Cache data storage if similar parameters already exists. If so, Cache data storage withdraw the convenient solution and send it to DM unit. Otherwise, Analysis module sends the parameters directly to the Reasoning module.

Reasoning Module. Reasoning module is responsible of carrying out the solution of the new situation to the system, by enabling objects to act autonomously depending on the state, the measurements and their environment. It is based on a multi agent system (MAS). Reasoning module in SADM-SmartObjects framework uses the BDI model [15], which is based on a theory of how humans

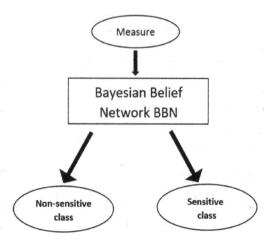

Fig. 3. Measure classification using BBN.

operate: objects have a set of beliefs about the world. They also have a set of desires that they plan to achieve. Finally, they have a set of intentions, which consist of the actions they are currently performing to achieve their desires [16]. Cognitive agents conceive solutions, then the supervisor which is a reactive agent adopts it. Figure 4 presentes a close-up look to Decision Making Unit.

Cache Data Storage. A memory storage inspired by the OS cache memory. It is where metadata on objects, virtual objects is stored. It aims to reduce the system response time by saving parameters and scenarios of previous situations. When the system input looks similar, automatically Cache data storage shows it up without a need to regenerate all the process.

3.3 Service Layer (Srv. Layer)

Service layer represents the higher layer which can be seen as a front-end one due to its relationship directly with users. It ensures the visualization of the different entities in IoT system, through a Graphic User Interface (GUI). The GUI enables users to monitor, manage, configure and manipulate objects.

Service layer communicate directly with Virtual Layer. Furthermore, Service Layer is seen as a social layer because it links this system with other systems, by ensuring communication and interaction with external parts. This is to say, it guarantees the openness and cooperation properties which are very fundamental for all IoT systems.

In order to improve the user experience, a GUI is provided in the framework SADM-SmartObject. This interface enables users to visualize and monitor:

- Virtual objects: GUI proposes a multiple managing options for users that allow a full control of these virtual objects: add, remove, edit,...

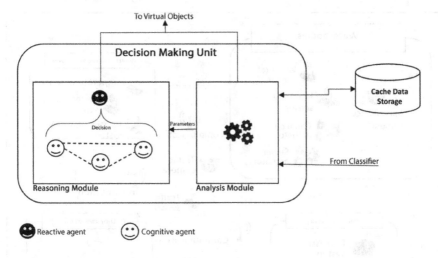

Fig. 4. Decision Making Unit.

- Solutions (DM results): User can visualize and manage the history of different solutions and Decision Making results proposed by the system.

GUI is able to create user profiles containing information about their preferences so that future estimates of preferences can potentially be derived, and solution will be adapted appropriately.

4 Case Study: Crisis Management

In recent years, several countries have experienced natural disasters (floods mainly in Algeria, Tunisia, France, etc.). Crisis management during a natural disaster is very delicate. It requires the involvement of several services and systems and the participation of several agents of the state to save people's lives and limit the damage. A smart city will certainly help managers to better manage the crisis.

We have therefore chosen to apply the idea of the proposed framework on a case study of crisis management during floods. In such a situation, all departments of the Ministries of the Interior, Defense, Health and Agriculture must work together to better identify problems, save the lives of persons and animals and minimize the damage. So, an IoT platform could help tremendously. Water Bodies are provided with various types of sensors, actuators and surveillance cameras, monitored by Water Bodies department's processing systems. All these equipments are in real-time communication with other equipments at the weather forecast services and authorities involved, in order to ensure a total collaboration between different entities (Fig. 5). Smart Objects will handle data processing and also decision-making.

Fig. 6 presents crisis management 'process' in SADM-SmartObject framework:

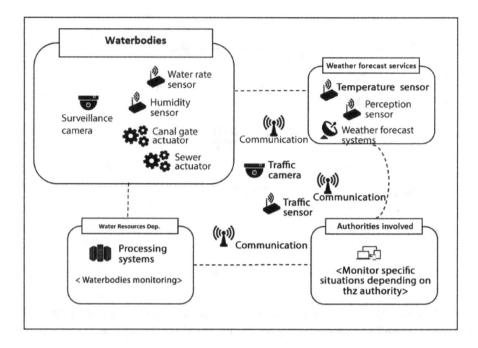

Fig. 5. Implementation aspects of crisis management scenario.

1. Sensors monitor weather forecast measurements: temperature, humidity, perception rate over a city, and also measurments from waterbodies: water rate of rivers, canals, water dom... All this informations are provided in real time.
2. Classifier receives the measurements coming from sensors, in order to derive s relevant parameters that will be used for the classifying process.
3. Classifier results on one of two main classes: Sensitive class and non-sensitive class, depending on a well defined threshold.
   - If it is a non sensitive class, there will be no action to take. it return back to 1.
   - If it is a sensitive class due to overrun the threshold, Analysis module parametrizes the measurements, then send a request for the appropriate existing solution scenario to Cache data storage.
   - If an existing solution is found, we go ahead to step 4.
   - If no solution is found, Analysis module triggers parameters to the Reasoning module in order to create a new suitable solution.
4. Virtual objects are evoked to execute the solution: a flood prevention and management mechanism is activated to properly control and deal with the situation.
5. A backup request for the generated solution is sent is sent to Cache data storage, at the same time of executing the solution and alerts are sent to civil protection services, national security, and local authorities, immediately.

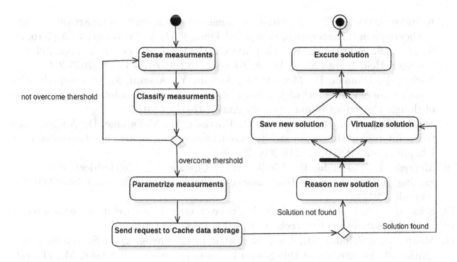

Fig. 6. Crisis management process.

5 Conclusion

The main purpose of this paper was to present the proposed framework SADM-SmartObjects based on a multi-agent system, offering a degree of intelligence for objects in an IoT environment. The framework has been applied here on a simplified case study to show the feasibility and explain the contributions. More research and studies can be investigated as a continuation of this work. One of them can be the validation of the proposed SMA architecture. For that, we are currently elaborating performance measurements with physical objects simulating crisis management system based on SADM-Smartobjects. The results will be published in the future.

References

1. ITU-T: Internet of Things Global Standards Initiative, International Telecommunication Union. http://www.itu.int/en/ITU-T/gsi/iot/Pages/default.aspx. Accessed 10 Feb 2019
2. Gubbi, J., Buyya, R., Marusic, S., Palaniswami, M.: Internet of Things (IoT): a vision, architectural elements, and future directions. Future Gener. Comput. Syst. **29**(7), 1645–1660 (2013)
3. Omale, G.: Gartner Identifies Top 10 Strategic IoT Technologies and Trends. Gartner. https://www.gartner.com/en/newsroom/press-releases/2018-11-07-gartner-identifies-top-10-strategic-iot-technologies-and-trends. Accessed 10 Feb 2019
4. García, C.G., Meana-llorián, D., G-bustelo, B.C.P., Manuel, J., Lovelle, C.: A review about smart objects, sensors, and actuators. Int. J. Interact. Multimed. Artif. Intell. **4**, 7–10 (2017)
5. Verma, P., Sood, S.K., Kalra, S.: Cloud - centric IoT based student healthcare monitoring framework. J. Ambient Intell. Humaniz. Comput. **9**(5), 1293–1309 (2018)

6. Kelaidonis, D., et al.: A cognitive management framework for smart objects and applications in the internet of things. In: Timm-Giel, A., Strassner, J., Agüero, R., Sargento, S., Pentikousis, K. (eds.) MONAMI 2012. LNICST, vol. 58, pp. 196–206. Springer, Heidelberg (2013). https://doi.org/10.1007/978-3-642-37935-2_15

7. Yachir, A., Djamaa, B., Mecheti, A., Amirat, Y., Aissani, M.: A comprehensive semantic model for smart object description and request resolution in the internet of things. Procedia Comput. Sci. **83**(Ant), 147–154 (2016)

8. Sánchez López, T., Ranasinghe, D.C., Harrison, M., McFarlane, D.: Adding sense to the internet of things: an architecture framework for smart object systems. Pers. Ubiquit. Comput. **16**(3), 291–308 (2012)

9. Manqele, L., Adeogun, R., Dlodlo, M.E., Coetzee, L.: Multi-objective decision-making framework for effective waste collection in smart cities. In: Global Wireless Summit (2017)

10. Sofia, K., Ben, L., El Bouaghi, O.: Multi-layer agent based architecture for internet of things systems. J. Inf. Technol. Res. **11**(4), 32–52 (2018)

11. Maamar, Z., Sellami, M., Faci, N., Ugljanin, E., Sheng, Q.Z.: Storytelling integration of the internet of things into business processes. In: Weske, M., Montali, M., Weber, I., vom Brocke, J. (eds.) BPM 2018. LNBIP, vol. 329, pp. 127–142. Springer, Cham (2018). https://doi.org/10.1007/978-3-319-98651-7_8

12. Maamar, Z., et al.: How to agentify the internet-of-things?. In: 2018 12th International Conference on Research Challenges in Information Science, pp. 1–6 (2018)

13. Lauria, E.J.M., Duchessi, P.: A Bayesian belief network for IT implementation decision support. Decis. Support Syst. **42**(3), 1573–1588 (2006)

14. Sheth, A.: Internet of things to smart IoT through semantic, cognitive, and perceptual computing. IEEE Intell. Syst. **31**, 108–112 (2016)

15. Fouad, H., Moskowitz, I.S.: Meta-Agents: Using Multi-Agent Networks to Manage Dynamic Changes in the Internet of Things. Elsevier Inc., Amsterdam (2019)

16. Stone, P.: Learning and multi agent reasoning for autonomous agents. In: IJCAI 2007, pp. 13–30 (2007)

Adjusting Population Size of Ant Colony System Using Fuzzy Logic Controller

Safae Bouzbita[✉], Abdellatif El Afia, and Rdouan Faizi

Smart Systems Laboratory, ENSIAS - Mohammed V University, Rabat, Morocco
Safae.bouzbita@gmail.com, a.elafia@um5s.net.ma, rdfaizi@gmail.com

Abstract. The population size has a very strong impact on the efficiency, solution quality, and computational cost in a Swarm Intelligence (SI). In Ant Colony System algorithm, and as a Swarm Intelligence and population size based algorithm, the number of ants plays a very important role in directing the colony toward a high quality solution within a reasonable time. In this paper, a Fuzzy Logic strategy for adjusting the number of ants during runtime is presented. The based indicators for this adjustment are: Iteration and Convergence Rate. Some experiments are conducted using Travelling Salesman Problems, and results show that modifying the number of ants has a crucial effect on the performance of the Ant Colony System algorithm especially on the quality of solution.

Keywords: Ant Colony System · Population size ·
Fuzzy Logic Controller · Parameters adaptation ·
Traveling Salesman Problem

1 Introduction

Over the last few years, researchers and scientists have paid a big attention to the artificial intelligence field on the purpose of improving and enhancing the human live. In artificial intelligence, Swarm Intelligence Algorithms (SIs) are considered as components that mimic biological procedures in order to solve problems with high complexity. A Swarm Intelligence algorithm is an optimization population based meta-heuristic method, where defining an optimal population size is considered critical to find optimal solution in an efficient time. One of the important Swarm Intelligence algorithms is the ant colony optimization method. Since the proposition of Ant System (AS) [1], several variants have been developed during the last decade to deal with NP-hard combinatorial optimization problems. As one of the most robust variants, the Ant Colony System (ACS) meta-heuristic. The specific characteristics of an Ant Colony System (ACS) algorithm are: (1) The use of a probabilistic transition rule to move from node to another, (2) removing an amount of pheromone from paths during building solutions, (3) addition of pheromone only to the global-best solution. Moreover, ACS algorithm has several parameters that require to be adjusted in order to enhance its performance. According to [2] ACS is a cooperative learning method, where a

© Springer Nature Switzerland AG 2019
N. T. Nguyen et al. (Eds.): ICCCI 2019, LNAI 11684, pp. 309–320, 2019.
https://doi.org/10.1007/978-3-030-28374-2_27

set of ants cooperate using deposited pheromone as indirect type of communication to share information in order to build solutions. However, the efficiency of an ACS algorithm is influenced by the given values of its parameters. Several learning approaches have been suggested in the literature in the seek of adapting the values of meta-heuristic parameters or to deal with combinatorial problems. For example in [3–14] researchers have used the well known Hidden Markov Modem (HMM) machine learning algorithm tune some meta-heuristic parameters as Ant Colony Optimization, Simulated Annealing and Particle Swarm Intelligence. Also, in [15–17] authors suggested the support vector machine learning algorithm to speed up branch-and-bound and cutting algorithm. While, other researches relied on self adaptive strategies to adapt parameters like in [18]. As one of those important parameters that affects the performance of the algorithm, we can cite the number of ants or the population size. In most applications, the recommended value of the number of ants equal to the number of cities and it remains fixed during the execution of the algorithm. Within this recommendation, a big number of cities requires a big number of ants, which can improve the search ability and the sufficiency of the algorithm but in return it increments the computational cost. While, a small number of ants speeds up the convergence of the algorithm but it could be falling into the optimum local solutions. To solve this problem, researchers have suggested different methods to find an appropriate value of population size in an Ant Colony Optimization algorithm. Some of them, preferred to analyse the effect of modifying the number of ants in ACS algorithm rather than defining the optimal number, in order to give some guidance to other researchers who try to tune the number of ants parameter [19]. Some others, discussed the increase of ants number in a drastically way, which they called a hyper populated Ant Colonies in the purpose to get a fast convergence and to limit the number of iterations [20]. On the Contrary of that, Liu et al proposed a self-adaptive control method, in which the number of ants decreased dynamically according to the found optimal solution at each iteration [21]. Regardless of the increase and the decrease of ants number, Liu et al confirmed that the population size is related to the number of cities, and according to that they defined a certain ranges to initialize the number of ants at the beginning of the algorithm [22]. In [23] authors studied the influence of number of ants versus the number of iterations, and concluded that the best number of ants is 10. In this paper, our contribution consists on the dynamic adjustment for the population size based on the number of iterations and the Convergence Rate performance measures using Fuzzy Logic Controller. The remain of this paper is structured as follows: Sect. 2 introduces the notion of Traveling Salesman Problem and Ant Colony System as solution for it. Section 3 describes the proposed adjustment method of population size using Fuzzy Logic Controller. In Sect. 4 the experimental results are reported and discussed. Finally, Sect. 5 resumes some conclusions about the proposed strategy.

2   Background

2.1   Travelling Salesman Problem

The Travelling Salesman Problem (TSP) is considered as one of the most complex combinatorial optimization problems studied in computer science. The TSP can be defined in two ways: The methodological and the theoretical ways. For the methodological way, the TSP is solved as integer linear programming problem with certain conditions. Where, the task is finding the shortest tour that visits all the cities in a given list of cities once and only once starting from one city and returning to the same city. Regularly, the TSP can be defined as follows: Minimize the objective function

$$f(x) = \sum_{i=1}^{n} \sum_{j=1}^{n} d_{ij} x_{ij}$$

Respecting constraints

$$\sum_{i=1}^{n} x_{ij} = 1$$

$$\sum_{j=1}^{n} x_{ij} = 1$$

$$x_{ij} = \begin{cases} 1 & if (i,j) \quad is \quad covered \quad in \quad the \quad tour, \\ 0 & otherwise \end{cases}$$

Where, n is the number of cities and d_{ij} is the distance between cities i and j. The TSP is then the optimization problem to find a Hamiltonian cycle that minimizes the tour's length. For the theoretical way, the TSP can be described as a complete graph $G = (N, A)$ with $N = 1, \ldots, n$ being a set of n nodes, also called cities, and $A = \{i, j\}$ $i \neq j$ is a set of arcs connecting the nodes. Each node i has a coordinates (x, y) and each arc (i, j) is assigned a distance d_{ij} between cities i and j. The distances between cities are usually stored in a matrix $D = (d_{ij})_{n*n}$, where $i, j = 1, \ldots, n$ and the diagonal d_{ii} elements equals to zero. For this minimization mission, $(n - 1)!$ possibilities of solutions have to be compared, which makes it very hard to be solved optimally in a polynomial time and then belongs to the NP-hard problems. Many heuristics and meta-heuristics have been proposed to find near optimal solution to this problem. The Ant Colony Optimization (ACO) meta-heuristic is one of the most powerful algorithms for solving the TSP.

2.2   Ant Colony System

Ant Colony System (ACS), is a cooperative learning approach extended from the original Ant System (AS) of ACO algorithms, that tends to increase the importance of exploitation of accumulated information collected by ants respecting exploration of search area when solving combinatorial optimization problems such as (TSP). For solving TSP by ACS, each ant from the population size n builds a solution in an iterative way. Informally, at the beginning of each iteration the n ants are randomly positioned on the graph of cities. Then, each ant selects the next city to visit by exploiting information about distance between cities and the pheromone levels on arcs connecting those cities. This is achieved using the following transition rules: The pseudo random proportional rule: with probability q_0, the city j for which the product between pheromone level and heuristic information is maximum is selected

$$j = argmax_{u \in J_k(i)} [\tau(i, u)][\eta(i, u)]^\beta \quad if \ q \leq q_0 \tag{1}$$

While, with probability $(1 - q_0)$ they resort to a biased exploration

$$p_{ij}^k = \begin{cases} \dfrac{\tau(i, j).[\eta(i, j)]^\beta}{\sum_{u \in J_k(i)} \tau(i, u)[\eta(i, u)]^\beta} & if \ \ j \in J_k(i) \\ 0 & otherwise \end{cases} \tag{2}$$

Where, $q0$ is a predefined parameter indicating the relative importance between exploration and exploitation ($0 \leq q0 \leq 1$) and q is a random number uniformly distributed in $[0, 1]$. Also, as an improvement over the traditional ACO algorithms, ACS uses a local pheromone update rule, every time an ant moves from city to another. This rule has the purpose to diminish the amount of pheromone from the visited arcs to encourage other ants to explore more solutions and not falling into the local optimum one.

$$\tau(i_k, j_k) := (1 - \xi)\tau(i_k, j_k) + \xi\tau_0 \tag{3}$$

Where, $\xi \in (0, 1)$ is a parameter called local pheromone decay parameter, and τ_0 is a very small constant that initializes the pheromone trails with value $1/(n.L_{nn})$, where n is the number of cities and L_{nn} is the length of a nearest neighbor tour. Moreover, in ACS algorithm only the best ant that constructed the tour with minimum cost is allowed to update the global pheromone matrix

$$\tau(i_k, j_k) := (1 - \rho)\tau(i_k, j_k) + \frac{\rho}{(L_{best})} \tag{4}$$

Where, $\rho \in (0, 1)$ represents the global pheromone decay parameter, and L_{best} is the length of best global tour.

2.3   Fuzzy Logic Controller

The concept of Fuzzy Logic was presented by Lotfy Zadeh in 1965, to represent ambiguous, uncertain, and approximate human decision making experience into a model understandable by machines and computers. In this context, a Fuzzy Logic System (FLS) can be viewed as a mapping of human reason and machines. Controllers that rely on FLS require three main steps:

– Fuzzification: convert crisp input variable into linguistic or fuzzy data using the so called Membership Functions (MFs)
– Fuzzy Inference Process: evaluate the fuzzy rules and combine the results using fuzzy set operation to obtain the fuzzy output
– Defuzzification: convert the obtained fuzzy output into a final crisp data according to the membership function of the output, using a defuzzifier method

Computers can handle only binary or crisp data such as '0' and '1'. In order to allow them to handle approximate data such as 'high' or 'Medium', the crisp data must be converted into a linguistic data using Membership Functions (MFs), many curves of Membership Functions exist for example Triangular, Gaussian and Trapezoidal Functions. Then, a set of fuzzy rules is created based on the problem data and an evaluation of fuzzy rules with a combination of the results of each rule are performed using fuzzy set operations (the most common used operations are max and min operations) to obtain a fuzzy output. At last, a defuzzifier method is performed to obtain a crisp value. The following diagram resume the main three steps of the proposed Fuzzy Logic Controller, with the use of Iteration and Convergence Rate as input variables and the population size as output variable (Fig. 1).

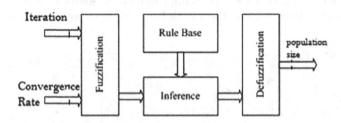

Fig. 1. Fuzzy Logic Controller diagram

3 Fuzzy Logic Controller for Adjusting Population Size

Nowadays, Fuzzy Logic became one of the most powerful tools for controlling and tuning parameters [25–29]. In fact, Fuzzy logic has the power of handling ambiguous and vague data (inputs) and making clear decisions (output) due to its similarity to the human being's thinking and reasoning [24]. In this paper, two input data are used in the controller method, which are: Iteration and Convergence Rate.

$$Iteration := \frac{Current\ \ iteration}{Total\ \ of\ \ iterations} \tag{5}$$

$$Convergance\ Rate := lim_{k \to \infty} \frac{|x_{k+1} - L|}{|x_k - L|} \tag{6}$$

Where, Current iteration is the number of elapsed iterations, and total of iterations is the total number of iterations required for running the algorithm, k is the number of iteration, x_{k+1} is the length of the current best tour, and L is the length of the best known tour. Equation 5 was taken From [30], in which the author proposed type-2 fuzzy logic system to dynamically adapt an Ant Colony System parameter. And the use of Convergence Rate expression as indicator for adapting the population size was inspired from [21, 22] works in which they used the Convergence Rate formula to control the population size for Ant Colony Optimization algorithms. Based on the literature [19, 23], the quality and the cost of obtained solutions from an ACO algorithm are influenced by the number of ants which is strongly related to the number of cities and the number of iterations. Therefore, the adjustment of the population size in this article was performed according to its relationship with the number of iterations and cities. Thus, a large number of ants could help in enhancing the solution quality but in return it decreases the convergence rate and increases the computational cost. However, the increase in the number of ants could be set off by lowering the number of iterations.

This approach was designed according to some previous knowledge; this is, in first iterations the algorithm needs a large number of ants to explore the search area, while at last iterations the redundant ants should be removed in order to reduce the travelling cost. Moreover, when the convergence rate tends to 1 this means that the best current solution is similar to the previous best found solution which means that there is no improvement in solutions is generated and the number of ants that guide the search is too high, so we need to reduce it.

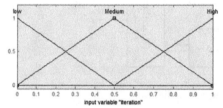

Fig. 2. Iteration input variable

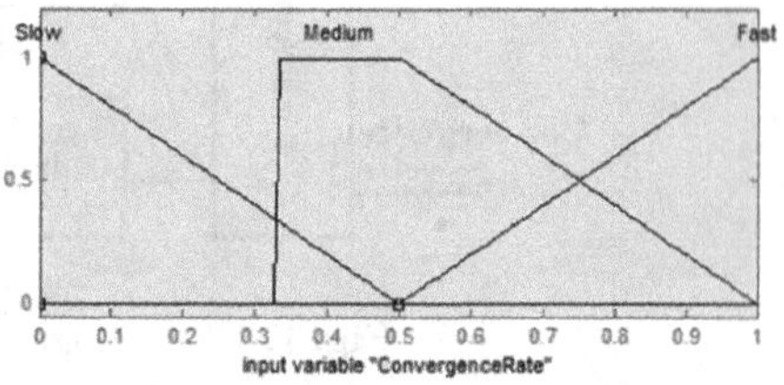

Fig. 3. Convergence rate input variable

Figure 2 shows the Iteration input variable granulated into three triangular Membership functions with a range from 0 to 1. Figure 3 shows the Convergence Rate input variable granulated into 2 triangular and one trapezoidal Membership functions with a range from 0 to 1. In Fig. 4 three triangular Membership functions of population size output variable are shown.

The mentioned Membership functions help us to represent a Fuzzy set graphically. In Fuzzy Logic, they mapped each element of input space to a membership value in [0,1] interval. Where, x-axis represents the input space or the universe of discourse, while the y-axis represents the degrees of membership in the [0,1] interval. The Membership function is usually denoted by the symbol $\mu_A(X)$, where A represents the Fuzzy set and X is the universe of discourse. In this context,

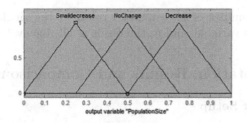

Fig. 4. Population size output variable

the denotation of Iteration membership functions is: $\mu_{Low}(X)$, $\mu_{Medium}(X)$, $\mu_{High}(X)$ where X is a crisp value for Iteration variable, and the denotation of Convergence Rate membership functions is: $\mu_{Slow}(X)$, $\mu_{Medium}(X)$, $\mu_{Fast}(X)$. We initialized the population size by: m = 0.6*n, which is recommended by [22], then the number of ants decreased during the runtime according to the proposed fuzzy system. Based on previous information, the fuzzy rules of the proposed approach can be described in the following table. The fuzzy rule set was developed to control the search abilities in ACS, in order to get the best performance and efficiency in a reasonable computational cost (Table 1).

Table 1. Fuzzy rule set for the fuzzy system with iteration and convergence rate as inputs

1) If Iteration is Low	and Convergence Rate is Slow	then No change
2) If Iteration is Low	and Convergence Rate is Medium	then small decrease
3) If Iteration is Low	and Convergence Rate is Fast	then decrease
4) If Iteration is Medium	and Convergence Rate is slow	then No change
5) If Iteration is Medium	and Convergence Rate is Medium	then No change
6) If Iteration is Medium	and Convergence Rate is Fast	then small decrease
7) If Iteration is High	and Convergence Rate is Slow	then decrease
8) If Iteration is High	and Convergence Rate is Medium	then small decrease
9) If Iteration is High	and Convergence Rate is Fast	then decrease

To evaluate the results of the individual fuzzy rules, the Min fuzzy set operator is adopted, according to Mamdani's conjunction operation (AND).

$$\mu_k = \min_{i,j=1,2,3} = \{\mu_i(x), \mu_j(y)\} \tag{7}$$

Where, k in the rule index, i and j are the indices for the input variables iterationLow, Medium, High and Convergence RateSlow, Medium, Fast.

For the defuzzification, we have used the centre of gravity algorithm according to the following equation:

$$\frac{\sum_{i=1}^{p} u_i \mu_i}{\sum_{i=1}^{p} \mu_i} \tag{8}$$

Where, p is the number of all evaluated rules, u_i the singleton membership function for output variable, and μ_i the result of all rule evaluation.

4   Experimentation, Results and Comparisons

4.1   Experiment Setup

The proposed fuzzy System is integrated in ACS to dynamically adjust the population size, and tested on some TSPs benchmarks TSPLIB described in Table 2. The algorithm was tested using the best known values of ACS algorithm parameters which are: $\beta = 2$, $\rho = 0.1$, $q_0 = 0.9$. The ants' initial position is set randomly on all experiments. The TSP benchmark instances used in this study were chosen from the TSPLIB [31] according to the most common used instances in the literature. The algorithm is developed on MATLAB. Each instance was ran for 1000 iterations.

4.2   Results and Comparisons

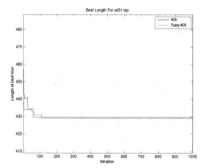
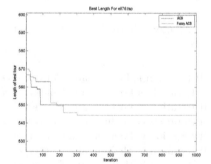

Fig. 5. Sample run on eil51.tsp   **Fig. 6.** Sample run on eil76.tsp

Figures 5 and 6 show the results from running both standard ACS and Fuzzy ACS algorithms on eil51.tsp and eil76.tsp TSPLIB instances. We can observe from the figures that is a kind of competition between the two algorithms in early iteration, but from certain iteration the Fuzzy ACS can outperform the standard one and reach better solutions. Figures 7 and 8 show the results from running both standard ACS and Fuzzy ACS algorithms on pr226.tsp and d198.tsp TSPLIB instances. As for Figs. 5 and 6 the obtained results show that the Fuzzy ACS achieves better solution in a considerable number of iterations. Table 2 summarizes the best found solutions from running the standards ACS and the hybridization between ACS and Fuzzy Logic in order to update the population size, in addition to the CPU time and the number of iteration in which the algorithm found this best solution (numbers between brackets).

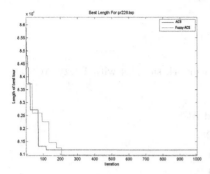
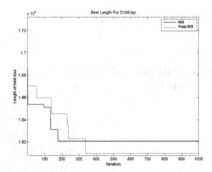

Fig. 7. Sample run on pr226.tsp   **Fig. 8.** Sample run on d198.tsp

Table 2. Summary of results of the standard ACS and ACSHMM algorithms on some TSP instances

Problem	Standard ACS		FuzzyACS		Best known solution
	Solution	CPUtime	Solution	CPUtime	
Eil51	434.5 [320]	134	428.8 [103]	201	426
St70	690 [244]	225	677 [243]	226.9	675
Eil76	565 [87]	181	545 [300]	237.3	538
Rat99	1229 [416]	1154.2	1221 [401]	712	1211
Eil101	660 [200]	316.78	636 [75]	361.1	629
Lin105	14524 [247]	699	14382 [208]	437	14379
Pr107	44620 [164]	403.6	44301.7 [84]	510.5	44303
Pr124	59159 [165]	472.2	59086 [30]	1101.5	59030
Rat195	2433 [230]	1832	2388 [114]	1400	2323
d198	16207	1637	15954 [325]	1612	15780
pr226	80764 [118]	5590	80470 [204]	2790	80369

From Table 2 we can observe that the results obtained from adapting the population size by the Fuzzy Logic controller can enhance the quality of solutions. So that some of the found solutions reached near best known ones. The experiment results also show that the needed time for testing the hybridization between Fuzzy Logic and ACS is a little more than testing the standard ACS alone. On the other hand, the Fuzzy ACS can find solutions in early iterations compared to the standard ACS algorithm. We can conclude from the results that modifying the population size of an Ant Colony System influences on the search ability.

5   Statistical Test

Table 3. Statistical validation for the TSP benchmark samples with Fuzzy ACS as control algorithm

TSP	Standard ACS
Eil51	2.32E-02
St70	3.45E-01
Eil76	8.07E-01
Rat99	5.4E-02
Eil101	1.05E-02
Lin105	2E-02
Pr107	2.75E-02
Pr124	4.89E-02
Rat195	4E-02
d198	3.02E-02
pr264	6.7E-03

To carry out the significance between the Fuzzy ACS and the standard ACS algorithms, a Wilcoxon Rank Test in a pair-wise comparison procedure was undertaken with $\alpha = 0.05$ as a significance level. The Wilcoxon Rank Test is a recommended method to compare dependent samples and value the significant differences. The following table represents the calculated p-value of the test.

From Table 3 we can observe that Fuzzy ACS approach can reach better solutions with level of significance of 5% compared to the standard ACS. Thus, the calculated p-value is under the significance level in most benchmark samples.

6   Conclusion

This paper proposed a dynamic adaptation of Ant Colony System' population size using the well known Fuzzy Logic Controller algorithm. The experiment results have proven that the size of population plays an important role to enhance the quality of solutions. Also, we can observe from the results that the proposed approach has a better search efficiency than the standard algorithm. Another point of strength of this proposed controller is its ability to be applied to any variant of ACO algorithms.

References

1. Dorigo, M., Maniezzo, V., Colorni, A.: The ant system: an autocatalytic optimizing process (1991)

2. Dorigo, M., Gambardella, L.M.: Ant colony system: a cooperative learning approach to the traveling salesman problem. IEEE Trans. Evol. Comput. **1**(1), 53–66 (1997)

3. Bouzbita, S., El Afia, A., Faizi, R.: A novel based hidden markov model approach for controlling the ACS-TSP evaporation parameter. In: 2016 5th International Conference on Multimedia Computing and Systems (ICMCS), pp. 633–638. IEEE (2016)

4. Bouzbita, S., El Afia, A., Faizi, R., Zbakh, M.: Dynamic adaptation of the ACS-TSP local pheromone decay parameter based on the hidden markov model. In: 2016 2nd International Conference on Cloud Computing Technologies and Applications (CloudTech), pp. 344–349. IEEE (2016)

5. Bouzbita, S., El Afia, A., Faizi, R.: Hidden markov model classifier for the adaptive ACS-TSP pheromone parameters. In: Talbi, E.-G., Nakib, A. (eds.) Bioinspired Heuristics for Optimization. SCI, vol. 774, pp. 153–169. Springer, Cham (2019). https://doi.org/10.1007/978-3-319-95104-1_10

6. Lalaoui, M., El Afia, A., Chiheb, R.: Hidden markov model for a self-learning of simulated annealing cooling law. In: 5th International Conference on Multimedia Computing and Systems (ICMCS) (2016)

7. Lalaoui, M., El Afia, A., Chiheb, R.: A self-tuned simulated annealing algorithm using hidden markov model. Int. J. Electr. Comput. Eng. **8**(1), 291–298 (2018)

8. Lalaoui, M., El Afia, A., Chiheb, R.: A self-adaptive very fast simulated annealing based on hidden markov model. In: 3rd International Conference of Cloud Computing Technologies and Applications (CloudTech) (2017)

9. Aoun, O., Sarhani, M., El Afia, A.: Investigation of hidden markov model for the tuning of metaheuristics in airline scheduling problems. IFAC-PapersOnLine **49**(3), 347–352 (2016)

10. Aoun, O., Sarhani, M., Afia, A.E.: Hidden markov model classifier for the adaptive particle swarm optimization. In: Amodeo, L., Talbi, E.-G., Yalaoui, F. (eds.) Recent Developments in Metaheuristics. ORSIS, vol. 62, pp. 1–15. Springer, Cham (2018). https://doi.org/10.1007/978-3-319-58253-5_1

11. El Afia, A., Sarhani, M., Aoun, O.: Hidden markov model control of inertia weight adaptation for particle swarm optimization. IFAC-PapersOnLine **50**(1), 9997–10002 (2017)

12. El Afia, A., Aoun, O., Garcia, S.: Adaptive cooperation of multi-swarm particle swarm optimizer-based hidden markov model. Prog. Artif. Intell. **8**, 1–12 (2019)

13. El Afia, A., Lalaoui, M., Chiheb, R.: A self controlled simulated annealing algorithm using hidden markov model state classification. Procedia Comput. Sci. **148**, 512–521 (2019)

14. Bouzbita, S., El Afia, A., Faizi, R.: Parameter adaptation for ant colony system algorithm using hidden markov model for TSP problems. In: Proceedings of the International Conference on Learning and Optimization Algorithms: Theory and Applications, p. 6. ACM (2018)

15. Kabbaj, M.M., El Afia, A.: Towards learning integral strategy of branch and bound. In: 2016 5th International Conference on Multimedia Computing and Systems (ICMCS), pp. 621–626. IEEE (2016)

16. El Afia, A., Kabbaj., M.M.: Supervised learning in branch-and-cut strategies. In: Proceedings of the 2nd International Conference on Big Data, Cloud and Applications, p. 114. ACM (2017)

17. Kabbaj, M.M., El Afia, A.: Adapted branch-and-bound algorithm using SVM with model selection. Int. J. Electr. Comput. Eng. (IJECE) **9**(4), 2481–2490 (2019)

18. Aoun, O., El Afia, A., Garcia, S.: Self inertia weight adaptation for the particle swarm optimization. In: Proceedings of the International Conference on Learning and Optimization Algorithms: Theory and Applications, p. 8. ACM (2018)
19. Alobaedy, M.M., Khalaf, A.A., Muraina, I.D.: Analysis of the number of ants in ant colony system algorithm. In: 2017 5th International Conference on Information and Communication Technology (ICoIC7), pp. 1–5. IEEE (2017)
20. Siemiński, A.: Using hyper populated ant colonies for solving the TSP. Vietnam J. Comput. Sci. **3**(2), 103–117 (2016)
21. Liu, Y., Liu, J., Li, X., Zhang, Z.: A self-adaptive control strategy of population size for ant colony optimization algorithms. In: Tan, Y., Shi, Y., Niu, B. (eds.) Advances in Swarm Intelligence. LNCS, vol. 9712, pp. 443–450. Springer, Cham (2016). https://doi.org/10.1007/978-3-319-41000-5_44
22. Liu, F., Zhong, J., Liu, C., Gao, C., Li, X.: A novel strategy of initializing the population size for ant colony optimization algorithms in TSP. In: 2017 13th International Conference on Natural Computation, Fuzzy Systems and Knowledge Discovery (ICNC-FSKD), pp. 249–253. IEEE (2017)
23. Fidanova, S., Marinov, P.: Number of ants versus number of iterations on ant colony optimization algorithm for wireless sensor layout. In: Proceedings of the Workshop of ICT for New Materials and Nanotechnologies, Bankya, pp. 90–93 (2013)
24. Bai, Y., Wang, D.: Fundamentals of fuzzy logic control—fuzzy sets, fuzzy rules and defuzzifications. In: Bai, Y., Zhuang, H., Wang, D. (eds.) Advanced Fuzzy Logic Technologies in Industrial Applications. Advances in Industrial Control, pp. 17–36. Springer, London (2006). https://doi.org/10.1007/978-1-84628-469-4_2
25. El Afia, A., Bouzbita, S., Faizi, R.: The effect of updating the local pheromone on ACS performance using fuzzy logic. Int. J. Electr. Comput. Eng. (IJECE) **7**(4), 2161–2168 (2017)
26. Olivas, F., Valdez, F., Castillo, O.: Ant colony optimization with parameter adaptation using fuzzy logic for TSP problems. In: Melin, P., Castillo, O., Kacprzyk, J. (eds.) Design of Intelligent Systems Based on Fuzzy Logic, Neural Networks and Nature-Inspired Optimization. SCI, vol. 601, pp. 593–603. Springer, Cham (2015). https://doi.org/10.1007/978-3-319-17747-2_45
27. Neyoy, H., Castillo, O., Soria, J.: Dynamic fuzzy logic parameter tuning for ACO and its application in TSP problems. In: Castillo, O., Melin, P., Kacprzyk, J. (eds.) Recent Advances on Hybrid Intelligent Systems. Studies in Computational Intelligence, vol. 451, pp. 259–271. Springer, Heidelberg (2013). https://doi.org/10.1007/978-3-642-33021-6_21
28. Lalaoui, M., El Afia, A., Chiheb, R.: Simulated annealing with adaptive neighborhood using fuzzy logic controller. In: Proceedings of the International Conference on Learning and Optimization Algorithms: Theory and Applications, p. 7. ACM (2018)
29. Amir, C., Badr, A., Farag, I.: A fuzzy logic controller for ant algorithms. Comput. Inf. Syst. **11**(2), 26 (2007)
30. Olivas, F., Valdez, F., Castillo, O., Gonzalez, C.I., Martinez, G., Melin, P.: Ant colony optimization with dynamic parameter adaptation based on interval type-2 fuzzy logic systems. Appl. Soft Comput. **53**, 74–87 (2017)
31. Reinelt, G.: TSPLIB—a traveling salesman problem library. ORSA J. Comput. **3**(4), 376–384 (1991)

Multi-swarm BSO Algorithm with Local Search for Community Detection Problem in Complex Environment

Youcef Belkhiri[1]([✉]), Nadjet Kamel[2], and Habiba Drias[1]

[1] University of Science and Technology Houari Boumediene, Bab Ezzouar, Algeria
belkhiri.youcef@gmail.com, hdrias@usthb.dz
[2] University Ferhat Abbas Setif 1, Setif, Algeria
nkamel@univ-setif.dz

Abstract. Discovering communities in complex environment is an interesting topic for many scientists. It becomes the mainstream issue in different research fields such as the web mining, biological networks and social networks. In this study, we propose a multi swarm version of Bee Swarm Optimization (BSO) algorithm for community detection problem with local search function called BSOCD-LS. The proposed algorithm considers the modularity Q for both local and global function. Additionally, the proposed method employs new technique to produce the reference solution and the taboo list to avoid stagnation. The experiments were carried out on real networks and compared to some representative methods. The results show that our proposed algorithm provide competitive results in term of modularity.

Keywords: Complex environment · Detection community ·
Local search · Bee optimization · Evolutionary algorithm ·
Multi swarm BSO algorithm · Modularity

1 Introduction

Complex system can be represented as complex networks such as social networks where individuals are the nodes and the relationships are represented by edges. The web is a network of pages which are interlinked by hypertext and in biological networks nodes represent the bio-chemical molecule, while edges represent the interaction between them. Recently, the majority of researches placed a major focus on understanding the evolution and the organization of such networks as well as the effect of network topology exerts on the dynamics and behaviors of the system [1–4]. Finding community structure in network is another challenge towards understanding the complex system they represent.

Detecting communities in complex network is similar to graph partitioning in graph theory and computer science and clustering in sociology [5,6]. A community can be viewed as a set of nodes which are strongly connected to each

© Springer Nature Switzerland AG 2019
N. T. Nguyen et al. (Eds.): ICCCI 2019, LNAI 11684, pp. 321–332, 2019.
https://doi.org/10.1007/978-3-030-28374-2_28

other and weakly connected the remaining nodes in the network. The existence
of relevant communities in a network is considered as a hot topic, making community detection a useful tool for interpreting network data and following their
evolutions.

Therefore, with the development and popularity of complex networks. new
techniques have been proposed, which can handle overlapping communities and
dynamic networks, where one node can belong to more that one community and
the networks evolve and change their structure along a time, a presentation of
the last efforts can be found in this recent survey [7]. However, disjoint community in static networks still remains an important topic in literature. Community
detection problem can be viewed as an optimization problem that aims to optimize an objective function to evaluate the quality of the communities. In [8]
Newman and Girvan have defined a metric, called modularity Q, to measure
this quality. The best quality that has the highest value of Q.

This paper is an extension of our earlier work presented in [9], in this earlier
work, a bee swarm algorithm was introduced to detect communities in complex
network. The algorithm is based on random behavior of bees whether to generate
initial solution or search space and at the end of the last iteration it selects the
solution with high score as the best found ever during the search. The current
works proposes multi swarm algorithm based on Bee swarm optimization that
incorporates some features to improve this approach and fill gaps. It uses a
guided solution to generate a promising initial solution, in each sub swarm some
bees perform a local search function to locate regions with potential to built
good solutions. The structure of this paper is organized as follows: in the next
section we define the concept of community detection and modularity function.
Section 2 describes some related approach to community detection. Section 4
presents BSO Algorithm and its origin. Section 4 presents the motivations and
the details of our proposed approach multi-swarm BSO algorithm with local
search for community detection problem in complex network called BSOCD-LS.
Section 5 provides the obtained results and their analysis. Conclusion is given in
Sect. 6.

2   Community Detection Problem

The community detection problem has been studied by several researches. It can
be viewed as dividing a network into P sub graphs that will help to understand
the topology of the network and determines the role of each individual. The
partitioning of a network must satisfy an objective function to evaluate the
community structures. The problem is NP-Hard [10] and is considered as an
optimization problem.

The community detection problem can be formulated as multi objective optimization problem such as [11,12]. Nevertheless, single optimization problem in
this field is still worthwhile and very used, which comforts our interest in the
single objective optimization issue. In literature, many objective functions were
introduced to measure the effectiveness of the community structures.

The next subsection, will describe the most widely accepted form used to discover community structures in complex networks, which is modularity maximization.

2.1 Modularity Measure

The modularity Q is a quantitative measure that was proposed by Newman in 2004 [8]. Maximizing the modularity is perhaps the most used paradigm for community detection. It consists in defining a benefit function that evaluates a division of an observed network into communities. Using this benefit function over possible divisions of a network and select the one that has the best score to be defined as the best division. Optimizing this measure in community detection problem is widely applied as exploited in BCALS [13], MDSTA [14], CDHC [15] and FN [16]. The modularity function expressed in Eq. (1) is presented in [8]. It defines a benefit function that returns a high value if the division of the network is good or a low value it is bad.

A network can be presented by an undirected graph $N = (V, E)$. V and E denote the sets of nodes and edges, respectively.

$$Q = \frac{1}{2m} \sum_{ij} (A_{ij} - \frac{k_i k_j}{2m}) s(c_i, c_j) \tag{1}$$

Suppose that A_{ij} is the adjacency matrix of N, if there is an edge between the nodes i and j, then $A_{ij} = 1$, otherwise $= 0$. $m = \frac{1}{2} \sum_{ij} K_{ij}$ denotes the total number of edges in the network, and $K_i = \sum_i A_{ij}$ is the degree of node I, $s(u, v)$ is equal to 1 if $u = v$ and 0 otherwise,c_i defines the community of the node I.

In [17] the Formula (1) was adapted to Formula (2). In this latter, the modularity is expressed as the sum of function f of all vertices. As we can see, foreach vertex a value is assigned to denote the belongingness to its community. Consequently, the sum of all the vertices value in the network will correspond to the global function Q.

$$Q = \frac{1}{2m} \sum_i f(i), \qquad f(i) = \sum_{j \in c_i} (A_{ij} - \frac{k_i k_j}{2m}) \tag{2}$$

From the idea proposed in [17], the global function Q is monotonically increased with local function f of each vertex. Here in Eq. (2) a local search of each vertex $f(i)$ is used to maximize the modularity Q by maximizing each vertex value. Assigning the vertex I to the community that provides a maximal value of $f(i)$ will lead to relevant community structures on networks. So, in the random procedure we try to maximize modularity as global function. However, in the second type of procedure we use Eq. 2 to perform a local search for each vertex to afford significant communities.

3   Related Work

Recently several methods have been developed to discover communities from complex networks. The most important approaches are found in [18]. In addition, approaches based on clustering thought have been used frequently in this domain due to their competitive results. Wang et al. proposed in [19] an improved algorithm based on k-means that selects K initial nodes randomly and afterwards assigns the remaining nodes to the most similar center nodes.

Khorasgani et al. proposed in [20] Top leader community detection algorithm, in which leader nodes are selected to be initial communities and the followers are affected to most common leader nodes according to its total number of links with its leader. The same idea is developed by Wang et al. in [21] to propose a new community detection algorithm based on distance centrality to form community structure. However, the proposed algorithm considers the nodes that have the highest value of distance centrality as initial communities, and then it measures the similarity between the center nodes and each other nodes in the network, and assigns each node to the most similar community. These methods require the size and the number of communities to provide relevant structures which is difficult to obtain. Therefore, we conclude that this type of methods is not efficient.

Based on top-leader and Distance centrality, authors in [13] proposed a new betweenness centrality with local search algorithm that relies on betweenness centrality measure to identify more appropriate initial communities and local function based on modularity Q to perform local search in the affectation of the remaining nodes in the network. This algorithm works without any prior information.

Authors in [22] proposed new method called BLDLP, based on the label propagation method using sensitivity parameter to achieve a desired community structures. Compared to the basic LPA, the results obtained showed the superiority of BLDLP.

Authors in [23] proposed an online framework for overlapping community detection problem in dynamic networks, they adapt clique percolation method CPM [24] and used label propagation to show the effectiveness of their approach. A presentation of the last efforts on dynamic networks can be found in this survey [7].

On the other hand, particle swarm intelligence was also adopted to enhance community detection problem by choosing an appropriate objective function which is often the modularity. For instance, bee swarm [25], genetic algorithm [26] and bat algorithm [27], have demonstrate to be powerful for problem solving. These algorithms yield optimal solutions or near-optimal solutions when the problem size is very large.

In [28], the authors proposed a multi swarm bat algorithm based on multiple cooperative strategies for rule association mining, the results show the ability of the multi swarm strategies to successfully overcome the state of art methods in term of time and quality.

4   Multi Swarm BSO Algorithm with Local Search for Community Detection Problem

This section presents the proposed algorithm based on parallel multi swarm BSO algorithm with local search called BSOCD-LS. From topologies proposed in [28], here, we intend to implement master slave topology with browsing technique to balance the exploration and the exploitation abilities. This approach is based on bee swam optimization algorithm (BSO) that was proposed by Drias in [29].

In the following, we present our proper modeling for community detection problem with bee swarm optimization. In particular, we describe the Solution representation, the master slave topology, the determination of the search area, the local search function and the objective function.

4.1   Solution Representation

A solution in community detection problem is formulated as a set of module; each module has a set of similar nodes V connected to each other. These modules represent communities. Each possible solution contains a number of communities and each community has its own nodes. First of all, BeeInit generates the Sref solution and from which other solutions will be created. The string based schema is adopted to represent solutions in our algorithm as shown in Fig. 1(a). The solution is represented by a string of values where the value is the community label and the indices are the nodes that belong to that community.

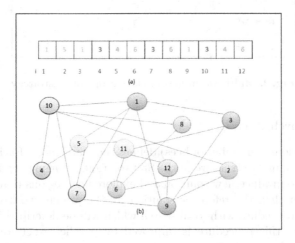

Fig. 1. Solution representation of the initial solution

The reference solution is considered to be the starting point of this algorithm. So, starting with a guided solution can lead to better results. The network shown in Fig. 2 contains 12 vertices. Consequently, the possible number of communities

PC = 6. The label community is only a nomination and does not represent the total number of communities in the network. As shown in Fig. 1, the nodes 6, 8 and 12 form community 6, and the network in this case is split only into 5 communities.

4.2 Master Slave Strategy

In this research, we are interested on multi population collaborative strategy called master slave strategy. One swarm which is responsible to generate the first Sref solution is called the master swarm and the other swarms represent slaves. All swarm are working in parallel way to communicate their optimal local solution to the master swarm to select new Sref solution. This strategy is illustrated in Fig. 2.

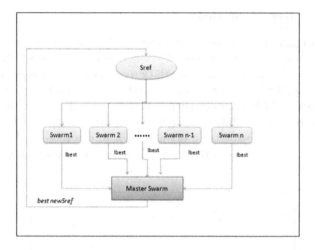

Fig. 2. Multi-swarm master slave cooperative strategy

4.3 The Search Area

A set of k solutions (k number of bees) defines the search area. Each bee tries to modify the community structure of the Sref solution, changing the label of some communities, to produce new solution and explore new regions that can provide solutions better than the reference solution. In the present work we propose a diversification procedure with local search which will be described in Algorithm 2. Furthermore, this procedure is improved by parallel execution during the construction of the search area.

The Diversification Procedure with Local Search. The most two positive points in this strategy are parallelization of the bees during the producing of the new solutions and the local search during the affectation of the nodes to their new communities to guaranty the maximization of the global function by maximizing the local function of each node. Each bee takes, at the same time (in parallel manner), the reference solution as the departure point to produce a new solution by altering its related nodes according to the diversification procedure. Each bee has its own nodes to modify their current communities if it guaranties the maximization of the global function by calculating the local functions of those nodes. In other words, if the modification of one node provides better global function than the precedent structure then it maintains this modification otherwise there is no need to change. With this strategy, we are certain that each bee at the end of its diversification procedure with local function, will offer a new solution with upper modularity than the reference solution. This procedure is based on the same concept in random diversification strategy to find the positions of nodes for each bee, however, the bees modify their current communities according to the local function f.

4.4   Parallel Bee Swarm Algorithm

Bee swarm algorithm was presented by Drias in [29]. The BSO algorithm for community detection [9] simulates the behavior of bees in nature. In each pass, bees are generated sequentially and randomly to form the population and selects the bee with high score to be the next reference solution. The BSO algorithm can be parallelized. Here, in BSOCD-LS the generation of sub-swarms and their bees are divided into multiple threads. All sub swarms are created in parallel instead of sequentially, which means that all bees are launched in parallel and apply the diversification procedure to reach their best local solution. In each sub swarm, bees are independents in their tasks, each bee has its own region to performs local search function and provide it best results. Once all bees finish their work they communicate their solution to select the best local solution in the sub swarm. At the end, each sub swarm communicates its best local solution to select the best global solution in the current iteration in order to choose the new reference solution.

4.5   Objective Function

The community detection problem is proved to be NP-hard which needs to optimize an objective function in order to furnish relevant community structures. In this paper we employ modularity Q to evaluate the obtained results. The result that has the highest value of Q is considered as the best result.

4.6   Pseudo Code Multi Swarm BSO Algorithm with Local Search for Community Detection

The main steps of our approach are summarized in Algorithms 1 and 2. This algorithm divides the initial population into equal sub swarms and uses technique of local search function to furnish an optimal solution based on modularity Q. this technique is called diversification procedure with local search (Algorithm 2).

At the beginning of the algorithm as shown in Algorithm 1, the initial solution is generated to represent the Sref solution. Form this solution N swarms are lunched in parallel, each swarm contains K bees that are executed in parallel applying the local search function detailed in Algorithm 2 to improve the Sref solution if possible. In Algorithm 2, for each bee before changing the community label of the concerned node, we calculate its new f(i) for each possible new community and choose the community that provide the maximum value of f(i), if the score of the new community is higher than the current one the node must change its community to the new one, otherwise, the node maintains its current community. Maximizing f(i) will guaranty the maximization of the global modularity Q. Therefore, each bee has to return a new solution with a new community structures at the end of its diversification procedure.

Algorithm 1: Master-Slave cooperative Strategy for community detection

Data: Sref, *SwarmN* , k // *SwarmN (slave populations)* is the total swarm number and k is
a number of bees
Result: *S** // Best Global solution
- Generate initial solution Sref
While (T< Max Iter) and (Optimal solution not found) **Do**
- **For** swarm = 1 **to** *SwarmN* (executed on parallel) **do**
  - **For each** bee in **Swarm do**
    - new Solution = Apply diversification procedure with local search
  - **end**
  - - send the best local solution to master population
- **end**
- Select the global best solution in master population to be the newSref
- new Solution = Sref
- Notify all slave populations with the new Sref solution
- Increase iteration number
end
  S* // **select the best Global solution**
end

Algorithm 2: The diversification Algorithm with local search

Data: Sref, *Cn* , k //*Cn* is number of communities actually exist and k is
a number of bees
Result: *S** // set of new solutions neighbors that forms search area
- **From** bee = 1 **to** K (executed on parallel) **do**
  - - i = bee ;
  - - new Solution = Sref ;
  - - j=1 ;
  - **while** *j < T* **do** //*T* length of Sref solution which is always total number of nodes.
    - -position=j
    - -pick the label community of the node *V* situated in position;
    - -Calculate local function *f(i)* of modularity of *V* for each community and select
      the community *C* that has the highest value;
    - - affect the node *V* to the community *C* that provides the highest value of *f(i)*.
    - - position= ((j*k)+i); // next position to jump to in new solution.
    - - j=j++;
  - **end**
  - - *S** = *S** +new Solution;
- **end**

Once all bees in each swarm return their new solution, each swarm communicate its best local solution to the master swarm in order to compare it with the other solutions. Master swarm will select the solution S that has the highest value of modularity Q to be the new Sref solution for the next iteration. This new solution will be stored in taboo list to avoid stagnation.

Finally, the solution S that has the maximum value of modularity Q in taboo list will be considered as the best solution of this experiment.

5   Experiments

In order to test the ability of our algorithm, multi swarm BSOCD-LS algorithm is tested on real world networks. Several methods have been selected to compare their results to those of our proposed approach. The proposed algorithms are coded in Java, and the experiments are carried out an $Intel®$ $Core^{TM}$ $i5 - 2450M$ CPU machine, 2.50 GHz, with 4 GB memory.

The comparison methods used in our experiments are BCALS [13], Top leader [20], distance centrality detection community [21], CDHC [15], FN [16], LPA [14] and BSOCD [9].

5.1   Real Data Sets

Here, the proposed algorithm was tested on real world networks, which are Zachary Karate Club [30] Dolphin Network [31], Football Network [32], Strike [33] and Polbooks [34].

To validate our approach, we have selected some real world networks, and the results are compared to other representative algorithms in Table 1. Usually, the community structure is unknown. Thus, based on the modularity function, the highest value is considered to be the best one.

Table 1. Comparison of modularity results

Q-value	Strike	Zachary	Dolphin	PolBooks	Football
FN	–	0.3807	0.5104	0.5020	0.5497
LPA	–	0.3646	0.4802	0.5006	0.5865
CDHC	–	0.373	0.477	–	0.602
TOP Leader	0.548	0.374	–	–	0.511
DCCD	0.561	0.371	0.4967	–	–
BCALS	0.5619	0.4197	0.5207	0.4430	0.5925
BSOCD	0.5515	0.4197	0.514	0.5180	0.604
BSOCD-LS	0.5619	0.4197	0.5247	0.5237	0.6045

As illustrated in Table 1. We can see that the outcomes of BSOCD and BSOCD-LS are close, however the BSOCD-LS is faster and more efficient than BSOCD, because this later relies on parallel execution of its bees to provide new solutions in the neighborhood and employs local search function to ensure the quality of new solutions in a small iteration number. In addition, compared to the selected approach, we can notice that BSOCD-LS achieves the highest value of modularity Q.

6   Conclusion

Bee swarm optimization algorithm is an algorithm that relies on population that represents the swarm, artificial bees are working together to generate relevant solutions with a high quality of nectar. BSO algorithm is widely applied in optimization problem and has proved to be efficient in such problems [25,35]. Our first adaptation of this algorithm in community detection problem, called BSOCD was successful. However, it has some weaknesses: the initial solution and search area are generated randomly and executed sequentially. In the current work, we have developed a parallel multi-swarm algorithm with local search function based on bee swarm optimization to uncover community structure.

This algorithm relies on local search function $f(i)$ based on modularity Q, k bees are working on parallel manner to reach faster the optimal solution than iterative execution, each bee optimizes its global function Q by maximizing the local function $f(i)$ for each nodes movements. The approach has been tested or real world networks, showing to be competitive with the state of the art methods.

As future works, we try to handle BSOCD-LS as multi objective optimization able to treat large data sets and improve its results.

References

1. Albert, R., Barabási, A.-L.: Statistical mechanics of complex networks. Rev. Mod. Phys. **74**(1), 47 (2002)
2. Albert, R., Jeong, H., Barabási, A.-L.: Internet: diameter of the world-wide web. Nature **401**(6749), 130–131 (1999)
3. Barabási, A.-L., Albert, R.: Emergence of scaling in random networks. Science **286**(5439), 509–512 (1999)
4. Newman, M.E.J.: The structure and function of complex networks. SIAM Rev. **45**(2), 167–256 (2003)
5. Johnson, D.S., Garey, M.R.: Computers and Intractability: A Guide to the Theory of NP-Completeness. Wiley Computer Publishing, Freeman, San Francisco (1979)
6. Scott, J., Carrington, P.J.: The SAGE Handbook of Social Network Analysis. SAGE Publications, Thousand Oaks (2011)
7. Rossetti, G., Cazabet, R.: Community discovery in dynamic networks: a survey. ACM Comput. Surv. (CSUR) **51**(2), 35 (2018)
8. Newman, M.E.J., Girvan, M.: Finding and evaluating community structure in networks. Phys. Rev. E **69**(2), 026113 (2004)
9. Belkhiri, Y., Kamel, N., Drias, H., Yahiaoui, S.: Bee swarm optimization for community detection in complex network. In: Rocha, Á., Correia, A.M., Adeli, H., Reis, L.P., Costanzo, S. (eds.) WorldCIST 2017. AISC, vol. 570, pp. 73–85. Springer, Cham (2017). https://doi.org/10.1007/978-3-319-56538-5_8
10. Gaertler, M., et al.: On modularity clustering. IEEE Trans. Knowl. Data Eng. **20**, 172–188 (2008)
11. Shi, C., Yan, Z., Cai, Y., Bin, W.: Multi-objective community detection in complex networks. Appl. Soft Comput. **12**(2), 850–859 (2012)
12. Zhou, Y., Wang, J., Luo, N., Zhang, Z.: Multiobjective local search for community detection in networks. Soft Comput. **20**, 1–10 (2015)

13. Belkhiri, Y., Kamel, N., Drias, H.: A new betweenness centrality algorithm with local search for community detection in complex network. In: Nguyen, N.T., Trawiński, B., Fujita, H., Hong, T.-P. (eds.) ACIIDS 2016. LNCS (LNAI), vol. 9622, pp. 268–276. Springer, Heidelberg (2016). https://doi.org/10.1007/978-3-662-49390-8_26

14. Zhou, X., Yang, K., Xie, Y., Yang, C., Huang, T.: A novel modularity-based discrete state transition algorithm for community detection in networks. Neurocomputing **334**, 89–99 (2019)

15. Yin, C., Zhu, S., Chen, H., Zhang, B., David, B.: A method for community detection of complex networks based on hierarchical clustering. Int. J. Distrib. Sens. Netw. **2015**, 137 (2015)

16. Newman, M.E.J.: Fast algorithm for detecting community structure in networks. Physical Rev. E **69**(6), 066133 (2004)

17. Jin, D., He, D., Liu, D., Baquerom, C.: Genetic algorithm with local search for community mining in complex networks. In: 2010 22nd IEEE International Conference on Tools with Artificial Intelligence, vol. 1, pp. 105–112. IEEE (2010)

18. Fortunato, S.: Community detection in graphs. Phys. Rep. **486**(3), 75–174 (2010)

19. Wang, Y.: An improved complex network community detection algorithm based on k-means. Adv. Intell. Soft Comput. **160**, 243–248 (2012)

20. Khorasgani, R.R., Chen, J., Zaïane, O.R.: Top leaders community detection approach in information networks. In: Proceedings of the 2010 International Conference on Knowledge Discovery and Data Mining (KDD 2010), Washington, DC, USA, pp. 1–9 (2010)

21. Wu, L., Bai, T., Wang, Z., Wang, L., Hu, Y. and Ji, J.: A new community detection algorithm based on distance centrality. In: 2013 10th International Conference on Fuzzy Systems and Knowledge Discovery (FSKD), pp. 898–902 (2013)

22. Jokar, E., Mosleh, M.: Community detection in social networks based on improved label propagation algorithm and balanced link density. Phys. Lett. A **383**(8), 718–727 (2019)

23. Boudebza, S., Cazabet, R., Azouaou, F., Nouali, O.: OLCPM: an online framework for detecting overlapping communities in dynamic social networks. Comput. Commun. **123**, 36–51 (2018)

24. Palla, G., Dernyi, I., Farkas, I., Vicsek, T.: Uncovering the overlapping community structure of complex networks in nature and society. Nature **435**(7043), 814 (2005)

25. Karaboga, D., Basturk, B.: A powerful and efficient algorithm for numerical function optimization: artificial bee colony (ABC) algorithm. J. Global Optim. **39**(3), 459–471 (2007)

26. Davis, L.: Handbook of Genetic Algorithms (1991)

27. Yang, X.-S.: A new metaheuristic bat-inspired algorithm. In: González, J.R., Pelta, D.A., Cruz, C., Terrazas, G., Krasnogor, N. (eds.) Nature Inspired Cooperative Strategies for Optimization (ICSO 2010), pp. 65–74. Springer, Heidelberg (2010). https://doi.org/10.1007/978-3-642-12538-6_6

28. Heraguemi, K.E., Kamel, N., Drias, H.: Multi-swarm bat algorithm for association rule mining using multiple cooperative strategies. Appl. Intell. **45**(4), 1021–1033 (2016)

29. Drias, H., Sadeg, S., Yahi, S.: Cooperative bees swarm for solving the maximum weighted satisfiability problem. In: Cabestany, J., Prieto, A., Sandoval, F. (eds.) IWANN 2005. LNCS, vol. 3512, pp. 318–325. Springer, Heidelberg (2005). https://doi.org/10.1007/11494669_39

30. Zachary, W.W.: An information flow model for conflict and fission in small groups. J. Anthropol. Res. **33**, 452–473 (1977)

31. Lusseau, D.: The emergent properties of a dolphin social network. Proc. R. Soc. Lond. B Biol. Sci. **270**(Suppl 2), S186–S188 (2003)
32. Girvan, M., Newman, M.E.J.: Community structure in social and biological networks. Proc. Natl. Acad. Sci. **99**(12), 7821–7826 (2002)
33. Michael, J.H.: Labor dispute reconciliation in a forest products manufacturing facility. Forest Prod. J. **47**(11/12), 41 (1997)
34. Books about us politics. http://networkdata.ics.uci.edu/data.php?d=polbooks
35. Karaboga, D.: An idea based on honey bee swarm for numerical optimization. Technical report, Technical report-tr06, Erciyes University, Engineering Faculty, Computer Engineering Department (2005)

Intelligent Management Information Systems

The Identification and Creation of Ontologies for the Use in Law Enforcement AI Solutions – MAGNETO Platform Use Case

Rafal Kozik[1,4], Michal Choras[1,4], Marek Pawlicki[1,4(✉)],
Witold Hołubowicz[4], Dirk Pallmer[2], Wilmuth Mueller[2],
Ernst-Josef Behmer[2], Ioannis Loumiotis[3],
Konstantinos Demestichas[3], Roxana Horincar[5], Claire Laudy[5],
and David Faure[5]

[1] ITTI Sp. z o.o., Poznan, Poland
mpawlicki@itti.com.pl
[2] Fraunhofer IOSB, Karlsruhe, Germany
[3] Institute of Communication and Computer Systems (ICCS), Athens, Greece
[4] University of Science and Technology, UTP, Bydgoszcz, Poland
[5] Thales Research & Technology, Palaiseau, France

Abstract. Every single day more and more organizations face the challenge of finding a way to support their conduct with data. The flooding amounts of data currently available vastly outweigh human capabilities, thus Big Data processing becomes a pressing issue. This problem is especially prevailing for Law Enforcement Agencies (LEAs), where massive amounts of critical data are collected from heterogenous sources, often by various entities in different countries. Ontologies have been developed into a predominant technique for establishing semantic interoperability among heterogeneous systems which transact information. In this paper we propose the Magneto ontology – a solution built as a crucial part of the Magneto project. It has been developed on top of well-established ontologies dealing with people, events and security incidents, bearing in mind the heterogenous nature of the myriad of data sources as the starting point. Examples of the building blocks, a classification of the sources of data, an overview of the application in a specific use scenario and a discussion on the future use of the ontology will be given.

Keywords: Ontology · Artificial intelligence ·
Common Representational Model · Semantic interoperability · Correlation

1 Introduction

Nowadays, Law Enforcement Agencies (LEAs) - similarly to other entities in different domains operating based on the mass volume of digitalised data - have to face problems related to big data processing, knowledge understanding and interoperability. It is clear that the common understanding of data between cooperating LEAs (or between LEAs and external parties), as well as flexible tools for information sharing and exchange are vital for effective and successful law enforcement and prosecution.

© Springer Nature Switzerland AG 2019
N. T. Nguyen et al. (Eds.): ICCCI 2019, LNAI 11684, pp. 335–345, 2019.
https://doi.org/10.1007/978-3-030-28374-2_29

There is a need to develop a common representational model for data used by LEAs. Therefore, in order to facilitate the law enforcement data representation, we propose our solution – so called MAGNETO ontology. The work presented in this paper is related to the first stage of collaborative research project MAGNETO (Technologies for prevention, investigation, and mitigation in the context of the fight against crime and terrorism), co-funded by the European Commission within Horizon 2020 programme. The main ambition of the project and the MAGNETO consortium is to empower LEAs (Law Enforcement Agencies) with the capability to process, manage, analyse, correlate and reason from large datasets characterized by heterogeneity. In particular, the technical goals defined by the Consortium are: development of solutions enabling the exploration of data from various sources, their indexing, enrichment through meta-information and contextualization, development of tools supporting semantic information fusion and inference based on processed data and development of a human-machine interface (HMI) enriching the situational awareness and operational capabilities of LEAs.

The goal of this paper is to present a flexible and sophisticated representational model for the data utilized by LEAs. The model is supposed to establish a common baseline for cooperation and information exchange for interoperable security systems.

The paper is structured as follows: Sect. 2 presents the current state of the approaches used to delineate and model the security-related knowledge, Sect. 3 addresses classification of the MAGNETO data sources and provides preliminary MAGNETO data model, while Sect. 4 discusses the future use of our ontology and Sect. 5 provides overall summary of our work.

2 Related Work

A multitude of models exist as an expression and representation of both semantic information and knowledge. Natural language, propositional logic, first-order logic, mathematical models, relational model, semantics nets or rules constitute merely several examples. Both in computer science and philosophy, ontologies share the attempt of representing concepts in order to model a specific domain. The representational primitives that are used are typically entities, ideas and events existing in the real world, with all their interdependent properties and relations, similarities and dissimilarities.

Ontologies are considered to be one of the pillars of the Semantic Web that provides standards to identify entities (*URIs*), express facts (*RDF*), express concepts (*RDFS*), share vocabularies, describe constraints (*OWL*), query knowledge (*SPARQL*), link data and publish data (*RDFa*). Ontologies have become a common approach when it comes to the task of ensuring semantic interoperability between heterogeneous systems exchanging information. Ontologies provide an abstraction layer in the Semantic Web to enable dialog and service negotiation between participating systems, ensuring that the participants have the same concept of the information exchanged.

In [1] the published Security Incident Ontology (SIO) is presented. This ontology was built to describe security relevant events on the campus of Ryerson University in Toronto. The light-weight ontology was built upon existing ontologies describing events, geolocation and timelines, people and their relations, The Event Ontology [2] was developed at Centre for Digital Music in Queen Mary University of London in October, 2004. This ontology is centred around the notion of an event, seen here as the way by which cognitive agents classify arbitrary time/space regions. This ontology has been proven to be suitable in a wide range of contexts, due to its simplicity and usability (i.e. conference talks, concerts, festivals). The ontology reuses Timeline [3] ontology for temporal predicate "event:time" and Geo RDF vocabulary [4] for spatial predicate "event:place". FOAF (Friend of A Friend) [5] is a lightweight ontology modelling persons, their activities and their relations to other persons and objects. It is a widely accepted vocabulary for representing Social Networks. Princeton WordNet (WN) is a lexical database for the English language [6, 7]. The SIO ontology was used to develop an infrastructure transforming textual notification of security incidents to a machine-readable representation. The SIO ontology specification and its Turtle version were made available by registering the dataset to Linked Open Data and adding it to the Linked Open Data Cloud.

The scope of this ontology is limited to security incidents at the university campus and handles only a small section that has yet to be covered by MAGNETO. Also based on the Event Ontology, a Forensic Complex Event Ontology has been developed for the analysis of video material at the Multimedia Vision Research Group of Queen Mary University of London. The ontology framework is a derivative of DOLCE foundational ontology and it is designed to represent events that forensic analysts commonly encounter in the investigation of criminal activities [8]. In the CAPER project, a conceptual structure of the cross-border organized crime has been developed by analysing the work of EUROPOL and its databases, resulting in a Europol Organized Crime Structure (OCS), which is a supranational structure embedding the specific natural structures, overcoming limitations due to non-harmonized criminal law systems [9]. The European LEA Interoperability Ontology (ELIO) aims at ensuring interoperability between the LEAs. ELIO is a lightweight ontology based on the taxonomy of OCS, implementing the concepts as classes and adding object properties for connecting the classes as "hasTechnique", "hasEssentialCondition", "hasCrime" and "hasCountry" [10]. Compared to the SIO ontology, the ELIO crimes concept is missing the embedded event concept of SIO, as a result the crimes are not assigned to agents, geo-location and time. The ELIO and MCO ontologies are not publicly available.

The Global Justice Extensible Markup Language (GJXDM) Data Model is an XML standard designed specifically for criminal justice information exchanges, providing law enforcement, public safety agencies, prosecutors, public defenders, and the judicial branch with a tool to effectively share data and information in a timely manner [11]. The Global Justice XML Data Model was the result of an effort by the justice and public safety communities to produce a set of common, well-defined data elements to be used for data transmissions. In 2005, the successor project National Information Exchange Model (NIEM) started, which was based on GJXDM, broadening the scope to include other federal and state agencies [12].

From our perspective, it is always important to use ontology in practice for reasoning and decisions, so that it can be termed as applied ontology [13].

3 MAGNETO Ontology

3.1 MAGNETO Data Sources Classification

The starting point for the MAGNETO Common representational model specification were the data sources. It is crucial from the perspective of the platform to comprehend the variety of possible data formats that will ingest the analyses. The data is to be sourced from a diverse spectrum of supported formats including structured documents (database exports, structured reports, lists, standardized descriptions), free (unstructured) text, pictures, audio sequences, video sequences, raw data. Those files will be drawn from an assortment of sources, including external LEA's, Police databases, surveillance systems/human sensors, Internet/OSIF (Open Source Information) content, telecon data, other databases.

The files will be drawn from an assortment of sources, including: External LEA's, Police Databases, Surveillance Systems/Human Sensors, standardized descriptions, the Internet/OSIF (Open Source Information) Content, Telecon data, other databases.

The Source Data is to only be stored in its initial location, thus protecting its integrity and assuring efficiency of use. Annotations based on the original data are more fitting to be served. The high-level overview of data source types has been listed in Fig. 1.

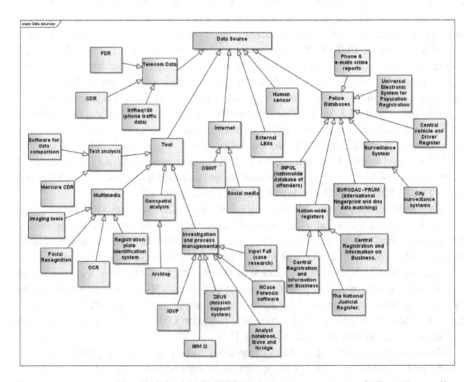

Fig. 1. Data sources identified for MAGNETO project use cases (arrows indicate "generalization" relation).

3.2   Building Blocks of CRM

The Common Representational Model (CRM) will be developed on top of several ontologies, taxonomies and classifications that will facilitate computational and data mining functionalities provided by various MAGNETO components.

Moreover, to bridge the gap between different taxonomies used within the project we propose to adopt several publicly available ontologies providing a common vocabulary and facilitating interoperability.

While developing the model we have decided to build its basis on top of several ontologies identified during the desktop research, namely: SIO (Security Incident Ontology), FOAF (Friend of a Friend) Vocabulary Specification and event ontology.

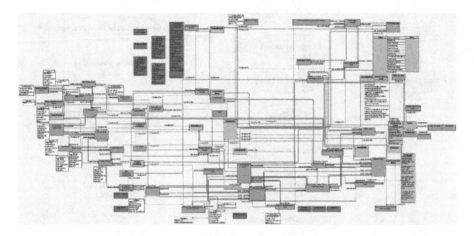

Fig. 2. A general overview of the preliminary version of CRM – intentionally left unreadable to present the scale of the model. It is not possible to fit the whole CRM on a printed page, but legible parts of it are presented in Figs. 6 and 7.

The Event Ontology shown in Fig. 3 describes events with a time and geo-location reference, involved agents/resources and a product generated by the event.

In the centre of the FOAF ("Friend of a Friend")-Ontology (see Fig. 4) is the concept of a Person, that is modelling the static attributes of a person and its relations to other persons, organisations and groups, and their activities in social networks.

The SIO Ontology (see Fig. 5) refines the event concept taken over from the Event Ontology by defining SecurityIncidents, and models persons as victims or subject of SecurityIncidents.

3.3   Validation of the Preliminary Version of the Ontology

To prove the applicability of the approach and test run selected ontologies an example of a use scenario was modelled. The graph (Fig. 2) depicts a situation involving an array of real-life situations and illustrates the relationships between certain agents and events. The graph itself might seem overly intricate, but considering the vast amounts

Fig. 3. General abstract classes of the Event Ontology

of information, evidence, detail and events LEA has gone through to finalize the case a certain degree of sophistication seems inevitable.

In order to validate the proposed preliminary version of the ontology, we have selected one of the use case scenarios. Specifically, we intended to examine to what extent it is capable of describing the context, key elements, and relations.

In Fig. 6 one can observe how the Investigation Event has multiple sub-events, namely the *SocialMedia* event, the *Interrogation* event and the *HouseSurvey* event.

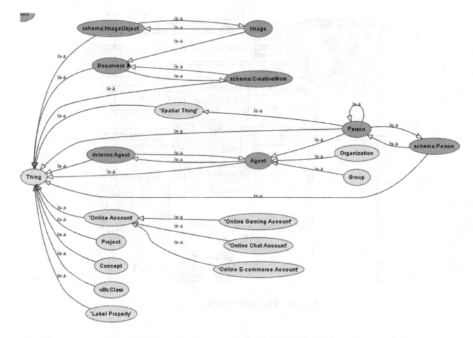

Fig. 4. General abstract classes of the FOAF Ontology

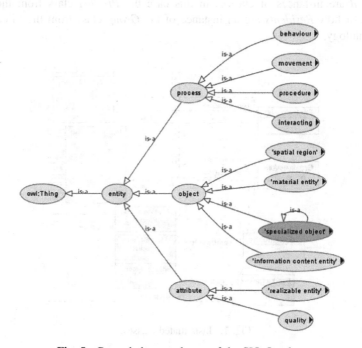

Fig. 5. General abstract classes of the SIO Ontology

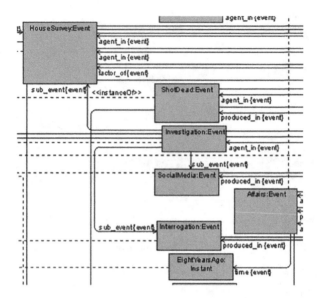

Fig. 6. The investigation event

Figure 7 demonstrates how specific individuals, like *Video_Evidence* or *Head-ShotWound* are instances of classes, in this case the *Product* class from the event ontology, or how *Residents* are an instance of the *Group* class from the FriendOfA-Friend ontology.

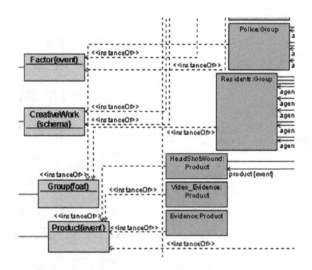

Fig. 7. Instantiated classes.

4 Discussion on the Future Use in Practice

The final product of the MAGNETO project will be a platform integrating all components, services and capabilities developed during the project (and mentioned in the Introduction). To enable communication, the exchange and fusion of information coming from different modules, the MAGNETO platform architecture, defined interfaces and the representational model that was described in the previous section need to be developed. In addition to the ability of representing knowledge and describing security events in a commonly understandable way, the goal of the MAGNETO representational model will be to support both anticipation and prediction of future trends (e.g. security threats) and to establish the common ground for reasoning and cognition to achieve situational awareness.

In addition, MAGNETO has as an ambition to monitor, study and contribute to the activities related to the standards of ISO/TC 292 "Security and Resilience" in the area of security aimed at enhancing the safety and resilience of society and to eventually propose the defined common representational model for standardization.

The ISO 22311 standard, originally prepared by ISO/TC 223 "Societal security" and later taken over by ISO/TC 391 "Societal and Citizen Security", was conceived for societal security purposes and specifies a common output file format that can be extracted from the video-surveillance content to allow different investigators to access digital video-surveillance content and perform its necessary processing.

Since the common data format introduced by the ISO 22311 standard is specific to the video content, it cannot be directly translated to a more general context of the MAGNETO project. Nevertheless, we mention the general principles that were followed during the standardization process that could be adapted to MAGNETO.

A list of minimum technical requirements has been established in order to assure the interoperability of different video-surveillance systems:

- All collected information should be referenced to Coordinated Universal Time (UTC).
- The data format should allow the file export of time slices of data coming from different sources and preserve the time correlation between the contents, whatever export process (removable media or data trans-mission) is used.
- The format should enable compatible, comparable processing of files exported by different systems (covering the same scene) with a common time base.
- The format should facilitate widely available, independent Operating Systems (OS) to allow for minimal processing, ensuring any combination of the following: video data and metadata display, direct access to the metadata without display of the videos, selection of content time slots or access to the sources defined by name or scene-location.

5 Conclusions

The preceding paper aimed to delineate the importance of creating an ontology to provide the semantic context to both the AI and the multitude of entities operating on similar data in the domain of law enforcement. The process of developing a common representational model growing out of several pre-existing ontologies, bridging the gaps between them, and building on top of them has been emphasized.

The main contribution of this document is the presentation and explanation of the proposed MAGNETO common representational model. A thorough analysis of the existing ontologies has been performed, an examination based both on expert knowledge and previous projects. The MAGNETO common representational model is thus created as an ontology, with one of the use cases modelled as a validation of the concept.

Acknowledgement. This work has been performed under the H2020 786629 project MAGNETO, which has received funding from the European Union's Horizon 2020 Programme. This paper reflects only the authors' view, and the European Commission is not liable to any use that may be made of the information contained therein.

References

1. Fani, H., Bagheri, E.: An Ontology for Describing Security Events (2015). https://doi.org/10.18293/seke2015-101
2. Raimond, Y., Abdallah, S.: "The event ontology," Centre for Digital Music, Queen Mary, University of London. http://motools.sourceforge.net/event/event.html
3. Raimond, Y., Abdallah, S.: "The Timeline Ontology," Centre for Digital Music, Queen Mary, University of London. http://motools.sourceforge.net/timeline/timeline.html
4. W3C Semantic Web Interest Group, "Basic Geo (WGS84 lat/long) Vocabulary," W3C Semantic Web Interest Group. http://www.w3.org/2003/01/geo/
5. FOAF Vocabulary Specification 0.99, Namespace Document, 14 January 2014. http://xmlns.com/foaf/spec/
6. Fellbaum, C.: WordNet: An Electronic Lexical Database. MIT Press (1998). http://wordnet.princeton.edu/
7. W3C WordNet RDF/OWL Files. https://www.w3.org/2006/03/wn/wn20/#wnjune06
8. Sobhani, F., Izquierdo, E., Piatrik, T.: Ontology-based forensic event detection using inference rules. Published in 2017 International Conference on Engineering, Technology and Innovation (ICE/ITMC) (2017)
9. CAPER WebSite: http://www.fp7-caper.eu/
10. González-Conejero, J., Varela Figueroa, R., Muñoz-Gomez, J., Teodoro, E.: Organized crime structure modelling for european law enforcement agencies interoperability through ontologies. In: Casanovas, P., Pagallo, U., Palmirani, M., Sartor, G. (eds.) AICOL-2013. LNCS (LNAI), vol. 8929, pp. 217–231. Springer, Heidelberg (2014). https://doi.org/10.1007/978-3-662-45960-7_16
11. Justice Information Sharing - Global Justice XML (Archive). https://it.ojp.gov/initiatives/gjxdm

12. NIEM - National Information Exchange Model, the official NIEM web site. https://www.niem.gov/
13. Choraś, M., Kozik, R., Flizikowski, A., Hołubowicz, W.: Ontology applied in decision support system for critical infrastructures protection. In: García-Pedrajas, N., Herrera, F., Fyfe, C., Benítez, J.M., Ali, M. (eds.) IEA/AIE 2010. LNCS (LNAI), vol. 6096, pp. 671–680. Springer, Heidelberg (2010). https://doi.org/10.1007/978-3-642-13022-9_67

Route Ontology in Value Recognition of Self-tour Planning Application

Daria Hołodnik[1](✉) ⓘ and Kazimierz Perechuda[2](✉) ⓘ

[1] Faculty of Physical Education and Physiotherapy,
Opole University of Technology, Prószkowska Street 76, 45-758 Opole, Poland
d.holodnik@po.edu.pl
[2] Wrocław University of Economics, Komandorska Street 118/120,
53-345 Wroclaw, Poland
kazimierz.perechuda@ue.wroc.pl

Abstract. In tourism information management there are two types of information networking that may assist the personalized self-tour planning: (1) tourist points of interest (regional attractions, activities and events) and (2) tourism services (hotel, gastronomy and transport). Therefore, the most important problem discussed in the paper is the integration of the tourism information networks for individual user optimization and personalization. In order to make this connection, there are overviewed three ontological approaches that lead to the recognition of tourist values. The object-based logic is explained as the first model, then the service-based model follows, with the experience-oriented model being discussed as the last one, thus going from the most passive way of self-tour planning to its most active form (through co-creation of the tourist route). The main focus of the latter approach is on designing two stages of the tourist experience that would manifest itself during the tour. Its operationalization is done by expert knowledge rooted in the tourist application functionality. The practical part of the paper deliberates the unique values that can be used to inform and enhance the smart and the intelligent tourist self-tour planner.

Keywords: Route-based ontology · Personalized tour · Tourist application ·
Value recognition · Experience design

1 Introduction

In computational sciences, ontology design is a process of designing an information structure and its proceedings. The technical way of defining ontology often contains however, the meanings and values which are perceived by the information users. Thus, looking upon them place the user perspective in the center of the ontology design [16]. Its focus is to identify and explain the relation between the logic of information streaming and the user experience driven by the usability of this process, so basically by the cognitive values. The moments when information is perceived will differ based on specific circumstances or even an individuals' previous or expected lived experiences. Diagnosing them requires, therefore, the contextualization of information use and the connection with life situations.

© Springer Nature Switzerland AG 2019
N. T. Nguyen et al. (Eds.): ICCCI 2019, LNAI 11684, pp. 346–356, 2019.
https://doi.org/10.1007/978-3-030-28374-2_30

Design of the tourism information networking can impact on the tourist value recognition and its application may play fundamental role in the e-tourism marketing [10], the tourism destination management [19], and in particular, in the self-tour digitalization [9, 23].

Because the self-guided tours are planned and organized by tourists' themselves and characterized by a highly personalized, individualized manner, the models of tourism information streams are extremely difficult to design and pattern [9]. Actually, the greatest challenge is a shift from the model of tourism information designing to the co-designing one [15], that as a result allows to reduce tourist uncertainty of the information use while composing own tours and experiences [17, 19].

The aim of the paper is thus, to examine the value recognition modelling in designing the self-tour application. To do so, the three ontological models are evaluated by their impact on solving self-tour problems.

2 Ontological Approaches to the Tourist Value Modelling

The diagnosis of route-based ontology is informed by the authors' practical and theoretical studies in tourism destination management [2, 19] and tourism networking marketing. Whereas, model design represented within this paper, is based on the figurative method of visualizing tourist value prediction [8].

Therefore, the theoretical conduction was constructed according to the postmodern formula: 'through theory making to practice prediction' and 'from practical thinking to theory visualization' [3]. The simultaneous use of the practical and theoretical approach has informed the new area of design studies [19] and has inspired a novel design framework for the tourist application.

At first there was an assumption that a process of ontological underpinning was rooted in tourist value recognition. The tourist cognitive value has been defined as the relationship between known (available and predictable tourism information design) and unknown particles (unavailable, but party predictable tourist travelling preferences) in respect to how information is perceived. Ontological studies in cognitive fields requires one to sketch new positioning, asymmetries, and movements in the 'game between', in order to expose the ready ontological patterns. Thus, through the modelling of the descriptive components there can be explored the tourist experience models [8, 11].

The ontology designs visualized on the Fig. 1 can be applied to information architecture by containing its animate aspects, so the context in which the tourism information is consumed, perceived, and later valued. The experience models are then relevant to the **tourist value recognition** in three different ontologies of information networking: from the object-based, through the services based, ending at the route-based one.

By following the first ontological model (Fig. 1-**Object ontology**), the value recognition is particularly related with the object-based information modelling [5], in tourism this is known as location-aware or context-aware points of interest [10-14].

In that way, some of the tourism objects can become particles of a tourist' travelling scenario [4, 8]. This type of gathering, collecting and matching information around tourism objects is mostly known and grounded in the georeferenced models or geographical-based ontology [13].

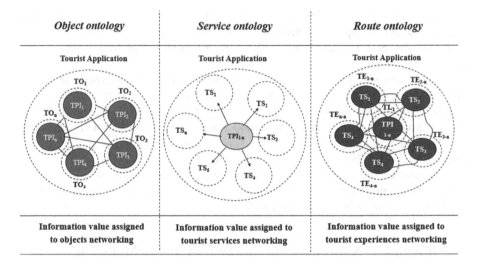

Fig. 1. Ontological intersection between information and tourist value modelling (Source: Author's own elaboration). Legend: TPI_1 – tourist point of interest, TO_{1-n} – tourism objects, TS_{1-n} – tourism services, TL_1 – tourist localization, TE_{1-n} – tourist experiences

However, the 'point to point' travelling is not very helpful from the self-tour planning point of view. Often, information about tourism objects and their networking's have been prepared with little knowledge of tourists' preferences motivation [10, 16] or tourist' context-based localization [11, 12]. In fact, it is a tourism information system that is able to navigate tourism sites but is not aimed to deliver solutions for the qualitative requirements current circumstances (e.g. connecting objects through the personal interests etc.). In this case, the self-tour planning remains a difficult task, and requires plans to be tailored to individuals' parameters of greatest impact such as: available tourist free time, variation of the tours, individual time of service consuming etc.

All this still lays at the tourists' hand and mind. Which is why the first model (Object ontology) is strongly linked with objectification logic [5], but lacks the personalization aspect [12] or the user-driven ontology [9, 16].

The second ontology (Fig. 1-**Service ontology**) is based on the tourism services design [17]. However, it is not possible to apply unless information about a tourists' past travelling activity was registered [7, 13]. This mechanism can be seen as an expansion of the previous ontology, whereby there is a greater association to related services placed around varied tourist objects [6, 13]. Still the tour planning and choosing processes must be undertaken entirely by the tourist, who in fact, must play a role of itinerary planner, leader and organizer. Some of the service choices however, can be actively stimulated and supported by the recommendation systems [1, 7, 13, 20].

The third ontology (Fig. 1-**Route ontology**) is based on integrating the personalized tourist points of interest [24] with tourism services. This can happen under the condition of involving tourist into the process of experience design (creating both, the individual tour and consumption model). This is a shift to the co-design ontology [15], wherein the chosen tourists' parameters become indicators of a tourist route. A parallel co-creation 'game' is played between tourist opportunities and tourist experience models, and indeed, it becomes a crucial relationship of composing information architecture for tourism 4.0 [21].

3 Route Ontology as a Base of Tourist Application

A practical aim of this paper is to identify the cognitive values of using tourist application based on the route ontology. So, it could work as the experience planner rather than simply having tourism information delivered through a mobile app as are provided by the e-travel advisors [10] or agencies [25].

The object- and service-route design varies from above-mentioned, because they have incorporated linear and topological logic of tour making, while route ontology is based on experience design and must be fundamentally aware of the tourist' value recognition models. Therefore, there are two distinguishable experience design stages conceived as the key of networking. Additionally, if one were to examine a large range tourist applications currently offered [22–24], two design and knowledge gaps are evident. The two gaps described in Fig. 2 include:

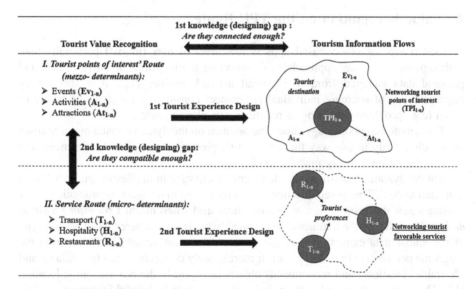

Fig. 2. Knowledge (designing) gaps in co-creating the tourist route by application (Source: Authors' own elaboration)

- the connectivity of object- and activity-based ontology (**1st knowledge gap**),
- the compatibility of objects and services of tourist interest (**2nd knowledge gap**).

While the first knowledge gap refers to the horizontal problem (connectivity between activities, events and attractions), the other demonstrates the vertical problem (compatibility between 1st and 2nd experience design) which is related to route planning as the key functionality of the innovative application.

An advantage of the route app is that tourists can be led through a specific line of attractions and a sphere of services. In the tourism market, some of the apps equipped with the 'route' function (e.g., Drive and Bike through California Wine Country, Historic Philadelphia, Tour the Streets of New Orleans' French Quarters etc. bicycle route, beer route, cultural route etc.) are offered. However, it is not the same functionality nature to the one is being discussed. The incorporation of the co-design process, which here is fundamental, enables tourist to create the own travelling strategy of the self-tour, while in the apps with 'ready routes' [24], he has been not participated in combining the route objects. Moreover, the active tour-planner is able to:

- match one preferences with the adequate service quality,
- estimate optimal route by both, its availability and attractiveness,
- cumulate the length of travel between objects and services,
- gives alternative options of the objects if one is not available.

In other words the route-based ontology, is generally expressing the modern trend of information networking in tourism destination marketing. But yet it has not been elaborated through its value proposition in the tourist experience design.

4   Value Recognition on the TPI' Route

A disadvantage of object-based apps is low level of user (tourist) personalization. Although there are new approaches to connecting tourist points of interest (TPI) and personal data gathered from user' social network profiles [12], it is still a very imprecise way of sourcing individual preferences considering the dynamic nature of travel (e.g., problems occurring in real-time tour planning, etc.).

Thus, route-based ontology should be oriented on the dynamic matching of tourism information. Only in this way the active co-shaping of tourist plans, preferences, and options can be realistically manifested (Fig. 3).

But the dynamic tourism means that a crucial question in implies in app is: 'what do you want to do?'. This posed question allows the tourist to navigate the true dilemma of visiting a new destination, that is: '**what, where and when might I do** *what I want to do* **here?**', replacing the traditional and typical 'what is offered here?'. The passive type of the tourist data extraction does not generate the most valuable answers from the long-time perspective (e.g. a day-tour or more), rarely connects tourist to available and 'desirable' locations, and recommends objects in regard to the nearest tourist location [13]. The tourist active app has been designed in a way to be helpful for tourists in their present time, place and circumstances, to achieve a greater effectiveness in associating the multi-object route with the tourism motives of the planner.

It is common for tourist to feel irritated, overwhelmed, ill-equipped, or uninformed when the planning process begins to get difficult or is taking too much time. Often, this is a function of too many 'information gaps' about connectivity between reaching a single TPI with another ones (to be matched are min.: disposition of tourist free time, opening hours and availability of TPI). When information is unreachable (not found at one source) or it becomes difficult to assemble or make sense of disparate pieces of information, tourists often make rash decisions, and undertake a 'spontaneous' or a

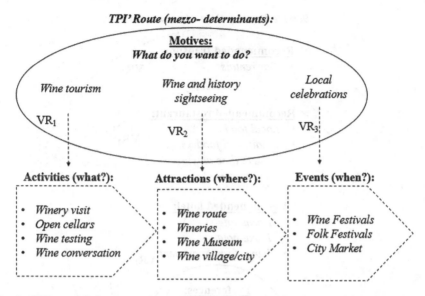

Fig. 3. TPI' routing in the tourist application (Source: Authors' own elaboration). Legend: VR_{1-3} – value recognition

risky tour, often forfeiting previously planned sites. The syndrome of the 'lost visit' is very disappointing and may bring about feelings of an unsatisfactory or unfulfilled experience. So, the key values to be recognized by the tourist app are: the TPI' selection up to the motives (what do I want to do?) and their availability up to the tourist time and location (where and when can I do that?).

Therefore, the mezzo-modelling illustrated on Fig. 3 identify and combine three spheres of a tourist time-spending model:

- **Activities** (key travelling activities related with wine tourism: winery visit, open cellars, wine testing, wine conversation),
- **Attractions** (sites assigned to the motives: wine route, wineries, wine museums and wine villages or cities)
- **Events** (event calendar assigned to the motives: wine festivals, folk festivals, city markets).

5   Value Recognition on the Service Route

The second stage of experience design (networking tourist service preferences) aims to diagnose the tourist model of consumption (Fig. 4.). Here there should be a set of consuming services that are compliment the TPI route (are located close to TPI and logically, rationally suits to them). Two filters can be used: (1) maximum acceptable distance from TPI and (2) he style of consumption, thus the identifying question is: 'where and how do you want to consume?

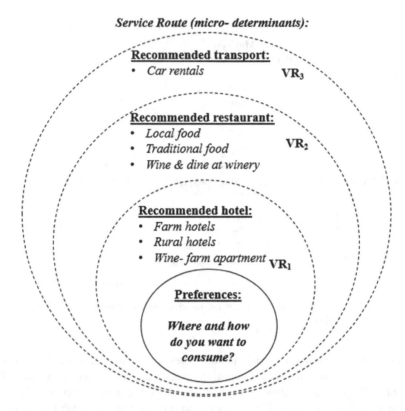

Fig. 4. Service routing in the tourist application (Source: Authors' own elaboration). Legend: VR_{1-3} – value recognition

Successfully supplementing the TPI route can be accomplished when the most necessary, but also the most compatible services, are added to it. Services should, at first, be logically separated in accordance with the already chosen model of time spending (TPI' route). If continuing the example of wine tourism drawn in Fig. 3, then the app should be able to make recommendations in at least three areas of services:

- **Accommodation** (recommendation should be: 'rural hotel, farm hotel or apartments at winery'-to be located close to the degustation place or at winery directly-**localization of activities** is the first vale recognition)
- **Food** (recommendation should be: 'local restaurants, traditional or wine & dine at winery'-to experience local wine and food pairing-**localization of attractions and events** as the second recognition),
- **Transportation** (recommendation should be: 'rental car'-to reach easily to rural areas-**localization of both, TPI and services** is the third vale recognition).

The second phase is more demanding in ontology design because of its qualitative character, and thus should be co-created by cross-disciplinary teams (e.g. tourism management experts, computer scientists, tourism psychologist) who together are able to diagnose and construct logical formulas of tourist 'optimal' service networks due to the cognitive values. To have access to individual preferences is one thing, but to match in a logical system of interpretation, is yet another thing. The more personalized tour is, the more importance plays service experience design (individual tourists do not depend on time as much as organized groups do). For this reason, the expertise knowledge of the tourism behaviorism and cognition is quintessential in modelling the meaningful and highly customized tourist models.

6 Value Verification in the Route Scenario

On the basis function of the application is the ability to create several possible scenarios for a tourist route (classified from the most reachable to the most unreachable in relation to the tourists' time disposition and the motives availability (Fig. 5).

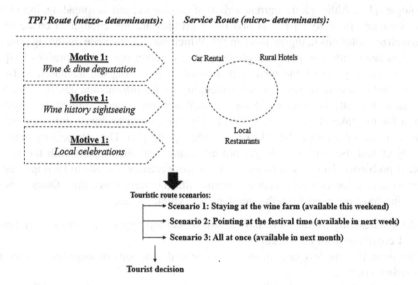

Fig. 5. Route scenarios in the tourist application (Source: Authors' own elaboration)

That means that the main analytical competences of future tourist applications are giving logical recommendations on how to combine what is offered, wished, and possible to do within a limited time period and the present conditions of the scenarios:

- **Scenario 1** (available now): 'Only some of the designed experiences are available in this time period',
- **Scenario 2** (short-term planning is required): 'Some of the designed experiences are available in short time perspective'
- **Scenario 3** (long-term planning is required): 'Some of the designed experiences are available in long time perspective'.

By following the generated scenarios a tourist can become familiar with the activities, events, attractions, and services that are possible to do and experience within a certain time perspective. Generally, the closer to present time, the less possible it is to match all items, due to TPI or services being occupied or unavailable. However, the tourist is gaining a complete view, not only into what the destination offers, but also into its attractiveness, connection, and recognition from personal point of view.

7 Conclusions

Solutions of information structuring in self-guiding tourism requires more complex and holistic ontology approaches. They have already begun to be developed through the combination of user-based and object-based ontologies [20].

The most frequent discussion among scholars in this area concerns the method of transforming information systems for new callings coming from the user driven ontologies [16]. Although the current arrival of ontological mix is spreading, individual data resources from social media and other profiles are not enough to create more personalized solutions in digital tourism [9]. Which insofar are made up through the *ex-post* data analyzing (e.g. past user preferences) to predict the *ex-ante* profiles [20].

This article provides the next step forward in exploring the advanced self-tour planner, but also informs why it is so challenging for the information designers [8, 18]. The main difficulty is to reconcile the recommendation systems (information system design for the sake of business profit [11, 13]) with the user-driven ontology (information systems design for the sake of individual profit [6]). The connectivity between the object and user ontology is yet not associated enough to dealt with the tourist context problems. Thus, the dimension of interconnectedness needs to be improved in order to design tourism information systems with the greater usability. Other conclusions that have emerged from the ontological 'symbiosis' are:

- the synthesizing picture of designing and modelling requires the cross-disciplinary and cognitive team co-working,
- the figurative models can mirror the logic and functions of cognitive values (in tourism context),
- the tourism information architecture can be done after the recognition of the tourist values (the modeling the self-tours of visitation and consumption),
- the exploration of the tourist problems in the motion-based, changeable and dynamic conditions are necessary in next generation of self-tourism.

Acknowledgment. "The project is financed by the Ministry of Science and Higher Education in Poland under the programme "Regional Initiative of Excellence" 2019–2022 project number 015/RID/2018/19 total funding amount 10 721 040,00 PLN".

References

1. Bahramiana, Z., Abbaspoura Ali, R.: An ontology-based tourism recommender system based on spreading activation model. In: The International Archives of the Photogrammetry, Remote Sensing and Spatial Information Sciences, vol. XL-1/W5 (2015)
2. Botterill, D., Platenkamp, V.: Key Concepts in Tourism Research. Sage Publishing Ltd., Los Angeles (2012)
3. Card, S.K., Mackinlay, J.D., Shneiderman, B.: Information visualization. In: Card, S.K., Mackinlay, J.D., Shneiderman, B. (eds.) Readings in Information Visualization: Using Vision to Think, pp. 1–34. Morgan Kaufmann, San Francisco (1999)
4. Carroll, J.M. (ed.): Making Use: Scenario-Based Design of Human-Computer Interactions. MIT Press, Cambridge (2000)
5. Chen, L., Nugent, C.: Ontology-based activity recognition in intelligent pervasive environments. Int. J. Web Inf. Syst. 5(4), 410–430 (2009)
6. Cheverst, K., Davies, N., Mitchell, K., Smith, P.: Providing tailored (context-aware) information to city visitors. In: Brusilovsky, P., Stock, O., Strapparava, C. (eds.) AH 2000. LNCS, vol. 1892, pp. 73–85. Springer, Heidelberg (2000). https://doi.org/10.1007/3-540-44595-1_8
7. Cho, Y., Kim, J.: Application of web usage mining and product taxonomy to collaborative recommendations in e-commerce. Expert Syst. Appl. 26(2), 233–246 (2004)
8. Dorrestijn, S., van der Voort, M., Verbeek, P.-P.: Future user-product arrangements: combining product impact and scenarios in design for multi age success. Technol. Forecast. Soc. Chang. 89, 284–292 (2014)
9. Fink, J., Kobsa, A.: User modeling for personalized city tours. Artif. Intell. Rev. 18, 33 (2002). https://doi.org/10.1023/A:1016383418977
10. García-Crespo, A., Chamizo, J., Rivera, I., Mencke, M., Colomo-Palacios, R., Gómez-Berbís, J.M.: SPETA: social pervasive e-tourism advisor. Telematics Inform. 26, 306–315 (2009)
11. Long, S., Kooper, R., Abowd, G.D., Atkeson, C.G.: Rapid prototyping of mobile context-aware applications. the cyberguide case study. In: Proceedings of the 2nd ACM International Conference on Mobile Computing. ACM Press, Rye (1996)
12. Makedos, K., Tryfona, N.: PLATIS: a personalized location-aware tourist information system. In: Proceedings of the Second ACM SIGSPATIAL International Workshop on Mobile Geographic Information Systems (2013)
13. Martínez, L., Rodríguez, R.M., Espinilla, M.: REJA: a georeferenced hybrid recommender system for restaurants. In: Proceedings of IEEE/WIC/ACM International Conference on Web Intelligence and Intelligent Agent Technology, pp. 187–190 (2009)
14. Moura, H., et al.: Developing a ubiquitous tourist guide. In: Proceedings of the 19th Brazilian Symposium on Multimedia and the WebMedia (2013)
15. Sanders, L., Stappers, P.J.: From designing to co-designing to collective dreaming: three slices in time. Interactions 21(6), 24–33 (2014)
16. Stojanovic, L., Maedche, A., Motik, B., Stojanovic, N.: User-driven ontology evolution management. In: Gómez-Pérez, A., Benjamins, V.R. (eds.) EKAW 2002. LNCS (LNAI), vol. 2473, pp. 285–300. Springer, Heidelberg (2002). https://doi.org/10.1007/3-540-45810-7_27
17. Stickdorn, M., Zehrer, A.: Service design in tourism: customer experience driven destination management. In: Clatworthy, S. (ed.) Proceedings of the 1st Nordic Service Design Conference, Oslo, Norway (2009)

18. Tolk, A., Diallo, S.Y., Turnitsa, C.D.: Ontology driven interoperability – M&S applications, whitepaper in support of the I/ITSEC Tutorial 2548, VMASC report, Old Dominion University, Suffolk, VA (2006)
19. Tussyadiah, I.P.: Technology and behavioral design in tourism. In: Fesenmaier, D.R., Xiang, Z. (eds.) Design Science in Tourism. TV, pp. 173–191. Springer, Cham (2017). https://doi.org/10.1007/978-3-319-42773-7_12
20. Zhou, T., Kuscsik, Z., Liu, J., Medo, M., Wakeling, J.R., Zhang, Y.: Solving the apparent diversity-accuracy dilemma of recommender systems. Nat. Acad. Sci. **107**(10), 4511–4515 (2010)
21. https://www.tourism4-0.org/
22. https://www.cntraveler.com/stories/2015-02-24/travel-apps-that-can-replace-your-tour-guide
23. http://selftour.guide/
24. http://selftour.guide/tours/napa-sonoma-valleys/
25. https://www.rome2rio.com/

The Extended Authentication Process in the Environment of the Laboratory Information and Management System

Pavel Blazek[1,2]([⊠]) [iD] and Ondrej Krejcar[1] [iD]

[1] Faculty of Informatics and Management, University of Hradec Kralove,
Hradec Kralove, Czech Republic
pavel.blazek@unob.cz, ondrej.krejcar@uhk.cz
[2] Faculty of Military Health Sciences, University of Defence in Brno,
Hradec Kralove, Czech Republic

Abstract. Laboratory information systems have evolved from applications designed to simplify or eliminate routine processes. Their further development follows the trend of interconnection with intelligent laboratory equipment. Laboratories of primary research are specific in many ways and commonly available information systems cannot be deployed there. Development of a new lab information and management system should be designed in order to ensure not only safe and secured operation but also modular requirements. Elements of data security can be successfully implemented on the basis of studies and standards which deal with this issue on a general level. The area of security should be viewed in the context of the lab as the whole. The mentioned type of laboratories processes a sensitive material, creates compounds of nonresearched properties, which are studied and results are subsequently published. It is obvious that the environment has to be secured at all levels. The following article describes a possible solution.

Keywords: Laboratory · Information system · Security · Authentication

1 Introduction

The development of laboratory information systems is generally based on the needs of laboratories to solve routine and repetitive tasks that computing can perform more quickly and efficiently [1]. Applications have been and are still being created for these purposes. Their connection creates a Laboratory Information System (LIS). The LIMS Laboratory Information Management System was created by adding management support functions.

Laboratories are most often divided according to their specialization. They can be distinguished by another key, whether they are clinical laboratories or primary research laboratories. From this point of view, information systems (IS) have a clearly defined framework. Their development is based on the needs of different disciplines [2]. A common feature is the need to consider a significant amount of legislation [3–8]. Their commercial success depends on meeting these criteria. However, under the conditions of primary research laboratories, these systems are hardly applicable.

© Springer Nature Switzerland AG 2019
N. T. Nguyen et al. (Eds.): ICCCI 2019, LNAI 11684, pp. 357–368, 2019.
https://doi.org/10.1007/978-3-030-28374-2_31

The main difference is the need for available functions higher variability [9]. The requirement is based on the main activity, research. The key distinction to this type of information system is security and secured data access.

2 Problem Definition

The system of biomedical data collection is more specific due to ethic and physical information sensitivity than systems of other branches. Legal rules, which limit data management and have to be respected during the development or selection of a particular information system (IS) [10], contribute to this situation. Formally, we can say that standard operating procedures of biomedical labs of primary research and clinical biochemical labs have the common base in good laboratory practice [11]. The difference lies in methods and goals, due to which information systems designated for clinical labs cannot be used exclusively in the labs of primary research [12]. The need to secure their content against unauthorized access and data theft makes it in some aspects challenging due to records on sensitive materials processing and producing compounds of nonresearched properties. In other words, it deals with keeping documentation comprising the valuable intellectual property of a particular organization. IS security [13], and its secured access at physical and data levels, has to be more sophisticated and more resistant. The academic environment of universities, where research is often carried out, is different from standard labs in terms of person's turnover, which places increased demands for security. Following ideas develop the study devoted to biomedical data security presented at conferences [14–17].

Problem solving of the user authentication and authorization in primary research labs is based on the real environment study. Two laboratories from Faculty of military health sciences University of Defense and from Faculty of Science University of Hradec Kralove were selected from the environment of the university campus of Hradec Kralove city. The Biological Research Center at the University Hospital was also selected to develop a real laboratory environment model. Their common feature is an environment that has a similar organization, but due to physical location, their security requirements are different It was this fact that was taken into account in their selection.

3 Related Works

Contrary to efforts to secure valuable information with passwords, we currently face the need of frequent authentication. The Internet is full of services, on which many routine activities of individuals, firms, and countries depend. Complexity which the IS has gained does not always allow the use of federative services for interconnection of related systems into the state of unified login so-called Single Sign-On. A great deal of login data and their forced changes lead users to facilitate the situation. Despite education and regular training [18], sharing accounts with co-workers or password administration in written or electronic form are impossible to eliminate entirely [19]. Even though only the logged-in user has access to particular equipment and a user profile, only imaginary security is concerned. More advanced users use applications which save inserted sensitive data in a coded form locally or in a cloud [20, 21]. A similar problem arises when a user applies the same password in different systems. Compromising any of them, a security incident in remaining systems may emerge without noticing. Security risk of password cracking is increased by the fact that a lot of browsers offer saving login data for automatic login on service providers websites without the password in order to simplify users' life. Unreasonable trust in applications and burden of users with the enormous number of login data lead to the fact that only some of them think about the form and place of passwords storing and if they cannot be stolen or misused, what level of risk compromising of protected data represent for an individual or a society [22].

4   Authentication Process

In general, authentication and authorization are the key pillars of intellectual property protection, whether it is information about the research and development or production process procedures. The process of authentication of a person accessing to a system and authorization of their permission have to be viewed from the perspective of the environment in which they are engaged. The information system primarily designated for administrative actions support is capable to operate on commonly available HW environments. Authentication of a user is based on entering the username and password while logging to the operating system of the work station eventually into the IS interface of the organization. These environments are somehow "blind" to the real identity of the logging person. Object identification is the act of trust set on the level of system security of the organization. It is based on the system of authentication supported by training of workers on following procedures which should prevent security incidents. Guidelines are to be elaborated for this purpose which is not always based on current standards and recommendations.

4.1   Password Authentication

A password, as the string of characters, has been historically the most frequently used method of a single-factor authentication accompanying humankind. Its electronic form, when a user types a sequence of characters on the terminal keyboard, has ensured access to different systems for decades. Password cracking depends on the combination of human as well as technical factors. They have to be brought into accord. The technical factor means an attempt to reach the password complexity, particularly in definition what characters and to what extent can be used for its creation. The human factor, because of brain capabilities, limits the boom of the technical factor [23]. In some systems, the password can reach the length of 16 up to 32 characters (MS Windows, Office365, Live), the length is not essentially limited in some applications (Facebook tested the password of 1000 characters), the others use only a block of first 8 characters and the rest is ignored (IOS). The password usable in practice has to be easily remembered, it means significantly shorter than the achievable maxima. A sufficient length is a concept which is defined with the number and parameters of used characters. It is derived from the technical capabilities of commonly available computing power. It should resist any attack for a defined period of time when the password is generated from the assumed characters in the range of the assumed number of characters. This group also comprises dictionary attacks when passwords are not generated but loaded from the list in the attempt of the breach. The passwords should not be created from known words, definitely not from the frequently used ones related to the person or the place of its engagement.

How easy or complicated is to crack the password keeping the above mentioned requirements depends on the number of characters of the virtual language and the number of characters used for the creation of the password [24]. The capacity of a virtual dictionary we can express for simplicity as a variant with repetition.

VVS(D, PZJ) = PZJ^Ds

Where:
VVS ... capacity of virtual dictionary
PZJ ... number of the characters language
and
D ... password length

For the language consisted of 62 characters, it means 218, 340, 105, 584, 896 possibilities, i.e. when we use capital letters of the alphabet and numbers (a–z; A–Z; 0–9). If we use commonly used special characters, the basic set of characters of the language is increased up to 78 and the number of possible passwords six times of previous value. The number of special characters is limited for users to those, which can be entered mainly from the Czech keyboard layout. After the detailed file exploration, it can be stated that approximately 1/3 of this way generated passwords do not meet the requirement of complexity which is not in compliance with a general model mentioned in [24] designated to authentication security. The calculation is based on recommendations for the use of a minimum password length of 8 characters [25] while keeping conditions of complexity. The complex password, which consists of a significant number of characters in combination with alphanumeric and special characters may resist with high probability to different types of attacks in the protected system allowing only a particular number of wrong attempts in a defined time interval with a forced time of validity.

4.2 Advanced Authentication Mechanism

The connection of a username and password with other elements is called multi-factor authentication. It could be a code saved on a removable medium or biometric data. Thanks to them we can verify the user identity with higher accuracy since copying them is very complicated. The method allows us to connect a particular person with an action or event in the system in real time. It is applied, for instance, in the three-factor authentication [1]. Within implementation, the unique identifier of a person, which belongs only to the verified person, is assigned to the name and password which can be divulged. Another parameter, which is assigned to the user in the system, is a code representing the scanned pattern which is compared during the process of authentication with the currently scanned code presenting a fingerprint, iris or retina image, face, hand geometry, voice pattern, and others [26]. Figure 1 describes this procedure.

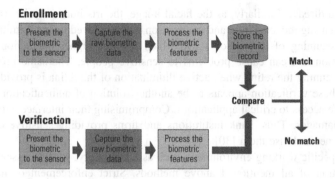

Fig. 1. General model comparing biometric data, source: [28]

Biometric markers are unique and confirmatory [27], however, they cannot be considered to be a separate element of authentication. They can be regarded as a similar identifier as it is the username. Efforts to compromise biometric records have been successful to some extent, however, they have not been only effective enough in comparison with attempts and money spent. It follows that they cannot be placed on the level of password. This finding is opposed in the material of the DELL [28], where the use of biometric elements is described in connection with strong authentication as the only verifying factor. If the password is regarded as the optional string of characters, it can be replaced in case of disclosure with another combination from the defined set of available characters. Biometric information is unique that is why it is not suitable for secured systems as a complex replacement of the combination of username and password. In addition to that, it is a strong identifier of the owner, therefore, it should be applied in really beneficial situations.

As given above, the use of biometric markers is connected with their loading and verification. Different variants have their pros and cons, which together with technical requirements for implementation identify the range of their application in practice [29]. The use of a particular variant also depends on physical conditions of implementation.

4.3   Authentication in the Lab

Authentication on the basis of fingerprints belongs to the oldest and the most widespread applications. It has relatively high accuracy, it is fast and user friendly. Quite a small sensor is needed for its usage. If we want to use the hand geometry, much larger sensors have to be taken into account, which does not matter in authentication of a person at the entrance to the building. Moreover, comparison of facial characteristic features descri-bed by their width to height ratio can be applied. Verification is based on photos or videos. The method is limited primarily by an image recognition sensor and lighting conditions, by wearing glasses, face expression and changes caused, for example by beard treatment. Comparing voice pattern with the voice of the identified person, a microphone only is used which is a cheap application independent on a language. The first disadvantage is that phrases having high volume patterns are used for comparison. The accuracy is strongly influenced by background noise and by the change of voice due to stress and disease. Similarly, as the facial image, the iris image can be used. It is a process of sensing reflected light and comparison with the saved image. Limiting can be a detailed scanning of the person's eye which requires higher interaction with the verified person and can cause problems to sensitive people. The same problem can appear in scanning the retina when active illumination of the retina is provided.

Multi-phase verification appears to be another solution of authentication which is used for safe access to critical applications. Compromising their interface could lead to extensive damages. Thus, bank institutions and firms providing sensitive data via a public data network use them [30].

In the specific working environment, such as a laboratory, we face essential limits for application of all mentioned above methods. Strict enforcement of improperly selected model would lead to failure of routine activities in real time or to the enormous burden of employees with extra activities, and as usual, it would lead to circumvention of deployed security procedures and to worsening the situation.

The use of biometrics is not complicated, however, it is difficult to apply in the lab environment due to the use of protective means. Fingerprinting cannot be taken through gloves, protective glasses can cause reflections which makes cornea scanning impossible. A mouth mask may mute voice. Furthermore, the mouth mask and glasses change facial physiognomy, so even recognition of the user's face is not a suitable way of identification.

Mentioned cooperating labs commonly use RFID card for user's identification. The only toxicology department is equipped with a one fingerprint reader at the entry to the lab.

4.4   Lab Environment Model

If we consider the lab as a building which is not formed only by rooms, where experiments are carried out, we are able to divide the given area into zones with a defined level of security. The situation will change and proportionate security can be achieved.

A number of zones come from the designation of the lab and substances, which are processed and stored there. Four zones, which are analyzed in details hereinafter, create the foundation. A worker moves there according to the phase of a work task and a daily schedule.

A simplified model of the workplace is divided to four zones. The lab staff is divided into seven group and the appropriate user permissions are declared for each of them.

- Lab management (head of laboratory)
- Suppliers (Suppliers and servicemen)
- Visitors (guests visiting the lab)
- Lab A1 – B2 (laboratory technician with authorization level indication)

The rights assigned to specific groups are shown in the Table 1.

In accordance with the model description in the following text full details of the lab operations are not given. Neither all eventualities of entrance variants and people movement are mentioned.

Table 1. A simplified model of the four-zones lab environment and assigned permissions

Staff group name	Zone No.			
	1	2	3	4
Lab management	A	A	A	AA
Lab A1	A	A	A	A
Lab A2	A	A	A	AA
Lab B1	A	A	A	AD
Lab B2	A	A	AA	AD
Suppliers	A	AA	AA	AA
Visitors	A	AA	AA	AD

Legend: A Access permitted, AA Accompanied access, AD Access denied

It is necessary to keep employees movement smooth and not to distract and bother them with unnecessary tasks. Passing through the zones is solved with contactless readers and mechanisms of automatic mechanical door control. The passage between the first and the second zone is an exception.

The first zone consists of an entrance hall with a reception where the staff, as well as visitors and suppliers, can enter from the outside area without any restrictions. After the authentication, the staff enters the inside laboratory area, the others are checked in by the reception clerk. If there is no reception clerk, the connection between the first and the second zone is provided by an intercom into the particular office or room.

The second zone consists of offices and utility rooms and is accessible through a couple of terminals which form a redundant element of entering people's primary control. Suppliers and Visitors can entry only to be accompanied by lab staff.

The third zone is a space where experiments and chemical agents are prepared. There is also a storeroom of chemicals and biological samples. Unlike the forth zone, no work with dangerous, toxic and psychotropic substances is performed there. All laboratory staff who participate in experiments are allowed to enter it.

Entering the fourth zone is allowed only for a limited number of employees. It is a place where dangerous substances are handled and stored. Space is separated by a door with an electric lock or frames which are able to identify passing people and let go through only the authorized ones.

Entering the lab from the outside area the user has to go through the reception, which means through the first zone, into the inside part of the working area, which means the second zone. The users are allowed to move freely through the cloakroom, the rest area and into the office where there is a base for their study, planning, and processing research outcomes on computers. In case they participates in a practical experiment, they are allowed to enter the laboratories, the third zone, pick up needed material and use laboratory devices and equipment. Optionally, the movement may be monitored in this space.

In the fourth zone, based on its size and disposition, movement of lab technicians is not necessary to restrict. Primarily, this place is designated for work with toxic substances and poisons. However, it is still necessary to keep the movement smooth in this workplace, which is space under a security regimen, including access to the material needed to conduct experiments. Manipulation with the material is under accurate records of processing and storing to prevent unauthorized manipulation, misappropriation or intoxication.

The space for the passage among zones is mainly emphasized. It is not a problem to use a combination of any of the above mentioned methods between the first and the second zone. The above mentioned restrictions related to biometrics are applied among inside zones. Therefore, the verification between the first and the second zone has to be maximally precise so that the movement among the rest of the zones can be based only e.g. on a single-factor authentication.

4.5 Robustness Requirement

For a practical realization in the above mentioned model, a connection of biometrics and chips with the range of approximately 50 cm seems to be technologically appropriate [31]. The employee can be identified by his fingerprint at the terminal between the first and the second zone. Subsequently, he is asked to put his personal chip on the reading and recording device. After reading the code it is compared with the record in the central security database. If they are the same, a new code is generated which is written down both in the chip and in the database. If the technology RFID Class 1 Gen 2 is used, 512 bites are available which allows up to 2512 different binary code variants. If we used the basic ASCII table where 512 characters coded by a pair of hexadecimal characters are, then we could realize a string of 64 ASCII characters. In accordance with the calculation in the part devoted to password security, the string is 8 times longer. To protect it, it is possible to realize its saving in a chip in the form of hash in accordance with the document NIST No. 2015-19181 [32] which defines SHA-3 as a standard.

People's movement in the laboratory is given by internal rules. Each laboratory has to have safety rules which among others define conditions of people's movement through the laboratory zones. In the rules for the simplified model, it can be one for assigning each account of a lab technician to the group allowing access to the lab of the appropriate level.

An authorized person with a new code enters the internal zones. If somebody owned a copy of the previous authentication of the observed person, he cannot use it. After the successful verification of the employee entering the laboratory, the system allows him other movement and manipulation with the material inside the zones according to an authorization level set for him. Leaving the workplace through registered passing to the first zone, the authorization for physical movement in the laboratory is locked. Door motion sensors along with the contactless chip and further to the safety system enable passing to other space and rooms. It would not happen at the entrance to the zones under a security regimen if there was an unauthorized person close to it. Simultaneous reading of two or more people's codes which security authority assesses dividedly for the particular zone results in the annulment of the entrance requirement.

Electronic systems run in laboratories are usually autonomous. The decentralized environment brings both duplicate management tasks and more complex and time-consuming security incident assessments, especially when composing a chronological sequence of events. It is given by searching for related data in different databases and completing them in a logical unit. The data due to differently set periods for saving records may not be complete. If we outline modern Laboratory information and management system as a complex environment, it can cover modules described in [17] and software interfaces for secure connection of the authentication system as shown in Fig. 2.

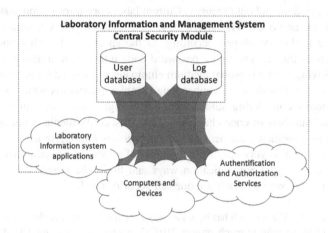

Fig. 2. LIMS – extended modular concept

Connection with a central verifying authority is their common feature. Modules designated for supporting different activities in a laboratory and security as well have united – centralized administration and moreover they can save records of defined events in the central log including time marks. Finding connections with a security incident is significantly simpler. The user is identified easily due to the only central user database and retrospectively easily monitored during the movement through the workplace, manipulation with material and devices, logging in to work stations and also during logging into the IS laboratory and manipulation with data.

It is not suitable to put the main information technology equipment and services to the laboratory environment. Laboratory staff shouldn't be disturbed by tasks not relating to their work. Servers and applications could be placed in the Cloud. However, for security reason or in case of connectivity lost is better to use dedicate server providing on-site verification of each user or device accessing information system sources.

5 Conclusion

To secure the physical space of a laboratory and intellectual property in the form of data records is indisputably necessary. Biomedicine is at the forefront. Laboratory researches and development of new procedures and medications is a competitive environment for laboratories. Undoubtedly, laboratories are places where there are agents which can change into weapons of mass destruction in the wrong hands and information which can be worth immensely. As mentioned above, it is necessary to think about laboratory security in a detached way, to see it as a connection of object security with personal and data security. Current laboratory information systems do not provide such an approach. The above described solution offers a simplified model which can be further developed according to the specifics of each laboratory. The strong point is to transfer creating a password code into the environment of technical equipment. Saving it on a personal medium eliminates a potential human factor failure. The employee is not made to remember long complex passwords which would not be possible to require considering numbers of code changes with every single leaving the workplace and numbers of code characters. Loss of security media is not considered a critical point as a biometric element of authentication is missing to use it successfully. The proposed system is very easy from the point of operation and administration view. It eliminates a variety of authentication ways and limits the range of possible user's sphere which is the way to reach a requested security level.

Acknowledgement. The research has been partially supported by the Faculty of Informatics and Management UHK specific research project 2107 Computer Networks for Cloud, Distributed Computing, and Internet of Things II. Thanks goes also to Mr. Martin Kulhanek, a diploma student, for some help in the paper preparation phase.

References

1. Jiang, Q., Khan, M.K., Lu, X., Ma, J., He, D.: A privacy preserving three-factor authentication protocol for e-Health clouds. J. Supercomput. **72**(10), 3826–3849 (2016). https://doi.org/10.1007/s11227-015-1610-x. ISSN 0920-8542
2. Kammergruber, R., Robold, S., Karliç, J., Durner, J.: The future of the laboratory information system – what are the requirements for a powerful system for a laboratory data management?. Clin. Chem. Lab. Med. (CCLM) **52**(11) (2014). https://doi.org/10.1515/cclm-2014-0276
3. ISO/IEC 17025 - General requirements for the competence of testing and calibration laboratories
4. ISO 9001 "Quality management"
5. Personal Information Protection and Electronic Documents Act, Second Session, Thirty-six Parliament, 48–49 Elizabeth II, 1999–2000, Statutes of Canada (2000)
6. Law on the Protection of Personal Information, promulgated by the Diet of Japan on May 30 (2003)
7. TSO (THE STATIONARY OFFICE): ITIL foundation handbook. 3rd ed. TSO, London (2012). ISBN: 978-0-11-331349-5

8. GAMP 5: A Risk-based Approach to Compliant GxP Computerized Systems. ISPE Headquarters, Tampa (2008). ISBN 1-931879-77-X

9. Prasad, P.J., Bodhe, G.L.: Trends in laboratory information management system. Chemometr. Intell. Lab. Syst. **118**, 187–192 (2012). https://doi.org/10.1016/j.chemolab.2012.07.001

10. Quo, C.F., Wu, B., Wang, M.D.: Development of a laboratory information system for cancer collaboration projects. In: IEEE Engineering in Medicine and Biology 27th Annual Conference (2005). https://doi.org/10.1109/iembs.2005.1617070

11. Ekins, S.: Computer Applications in Pharmaceutical Research and Development, pp. 57–61. Wiley, Hoboken (2006). ISBN 0-471-73779-8

12. Hu, Y.: Development of information management system used in laboratory advanced materials research. In: Engineering in Medicine and Biology Society, IEEE-EMBS 2005, 27th Annual International Conference, Shanghai, pp. 2859–2862. IEEE (2012). https://doi.org/10.4028/www.scientific.net/AMR.605-607.2518. ISBN: 0-7803-8741-4

13. Haas, S., Wohlgemuth, S., Echizen, I., Sonehara, N., Müller, G.: Aspects of privacy for electronic health records. Int. J. Med. Inf. **80**(2) (2011). https://doi.org/10.1016/j.ijmedinf.2010.10.001

14. Blazek, P., Kuca, K., Jun, D., Krejcar, O.: Development of information and management system for laboratory based on open source licensed software. In: Núñez, M., Nguyen, N.T., Camacho, D., Trawiński, B. (eds.) ICCCI 2015. LNCS (LNAI), vol. 9330, pp. 377–387. Springer, Cham (2015). https://doi.org/10.1007/978-3-319-24306-1_37

15. Blazek, P., Kuca, K., Jun, D., Krejcar, O.: Development of information and management system for laboratory based on open source licensed software with security logs extension. J. Intell. Fuzzy Syst. **32**(2), 1497–1508 (2017). https://doi.org/10.3233/jifs-169145

16. Blazek, P., Kuca, K., Krenek, J., Krejcar, O.: Increasing of data security and workflow optimization in information and management system for laboratory. In: Rojas, I., Ortuño, F. (eds.) IWBBIO 2017. LNCS, vol. 10208, pp. 602–613. Springer, Cham (2017). https://doi.org/10.1007/978-3-319-56148-6_54

17. Blazek, P., Kuca, K., Krejcar, O.: Concept of a module for physical security of material secured by LIMS. In: Rojas, I., Ortuño, F. (eds.) IWBBIO 2018. LNCS, vol. 10813, pp. 352–363. Springer, Cham (2018). https://doi.org/10.1007/978-3-319-78723-7_30. ISBN 978-3-319-78722-0

18. Mamonov, S., Benbunan-fich, R.: The impact of information security threat awareness on privacy-protective behaviors. Comput. Hum. Behav. **83**, 32–44 (2018). https://doi.org/10.1016/j.chb.2018.01.028. ISSN 07475632

19. Rudolph, M., Feth, D., Polst, S.: Why users ignore privacy policies – a survey and intention model for explaining user privacy behavior. In: Kurosu, M. (ed.) HCI 2018. LNCS, vol. 10901, pp. 587–598. Springer, Cham (2018). https://doi.org/10.1007/978-3-319-91238-7_45. ISBN 978-3-319-91237-0

20. Liang, K., et al.: A secure and efficient ciphertext-policy attribute-based proxy re-encryption for cloud data sharing. Future Gener. Comput. Syst. **52**, 95–108 (2015). https://doi.org/10.1016/j.future.2014.11.016. ISSN 0167739X

21. Rao, Y.S.: Privacy-preserving decentralized key-policy attribute-based encryption schemes with fast decryption. In: Jajodia, S., Mazumdar, C. (eds.) ICISS 2015. LNCS, vol. 9478, pp. 521–531. Springer, Cham (2015). https://doi.org/10.1007/978-3-319-26961-0_31. ISBN 978-3-319-26960-3

22. Rasmussen, L., Maddox, C., Harten, B., White, E.: A successful LIMS implementation: case study at southern research institute. J. Assoc. Lab. Autom. **12**(6), 384–390 (2007). https://doi.org/10.1016/j.jala.2007.08.002. ISSN 15355535

23. Pavlik, J., Komarek, A., Sobeslav, V.: Security information and event management in the cloud computing infrastructure. Comput. Intell. Inf. 209–214 (2014). https://doi.org/10.1109/cinti.2014.7028677

24. Hub, M., Capek, J., Myskova, R., Roudny, R.: Usability versus security of authentication. In: International Conference on Communication and Management in Technological Innovation and Academic Globalization-Proceedings, Puerto De La Cruz, Spain, pp. 34–38 (2010). ISBN 978-960-474-254-7

25. Brumen, B., Taneski, V.: Moore's curse on textual passwords. In: 38th International Convention on Information and Communication Technology, Electronics and Microelectronics (MIPRO) IEEE, pp. 1360–1365 (2015). https://doi.org/10.1109/mipro.2015.7160486. ISBN 978-9-5323-3082-3

26. Hoober, S.: Design for Fingers and Thumbs Instead of Touch. UXmatters. Accessed 24 Aug 2017

27. Jain, A.K., Ross, A., Prabhakar, S.: An introduction to biometric recognition. IEEE Trans. Circuits Syst. Video Technol. 14(1), 4–20 (2004). https://doi.org/10.1109/tcsvt.2003.818349. ISSN 1051-8215

28. The Role of Biometrics in Enterprise Security. http://www.dell.com/downloads/global/power/ps1q06-20050132-Tilton-OE.pdf. Accessed 5 Feb 2018

29. Potter, R., Weldon, L., Shneiderman, B.: Improving the accuracy of touch screens: an experimental evaluation of three strategies. In: Proceedings of the Conference on Human Factors in Computing Systems, CHI 1988, Washington, DC, pp. 27–32 (1988). https://doi.org/10.1145/57167.57171

30. Liu, T., Wang, Y.: Beyond scale: an efficient framework for evaluating web access control policies in the era of big data. In: Tanaka, K., Suga, Y. (eds.) IWSEC 2015. LNCS, vol. 9241, pp. 316–334. Springer, Cham (2015). https://doi.org/10.1007/978-3-319-22425-1_19. ISBN 978-3-319-22424-4

31. Al-Saggaf, A.A.: Key binding biometrics-based remote user authentication scheme using smart cards. IET Biometrics 7(3), 278–284 (2018). https://doi.org/10.1049/iet-bmt.2016.0146. ISSN 2047-4938

32. Announcing Approval of Federal Information Processing Standard (FIPS) 202, SHA-3 Standard: Permutation-Based Hash and Extendable-Output Functions, and Revision of the Applicability Clause of FIPS 180-4, Secure Hash Standard

Effect of Implementation of the 5S Practices on Working Conditions and Health of Employees

Anna Cierniak-Emerych$^{(\boxtimes)}$ ⓘ and Robert Golej$^{(\boxtimes)}$ ⓘ

Wrocław University of Economics, Wrocław, Poland
{anna.cierniak-emerych, robert.golej}@ue.wroc.pl

Abstract. With the Fourth Industrial Revolution, radical transitions are being observed in manufacturing systems. The use of robots and automation leads to changes in the structure of employment in the economy. The number of employees in the service-providing sector and creative industries will be increasing and this creates new research space, especially in the area of the effect of working conditions on workers' health and their creativity. The aim of this study is to identify the nature of the relationship between working conditions and the way and scope of implementation of 5S practices. This means identification of the objectives set for the implementation of 5S in the perspective of working conditions and undertaking an analysis of their potential and actual impact on the health and creativity of employees.

Keywords: Lean management · Working conditions · 5S · Creativity

1 Introduction

Changes taking place in requirements concerning working conditions are driven by many variables. One of them is self-awareness of employees and their organizations in terms of the necessity to use basic solutions ensuring occupational health and safety, and complex personnel policies ensuring fairness of working conditions, often developed at a philosophical-ethical or economic level, in order for these guidelines to be operationalized by management practice [1]. Therefore, the problems of working conditions for employees do not only concern the enterprise which employs the employee, but they are also part of the socio-economic governance that ensures its sustainability [2]. The predicted results of Industry 4.0 in the sphere of employment are not unambiguous [3]. The fourth industrial revolution can causes that the typical activities of industrial production will be carried out by automated production lines, in which the human work will be small. Industry 4.0 may cause an increase in the demand for qualified employees and improvement of working conditions. There are many papers related to technological aspects of Industry 4.0 (IoT, Artificial Intelligence) [e.g. 4–6], however the human resources management issues (especially in terms of quality management) are also still very important and often marginalized in the literature of subject. One should expect, as is already observed, that the services sector will grow and the role of creative industries will increase. Industry 4.0 will force an increase in

© Springer Nature Switzerland AG 2019
N. T. Nguyen et al. (Eds.): ICCCI 2019, LNAI 11684, pp. 369–382, 2019.
https://doi.org/10.1007/978-3-030-28374-2_32

the interest of researchers in shaping the working conditions of positively stimulating employees towards creative attitudes while simultaneously taking care of their mental and physical health.

The aim of this study is to identify the nature of the relationship between working conditions and the way and scope of implementation of 5S practices. The analysis the problems arising at the interface between lean manufacturing and working conditions is the main subject of the researches. Frequent practice is the transfer of LM principles and the adaptation of LM tools such as 5S to non-production areas. [7, 8] A question can be asked if such an approach is justified in the case of: creative industries, R & D departments and other organizational units whose aim is to create innovative solutions such as: algorithms, business models, products, sales models and others. Proponents of "ordering everything" states that orderly reality organizes thinking, but the issue related to activate the mind to look for new, unconventional solutions is used in practice in a very small degree. Rather, the organization do not orientate towards increasing productivity and improving "what is" [9]. This concept can be a hidden internal blockade of novelty. Another problem is if the organization wants to be creative, is it going to be a "mess" and what is the acceptable level of clutter and at what positions? The main contribution of the paper is the attempt to answer the question whether in selected manufacturing companies (companies from Lower Silesia in Poland), which implemented at least LM elements, the widely understood working conditions were taken into account when implementing solutions for lean manufacturing. Researches are also related to the effects on the physical and mental health of workers before and after the implementation of lean methods studied. Also the impact of working conditions on the creativity of employees taken into account when using 5S is discussed.

2 Theoretical Background

2.1 5S Practice as a Tool for the LM Concept

In Poland, the lean management concept is usually described as "lean production", "lean manufacturing", "lean management" or "lean organization" [10].

Acting according to the 'lean' concept means the most efficient use of available materials and company resources to achieve the best possible results. This mainly means a series of activities aimed at eliminating waste in the broad sense of the term, not only that occurring during the manufacturing process, but also from the entire area around it, including the network of logistic connections [10].

In Japan, three types of waste have been enumerated [11]:
muda (futility) - when production exceeds demand,
mura (unevenness) - sometimes production exceeds demand, sometimes it does not,
muri (unreasonableness) - when demand exceeds production.

This is one of several waste classifications, termed 3M or 3MU. It aims to optimise the consumption of human resources, machinery, equipment and materials needed for manufacturing of products, and delivering them in a timely manner. This method identifies seven basic types of waste: overproduction, excess inventory, improper transport, defects, unnecessary processing, unnecessary downtime, excessive traffic.

Therefore, the improvement in production efficiency requires their identification and elimination of their causes. The literature indicates the entire range of LM tools from basic TPM, through SMED, JiT, 5S. It is worth mentioning here that among a wide range of these tools, the 5S system is considered to be particularly related with shaping and even improving working conditions, as already mentioned above. The 5S system (practice) is considered to be a tool used to support solving problems related to work organization [8]. As it is emphasized, this helps not only enhance the work organization but also improve the conditions and safety at work [12]. Therefore, attempts are being made to extend this system with another S, i.e. safety, viewed as safe and healthy working conditions. Consequently, the concept of 5S+1 or even 6S [7, 13, 14] has emerged. The 5S practices, as argued by Zimon, have an especially positive effect on physical working conditions, thus offering opportunities to minimize the costs of reorganization [9] at workstations. The reference to 5S requires consideration of [8, 15]:

- seiri, as sorting and elimination of what's unnecessary,
- seiton, as an expression of systematization, setting in order and segregation,
- seiso, as sweeping and cleaning category,
- seiketsu, which favours standardization and thus order,
- shitsuke, relating to self-discipline.

As a consequence of using 5S practices, safe working conditions result directly from the essence of the discussed system. 'Good organization in and around your own workplace' [16, 17] which is the term used to define the 5S system, also means management that is safe for human, taking into account meeting human interests in this respect.

2.2   Working Conditions: Their Components and Importance at Work

The analysis of the literature on the subject leads to the conclusion that in practice we are dealing with a very enigmatic approach to the definition of working conditions, which probably inspires some authors to consider the conditions we are interested in mainly or exclusively in terms of their components. Consequently, the conditions discussed are most often considered to be divided into two main groups, i.e. physical and non-physical components, within which individual items are additionally distinguished. The physical components include physical, material, chemical and biological elements such as e.g. workstation and room equipment, lighting, microclimate, noise, etc. The non-physical components mean e.g. working time, interpersonal relations, and social and living activities [1]. The importance of working conditions is also reflected in the fact that the European Foundation for the Improvement of Living and Working Conditions decided to clarify this category [18]. The foundation defines working conditions as a set of factors that relate to the working environment and the aspects of the employee employment. This includes the following issues:

- work organization and worker activity (type of work);
- training, development of skills and competences, employability (neologism);
- health, safety and well-being;
- working time and work-life balance.

Broader information about how the concept of working conditions is viewed by this organization can be demonstrated by the answers to the questions asked in the surveys conducted in the five-year cycles since 1991. The last survey was conducted in 2015. In consecutive editions, the scope of the study was specified and extended [19].

The analysis of the literature on the subject leads to the conclusion that the definition of working conditions has not changed drastically over the last dozen or even several dozen years. Only the scope of the problems to be dealt with was extended. Health and safety are increasingly often emphasized not only from the standpoint of physical health, but also from the psychosomatic and mental perspective. Hence the extension of the concept of working conditions to all factors that affect mental health, from interpersonal relations to the application of CSR and lean management.

When defining the concept of working conditions, definitions which are most often indicated (one of them being quoted above) have been proposed by organizations dealing with working conditions and safety. However, the literature sometimes separates the concept of safety from working conditions. Most often, when considering working conditions, researchers also point to work safety. If the emphasis is on safety, the risks mostly concern physical health. If the focus is placed on the working conditions, then the subject matter is much broader. The studies published by researchers dealing with working conditions have also used the notion of the quality of the working environment, in a way separating working conditions from the sphere of physical effects and the quality of the working environment as a set of factors affecting mental health [20]. According to many authors [21], the quality of the working environment consists of many elements, including: the level of trust in the organization, fairness in the organization, feeling of support from the organization and support from superiors. However, as usually, the reality is much more complex as it turns out that research demonstrated the psychosomatic character of human health. Mental health affects physical health, whereas physical health affects mental. The first and fundamental field of interest for researchers that examine working conditions was the area of occupational health and safety hazards, i.e. the analysis of the effect of working conditions on physical health (accidents and occupational diseases). Next, the researchers focused more on the effect of working conditions on health in a broader sense, not only in physical, but also in mental terms. In literature, however, these terms are often used interchangeably and defined for research purposes. Nowadays, working conditions should be identified with the broadly understood working environment.

Mental tension should be defined as 'a term associated with an affective rather than cognitive area, and that has all the negative effects, and all the pollution associated with professional activity' [22]. In this vein, Karasek [23, 24] shows that work complexity and social support counterbalance the negative effects of excessive psychological demand. This has been demonstrated in empirical studies [e.g. 25, 26]. Research can therefore be done to identify factors that affect working conditions or, more anthropologically, their changes, and the strength of their effect on physical and mental health, well-being, productivity, creativity, etc. The focus of this paper was on the correlations between working conditions and the implementation of the lean management concept. In particular, the aim was to examine the employers' and employees' awareness of the benefits and limitations of working conditions and, as a result, of the health and safety of employees following the use of specific lean management tools.

2.3 Effect of Lean Management on Working Conditions, Employees' Health and Their Creativity

Health

Analysis of Polish literature reveals a peculiar manifestation of enthusiasm and uncritical approach to LM and the consequences of using its tools, including the perspective of shaping working conditions that is the focus of the present study.

However, if one looks critically at the objectives and tasks of LM which are commonly discussed in literature, it can be observed without much insight that the dominant objective of LM is to improve only the efficiency of production, and ultimately its effectiveness. Human is reduced to the role of a 'bio-robot', whose goal is to bring the highest efficiency while self-limiting unnecessary downtime or excessive movements. Limiting downtime may mean increased time pressure, increased speed of performing activities, and reduced micro-rest. Timing and layouts are often defined in the light of performance radicalization, forcing an increase in work intensity and inappropriate, painful and tedious postures or increasing the risk of injuries and accidents caused by physical fatigue or fatigue related to the lack of concentration caused by mental fatigue. It would seem that the reverse U theory, which clearly explains that no extremes of the explanatory variable give an optimal long-term effect to the explained variable, is unnoticed [27–29]. It cannot and must not be denied that many LM solutions such as 5S allow for the improvement in material conditions and safety at work. However, research on the impact of working conditions on mental health and psychosomatic health is now becoming the subject of more and more frequent explorations. Science has not developed any certainties and paradigms in this area yet.

Against this background, however, foreign literature already contains studies indicating negative aspects of the implementation of LM tools for the health and life of employees [30]. In the United States, the degradation of workers' health took place earlier than in the European Union, and lasted from the mid-1980s to the mid-1990s, because the first forms of production organization based on the LM concept were implemented in that country [31–33]. Research revealed that this phenomenon reached Europe in the 1990s [34–37]. In the mid-1990s the number for accidents at work and occupational diseases in the United States began to decline. It seems that this is because, among other things, the role of the organization responsible for occupational safety and health (OSHA) has been reinforced [38]. Studies have identified correlations between several main factors of working conditions that have led to the deterioration of health status of employees. These factors included [25, 39, 40]:

- repetitive work, its intensity,
- teamwork, the pace of work depends on the work of colleagues and machines,
- rotating schedules,
- compliance with quality standards, sitting position.

In the era of Industry 4.0, (IoT, Artificial Intelligence), the influence of working conditions on the mental health of employees is becoming more and more important. This area is increasingly being studied.

In conclusion of the theoretical considerations and achievements of the researchers in this area, it should be noted that the LM concept in its basic version, in a way emerging from the war economy, was essentially oriented towards production efficiency and, in particular, towards machine efficiency; man ceased to be the focal point of this concept. It became an inspiration for the analysis of the links between the implementation of the LM concept tool in the form of 5S and its results in the area of shaping working conditions in selected examples of enterprises.

Creativity

Riposte Albert Einstein [41]: "If a cluttered desk is a sign of a cluttered mind, is it a sign of what is empty?" has become the favorite motto of the mess. According to American scientists, the disorder on the desk is to stimulate the mind for hard work. Experiment of researchers Vohs, Redden, and Rahinel [42] showed that people working in disordered rooms invented more uses of the ping-pong ball. Another experience of the same researchers proved that disorder encourages people to leave the beaten path and try new things. The experiment consisted of choosing a fruit smoothie. The respondents in a neat environment preferred classic drinks, while the participants introduced into the disordered rooms decided on new combinations. Researchers Vohs, Redden, and Rahinel [42] concludes that: orderly environments promote convention and healthy choice, which can improve life, helping people abide by standards and increase well-being; disordered environments stimulate creativity, which is of great importance for culture, art and business (eg creative industries).

Fondness for order is conducive to conservatism, and creativity does not like him very much. New ideas are often the result of associating distant elements, finding common features of very different objects, so chaos can provoke you to look for similarities where you would not expect them to be found. A combination of seemingly mismatched elements can be a simple solution to a complex problem. Abrahamson and Freedman [43] argue that "Organizing and over-organizing entail high costs that we do not notice, while ignoring the fact that people or disordered organizations are often more effective, creative and flexible."

In practice, this means that not all workplaces in the organization are the same. We should apply such methods of shaping working conditions that will stimulate the implementation of specific goals while limiting the negative impact of working conditions on the physical and mental health of employees. It is therefore possible to deliberately and intentionally shape the order of the work environment to achieve the expected behaviors of employees. Responsible and safe in production processes and unconventional in creative activities. Similarly, in this case we can recall the curve of an inverted U. According to this theory, none of the extremes is correct. Extreme disorder will not improve creativity, just like extreme ordering. The 5S method seems too restrictive for creative activities, but some sort of ordering is necessary. This requires a flexible approach and adapting the 5S method to a specific situation, the placement of employees and alignment of their temperaments.

3 Research Methodology

The literature review indicates a cognitive gap in the relationships between physical and non-physical working conditions in the broad sense of the term, and the way 5S practices are implemented. Four research questions were asked in the study. The first question was: Were the widely understood working conditions taken into account when implementing solutions of lean manufacturing in companies in Lower Silesia which implemented at least LM elements? The second question was: Were the effects on the physical and mental health of workers before and after the implementation of lean methods studied? Was the impact of working conditions on the creativity of employees taken into account when using 5S? Does the shaping of working conditions using the 5S method take into account the goals and specificity of work in different positions? The next part was based on the empirical material related to lean management (LM) implementations collected in three manufacturing companies in Lower Silesia which implemented LM in the form of 5S practices in 2017–2018.

Given the qualitative nature of the problems discussed, the case study method was chosen to present them, with a greater focus on their in-depth understanding. This was aimed to find what can be only suggested by qualitative results [44]. Data sources concerned the analysis of documents concerning the implementation of the 5S system in enterprises of three manufacturing enterprises[1]. These implementations were made in 2017–2018. Participant observation and free-form interviews with managers and employees involved in the implementation of the system were also used. More specifically, an in-depth interview (IDI) was used, which is the direct method of the primary survey, with the respondent being an active object of the measurement, and the interviewees being in direct contact with the interviewers (*conversation*) [45].

The analysis was conducted using a descriptive method. The main objective of the study was to determine whether the implementation of the LM concept has taken into account the consequences of its implementation for the physical and mental health of employees. In the enterprises surveyed, the 5S method was the basic tool to reduce waste. This method was used first. Other LM methods have not yet been implemented.

4 Results. Analysis of the Effects of LM Implementations on Working Conditions

Implementation of the 5S practice did not differ significantly in the surveyed entities. The market on which they operate is stable and competitive. Work organization in the enterprise consists in division of duties, in which specific tasks are assigned to specific areas and employees. This consists in managing the tasks and activities in such a way that the organization functions efficiently, nobody performs the same tasks twice, and people with adequate competences perform work at specific positions.

---

[1] The enterprise did not give the consent to use the enterprise name.

The Implementation of the 5S System Started with the Identification of Problems. It was done mainly through observation and interviews with employees. This has allowed for obtaining information that provides a picture of the company from within and allows for the identification of irregularities and shortcomings in the company. It should be noted that the criterion of evaluation of what is correct and what is not was indicated in the 5S method itself.

The first problem that was addressed was the untidiness in the offices. There were many papers and binders, loosely arranged materials such as pens, staplers and briefcases that were not needed during the work and only generated the excess mess. Furthermore, there was no space for clothes or umbrellas. There were also things in the office that imitate real objects. For example, empty boxes, which sometimes serve as chairs, should be removed and replaced by real chairs. There is also no properly functioning information board. All this translates into longer times of searching for items the employee needs, stumbling over various things or changing the place of documents from one place to another. Another problem was the objects placed in the corridor between the office rooms and the production hall. Often were standing their various items needed in production but making employees difficult to move.

A mess was also noticed at the place of production process. Having been used, tools are put back in various places. If one intends to use them again, they look for them or ask other colleagues where they are. This leads to a substantial waste of time.

Another weak point that should be analysed is the shelving in the production hall. Many shelves are in the right places, but the problem is what is placed on them. There are all kinds of tools, resources and personal protections, used for work. However, they are arranged randomly and poorly labelled. Personal protections are in one box. If one wants to find, for example, safety glasses, they have to search the cardboard box because the glasses are mixed with gloves or earplugs protecting against noise. It is also important that measuring instruments should be kept in their fixed locations. Although currently they are stored in one container, the access to them is difficult since.

Another area that may cause confusion in the company is the unarranged documents. They concern mainly the information about what assortment is currently in production and what activities have been performed so far. These are important messages and notes for food production. Therefore, they should always be easily accessible and one should pay attention to how they are stored. It is important that all materials are arranged and always in their place. This ensures that every employee who starts his or her change can easily analyse the situation in production process, so that he or she does not waste time on searching for the necessary information. Another shortcoming was observed in employee uniforms. They do not wear suitable workwear that can provide quick access to small but essential tools. This means that an employee who needs to cut the film covering the box must either carry a knife in his pockets or waste time by going to the shelf with the appropriate equipment. Another area worth looking at is the information boards. These have been introduced, but some shortcomings can be noticed. Removing some of them will make work much easier and more efficient. One can see sheets of paper peeling off the wall, which makes it difficult to read the information contained on them. The observation also reveals that employees have no place to write down their own notes. This results in writing down information on coloured sheets of paper and putting them in the document sleeves, which also makes it difficult to read the basic data. The fact that pens and markers also do not have their own fixed location is also noticeable.

During the observation of the work flow, a general untidiness was also noticed, which after the end of the shift was attempted to be cleaned up. However, such behaviour is inconsistent with the lean management philosophy. With this approach, workers have to waste time by putting things back, and they could have done so earlier, when they were in the place and putting away the tool would not require additional time. Things which should not be present in the company were also observed. They only wasted space and did not bring anything constructive to the operation. Such items should be moved or disposed of completely.

Implementation

The 5S method was implemented with the support of: shadow boards, red and green cards, plastic boxes with ready labels that can be written down, sets of coloured notes, information boards, several binders and folders, posters and 5S instructions. The necessary cleaning equipment and new working clothing were used.

As part of the implementation, a **selection** was made, consisting in that all employees working in the Production, Laboratory and Office Departments marked items with red and green labels, photographed their workstations and placed objects with red cards in appropriate places. Furthermore, office workers tidied their workstations by arranging all materials in a logical and orderly way, using binders, folders, etc. at the same time. The employees were given new work clothes that have pockets for small, most needed tools such as gloves, knives, or protective earplugs. Another effect of the 5S implementation is **systematization**. The tools on the workstations were arranged. One shadow board was placed to contain the most commonly used objects on them and the second was used to contain the daily cleaning equipment. The shelves were tidied up and clearly marked boxes were introduced, in which objects were segregated according to their purpose. Furthermore, auxiliary lines were painted in the production hall. This helps to always find the place where to put the forklift, where to put the pallets, and where to put the dirty or washed kegs. Information boards with production schedule and employee work schedule were introduced. The fourth S, **standardization**, consisted in the development of documents which would enable all procedures to be regulated. The collected photographs were printed and attached to the rest of the documents and instructions. The employee responsible for the implementation of lean management developed instructions on how to avoid mess, how to perform cleaning work, what methods to use for control and motivation and how to build 5S checklists. **Self-discipline**: the main activities that will be implemented include continuous improvement of cleaning methods, caring for the order in the workplace, following the rules and principles developed during the implementation of the 5S method.

In the other two companies, very similar problems and small differences were observed in the way 5S practices were implemented. Due to the volume limitation of this study, only one company was described in detail.

5 Conclusions

The analysis presented in this paper allowed for drawing conclusions on taking into account and conscious shaping of working conditions while designing and implementing LM solutions in light of ensuring employee creativity and their health in physical and mental terms. It was identified based on the interviews that most of the activities were aimed at improving efficiency by reducing waste of time. With regards to the question whether working conditions were taken into consideration during implementation of 5Ss the working conditions were not indicated as the aim of this implementation. It was not ensured that work does not lead to negative changes in the mental health status of the employee or his/her creativity. It should be emphasized that the implementation work was not supervised by an OHS expert. It can be stated that physical working conditions were unintentionally improved by removing unnecessary items and setting up places for individual materials, tools and devices. The interviews show that the places for specific items were not always correctly indicated. While obtaining the effect of standardization and systematization, ergonomics and process optimization resulting from the identification of location of individual activities and required resources were underestimated. The implementations did not validate the results of the implementation in terms of the effect of the changes on employee health, their creativity, their well-being at work or the level of stress they experienced.

It was commonly believed in the examined processes of the 5S implementation, that the 5S system itself 'knows best' which work environment is best for everyone. This conviction is revealed in the language of the statements. Such a belief may have its source in the philosophy of Confucianism, in which order is a superior and somehow heavenly value. Therefore, order, standardization, systematization are perfect and they introduce perfection. The logical consequence of such an approach is that perfection means uniformity. Such a view can, and should, be disputable. One of the reasons for progress is the tension resulting from diversity. Diversity also means a different level of arrangement considered by a particular person as an order. Obviously, as a form of place where group activities are performed, company cannot accept excessive disorder. The study found that with the implementation of the 5S principles, the employees felt: fear that they will not be able to cope with the new requirements; fear that they will not adapt to the new order, that they will have to look for something for a longer time, with the current state considered good; fear that the cleaning process will take additional time and they will not perform their basic assignments; fear that the cleaning will have to be carried out after the working time agreed with the employer (without appropriate overtime); the fear that the working environment will start to resemble a sterile laboratory, more like a dissecting laboratory than a living and diverse environment; the fear that the sources of creative inspiration, like a ball from the second grade of the primary school lying on a desk, will disappear; the joy that there will finally be order and everyone will know where the office clips are. Another effect of standardization and systematization is that the workplace was depersonalized in favour of its standardization, which means for the employee and the employer:

- easier preparation of a new employee for the position, shortening the training time to the level of expected efficiency,

- maladjustment of the workplace to physical characteristics of individual people; for example, the person 200 cm tall needs different ergonomics of sitting at a table than a person 150 cm tall,
- exclusion of people with reduced mobility from work,
- inspiring a sense of substitutability among employees, which leads to a reduction in their motivation and self-esteem,
- fear for losing the job.

Further interviews showed that the feeling of anxiety did not disappear but it was replaced by a habit that weakened its effect. They showed that the 5S method, considered an important component of the lean management approach, was implemented in a way that raised a lot of concerns among employees. The health, mental well-being and creativity of employees was not taken into account during the implementation of 5S. Furthermore, there is a noticeable improvement in occupational safety, which is often an unintended outcome of cleaning up the working environment.

6 Summary

The results of the study encourage development of such solutions in the 5S system that, on the one hand, will ensure occupational safety and health, and on the other hand, will provide a level of workplace organization that will guarantee a certain level of its personalization. Such a solution may be offered by the adaptation of 5S principles to individual employees. It can be said that this would mean the development of the 5S+P concept. Furthermore, many negative emotions and behaviours can be avoided by indicating a broader vision of the production system and the place of individual employees in this system. In the case of planned employment reductions, the ways of supporting employees in obtaining new jobs or increasing their competences should be indicated. Detailed LM methods should be introduced only after both the appropriate level of knowledge and sense of safety of employees have been ensured.

An important problem in conducting further research is the distinction between physical and non-physical factors in the light of physical and mental health. There may be physical conditions that affect mental health, but there may also be non-physical conditions that influence physical health. The question also arises as to whether health should be considered as psychosomatic, so that conditions may have a greater impact on physical or mental health. These considerations may be very important in the light of the changes brought about by the Fourth Industrial Revolution. At present, changes are occurring in the labour market, with more and more work provided in the service-providing sector, where working conditions and health problems will shift the emphasis from physical conditions to non-physical conditions and from physical to mental, or at least psychosomatic, health.

Acknowledgment. "The project is financed by the Ministry of Science and Higher Education in Poland under the programme "Regional Initiative of Excellence" 2019–2022 project number 015/RID/2018/19 total funding amount 10 721 040,00 PLN".

References

1. Cierniak-Emerych, A.: Europejskie standardy praw człowieka i warunków pracy [eng. European standards of human rights and working conditions]. Wyd. IB-iS, Wrocław (2005)
2. Gawrycka, M., Szymczak, A.: Praca jako dobro indywidualne i społeczne, [eng.Work as an individual and societal good], Studia Ekonomiczne. ZN Uniwersytetu Ekonomicznego w Katowicach, Nr 214, pp. 276–287 (2015)
3. Bendkowski, J.: Zmian w pracy produkcyjnej w perspektywie koncepcji Przemysł 4.0 [eng. Changes in production work in the perspective of the Industry 4.0 concept], ZN Politechni Śląskiej, Organizacja i zarzdzanie 1990(112), pp. 21–33 (2017)
4. Waris, M.M., Sanin, C., Szczerbicki, E.: Community of practice for product innovation towards the establishment of industry 4.0. In: Nguyen, N.T., Hoang, D.H., Hong, T.-P., Pham, H., Trawiński, B. (eds.) ACIIDS 2018. LNCS (LNAI), vol. 10752, pp. 651–660. Springer, Cham (2018). https://doi.org/10.1007/978-3-319-75420-8_61
5. Komninos, A., Frengkou, E., Garofalakis, J.: Predicting user responsiveness to smartphone notifications for edge computing. In: Kameas, A., Stathis, K. (eds.) AmI 2018. LNCS, vol. 11249, pp. 3–19. Springer, Cham (2018). https://doi.org/10.1007/978-3-030-03062-9_1
6. Angin, P., Mert, M.B., Mete, O., Ramazanli, A., Sarica, K., Gungoren, B.: A blockchain-based decentralized security architecture for IoT. In: Georgakopoulos, D., Zhang, L.-J. (eds.) ICIOT 2018. LNCS, vol. 10972, pp. 3–18. Springer, Cham (2018). https://doi.org/10.1007/978-3-319-94370-1_1
7. Becker, J.E.: Implementing 5S to promote safety and housekeeping. Prof. Saf. **46**(8) (2001)
8. Gapp, R., Fisher, R., Kobayashi, K.: Implementing 5S within a Japanese context: an integrated management system. Manag. Decis. **46**(4) (2008)
9. Zimon, D.: Rola jakości w logistyce produkcji, PiZ **13**(12) (2012)
10. Walentynowicz, P.: Uwarunkowania skuteczności wdrażania Lean Management w przedsiębiorstwach produkcyjnych w Polsce [eng.Determinants of the effectiveness of Lean Management implementation in production enterprises in Poland], WUG, Gdańsk (2013)
11. Kornicki, L., Kubik, S.Z.: Identyfikacja marnotrawstwa na hali produkcyjnej [eng. Identification of waste on the production floor]. ProdPress.com, Wrocław (2008)
12. Karaszewski, R.: Nowoczesne koncepcje zarządzania jakością [eng.Modern concepts of quality management], Wyd. TNOiK. SWU "Dom organizatora", Toruń (2009)
13. Gajdzik, B.: Word Class Manufacturing in metallurgical enterprise. Metalurgija **52**(1) (2013)
14. Junewick, M.A.: Lean Speak. The Productivity Business Improvement Dictionary. Productivity Press, New York (2002)
15. Szatkowski, K.: Nowoczesne zarządzanie produkcją. Ujęcie procesowe [eng. Modern production management. Process shot], Wydawnictwo PWN, Warszawa (2014)
16. Aluchna, M., Płoszajski, P. (red.): Zarządzanie japońskie. Ciągłość i zmiana [eng. Japanese management. Continuity and change], SGH w Warszawie, Warszawa (2008)
17. Dziuba, S.Z., Godyń, M.: Identification of significant discrepancies occurring in the process of cable production using selected quality management tools. In: Borkowski, S., Ingaldi, M. (eds.) Toyotarity. Management of Technology, pp. 153–165. Aeternitas Publishing House (2014)
18. EUROFOUND: Working conditions (2019). https://www.eurofound.europa.eu/pl/topic/working-conditions. Accessed 04 Mar 2019
19. EUROFOUND: European Working Conditions Surveys (EWCS) (2015). https://www.eurofound.europa.eu/pl/surveys/european-working-conditions-surveys/sixth-european-working-conditions-survey-2015. Accessed 04 Mar 2019

20. Cropanzano, R.M.M.: Social exchange theory. Interdisc. Rev. J. Manag. **31**(6), 874–900 (2005)

21. Krot, K., Lewicka, D.: Wpływ jakości środowiska pracy na zachowania pracowników [eng. Impact of the quality of the work environment on the behavior of employees], Zarzadzanie. 4 (39) ZN Uniwersytetu Szczecińskiego. Studia i Prace Wydziału Nauk Ekonomicznych i Zarządzania, pp. 95–109 (2015). https://doi.org/10.15611/pn.2017.463.25

22. Sperandio, J.C.: La psychologie en ergonomie. Presse Universitaire de France, Paris (1980)

23. Karasek, R.: Job demands, job decision latitude, and mental strain: implications for job redesign. Adm. Sci. Q. **24**(2) (1979)

24. Karasek, R., Theorell, T.: Healthy Work: Stress, Productivity, and the Reconstruction of Working Life. Basic Books, New York (1991)

25. Stock, S., Messing, K., Tissot, F., Seifert, A.M., Vézina, N.: Les troubles musculo-squelettiques, la détresse psychologique et les conditions de travail au Québec : relations complexes dans un monde du travail en mutation [eng.Musculoskelettical disorders, mental distress and working conditions in Quebec: complex relationships in a changing world of work]. Santé, Société et Solidarité **5**(2), 45–58 (2006)

26. Cottini, E., Lucifora, C.: Mental health and working conditions in Europe. Ind. Labor Relat. Rev. **66**(4), 958–988 (2013)

27. Czakon, W.: Równowaga a wzrost – relacja odwróconego U w naukach o zarządzaniu [eng. Balance and growth - the relation of inverted U in management sciences], Przegląd Organizacji, pp. 7–10 (2012)

28. Ang, S.: Competitive intensity and collaboration: impact of firm growth across technological environments. Strateg. Manag. J. **29**, 1057–1075 (2008)

29. Uzzi, B.: Social structure and coopetition in interfirm networks: the paradox of embeddedness. Adm. Sci. Q. **42**, 35–67 (1997)

30. Valeyre, A.: Les conditions de travail des salariés dans l'Union européenne à quinze selon les formes d'organisation [eng. Working conditions of employees in the EU-15 according to the forms of organization], Travail et Emploi, 112/11-12, 2007, pp. 35–47 (2007). http://journals.openedition.org/travailemploi/2185, https://doi.org/10.4000/travailemploi.2185

31. Askenazy, P.: Innovative workplace practices and occupational injuries and illnesses in the United States. Econ. Ind. Democracy **22**(4), 485–516 (2001)

32. Brenner, M., Fairris, D., Ruser, J.: 'Flexible' work practices and occupational safety and health: exploring the relationship between cumulative trauma disorders and workplace transformation. In: Social Science Research Network, ID 333762 SSRN Scholarly Paper (2001)

33. Fairris, D., Brenner, M.: Workplace transformation and the rise in cumulative trauma disorders: is there a connection? J. Labor Res. **22**(1), 15–28 (2001)

34. Daubas-Letourneux, V., Thébaud-Mony, A.: Blind spots in our knowledge of industrial accidents. Travail et Emploi **88**, 25–42 (2001)

35. Daubas-Letourneux, V., Thébaud-Mony, A.: Organisation du travail et santé dans l'Union Européenne [eng. Work organization and health in the European Union]. Travail et Emploi **96**, 9–35 (2003)

36. Datta, G.N., Kristensen, N.: Work environment satisfaction and employee health: panel evidence from Denmark, France and Spain, 1994–2001. Eur. J. Health Econ. **9**, 51–61 (2008)

37. Bertrand, T., Stimec, A.: Santé au travail [eng. Health at work]. Revue Française de Gestion **214**, 127–144 (2011)

38. Askenazy, P.: La santé et la sécurité dans les entreprises américaines. [eng.Occupational health and safety in American companies]. Actes de la recherche en sciences sociale **163**, 72–89 (2006)

39. Askenazy, P., Caroli, E.: Pratiques innovantes, accidents du travail et charge mentale : résultats de l'enquête française. Conditions de travail 1998. [eng. Innovative practices, work place accidents and mental strain: the results of a French study entitled, 1998 working conditions]. Perspectives interdisciplinaires sur le travail et la santé 5(1) (2003)

40. Gollac, M.: L'intensité du travail [eng.Work intensity].Revue économique 56(2), 195–216 (2005)

41. Fedirko, J.: Einsteiniana, Alma Mater, no. 114, maj (2009)

42. Vohs, K.D., Redden, J.P., Rahinel, R.: Physical order produces healthy choices, generosity, and conventionality. Whereas Dis. Produces Creativity Psychol. Sci. 24(9), 1860–1867 (2013). https://doi.org/10.1177/0956797613480186

43. Abrahamson, E., Freedman, D.H.: A Perfect Mess: The Hidden Benefits of Disorder. Little, Brown, New York (2007)

44. Wójcik, P.: Znaczenie studium przypadku jako metody badawczej w naukach o zarządzaniu, [eng.The importance of a case study as a research method in management sciences], "e-Mentor" 48(1), 17–22 (2013)

45. Kaczmarczyk, S.: Badania marketingowe. Metody i techniki [eng.Marketing research. Methods and techniques], PWE, Warszawa (1999)

Advanced Data Analysis in Multi-site Enterprises. Basic Problems and Challenges Related to the IT Infrastructure

Helena Dudycz[1](✉) ⓘ, Paweł Stefaniak[2] ⓘ, and Paweł Pyda[3] ⓘ

[1] Wrocław University of Economics, Wrocław, Poland
helena.dudycz@ue.wroc.pl
[2] KGHM Cuprum Research and Development Centre, Wrocław, Poland
pkstefaniak@cuprum.wroc.pl
[3] KGHM Polish Cooper S.A., o/COPI,
KGHM Polska Miedź S.A., Lubin, Poland
pawpyd@gmail.com

Abstract. The aim of the paper is to present the results of a study on the existing IT infrastructure in large, multi-site enterprises in the context of conducting data analysis for the needs of managerial staff. The paper describes approaches to data analysis in this type of enterprises, indicating the problems arising from their IT infrastructures. Also included in this paper are conclusions of the study, which concern, among other things, the challenges faced by multi-site enterprises. Firms of this kind operate in a competitive market, therefore to be able to maintain their position of well-established players, they must take action to implement advanced data analysis. One of such actions is modification and expansion of the enterprise's IT infrastructure, including the implementation of Big Data solutions. The contribution of this paper is the analysis of IT infrastructure in large, multi-site enterprises and conclusions from this examination in the context of advanced data analysis for the needs of the managerial staff.

Keywords: Advanced data analysis · IT infrastructure · Multi-site enterprise · Big Data

1 Introduction

Many large industrial enterprises conduct their business activity in a turbulent and volatile market, which translates into the uncertainty of their operation. In such circumstances, enterprise management must constitute a future-oriented decision-making process. This requires access to information describing not only the current situation of the enterprise but also the execution of numerous advanced predictive analyses concerning future situations. Not only should these analyses provide information about potential threats, but insights in possible development opportunities. Such information (so-called weak signals) is often crucial for enterprises, but difficult to obtain. This requires an advanced analysis of data from databases maintained in both the enterprise and its environment. The market situation also forces them to be performed in real time, based on up-to-date data and not only on data aggregated in data warehouses. This

© Springer Nature Switzerland AG 2019
N. T. Nguyen et al. (Eds.): ICCCI 2019, LNAI 11684, pp. 383–393, 2019.
https://doi.org/10.1007/978-3-030-28374-2_33

requires building a proper IT infrastructure in the enterprise, including Big Data tools, as well as applying analytical systems which contain advanced methods and algorithms of machine learning.

In the case of large industrial enterprises, production is increasingly often carried out and controlled using tools such as micro-controllers (to control machines) or digitally controlled machines connected to the Internet (using the Internet of Things technology). Due to the growing amount of data processed and services related to cybersecurity, the use of this type of data for analytical purposes requires enterprises to design appropriate IT infrastructure, implement appropriate IT tools, and introduce organisational changes. The execution of such IT infrastructure also requires that data analysis should be taken into consideration, based on collected historical production data enabling the identification of factors that determine the course and outcome of the process as well as the prediction of unplanned events or machinery failures.

The research conducted into the analysis of the existing infrastructure in a multi-site, territorially extensive enterprise, where the technological process consists of many sub-processes conducted sequentially and/or in parallel, shows that what we are dealing with is a situation where individual plants apply distributed and diverse IT systems. It also turns out that the IT infrastructure in such enterprises is insufficient to perform advanced data analysis for the purpose of the management's decision-making. Information assets are often hidden because they are located in enterprise facilities' local databases, which is why enterprises interested in improvements including the quality of decision-making at the Management Board level should be inclined to develop their IT infrastructure with a holistic view of business operations in mind.

The aim of the paper is to present the existing IT infrastructure in large industrial enterprises in the context of conducting data analysis for the needs of managerial staff. The structure of the paper is as follows. First, the development of IT systems in the context of data analysis supporting enterprises' managerial staff was briefly discussed. The next section, based on the research conducted, characterises large, multi-site enterprises' approaches to data analysis resulting from the IT infrastructures owned by them. The paper ends with a summary including conclusions from the research with respect to the challenges related to the development of IT infrastructures in multi-site enterprises as well as information on the areas in which the research should be continued.

2   Development of IT Systems Supporting Data Analysis

One of the basic objectives of the implementation of information and analysis systems is to support enterprises' management on the decision-making process, which may translate into increased management efficiency and competitiveness on the market. For over a decade, we have been observing the development of Business Intelligence (BI) systems, whose main objective is to provide access to relevant data at the right time to enable actively making decisions which are optimal at a given moment [1]. Users of these systems receive both standard and ad hoc reports, but it is only their knowledge that determines the correct interpretation of the information contained in them.

Initial BI systems were designed primarily for people who could understand data models and had the time to build various analysis scenarios and then pass the information on to those who needed it [2]. In literature is described that since 2005, we have been dealing with a generation of systems called Business Intelligence 2.0 [3, 4]. A system of this kind is characterised by such properties as real-time event control and analysis, instant access to information at various levels of enterprise management, predictive analysis, improved interactive visualisation, ontologies, semantic information search, as well as common and mobile access to data [5]. This system is focused on the semantic analysis of data, using data and information from multiple sources (including external sources). One of the main artefacts to create a semantic network is the ontology, which is used to create the necessary knowledge models for defining and explaining functionalities in analytical tools [6]. This development of systems, resulting from, among other things, the emergence of new data sources which come from the enterprise's environment, new technologies, and new concepts of data management, was important in the creation and development of Enterprise 2.0. There are also BI solutions and modules of data analysis dedicated to industrial enterprises [7, 8].

The enormous development of information technologies, in particular technologies for generating, storing, and processing data, has caused the amount of digital data stored in enterprises to grow year by year. It contains a wealth of valuable information that can be discovered using appropriate methods [9]. In addition, the creation of the Internet of Things technology, which is starting to be used in industrial enterprises, has led to the generation of additional enormous amounts of data resulting from the communication of various types of devices. In combination with a very big amount of data created in large enterprises and their environments, it became a reason for the creation and development of various types of IT solutions allowing the analysis of such enormous amounts of accumulated data [10]. In the literature, particular attention is paid to Big Data tools and solutions that support data mining methods in processing very large data sets, e.g. Hadoop, HBase and MongoDB [10, 11]. In order to implement advanced analytics and Big Data tools in a enterprise, one needs to know the following:

- Big Data is not only a matter of technology but also of using large data sets to improve the safety and efficiency of work.
- The basic success factor, in an area involving the work of both people and computers, is decisions made by specific employees based on the conclusions of data analysis.
- Any solution using machine learning methods must be primarily geared towards business benefits based on hypotheses of the potential impact of selected data instead of an analysis of all data available. Identification and rejection of irrelevant data is already a good way to success.
- It is irrelevant how imperfect the data is at present. Even incomplete data can provide revealing conclusions using advanced data analysis methods.

The concept of Big Data is often associated with Data Science, whose main task is to enable both people and computers to learn from accumulated data [12, 13]. The main goal of Data Science is to use computers to automatically process and analyse large data sets. Data Science is about how to select data and how to use it to acquire knowledge that can then be used to make decisions, predict the future, or understand the past [12, 14].

The currently implemented advanced data analysis, using the capabilities of Big Data tools, includes methods of data mining and machine learning, which allow one to see patterns hidden in data [11, 15]. The result of using these methods is models that create a certain set of rules established on the basis of data analysed. Its accuracy and reliability can be measured and objectively assessed before it is put into practice.

3 Data Analyses in Multi-site Industrial Enterprises

3.1 Development of the IT Infrastructure in Large, Multi-site Enterprises

Many large industrial enterprises, whose organisational structure includes more than a dozen (sometimes even several dozen) territorially dispersed facilities, have a very extensive IT infrastructure, comprising several (in some cases even more than a dozen) IT systems to support the production activity and an enormous number of various IT tools. This stems from the fact that the operation is based on a number of domain-specific systems. Some of them are standard software solutions supplied by leading manufacturers (e.g. the IT system produced by the enterprise SAP), to which all branches of the enterprise have common access. The production activity of such enterprises determines their use of IT systems including those adapted to specific business needs. Some of them are applied at one branch only but there are also systems used by several branches. The existence of such an IT structure is characteristic for large enterprises, operating for at least 20–30 years and constantly developing and trying to compete on the market. Enterprises of this type characteristically feature openness to IT solutions that support both the production process and managerial staff on the management of the company. Therefore, they constantly develop their existing IT systems and implement new solutions that support the implementation of existing and newly developed business processes. This results in a situation where there are dedicated IT systems in the facilities, obtaining data from various sources and often collecting data in databases according to different standards. On the basis of databases maintained in the facilities, reports are created for a given facility's management. On the other hand, reporting to the Management Board is often a combination of reports from different systems and data sources.

Figure 1 features a diagram presenting a scheme of creating reports for the Management Board on the basis of various IT systems implemented in the facilities. With such an IT system infrastructure in the enterprise, the following problems with data analysis for the Management Board can be formulated. Since the data in the facilities is often collected in different standards and IT systems, there may be a problem with its availability and reliability at the level of the Management Board. Data analyses are carried out within facilities for their managerial staff. The reports created are dedicated to specific production departments, so they may have different structures, contain data from different periods, etc., which may limit the possibility of comparing it at the level of the enterprise's Management Board. Differences in the reports created by specific facilities for the Management Board may result from the algorithm used to generate management information, which may in one case be too general and based on selected data, while in another case including large amounts of detailed data. This kind of situation may also affect the quality of the data on the basis of which the analysis of such data, providing key information to the Management Board, should be conducted.

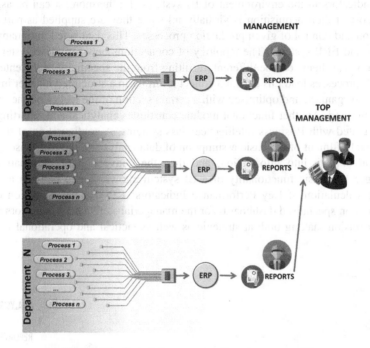

Fig. 1. Distributed data sources (Source: own work)

In summary, in large, multi-site enterprises, IT systems at individual facilities were implemented at different times. Additionally, these are various solutions provided by many IT enterprises. Therefore, both at the level of databases and at the level of reports developed between these IT systems, there are differences between terms (the so-called uniform data dictionary problem is observed in the enterprise's IT systems). These differences may concern using different words to designate the same as well as the use of the same terms, but the context of their meaning is different.

3.2 Implementation of Data Warehouses and Business Intelligence Systems to Support Data Analysis

Data warehouses and Business Intelligence systems are implemented in order to improve and execute data analysis and report development across the entire enterprise on the basis of data contained in the facilities' various databases. This makes it possible, among other things, to standardise the enterprise's dictionary of business terms.

Figure 2 shows a general scheme illustrating the data collection and processing infrastructure of a industrial enterprise where a data warehouse and a BI system were implemented. The basic data, which constitutes the largest amount of data concerning production facilities, comes from SCADA industrial automation systems as well as various reporting systems and flat files. Industrial automation systems are a very attractive source of data for the implementation of computation procedures for controlling indicators in the environment of BI systems. Furthermore, it can be assumed that the cost of their acquisition is virtually nil since they are supplied as part of the supervision and control of given production processes. This data is fed into many local databases and ERP systems. The topology of connections between these systems and the data fusion scheme can be different, resulting from the specificity of the enterprise. Then ETL processes load this data and collect it further in a structured manner in a data warehouse, organised and optimised with a certain section of the reality of one or more facilities in mind. Another functional module constitutes analytical and reporting tools fully integrated with Business Intelligence class systems. A configuration of this kind enables the fulfilment of the basic assumption of data analysis in the enterprise, i.e. the conversion of data into information, and then the conversion of information into knowledge. The basic functionality of a BI system allows you to perform analyses, reporting, calculation of Key Performance Indicators (KPI), and presentation of key information on specialised dashboards for the managerial staff. These indicators are the basis of decision-making both at strategic as well as tactical and operational levels.

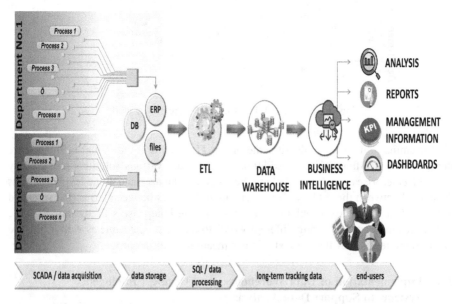

Fig. 2. Typical data flow and the process of extraction of management information in an enterprise (Source: own work)

Modern managerial support systems often utilize visualization as a fundamental form of presenting information. Most existing Business Intelligence systems provide various functionalities for data aggregation and visualization. Visualization in BI systems evolves from simple static objects to iterative, collaborative processes, which are able to create new knowledge dynamically. An important function of business-oriented system is the visualization of the calculated KPIs.

In industrial enterprises, operational data comes mainly from SCADA industrial automation systems. Another source of information is the operational supervision responsible for reporting on production. This is information entered manually, using template-based forms, as well as various types of tabular breakdowns, or even simple telephone reports, which are also used in ERP systems to record individual production processes. As for more advanced data analysis, it is carried out mainly using a BI system. In many enterprises, this analysis boils down to basic, general KPI's concerning the whole enterprise.

On the IT market, there are many extensive Business Intelligence systems, or single information and analysis modules as well as decision support systems that process data stored in a data warehouse. The usefulness of this type of IT solutions in an enterprise depends on the needs of its managerial staff, which are determined by factors including the size of the enterprise and its IT infrastructure.

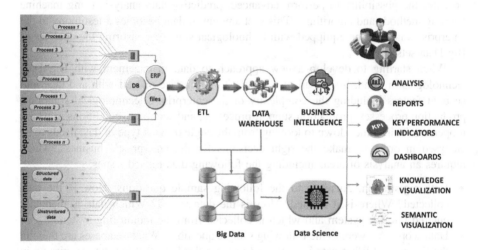

Fig. 3. Data flow scheme in IT infrastructure including Big Data solutions (Source: own work)

3.3   The Need to Conduct Advanced Data Analyses

In large industrial enterprises, the amount of accumulated data on both operational and financial activities is very large. Nevertheless, it is still used to a limited extent for the purpose of analysis. Currently, there are already modules containing data mining algorithms in Business Intelligence class solutions, making it possible to discover hidden knowledge in enterprises' data. Very often, however, these are algorithms of the black box type, without the possibility of flexible adjustment of models to specific use scenarios, or ones that are suboptimal in terms of data modelling, time series analysis, predictive analytics, etc. At some point, data analysis in a large, multi-site enterprise using the existing IT infrastructure reaches a critical moment, where:

- data management becomes more difficult due to its growing amount,
- forecasting patterns requires applying more sophisticated statistical methods and/or the use of artificial intelligence methods and techniques,

- predictive models require the discovery and consideration of a more complex hierarchy and cause-effect relationships,
- maintaining competitiveness on the market requires access to more detailed data, including environment data, in order to obtain a much more accurate description of reality,
- the assumptions of analytical models should be updated on the basis of continuous multidimensional analyses of historical data.

Many large enterprises operate in an international, volatile, and competitive market. This situation forces such enterprises' analysts to perform complicated calculations using advanced models, based on the data in the enterprise but also in its environment. The task of performing such analyses requires the modification of the enterprise's IT infrastructure in the enterprise so that it allows advanced data analysis (Fig. 3). All the more so that the data available (its volume and abundance) in this type of enterprises provides the possibility to perform advanced, predictive data analysis using machine learning methods and algorithms. This vast amount of data becomes a testimony to the enterprise's need to be equipped with technological solutions ensuring the analysis of Big Data sets.

When starting to develop a new approach to data management with Big Data technologies in mind, first of all, it is crucial to familiarise oneself with and take into account factors including the complexity of the enterprise's technological solutions, production processes, production support processes, and economic conditions in which it operates. This comes down to looking from the angle of what type of data needs to be analysed in order to make the right decisions for the enterprise's business, which requires an analysis of areas including the following data-related issues:

- Data registration. Answers to the following sample questions: How is the data collected? Where is it created? How is the data stored? Which data is manually entered into the system and which is collected from the monitoring systems?
- Data scope. Answers to the following sample questions: What databases are there in the enterprise? What data is contained in these databases? What data is missing in the databases but needed to analyse the enterprise's position on the market?
- Data infrastructure and archiving. Answers to the following sample questions: How is the data stored? What is the structure of this data? What is the data's storage infrastructure?
- Data availability. Answers to the following sample questions: What is the availability of key data at the level of the enterprise's Management Board? What is the availability of data at the level of the enterprise facilities' management? How much time does it take to obtain the necessary data and ad hoc reports?
- Data quality. Answer the following example questions: Can data gaps occur? Can there be erroneous data? What are its main causes? Are there ways to recreate "lost" information (interpolation, alternative algorithms)?
- Analysis. Answer the following example questions: What type of analysis can be carried out on the basis of data available? Is it possible to carry out analyses taking into account the enterprise's situation on the market?

Analysis of the existing IT infrastructure in an enterprise allowing for the above-mentioned aspects makes it possible to verify whether its IT systems are capable of providing the required functionality. In addition, it allows a preliminary assessment of the extent to which it is necessary to improve the consistency and quality of data and to define a concept for a data integration architecture to enable Big Data analyses (particularly if there are different data standards between analogous systems and/or enterprise facilities).

4 Conclusions and Future Works

The paper presents conclusions from the examination of IT infrastructures existing in multi-site industrial enterprises in the context of data analysis for the needs of the managerial staff (in particular for the Management Board). As the study has shown, the IT infrastructure in this type of enterprises is affected by how long the enterprise has been operating and what IT systems were needed to support both its production and business processes. For example, in an enterprise established in the 1960s, we observe solutions which were implemented gradually along with the technological evolution, i.e. starting with single-module transaction systems sufficient to perform data analysis for the needs of a specific facility. Such systems, which have been continuously modified and improved, are still in use. These are most often solutions dedicated to a specific production or business process. Next, multi-module transactional systems (ERP class) were implemented, supporting data analysis for the needs of the facility and generating reports for the enterprise's Management Board. The next stage is the implementation of a data warehouse and BI systems so that the Board of Directors receives reports on the analysis of key parameters evaluating the enterprise's operation. This means that we see a variety of IT solutions in these enterprises affecting the approach to the applied analysis of data used by the enterprise's Management Board. Nowadays, decision-makers want not only to look at static reports or even ad hoc reports, but want also easy-to-use tools to assess goals and key performance indicators to identify any chances of advancement and threats of breakdown [16]. The usefulness of the BI system is related to the provision of required information at the right moment, because this system should be focused on the semantic analysis of data, using data and information from multiple sources (including external sources).

Upon the analysis of large, multi-site enterprises with IT infrastructures that also include implemented data warehouses and BI systems, it can be concluded that the IT systems applied in these enterprises enable efficient handling of business processes in terms of storage, processing, analysis, integration, and sharing of data in the form of reports. The global tendency indicates that we should expect an upward trend in demand for the collection and processing of large amounts of data in real time. This will be a consequence of the implementation of new IT systems using the Internet of Things technology related to the handling and analysis of data from industrial devices (production machines, water pumps, transport systems, ventilation/air conditioning, sensors of environmental parameters, including toxic gases, etc.). In addition to typical structural data, there is also a need to collect unstructured data, such as images from CCTV cameras or sounds produced by machinery. To analyse this type of data, we could employ algorithms, methods and tools of artificial intelligence, data mining, and machine learning. They are able to process and analyse signals (e.g. image recognition) in real time and, on that basis, to take appropriate decision-making steps.

In the age of the fourth industrial revolution [17], many industrial enterprises reach a critical point where being a world leader and/or a major player in a given industry forces businesses into implementing modern technological solutions, and thus the modification and adjustment of their IT infrastructures to collect and analyse large data sets (Big Data) using machine learning techniques. In practice, there is a growing interest among industrial enterprises in the use of IoT techniques to support the implementation of production processes and centralisation of enterprise analytics through the development of an Analytical Centre. Achieving this requires enterprises to introduce a uniform standard of registration, transmission, and collection of data, ensure an appropriate layer of communication, and create a computational cluster as well as analytical tools for the analysis of large sets of streaming and historical data for the purpose of building knowledge in the enterprise.

Research into advanced data analysis in large, multi-site industrial enterprises will focus on four aspects. Firstly, the development of assumptions for the construction of a data and service management centre allowing for, among other factors, trends resulting from the Industry 4.0 concept. Secondly, the design of an IT infrastructure for processing and managing data and services by adopting SOA Governance solutions. Thirdly, the design of analytical process automation using SOA services. Lastly, the development of a concept for extending the IT infrastructure by adding Big Data and advanced data analysis tools for this type of enterprises.

References

1. Lasi, H.: Industrial intelligence–a BI-based approach to enhance manufacturing engineering in industrial companies. In: Proceedings of the 8th CIRP Conference on Intelligent Computation in Manufacturing Engineering (CIRP ICME), Gulf of Naples, Italy, vol. 12, pp. 384–389 (2012)
2. Raden, N.: Business Intelligence 2.0: Simpler, More Accessible, Inevitable (2007) http://www.informationweek.com/news/software/bi/197002610
3. Nelson, S.: Business Intelligence 2.0: Are we there yet? SAS Global Forum (2010). http://support.sas.com/resources/papers/proceedings10/040-2010.pdf
4. Trujillo, J., Maté, A.: Business intelligence 2.0: a general overview. In: Aufaure, M.-A., Zimányi, E. (eds.) eBISS 2011. LNBIP, vol. 96, pp. 98–116. Springer, Heidelberg (2012). https://doi.org/10.1007/978-3-642-27358-2_5
5. Neumayr, B., Schrefl, M., Linner, K.: Semantic cockpit: an ontology-driven, interactive business intelligence tool for comparative data analysis. In: De Troyer, O., Bauzer Medeiros, C., Billen, R., Hallot, P., Simitsis, A., Van Mingroot, H. (eds.) ER 2011. LNCS, vol. 6999, pp. 55–64. Springer, Heidelberg (2011). https://doi.org/10.1007/978-3-642-24574-9_9
6. Dudycz, H., Korczak, J.: Process of ontology design for business intelligence system. In: Ziemba, E. (ed.) Information Technology for Management. LNBIP, vol. 243, pp. 17–28. Springer, Cham (2016). https://doi.org/10.1007/978-3-319-30528-8_2

7. Stefaniak, P., Wodecki, J., Zimroz, R.: Maintenance management of mining belt conveyor system based on data fusion and advanced analytics. In: Timofiejczuk, A., Łazarz, B.E., Chaari, F., Burdzik, R. (eds.) ICDT 2016. ACM, vol. 10, pp. 465–476. Springer, Cham (2018). https://doi.org/10.1007/978-3-319-62042-8_42

8. Stefaniak, Pawel K., Zimroz, R., Sliwinski, P., Andrzejewski, M., Wyłomanska, A.: Multidimensional signal analysis for technical condition, operation and performance understanding of heavy duty mining machines. In: Chaari, F., Zimroz, R., Bartelmus, W., Haddar, M. (eds.) Advances in condition monitoring of machinery in non-stationary operations. ACM, vol. 4, pp. 197–210. Springer, Cham (2016). https://doi.org/10.1007/978-3-319-20463-5_15

9. Grus, J.: Data Science from Scratch. O'Reilly, Sebastopol (2015)

10. Eaton, Ch,, Zikopoulos, P. C.: Understanding Big Data: Analytics for Enterprise Class Hadoop and Streaming Data. McGraw-Hill Osborne Media (2011)

11. Dean, J.: Big Data, Data Mining, and Machine Learning. Wiley, Hoboken (2014)

12. Cady, F.: The Data Science Handbook. Wiley, Hoboken (2017)

13. Chen, H., Chiang, R.H.L., Storey, V.C.: business intelligence and analytics: from big data to big impact. MIS Q. 36(4), 1165–1188 (2012). https://doi.org/10.2307/41703503

14. Ozdemir, S.: Principles of Data Science. Packt, Birmingham (2016)

15. Wu, X., Zhu, X., Wu, G.-Q., Ding, W.: Data mining with big data. IEEE Trans. Knowl. Data Eng. 26(1), 97–107 (2014). https://doi.org/10.1109/TKDE.2013.109

16. Dudycz, H., Nita, B., Oleksyk, P.: Application of ontology in financial assessment based on real options in small and medium-sized companies. In: Ziemba, E. (ed.) AITM/ISM -2018. LNBIP, vol. 346, pp. 24–40. Springer, Cham (2019). https://doi.org/10.1007/978-3-030-15154-6_2

17. Gilchrist, A.: Industry 4.0: The Industrial Internet of Things. Apress, Berkeley, CA (2016). https://doi.org/10.1007/978-1-4842-2047-4

Data Sources for Environmental Life Cycle Costing in Network Organizations

Michał Śnierzyński[1], Marcin Hernes[1](✉) ⓘ, Andrzej Bytniewski[1] ⓘ,
Małgorzata Krzywonos[1] ⓘ, and Jadwiga Sobieska-Karpińska[2]

[1] Wrocław University of Economics,
ul. Komandorska 118/120, 53-345 Wrocław, Poland
{michal.snierzynski,marcin.hernes,andrzej.bytniewski,
malgorzata.krzywonos}@ue.wroc.pl
[2] The Witelon State University of Applied Sciences in Legnica,
ul. Sejmowa 5A, 59-220 Legnica, Poland
jadwiga.sobieska.karpinska@gmail.com

Abstract. Environmental Life Cycle Costing (ELCC) is a summary of all costs related to the product life cycle that are covered directly by one or more entities engaged in this life cycle (e.g. by the supplier, producer, user or consumer as well as all persons involved in the "end of life" phase), increased by the costs of environmental impact. Its correct implementation depends on the quality of data. In assessing the quality of the data, such characteristics as unambiguity, objectivity, timeliness, time stamping, granularity, the occurrence of duplicate data, completeness, availability, precision, interpretability, integrity, and coherence, are taken into account. Thus, the quality of data depends largely on the sources of their acquisition. Due to the extensive information scope of the ELCC, data sources located in network organizations may be relevant. Significant problems are: identifying business processes performed in network organizations and recognizing the features of network organizations in order to improve the ELCC calculations. The aim of this paper is to identify the data sources for ELCC in network organizations. The obtained results can be used, for example, to calculate ELCC automatically by means of artificial intelligence tools.

Keywords: Environmental Life Cycle Costing · Network organizations · IT systems · Data acquisition

1 Introduction

Environmental Life Cycle Costing (ELCC) method was developed by the Society of Environmental Toxicology and Chemistry between 2002 and 2005 [1, 2]. Officially, ELCC was published in 2008; however, before and after 2008, there were several studies which described various aspects of ELCC [2]. Environmental Life Cycle Costing (ELCC) is a summary of all costs associated with the product life cycle that are covered directly by one or more entities engaged in this life cycle (e.g. supplier, producer, user or consumer as well as all persons involved in the "end of life" phase), increased by the costs of environmental impact [3, 4]. These costs must be related to real cash flows [1].

© Springer Nature Switzerland AG 2019
N. T. Nguyen et al. (Eds.): ICCCI 2019, LNAI 11684, pp. 394–405, 2019.
https://doi.org/10.1007/978-3-030-28374-2_34

Hunkeler et al. [1] provided a classification of LCC into three main approaches: Conventional (C-LCC), Environmental (E-LCC), and Societal Life Cycle Costing (S-LCC) - which differ mainly in terms of perspective, costs included, and potential uses.

Most of the C-LCCs have a single stakeholder (producer or consumer) perspective and assess decisions concerning products or investments requiring high initial capital [5]. In situations when managers want to implement new production technologies, there is a lack of comprehensive tools to support these decisions, both in terms of cost and sustainability [6]. That is the reason why there is a need to develop tools that support personnel management. The general framework of the ELCC is based on the physical life cycle of the product, which requires an analysis of at least four main stages. When implemented in an enterprise, they may be subject to further specification and clarification. These stages include [7]:

- research and development;
- production;
- use and maintenance;
- management during the liquidation and utilization phase.

The ELCC introduces (in each of these stages), in contrast to the traditional LCC, the so-called environmental costs, i.e. costs associated with the impact that economic activities have on the environment. Among them, fees for using the environment, environmental taxes, costs of emission control, costs of advertising for organic products, costs of compensation for environmental pollution, costs of medicines, and health-related stays. According to the conceptual assumptions of the ELCC, these costs should be separately recorded separately in group 5 and separated in the profit and loss account. In practice, this generates additional work, which in turn increases employment and other related costs. Very often, the separation of environmental costs from the operational costs is based solely on employee estimations and experience [8]. ELCC also analyzes consumer generated costs, as well as, for example, landfill and recycling fees. It takes into account all environmental costs increased by external costs and the potential for them occurring in the future [1]. ELCC utilizes the steady-state cost model. It means that no discounting and depreciation was taken into account [9].

The environmental life cycle costing was created as a technique complementing the environmental Life Cycle Assessing (LCA) [10]. LCA is a standardized method of assessing the environmental impact of a product and resource consumption throughout its life cycle [2].

The result of conducting the ELCC is a comparison of all costs related to the life cycle of the product, which is carried out directly by one or more entities involved in that life cycle - the list may refer to actual or planned costs, e.g., for various alternative materials used in production. LCC formulation involves selecting appropriate methodology. This formulation comprises of eight steps [11]:

(1) Establishment of operation profiles (OP): this step describes the periodic cycle when the equipment will operate and also when it will not be working.
(2) Establishment of utilization factors: These factors indicate in what way the equipment will be functioning within each mode of the OP.
(3) Identification of all the cost elements.

(4) Determination of the critical cost parameters: factors which control the degree of the costs incurred during the life of the equipment.

(5) Calculation of all costs at current prices.

(6) Escalation of current costs at assumed inflation rates.

(7) Discounting of all costs to the base period: By considering the time value of the money, cash flows occurring in different periods should be discounted back to the base period to ensure comparability.

(8) Summing up discounted cost to establish the net present value (NPV).

Net present value (NPV) and internal rate of return (IRR) were the most common indicators for long-term investment (orchards and plants) with a classic LCC or ELCC. However, as indicated by de Menna et al. [5] these financial indexes usually imply a single actor perspective, rather than a systemic one.

Considering the broad scope of the ELCC, it can be noticed that its correct implementation depends on the quality of available. In assessing the quality of data, characteristics such as unambiguity, objectivity, timeliness, time stamping, granularity, occurrence of duplicate data, completeness, availability, precision, interpretability, integrity, and coherence, are taken into account. Thus, the quality of data depends largely on the sources of their acquisition. Due to the vast information scope of the ELCC, data sources located in network organizations may be relevant. Serious problems are indicating business processes performed in network organizations and recognizing the features of network organizations in order to improve the ELCC calculations and to identify the data sources in IT systems that are being used in these organizations. The main aim of this paper is to identify the data sources for ELCC in network organizations. These data sources can be used, for example, to calculate ELCC automatically by means of artificial intelligence tools.

The existing papers are focused mainly on models and methods of conducting the ELCC however, there are no publications related to data acquisition. Therefore the identification of data sources for performing ELCC is this paper's main contribution to the ELCC research area. The issue was analyzed and discussed on the basis of secondary sources of information and own research. The source data consisted of scientific materials associated with the ELCC, network organizations, IT systems, and data acquisition.

The following research methods were used to achieve the goal of this paper: analysis of the source literature, observation of phenomena based on the practical experience of authors related to working in network organizations and implementing IT systems in these organizations as well as induction and deduction methods.

The first part of the paper describes the state-of-the-art and basic notions within the field of research. Next, the main business processes performed in network organizations concerning ELCC have been identified. The last part of the paper was devoted to presenting the data sources within particular ELCC cost categories; discussion, and conclusions.

2 Related Works

The literature search was performed on the ScienceDirect website with using keywords "environmental life cycle costing". Within the keywords, titles, and abstracts, we have obtained only 67 references within the period 1999–2019. In Scopus, within the period 2010–2019, we have obtained only 27 references. When we added "environmental life cycle costing" AND "data acquisition"; "environmental life cycle costing" AND "data source", "environmental life cycle costing" AND "data collection", "environmental life cycle costing" AND "network organization" to the keyword combination in both databases we do did not receive any references. Only one reference has been found when the combination of "environmental life cycle costing" AND "data collection" has been used [12], and one reference has been obtained when the combination of "environmental life cycle costing" AND "information technology" has been used to perform a search within the keywords, titles, and abstracts. On this basis, we concluded that the subject undertaken by this study is rare and worthy of investigation. Hunkeler et al. [1] divided costs into several categories: economic cost categories, life cycle stages, activity types, and other cost categories. Economic cost categories are related to the general type of cost, such as market costs, budget costs, and social costs. Life cycle stages categories relate to the segments of the supply chain analyzed, from product design and development to material extraction, use phase, and end of life. Activity types categories are a detailed specification of stages, including processes involved. Other cost categories are particular cost items within activities and stages [5, 13].

It should be noted that in modern economic systems, traditionally structured enterprises still exist, but they are starting to play increasingly smaller role. New business models are emerging, the structure of which is most often a complex compilation of traditionally defined models of organizational structures. The network organization is considered to be the most effective organizational form, created voluntarily and one that is subject to continuous reconfiguration of the structure of its entities, i.e., business units or their separate parts and physical persons [14–16]. It is interconnected by various relations (e.g., intellectual, economic, and social), but also allows for autonomy in these relations, partnership, and trust in using the network resources. It enables their active cooperation, exchange of knowledge, experience, and resources, as well as improvement in competences and team (joint) decision-making and creating added value that is competitive in a turbulent global environment. Cooperating industrial units are perceived by the market as one enterprise. It must be emphasized that although network organizations have been operating on the market for a long time, information technology is a factor conducive to their creation.

Various entities conduct joint business activities in order to achieve complementarity and are territorially dispersed, in order to benefit from globalization for this reason appropriate integration and improvement of solutions within their IT systems is required. It is also necessary to create and improve the architecture of the distributed systems, which is a factor conducive to the increase in the efficiency of units and their networks in the provision of services (individual and integrated) focused on the needs of clients (individual and institutional).

Summing up the above issues, one can conclude that there are many publications about concepts and methods for calculating the ELCC, but to the best of authors' knowledge, there is a cognitive gap concerning data sources in network organizations' IT systems needed for ELCC calculations. These sources are necessary to be able to automatically calculate ELCC by means of IT systems (artificial intelligence tools can be very helpful for this purpose). Therefore, the identification of data sources in network organizations' IT systems, which can be then processed in ELCC using automatic calculations, is a significant research problem.

3   Identification of Main Business Processes in Network Organizations in Relation to ELCC

Network organizations are characterized by certain features, which facilitate the ELCC calculations. These features include:

- Basic information infrastructure. Very often, the leader of network organization provides hardware and software architecture necessary to exchange information between organizations functioning in the network structure.
- Automation of information flows. The electronic information processing is performed; the documents in paper form are eliminated.
- The real-time information flow (the stream of information) between particular organizations.
- Easier access to data because there is direct access of every organization to the standard information system.
- Creating a new knowledge value, reducing the costs of acquiring additional knowledge from other organizations.
- Exchange of experiences in the field of business processes, improvement or innovations.
- Reducing the environmental costs of new technologies, because these costs are distributed among all of the organizations in the network.
- Carrying out business processes is based on trust and access to the know-how of all entities in the network organization.
- Lower environmental costs of the product, because organizations influence each other in terms of minimalizing these costs.
- Lower costs of utilization and repairs (costs divided among several entities).
- Distribution of the divestment costs (e.g., old technology) among several entities.
- Joint coverage of investment costs, e.g. technology costs - licenses, technology development.
- Lower probability of particular organization being renamed, a higher level of entity identification.
- High possibility of personalization of information systems.
- Standardization of data semantics and information security processes.
- Sharing the material, non-material and human resources without limitations.
- High possibility of providing the manufacturing orchestration (services-oriented manufacturing).

- Facilitation related to the standard supply chain management in both, physical and information flows.
- Increasing the level of employee responsibility.
- Building strategic relationships between organizations and the expedited process of finding partners.
- High responsibility awareness of the cooperating teams.
- Current efforts at increasing customer awareness.
- Facilitation of the presumption process. Prosumer can participate in improving the product throughout its entire environmental cycle.
- Open access to changing information technologies.
- Joint efforts to increase programs aimed at pro-ecological behavior.
- Conventional ways of motivating producers to take greater environmental responsibility.

These features allow for the integration of the business processes carried out in network organizations. The identification of essential processes occurring in network organization is vital to identify the data sources of ELCC. The analysis of business processes has been performed based on references [e.g., 17–20] as well as the experience of authors related to analysis, design, and implementation of management information systems in business organizations. There are many criterions used to classify business processes. According to this criterion [21], the following processes are performed in the network organizations:

1. Basic processes are processes which directly generate an added value, the customer sees them most easily and through these processes he evaluates the quality and efficiency of the entire company; they include:

   - "input" logistics, which includes activities related to the preparation of production and "output" logistics, which includes sales activities; these processes in network organizations are integrated into the supply chain management process; it includes material, information and cash flows; effective supply chain management reduces costs and the time of the entire supply, production, and distribution cycle;
   - manufacturing is a material and economic system, which is used to produce products and services that meet the needs of consumers; it consists of a group of sockets or workstations; this is a process of transforming semi-finished products and input raw materials (entry vectors) into finished products that are suitable for use; final products (output vectors) are ready for sale and are one of the components of the production system; in addition to the products, the production waste is also generated and can be re-used, sold or appropriately disposed of;
   - marketing is a social process in which individuals and groups obtain what they need through creating, offering and free exchange of goods and services that have value,
   - after-sales services - are all contacts with a customer who has already made purchases; complaints, exchanges, or returned goods.

2. Auxiliary processes indirectly generate added value; the client has poor under-standing of their quality, and therefore, they have a low impact on shaping the external image of the organization, they include:

   - quality control - the main task of the quality control process during production is to control of the supplied production materials, technical documentation and qualifications and rights of employees,
   - maintenance - is a comprehensive process of ensuring the availability of efficient machines to be engaged in the production process. It includes three sub-processes: preparation of machines for work, repair and conservation;
   - financial accounting - is a process of measurement and registration of economic events, as well as monitoring the financial situation of the business entity;

3. Management processes - have a strategic impact on how to generate value added; regulate essential and auxiliary processes; their main task is to define the mission, strategy, and principles of operation of the entire organization, including monitoring the effectiveness of processes, they include:

   - general organization management - relies on making decisions that ensure the use of specific resources to achieve the desired goals set by the owner of the organization, and on coordinating the activities of people involved in this activity to achieve results that are difficult to achieve alone,
   - human resources management - strategic process, subjectively treating the employees - taking into account their needs, expectations and optimally using this resource in the right place and time under both quantitative and qualitative assessment, following the objectives, and the mission of the organization,
   - customer and supplier relationship management - relies on building customer and supplier loyalty towards the company by developing long-term relationships profitable for both parties, using the latest achievements in information pro-cessing technology,
   - knowledge management - include all processes enabling the creation, dissemi-nation, and utilization of knowledge to achieve its goals; it takes the form of an interactive model with multidirectional interactions between its various ele-ments: knowledge creation, dissemination of knowledge and application of knowledge,
   - environmental management - purposeful action aimed at maintaining and improving the state of the natural environment influenced by human activity; environmental management must be integrated with the general management process.

The processes performed in network organizations allow for streamlining the flow of data, which leads to lowering the costs and faster data acquisition for ELCC in com-parison to traditional organizations. The features of network organizations facilitate the ELCC calculating. However, to automate this process, the real-time data from IT systems running in network organizations are needed. The problem of identification of data sources is characterized in the next section of this paper.

4   The Data Sources' Indication

The business processes described in the previous section are mapped to the IT systems running in network organizations. The financial accounting system is mainly focused on the acquisition prices, depreciation, and residual value of assets. These values are collected by means of applicable accounting rules and procedures (GAAP/IFRS/local accounting standards). It is natural that the usage of classical accounting is not suitable when assessing the actual costs and benefits associated with the asset. The reason for that is the complexity of investment opportunities.

The practical use of LCC is still limited to its complexity assumption. Therefore, in order to calculate ELCC data from financial-accounting is insufficient. The data from other systems, running in a network organization, are also needed. These systems include:

- Enterprise Resource Planning (ERP),
- Computer Aided Design (CAD),
- Supply Chain Management (SCM),
- Customer Relationship Management (CRM).

Table 1 Presents data sources (systems, ERP's sub-systems, and modules) associated with the main categories of Life Cycle Costs (these categories have been determined in [22, 23]).

Table 1. Data sources for ELCC

Category of costs	Costs	Data sources – systems or sub-systems and modules of ERP system
Investment (acquisition) costs	Cost of design and survey	Computer Aided Design, Technical Production Preparation (structural cart of product-bill of materials), technological cart of product, Supply Chain Management (e.g., invoices from the supplier include the division into positions itemizing costs)
	Cost of the project (e.g., buildings, machinery, land, equipment)	Fixed Asset sub-system
	Costs related to managing document's lifecycle	Workflow, Document Management System
	Cost of land or workshop increases if additional investments are required	Fixed Asset sub-system, Logistics subsystem
	Related cost associated with the placement of buildings/machinery/equipment	Maintenance sub-system
	Other costs	Logistics sub-system, fixed assets sub-system, human resources management sub-system, Supply Chain Management
	Other investments	
	Operating costs associated with preparing assets and realization of assets	Human resource management sub-system, Logistics sub-systems (e.g., materials, energy)

(*continued*)

Table 1. (*continued*)

Category of costs	Costs	Data sources – systems or sub-systems and modules of ERP system
Operation costs	Cost of materials and energy supply	Logistics sub-system, Supply Chain Management
	Cost of water and wastewater	Logistics sub-system, Supply Chain Management
	Cost of waste disposal	Logistic sub-system, Supply Chain Management
	Service fees, insurance	Financial-accounting sub-system, external systems of public entities
	Payroll costs	Human resource management sub-system
	Costs related to security and safety	Logistic sub-system, Human Resources Management
	Cost of cleaning	Logistic sub-system, Human Resources Management, Supply Chain Management
	Administrative charges	Financial-accounting sub-system, external systems of public entities
Maintenance costs	Services; general inspection; warranty inspections	Customer Relationship Management sub-system, Human Resources Management, Logistics sub-systems
	Plan of maintenance; downtime; break time	Maintenance sub-system
Renewal costs	Repair services	Customer Relationship Management sub-system, Human Resources Management, Logistics sub-systems
	Divestment	Fixed Asset sub-systems, Supply Chain Management, Human Resource Management, Logistics sub-systems (materials required to carry out divestment)
	Cost of disposal of the building/machinery/equipment Cost of recycling materials or raw materials	Supply Chain Management, Customer Relationship Management sub-system

Financial-accounting sub-systems provide data associated with all kinds of cost categories. More details pertaining to costs can be found in the remaining sub-systems. The completeness of data may differ between sources, so when possible, one source should be used, or data integration method can be applied. The data sources mentioned in Table 1 can be used for calculating the ELCC considering both real and predicted costs (multiple-variants of calculating the ELCC).

5   Research Implications

In network organizations, the components used in the production process are jointly designed. It reduces the number of resources (manpower, energy, fuel, and environmental pollution) - the PSA concern (using the common frame - floors for various car models) can be mentioned as an example. In network organizations, the process of distributing the manufactured components used in the production process of various organizations is also optimized and rationalized. In consequence, consumption of resources is reduced. Marketing campaigns, repairs and maintenance are all organized jointly by the producers. The process of rendering products manufactured by network organizations is organized in a similar way in order to reduce the costs of utilization. Network organizations jointly contribute to bearing social costs caused by the use of their products and are interested in making the costs as low as possible.

Data sources in network organizations' IT systems serve as the basis for calculating the ELCC. They should be used in the ELCC automatic calculation module, which can be set in the financial-accounting sub-system of ERP. The existing ERP systems do not include such a module. The indicated data sources can be set to description function during module analysis and design phase (users' requirements analysis). The functions can be related to a particular category of costs. Another critical aspect is the analysis of integration technologies (e.g., common database, API, web services, Enterprise Service Bus); however, it depends on particular systems running in particular network organizations. Of course, to develop an ELCC automatic calculation module, other determinants should also be taken into consideration. The fundamental issue is the European Union law that refers to ELCC. Current directive requires [24] that where ELCC is used, the calculation method, and the data to be provided by tenderers are required to be set out in the procurement documents. Specific rules also apply to methods of assigning costs to environmental externalities, which aim to ensure that these methods are fair and transparent. ELCC makes good sense regardless of a public authority's environmental objectives. By applying ELCC, public purchasers take into account the costs of resource use, maintenance, and disposal, which are not reflected in the purchase price. Often this will lead to 'win-win' situations whereby a greener product, work, or service will have an overall lower price. The following areas have the most potential for savings over the life cycle of a product, work, or service [23]:

– Savings on energy, water, and fuel consumption,
– Savings on maintenance and replacement,
– Savings on disposal associated costs.

Other than recovery issues, prolonging the life of the product, producer and consumer responsibility, encouraging manufacturers, and incentives for customers are fundamental ELCC issues.

6 Conclusions

Identification of the data sources for ELCC in network organizations is a process that is critical for the design and development of the automatic ELCC calculation method. This paper presents general issues related to this problem. The detailed analysis of particular IT systems running in network organizations should be carried out.

There are also limitations for data acquisition when performing the ELCC that are related to unavailability of some types of data. For example, in CRM sub-system information about clients, or activities related to recyclable materials (e.g., bottles,) is not available. It is necessary to extend the CRM system to these aspects. Also, the large variability of network organizations and entities outside of the organization is a fundamental problem.

The ELCC calculation is a necessary step involved in caring for the environment for the sake of future generations. Trustworthiness and awareness of companies is of crucial importance. In other words, network organizations should effectively operate within the environment. Increasing numbers of programs focused on pro-ecological behavior are needed.

Future research works can be focused, for example, on developing the method for automatic ELCC calculation and on application of artificial intelligence tools (e.g., cognitive or deep learning technologies) to support this method (e.g., for predicting environmental costs of different kinds of substitute materials to be used for product development).

Acknowledgment. "The project is financed by the Ministry of Science and Higher Education in Poland under the programme "Regional Initiative of Excellence" 2019–2022 project number 015/RID/2018/19 total funding amount 10 721 040,00 PLN".

References

1. Hunkeler, D., Lichtenvort, K., Rebitzer, G.: Environmental Life Cycle Costing, pp. 9–16. CRC Press, Boca Raton (2008)
2. Miah, J.H., Koh, S.C.L., Stone, D.: A hybridised framework combining integrated methods for environmental life cycle assessment and life cycle costing. J. Cleaner Prod. **168**, 846–866 (2017)
3. Núñez, M., Civit, B., Muñoz, P., Pablo Arena, A., Rieradevall, J., Anton, A.: Assessing potential desertification environmental impact in life cycle assessment. part 1: methodological aspects. Int. J. Life Cycle Assess. **15**(1), 67–78 (2010)
4. Biernacki, M.: ELCC costing and eco-marketing in business operations. Research Papers of the Wroclaw University of Economics, p. 480 (2017)
5. De Menna, F., Dietershagen, J., Loubiere, M., Vittuari, M.: Life cycle costing of food waste: a review of methodological approaches. Waste Manage. **73**, 1–13 (2018)
6. Kianian, B., Kurdve, M., Andersson, C.: Comparing life cycle costing and performance part costing in assessing acquisition and operational cost of new manufacturing technologies. Procedia CIRP **80**, 428–433 (2019)
7. Payen, S., Basset-Mens, C., Perret, S.R.: LCA of local and imported tomato: an energy and water trade-off. J. Clean. Prod. **87**(15), 139–148 (2015)

8. Dijkman, T.J., Basset-Mens, C., Antón, A., Núñez, M.: LCA of food and agriculture. In: Hauschild, M., Rosenbaum, R., Olsen, S. (eds.) Life Cycle Assessment. Springer, Cham (2018). https://doi.org/10.1007/978-3-319-56475-3_29

9. Luo, L., Van Der Voet, E., Huppes, G.: Life cycle assessment and life cycle costing of bioethanol from sugarcane in Brazil. Renew. Sustain. Energy Rev. 13(6–7), 1613–1619 (2009)

10. Martinez-Sanchez, V., Tonini, D., Møller, F., Astrup, T.F.: Life-cycle costing of food waste management in Denmark: importance of indirect effects. Environ. Sci. Technol. 50(8), 4513–4523 (2016)

11. Durairaj, S.K., Ong, S.K., Nee, A.Y.C., Tan, R.B.H.: Evaluation of life cycle cost analysis methodologies. Corp. Environ. Strategy, Vol. 9, No. 1, 30–39 (2002)

12. Hall, M.R.: The sustainability price: expanding environmental life cycle costing to include the costs of poverty and climate change. Int. J. Life Cycle Assess. 24(2), 223–236 (2019)

13. Schau, E.M., Traverso, M., Finkbeiner, M.: Life cycle approach to sustainability assessment: a case study of remanufactured alternators. J. Remanufact. 2(1), 5 (2012)

14. Knoke, D.: Changing Organizations: Business Networks in the New Political Economy. Routledge, New York (2018)

15. Ellison, N.B., Gibbs, J.L., Weber, M.S.: The use of enterprise social network sites for knowledge sharing in distributed organizations: the role of organizational affordances. Am. Behav. Sci. 59(1), 103–123 (2015)

16. Ding, K., Jiang, P., Leng, J., Cao, W.: Modeling and analyzing of an enterprise relationship network in the context of social manufacturing. Proc. Inst. Mech. Eng. Part B: J. Eng. Manufact. 230(4), 752–769 (2016)

17. Goldstein, A., Johanndeiter, T., Frank, U.: Business process runtime models: towards bridging the gap between design, enactment, and evaluation of business processes. Inf. Syst. E-Bus. Manage. 17, 27 (2019)

18. Engel, R., et al.: Analyzing inter-organizational business processes. Inf. Syst. E-Bus. Manage. 14, 577 (2016). https://doi.org/10.1007/s10257-015-0295-2

19. Prajogo, D., Olhager, J.: Supply chain integration and performance: the effects of longterm relationships, information technology and sharing, and logistics integration. Int. J. Prod. Econ. 135, 514–522 (2012)

20. Hajdul, M., Kawa, A.: Global logistics tracking and tracing in fleet management. In: Nguyen, N.T., Trawiński, B., Kosala, R. (eds.) ACIIDS 2015. LNCS (LNAI), vol. 9011, pp. 191–199. Springer, Cham (2015). https://doi.org/10.1007/978-3-319-15702-3_19

21. Grajewski, P.: Cultural determinants of the process-oriented organization. Management 16 (1), 377–386 (2012)

22. Daylan, B., Ciliz, N.: Life cycle assessment and environmental life cycle costing analysis of lignocellulosic bioethanol as an alternative transportation fuel. Renew. Energy 89, 578–587 (2016)

23. Spickova, M., Myskova, R.: Costs efficiency evaluation using life cycle costing as strategic method. Procedia Econ. Finance 34, 337–343 (2015)

24. Directive 2014/24/EU and Article 83(2) of Directive 2014/25/EU

Artificial Intelligence in Cybersecurity: The Use of AI Along the Cyber Kill Chain

Iwona Chomiak-Orsa[1] , Artur Rot[1(✉)] , and Bartosz Blaicke[1,2]

[1] Wroclaw University of Economics, Wroclaw, Poland
artur.rot@ue.wroc.pl
[2] McKinsey & Company, Berlin, Germany

Abstract. The current challenge with defense against cyberattacks is that the speed and quantity of threats often outpace human-centered cyber defense capabilities. That is why a new Artificial Intelligence driven approach may enhance the effectiveness of security controls. However, it can also be used by adversaries to create more sophisticated and adaptable attack mechanisms. Distinguishing three key AI capabilities (knowledge acquisition, human-like perception and decision making), the goal of this paper is to assert where within the cyber kill chain have AI capabilities already been applied, and which phase holds the greatest near-term potential given recent developments and publications. Based on literature review, authors see the strongest potential for deploying AI capabilities during the reconnaissance, intrusion, privilege escalation and data exfiltration steps of the cyber kill chain with other uses being deployed in the remaining steps.

Keywords: Cybersecurity · Artificial Intelligence · AI · Security controls · Cyber kill chain

1 Introduction

Cybersecurity is a field that has been gaining significant attention among IT professionals and the general public. One of the reasons for this interest is due to the rising prominence of cyberattacks and their growing impact, as they are now considered one of the top five global risks by the World Economic Forum [1]. Moreover, cyberattacks are becoming increasingly dangerous: they are growing in quantity at 34% per year [2] are becoming more sophisticated (e.g. the recent Triton attack that could override itself to cover its tracks [3]) and a single attack (e.g. NotPetya) can easily affect computers in more than 100 countries worldwide [4]. Unfortunately, the defense perimeter is enormous, and attackers only need a single-entry vector to be successful. Therefore, not only many attacks remain in stealth mode with average time of detection being multiple months, but many more are believed to pass completely unnoticed [5].

Cybersecurity is also no longer an "IT only" problem, as attacks have crossed the digital-physical barrier already in 2010. Modern cyberattacks can have physical consequences or be used as targeted military weapons, potentially more effective than traditional warfare, as showcased by Stuxnet used to sabotage the Iranian nuclear program [6].

© Springer Nature Switzerland AG 2019
N. T. Nguyen et al. (Eds.): ICCCI 2019, LNAI 11684, pp. 406–416, 2019.
https://doi.org/10.1007/978-3-030-28374-2_35

All that creates additional pressure for businesses to remain resilient. However, shortage of adequate talent, and the inability of human analysts to process all the incoming potential breach indicators mean that defense measures are far from matching existing demand, and will not do so for the foreseeable future [7]. The industry is clearly becoming aware of the ongoing difficulty of detecting advanced threats [8], as shown by the persistent prominence of themes such as "security incident," "threat actor," and "malware" during last decade of RSA Conferences.

This is exactly where the core promise of Artificial Intelligence (AI) within cybersecurity comes into play. The potential to combine human ingenuity with the speed and effectiveness of machines through the use of applied AI (focused on a specific set of tasks) and, at a later stage, with general AI (where machines can perform general intelligent actions across a wide set of tasks) can be a game changer for the defense community. However, it also means that the malicious actors will start to use the same tools to increase the sophistication of their attacks, forcing swift adoption of AI powered tools among the long tail of adopters if they do not want to get left behind.

Therefore, the main goal of this paper is to assess where within the cyber kill chain framework can AI capabilities be deployed. A second question is, which steps hold the greatest near-term transformative potential - as demonstrated by recent development and publications - that could change how both sides approach the issue. The proprietary contribution of this paper is the use of full cyber kill chain to analyze the potential applications as well as identification and segmentation of existing commercial solutions within that framework. Such understanding could help early adopters assess where to focus their deployment efforts first.

2   AI Capabilities Framework

Artificial Intelligence is a broad term that describes how machines can perform tasks that have historically required skills considered uniquely human. It includes being able to analyze and understand data, to use language and to creatively solve complex problems without following a preprogrammed algorithm. Machine Learning (ML) is another term that is often used interchangeably with AI, but in fact is a subset of all the potential techniques used to develop AI tools that is considered state-of-the-art [9]. In short, it can be described as a method to train a computer by feeding large amounts of information to the algorithm, allowing it to consume that data, iterate to adjust itself, and thus improve over time. In addition, one can also group Artificial Intelligences based on the split between applied and general AI, as mentioned in the previous chapter.

For the purposes of this paper, the capabilities that an AI can provide are grouped into three categories related to knowledge, perception and decision making, as introduced in [10].

- KNOW - capabilities related to data analysis, knowledge representation and insight generation. These include data clustering and visualization tools leveraging AI such as Qymatix or applied AI for identity analytics, e.g. based on user behavior analytics (UBA).

- SENSE - natural language processing, machine vision and speech recognition systems. Core examples include modern digital assistants such as Apple's Siri, Microsoft's Cortana or Amazon's Alexa as well as translation systems such as Google's Translate, DeepL or video processing and face recognition systems such as the one developed by Facebook to identify people on uploaded photos.
- ACT - automated decision making and expert systems. These can vary from recommendation engines that are used by retailers to suggest the next purchase for a user, to more sophisticated applied AI solutions such as IBM's Watson Security Operation Center (SOC) that can semi-autonomously run part of a security operation at a company [11].

Together, these three capabilities represent the main use cases of applied AI that we will explore further, in conjunction with a sequence of steps called the cyber kill chain that a typical malicious actor is following to perform a cyber-attack.

3   Recent AI Advancements in Cybersecurity and Related Work

Researchers and businesses have already proven that the above-mentioned concepts can be successfully applied to cybersecurity as described in [12] and [13]. In addition, [13] have already looked at the cyber kill chain concept but simplified the analysis by aggregating all domains into four broader concepts. This work is expanding on that approach. Deployments of AI within cybersecurity that are currently commercially available focus on curating vast amounts of data and supporting security analysts in performing their jobs more efficiently and accurately. Automated systems are also using behavior modeling to learn from previous threats and risks and predict what future attack scenarios might look like [14]. However, there are other, more sophisticated concepts being tried out, such as "cyber immune system" that can adapt to changing circumstances.

Moreover, both defense as well as attack methods can benefit from AI. A selective reference library is already being developed by IBM Security to provide a sample implementation library for rapid crafting and analysis of attacks and defense methods for machine learning models including many state-of-the-art classifiers [15].

However, the advancement of AI as a field gives rise to questions regarding its influence in the long term. We already see that some of the applied AI systems can be better than humans, especially in clearly defined and computationally intense problem-solving, including board games (both Chess and Go world champions have been beaten by AI systems) or popular shows such as Jeopardy. An expert survey shows that fast advancements in AI will continue for the next three decades, with the expectation that a superintelligence might emerge in less than 30 years. The experts also estimate that there is about one in three chance that such development turns out 'bad' or 'extremely bad' for humanity [16]. Thus, we will continue to see new use cases and innovations in the fields we thought of as strictly human, such as AI-created artwork that is being sold on auctions [17] or in terms of cybersecurity increasing use of AI to substitute people-intense processes, to a point where they can act on their own. However, due to the sensitive nature of cybersecurity controls, this adds another layer of consideration (not relevant yet) when deploying more and more intelligent systems that will have autonomous decision-making capabilities. As a society we still lack legal, regulatory or even moral frameworks for how to handle consequences of actions undertaken by an Artificial Intelligence.

4 Cyber Kill Chain Framework in Relation to AI

Cyber kill chain is a framework that is widely used and recognized within the cybersecurity community to describe a sequence of steps that most attacks follow. It has been initially introduced by Lockheed Martin based on a military approach [18] but has been heavily modified since. For the purpose of this paper, we are using a modified version proposed by Varonis [19] that expands on the original concepts with anti-forensics and lateral movement steps that are much more common nowadays.

The framework in Table 1 follows eight steps, from gaining access through initial gathering of information and actual attack using discovered vulnerabilities (phases 1–3), followed by advancing deeper into the organization's systems by increasing privileges, exploring additional attack tactics and hiding actions (phases 4–6), and finally potential disruption of services and exfiltration of data (phases 7–8). For each intersection of the steps and the AI capability the authors indicate their subjective relevance in terms of direct applicability of currently available and proposed solutions to solve the issues represented at each step.

Table 1. Current relevance at the intersection of cyber kill chain steps and AI capabilities.

	Recon	Intrusion	Exploitation	Escalate access	Lateral moves	Obfuscation	DoS	Data exfil.
KNOW	High	High	Low	High	High	High	Low	Low
SENSE	High	High	Low	High	Low	Low	Low	High
ACT	Low	High	High	Low	Low	Low	High	High

The estimated potential of current and proposed AI solutions is highest in the early steps of the cyber kill chain, specifically reconnaissance, intrusion, and privilege/access escalation, but also in the last step used to exfiltrate data. There are valid use cases among other steps, as described below, but based on the analysis of existing and upcoming capabilities authors expect to see the biggest gains in these four steps and thus would suggest these as the most promising for further research.

Subsequent chapters will describe in more detail the intersection of each step with the relevant AI capabilities as depicted in Table 1, together with recent usage examples and proposed solutions.

4.1   Reconnaissance

The initial step is reconnaissance. Typically one of the longest phases, lasting days, weeks, or even months, as the attacker collects as much data as possible for the subsequent attack. This data can include personal information (e.g. email, coworker names, personal preferences) and system information (e.g. operating system, installed applications, including versions). Attackers often rely on passive methods so as to not alarm the potential victim, a strategy that requires more time and patience. However, faced with time constraints, many malicious actors follow a direct or active intelligence gathering approach, with penetration testing, social engineering, or even physical scouting while being disguised e.g. as a delivery person - as done by a well-known hacker Kevin Mitnick, to find passwords written down on post-it notes [20].

Open Source Intelligence (OSINT) collection is one of the key methods that hackers who want to stay invisible use, because it relies exclusively on publicly available information. However, the ability to correlate seemingly insignificant pieces of information across various sources, including the deep and dark web content, can result in very powerful datasets. If such collection is done by being even more active - through inquiries that leave a data trace or create subsequent discussions - it can be captured and correlated by companies using AI. Such services deliver customized cyber threat insights allowing companies to identify potential threats multiple times faster than when relying on analysts [21].

Finally, advancements in the field of Artificial Intelligence have improved the capabilities of face recognition. AI systems typically create a "faceprint" by measuring distances between multiple points of the face to create a unique identifier. Combined with vast amounts of photos and videos available online this could be used to identify, via facial recognition, any known hackers trying to perform physical reconnaissance. It was even suggested that the recent "10 Year Challenge" on social media that prompted people to upload their current photo next to their photo from 10 years prior was a plot to create a large database to train facial recognition algorithms on how to handle age progression and age recognition [22]. These kinds of systems are also increasingly more affordable, as researches from India have already provided a complete IoT facial recognition security system description that could be used as a blueprint for developing in-house systems [23].

4.2   Intrusion

The second step is where the initial breach happens, based on the information gathered previously. Malicious actors would often use malware (e.g. delivered via email using phishing) or known vulnerabilities to inject the code to gain access, but they can also use compromised credentials.

Phishing as an initial way to compromise the system is widely used, as deceiving people is significantly easier than defeating software and hardware security systems. To support malicious actors in such endeavors, in 2016 a pair of researchers introduced a neural network capable of learning how to tweet phishing posts targeting specific users. It uses clustering to identify high value targets based on their level of social engagement, so that it first identifies the best target to approach and then prepares tailored content to share with them. These two capabilities, combined, became "the first automated end-to-end spear phishing campaign generator for Twitter" [24].

To prevent the intrusion in the first place, companies such as EndGame or SentinelOne develop machine learning models to detect malicious activity. Some vendors have created AI-powered chatbots that can support human analysts in creating and understanding specific queries, while others focus on correlation of alerts and events to filter through the noise as much as possible [25]. Companies have even released open-source datasets that can be used to train machine learning classifiers to detect malware via static analysis as a way to support the community.

4.3 Exploitation

The third step is all about using the newly gained access to the system to further increase the foothold of the attacker within the environment. Attackers will often use additional tools to find vulnerabilities, modify security certificates, or create customized scripts to gain better control and insights.

To deal with attackers that have already compromised the corporate environment, there are tools such as DarkTrace, which use AI-based security monitoring modeled on the human immune system. The system works by first learning what is considered 'normal behavior' for every user and device in the environment. Without presuming to judge what activity is 'malicious' and what isn't, the AI system independently learns to detect significant deviations from the norm. This is where the second part of the system takes over, acting like a digital antibody. It intelligently generates adequate response to the identified anomaly, with the reaction times significantly faster than any human analyst [26] (as stated by the company itself). These solutions, while already available on the market, are still very fresh. However, when they mature and are deployed at a larger scale, they could become "game changers" for the entire cybersecurity industry.

4.4 Privilege Escalation

Following the exploitation phase, the attacker tries to gain access to additional data and other parts of the system, by escalating their privileges from the regular user account that is typically compromised first, into a power user or ideally an administrator account that would offer maximum access.

One way to gain further access is to check if current administrator accounts might be using weak passwords that can be easily guessed. Researchers have already applied Generative Adversarial Networks as an attempt to discover rules and restrictions based on leaked passwords datasets. After performing such training, the AI-based system called PassGAN could generate intricate passwords (more complex than created by rules-based generators) and significantly accelerate password guessing attacks. The use of AI improved the state-of-the-art tools success rate by matching additional 51–73% passwords without any additional human input [27].

Instead of targeting systems, malicious actors are also trying to "break people" through social engineering. These types of attacks often involve the use of deception to convince employees to provide accesses, divulge passwords or follow dangerous procedures imitating legitimate IT department queries. It is already possible to detect such attacks through natural language processing of dialogs and conversations and subsequent keyword and semantic analysis [28]. However, adding AI capabilities like automated transcription of calls in near real time and allowing the neural network to learn overtime would improve the effectiveness of such solutions in line with their increasing scale.

4.5   Lateral Movement

After obtaining admin credentials, attackers can further explore the interconnected systems and assets in search for sensitive data (including email servers, structured databases and unstructured data) and additional access credentials. During this phase attackers would often use the same tools as an IT department, making it difficult to differentiate legitimate activities from malicious ones.

However, SentinelOne, a cybersecurity company, has developed an AI-driven engine to identify actions that are often driven by scripts with automatic spreading capabilities. The technology uses low level monitoring to gain overview of operations across all the machines. With the full context, it can identify the anomalies in usage of various techniques to move around the network alerting the security team [29].

4.6   Obfuscation

After learning as much as possible about the system and spreading to different parts of the environment, attackers (especially if they want to stay hidden) will try to conceal their presence and mask all the past and current activities to avoid detection as long as possible. This means that log files will be thoroughly cleaned, time stamps for certain activities might be modified, and false forensic evidence may even be planted to mislead potential investigators.

Insiders can often become just as much a threat as external attackers. Disgruntled employees already have most of the accesses they need to cause damage, but they will try to cover their tracks. Therefore, log correlation and other more sophisticated methods are used to detect if files have been tampered with, or if there are any changes between current and historical log that should not have appeared [30]. Tools such as detection of anomalies using dynamic rule creation have already been proposed [31] to compensate for these kinds of activities.

Authors of malware make it more sophisticated as well. Malware files are now capable of meta-morphing, which means that while the functions remain the same, the appearance - or, more precisely, the generated code - can be highly diverse. Such techniques prevent signature-based protection mechanisms from identifying the file as malicious, and obfuscate its real identity. Researchers have proposed a non-signature-based way to identify such malware using a statistical detector that can augment existing antivirus solutions [32].

4.7   Denial of Service

This phase is focused on operations disruption so that legitimate users can't access or use the system as intended. In most cases it is optional (or considered last resort effort following discovery, preventing further identification of the perpetrators) as not all attacks are focused on interrupting victims' operations. In addition, such visible consequences often lead to increased scrutiny and discovery of the breach itself, cutting off the attackers from the target. There are, however, instances where disruption of operations is the precise goal of the attack. This includes cases when the distributed denial of service (DDoS) attack floods servers with so much connections or data requests that it cannot process legitimate users (often used against websites), or ransomware infections that prevent users from accessing files on their computers.

While the DDoS attacks have been around for years, AI has made the botnet creation and management easier, as it can improve identification and engagement of target devices for recruitment into the botnet and subsequent monetization [33]. Because modern botnets can use various devices, including IoT nodes (as evident in the Mirai-botnet attack using home routers as zombie-nodes), they are increasingly more difficult to detect and destroy. However, machine learnings have been proposed as one of the more effective techniques used for their detection [34].

4.8 Data Exfiltration

The final step is to access and copy or transfer data from its original location to a secure server or into the hands of the perpetrators. It is then possible to further analyze the dataset, try to extort ransom from the target, sell it on the dark web or even use it for national intelligence purposes.

If the perpetrators are attacking remotely, it is likely they will have to move the data through the existing corporate network onto a server in the Internet to obtain a copy. It is possible to find anomalies such as a large number of low bandwidth connections from multiple hosts (trying to remain stealthy) or establishing encrypted tunnels to locations that do not have a geo-tag near a legitimate location. It has also been proposed that when attackers are using DNS data tunnels to malicious web domains, a decision technique that sequentially accumulates evidence under uncertainty conditions could be implemented as a potential remedy [35].

In addition, making a full circle from their first step – reconnaissance - if the attackers are trying to physically take the data it is possible to use CCTV cameras to monitor traffic in the restricted zones such as a sensitive data center, or even use facial recognition to identify the perpetrators (when only legitimate users are able to access the data). Of course, these additional measures should only be applied to the most valuable information assets such as key intellectual property etc.

5   Conclusions

Artificial Intelligence is here to stay, and as described in this paper it is already well established across many steps of the cyber kill chain. Current benefits vary, from early threat recognition, through implementation of adaptable security solutions, to supporting attackers in their malicious activities. Additional use cases and increases in efficiency will further strengthen the role AI technology plays in the cybersecurity space, forcing both sides to adopt it even more.

The authors envision that in the near future, the use of AI will continue to be mostly visible during reconnaissance, infiltration, privilege escalation and data exfiltration phases, as this is where most of the current solutions operate. However, with cyber-security being a rapidly changing field it is possible that advancements will soon uncover new uses that will further support remaining steps. Our hope is that this paper, by segmenting commercial solutions based on actual use cases, can help decision makers when deploying AI capabilities in their environments. The authors also intend to continue exploring the topic through additional work as part of holistic cybersecurity improvement model for large organizations.

Aside from the fear of where the development of AI can lead to, there are also additional drawbacks that should be considered before implementation. First of all, these systems are not yet fully autonomous, so without a well qualified personnel they will not be able to function as intended. Secondly, potential data privacy issues can arise if an AI can fully leverage all of the available information. Thirdly, once an AI is capable of making its own choices, we lack any regulatory or ethical frameworks to guide the decision process, which in the security context could mean contacting the authorities or raising red flags that the company or operator of the system might not have advised at that time.

However, while many of the described solutions are already being deployed, the authors agree with the perspective of Walter Isaacson (biographer of the digital era innovators) that the hype related to Artificial Intelligence has not yet caught up fully to reality. So far, the best possible outcomes seem to be coming from a symbiotic rela-tionship between man and machine, or joint work where human capabilities are aug-mented and can guide the machine towards the solution in a much faster and detailed manner [36].

Acknowledgments. The project is financed by the Ministry of Science and Higher Education in Poland under the programme "Regional Initiative of Excellence" 2019–2022 project number 015/RID/2018/19 total funding amount 10 721 040,00 PLN.

References

1. World Economic Forum (WEF) - The Global Risks Report 2019. http://www3.weforum.org/docs/WEF_Global_Risks_Report_2019.pdf. Accessed 27 Jan 2019
2. United States Government Accountability Office (US-GAO) Information Security - Agencies Need to Improve Controls over Selected High-Impact Systems. https://www.gao.gov/assets/680/677293.pdf. Accessed 21 Jan 2019
3. Venkatachary, S.K., Prasad, J., Samikannu, R.: Cybersecurity and cyber terrorism - in energy sector – a review. J. Cyber Secur. Technol. **2**, 111–130 (2018)
4. Jasper, S.: Russia and ransomware - stop the act, not the actor. The National Interest, November 2017
5. Verizon Data Breach Investigations Report 10th Edition. http://www.verizonenterprise.com/verizon-insights-lab/dbir/tool/. Accessed 22 Jan 2019
6. Zetter, K.: Countdown to Zero Day. Stuxnet and the Launch of the World's First Digital Weapon. Random House, New York (2014)

7. Libicki, M., Senty, D., Pollak, J.: Hackers wanted: an examination of the cybersecurity labor market. RAND National Security Research Division, Santa Monica, California, USA (2014)
8. Baker, W., Jacobs, J.: Abstractions of security - mining a decade of RSA. In: RSA Conference, San Francisco (2018)
9. Forbes - What Is the Difference Between Artificial Intelligence and Machine Learning? https://www.forbes.com/sites/bernardmarr/2016/12/06/what-is-the-difference-between-artificial-intelligence-and-machine-learning/. Accessed 21 Mar 2019
10. Brashear, J., Shacklady, J., Sinclair, A.: The New Normal - Exponential Growth Powered by AI. Accenture Strategy Press (2016)
11. IBM QRadar Advisor with Watson. https://www.ibm.com/downloads/cas/52GBXLK8. Accessed 06 Mar 2019
12. Muppidi, S., Lodewijkx, K.: AI and cybersecurity – applications of artificial intelligence in security understanding and defending against adversarial AI. https://www.rsaconference.com/writable/presentations/file_upload/spo2-t07-ai_and_cybersecurity_-_applications_of_artificial_intelligence_in_security-understanding_and_defending_against_adversarial_ai.pdf. Accessed 18 Mar 2019
13. Wirkuttis, N., Klein, H.: Artificial intelligence in cybersecurity. Cyber Intell. Secur. 1(1), 103–119 (2017)
14. Goosen, R., Rontojannis, A., Deutscher, S., Rogg, J., Bohmayr, W., Mkrtchian, D.: Artificial intelligence is a threat to cybersecurity. it's also a solution. https://www.bcg.com/publications/2018/artificial-intelligence-threat-cybersecurity-solution.aspx. Accessed 21 May 2019
15. IBM Adversarial Robustness Toolbox (ART v0.7.0). https://github.com/IBM/adversarial-robustness-toolbox. Accessed 05 Apr 2019
16. Müller, V.C., Bostrom, N.: Future progress in artificial intelligence: a survey of expert opinion. In: Müller, V.C. (ed.) Fundamental Issues of Artificial Intelligence. SL, vol. 376, pp. 553–570. Springer, Cham (2016). https://doi.org/10.1007/978-3-319-26485-1_33
17. Dezeen – Christie's sells AI-created artwork painted using algorithm for $432,000. https://www.dezeen.com/2018/10/29/christies-ai-artwork-obvious-portrait-edmond-de-belamy-design/. Accessed 20 May 2019
18. Lockheed Martin – gaining the advantage – applying cyber kill chain methodology to network defense. https://lockheedmartin.com/content/dam/lockheed-martin/rms/documents/cyber/Gaining_the_Advantage_Cyber_Kill_Chain.pdf. Accessed 27 Feb 2019
19. Hospelhorn, S.: Varonis - what is the cyber kill chain and how to use it effectively. https://www.varonis.com/blog/cyber-kill-chain/. Accessed 07 Mar 2019
20. Mitnick, K.: Art of Invisibility - He World's Most Famous Hacker Teaches You How to Be Safe in the Age of Big Brother and Big Data. Little, Brown and Company, Boston (2017)
21. Recorded Future - How Artificial Intelligence Is Shaping the Future of Open Source Intelligence. https://www.recordedfuture.com/open-source-intelligence-future/. Accessed 29 Mar 2019
22. Kharkovyna, O.: Facial recognition and AI - latest developments and future directions. https://becominghuman.ai/facial-recognition-and-ai-latest-developments-and-future-directions-39d22201d88b. Accessed 14 Mar 2019
23. Balla, P.B., Jadhao, K.T.: IoT based facial recognition security system. In: 2018 International Conference on Smart City and Emerging Technology (ICSCET), India (2018)
24. Seymour, J., Tully, P.: Weaponizing data science for social engineering – automated E2E spear phishing on Twitter. In: DEFCON Conference (2016)
25. Zelonis, J., Balaouras, S., Cyr, M., Dostie, P.: The forrester MITRE ATT&CK evaluation guide (2019)

26. Heinemeyer, M.: Thwarting an invisible threat - how AI sniffs out the Ursnif trojan. https://www.darktrace.com/en/blog/thwarting-an-invisible-threat-how-ai-sniffs-out-the-ursnif-trojan/. Accessed 26 Mar 2019
27. Hitaj, B., Gasti, P., Ateniese, G., Perez-Cruz, F.: PassGAN - a deep learning approach for password guessing. In: NeurIPS 2018 Workshop on Security in Machine Learning (2018)
28. Sawa, Y., Bhakta, R., Harris, I.G., Hadnagy, C.: Detection of social engineering attacks through natural language processing of conversations. In: IEEE Tenth International Conference on Semantic Computing - ICSC (2016)
29. SentinelOne announces lateral movement detection engine. https://www.sentinelone.com/press/sentinelone-announces-lateral-movement-detection-engine-catch-unauthorized-network-movement-malicious-actors/. Accessed 04 Mar 2019
30. Ambre, A., Shekokarb, N.: Insider threat detection using log analysis and event correlation. Procedia Comput. Sci. **45**, 436–445 (2015)
31. Breier, J., Branišová, J.: A dynamic rule creation based anomaly detection method for identifying security breaches in log records. Wireless Pers. Commun. **94**, 497–511 (2017)
32. Kuriakose, J., Vinod, P.: Unknown metamorphic malware detection - modelling with fewer relevant features and robust feature selection techniques. IAENG Int. J. Comput. Sci. **42**, 139–151 (2015)
33. Stone, M.: Fight fire with fire: how AI plays a role in both stopping and committing DDoS attacks. https://securityintelligence.com/fight-fire-with-fire-how-ai-plays-a-role-in-both-stopping-and-committing-ddos-attacks/. Accessed 14 Mar 2019
34. Baruah, S.: Botnet detection: analysis of various techniques. Int. J. Comput. Intell. IoT **2**, 7 (2019)
35. Mc Carthy, S.M., Sinha, A., Tambe, M., Manadhata, P.: Data exfiltration detection and prevention: virtually distributed POMDPs for practically safer networks. In: Zhu, Q., Alpcan, T., Panaousis, E., Tambe, M., Casey, W. (eds.) GameSec 2016. LNCS, vol. 9996, pp. 39–61. Springer, Cham (2016). https://doi.org/10.1007/978-3-319-47413-7_3
36. Isaacson, W.: Innovators - How a Group of Hackers, Geniuses, and Geeks Created the Digital Revolution. Simon & Schuster, New York (2015)

Ontology-Based Representation of Crisis Response Situations

Walid Bannour[1]([⊠]), Ahmed Maalel[1,2],
and Henda Hajjami Ben Ghezala[1]

[1] National School of Computer Sciences, RIADI Laboratory,
University of Manouba, 2010 Manouba, Tunisia
walid.bannour@ensi-uma.tn, {ahmed.maalel,
henda.benghezala}@ensi.rnu.tn
[2] Higher Institute of Applied Science and Technology,
University of Sousse, 4003 Sousse, Tunisia

Abstract. Crisis situations are highlighted by the involvement of various emergency response organizations aiming at saving lives and reducing crisis impacts. However, this variety makes communication and information sharing challenges rise. The use of semantic Web technologies has been recognized as a suitable solution to address these challenges. This paper proposes an ontology-based representation of crisis situations providing a unified and sharable knowledge base between crisis response stakeholders. The developed ontology, named CROnto (Crisis Response Ontology), merges three pertinent aspects of the domain of crisis response. First, crisis features which represents crisis characteristics. Second, crisis effects which describes the various impacts that could be engendered by a disaster. Third, crisis response which represents strategic response plans. For the purpose of evaluating CROnto ontology, we adopt criteria-based evaluation approach.

Keywords: Knowledge representation · Ontology · Crisis response

1 Introduction

Natural disasters (e.g., South Asia tsunami, Katrina hurricane and Nepal earthquake) or Man-made disasters (e.g., 9/11 terrorist attack and Bhopal gas leak) are dynamic and complex events that consequently involve complicated management tasks. In such crisis situations, various stakeholders from different response organizations need to work together simultaneously aiming at reducing crisis impacts. Information sharing and coordination are key factors to effectively respond to a crisis [1]. Nevertheless, each response organization (e.g., fire department, medical units and Police) has its own domain vocabulary and its proper information system. This raises information exchange and communication challenges since the semantics of data could be heterogeneous [2]. For instance, the word "vehicle" could mean a "fighting truck" or "fire engine" for firefighters contrary to medical staff that use the word "vehicle" to design an "ambulance". Thus, there should be a common definition of concepts and relationships between these concepts to overcome semantic interoperability problem

© Springer Nature Switzerland AG 2019
N. T. Nguyen et al. (Eds.): ICCCI 2019, LNAI 11684, pp. 417–427, 2019.
https://doi.org/10.1007/978-3-030-28374-2_36

[2, 3]. In order to resolve this issue, many researchers has suggested the use of ontologies since they provide a unified explanation of concepts and relationships of a domain of interest on the one hand, and make them sharable between various users in a machine-readable format on the other hand [2, 4]. Regarding crisis response domain, ontologies can improve coordination and interaction between the involved responders and can also facilitate emergency data integration and querying [5].

In this paper, we propose an ontology for crisis response domain, named CROnto, which provides a common and unified vocabulary to overcome communication and information exchange problems and make knowledge sharing easy between crisis response stakeholders. In addition, the proposed ontology aims to assist crisis managers in decision making process. In fact, it constitutes the unified knowledge base for our future crisis response decision support system.

Our proposed ontology covers the following main aspects: (1) crisis features which describes crisis characteristics, (2) crisis effects which represents the various impacts that a disaster could engender on different vulnerable objects and (3) crisis response which represents response plans, their corresponding tasks, responders, their related actions and the needed resources. More specifically, crisis features and effects are represented via domain ontology, while crisis response strategies are described via task ontology. Regarding ontology development process, we adopted the step-by-step ontology development process proposed by Haghighi et al. [5] which is outlined in Sect. 3. Domain knowledge has been acquired from the most prominent existing models in literature in the field of crisis management and with the help of 3 experts from the fire department of Mahdia, Tunisia. With regard to CROnto ontology evaluation, we adopted criteria-based evaluation approach [6] to verify its design and content.

The rest of this paper is organized as follows: existing prominent ontologies in literature representing crisis management domain knowledge are outlined in Sect. 2. CROnto ontology development process is detailed in Sect. 3. The evaluation of our ontological model is presented in Sect. 4. Finally, Sect. 5 concludes the paper and presents our future work.

2   Related Work

The use of semantic Web technologies has grown in the domain of emergency management since it is suitable to tackle interoperability and information sharing challenges [2]. Several ontological models have been proposed in the literature to overcome these issues. Kontopoulos et al. [7] proposed an ontology for climate crisis management in order to facilitate decision support during climate-related disasters. Their constructed ontology constitutes the knowledge base of their decision support system developed in the context of the beAWARE EU-funded project [8] that aims to support natural disaster forecasting and management. Their proposed ontology mainly covers the following aspects: crisis representation, crisis impacts, sensor analysis and first responders' unit allocations. They did not represent physical resources needed to perform a mission. Besides, their developed ontology only covers natural disasters types.

"EmergencyFire" ontology proposed by Bitencourt et al. [9] represent emergency response protocols related to fire disasters in buildings. The aim of their work is to contribute to the tactical and strategic planning of involved organizations. With the aid of a number of experts from the Military Department of Firefighters in Bahia State in Brazil, the authors included various concepts specific to fire emergency domain such as fire classes and combustion elements.

Barros et al. [10] developed EDXL-RESCUER ontology which is considered as the conceptual model of the RESCUER (Reliable and Smart Crowdsourcing Solution for Emergency and Crisis Management) project [11] that aims to support security forces in emergency situations. The authors developed EDXL-RESCUER ontology to resolve interoperability problems between legacy systems and the RESCUER project.

Haghighi et al. [5] proposed a Domain Ontology for Mass Gatherings (DO4MG) that constitutes the knowledge base of their intelligent decision support system in medical emergencies for mass gatherings. The DO4MG ontology aims to resolve inconsistencies and to increase communication efficiency between medical emergency personnel. Their ontological model contains particular concepts related to mass gathering domain such as the type of gathering, the environmental factors and emergency management planning.

MOAC (Management Of a Crisis Vocabulary) [12], a relevant lightweight vocabulary that provides terms in order to let practitioners and professionals link crisis management activities together as Linked Data. The reason behind creating MOAC vocabulary is to publish humanitarian agencies data as open source instead of being kept in spreadsheets, PDFs and word documents. To achieve this work, many contributions have been made by different stakeholders: the Global Shelter Cluster [13], the United Nations Office for the Coordination of Humanitarian Affairs (UN OCHA) [14] and the Ushahidi platform [15].

To effectively exchange information between organizations involved in disaster management that have different vocabularies at human language and IT levels, Babitski et al. [16] developed a set of ontologies that cover the description of damages, resources and the connection between them. Their core ontology is considered as a part of a prototype that aims to integrate information from different stakeholders.

Bénaben et al. [17] proposed a prominent UML-based metamodel for crisis situations as part of the French ISyCri project. This latter aims to support interoperability between crisis response stakeholders' information systems and to coordinate their activities through a collaborative process. Their built metamodel is composed of 3 packages: crisis characterization which describes a crisis, studied system which refers to objects affected by a crisis and the treatment system that represents crisis response procedures and describes collaborative processes. This reference metamodel was further translated into an OWL-DL (OWL-Description Language) ontology.

None of the above mentioned works has proposed an ontological model to represent crisis response strategies. This motivated us to develop domain ontology to represent crisis features and effects and task ontology to describe crisis response strategies, thus contributing to strategic planning.

3   CROnto Ontology Development

Since modeling crisis situations requires joint efforts of experienced persons with different viewpoints, we have adopted a collaborative ontology design approach [18]. In addition, aiming at supporting crisis managers in decision making process, we have relied on our personal imagination and creativity, thus following inspirational ontology design approach [18].

Regarding CROnto ontology development methodology, we have followed the ontology development process proposed by Haghighi et al. [5] (see Fig. 1) since it contains the common steps of the most known ontology development methodologies in the literature [5]. The next subsections detail CROnto ontology process phases.

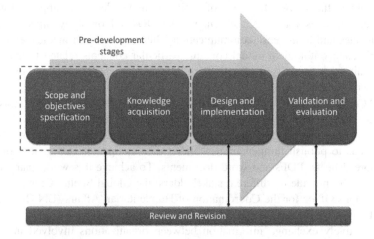

Fig. 1. Ontology development and evaluation process adapted from [5]

3.1   Pre-development Stages of CROnto

Scope and Objectives Specification. The scope of our ontology is the crisis response domain. Therefore, the main users of our ontology are involved emergency response organizations such as civil protection department (i.e., fire department), emergency medical services (EMS), Police and other crisis response teams.

The main objectives of our ontology are:

- Specification of a common vocabulary between different stakeholders. Due to the fact that every response organization has its own vocabulary, CROnto ontology constitutes a unified knowledge base that aims to overcome interoperability problems and to enhance interaction and communication between these various organizations.
- Enhancing crisis managers decision making quality during disaster response phase. Actually, CROnto ontology constitutes the knowledge model on which our future intelligent decision support system reasons. This latter aims to improve crisis

managers' situation awareness and to suggest up-to-date strategic response plans. Integrating CROnto ontology into such a system can help to overcome terminology inconsistencies between the various system users i.e., responders.

Knowledge Acquisition. After identifying the scope and the objectives of our ontology, we move to the second step of the pre-development stage i.e., knowledge acquisition. This step includes exploration, extraction and derivation of knowledge from the domain of interest. Many resources have been used to acquire domain knowledge which is in our case the crisis response domain. Regarding concepts, we used terminologies from prominent existing ontologies e.g., [10], [13] and metamodels e.g., [17, 19] from literature. The list of the extracted concepts is depicted in Table 1. With regard to taxonomy, we used SoKNOS ontology [16] to categorize resources and the models of [7, 17] to categorize vulnerable objects exposed to risk.

In addition, in order to acquire domain terminology, we referred to a public report related to disaster risk reduction from the United Nations General Assembly [20], a glossary of humanitarian terms from the World Health Organization (WHO) [21] and government manuals such as the guide to emergency management of the US Federal Emergency Management Agency (FEMA) [22]. Besides the resources mentioned above, we gathered domain knowledge from experts who work in the field of crisis management. We made a first interview with 3 experts working in the regional fire department of Mahdia in Tunisia.

Table 1. List of extracted crisis response concepts from literature

Source	Concepts
Bénaben et al. [17]	Risk, Good, Natural site
Kontopoulos et al. [7]	Asset, Living being, Educational facility
Babitski et al. [16]	Accessory, Clothing, Device, Weapon, Material, Pharmaceutical product
Othman et al. [19]	Exposure

3.2 Design and Implementation

CROnto ontology is implemented with Protégé 5.5.0 ontology editor [23] and is saved as an OWL (Web Ontology Language) file [24]. OWL is a common ontology language which defines and describes classes, subclasses and properties i.e., object properties, datatype properties and annotation properties. In the following subsections, we present our ontological model in relation to the key aspects of the crisis response domain knowledge i.e., crisis features, crisis effects and crisis response. For reasons of brevity, not all object properties and datatype properties will be discussed.

Crisis Features Representation. The ongoing disaster is represented by the class *"Disaster"* (see Fig. 2). A disaster could lead to another disaster. Each disaster has a type defined by the class *"Disaster_Type"*. This latter has 2 subclasses: *"ManMade_Disaster"* which represents any type of disaster that results from human decisions and *"Natural_disaster"* which represents any type of disaster resulting from natural causes. For instance, the last disaster that hit Tunisia territories (*Disaster18_CapBon*) is of type *Flood*. Besides, each disaster has a risk factor represented by the class *"Risk"*. More specifically, a risk is defined by the probability of occurrence and the severity level of a disaster. These 2 features are represented by *"Disaster_Occurence_probability"* and *"Disaster_Severity_Level"* datatype properties. Moreover, each disaster has one or more locations defined by the class *"Location"*. It contains *"Longitude"* and *"Latitude"* datatype properties. For example, the aforementioned flood disaster hit the regions of *Nabeul, Beni Khalled* and *Bouargoub*. In addition, each location has specific weather condition parameters represented via *"Weather_Condition_Parameter"* class. This latter is subdivided into 4 subclasses: *"Wind_Direction"*, *"Wind_Speed"*, *"Temperature"* and *"Precipitation"*. For instance, the region of *Nabeul* has Precipitation_1, an individual of the class *"Precipitation"* as a weather condition parameter.

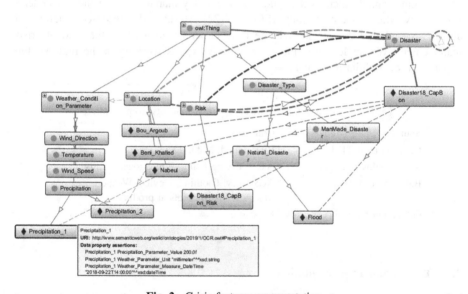

Fig. 2. Crisis features representation

Crisis Impacts Representation. The strike of a disaster engenders multiple impacts on various vulnerable objects. In our ontology, crisis effects are modeled by the class *"Impact"* and crisis vulnerable objects are modeled via the class *"Exposure"* (see Fig. 3). Since there are various kinds of impacts, we have modeled them into 2 subclasses: *"Casualties"* and *"Damage"*. Regarding *"Casualties"* class, it refers to any kind of impact that could be produced on a human or an animal such as *Death* and *Injury*. Concerning *"Damage"* class, it represents all various physical harms that could affect a non-living organism such as *"Collapsed_Structure"*, *"Blocked_Road"* and

"Compromised_Bridge". Here we note that we used MOAC terminology [12] to represent *"Damage"* class individuals.

With regard to the class *"Exposure"*, it has "Asset" and "Living_Being" as subclasses. "Asset" describes non-living organisms and could be either *"Good"* (e.g., *"Bridge"*, *"Dam"* and *"Road"*) or *"Natural_Site"* (e.g., *"Forest"*, *"River"* and *"Sea"*). However, "Living_Being" describes living organisms and could be either *"Person"* or *"Animal"*. For more clarity in Fig. 3, we have surrounded all classes and instances related to crisis exposure with a blue line and those related with crisis impacts with a red line (see the colored version of the paper).

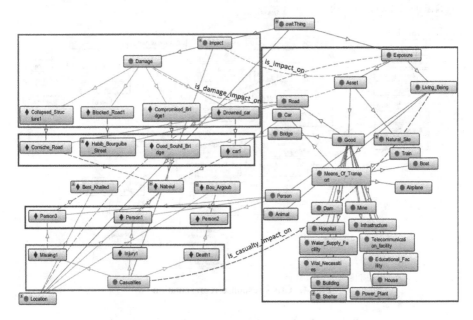

Fig. 3. Crisis effects representation (Color figure online)

"Is_impact_on" object property relates *"Impact"* class (Domain) and *"Exposure"* class (Range). More specifically, since we modeled both impact types and exposure categories, we divised *"is_impact_on"* object property into 2 subproperties: *"is_casualty_impact_on"* which relates "Casualties" class (Domain) and *"Living_being"* (Range) and *"is_damage_impact_on"* which links *"Damage"* class (Domain) to *"Asset"* class (Range). For instance, *Death1* is a casualty impact on *Person1* and *Compromised_bridge* is a damage impact on *Oued_Souhil_Bridge*.

Crisis Response Representation. Crisis response strategies are modeled as a task ontology [25] since it describes problem solving structure and can be shared. As shown in Fig. 4, a disaster Impact (class *"Impact"*) triggers (object property *"triggers"*) a response plan (class *"Response_Plan"*). Moreover, this latter describes a set of tasks (class *"Task_of_Plan"*) to perform in order to reduce crisis effects. Each task involves an emergency response organization (class *"Responder"*), an action to perform (class

"Action_of_task") and a set of required resources (class *"Resource"*). More specifically, a responder performs an action (via object property *"performs_action"*) which
requires a set of resources (via object property *"requires_resource"*). For instance, as
shown in Fig. 4, Evacuation Plan (*"Response_Plan"*) has set of tasks e.g.,
Evac_Task_6 (*"Task_of_Plan"*) which involves Civil Protection Brigade of Nabeul
(*"Responder"*). This latter performs Victim Transportation action (*"Action_of_Task"*)
which requires Lorry and Rescue Helicopter resources (*"Resource"*).

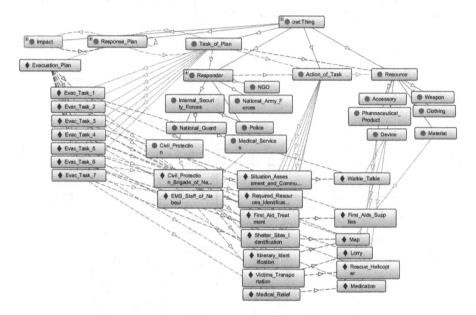

Fig. 4. Crisis response representation

Regarding *"Responder"* class, it contains *"Internal_Security_Forces"*, *"Nationa-
l_Army_Forces"*, *"Medical_Services"* and *"NGO"* i.e., Non-Governmental Organizations subclasses. Internal security forces consist of civil protection forces i.e., fire
brigades (class *"Civil_Protection"*), Police agents (class *"Police"*) and National Guard
brigades (class *"National Guard"*). With regard to resources, they are classified into 6
categories: *"Device"*, *"Material"*, *"Accessory"*, *"weapon"*, *"clothing"* and *"Phar-
maceutical_product"* [16].

4   CROnto Ontology Evaluation

Several ontology evaluation approaches have been proposed in literature to assess
whether the ontology has properly represented certain domain knowledge. Studying the
most common evaluation approaches has conducted us to choose the criteria-based
evaluation approach [6, 26, 27]. This approach uses a set of criteria to verify ontology
design and content. We selected a list of criteria among those which are outlined in the

work of Yu et al. [6]. These criteria are: clarity, consistency, conciseness and correctness. The next subsection details each criterion.

4.1   Clarity

Gruber [26] declared that the defined ontology terms "should effectively communicate the intended meaning" eliminating any subjectivity or ambiguity aspects. The author added that all defined terms should be formally defined and these definitions should be documented in natural language. In our context, the feedbacks of the interviewed domain experts have helped us to verify ontology clarity and more specifically to omit or replace any ambiguous term. For instance, we had "Actor" as a key concept which represents emergency response organizations. During an interview with civil protection agents, they agreed that this term does not deliver its intended meaning and should be replaced with the term *"Responder"*. Regarding formal definition of ontology terms, most of CROnto ontology terms have their formal definitions since they were extracted from literature and from government manuals. For example, the term *"Disaster"* is defined as "A serious disruption of the functioning of society, causing widespread human, material or environmental losses" [28].

4.2   Consistency

Consistency or coherence [26] means that ontology concepts should have logical consistency. Any contradiction between explicit or inferred axioms and their definitions makes the ontology incoherent [26]. As an example, the class *"Shelter"* which is defined as any public building that could be temporary converted into a refuge during disasters was a subclass of both *"Asset"* and *"Resource"*. However, the inferences were inconsistent because resources are defined as items proper to responders in order to use them to perform response actions. Nevertheless, it is not the case for the *"Shelter"* concept. So, we removed it from "Resource" subclasses.

4.3   Conciseness

According to Gómez-Pérez [27], an ontology is concise if it doesn't include unnecessary or useless definitions besides explicit redundancies between definitions. For instance, regarding CROnto ontology, it included 2 classes "Infrastructure_Damage" and "Vital_Lines_Damage" as subclasses of the class *"Impact"*. "Infrastructure_Damage" represented all damages that harm the infrastructure (e.g., collapsed structure and unstable structure) and "Vital_Lines_Damage" described any damage that hits water supply facilities or electricity power plants. Since we realized that categorizing damages is unnecessary and useless for our ontology, we have melted "Infrastructure_Damage" and "Vital_Lines_Damage" classes into one class *"Damage"*.

4.4   Correctness

Correctness refers to the correspondence of real world entities and properties with ontology concepts and properties [6]. This criterion has been carefully considered in

CROnto ontology development and validation. As an example, domain experts' feedback has led us to add the concept *"Weather_Condition_Parameter"* since it constitutes a key factor in crisis response operations. More specifically, response tasks depend on weather condition parameters. In other words, it may increase the complexity of a crisis, thus increases response tasks complexity.

5 Conclusion

This paper presents an ontology for crisis response domain. The main objectives of the proposed ontological model are twofold: overcoming semantic interoperability problem between different emergency response organizations and providing a unified and sharable knowledge base. More specifically, CROnto ontology represents 3 main aspects of the crisis response domain: crisis features, crisis effects and crisis response strategies aiming at contributing to strategic planning. The resulting ontology was evaluated based on criteria-based approach to check its design and content.

Regarding future work, CROnto ontology actually constitutes the backbone of our future crisis response decision support system. The objectives of this latter are twofold: (1) enhancing crisis managers' situation awareness by providing up-to-date situational crisis information through ontology querying mechanisms and (2) suggesting up-to-date and dynamic response plans. The next step is to propose a semi-automatic ontology population method. This step will be performed via a mobile crowdsourcing solution adding a new contribution to our work.

References

1. Diniz, V.B., Borges, M.R., Gomes, J.O., Canós, J.H.: Decision making support in emergency response. In: Encyclopedia of decision making and decision support technologies. pp. 184–191. IGI Global (2008)
2. Liu, S., Brewster, C., Shaw, D.: Ontologies for crisis management: a review of state of the art in ontology design and usability. In: ISCRAM (2013)
3. Fan, Z., Zlatanova, S.: Exploring ontologies for semantic interoperability of data in emergency response. Appl. Geomat. **3**, 109–122 (2011)
4. Grimm, S., Abecker, A., Völker, J., Studer, R.: Ontologies and the semantic web. In: Domingue, J., Fensel, D., Hendler, J.A. (eds.) Handbook of Semantic Web Technologies, pp. 507–579. Springer, Heidelberg (2011). https://doi.org/10.1007/978-3-540-92913-0_13
5. Haghighi, P.D., Burstein, F., Zaslavsky, A., Arbon, P.: Development and evaluation of ontology for intelligent decision support in medical emergency management for mass gatherings. Decis. Support Syst. **54**, 1192–1204 (2013)
6. Yu, J., Thom, J.A., Tam, A.: Evaluating ontology criteria for requirements in a geographic travel domain. In: Meersman, R., Tari, Z. (eds.) On the Move to Meaningful Internet Systems. LNCS, pp. 1517–1534. Springer, Heidelberg (2005). https://doi.org/10.1007/11575801_36
7. Kontopoulos, E., et al.: Ontology-based representation of crisis management procedures for climate events. In: Boersma, K., Tomaszewski, B. (eds.) ISCRAM 2018 Conference Proceedings – 15th International Conference on Information Systems for Crisis Response and Management, pp. 1064–1073. Rochester Institute of Technology, Rochester (2018)

8. beAWARE Project Homepage. https://beaware-project.eu/
9. Bitencourt, K., Durão, F.A., Mendonça, M., Santana, L.L.B.D.S.: An ontological model for fire emergency situations. IEICE Trans. Inf. Syst. **101**, 108–115 (2018)
10. Barros, R., Kislansky, P., Salvador, L., Almeida, R., Breyer, M., Pedraza, L.G.: EDXL-RESCUER ontology: conceptual model for semantic integration. In: ISCRAM (2015)
11. RESCUER Project Homepage. http://www.rescuer-project.org/
12. Limbu, M., Wang, D., Kauppinen, T., Ortmann, J.: Management of a crisis (MOAC) vocabulary specification. http://observedchange.com/moac/ns/
13. Shelter Cluster Homepage. https://www.sheltercluster.org/
14. UNOCHA Homepage. https://www.unocha.org/
15. USHAHIDI Homepage. https://www.ushahidi.com/
16. Babitski, G., Probst, F., Hoffmann, J., Oberle, D.: Ontology design for information integration in disaster management. GI Jahrestag. **154**, 3120–3134 (2009)
17. Bénaben, F., Hanachi, C., Lauras, M., Couget, P., Chapurlat, V.: A metamodel and its ontology to guide crisis characterization and its collaborative management. In: Presented at the Proceedings of the 5th International Conference on Information Systems for Crisis Response and Management (ISCRAM), Washington, DC, USA, May 2008
18. Holsapple, C.W., Joshi, K.D.: A collaborative approach to ontology design. Commun. ACM **45**, 42–47 (2002)
19. Othman, S.H., Beydoun, G., Sugumaran, V.: Development and validation of a disaster management metamodel (DMM). Inf. Process. Manag. **50**, 235–271 (2014). https://doi.org/10.1016/j.ipm.2013.11.001
20. UN General Assembly: Report of the open-ended intergovernmental expert working group on indicators and terminology relating to disaster risk reduction, p. 41. UN General Assembly, New York, USA (2016)
21. World Health Organization: ReliefWeb glossary of humanitarian terms (2008)
22. Blanchard, B.W.: Guide to emergency management and related terms, definitions, concepts, acronyms, organizations, programs, guidance, executive orders and legislation: a tutorial on emergency management, broadly defined, past and present. Federal Emergency Management Agency, USA (2008)
23. Protégé: A free, open-source ontology editor and framework for building intelligent systems (2013)
24. McGuinness, D.L., Van Harmelen, F.: OWL web ontology language overview. W3C Recomm. **10** (2004)
25. Mizoguchi, R., Vanwelkenhuysen, J., Ikeda, M.: Task ontology for reuse of problem solving knowledge. Very Large Knowl. Bases Knowl. Build. Knowl. Shar. **46**, 45 (1995)
26. Gruber, T.R.: Toward principles for the design of ontologies used for knowledge sharing? Int. J. Hum. Comput. Stud. **43**, 907–928 (1995). https://doi.org/10.1006/ijhc.1995.1081
27. Gómez-Pérez, A.: Towards a framework to verify knowledge sharing technology. Expert Syst. Appl. **11**, 519–529 (1996)
28. Mohamed Shaluf, I.: Disaster types. Disaster Prev. Manag. Int. J. **16**, 704–717 (2007)

Software Quality Improvement by Application of a Component-Based Software Meta-Architecture

Tomasz Skalniak[1] , Artur Rot[2(✉)] , and Wieslawa Gryncewicz[2]

[1] Leipzig University, Leipzig, Germany
skalniak@wifa.uni-leipzig.de
[2] Wroclaw University of Economics, Wroclaw, Poland
{artur.rot,wieslawa.gryncewicz}@ue.wroc.pl

Abstract. Designing software is a complex process which requires a lot of knowledge and experience. Every software has a high-level architecture which can be represented as a set of taken design decisions. Software meta-architectures, architectural styles, and reference models are commonly used tools which help to shape the software architectures by delivering sets of already taken, and validated design decisions. The STCBMER is a component-based software meta-architecture founded on a set of simple pieces of architectural knowledge, called architectural principles. The authors of this publication have defined the STCBMER and its principles in previous works. The main aim and the contribution of this paper is to look for a correlation between a component-based software meta-architecture (STCBMER) and software quality attributes.

Keywords: Meta-Architecture · Software quality · Software improvement · Reference models

1 Introduction

All the existing software systems are built after taking a set of design decisions [4]. A set of taken design decisions is one of the ways of how to represent a software architecture [1, 5]. The software architecting process [2] is a complex, iterative process of taking and documenting the design decisions. The taken design decisions can be wrong [1], and if not noticed fast enough, the costs of handling the bad consequences can be high. That's why concrete software architectures are often based on more abstract models: meta-architectures, software reference models, or sets of architectural styles. The high-level Software Meta-Architectures (SMA) are usually based on the well-known, approved by practitioners, sometimes standardized pieces of Architectural Knowledge [3]. Pieces of the Architectural Knowledge can be captured as simple architectural principles (AP), guidelines, or rules [6–8]. Selecting concrete APs as basis for a SMA means taking design decisions. If a SMA is validated and proved, it brings to a concrete software architecture (SA) a set of already taken design decisions, this means that the software architecting process is simpler, and the risk of taking wrong choices is smaller. Making design decisions means choosing how to resolve a problem, how to model a software

© Springer Nature Switzerland AG 2019
N. T. Nguyen et al. (Eds.): ICCCI 2019, LNAI 11684, pp. 428–439, 2019.
https://doi.org/10.1007/978-3-030-28374-2_37

element in a concrete way. Design decisions are taken after having many potential choices. Not always there is only one correct choice, usually decision of which choice to select is based on a concrete case's context. For example, sometimes software security is more important than the user experience. Choices selected by taking design decisions are corresponding with concrete software requirements. Some of the software requirements are quality-related. To describe the needed software quality levels, quality software models can be used. Software quality models are usually "multi-dimensional" in the sense that there are different types (dimensions, attributes) of software quality. Sometimes focusing on achieving one concrete software quality attribute means decreasing a second one, usually choosing between different software quality attributes means a trade-off. The aim and contribution of this paper is to show a correlation between concrete APs of a concrete SMA and the software quality. Knowing the correlation between the SMA and its APs and the different types/attributes of software quality can make a decision of choosing the right SMA more reliable, secure and clear.

2 Related Research

Component-based software meta-architectures, architectural principles, software complexity and software quality are the research fields of the authors of this publication [7–9, 12]. This research paper is a continuation of the previous authors works. The authors of the publication have successfully applied and validated the research artifacts from the previous articles (including the STCBMER meta-architecture and its principles, which were described in [8] in details) in various real-life contexts, in particular in the field of the electronic service markets, independent living, quality of life, etc. The current research document brings a new contribution to the software meta-architectures and software reference models by showing a correlation between the well-known elements of architectural knowledge (architectural principles) and software quality attributes. The research problem of creating the right, modern software meta-architectures and reference models is easier to approach if the correlation between the meta-architectures and the software quality is known. This correlation was expected, but never before described for the STCBMER. Knowing which attributes of software quality is supported by a concrete software meta-architecture is a great value for the software architects, researchers and practitioners. This knowledge is especially needed when it comes to select a concrete software meta-architecture to build a concrete software solution. In addition, the found, strong correlation between the architectural knowledge (in the form of architectural principles) and the software quality is an additional proof showing a great value of having the architectural knowledge which was retrieved, documented and made public available. Even the simplest rules seem to be strictly connected with software quality which is always an important aspect when it comes to design and build software. In the modern, complex software systems, in times of distributed software, cloud computing, software virtualization, systems integration, service-oriented, resultant architectures [9], platform and infrastructure as a service approaches, there is an important need of building new, modern meta-architectures based on good sets of architectural principles. The current state of the architectural knowledge is getting bigger and bigger with the growth of complexity of the software engineering and architectural models and new principles.

3 STCBMER as a Component-Based Software Meta-Architecture

3.1 STCBMER Layers

The authors of this publication, together with other co-authors, in a series of already published papers, have proposed and validated the STCBMER (Smart Client-Template-Controller-Bean-Mediator-Entity-Resource) [7–9] as a SMA for component-based, service-oriented software. STCBMER is represented as a set of layered, high-level components, theirs relationships (graph representation), and a set of underlying design decisions captured as simple APs.

The Fig. 1 presents the STCBMER layers, components, and the components relationships. The STCBMER model contains data layer (Utility Data Sources), Business Logic layer, Application Logic layer, and the Smart Client Logic Layer. The Utility Data Sources is a component which stores all the data of different kinds, e.g.: relational databases, non-relational databases, data files, web-based data sources, etc. The Business Logic layer contains components which are needed to store, process and expose business entities. The Application Logic layer contains components which together enable to create an application, including connecting to the Business Layer, processing application entities, handling UI and potentially serving web resources if application supports web environment. The Smart Client Logic layer contains components creating a web application which can be run in a web browser. All the STCBMER layers communicate with each other based on the REST interface [10]. The layered STCBMER architecture stack enables to separate applications, business logic and data. For example, one Business Logic layer can be prepared to serve the business logic to many applications (Application Layers).

3.2 STCBMER Architectural Principles

The STCBMER meta-architecture is not only a graph of interconnected components, but also a set of APs presented in Table 1. They were precisely described in previous authors work (see [8]).

The DDP (Downward Dependency Principle) states that the main dependency structure is top-down. Objects in higher layers depend on objects in lower layers. Therefore, lower layers should be more stable (should changeless) than higher layers. Interfaces, abstract classes, dominant classes and similar devices should encapsulate stable layers in the way that there is possibility to extend them when it is needed.

The UNP (Upward Dependency Principle) supports low coupling in a bottom-up communication between layers achieved by asynchronous communication (based on event processing). Objects in higher layers play a role of subscribers, sometimes called as observers, for state changes in lower layers. When an object (publisher) in a lower layer changes its state, it sends notifications to its subscribers. The subscribers can also communicate with the publisher so that their states are synchronized with its state.

The NCP (Neighbor Communication Principle) principle limits the DDP principle. It guarantees that objects can communicate with non-neighboring layers. It is possible only by utilizing chains of message passing through neighboring layers. To enforce the

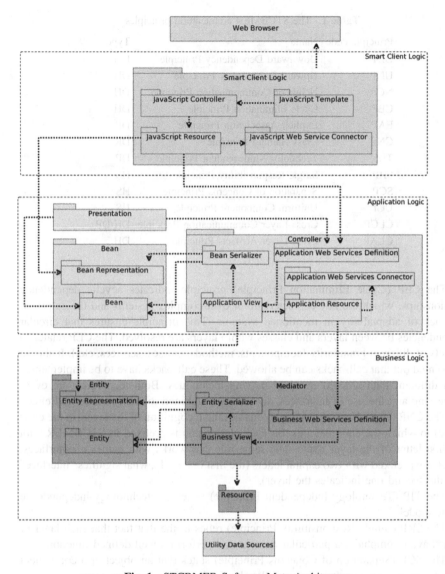

Fig. 1. STCBMER Software Meta-Architecture

NCP principle, the message transferred between distant objects uses forwarding or delegation. It can be also observed that in multicompound cases, a special acquaintance layer can be applied to group interfaces to assist in collaboration that engages non-neighboring layers.

The EAP (Explicit Association Principle) presents permitted message, which is transferred between the objects. The EAP refers to the associations, which are established on directly collaborating classes of objects. Associations resulting from DDP are unidirectional (otherwise they would create circular dependencies). It is worth to emphasize that not all associations between classes are due to message transferring.

Table 1. The STCBMER architectural principles

Principle code	Name	Type
DDP	Downward Dependency Principle	DH
UNP	Upward Dependency Principle	DH
NCP	Neighbor Communication Principle	DH
CEP	Cycle Elimination Principle	DH
EAP	Explicit Association Principle	DP
CNP	Class Naming Principle	DR
TIP	Technology-Independent Principle	DP
SRP	Single Responsibility Principle	HS
SCP	Separation of Concerns Principle	HS
UCP	Uniform Component Principle	HS
CLCP	Cross-Layer Communication Principle	DH/DP
CLAP	Cross-Layer Artifacts Principle	DH

The CEP (Cycle Elimination Principle) principle indicates acyclic dependency relationships, which are key characteristic of over-complex systems and the culprit of the lack of adaptability in mentioned systems. This principle ensures that circular dependencies between layers and classes within layers are resolved. The CEP relates to objects of different granularity (components, methods, classes, services, etc.). It should be pointed out that call-backs can be allowed. These call-backs have to be implemented with different than straight message passing techniques. Both techniques are event processing and the use of interfaces, sometimes combined to achieve a desired effect.

The CNP (Class Naming Principle) enables the recognition of the layer (in the class name) to which the class belongs. So each class name is prefixed in STCBMER with the first letter of the layer name. The same rule can works with names of interfaces, which are prefixed with two capital letters (the first one is "I", what signifies "interface" and the second one indicates the layer).

The TIP (Technology-Independent Principle) states the technology-independence of the model.

The SRP (Single Responsibility Principle) relies to the that fact that each layer or pillar have to emphasis a particular domain and perform a well-defined function.

The SCP (Separation of Concerns Principle) states that an object or a component have to be independent from internal details of other objects or components.

The UCP (Uniform Component Principle) states that mixing different types of components in the same logical layer is not allowed.

The CLCP (Cross-Layer Communication Principle) states that it should be clear how components communicate with each other, and that the model has to be created on an open structure, taking into account industry best practices.

The CLAP (Cross-Layer Artifacts Principle) states that crosscutting code have to be separated from the system as far as possible and grouped in pillars.

The STCBMER architectural principles are attached to four AP classes [8]. Dependencies Handling (DH) describes dependencies which can be formed between architecture elements. Development Rules (DR) presents the way of development and maintenance of the system's code. Holonic Structure (HS) refers to the nature of the model's elements and it shows how the architecture decomposes to these elements. Design Patterns (DP) includes all design patterns and best practices, which influence the possible shape of the architecture.

4 Software Quality Model

SQuaRE ISO/EIC 25010 International Standard [11] is a "System and software quality model" which defines software quality as a multidimensional value. SQuaRE defines two main types of systems and software quality: "quality in use" and "product quality".

Table 2. The SQuaRE product quality model

Quality attribute	Sub-attributes
Functional suitability	Functional completeness, Functional correctness, Functional appropriateness
Performance efficiency	Time behavior, Resource utilization, Capacity
Compatibility	Co-existence, Interoperability
Usability	Appropriateness recognizability, Learnability, Operability, User error protection, User interface aesthetics, Accessibility
Reliability	Maturity, Availability, Fault tolerance, Recoverability
Security	Confidentiality, Integrity, Non-repudiation, Accountability, Authenticity
Maintainability	Modularity, Reusability, Analysability, Modifiability, Testability
Portability	Adaptability, Installability, Replaceability

The quality in use model composed of 5 characteristics (and few sub-characteristics) that communicate the outcome of interaction when a product is used in a particular context of use. The product quality model is composed of 8 characteristics (and few sub-characteristics) connected with static properties of software and dynamic properties of the computer system (see Table 2). The scope of this publication is limited only to the product quality, quality in use model is not taken into consideration.

5 STCBMER Architectural Principles and the Supported Quality Attributes

As shown in Table 1, the STCBMER architectural principles are of different classes. Some of them are regulating the rules of possible dependencies between architecture components (DH), some are related to the implementation (DR), some are the rules of what the architecture components should contain, and how to decompose the system logic, and finally some of the architectural principles are just well known, simple design patterns, and best practices. The architectural principles are of different kinds, and applying some of them can strengthen or weaken concrete software quality attributes. Usually a design decision as a step in software architecting process is a trade-off – in concrete cases, some software quality attributes are more important than others, and usually improving one means decreasing other.

Looking at definitions of the SQuaRE quality attributes, and on definitions of the STCBMER architectural principles, correlation between applying concrete principles, and strengthening concrete quality attributes can be observed.

The CNP gives possibility to recognize the layer in the class name to which the class belongs. To this aim, each class name is prefixed in with the first letter of the layer name. Such a definition of CNP very concretely relates to Maintainability defined in SQuaRE as "a degree of effectiveness and efficiency with which a product or system can be modified by the intended maintainers". The more readable and understandable the code is (CNP), the easier and more with higher efficiency a product or system can be modified. It means that just by definition the CNP supports the SQuaRE Maintainability.

The CEP principle says that no cycles are allowed in the graph representation of the SMA. Figure 2 presents a simple cycle between architecture components. Between the A and B components, there are two dependencies defined: A depends on B, and B depends on A. It means that after a change in A component, B component can behave differently since it depends on the new implementation of A. The change in B can be not wanted, in worst case can introduce a bug or maybe even make B not buildable or not deployable. In such a case, (and only if the not wanted effect in the B component is noticed on time) a fix to the B component should be introduced. But the fix in the B component can introduce a not wanted change in the A component. It means that having a cycle in SMA always makes stability of the system as a hard to achieve quality, especially after introducing changes in the components from the cycle. CEP means having less probability that a change in one component can influence a second one. Since SQuaRE Modifiability is defined as "a degree to which a product or system can be effectively and efficiently modified without introducing defects or degrading existing product quality", by definition the CEP heavily supports the SQuaRE Modifiability quality attribute. If circular dependencies were acceptable in a SMA, efficiency of identifying parts to be modified to introduce a change would be lower since circular dependencies can introduce infinite loop of dependencies. Since SQuaRE Analysability is defined as "a degree of effectiveness and efficiency with which it is possible to identify parts to be modified", the CEP supports the SQuaRE Analysability. Supporting Modifiability and Analysability means - by definition of Modifiability as a sub-attribute – supporting the SQuaRE Maintainability.

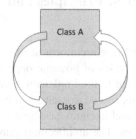

Fig. 2. Circular dependency

The DDP principle says that the dependencies between layers can only be directed from stack's top to bottom. The lowest layer is the one which is the most stable one, the highest layer is the less stable one. If layers are forming a stack, we always know that the higher layers depend on the lower layers, so after modifying lower layers, we know from DDP that the higher layers might require change as well. Since SQuaRE Analysability is "a degree of effectiveness and efficiency with which it is possible to identify parts to be modified", DDP supports SQuaRE Analysability. At the same time, thanks to the layers stack, if the change is introduced to the highest layer, lower layers are not touched. Since SQuaRE Modularity is defined as "a degree to which a system or computer program is composed of discrete components such that a change to one component has a minimal impact on other components", DDP supports SQuaRE Modularity.

TIP means building technology-independent SMA. If SMA is technology-independent, the system based on such a SMA cannot produce or depend on technology-specific solutions. Thanks to that systems based on SMA containing TIP should be more integrate able and connectable with other systems, because the technology barrier is as low as possible. At the same time, the CLCP principle says that the components communication should be clear and understandable, and that the architecture model should be open and follow the industry best practices. The more the communication between components is clear, and based on industry standards, the easier it is to replace such a component with a different one or to reuse it. Since the SQuaRE Reusability means "a degree to which an asset can be used in more than one system, or in building other assets", TIP and CLCP support the Reusability. TIP supports it because easier integration using technology-independent interfaces means that systems based on SMA with TIP, could be used to build other systems. CLCP supports Reusability for a similar reason: if the communication between components is based on open structure and is understandable, the potential of reusing the system in different context is higher. What is more, since the SQuaRE Replaceability means "a degree to which a product can replace another specified software product for the same purpose in the same environment", it can be easily observed that the TIP and CLCP also support Replaceability. TIP supports it because being technology-independent makes it easier e.g. to replace some module with a different one having the same interface, but different implementation. CLCP supports Replaceability for a similar reason: if the communication between components is based on open structure and is understandable, the process of replacing the system's components with different ones is easier than if the components communication would not be understandable, open, and based on industry best practices.

The SRP says that the SMA elements should have a single responsibility. This means that when one of the system functions should be modified, if such a function is implemented inside a set of SRP components which are only responsible for one function, it might happen that the required change would only touch the function-specific component. If SRP wasn't be followed, and every component could be responsible for many functions, it would be harder to analyze which components should be changed to achieve the function goal. That is why, since SQuaRE Analysability means "a degree of effectiveness and efficiency with which it is possible to identify parts to be modified", SRP supports SQuaRE Analysability. Supporting the SQuaRE sub-attribute Analysability means also supporting the more general Maintainability.

The CNP gives possibility to recognize in the class name the layer to which the class belongs. Following the CNP makes the code more readable, and more understandable. What is more, looking just at a class name, it is clear to which layer it belongs to. It makes introducing the needed changes in the system easier, since the classes can be recognized and classified faster than without the prefixes in the class names. This means that locating the places to be changed is easier if the CNP is followed. Since the SQuaRE Analysability means "a degree of effectiveness and efficiency with which it is possible to identify parts to be modified", CNP supports the Analysability.

The SCP is a "separation of concerns principle" stating that an object or a component shouldn't depend on internal details of other objects or components. In other words, SCP is an encapsulation principle. If components would depend on internal implementation of other components instead of keeping the communication based on contracts and interfaces, a change in the internal implementation of a component could change or even brake a component depending on it. It means that since SQuaRE Modifiability is defined as "a degree to which a product or system can be effectively and efficiently modified without introducing defects or degrading existing product quality", SCP supports the Modifiability.

6 Conclusions and Future Work

The analysis of the software quality attributes definitions and the definitions of the STCBMER architectural principles has shown that SQuaRE Maintainability and Portability are the quality types supported by STCBMER. The results of the comparative evaluation of the SQuaRE quality attributes definitions, and STCBMER architectural principles is presented in Table 4. The stars (*) in the table cells means that the correlation between a given quality attribute and an architectural principle was found. Every found correlation means that a concrete quality attribute is positively supported by a given architectural principle. This means that the software based on the STCBMER meta-architecture and following its principles should - to some extend - be maintainable and portable.

Table 3. SQUARE quality attributes and STCBMER architectural principle classes correlation

		DH	DP	HS	DR
Maintainability	Modularity	1			
	Reusability	2	1		
	Analysability	2		1	1
	Modifiability	1		1	
	Testability				
Portability	Adaptability				
	Installability				
	Replaceability	1	1		

Table 4. The STCBMER and SQUARE Correlation

		DDP (DH)	UNP (DH)	NCP (DH)	CEP (DH)	EAP (DP)	CNP (DP)	TIP (DP)	SRP (DP)	SCP (HS)	UCP (HS)	CLCP (DH/DP)	CLAP (DH)
Maintainability	Modularity	*											
	Reusability							*				*	
	Analysability	*			*	*		*					
	Modifiability				*						*		
	Testability												
Portability	Adaptability												
	Installability												
	Replaceability							*				*	

The authors of this publication didn't find a correlation between other types of software quality (e.g. software security), however this doesn't mean that the other types of software quality are not supported by STCBMER. It also doesn't mean that the other types of the software quality are lowered just by using STCBMER. If the correlation is not presented in the Table 4, it only means that the authors of the publication didn't notice it by evaluating and comparing the definitions of both SQuaRE quality attributes and STCBMER principles. Table 3 shows a correlation between four STCBMER architectural principle classes (Table 1) and the supported SQuaRE quality attributes. The numeric values in the cells of Table 3 represent by how many STCBMER Aps a given quality attribute is supported. SQuaRE Maintainability is a quality attribute which is widely supported by STCBMER APs. Only the Maintainability/Testability support is not observed, however this doesn't mean that the STCBMER doesn't support the Testability, the missing correlation was just not clear enough to be mentioned. All the Maintainability sub-characteristics are covered by DH principles. It can be observed that the DH class (50% of all STCBMER principles) is the one which support the biggest number of SQuaRE quality attributes, however all the other AP classes (DP, HS, DR) also support the SQuaRE Maintainability. DH principles are the ones which regulate what kind of dependencies between layers and components are allowed in STCBMER. Most of the Maintainability support come from the DH principles (6 out of 10 supporting principles are of DH class). Table 3 shows a clear correlation between SQuaRE Maintainability and the APs of the DH class. It illustrates the fact that dependencies between software layers and components are strictly correlated with software maintainability. Tables 4 and 3 show that SQuaRE Maintainability is not the only software quality attribute supported by STCBMER architectural principles, Portability is also supported (by two different APs of two different principle classes: DH, DP).

The authors of this publication have analysed the correlation between the STCBMER software meta-architecture with its APs and the SQuaRE software quality attributes. It occurred that there are some SQuaRE quality attributes which are supported by STCBMER architectural principles. But the presented correlation is not measured "in numbers". The limited scope of this publication doesn't allow to focus on each found correlation and to analyse it deeper. Measuring the exact correlation is one of the potential, related work areas, and can be a field of a future analysis. Supporting one software quality attribute usually means lowering a different one. Supporting the required software quality attributes means usually losing some quality in less important quality types. For example sometimes the system performance efficiency can be lowered if the system security is one of the crucial qualities. The authors of the paper didn't focus on the trade-offs which have to be made to support concrete quality attributes. Maybe STCBMER, by supporting maintainability and portability lowers quality of other software quality characteristics. This topic is related to the presented work, and can be a field of a future analysis.

Acknowledgments. The project is financed by the Ministry of Science and Higher Education in Poland under the programme "Regional Initiative of Excellence" 2019–2022 project number 015/RID/2018/19 total funding amount 10 721 040,00 PLN.

References

1. Bosch, J.: Software architecture: the next step. In: Oquendo, F., Warboys, B.C., Morrison, R. (eds.) EWSA 2004. LNCS, vol. 3047, pp. 194–199. Springer, Heidelberg (2004). https://doi.org/10.1007/978-3-540-24769-2_14
2. Babar, M.: A web-based system for managing software architectural knowledge. In: Yao, J. (ed.) Web-Based Support Systems, pp. 305–332. Springer, London (2009). https://doi.org/10.1007/978-1-84882-628-1_14
3. Babar, M.: Supporting the software architecture process with knowledge management. In: Babar, M., Dingsyr, T., Lago, P., van Vliet, H. (eds.) Software Architecture Knowledge Management, pp. 69–86. Springer, Heiderberg (2009). https://doi.org/10.1007/978-3-642-02374-3_5
4. Lee, L., Kruchten, P.: Visualizing software architectural design decisions. In: Morrison, R., Balasubramaniam, D., Falkner, K. (eds.) ECSA 2008. LNCS, vol. 5292, pp. 359–362. Springer, Heidelberg (2008). https://doi.org/10.1007/978-3-540-88030-1_37
5. Kruchten, P., Lago, P., van Vliet, H.: Building up and reasoning about architectural knowledge. In: Hofmeister, C., Crnkovic, I., Reussner, R. (eds.) QoSA 2006. LNCS, vol. 4214, pp. 43–58. Springer, Heidelberg (2006). https://doi.org/10.1007/11921998_8
6. Martin, Richard A., Robertson, Edward L., Springer, J.A.: Architectural principles for enterprise frameworks: guidance for interoperability. In: Bernus, P., Fox, M. (eds.) Knowledge Sharing in the Integrated Enterprise. ITIFIP, vol. 183, pp. 79–91. Springer, Boston, MA (2005). https://doi.org/10.1007/0-387-29766-9_7
7. Maciaszek L., Skalniak T., Biziel, G.: A meta-architecture for service-oriented systems and applications. In: Fourth International Symposium on Business Modeling and Software Design, pp. 20–28. ScitePress (2014)
8. Maciaszek, L., Skalniak, T., Biziel, G.: Architectural principles for service cloud applications. In: Shishkov, B. (ed.) Business Modeling and System Design, vol. 220, pp. 1–21. Springer, Cham (2015). https://doi.org/10.1007/978-3-319-20052-1_1
9. Maciaszek L., Skalniak T.: Confluent factors, complexity and resultant architectures in modern software engineering: a case of service cloud applications. In: Fifth International Symposium on Business Modeling and Software Design, pp. 37–46. ScitePress (2015)
10. Fielding, R.T.: Architectural Styles and the Design of Network-Based Software Architectures. PhD thesis, University of California, Irvine (2000)
11. ISO/IEC. ISO/IEC 25010 - Systems and software engineering - Systems and software Quality Requirements and Evaluation (SQuaRE) - System and software quality models (2011)

12. Skalniak T., Kutera R., Gryncewicz W.: Towards an architecture of electronic service market system – requirements analysis and evaluation. In: Ganzha, M., Maciaszek, L., Paprzycki, M. (eds.) Communication Papers of the 2017 Federated Conference on Computer Science and Information Systems, FedCSIS, Prague (2017)
13. Labidi, N., Chaari, T., Bouaziz, R.: Towards an automatic intention recognition from client request. In: Nguyen, N.-T., Manolopoulos, Y., Iliadis, L., Trawiński, B. (eds.) ICCCI 2016. LNCS (LNAI), vol. 9875, pp. 163–172. Springer, Cham (2016). https://doi.org/10.1007/978-3-319-45243-2_15

Intelligent Sustainable Smart Cities

Real-Time Learning of Power Consumption in Dynamic and Noisy Ambient Environments

Fabrice Crasnier[1,2]([⊠]), Jean-Pierre Georgé[1]([⊠]), and Marie-Pierre Gleizes[1]([⊠])

[1] University Toulouse III - Paul Sabatier - IRIT,
118 route de Narbonne, 31062 Toulouse Cedex 9, France
{fabrice.crasnier,jean-pierre.george,marie-pierre.gleizes}@irit.fr
[2] Société SCASSI, 209 rue Jean Bart, 31670 Labege, France
fabrice.crasnier@scassi.com

Abstract. The usual approach to ambient intelligence is an expert modeling of the devices present in the environment, describing what each does and what effect it will have. When seen as a dynamic and noisy complex systems, with the efficiency of devices changing and new devices appearing, this seems unrealistic. We propose a generic multi-agent (MAS) learning approach that can be deployed in any ambient environment and collectively self-models it. We illustrate the concept on the estimation of power consumption. The agents representing the devices adjust their estimations iteratively and in real time so as to result in a continuous collective problem solving. This approach will be extended to estimate the impact of each device on each comfort (noise, light, smell, heat...), making it possible for them to adjust their behaviour to satisfy the users in an integrative and systemic vision of an intelligent house we call *QuaLAS: eco-friendly Quality of Life in Ambient Sociotechnical systems*.

Keywords: Ambient intelligence · Multi-agent systems · Complex systems · Collective learning

1 Introduction and Context

Miniaturization of technologies has gradually transformed our living spaces into pervasive environments with a sufficient level of perception to seamlessly interact with them, and where people now expect intelligent automation of their comfort. An ambient environment is made up of a multitude of heterogeneous devices, some measuring its physical characteristics while others act on its physical properties. Knowing how to operate such a complex and interconnected system is a first level of learning that is often left to experts in the field, as it currently requires specific modelling frameworks.

On the contrary, we propose to use an autonomous and local multi-agent adaptation approach so as to provide ambient sociotechnical systems immersed

N. T. Nguyen et al. (Eds.): ICCCI 2019, LNAI 11684, pp. 443–454, 2019.
https://doi.org/10.1007/978-3-030-28374-2_38

in dynamic environments with real-time learning capacities. The main gap with existing techniques is the broader idea that, to fully understand and control a real-world complex systems, it is necessary to use an Artificial Intelligence approach that is itself a complex system [3]. We illustrate this concept with electrical consumption, which is similar to all other forms of learning about impacts of devices (on temperature, noise, light, smell...) with some slight modifications.

Below, after defining the concepts of the intelligent ambient environment, we explain why we decided to base our work on intelligent housing using a multi-agent approach. In Sect. 2, we present the multi-agent system allowing us to consider the self-modelling and simulation of electricity consumption by ambient socio-technical devices. Section 3 details some experiments and analyses them.

1.1 The Ambient Environment

As early as the 70's, home automation was described [6] as consisting of knowing and then controlling an environment using a number of detectors such as thermometers, hygrometers, radars and all kinds of electronic systems. In this representation, electronic devices are omnipresent in the environment but an operator remains in control of the execution of all tasks that act for his personal comfort. With technological developments, advances in information technology and in particular network interconnections, this vision evolved towards ubiquitous computing: computer devices are omnipresent, to such an extent that they gradually disappear to become one with the host environment. *"The most profound technologies are those that disappear. They weave themselves into the fabric of everyday life until they are indistinguishable from it"* [7].

In recent years, the number of connected objects in our personal and professional environment has increased steadily, in particular for *Industry 4.0* and *Smart Cities*. Figures of nearly 50 billion connected objects are announced for the beginning of 2050 with a spread within the new habitats averaging 250 home automation objects per household.

Research using ambient environments continues today with the advent of *smart-**[1]. A particular interest is the focus on user *comfort* and environmental impact. Research such as [2] aims at determining the influence of the behaviour of the occupants on the thermal and visual comfort of this environment, as well as the impact on the energy performance of the building. To carry out these experiments, four offices were instrumented with sensors to detect environmental physical variables, as well as operations on blinds and windows.

[4] shows the difficulty of observing a highly dynamic environment with humans at the centre of the activity and designs a system capable of observing the recurrent actions of users so as to establish in which contexts these actions are performed in order to supplant the user if a similar situation arises.

[5] focuses on human activity in relation to residential power consumption. His approach is based on the SMACH platform [1] to simulate human behaviour

---

[1] Cities, grids, homes, environments...

in the habitat, which makes it possible to simulate the daily activity of households. It is defined as a set of inhabitants, tasks and electrical appliances. The central element is the notion of task. These tasks involve the use of energy-using household appliances, which are predefined in an environment for residents to use. This model, although scalable, requires a knowledge of the characteristics of the devices that will be added to the environment.

1.2   The Intelligent Ambient Environment

The combination of ubiquitous computing and artificial intelligence has given rise to a new field of research, that of ambient intelligence (AmI). The idea is that it is possible to continuously analyze the environment, learn about the user-environment interaction and model their activities. This provides an ability to discern situations, contexts or problems and dynamically adapt to them. It is noteworthy that, probably given the growing maturity of technology, there was a rapid interest from the industry in a domestic setting, as can be seen with the Philips HomeLab[2] inaugurated in 2002.

The European Commission, through ISTAG (Information Societies Technology Advisory Group) has been promoting the concept of ambient intelligence and providing guidelines for a unified vision of AmI. In 2001 the group imagined four illustrating scenarios[3], showing different situations of use but all four integrate in depth the relationship between human needs and comforts, and their intelligent environment. ISTAG defends the idea that ambient intelligence should be attentive to the specific characteristics of each individual, adapt to the needs of users, be able to respond intelligently to spoken or gestural indications, and even engage in dialogue. It must be non-intrusive and most often invisible. Finally, it should not involve a long period of learning for the user and should be usable by ordinary people.

The purpose of our research is to enable an intelligent house to learn its *eco-citizenship function*, enabling it to minimize consumption costs when making decisions while remaining within the constraints imposed on it. But like Smart Grids, learning how to use electricity in a Smart Home (that can be integrated into Smart Buildings) is not a naive subject as current devices do not (or seldom, or not reliably) provide their own instantaneous consumption. It is also unreliable to estimate that the manufacturer's indications will be sufficient to predict the power consumption of each device in real time. It is also unrealistic to suppose that a device is always constant without degradation. Moreover, providing a complete set of new fully integrated devices would have a strong monetary and resources consumption impact. This is not eco-friendly, at a time when devices are being reconditioned to give them a second life.

Our work aims at showing how it is possible to take an existing environment with its devices and enhance it with artificial intelligence so as to have sufficient

---

[2] https://www.noldus.com/default/philips-homelab.

[3] Scenarios for ambient intelligence in 2010 (ISTAG 2001 Final Report) (2001) by K. Ducatel, M. Bogdanowicz, F. Scapolo, J. Leijten, J. C. Burgelma.

elements to perceive, decide and produce adequate actions. In this context of activity, we assume that the main electricity meter provides the overall electricity consumption of the house and each device has only the ability to provide its operating condition as on/off (or it can be deduced, or the user has to indicate this). This minimalist information, which can be integrated at low cost into the habitat, has to still enable devices to learn their electricity consumption in order to participate in the function of minimizing habitat consumption.

1.3   Why a Multi-agent Approach?

In a real and evolving ambient environment, devices appear according to needs, operate intermittently over time, and disappear according to their obsolescence. Learning their power consumption can be seen as the resolution of a simple linear system. As shown in Fig. 1, to perform these calculations, it is necessary to create a linear system composed of p non-collinear equations p_i with n unknown variables d_k, where p_i represents a perception of the environment at a time t and d_k the power consumption of a device. Each perception p_i forms an equation where the consumption of each device is weighted by 0 or 1 corresponding to their operating state (on/off) at a time t and where the total consumption is known. This results, to be solvable, in an invertible square matrix ($p = n$) of rank n.

Perception \ Devices	1	2	3	Power consumption (Watts)
p[1]	ON	ON		352
p[2]		ON	ON	542
p[3]	ON		ON	925

$$S = \begin{cases} 352 = d1 + d2 \\ 819 = d2 + d3 \\ 925 = d1 + d3 \end{cases} \qquad M = \begin{pmatrix} 1 & 1 & \square \\ \square & 1 & 1 \\ 1 & \square & 1 \end{pmatrix} \begin{pmatrix} 352 \\ 819 \\ 925 \end{pmatrix}$$

Fig. 1. Environmental perception set

As the overall consumption of the environment is equal to the sum of the devices in operation, the equation allowing us to solve the problem can be expressed as:

$$GlobalConsumption_t = \sum_{k=1}^{n} DeviceState_{k,t} * DeviceConsumption_k, t$$

Unfortunately, the formal solution of a system of linear equations is possible only in an ideal theoretic situation as it does not meet several of the requirements of a realistic ambient socio-technical system: (1) supporting dynamics[4];

---

[4] Adding devices, changing or removing some.

(2) supporting noisy data[5]; (3) proposing a solution at any time[6]; (4) having an acceptable resolution time for the studied environment[7].

The Adaptive Multi-Agent Systems (AMAS) approach we propose enables the design of decentralized systems whose objective is to solve complex, incompletely specified problems, and for which there is no acceptable algorithmic solution already known [3]. According to this approach, the designer defines the local behaviour of each of the agents composing the system so as to obtain a global organization of these agents that produces an *adequate collective function*[8]. This organization between agents results from interactions between the multi-agent system and its environment, and by continuously and locally adapting to its dynamics, it is thus able to manage (and learn from) unforeseen events. The increasing complexity of ambient environments with the appearance of billions of devices favours the design of decentralized intelligent systems with self-* properties[9]. These systems consist of a set of autonomous and interacting agents, leading to the emergence of a collective behaviour. Thanks to their self-* properties, these systems are capable of adapting to and managing dynamics due to endogenous and exogenous changes. This approach has already shown interesting results in Ambient Intelligence [4].

2   A Power Consumption Estimation MAS

Our research aims at enabling each device in an ambient environment to continuously estimate its own power consumption. The multi-agent consumption system model presented in Fig. 2 shows the environmental perception capabilities, i.e. the overall electricity consumption of the environment as well as the operating states of the actual devices (roller shutter, radiator, ceiling lamp, loudspeaker...). It is composed of an *Estimation agent* and *Device agents*. An Estimation agent processes the perceived data and solicits the Device agents representing real ambient socio-technical devices within the MAS in order to obtain an estimate of their electricity consumption.

The Consumption MAS achieves this objective by minimizing the observed error between the overall consumption and the sum of the electricity consumption estimates provided by the Devices agents. The evolution of the system is carried out by comparing the successive situations provided by the environment. A *situation* consists only of a perception of the overall consumption of the environment as well as the operating states of the actual devices (on/off).

2.1   The Estimation Agent

The Estimation agent is responsible of minimizing this power estimation error. To achieve its objective, the Estimation agent constantly cooperates with the

---

[5] Due to imprecise or low-quality sensors.

[6] Even partial or imprecise, possibly linked with a certainty coefficient or trust.

[7] The solver has to start learning in real time and not wait for a specific data set.

[8] Result or behaviour of the system considered satisfactory by an external observer.

[9] Self-stabilizing, self-organizing, self-observation, self-optimizing, self-managing...

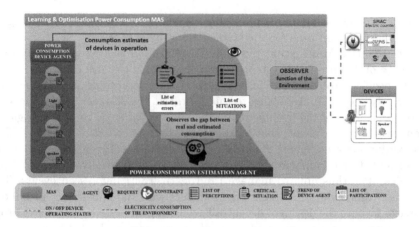

Fig. 2. Model of the multi-agent consumption system

Device agents by providing them with the necessary elements to improve their consumption evaluation (i.e. feedback). It receives new data from the environment whenever changes occur.

At time t, the Estimation agent perceives information from the ambient environment that we will call a *situation* S_i (see Fig. 3). It simply consists of the overall power consumption of the environment as well as the operating states (on/off) of the actual devices.

Devices \ Situations	1	2	3	4	5	6	7	8	9	10	Power consumption (Watts)
S[1]	ON					ON	ON	ON			741
S[2]	ON		ON	ON				ON	ON		1113
S[3]	ON			ON		ON		ON			953
S[4]	ON			ON		ON	ON	ON		ON	1392
S[5]		ON	ON					ON	ON	ON	1207
S[6]		ON				ON		ON	ON	ON	1372

Fig. 3. Footprints of the environment called *situations*

The Estimation agent calculates the estimation error, which represents all the errors made collectively by the Device agents at the time of their power consumption estimation:

$$Error = \sum_{k=1}^{n}(EstimatedDeviceConsumption_k) - GlobalConsumption$$

This is done for each situation (Fig. 4). The red/left bars indicate the overall power consumption of a situation and the blue/right bars represent the sum of the power consumption estimates made by the Device agents.

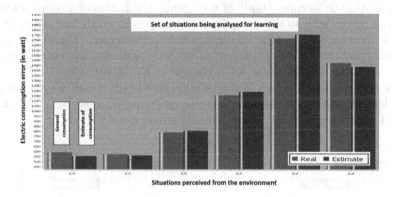

Fig. 4. Real versus estimated power consumption (Color figure online)

The Estimation agent consecutively memorizes the situations as the environment changes, thus forming a knowledge base of situations (Fig. 5). If the error is positive, the devices have collectively overestimated the value of the consumption and if the error is negative, they have underestimated it.

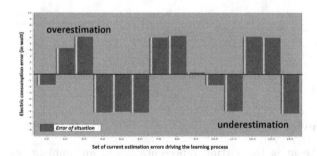

Fig. 5. Representation of errors in a knowledge base of 14 situations

In addition, the Estimation agent evaluates the convergence of consumption errors after each addition of a situation in the knowledge base (representing a *learning phase*), its approach to zero indicating that a collective solution is found. It is important to note that this solution, although already interesting for the user, is not necessarily indicating the exact real consumption of the devices, as a sufficient number of different situations is needed to have a unique mathematical solution. Nevertheless, its approach to zero indicates that the Estimation agent is ready to integrate a new environmental situation in the knowledge base, as it is no longer sufficient to progress.

As long as the convergence of the maximum error is not close to zero, the Estimation agent requests of the Device agents to re-evaluate their consumption estimates. At each learning step[10] of the agents, the Estimation agent provides the Device agents with all the errors for the situations in which they are involved.

Once the convergence of the maximum error is close to zero (Fig. 6), a learning phase ends and the Estimation agent integrates a new environmental situation (if it is available, else it waits for a change in the environment). The latter disrupts the balance of errors if the solution previously found was not exact. A new learning phase begins until there are no more disruptions in the errors observed, indicating that all device estimations are exact.

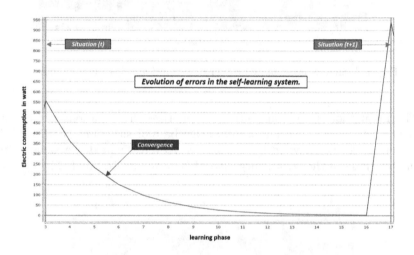

Fig. 6. Convergence between two perceptions

2.2   The Device Agent

The Device Agent is the virtual representation of an ambient socio-technical device of the environment within the Consumption MAS. Its nominal behaviour (its goal) is the learning of its power consumption and its cooperative behaviour is to help the Estimation agent to solve the consumption errors it observes.

The Device agent perceives the data provided by the Estimation agent, containing the estimation errors for all the situations in which it is active. As we indicated (Fig. 5), this information consists of positive and negative errors, and the Device agent will determine the maximum overestimation $C+$ and underestimation $C-$ errors. Its goal is then to minimize these *critical situations* but it can not usually do it by itself: changing its power consumption estimation will

---

[10] Or life cycle of the agents: perceive, decide, act.

either increase both $C+$ and $C-$ or decrease both, and the other active devices are also responsible of the error. Thus, it will mainly equilibrate them (trying to reach $C_+ + C_- = 0$) by calculating a value α allowing the balancing of these situations, such that:

$$(C_+ + \alpha) + (C_- + \alpha) = 0, \text{ which is: } \alpha = -\tfrac{1}{2}(C_+ + C_-)$$

Figure 7 shows an example for a Device agent analyzing 4 situations. The Device agent calculates the equilibrium point between the two extreme situations in order to obtain a maximum minimization (M) while collectively reducing their difference (E).

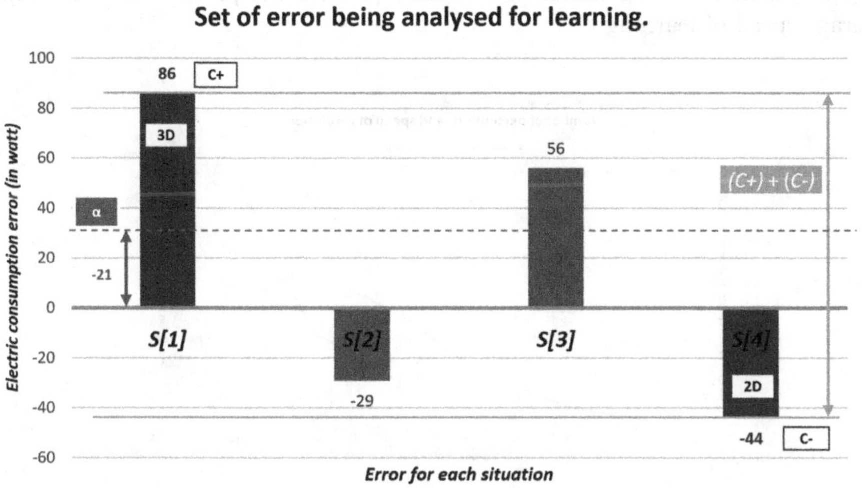

Set of error being analysed for learning.

Fig. 7. Example of a minimization function.

The Device agent is able to determine the number of participants in the most critical situation that will possibly[11] help. Since it shares the problem solving with them, it can adjust its participation as follows:

$$\alpha = -\tfrac{1}{2}(C_+ + C_-)\tfrac{1}{k}, \text{ with } k = numberOfParticipatingAgents$$

The agent Device modifies its electricity consumption estimation at each learning cycle by adding the result of its minimization function, and transmits the new estimation to the Estimation agent. He also creates a history of his previous estimates to determine if he has a cyclical behaviour, thus indicating his inability to improve his estimation. It also transmits this information to the Estimation agent.

---

[11] It is uncertain as some agents may be part of other more critical situations.

3   Experiments and Results

We subjected our power consumption learning model to various non-noisy and noisy environments consisting of 5, 10, 20, 20, 30, 30, 40, 50 ambient devices respectively in order to observe its ability to pass certain scales (Fig. 8). We consider that the problem is solved if all devices have reached a learning error of less than 1%. Each learning scenario is repeated 10 times to obtain an observation average that reflects reality. Indeed, since perceptions of the environment are random, in some cases, some perceptions do not serve any useful purpose in learning and even disrupt the system, but they are part of the perceptions generated by the environment. It is therefore important to show the system's ability to take this disruption into account. We can study the average number of perceptions of the environment necessary to solve the problem as well as its average speed of learning.

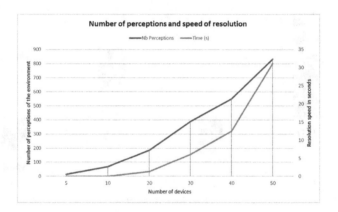

Fig. 8. Number of perceptions and speed of resolution

We can observe in real time how an agent adjusts its estimation. In Fig. 9 with 10 devices for instance, an agent appears in the environment as soon as the multi-agent system is started and progresses towards a limit of about 350 watts, which is its real power consumption.

With 15 devices, we show that the worst device error converges both in a non-noisy (Fig. 10) and a noisy (Fig. 11) environment.

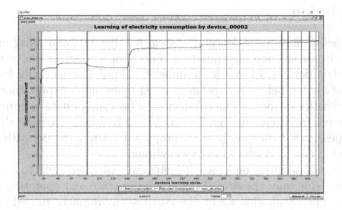

Fig. 9. Learning of electricity consumption by a device

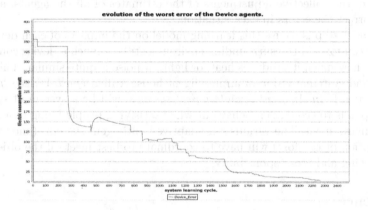

Fig. 10. Evolution of the worst error of the device agents without noise

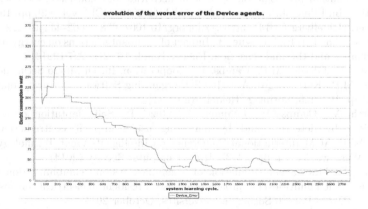

Fig. 11. Evolution of the worst error of the device agents with noise

4   Conclusion

We presented a multi-agent learning system for dynamic and noisy intelligent ambient environments and illustrated the concept on estimating power consumption of electric devices. Research on ambient habitat has generally focused on the study of human behaviour and most often relies on an expert knowledge of the characteristics of socio-technical devices. This type of data is currently not available in real environments (and seems generally unrealistic with all the new devices appearing all the time), so we propose a learning model with minimal resources, that can be deployed in any environment.

Thus, the self-adaptive multi-agent system we described seeks to achieve this objective by using only the overall power consumption and operating status of the devices. The Estimation agent observes the environment in real time as it changes and requests new estimates from Device agents until real and estimates match. The learning of the power consumption of each Device agent emerges as a result of the collective adjustments of the estimates of all the agents, as they try to correct the errors in each situation.

The next step is to use this learning model on the impacts of each device on physical comforts of the surrounding environment: how much a device consumes power or how much it produces heat, or light, or noise is quite similar. This integrative and systemic vision of an intelligent house, called *QuaLAS: eco-friendly Quality of Life in Ambient Sociotechnical systems*, will be a system of systems that responds to eco-citizen behaviour while satisfying people living in an ubiquitous environment. The various self-adaptive multi-agent systems (one for each consumption or comfort) will have to coordinate to best meet all the objectives of well-being and eco-responsibility.

References

1. Amouroux, É., Huraux, T., Sempé, F., Sabouret, N., Haradji, Y.: SMACH: agent-based simulation investigation on human activities and household electrical consumption. In: Filipe, J., Fred, A. (eds.) ICAART 2013. CCIS, vol. 449, pp. 194–210. Springer, Heidelberg (2014). https://doi.org/10.1007/978-3-662-44440-5_12
2. Bonte, M., Thellier, F., Lartigue, B.: Impact of occupant's actions on energy building performance and thermal sensation. Energy Build. **76**, 219–227 (2014)
3. Georgé, J.P., Gleizes, M.P., Camps, V.: Cooperation. In: Di Marzo Serugendo, G., Gleizes, M.P., Karageorgos, A. (eds.) Self-organising Software. Natural Computing Series, pp. 193–226. Springer, Heidelberg (2011)
4. Guivarch, V., Camps, V., Péninou, A., Glize, P.: Self-adaptation of a learnt behaviour by detecting and by managing user's implicit contradictions. In: IEEE/WIC/ACM International Conference on Intelligent Agent Technology (IAT 2014), Warsaw, Poland, pp. 24–31. IEEE Computer Society (2014)
5. Huraux, T.: Multi-agent simulation of a complex system: combining domains of expertise with a multi-level approach - the case of residential electrical consumption. Ph.D., UPMC - Paris 6 Sorbonne Universités, October 2015
6. Sarda, P.: La maison de l'an 2000. INA - reportage TF4, October 1979. https://www.ina.fr/video/CAA7901376201
7. Weiser, M.: The computer for the 21st century. Sci. Am. **265**(3), 66–75 (1991). http://www.ubiq.com/hypertext/weiser/SciAmDraft3.html

Quaternion Entropy to Analysis of Downhill Skiing Data - Preliminary Study

Agnieszka Szczęsna[1]($\boxtimes$) and Mateusz Janiak[2]

[1] Institute of Informatics, Silesian University of Technology, Gliwice, Poland
agnieszka.szczesna@polsl.pl
[2] Polish-Japanese Academy of Information Technology, Warsaw, Poland
mjaniak@pjwstk.edu.pl

Abstract. Nonlinear techniques are extremely useful to analyze the human movement within sport context. One of the most popular metric of process complexity is entropy. This work concerns application of quaternion approximation entropy for analysis of human motion during downhill skiing. Skier motion is represented as time series of orientations of two skies and chest. Orientations are coded as unit quaternions. Such approach was used to quantify chaotic behaviour in context of regularity in time series. The preliminary study discussed the results obtained from IoT system consists of three inertial measurement sensors (IMU) and smartphone.

Keywords: Quaternion entropy · Approximate entropy · Motion data analysis · Orientation · Downhill skiing data

1 Introduction

Complex processes can be analysed by nonlinear dynamical tools. This is a powerful approach used for understanding biological processes. One of the most used metric of system complexities is the Kolomogorov entropy. For application on short and noisy signals the approximate [1, 2] and sample entropy [3], as family of statistics were proposed. Thus, a low value of such defined entropy reflects a high degree of regularity, as shows different applications to analysis biomedical signals, for example cardiovascular [3–6] and EEG [7–10] time series.

In [11,12], authors analyse the gait data to identifying the presence of deterministic chaos by mean of the largest Lyapunov exponent (LLE). Entropy is also used for gait data analysis. Here, the input time series consisting of spatio-temporal parameters like step time, length, width and stride intervals [13,14], COP (center of pressure) trajectory [15] or segments acceleration signals [16,17].

Nonlinear techniques are extremely useful to analyze the human movement within sport context. One of application is analysis of human movement variability [18,19]. In [20] entropy-based techniques are considered to measure, analyse and evaluate the human performance variability under three different case

© Springer Nature Switzerland AG 2019
N. T. Nguyen et al. (Eds.): ICCCI 2019, LNAI 11684, pp. 455–463, 2019.
https://doi.org/10.1007/978-3-030-28374-2_39

studies: golf, tennis, and soccer. The analysis is based on trajectory but to computation position vector is treated as three separate signals (coordinate values x, y and z). The complexity of movement of a rock climber's center of mass (COM) during an ascent has been described as geometric entropy. It has been proposed that lower geometric entropy could represent more fluid and economical movement during climbing [21,22]. Chaos theory is also used for assessment of balance based on COM trajectory [23].

In [24] the new quaternion, approximate entropy to analysis of human gait data was proposed. The input time series were the segments orientations in time during the gait. This work concerns application of quaternion approximation entropy $ApQuatEn$ for unit quaternion time series represented orientations of two skies and skier chest during downhill skiing. Such approach was used to quantify chaotic behaviour in context of regularity in time series. The preliminary study discussed the results obtained for data of 6 skiers grouped in terms of skills on three levels. Data was obtained from IoT system consists of three inertial measurement sensors (IMU) and smartphone.

Based on actual knowledge, there is no proposition to compute entropy for analysis downhill skiing data based on unit quaternions time series. Described conception allows to process correlated data and obtain results taking into account rotations in 3D.

2   Materials and Methods

2.1   Quaternion Approximate Entropy

The o orientation indicates the orientation of the rigid body defined in the reference system (also named as the reference frame). Rotation means a change in orientation, $o_1 \rightarrow o_2$. The group $SO(3)$ (special orthogonal group) contains all rotations around the origin of the Euclidean coordinate system $\mathbb{R}^3$. Rotations can be described by orthogonal matrices, three Euler angle (usually referred to as roll, pitch and yaw) and unit quaternions [25,26].

Let us assume that input a motion signal consists of quaternions: $q_1, q_2, \ldots, q_n$ where $q_i \in \mathbb{H}_1$ (where $\mathbb{H}$ is a quaternion algebra) and $n = 2^k$ for some $k \in \mathbb{N}$. Furthermore, the signal is processed by the selective negation (hemispherization), that is, every quaternion q_i $(i > 1)$ is converted to $-q_i$ if $\langle q_i, q_{i-1} \rangle < 0$, because of duality of unit quaternions which represent rotations. It satisfies the requirement according to which two adjacent quaternions are located on the same hemisphere.

The time series signal of measurements is equally spaced in time, the sequence of m-elements vectors can be defined as $x(1), x(2), \cdots, x(N - m + 1)$, where $x(i) = [q_i, q_{i+1}, \cdots, q_{(i+m-1)}]$. Next for each i and j, $1 \leqslant i \leqslant N - m + 1$, and $1 \leqslant j \leqslant N - m + 1$,

$$C_i^m(r, N) = \frac{\#(d[x(i), x(j)] \leqslant r)}{(N - m + 1)} \tag{1}$$

where $\#$ is the number of elements in set, r is vector comparison distance and m is the dimension of created and compared vectors. The distance d is defined in (3).

Quaternions are of unit length, which means they are located only on a hypersphere $\mathbb{H}_1$. Thus, to compare rotations, the cosine distance between related quaternions was used. Such metric is reflected by angles between vectors formed by quaternions' components. The scalar product $\langle q_1, q_2 \rangle$ can be used to accomplish the task:

$$d_{cosine}\left(q_i, q_j\right) = \frac{1 - \langle q_i, q_j \rangle}{2}. \tag{2}$$

The distance between two quaternions $|q_{i+k-1}, q_{j+k-1}|$ is defined as d_{cosine}, so the equation is:

$$d\left[x(i), x(j)\right] = \max_{k=1,2,\cdots,m} \left(d_{cosine}\left(q_{i+k-1}, q_{j+k-1}\right)\right). \tag{3}$$

We can define $\Phi^m(r)$ as

$$\Phi^m(r, N) = (N - m + 1)^{-1} \sum_{i=1}^{N-m+1} \log\left(C_i^m(r, N)\right). \tag{4}$$

After fixing m and r we obtain definition of approximate quaternion entropy:

$$ApQuatEn(m, r) = \lim_{N \to \infty} \left[\Phi^m(r, N) - \Phi^{m+1}(r, N)\right]. \tag{5}$$

Given N samples, we can define the following formula as statistics:

$$ApQuatEn(m, r, N) = \Phi^m(r, N) - \Phi^{m+1}(r, N). \tag{6}$$

2.2   Downhill Skiing Data

Time series were extracted from freely downhill skiing based on data from IoT system (Snowcookie system[1]). System consists of three inertial measurement sensors (IMU) one on each ski and one on skier chest. Additional from smartphone the GPS position, GPS velocity and atmospheric pressure are available. Based on IMU signals as a result the quaternion orientation of sensors can be obtained. The accuracy of orientation depends of many factors, like dynamic of motion, temperature, staring calibration. Estimated average error is about $8°$ [27]. Orientation data was recorded with 50 Hz frequency. Figure 1 presents the coordinate system of three sensors after calibration available in the Snowcookie system. The x axis is directed along the ski, the z up, and y on the left according to right-handed coordinate system. The example orientations of left ski during turns, converted from unit quaternions to three Euler angles, are presented in Fig. 2. For acquisition the following models of Apple iPhone were used: iPhone 6+, iPhone 6, iPhone 8+.

Six skiers (3 women and 3 men) participated in the experiment. Skiers were classed on the basis of skills into three groups: two skiers with level 4, two skiers with level 7 and two skiers with level 9. The level was determined according to

---

[1] The Snowcookie system https://snowcookiesports.com.

Fig. 1. Coordinate system of three sensors (based on the Snowcookie system documentation).

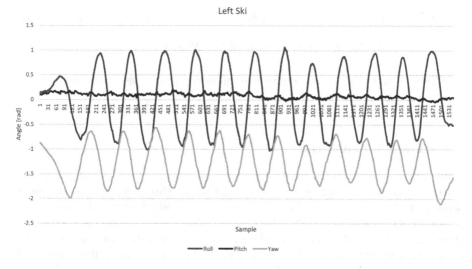

Fig. 2. Orientations of left ski during turns presented as three Euler angles.

the 9-point scale developed by Professional Ski Instructors of America (PSIA), where level 1 determines beginner and level 9 racer skier. The downhill data described runs was obtained from different slopes and days. For experiment the sequences of 25–30 parallel turns series were cut off from runs data. Finally the 184 sequences were used. The mean velocity of all turns was 9.5450 [m/s] (standard deviation 2.3750). The input data characteristics is presented in Table 1.

Based on data from the Snowcookie system, for the purpose of calculations *ApQuatEn*, a text file (csv format) was created for each run of a given skier. Created file has following structure:

timestamp;
turn number;
chest orientation quaternion;
right ski orientation quaternion;
left ski orientation quaternion;
GPS velocity

Table 1. The input data characteristics.

Level	Skiers	Turns sequences	Mean velocity [m/s]
Level 4	1 man, 1 woman	49	7.3556
Level 7	1 man, 1 woman	64	9.2103
Level 9	1 man, 1 woman	71	11.3373

3   Results and Discussion

Samples of 25–30 series of parallel turns are unit quaternion time series for each sensor (left ski, right ski and chest). For each time series, the *ApQuatEn* value was calculated. The set of 25–30 turns was chosen based on results presented in Fig. 3. Entropy was quantified on data in increments of samples of 5 turns. The value of entropy stabilize between twenty-fifth and thirtieth turn.

To experiments the $m = 2$ was used. Typically, it is suggested that for clinical data, the length of vectors m is to be set at 2 for approximate entropy *ApEn* algorithm [2]. The value of threshold r was defined as mean values of distance d_{cosine} between each following q_i and q_{i+1} quaternion in time series. This is same formula was used in [24] for analysis of gait data. All computations were performed using Matlab software. The implementation is based on psedocode presented in [13].

The Pearson correlation coefficient between values of entropy for chest to left ski is 0.13, chest to right ski is 0.19 and left to right ski is 0.59. Entropy values of two skies during turns are correlated. Orientations of chest during downhill skiing change in smaller range that orientations of skies. In Fig. 4 the box plots of mean entropy of left and right ski are presented. The values are grouped based on skill level of skiers. The more advanced skier (higher level), the lower entropy values with smaller range of values. Smaller entropy values indicate a greater repeatability of the orientations in the input time signal. This means that skiers with a higher level, have better skis control and are not susceptible

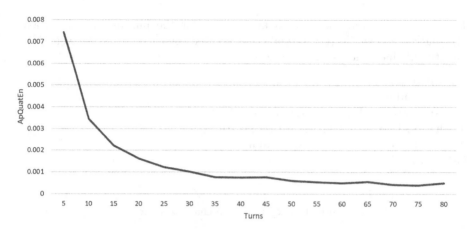

Fig. 3. The value of entropy for right ski $ApQuatEn$ ($m = 2$, $r = mean(d_{cosine})$) in relation to numbers of turns (skier with level 9).

to local perturbations, such as bumps, obstacles, icing. The obtained data did not allow to indicate statistically significant differences between levels. This will be examine in next experiments. The result median values of entropy are presented in Table 2.

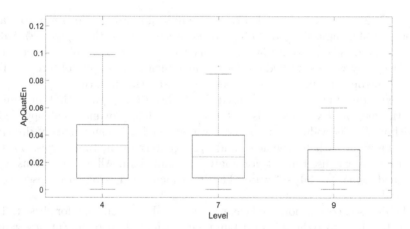

Fig. 4. Box plot of mean entropy of left and right ski $ApQuatEn$ ($m = 2$, $r = mean(d_{cosine})$).

Table 2. The median values of result *ApQuatEn* for skies (mean value of entropy for left and right skies) and chest sensors.

	Left and right ski	Chest
Level 4	0.0327	0.0363
Level 7	0.0243	0.0208
Level 9	0.0148	0.0015

This is also confirmed by the value of the Pearson correlation coefficient (Table 3) for the entropy value and the average GPS velocity values in a series of turns. Where the entropy values for skies are strong correlated with velocity for skiers with level 4 and 7. And for skiers with level 9 there is no correlation. So the velocity does not affect the repeatability of movement. The advanced skiers can ski in this same way beside of velocity.

Table 3. The Pearson correlation coefficient for values of *ApQuatEn* for skies (mean value of entropy for left and right skies) and chest sensors in correlation to mean value of velocity in turns series for three groups of skiers (level 4, 7 and 9).

	Left and right ski	Chest
Level 4	0.8860	0.0796
Level 7	0.8797	0.2455
Level 9	0.0165	0.2022
All	0.8962	0.2769

4   Conclusions

This work concerns application of the quaternion approximation entropy *ApQuatEn* for unit quaternion time series represented orientations of skies and skier chest during downhill skiing. The entropy value can be used to quantify chaotic behaviour in context of regularity in time series. The preliminary study discussed the results obtained for data of 6 skiers, freely skiing on different ski slopes. For consideration, was taken only data of parallel turns (skidding or carving). Orientations of sensors placed on two skis and skier chest were obtained from IoT system. It was confirmed that all considered time series are characterized by positive values of entropy, indicated chaotic behaviour.

The preliminary results show some interesting relationship between the skier's skill level and the values of entropy. This requires further research on a wider group of participants. For a detailed analysis, it is required to have the same conditions (slope, type of snow) during the experiment.

Acknowledgments. Publication partially supported by the Rector's grant in the field of scientific research and development works, Silesian University of Technology (Gliwice, Poland), grant number 02/020/RGJ/18/0125 (2018–2019) (ASz).

Publication partially supported by project "Innovative IT system to support alpine skiing and biathlon training, with the functions of acquisition of multimodal motion data, their visualization and advanced analysis using machine learning techniques, Snowcookie PRO", Smart Growth Operational Program 2014–2020, POIR.01.01.01-00-0267/17 (2018–2020) (MJ).

References

1. Pincus, S.: Approximate entropy (ApEn) as a complexity measure. Chaos Interdisc. J. Nonlinear Sci. **5**(1), 110–117 (1995)
2. Pincus, S.M., Huang, W.M.: Approximate entropy: statistical properties and applications. Commun. Stat. Theory Methods **21**(11), 3061–3077 (1992)
3. Richman, J.S., Moorman, J.R.: Physiological time-series analysis using approximate entropy and sample entropy. Am. J. Physiol. Heart Circulatory Physiol. **278**(6), H2039–H2049 (2000)
4. Pincus, S.M., Viscarello, R.R.: Approximate entropy: a regularity measure for fetal heart rate analysis. Obstet. Gynecol. **79**(2), 249–255 (1992)
5. Kaplan, D., Furman, M., Pincus, S., Ryan, S., Lipsitz, L., Goldberger, A.: Aging and the complexity of cardiovascular dynamics. Biophys. J. **59**(4), 945 (1991)
6. Liu, C., Liu, C., Shao, P., Li, L., Sun, X., Wang, X., Liu, F.: Comparison of different threshold values r for approximate entropy: application to investigate the heart rate variability between heart failure and healthy control groups. Physiol. Meas. **32**(2), 167 (2010)
7. Abásolo, D., Hornero, R., Espino, P., Poza, J., Sánchez, C.I., de la Rosa, R.: Analysis of regularity in the EEG background activity of Alzheimer's disease patients with approximate entropy. Clin. Neurophysiol. **116**(8), 1826–1834 (2005)
8. Zhang, X.S., Roy, R.J., Jensen, E.W.: EEG complexity as a measure of depth of anesthesia for patients. IEEE Trans. Biomed. Eng. **48**(12), 1424–1433 (2001)
9. Kannathal, N., Choo, M.L., Acharya, U.R., Sadasivan, P.: Entropies for detection of epilepsy in EEG. Comput. Methods Programs Biomed. **80**(3), 187–194 (2005)
10. Acharya, U.R., Molinari, F., Sree, S.V., Chattopadhyay, S., Ng, K.H., Suri, J.S.: Automated diagnosis of epileptic EEG using entropies. Biomed. Signal Process. Control **7**(4), 401–408 (2012)
11. Piórek, M., Josiński, H., Michalczuk, A., Świtoński, A., Szczęsna, A.: Quaternions and joint angles in an analysis of local stability of gait for different variants of walking speed and treadmill slope. Inf. Sci. **384**, 263–280 (2017)
12. Josiński, H., Michalczuk, A., Świtoński, A., Mucha, R., Wojciechowski, K.: Quantifying chaotic behavior in treadmill walking. In: Nguyen, N.T., Trawiński, B., Kosala, R. (eds.) ACIIDS 2015. LNCS (LNAI), vol. 9012, pp. 317–326. Springer, Cham (2015). https://doi.org/10.1007/978-3-319-15705-4_31
13. Yentes, J.M., Hunt, N., Schmid, K.K., Kaipust, J.P., McGrath, D., Stergiou, N.: The appropriate use of approximate entropy and sample entropy with short data sets. Ann. Biomed. Eng. **41**(2), 349–365 (2013)
14. Costa, M., Peng, C.K., Goldberger, A.L., Hausdorff, J.M.: Multiscale entropy analysis of human gait dynamics. Phys. Stat. Mech. Appl. **330**(1–2), 53–60 (2003)

15. Ramdani, S., Seigle, B., Lagarde, J., Bouchara, F., Bernard, P.L.: On the use of sample entropy to analyze human postural sway data. Med. Eng. Phys. **31**(8), 1023–1031 (2009)
16. Bisi, M., Stagni, R.: Complexity of human gait pattern at different ages assessed using multiscale entropy: from development to decline. Gait Posture **47**, 37–42 (2016)
17. McGregor, S.J., Busa, M.A., Skufca, J., Yaggie, J.A., Bollt, E.M.: Control entropy identifies differential changes in complexity of walking and running gait patterns with increasing speed in highly trained runners. Chaos Interdisc. J. Nonlinear Sci. **19**(2), 026109 (2009)
18. Caballero, C., Barbado, D., Moreno, F.J.: Non-linear tools and methodological concerns measuring human movement variability: an overview. Eur. J. Hum. Mov. **32**, 61–81 (2014)
19. Stergiou, N., Decker, L.M.: Human movement variability, nonlinear dynamics, and pathology: is there a connection? Hum. Mov. Sci. **30**(5), 869–888 (2011)
20. Couceiro, M.S., Clemente, F.M., Dias, G., Mendes, P., Fernando, M.L.: On an entropy-based performance analysis in sports. In: 1st International Electronic Conference on Entropy and Its Applications, Multidisciplinary Digital Publishing Institute (2014)
21. Watts, P.B., Drum, S.N., Kilgas, M.A., Phillips, K.C.: Geometric entropy for lead vs top-rope rock climbing. Int. J. Exer. Sci. **9**(2), 6 (2016)
22. Sibella, F., Frosio, I., Schena, F., Borghese, N.: 3D analysis of the body center of mass in rock climbing. Hum. Mov. Sci. **26**(6), 841–852 (2007)
23. Buchecker, M., Sattlecker, G., Birklbauer, J., Wegenkittl, S., Lindinger, S.J., Müller, E.: Effects of fatigue on postural control strategies during biathlon shooting-a nonlinear approach. In: Science and Skiing VI, Meyer & Meyer Verlag, Aachen, pp. 495–504 (2013)
24. Szczęsna, A.: Quaternion entropy for analysis of gait data. Entropy **21**(1), 79 (2019)
25. Hanson, A.J.: Visualizing Quaternions. Morgan Kaufmann, San Francisco (2005)
26. Goldman, R.: Understanding quaternions. Graph. Models **73**(2), 21–49 (2011)
27. Szczęsna, A., et al.: Inertial motion capture costume design study. Sensors **17**(3), 612 (2017)

Modelling of Vehicles Movements
for the Design of Parking Spaces

Miroslava Mikusova[1($\boxtimes$)] and Jamshid Abdunazarov[2]

[1] Faculty of Operation and Economics of Transport and Communications,
Department of Road and Urban Transport, University of Žilina,
Univerzitná 8215/1, 010 26 Žilina, Slovakia
mikusova@fpedas.uniza.sk
[2] Faculty of Auto Transport, Department of Land Transport Systems,
Jizzakh Polytechnic Institute, Islam Karimov Avenue 4, Jizzakh, Uzbekistan

Abstract. Nowadays, in all cities there is an acute problem of lack of parking spaces. The number of vehicles is significantly growing not only in megacities but also in small cities, and there are no more parking places. The pace of solving this problem is several times slower than the speed of transport growth among the citizens. Presented research is focused on determination of the optimum sizes of parking place for designed vehicles as an element of the roads. On example of passenger cars and trucks are determined optimum parking places. The results of research on dimensioning parking spaces are recommendations that should be used for the design of objects of transportation infrastructure.

Keywords: Passenger car · Truck · Auto train · Trajectory · Parking space · Turning radius of vehicles

1 Introduction

Trends in the size of cars in traffic flow, an acute shortage of parking space requires a more careful attitude to the design of the size of parking place and parking space [1–3]. Unfortunately, the design of parking does not take into account the composition of the traffic flow that takes shape on a specific road, transport infrastructure object (requirements are obvious here, in the USA where the size of cars is larger than in Europe, the size of parking space is larger), the duration of parking is not taken into account short-term parking near shops, banks, etc., requires more space for maneuvering upon arrival and departure from the parking space than during long-term parking) [4–7]. The most acute problem manifested itself when a ban was imposed on the transit movement of vehicles weighing more than 12 tons in the daytime along the Moscow Ring Road (Resolution of the Mayor of Moscow dated November 15, 2012 No. 650-PP "On Amendments to Legal Acts of the Government of Moscow" [8]). According to the Moscow mayor's office, more than 150 thousand trucks with a maximum weight of more than 3.5 tons are moving through the city streets during the daytime. About 40 thousand trucks arriving daily from the regions.

© Springer Nature Switzerland AG 2019
N. T. Nguyen et al. (Eds.): ICCCI 2019, LNAI 11684, pp. 464–475, 2019.
https://doi.org/10.1007/978-3-030-28374-2_40

At the Moscow Ring Road, large trucks make up 30% of the flow, half of which are transit and do not serve the needs of the capital [9]. At this time, there was no experience in designing parking place for cars arriving in Moscow or following in transit.

In the domestic regulatory and procedural documents, the dimensions of parking spaces for road infrastructure facilities are defined in the Methodological Recommendations of the SRC MDRS MIA [10], IRM 218.4.005-20101 и SS P 52289-20042. The dimensions in these documents were borrowed from the Handbook for Automobile Transportation and Traffic Management [11] published in the USSR in 1981, which, in turn, was a translation of the American Road Traffic Management Handbook of 1965 and the recommendations given in the third edition of the Transportation and Traffic Engineering Handbook [12].

Requirements for parking geometry in regulatory documents contain ambiguous, sometimes contradictory information that may adversely affect the level of road safety [13]. Thus, in the "Methodological recommendations on the design and equipment of highways to ensure traffic safety" [14], the turning radius of passenger cars is 8 m, and for truck is 9–12 m. When approximate calculation of the total area of coverage in parking place, including the area of maneuvering and parking, it is recommended to proceed from the average area per one passenger car of 25 m^2, on a truck −40 m^2. At the same time, in the album of typical projects "Cross-sectional profiles of highways passing through settlements" (TP503-0-47.86) 4, the average parking area for a truck should be 92.4 m^2, not 40 m^2, as stated in the methodological recommendations. The dimensions of the parking space given in the Regulations for the placement of multifunctional zones of road service on roads [15] take into account the size of modern cars, but this is not enough to develop a complete planning solution, since the parking maneuvers are not taken into account, and only the dimensions of the parking space are given. The passenger car and truck sizes used in the United States correspond to a parking angle of 45°, while it is indicated that at angles of 30°, the width of the passages can be reduced to 6.0 m, and the width of each parking space - by 30 cm. For large trucks, the length of the longitudinal parking space must be at least 41 m, width by 5.2 m. The same values are specified in the regulations of the United Arab Emirates for large trucks on parking spaces [16].

At the Department of Survey and design of roads MADI have been conducted research to justify the size of parking spaces for vehicles, taking into account the characteristics for modern traffic on the roads of the Russian Federation.

This research work included: monitoring parking maneuvers, studying the real situation when setting up parking spaces and modeling parking maneuvers of passenger cars and trucks using the AutoTURN software, which allows to simulate the movement and maneuvering of vehicles at speeds up to 60 km/h, and also to model three-dimensional movement on a 3D surface, localize modeling for various groups of vehicles; graphically represent the dynamic dimensions indicating the dynamic dimensions of the vehicles (external and internal wheels, characteristic points of the body); create vehicle reversal patterns [17]. In the study of the authors, it was found that the difference in AutoTURN data of the values of these parameters in comparison with the experimental values does not exceed 4.07%, that in the presence of a very similar nature of those and other curves, it can be considered valid and this makes it possible to use the results obtained on the software AutoTURN, and use this program when determining the dynamic size of cars.

Parking space for vehicles includes parking spaces for vehicles and a maneuvering area, designed for the entrance to parking spaces, exit and setting cars. The dimensions of the parking space must ensure unhindered entry, opening the doors of the vehicles, unloading or loading luggage, and then unimpeded exit without hitting other vehicles [18].

The dimensions of the car parking space determine its type and size (length, width, turning radius of the inner rear wheel, overhang, base, gauge). To be able to bypass and open the doors of the car, the parking dimensions should be 0.5 m larger than the corresponding dimensions of the designing vehicles [19–22].

The "Methodological guidelines for the design and equipment of highways to ensure traffic safety" [23] indicated that parking at large recreation areas, at roadside catering establishments, motels and campgrounds should be placed between the highway and buildings with vehicle separation by types and sizes. Parking areas for trucks and passenger cars should be demarcated and provide for each type of vehicle a separate entrance to the appropriate temporary parking area.

In this case, passenger cars and buses are recommended to have on the left, and trucks on the right in the direction of travel [24].

It is recommended to place the parking of trucks parallel to the axis of movement, while parking of passenger cars mainly should be arranged according to an oblique angle at an angle of 45°–60°. For long stays in the parking place, as well as in cramped conditions, when the parking place have one exit, it is recommended to install vehicles perpendicular to the direction of the axis of movement. Recommendations are given for the designation of the average area of coverage for one vehicle, taking into account the area of the exit and entry zones and the area of the parking space itself.

2   Modelling of the Movement of Vehicles

The dimensions of the parking spaces of cars are determined depending on the type of car and its parameters (length, width, radius of rotation of the inner rear wheel, the outer point of the front bumper, base, and gauge). To be able to bypass and open the doors of the car, the parking dimensions must be 0.5 m larger than the corresponding dimensions of the design vehicle. To determine the width of the maneuvering of parking spaces, the authors took into account the minimum turning radius of the design vehicle and its dynamic size. To do this, studies have been conducted by authors, which allowed us to determine these characteristics [25, 26]. In the study, the width of the passage was determined as follows. When designing the parking space and the entrance vehicles at parking spaces, the following schemes and provisions were applied in the calculations:

1. the road train leaves the parking space in the forward direction;
2. auto train drives backwards in a parking space;
3. road train drives forward;
4. the road train leaves the parking space in reverse.

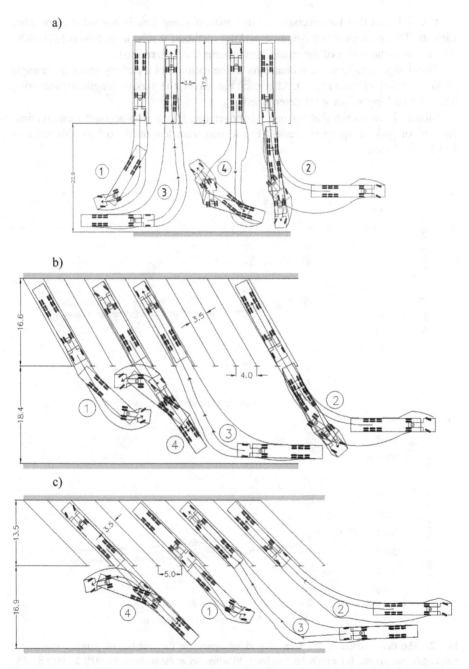

Fig. 1. Maneuvering schemes for a train (16.5 m) in a parking. (a) the location of the parking space at an angle of 90°; (b) the location of the parking space at an angle of 45°; (c) the location of the parking space at an angle of 60°. 1 - way forward; 2 - backing; 3 - forward ride; 4 - reversing

It was found that for reversing a large maneuvering lane is needed than in other variants. This maneuver is a common parking method for road train drivers [27]. With this in mind, the width of the maneuvering strip was determined.

The design vehicle made a maneuver at the location of a parking space at an angle of 90°, 60° and 45° (see Fig. 1). After each maneuver, the parking length, maneuvering lane, and parking width were determined.

Studies have shown that for one passenger car, taking into account maneuvering, 28.7 m² of parking space is needed. For a road train length of 16.5 m, this value is 143.1 m² of area.

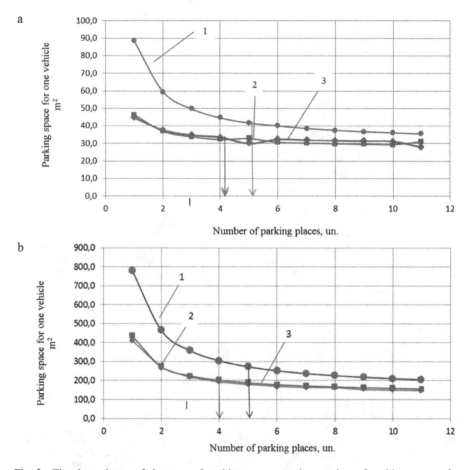

Fig. 2. The dependence of the area of parking space on the number of parking spaces for passenger cars (a) and for a train 16.5 m long (b) when set at the corners: 1 - 90°; 2 - 60°; 3 - 45°

From Fig. 2 it follows that with more than five parking spaces, the area of parking space for one vehicle does not increase (depending on the angle). When the parking space is located at an angle of 90°, and if there are less than 5 parking spaces in the parking, the parking space is reduced by one car. At the location of parking spaces at angles of 60° and 45°, the indicator is 4 parking spaces. Similar values are obtained for cars and for trucks. Proceeding from this, it can be concluded that, when parking places at an angle of 90°, designing less than five parking spaces is ineffective for any type of car, and if placed at angles of 60° or 45°, up to four parking spaces are considered ineffective.

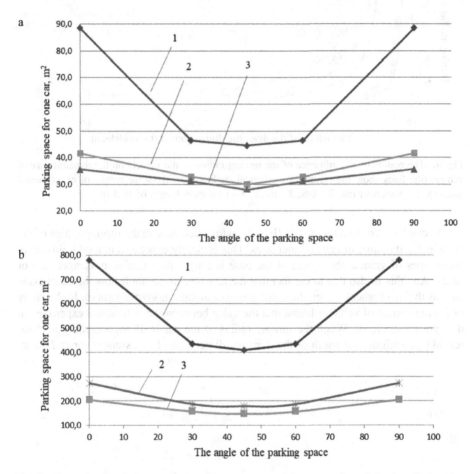

Fig. 3. Dependence of the required parking space at different angles of the installation for passenger cars (a) and for a train 16.5 m long (b): 1 - one vehicle; 2 - 5 vehicles; 3 - 11 vehicles

From Fig. 3 follows that at the location of parking spaces at an angle of 45°, less space is required than at an angle of 60° or 90°. These values do not affect the number of parking spaces; moreover, these values are the most effective indicator when maneuvering cars on a parking lot [28].

The results of theoretical and experimental studies by the author of the influence of the turning radius on the width of the dynamic dimension are shown in Fig. 4.

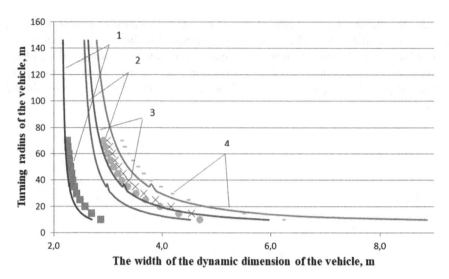

Fig. 4. The results of the influence of the turning radius of the vehicle on the dynamic size of vehicle (the lines show the results of theoretical studies, dots show the results of experimental studies). 1 - passenger car; 2 - bus; 3 - truck; 4 - road train length of 16.5 m

As can be seen from the results (Fig. 3), with a decrease in the turning radius of the vehicle, the dynamic dimension increases. This is clearly expressed in road trains, as in these types of vehicle the length of the base is longer than that of passenger cars or buses. And this is also due to the fact that the rear wheels do not follow the exact same path as the front wheels when the vehicle moves along a horizontal curve. In the study of the movement of vehicles found that the value between theoretical and experimental data are insignificant. When the turning radius of the car is 45 m, according to theoretical calculations, the width of the dynamic dimension of a passenger car is 2.25 m.

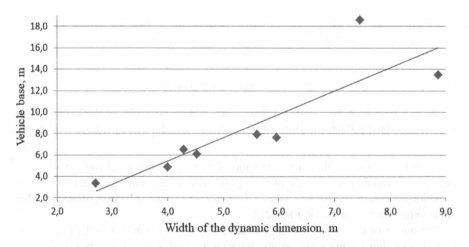

Fig. 5. Dependence of the dynamic dimension of the vehicle on its base

And the experimental data show 2.34 m. The greatest difference is noted for buses with a base of 6.1 m. If the theoretical dynamic dimension was 2.86 m, the experimental data show its values equal to 3.19 m with a turning radius of 45 m. The change in the dynamic dimension is typical for all types of vehicles, but its greatest changes are noted for road trains. With a turning radius of 45 m, according to theoretical calculations, the dynamic size of the train is 3.48 m, and according to the result of the survey it shows 3.64 m.

As follows from Fig. 5, the dynamic dimension of cars depends on the length of the base of cars. With the increase in the length of the base of the vehicle width of the dynamic dimension increases. The equations defining this dependence correspond to a straight line with the equation $y = 2,1774x - 3,2676$. The correlation coefficient is $R = 0.74$.

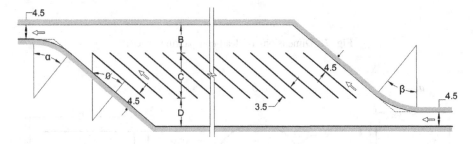

Fig. 6. Elements of breakdown of parking space for trucks. $\alpha - \beta$ – parking angle; $\emptyset$ – vehicle installation angle; B – D – maneuvering strip; C – parking module length

Table 1. Sizes of parking spaces at different corners of the parking of trucks

Installation angle, degree		Sizes of parking spaces, m (see Fig. 9)			
Ø	α	β	B	C	D
A 16					
30	30	30	7,5	12,0	7,5
35	35	35	8,5	13,0	8,5
40	40	40	8,7	13,5	8,7
45	45	45	9,5	15,5	9,5
A 20					
30	30	30	8,0	13,0	8,0
35	35	35	9,0	15,5	9,0
40	40	40	9,2	16,5	9,2
45	45	45	10,0	17,7	10,0

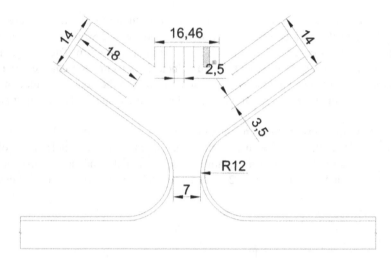

Fig. 7. Dimensions of dead-end parking spaces

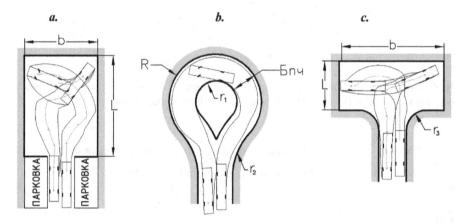

Fig. 8. Schemes of turning platforms on the territory of the road service facilities of the dead-end (a) circular (b) and T-shaped (c) type

3   Conclusions

Based on the above data, we can draw the following conclusions:

1. Less than 5 parking places at an angle of 90° is economically inefficient for any type of vehicle.
2. When located at angles of 60° or 45°, up to 4 parking places are considered to be economically inefficient.
3. On the dynamic size of the car affects the length of the base of the car. With an increase in the distance of the base length, the width of the dynamic dimension increases.

4. When determining the size of parking spaces should be taken into account the dynamic size of vehicle.

The following types of design vehicles were recommended as most frequently encountered on the roads: passenger car (P); city bus (CB); bus (B); articulated bus (AB); truck (T); road train consisting of truck tractor and semi-trailer (A16); road train consisting of a truck and a trailer (A20).

Considering the foreign experience of organizing parking spaces for large-sized vehicles, which provides for entry and exit to a parking without reversing, as a result of research, it is recommended to take the dimensions of parking spaces in accordance with the values in Table 1 and Fig. 6.

For servicing two-way traffic at road service facilities, the authors recommend dead-end parking spaces for semi-trailer (A16) (see Fig. 7).

If necessary, the organization of the reversal of vehicles, provide turning areas (Fig. 8), the dimensions of which are presented in Table 2.

Acknowledgment. This paper was supported by the Project 586292-EPP-1-2017-1-PL-EPPKA2-DBHE-JP - INTRAS - Intelligent Transport Systems: New ICT – based Master's Curricula for Uzbekistan, co-funded by the ERASMUS + scheme under grant agreement no. 2017-3516/001-001.

References

1. Mikusova, M., Gnap, J.: Experiences with the implementation of measures and tools for road safety. CIT 2016: XII congreso de ingenieria del transporte, Valencia, Spain, pp. 1632–1638 (2016)
2. Horalek, J., Sobeslav, V.: Analysis of software routing solution based on mini PC platform for IoT. In: Nguyen, N.T., Pimenidis, E., Khan, Z., Trawiński, B. (eds.) ICCCI 2018. LNCS (LNAI), vol. 11055, pp. 455–466. Springer, Cham (2018). https://doi.org/10.1007/978-3-319-98443-8_42
3. Mikusova, M., Torok, A., Brida, P.: Technological and economical context of renewable and non-renewable energy in electric mobility in Slovakia and Hungary. In: ICCCI 2018 - 10th International Conference on Computational Collective Intelligence - Special Session on Intelligent Sustainable Smart Cities, pp. 429–436 (2018)
4. Jamroz, K., Budzynski, K., Kustra, W., et al.: Tools for road infrastructure safety management - Polish experiences. In: 17th Meeting of the EURO-Working-Group on Transportation, Transportation Research Procedia, vol. 3, pp. 730–739 (2014). https://doi.org/10.1016/j.trpro.2014.10.052
5. Jankowska, D., Mikusova, M., Wacowska-Slęzak, J.: Mobility issues in selected regions of poland and slovakia – outcomes of international project SOL (Save Our Lives) survey. Periodica Polytech. Transp. Eng. **43**(2), 67–72 (2015). https://doi.org/10.3311/pptr.7580
6. Mikusova, M.: Joint efforts needed to prevent traffic accidents, injuries and fatalities. Saf. Secur. Eng. V, 503–514 (2013). https://doi.org/10.2495/safe130451
7. Mikušová, M.: Value of networking in transport policy related to the road safety. In: Mikulski, J. (ed.) TST 2011. CCIS, vol. 239, pp. 70–77. Springer, Heidelberg (2011). https://doi.org/10.1007/978-3-642-24660-9_8

8. Information and legal portal Garant. Electron. Dan. (2018). http://www.garant.ru/hotlaw/moscow/430367. Accessed 27 Jan 2018

9. Buranov, I.: Mayor shifted the burden of responsibility to the region. Newspaper "Kommersant", vol. 218 (5003) (2012)

10. Monitoring compliance with the norms, rules and standards when designation and construction of roadside facilities (service facilities). Methodical recommendations. SIC STSI of the Ministry of Internal Affairs of Russia, p. 28 (2004)

11. Rankin, V.U.: Automobile Transportations and the Organization of Traffic. Reference book. Per. from English, Rankin, V.U., Klafey, P., Halbert, S., et al. Transport, p. 592 (1981)

12. Baerwald, J.E.: Transportation and Traffic Engineering Handbook, 3rd edn., p. 717. Institute of Traffic Engineers, Washington (1965)

13. Mikusova, M.: Crash avoidance systems and collision safety devices for vehicle. DYN-WIND2017, vol. 107, Article num. 00024. https://doi.org/10.1051/matecconf/2017 10700024

14. Design and equipment of highways to ensure traffic safety. Methodical recommendations. Transport (1983)

15. Regulations for the placement of multifunctional road zones of the service on the highways of the State company "Russian highways" (Approved by the order of the State company "Russian highways" 24 June 2013 No. 114). http://www.rhighways.ru/for_investor/road_service/multifunctionalroad_service_area/. Accessed 18 Dec 2018

16. Machado, L., Merino Dominguez, E., Mikusova, M.: Proposta de índice de mobilidade sustentável: metodologia e aplicabilidade. Cadernos Metrópole, 14(July–December) (2012). ISSN 1517-2422. http://www.redalyc.org/articulo.oa?id=402837818011. Accessed 18 Jan 2019

17. AutoTURN. Advanced vehicle simulations, Transoftsolution. http://store.softline.ru/transoft/transoft-autoturn. Accessed 18 Sept 2018

18. Help for guests. Guidelines. Elektron. Data (2013). http://www.gosthelp.ru. Accessed 18 Dec 2018

19. Mikusova, M., Zukowska, J., Torok, A.: Community road safety strategies in the context of sustainable mobility. Commun. Comput. Inf. Sci. **897**, 115–128 (2018)

20. Abdunazarov Nurmuhumatovich, J., Mikusova, M.: Application of GIS in automobile-road sector (Using the ArcGIS example). In: CMDTUR 2018 - Proceedings of 8th International Scientific Conference, pp. 324–327 (2018)

21. Callejas-Cuervo, M., Valero-Bustos, H.A., Alarcón-Aldana, A.C., Mikušova, M.: Measurement of service quality of a public transport system, through agent-based simulation software. In: Huk, M., Maleszka, M., Szczerbicki, E. (eds.) ACIIDS 2019. SCI, vol. 830, pp. 335–347. Springer, Cham (2020). https://doi.org/10.1007/978-3-030-14132-5_27

22. Zukowska, J., Mikusova, M., Michalski, L.: Integrated safety systems - the approach toward sustainable transport. In: Archives of Transport System Telematics, vol. 10, no. 2, pp. 44–48 (2017). ISSN 1899-8208

23. The Methodical recommendations on designing and equipping the highways for road safety, Minavtodor RSFSR, M.: Transport (1983)

24. Alsobky, A., Hrkút, P., Mikušová, M.: A smart application for university bus routes optimization. In: Kováčiková, T., Buzna, Ľ., Pourhashem, G., Lugano, G., Cornet, Y., Lugano, N. (eds.) INTSYS 2017. LNICST, vol. 222, pp. 12–20. Springer, Cham (2018). https://doi.org/10.1007/978-3-319-93710-6_2

25. Abdunazarov, J.N.: Justification the parameters of design vehicles for the design geometric elements of highways, PhD's thesis, Moscow, MADI, p. 143 (2015)

26. Mikusova, M.: Sustainable structure for the quality management scheme to support mobility of people with disabilities. Procedia Soc. Behav. Sci. **160**, 400–409 (2014). https://doi.org/10.1016/j.sbspro.2014.12.152

27. Mikusova, M.: Proposal of benchmarking methodology for the area of public passenger transport. Periodica Polytech. Transp. Eng. **47**(2), 166–170 (2019). https://doi.org/10.3311/PPtr.10271

28. Abnunazarov, J., Mikusova, M.: Testing trajectory of road trains with program complexes, The Archives of Automotive Engineering – Archiwum Motoryzacji, AMO-00003-2018-02

The Importance of Rehabilitation for Disabled Citizens in SMART Cities

Libuše Svobodová$^{(\boxtimes)}$

University of Hradec Kralove, Rokitanskeho 62, 50003
Hradec Kralove, Czech Republic
libuse.svobodova@uhk.cz

Abstract. Innovations in technology over the last two decades have become a means to empower individuals with disabilities by becoming a tool for independence. The paper deals with the issue of rehabilitation and the development of computer literacy in our country with focus on the disabled citizens. Selected issues from Strategic framework for employment policy by 2030 in the Czech Republic are presented and examined. The aim of the paper is to identify key issues of rehabilitation, present model of coordinated rehabilitation on the free labor market by disabled citizens in the connection with future trends on the Czech market. This aim serves as a starting point for the reaching of the sub-goal, which deals with realization of interconnected and collaborative system of rehabilitation. Even education does not solve everything, people also need to improve on ICT and digital competences that are one of the part of smart cities in daily life. In professional life is spoken about Industry 4.0 and Work 4.0.

Keywords: Education · Rehabilitation · SMART city · Work 4.0

1 Introduction

The goal of the article is the analysis of the rehabilitation and digital literacy of people with disabilities and economic policy proposal of their life-long education in the era of Smart Cities. The value added is in the field of economic policy, smart education and a better life for people with disabilities. Citizens with disabilities are the part of the economic system. They can stay at home and do nothing or they can be part of the work environment and focus on outputs of the institutions and other goals. Citizens with disabilities are part of the current social system not only in the Czech Republic and they get social contributions and benefits. The most of the rehabilitation activities are unnecessarily finished at this point in the most cases. A lot of citizens with disabilities wouldn't get only social contributions but they would like to be legitimate part of the society in the companies and create values. Those individuals may use rehabilitation parts as are rehabilitation pedagogical, social and working. Experts will help to identify the possibilities and abilities of a disabled citizen and help to find opportunities for further education and retraining followed by employment in these parts of the imaginary chain of coordinated rehabilitation. The result is maximum self-sufficiency and a good sense of awareness of values in family with disabled and society. This is the ideal system that, unfortunately, does not work today.

© Springer Nature Switzerland AG 2019
N. T. Nguyen et al. (Eds.): ICCCI 2019, LNAI 11684, pp. 476–487, 2019.
https://doi.org/10.1007/978-3-030-28374-2_41

In 2014, Vyskočil stated in the Background for Government Policy Against NGOs by 2020 [1] that social business is a concept and phenomenon that gains popularity and raises the interest of the academic and professional public. It is important not only in the Czech Republic, but also abroad. In the concept of social business are often perceived indefinite activities, but always, as it is given by the name "social business", they are socially oriented and publicly beneficial, which can be considered as universal solver of social problems.

Čeledová and Čevela [2] dealt with the different breakdowns and perceptions of the rehabilitation process (Jesenský [3], Švestková [4], Novosad [5], Votava [6], Pfeiffer [7]). They carried out the research in rehabilitation, complete, comprehensive, complex rehabilitation, until they came to coordinated rehabilitation, which they consider to be the most important. They also refer to Maslow's pyramid needs, which coordinated rehabilitation gradually helps to fulfill.

1.1 Smart City × Social Aspects

In Komninos' definition from 2006 a smart city is defined as "territories with high capacity for learning and innovation, which is built—in the creativity of their population, their institutions of knowledge creation, and their digital infrastructure for communication and knowledge management" [8].

Giffinger et al. [9] considers "Smart" as a mean of a prospective performing taking into account the development aware, flexible, transformable, synergistic, individual, self-decisive and strategic aspects for smartness achieving. According to Giffinger et al. [9], Smart City is used to establish the smartness in industrial, educational, governmental sectors without forgetting the use of modern technologies in daily life, which means that there are significant activity's realms to the Smart City term, the thing that brought R. Giffinger identify 6 characteristics which are: "Smart Economy, Smart Environment, Smart Governance, Smart Living, Smart Mobility and Smart People".

To make things easier to understand, we can consider that the city is just a system that gathers many systems. Thus, we can define the city as a "System of Systems". So to get to Smart City, we just bring the intelligence to systems. The significance of the Smart City is the city that receives many contribution technologies from lots of companies by giving innovated products for the city markets to realize this intelligence, without forgetting innovations developing history evoked from traffic flows to the wireless technologies in order to precise and control parameters and, consequently, the individual choices to build smartness in various sectors [10].

Smart Economy is described by innovative, entrepreneurial, productive, flexible economy, trademarks and the integration in all markets types. For Smart People, we find the development of HL regarding their education and quality of social interaction. Smart Governance includes all political, administrative and public services aspects. We can also describe Smart Mobility by the wide accessibility, ICTS availability and new systems sustainability, Smart Environment that can be obtained thanks to acting on attractive natural conditions and environmental protections plans, as well as Smart Living that includes all quality of life aspects [10].

In 2008, the Council of Europe [11] identified 12 principles of good governance at local level. They include: fair conduct of elections, representation, and participation;

responsiveness; efficiency and effectiveness; openness and transparency; rule of law; ethical conduct; competence and capacity; innovation and openness to change; sustainability and long-term orientation; sound financial management; human rights; cultural diversity and social cohesion; accountability. The implementation of most of the above-mentioned principles can be supported, which is easy to notice, due to implementation of the concept of smart city.

In Poland were the following areas recognized as the ones with the highest convergence of Smart city: education, participation, social inclusion, GDP growth, financial services, infrastructure, research and development, economic innovation, entrepreneurship, employment, sustainable agriculture, industry, adaptation to climate change, and pollution. Activities in the scope of urban policy in Poland are focused on the improvement of the development conditions of Polish cities, and the first of them is the dissemination of the principles of public participation in decision-making and management of cities and their functional areas. The above-mentioned activities include the project initiated by the Ministry of Development entitled Human Smart Cities—smart cities co-created by the inhabitants [12]. Among others, this project includes the thematic area defined as "Innovative solutions aimed at supporting the social participation, as an element necessary for an intelligent city co-created by the inhabitants (3.0 Human Smart City)" [13].

Deloitte presents three key differentiators of a smart city [22]:

- Quality of life
- Economic competitiveness
- Sustainability

Economic competitiveness is presented as cities have long been important centers of trade and commerce, leveraging the proximity of so many diverse citizens to help drive an innovative economy. A smart city is a business-friendly city, ensuring that jobs and tax revenue form a healthy economic platform.

Cities function as 'engines of economic growth' and dominate local and national economies [23]. In paper was presented Smart City System building blocks that are: Smart people, smart economy, smart mobility, smart environment, smart living and smart governance. To transform itself into a smart city, a city has many areas in which it can act. Six basic directions for action will enable it to direct its objectives along this route, according to the definition of smart cities given by Boyd Cohen, an urban development researcher [24].

1. The smart economy: it is a city that wants to position itself as a capital of the new economy and innovation as well as a centre that draws people to it.
2. Smart governance: it is a city whose public services have entered the digital era with efficient online services, wifi and the use of digital data produced in the city.
3. The smart environment: it is a city which reconciles its roles as a living space, for mobility, an economic centre… while reducing its footprint on the planet (reduced consumption of energy and natural resources and reduced polluting emissions).
4. Smart mobility: it is the city which organises itself to offer an alternative to car congestion and pollution by promoting the effectiveness of means of collective and sustainable travel.

5. The smart population: it is a city which fosters the development of its citizens by levelling out inequalities and encouraging them to acquire skills.
6. The smart living environment: it is a city which pushes itself up to the highest level in terms of health and safety for example.

All of those mentioned parts of Smart city are connected with disabled citizens.

How can cities be made more accessible for disabled people? was discussed on April 2016 [25]. For the roughly 80 million EU citizens who have some form of disability, navigating the bustling maze of a city can pose all sorts of challenges. People with disabilities would often like to be more mobile and independent.

2 Methodology and Goals

This paper discusses the issue of education and the development of computer literacy in our country with focus on the disabled citizens in the work and education rehabilitation. Habits of future education and work in the context of industry 4.0 and work 4.0 are analysed.

- Latest data from the Czech national statistical office on the development of future education by disabled citizens are presented.
- Data from Strategic framework for employment policy by 2030 in the Czech Republic that focus on disabled people and digital Czech Republic are presented.

The aim of the paper is to identify key issues of further education of disabled citizens in the connection with future trends in the Czech market. This aim serves as a starting point for the reaching of the sub-goal, which deals with realization of interconnected and collaborative system of rehabilitation.

Literature review encompasses following areas: definitions to key expressions relevant to the scope of the paper like disabled citizens, rehabilitation, smart city, smart economy, social aspects etc.

The article is based on primary and secondary sources. The secondary sources provide information about rehabilitation, education and work, professional literature, information collected from professional press, web sites, discussions and previous participation at professional seminars and conferences related to the chosen subject. It was then necessary to select, classify and update accessible relevant information from the numerous published materials that provide the basic knowledge about the selected topic.

The main part of the article is based on the proposal of model of rehabilitation in the Czech Republic as solution that will led to gain knowledge and experience that will support all parts of rehabilitation and stakeholders in the context of disabled citizens in the Czech Republic. The article does not aim to provide one niche solution. The aim is to prepare ideas, resources and explanations justifying the need of education in ICT competencies. Potential solutions and recommendations will be discussed with experts in the field.

3   Use of Technologies and Education by People with Disabilities

Data from the national statistical office are presented. Data refer to utilization of information and communication technologies by individuals, esp. disabled citizens.

From 9 July 2018 to 18 January 2019, a selection survey on the lives of people with disabilities is being carried out throughout the Czech Republic under the abbreviation VŠPO 2018. VŠPO was in progress in 2013. Focus is not on data from doctors, but disabilities are directly asked in the Czech Republic. The investigation will be able to better understanding with which barriers and complications the people with disabilities are living. Within the Czech Republic, experienced interviewers of the Czech Statistical Office will address 9,000 pre-selected households in which is at least one person aged 15 or over with disabilities. Their responses will help get very valuable aggregate statistics and data that are not available from other sources. These data can serve, for example, as a basis and argument for enforcing legislative changes aimed at removing barriers and improving the current situation of persons with disabilities in the Czech Republic [14].

Since 2016, there are more households in the Czech Republic equipped with internet access rather than with a computer. In the Q2 of 2017 internet access was already used by 77% of households (3.4 million). In the past ten years, the number of households with internet access has increased by two million – in 2007 internet access was used by a third of Czech households (1.4 million).

Internet has become widely available to the general public, both in terms of accessibility as well as cost. A boundary was crossed in 2007, when for the first time a majority (55%) of households in the EU28 had internet access. This proportion continued to increase, passing three quarters in 2012, and four fifths in 2014. By 2017, the share of EU28 households with internet access had risen to 87%, some 32 per cent higher than in 2007. The fast growth of computer users in the Czech Republic is already over. However, this does not apply to all groups of citizens. In the past few years, the fastest growing number was the number of persons using a computer at the age of retirement or early retirement. In 2007, not even 8% of pensioners were using a computer; in 2017 this number increased to 36% of them [15].

Adult Education Survey was done in 2016 in the Czech Republic. It was focused on approaches and attitudes towards further education. We will focus on results aimed at involvement in further education and willingness to engage in education by economic status, people with disabilities.

Men who achieve higher participation in (non-formal) education than women generally do not declare their willingness to participate in education beyond what they have already completed, participate in any education at all if they did not join any educational activities during the period under review. 7% of disabled woman and 3% of disabled man participated in education and did not want to participate more. 4% of disabled woman and 2% of disabled man participated in education and wanted to participate more. 11% of disabled woman and 10% of disabled men did not participate in education but wanted to participate. Finally, 78% of women and 85% men did not participate and did not want to participate [16].

Group of disabled people is that who have to initiate their education, including career-oriented ones, usually by themselves, complicated by their involvement in external barriers such as health problems, lack of time to care for a family member, or lack of finances. From the results is evident that disabled women are not only more involved (mainly in non-formal) education, but their overall interest in education is higher (according to the general level of the declaration). Overall, however, the level of involvement in education among disable pensioners is relatively low [17].

The most significant difference disabled with other economic groups was recorded for health and age-related reasons. While for the other categories the highest response was 9%, it was 36% for disabled. Interestingly, only 7% of old-age pensioners said the same answer. Those who participated in formal or informal learning, 3% wanted to participate more, and 5% did not want to participate more. Those who did not participate in the education process were 10% willing to participate and 82% did not want to participate [16].

4 Proposal of Potential Solution and Strategic Framework for Employment Policy in the Czech Republic

We were asked by the company CPRHK s.r.o. from social business to prepare concept of collaborative rehabilitation with focus on work rehabilitation, keeping existing employees and adaptation to market developments. One of the development are changes in the economy and more and more use technologies in the companies. Concept of Industry 4.0 is expecting people educated in the field of ICT [18].

4.1 Strategic Framework for Employment Policy by 2030 in the Czech Republic

It appears that the modern labor market requires a more complex approach for some groups of disadvantaged people, which is not applicable in the current system to the necessary extent. One of them is further education and retraining. The main problem with retraining remains, in particular, their ability to respond to labor market demands, especially in the situations of dynamically changing skill needs. However, employers and workers are not satisfied with retraining and their process. Therefore document action plan of work 4.0 in the Czech Republic was done. Being aware of these new trends, and the Industry 4.0 Initiative, the Ministry of Labor and Social Affairs in 2016 develop a research study, Work Initiatives 4.0 ("Work 4.0"). The main effort of the Ministry of Labor and Social Affairs in this area is to analyze the current situation and future labor market trends related to the 4th Industrial Revolution and to prepare scenarios and measures to respond adequately to these changes. Addressing the impact of the 4th Industrial Revolution, digitization of state administration and the economy on society is a complex issue and, by its very nature, multiresort with regard to the spheres of social and economic life that interferes. For this reason, on the basis of Government Resolution No. 629/2018, program Digital Czech Republic was created, which is an umbrella strategic cross-sectional document. The process of setting up and implementing the program is coordinated by the Government Council for the Information Society. The Digital Czech Program consists of three basic pillars:

- Czech Republic in Digital Europe
- Information Concept of the Czech Republic
- The Digital Economy and Society

No less important role, such as the actual impacts of technological change, will be the demand for some services and the public sector's response to it in the future market.

The upcoming topic in the coming decade will be, in particular, to promote the adaptability of workers and their employers to new conditions and to significantly enhance the role of lifelong learning, including the employment of substantial further education. Further education will not be influenced only in terms of content or meaning in terms of acquiring skills and competencies for remaining or retention on the labor market, but the role of its actors will change as a result of changes in the organization of work.

We can expect to strengthen the role of competences, especially key transferable, and the emphasis on higher education and skills flexibility and the ability to work with ICT technologies and related digital literacy.

Qualitative labor market changes in the future carry the risk of an increased threat to some groups. First of all, it is about elderly people whose population is characterized by both a lower level of digital competences and a lower level of formal education. Although in the long run it can be expected that people with a certain experience in using ICT will be moving to older age groups, it is an undeniable fact that older people (at any given time) are less adaptable. At the same time, technological progress is very dynamic and dramatically transforms the set of necessary digital competences, which older generations can no longer respond adequately. Disabled citizens are very often in this group.

National Concept of Cohesion Policy Implementation includes also one of the following sub-area: to increase the participation of disadvantaged groups (also disabled citizens) in the labor market through personalized services and their more effective activation (including better targeting of active employment policy) [17].

4.2   Proposal of Potential Solution in Rehabilitations

In the Czech Republic is nowadays closed and competitive system between particular rehabilitations. They are not linked and they do not co-ordinate collaborate, see Fig. 1.

The aim of the future work is to link individual issues of rehabilitation so that they do not work only separately, but that citizens who have health or other problems get information in time and at the right place, what to do next and where to turn to "off" their partial, or complete dependence and become more self-sufficient. It is important to know each other in this "chain", to learn about the reasons for our behavior and the negotiation, the possibilities and barriers to the legislation and the economy of our activities. The proposed solution is presented in Fig. 2. Solution depend on the next key factors: the interest about education and retraining, the possibilities and equipment of disabled, money for the necessary changes in the process of retraining, content and type of retraining.

Fig. 1. Rehabilitation in the Czech Republic nowadays [according to 18]

It might be motivating do not study only from the printed materials, but to inter-connect it with electronic materials and to use elements of blended learning for dis-abled. Education may be realized in the companies where are disabled citizens working, in the special centers or from home. There are more possible ways which might be adopted, firstly learning management system on the virtual platform, secondly communities in social networks or special website or others. All solutions are signif-icantly different and have their pros and contras.

Disabled depended citizen is at the bottom. Between health and education reha-bilitation are doctors and the Czech social security administration. Between education and social rehabilitation are regions and cities. In the next step is the Chamber of Deputies Parliament of the Czech Republic and Integrated Portal of the Ministry of Labour and Social Affairs of the Czech Republic. At the top after all parts of reha-bilitation is disabled citizen that is supported and self-sufficient.

4.3 Computer Literacy, Industry 4.0, Work 4.0 and Disabled Citizens

Computer literacy ranks among not only useful but also already essential skills. Computer literacy like traditional literacy involves understanding text and visual symbols, and then it includes technical skills to use a computer and other related technology. Definition on computer literacy was taken from the online dictionary Business dictionary: Level of familiarity with the basic hardware and software (and now Internet) concepts that allows one to use personal computers for data entry, word processing, spreadsheets, and electronic communications. Read more: [19].

Maresova et al. [20] provide an overview of studies dealing with Industry 4.0 from the business and economic perspectives. A scoping review is performed regarding business, microeconomic and macroeconomic economic problems. Poor, Basl [26]

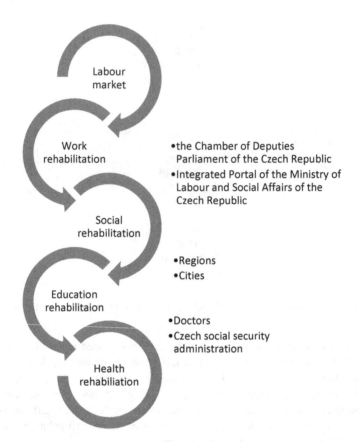

Fig. 2. Model of rehabilitation in the Czech Republic – proposed solution [according to 18]

focused on the processes of Industry 4.0 implementation in the Czech Republic. Vokoun et al. [27] focused on the strategic importance of human resources management and the roles of human capital investment and education and Novák et al. [28] focused on institutional analysis of the contemporary regional labour market in the Czech Republic.

Employment growth in the Czech Republic is mainly due to a large increase demand for workers in the manufacturing industry, which employs more men and women than in the EU 28 and more than in tertiary sector. This employment growth causes shortages of qualified labors on the market. In August 2016 the Government of the Czech Republic approved Initiative Industry 4.0, which aims to strengthen the competitiveness of the Czech Republic [21].

5 Conclusion and Discussion

Strategic framework for employment policy by 2030 in the Czech Republic [17] focus on the changes on the work market. It is expected that market will need more computer literacy educated people in the concept Work 4.0. Disabled citizens are mentioned in the plan as one of the group that can undergo further education in the computer literacy field to operate with advanced technologies and to use market gap.

Not only from professional practice, attendance at expert conferences, meetings and discussions, but also from the obtained professional resources, shows that in the area of social entrepreneurship there is place for innovation and to improve and make more effective the cooperation between the individual and the participants in the rehabilitation process. For disabled is important to participate in streamlining communication so that they do not only work separately but as a whole, so that the rehabilitated people get the best support for their involvement not only in the work process but also in the personal life. Connected topic "smart education" and disabled is not often solved in the professional literature. Only one article on this connected topic is presented in the database Scopus. Voronov et al. [29] describes the development of the software package "Surdotelephone" with the help of intelligent data processing technologies, such as machine learning methods, to help people with hearing impairments who receive distance education. Nemec, Chan [30] describes challenges for hiring, training, and supervising psychiatric rehabilitation service providers for positions that involve the use of digital health technology. Purpose of the paper is adoption and implementation of any new technology or technique requires workforce development. Both of those articles are interesting for some groups of disabled citizens that would like to undergone coordinated rehabilitation process. The suggested model (Fig. 2) presents interconnected process of rehabilitation that is recommended. Critical factors of success are communication effort and channels between individual stakeholders in the rehabilitation process and also finances are too important. Next factors are development on the labor market, competencies of disabled in the digital era and also quality of life. In the process of education rehabilitation may be used hybrid learning as a way to educate people became full smart cities residents [31].

It is desirable to raise stakeholders' interest and to make suggestions as if they were theirs. Nowadays is in the Czech Republic used closed and competitive system between particular rehabilitations. It is possible to recommend to realize interconnected and collaborative system of rehabilitation and to interconnect all links.

Acknowledgement. The paper is supported by the project SPEV 2019 at the Faculty of Informatics and Management of the University of Hradec Kralove, Czech Republic. In addition, the authors thank Anna Borkovcova for her help with the project.

References

1. Vyskočil, M.: Background to Government Policy Against NGOs by 2020, Social Entrepreneurship, 2014. https://www.vlada.cz/assets/ppov/rnno/dokumenty/studie_vyskocil_pro_web.pdf. Accessed 10 Feb 2019

2. Čeledová, L., Čevela, R.: Coordination of comprehensive rehabilitation. Praktický lékař **91** (11), 653–656 (2011)
3. Jesenský, J.: Introduction to the Rehabilitation of People with Disabilities. Karolinum, Praha (1995)
4. Novosad, L.: Fundamentals of Special Counseling. Portál, Praha (2000)
5. Pfeiffer, J., Votava, J.: Rehabilitation with Using Technology. Avicenum, Praha (1983)
6. Švestková, O., Hoskovcová, S.: New approaches to the look at disabled citizen and international classification of functional abilities, disability and health. E-Psychologie **4**(4), 27–40 (2010). http://e-psychologie.eu/clanek/106
7. Votava, J., Kol, A.: Comprehensive Rehabilitation of People with Disabilities. Karolinum, Praha (2005)
8. Komninos, N.: The architecture of intelligent cities. In: Intelligent Environments, vol. 6, pp. 53–61. 64 (2006)
9. Giffinger, R., Fertner, C., Kramar, H., Meijers, E.: Smart Cities: Ranking of European Medium-Sized Cities., Vienna University of Technology (2007)
10. Arroub, A., Zahi, B., Sabir, E., et al.: A literature review on smart cities: paradigms, opportunities and open problems. In: International Conference on Wireless Networks and Mobile Communications (WINCOM), pp. 180–186 (2016)
11. COEFLGR. 12 Principles of Good Governance and European Label of Governance Excellence (ELoGE); Council of Europe: Brussels, Belgium (2008)
12. Ministerstwo Inwestycji i Rozwoju HUMAN SMART CITIES. Smart Cities Co-Created by Residents. https://www.popt.gov.pl/strony/o-programie/wydarzenia/konkurs-dla-samorzadow-human-smart-cities-inteligentne-miasta-wspoltworzone-przez-mieszkancow/. Accessed 15 Nov 2018
13. Ministerstwo Inwestycji i Rozwoju Regulamin Konkursu Human Smart Cities. https://www.popt.gov.pl/media/56932/Regulamin_konkursu_Smart_Cities_final_maj_2018.doc. Accessed 15 Nov 2018
14. Selection survey of people with health restrictions – VŠPO. https://www.czso.cz/csu/vykazy/vyberove-setreni-osob-se-zdravotnim-omezenim-vspo
15. Use of Information and Communication Technologies in Households and Individuals (2018). https://www.czso.cz/csu/czso/vyuzivani-informacnich-a-komunikacnich-technologii-v-domacnostech-a-mezi-jednotlivci. Accessed 10 Feb 2019
16. Adult Education in the Czech Republic (2016). https://www.czso.cz/csu/czso/vzdelavani-dospelych-v-ceske-republice-2016. Accessed 10 Feb 2019
17. Strategic framework for employment policy by 2030 in the Czech Republic
18. Work Rehabilitation Center, Newsletter, 3 March 2018. http://www.cprhk.cz/ke-stazeni/newsletter/2018-03-newsletter.pdf. Accessed 10 Feb 2019
19. Computer literacy. http://www.businessdictionary.com/definition/computer-literacy.html. Accessed 10 Feb 2019
20. Maresova, P., Soukal, I., Svobodova, L., et al.: Consequences of industry 4.0 in business and economics. Economies **6**(3), 46 (2018)
21. Hedvicakova, M., Svobodova, L.: The labor market of the Czech Republic in the context industry 4.0. In: 20th International Colloquium on Regional Sciences, pp. 303–310 (2017)
22. Smart Cities of the Future - From vision to reality. https://www2.deloitte.com/us/en/pages/consulting/solutions/smart-cities-of-the-future.html
23. Vinod Kumar, T.M. (ed.): Smart Economy in Smart Cities. ACHS. Springer, Singapore (2017). https://doi.org/10.1007/978-981-10-1610-3
24. What is a smart city? https://smartcity.brussels/the-project-definition

25. How can cities be made more accessible for disabled people? 5 April 2016. https://www. debatingeurope.eu/2016/04/05/how-can-cities-be-made-more-accessible-for-disabled-people/#.XLTr9ugzY2w
26. Poor, P., Basl, J.: Czech republic and processes of industry 4.0 implementation. In: Annals of DAAAM and Proceedings of the International DAAAM Symposium, vol. 29, no. 1, pp. 0454–0459 (2018)
27. Vokoun, M., Caha, Z., Straková, J., Stellner, F., Váchal, J.: The strategic importance of human resources management and the roles of human capital investment and education. Sci. Pap. Univ. Pardubice Ser. D **25**(42), 258–268 (2018). Faculty of Economics and Administration
28. Novák, V., Vokoun, M., Stellner, F., Vochozka, M.: Institutional analysis of the contemporary regional labour market in the Czech Republic. E a M: Ekonomie a Management **19**(3), 4–19 (2016)
29. Voronov, V.I., Genchel, K.V., Voronova, L.I., Travina, M.D.: Development of a software package designed to support distance education for disabled people. In: Proceedings of the 2018 IEEE International Conference "Quality Management, Transport and Information Security, Information Technologies", IT and QM and IS 2018, pp. 746–751 (2018)
30. Nemec, P.B., Chan, S.: Behavioral health workforce development challenges in the digital health era. Psychiatr. Rehabil. J. **40**(3), 339–341 (2017)
31. Svobodová, L., Hedvicakova, M.: Use of smart technologies for hybrid learning as a way to educate people became full smart cities residents. In: Nguyen, N.T., Pimenidis, E., Khan, Z., Trawiński, B. (eds.) ICCCI 2018. LNCS (LNAI), vol. 11056, pp. 419–428. Springer, Cham (2018). https://doi.org/10.1007/978-3-319-98446-9_39

Cybersecurity Analysis of IoT Networks

Josef Horalek and Vladimir Sobeslav[(✉)]

Faculty of Informatics and Management, University of Hradec Kralove,
Hradec Kralove, Czech Republic
{josef.horalek,vladimir.sobeslav}@uhk.cz

Abstract. The goal of the article is to introduce the security risks connected with intelligent IoT networks and the recommendation of their elimination and the way to sustain them at an adequate level. Recommendations are related to general architecture of IoT for the risk management that presents one of many views for risk managements and their mitigation using standard and obligatory methods. These methods are practically tested within recommendations of general access for elimination of the cybernetic risks within IoT network solutions build on standard and generally accessible components.

Keywords: CIA triad · Parkerian hexad, IoT · MQTT · IoTWF · OneM2M · IoT-A

1 Introduction

During security solutions within Information and Communication Technologies (ICT) and Industrial Control System (ICS) technical and organizational security measures are set and their task is to fully eliminate or minimize security risks whose overall risks, defined by the risk analysis, reach beyond the acceptable set of values. During the application of the cyber security, the principles known as triads are implemented. Among the most used ones is CIA (Confidentiality, Integrity, Availability) triad combined with elements of the cyber security including People, Technology, Process combined with the cyber security life cycle Prevention, Detection, Reaction [1]. Security model Parkerian hexad [2–4] that extends CIA triad with Possession/Control, Authenticity and Utility is often used today. Utilization of these standardized approaches during employment of the cyber security is dependent on the used standard, model and architecture of intelligent networks. Among the most used architectures employed for the intelligent networks is OneM2M Standardized Architecture whose goal is to implement a single solution that will be simply applicable for IoT components already in use and simultaneously using horizontal structuring and REST. Simultaneously, it will abstract a great scale of devices, technologies and protocols by putting them into single and general result [5, 6]. Another important seven-layered referential model is IoTWF Standardized Architecture that provides clean, simplified view and deals with often overlooked sub-fields such as edge computing, data storage or access control [5, 7]. Another project trying to come up with a referential model that would help integration of a large amount of heterogeneous technologies found in IoT systems and help to narrow the connection among individual

© Springer Nature Switzerland AG 2019
N. T. Nguyen et al. (Eds.): ICCCI 2019, LNAI 11684, pp. 488–499, 2019.
https://doi.org/10.1007/978-3-030-28374-2_42

parts of the systems is IoT-A [5, 8]. The wide extent of diversification of approaches to architecture of intelligent IoT networks from the risks' point of view leads to division of approaches and acceptance of relevant and obligatory measures. Model solutions introduced below unequivocally prove that risks connected to the cyber security is possible to lower and keep in acceptable extent using generally used intelligent components for IoT networks.

2 General IoT Architecture for Risk Management

Despite the attempts for unified approach to architecture and unified model for intelligent IoT networks there is not a clearly defined general model based on which the risks using threats can be identified in individual layers. In the fact the only agreement is that architecture should be, like a reference model for creation of computer networks ISO/OSI, divided into several layers where each layer should be independent and easily replaceable if necessary. Similarly to ISO/OSI model, it is convenient to work with an abstract model that generally describes individual functionalities of each suggested layer and avoids description of specific implementation or suggestion of individually used protocols. The layers question can be solved from [9] where one of the easiest and most basic models describing architecture and three basic layers (Perception layer, Transportation layer and Application layer) is proposed. From the cyber security management point of view, it is recommended according to [10] to add Service layer. Dangers connected to Communication between layers, that are presented as fifth virtual layer, cannot be overlooked.

Application layer – with this layer different business process services work, examination and attempts to understand data take place here together with sorting and processing of intelligent data acquired from prior layer. Application layer can distinguish valid data, corrupted data or data used to overload the system. This layer should also be able to edit data, so they are usable by other services such as various mediators, cloud services or for example application service.

Great risk in application layer is incorrect configuration of remote access therefore danger of system configuration changes from the attacker's side. With incorrect security of service applications service information such as log files or passwords and cryptographic keys can leak. In case of incorrect security of driving applications wrong functionality of systems can happen due to abuse of faulty configuration.

Service layer – the main task of the service layer is to provide mediator that mediates some of the important functionalities in lower layers of model to the third-party applications or applications and services working in application layer. This service provision is based on expositions of standardized API.

Main security risks in this layer are provision of correct authorization and access control, sensitive and personal data leaking and abuse of provided services (for example overload, DoS attacks, recording of inappropriate information or slipping of false information).

Transportation layer – the main task of Transportation layer is data transfer to one of the data storages where they are saved for later use, or to provide data to one of the applications working at the highest layer.

Security risks of Transportation layer are tightly connected with security risks of individual protocols used for communication (mostly wireless). Most common security issue with communication protocols is possibility of transferred data surveillance which can cause leakage of sensitive data or cracking of security in use. Another issue is common DoS attacks.

Perception layer – the main task of perception layer (sometimes described as physical layer) is surveillance, information gathering and ability to control individual objects in this layer. Described layer can be divided into two parts – perception node (sensors, actuators, smart object and other physical devices) and perception network, which task is to connect individual physical devices and enable their communication and data exchange and enable transfer of collected data to higher layers of model.

In this layer there are specific security dangers; non-functioning or attack (program or physical) on any of the end devices can cause credibility of the data breach, DoS type attack or Flooding, leaking of sensitive user information, routing problem or abuse of cryptographic keys.

Communication between layers – finally it is necessary not only to examine functionalities found in individual layers of introduced models but also focus on communication undergoing between individual layers. There are security risks which cannot be ignored, for example the possibility of sensitive information leaking because it is not secured while switching between individual layers, wrong authorization conversion of individual entities (the user might not have same level of access to information in different layers) or mishandling of information that are duplicated when used in more layers at once.

3 Model Solution Proposal

The main task of the present solution is to introduce easy a universal model of hardware-software architecture that, with the help of commonly available devices such as Raspberry Pi or Arduino and freely attainable technologies, simulates real instances of use, that are visible in already existing solution for networks of Internet of Things type Fig. 1.

Basic preview of prepared architecture shows that there are one or more central components in the network that feature sufficient computing performance for the execution of role of the central server. The task of the central server is network communication control, reception, processing, forwarding of data and executing computing or high-energy using operations such as authorization of individual elements in network, generating and management of certificates or cypher keys. The rest of the elements in the network are energetic and computing restricted devices which task is to either gather surrounded data and information with help of set sensors or to execute appropriate tasks based on received data or commands with help of set actuators. These devices either have a microcontroller or they are directly physically connected to the neighbouring device that have their own microcontroller. The elements with a type of microcontroller and a communication model are capable of communication and data exchange with central server using suitable wireless technology.

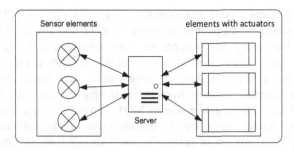

Fig. 1. Visualization of architecture

3.1 Utilization of Hardware Elements

For realization and testing of proposed architecture Arduino, Raspberry Pi and ESP8266 were used.

Arduino was used as a client device in two board variants. The first of them was version labelled UNO that uses only 32 kB flash memory for data storage and 2 kB RAM memory, the second one was version labelled MEGA that features higher performance being 256 kB of flash memory and 8 kB RAM.

Raspberry Pi was used, thanks to relatively high computing performance and Linux operation system, as the central server. Specifically, the Raspberry Pi 3 Model B by Broadcom company was used; it uses a quadcore processor with 1.2 GHz frequency, 1 GB DDR3 RAM, internal storage with 32 GB capacity and it can communicate with its surrounding thanks to Wi-Fi or Bluetooth LE technology. As the operational system Raspbian version 4.9.41. was used.

ESP8266 is a programmable microchip by Espressif Systems company; it has complete support of TCP/TP stack and communicational Wi-Fi standard. Within introduced solution microchips ESP8266 with 4 MB flash memory and 96 kB operational memory were used. It is important to consider that the installed Wi-Fi model uses more than a half of total memory capacity to work properly therefore <45 kB operational memory is available for user programs.

3.2 Solution for Network Communication

The decision to use described HW elements influenced the choice of network protocols, mostly because ESP8266 microchips which manage the wireless communication can work only with IP stack and Wi-Fi communicational standard. However, because it is expected that IoT type solution will be eventually at least partially connected to Internet network, it should not cause problems. For these reasons it was possible to choose from the pool of protocols in transportation and application layer. The decision to use Internet network seems clear because it functions for a long time based on combination of transportation protocol TCP and application protocol HTTP often combined with REST. However, because of big direction connected with these protocols, using them in networks with limited computing devices is not recommended. For these reasons two reduced protocols that are often used in already existing solutions of IoT type were used – MQTT protocol that in transportation layer uses reliable TCP protocol and implements suggested model publish/subscribe. MMQT was also used because in the introduced architecture it is not possible to ensure reliable connection between individual ending elements and the central server, and the set solution does not need to use protocol to manipulate the data. Another factor was the fact that for the functionality purpose of set architecture the more suitable was the publish/subscribe model than the request/response one. The negative side to MQTT protocol comes from the concept designed to be the simplest and to be effective and used without problems with devices that feature very small amount of calculating and memory sources. This limits possibilities for security and it is necessary to deal with higher security at the application level. MQTT protocol offers authentication feature; for devices connected to MQTT broker at its basic form it provides a protocol with the possibility to use unique client identificatory, client user name and password. These attributes are sent as a part of CONNECT packet head. The first potential security problem while using this type of authentication is that till the 3.1.1. protocol version which officially recommended passwords to be maximally 12 characters long and specific identifiers to not be longer than 23 characters, and in consequences. |This made it impossible to use sufficient safety series. The newer version of protocol does not require these suggestions and it should not cause serious security risks. Another risk while using authentication implemented in MQTT protocol is that CONNECT packets which parts are authentication attributes are sent between a client device and broker without any system of cyphering, therefore in form of simple text. Therefore, if anyone manages to catch packet send in this form, they can use these attributes to false authentication of the device and endanger integrity of the solution. If we want to use built-in authentication mechanism safely, it is necessary to implement cyphering of sent packets in lower layers of architectonic model. Because the wireless communication is considered dangerous, the only solution is solution implementation in the transportation layer. This solution is often implementation of TLS protocol (or IPSEC or TDLS) Fig. 2.

```
▶ Frame 28: 149 bytes on wire (1192 bits), 149 bytes captured (1192 bits) on interface 0
▶ Ethernet II, Src: 00:00:00_00:00:00 (00:00:00:00:00:00), Dst: 00:00:00_00:00:00 (00:00:00:00:00:00)
▶ Internet Protocol Version 6, Src: ::1, Dst: ::1
▶ Transmission Control Protocol, Src Port: 33660, Dst Port: 1883, Seq: 1, Ack: 1, Len: 63
▼ MQ Telemetry Transport Protocol
  ▼ Connect Command
    ▶ 0001 0000 = Header Flags: 0x10 (Connect Command)
      Msg Len: 61
      Protocol Name: MQTT
      Version: 4
    ▶ 1100 0010 = Connect Flags: 0xc2
      Keep Alive: 60
      Client ID: mosqpub|8195-raspberryp
      User Name: Test user
      Password: Test password
▶ Frame 48: 178 bytes on wire (1424 bits), 178 bytes captured (1424 bits) on interface 0
▶ Ethernet II, Src: 00:00:00_00:00:00 (00:00:00:00:00:00), Dst: 00:00:00_00:00:00 (00:00:00:00:00:00)
▶ Internet Protocol Version 6, Src: ::1, Dst: ::1
▶ Transmission Control Protocol, Src Port: 58638, Dst Port: 8883, Seq: 2626, Ack: 3457, Len: 92
▼ Secure Sockets Layer
  ▼ TLSv1.2 Record Layer: Application Data Protocol: mqtt
      Content Type: Application Data (23)
      Version: TLS 1.2 (0x0303)
      Length: 87
      Encrypted Application Data: 64dc4d24f4ad9d71a0615cadb779664061812e993b2e2b54...
```

Fig. 2. Comparing the CONNECT packet using the MQTT protocol itself and using MQTT in combination with the TLS implementation in the transport layer

If the authentication process was successfully implemented, it is possible to authorize a client for reading and recording into the chosen set of existing topics that are managed in server using ACL of files. The file should be, similarly to other files of the same type, saved on the server in the way that no unauthorized person should be able to change the content.

In special cases when it is not possible to use security mechanism of the transportation layer for the implemented solution (in Internet of Things type networks it is mostly because of insufficient calculating performance on client's or server's devices), it is possible to use content cyphering of PUBLISH packets in the application layer. For this model simple symmetrical cyphering can be utilized (i.e. AES) for its calculating simplicity, for providing end-to-end cyphering data, or for providing cyphered communication through MQTT protocol in settings with very limited computing resources; alternatively, it provides a possibility to add another security layer to setting where it is necessary to have maximal security of transferred data. One of the security risks is necessity for installation and management of cyphered keys in individual client devices or alternatively ensuring unproblematic exchange or invalidation of the keys that opens way to unwanted or deliberate administrator mistakes. Unlike with TLS protocol use we are not able to 100% verify originator of the sent data and our solution can potentially become subject for man-in-the-middle or replays attack attacks.

4   Model Solution Implementation

Clear identification of client devices – to ensure the possibility of clear identification of the end devices is one of the key functions for correct functionality of the implemented solution. Thanks to this quality, it is possible to keep renewable session for MQTT broker connection and therefore ensure reliable exchange of data even through unreliable connection or during malfunction or temporary shutdown of some of the end devices. Clear identification is also crucial for reliable and functional implementation of authorization and authentication processes. Because suggested solution for wireless communication uses technology using IP stack and work with IP addresses would be possible, it is not a flexible approach in the case of changing communication technologies usual in solutions of IoT types. Therefore, it was necessary to choose an attribute that was not dependant on the choice of the communication technologies to ensure clear identification of the end devices. As a solution for ESP8266 type microchips chosen for securing the communication services, utilization of MAC addresses of individual devices has been proposed. However, because the first part of MAC address is assessed for identification needs of microchip producer identical with most of the devices of this type, only last three bytes of MAC address device will be used in this solution for identification.

Server device setting – the central server element plays the main role. in implemented architecture. The proposed solution utilizes MQTT broker whose task is to manage connections of individual clients and their authentication and authorization, messages reception that the clients publish in individual topics and assurance of subsequent publication of the messages to all clients that lawfully registered for their subscription. The device ensuring this function is Raspberry Pi on which the solution based in Eclipse Mosquitto project was implemented. The principal reason for this implementation was openness of the source code. Thanks to this, the implementation is accessible to public audit and therefore it is possible to prevent security risks that could be hidden deep in the source code, or to react quickly to them. Another advantage is the possibility of fast creation of client test devices inside the system terminal. Consequently, the testing of any newly used or changed configuration is easier. Installation of Mosquitto broker is standard as installation of software packet for Debian, whose part is the broker, which can be turned on as the user programme or as the system service.

Authentication configuration of client devices – in its basic version MQTT protocol is capable of executing authentication of connected end devices with the help of transferred user name in combination with the password. Implementation of MQTT broker Mosquitto in default version supports only definition of authentic pairs of user names and passwords in form of file loaded from the file system of server device which content is adjusted so the user passwords are cyphered. Because this file containing sensitive data is saved directly on the server device, it is better for the reduction of security risks not to enable reading and other manipulations with the file by users other than the user using Mosquitto broker instances.

If the character of solution required possibility of some definition of the authentic users (i.e. from cyphered data table or from question about privileged web server that secures other types of authentication in network), it is possible to extent Mosquitto with some of the freely available authentication plugins that implement required definition system. To turn on the authentication of the client devices on Mosquitto broker, it is necessary to define the way in the configured file to the file containing the list of allowed users with following command password_file <path> and afterwards order the broker to use the file to authenticate every new connected client device. This can be achieved by configurations command allow_anonymous false Fig. 3.

Fig. 3. Authentication file

Authorization of client devices – another possibility for security that is available in MQTT protocol is authorization of connected client devices. Mosquitto enables authorization of connected client devices to entry and reading of data only in topics to which permission was given. In basic version of Mosquitto broker this can be achieved by defining simple rules to the classic ACL file. Every rule written in ACL file grants the client device one or two permission to specific topic and permission can be given for reading, writing or both. Rules themselves are divided into three independent sections in ACL file. In the first section there are general rules and these rules define authorization of all users that connected anonymously and therefore did not give broker their user name and password.

Communication setting through TLS – in the solution the authentication and authorization systems are used with help of user name and password. For their safe use it is necessary to implement cyphered communication in transportation layer; in this case with the help of TLS protocol. The first problem that needs to be solved during the implementation of communication through TLS protocol is the choice of reliable certification authority that will guarantee the origins of certificates that will identify individual devices. However, because for our solution, it is not necessary to use publicly recognized authorities; personal certification authority was chosen to sign individual client and server certificates with help of OpenSSL software package.

Client devices setting – client devices Arduino IDE developer settings was used to program; after that library package extension Arduino Core for ESP8266 Wi-Fi chip was added. This enabled writing of firmware controlling microchips ESP8266. Pre-compiled firmware NodeMCU was also used, and individual user programmes were written with the help of script language LUA that places high demands on already limited RAM memory capacity.

Connection of Wi-Fi network type device – because the communication that uses standard Wi-Fi is one of the main functionalities, it is enough to import one of the service classes of used library, for Arduino Core it is specifically "ESP8266WIFI" class, then to define SSID access point and password to access the network. Then it is recommended to pre-set the behaviour of the microchip to client regime, in the opposite case the chip would try to behave like a client and it would draw excessive amount of already limited calculating resources as shown in the code below.

```
#include <ESP8266WiFi.h>
const char *ssid="SSID";
const char *pass="PASS";
void setup_wifi(){
    // set wifi to client mode
    WiFi.mode(WIFI_STA);
    WiFi.begin(ssid, pass);
    While (WiFi.status() !=WL_CONNTECTED){
        Delay (500)
    }}
```

Communication with MQTT broker – important functionality necessary for putting the client device into operation is correct and functional communication with server broker while using MQTT protocol. For this the simple library PubSub Client was created which enables to make connection to MQTT broker and to send any message to chosen topic. Except for message publication, the device can subscribe to any topic and accept messages that were published by other clients in this topic. Library itself can connect to broker or use one of the implemented service class that is able to create secure connection through TLS protocol according to the example below.

```
#include <PubSubClien.h>
const char * mqtt_broker="XXX.XXX.XXX.XXX";
const uint16_t * mqtt_broker_port=1883;
const char * mqtt_topic="/temperature";
const char * device_name="ESP8266";
const char * mqtt_message="Hello!";
        //defining collback before client initialization
Void msg_callback(char* topic, byte* payload, unsigned int
length);

PubSubClient    pubsubClinet(mqtt_broker,    mqtt_broker_port,
msg_vallback, WifiClient);
Void do_broker_connection() {
        if (!pubsibClinet.connected() {
            while (!pubsibClinet.connected() {
            pubsibClinet.connected(device_name);)
            pubsibClinet.subscribe(mqtt_topic);
            pubsibClinet.publish(mqtt_topic, mqtt_message);}
        pubsubClient_loop(); }
    void msg_callback(char* topic, byte* payload, unsigned int
lenght] {
        for (int i=0; i<length; i++){
        serial.print ((char]payload[i]);}
    Serial.println();}
```

Setting of TLS on client's side – TLS protocol will be used to secure communication on transportation layer. If the protocol is correctly and completely implemented, it is possible to safely verify the identity of individually connected client devices but also of the server itself that runs on MQTT broker instances. This way the reliability and integrity of every message is secured. With correct implementation of TLS protocols in devices used in IoT type solution for the reasons of high calculating and data demands used in cryptographic algorithms added to direction because of installation and subsequent management of client and server certificates. The problem of calculating and data demands can be suppressed by using one of the libraries which are implemented in the way for them to be possibly used in devices such as microchips ESP8566. The following three free access libraries were tested:

- **embedTLS** – is the first tested library available in pre-compiled nodeMCU firmware. This library uses LUA script language and because of the high demand on RAM the implementation experiment that would be able to communicate with client and server authentication was not successful.
- **BearSSL** – this library has a potential to become the primary TLS tool available in Arduino Core for ESP8266 library package, however, its employment is still in testing phase. The advantage of this library is the possibility of choice between classical implementation using RSA algorithm or alternatively using algorithm over elliptic curves. At the time of testing the library was not completely functional therefore the safe and reliable use was not possible.

- **axTLS** – the library is implemented as a default solution for TLS communication in Arduino Core for ESP8266 packet. Using this library communication between broker and client device was fully provided with functional verification of server and client certificates.

AxTLS library is implemented in Arduino Core as part of the WifiClientSecure service class that secures safe communication. The library has a lot of properties and thanks to them an unproblematic and safe management with low-performance devices is possible. The properties are for example extremely small memory print of the library itself, session resumption support (in other words it is not necessary to undergo memory demanding handshake process during every connection loss), optional size of used cyphered keys, etc. From the security viewpoint is it necessary to mention that the library can run TLS version of 1.2 protocol, which is currently considered safe. A drawback is that there is support of only one cypher algorithm packet (in this case RSA) and with that is connected zero possibility for optimization in area where, under different circumstances, we could for example save up by using algorithms based on elliptic curves.

For identity verification the library uses classical X509v1 type certificates. The certificate can be loaded into the memory either in form of byte field or ASCII series (in TLS protocol terminology – DER or PEM format certificates).

Last but not least, while using the certificates it is necessary to take care of their safe creation as well as to pay attention to their safe storage using device featuring special chip used for sensitive information saving that guarantees that they cannot be read retrospectively not even in the case that the attacker has physical and unrestricted access to the device.

5 Conclusion

The aim of the article was to introduce a new view to the cybernetic risks solutions in intelligent IoT networks. To reach the defined goal it was necessary to first define and set general architecture of IoT networks from the viewpoint of risk control when the layer viewpoint was used with analysis of individual risks per individual layer. This approach allows to suggest an effective complex solution with optimization of accepted mitigation measures per individual layer including their substitution when it is not technically or organizationally possible to realize set measures in a particular model layer.

For practical testing and verification of the chosen approach a general model of intelligent IoT network have been created using standard and commonly accessible HW technologies commonly implemented for IoT such as Arduino, Raspberry Pi 3 Model B platforms and programmable microchip ESP8266. Exchange of data itself in the present solution have been realized while using lightweight MQTT protocol that uses proposed publish/subscribe model and is designed for employment in networks with restricted calculating and data tools.

Possibilities of security were introduced and illustrated. They are a part of the basic version of MQTT protocol such as the user authentication using the user name and password and their authorization with individual data sources with help of rules defined in ACL file, as well as using another supporting tools that have restricted possibilities for security of this protocol widening it with more security layers. One of the tools was deployment of TLS protocol in the transportation layer of the model. Functional deployment of this protocol including functioning client and server authentications presented a challenge with chosen and performance limited hardware elements, but it was solved after a few unsuccessful attempts by using lightweight axTLS library.

The result proves suitability of layered IoT model for risk management and real demand for standard of cyber security in environment of intelligent IoT networks while using limited performance equipment. This leads to the result that it is not necessary or relevant to demand commercial elements or advanced IoT security methods, or to implement them and it is possible to achieve that IoT networks are not perceived as security risks, but fulfil security standards in ICT world.

Acknowledgment. This work and the contribution were supported by a Specific Research Project, Faculty of Informatics and Management, University of Hradec Kralove, Czech Republic. We would like to thank Mr. L. Mercl, a doctoral student, and Mr. J. Rydl, a graduate, of Faculty of management and informatics, University of Hradec Kralove, for the practical verification of the proposed solutions and close cooperation in the solution.

References

1. Andress, J.: The basics of information security: understanding the fundamentals of InfoSec in theory and practice. Second edition. Boston: Elsevier/Syngress, Syngress is a imprint of Elsevier (2014). ISBN 9780128007440
2. Rjaibi, N., Rabai, L.B.A.: Developing a novel holistic taxonomy of security requirements. Procedia Comput. Sci. **62**, 213–220 (2015). https://doi.org/10.1016/j.procs.2015.08.442. https://linkinghub.elsevier.com/retrieve/pii/S1877050915025776. Accessed 11 Feb 2019, ISSN 18770509
3. Li, S., Tryfonas, T., Li, H.: The Internet of Things: a security point of view. Internet Res. **26** (2), 337–359 (2016)
4. Li, S., Xu, L.D., Romdhani, I.: Securing the Internet of Things. Syngress, Cambridge (2017). ISBN 9780128044582
5. Hanes, D., Salgueiro, G., Grossetete, P., Barton, R., Henry, J.: IoT Fundamentals: Networking Technologies, Protocols, and Use Cases for the Internet of Things. Cisco Press Fundamentals Series. Cisco Press, Indianapolis (2017). ISBN 9781587144561
6. Anton-Haro, C., Dohler, M.: Machine-to-machine (M2M) Communications: Architecture, Performance and Applications. Woodhead Publishing Limited, Cambridge (2015). Woodhead Publishing series in electronic and optical materials, no. 69. ISBN 9781782421023
7. Gubbi, J., Buyya, R., Marusic, S., Palaniswami, M.: Internet of Things (IoT): a vision, architectural elements, and future directions. Future Gener. Comput. Syst. **29**(7), 1645–1660 (2013). https://doi.org/10.1016/j.future.2013.01.010. Accessed 2019-02-09, ISSN 0167739X
8. Pisching, M.A., Junqueira, F., Santos Filho, D.J., Miyagi, P.E.: An architecture for organizing and locating services to the industry 4.0. In: 23rd ABCM International Congress of Mechanical Engineering Rio de Janeiro Dezembro, pp. 1–8 (2015)

9. Jing, Q., Vasilakos, A.V., Wan, J., et al.: Wireless Netw. **20**, 2481 (2014). https://doi.org/10. 1007/s11276-014-0761-7

10. Hosenkhan, R., Pattanayak, B.K.: A secured communication model for IoT. In: Satapathy, S. C., Bhateja, V., Somanah, R., Yang, X.-S., Senkerik, R. (eds.) Information Systems Design and Intelligent Applications. AISC, vol. 863, pp. 187–193. Springer, Singapore (2019). https://doi.org/10.1007/978-981-13-3338-5_18

Using Wavelet Transformation for Prediction CO₂ in Smart Home Care Within IoT for Monitor Activities of Daily Living

Jan Vanus, Alice Krestanova, Jan Kubicek$^{(\boxtimes)}$, Ojan Gorjani,
Marek Penhaker, and David Oczka

Department of Cybernetics and Biomedical Engineering,
Faculty of Electrical Engineering and Computer Science, VSB–Technical
University of Ostrava, 17. Listopadu 15, Ostrava, Czech Republic
{jan.vanus, alice.krestanova.st, jan.kubicek,
ojan.majidzadeh.gorjani.st, marek.penhaker,
david.oczka}@vsb.cz

Abstract. In Smart Home Care (SHC) rooms from the measured operational and technical quantities for monitoring activities of every day of life for support of independent life for elderly people. The proposed algorithm for data processing (predicting the CO_2 course using neural networks from the measured temperature indoor T_i (°C), temperature outdoor T_o (°C) and the relative humidity indoor rHi (%)) was applicated, verified and compared in MATLAB SW tool and IBM SPSS SW tool with IoT platform connectivity. In the proposed method, a stationary wavelet transformation algorithm was used to remove the noise of the resulting predicted waveform of expected process. Two long-term experiments were performed (specifically from February 8 to February 15, 2015, from June 8 to June 15, 2015) and two short-term experiments (from February 8, 2015 and from June 8, 2015). For the best results of the trained ANN BRM within the prediction of CO_2, the correlation coefficient R for the proposed method was up to 90%. The verification of the proposed method confirmed the possibility to use the presence of people of the monitored SHC premises for rooms ADL monitoring.

Keywords: Smart Home Care (SHC) · Monitoring · Prediction ·
Trend detection · Artificial Neural Network (ANN) ·
Bayesian Regulation Method (BRM) · Wavelet Transformation (WT) ·
SPSS (Statistical Package for the Social Sciences) IBM ·
IoT (Internet of Things) · Activities of Daily Living (ADL)

1 Introduction

In this time, in population increase interesting about modern technologies with focused to automation. User can manage operational and technical things easily in environment along with providing support for the independent housing of elderly persons and disabled people in buildings indicated as Smart House Care (SHC), from this reason we make visualization of the technological process as required by the users. IT can be possible to

© Springer Nature Switzerland AG 2019
N. T. Nguyen et al. (Eds.): ICCCI 2019, LNAI 11684, pp. 500–509, 2019.
https://doi.org/10.1007/978-3-030-28374-2_43

monitoring life of senior citizens with using sensors. These sensors are used for the common management of the operational and technical functions in Smart House Care.

In simple words, the IoT is using for sending data and receiving data in objects, too. The main contribution of the article is to verify the assumption of improving the accuracy of the CO$_2$ prediction method using ANN BRM with the Wavelet Transformation filter algorithm to remove additive noise from the predicted CO$_2$ course.

2 Related Work

The visualization has got a sensor data, which are situating in the building for sensing the duration of the activities [1]. Fleck describes a method, which it has got a core in intelligent cameras for monitoring of all day and supervision of elderly people. For display information about life in intelligent home is using visualization, when it includes evaluation of the place where senior is and sensing his activities [2]. In this time, processing of big data of measured quantities using Soft Computing Methods (SC) [3, 4], which are available for Big Data Analysis within the IoT platform [5, 6].

The Internet of Things, known briefly as the IoT, can be seen as an integration layer that creates links between several physical devices, sensors, actuators and regulators [7]. For example, Xu et al. uses IoT for real-time system design for micro-environment parameters such as temperature, humidity, PM10 and PM2.5 [8]. Min et al. has proposed the use of the IoT for observation of discrete manufacturing [9].

Wang et al. is viable Internet of Things monitoring system that combines wireless sensor network, embedded development, GPRS communication technology, web service, and Android platform for mobile [10].

Windarto et al. represent an application of IoT by implementing automation of lights and door in a room [11]. Coelho et al. used IoT to collect data from multiple heterogeneous sensors that were providing different types of information a variety of locations in a smart home [12]. Data collection in these examples usually leads in big data. Data collection in this kind of examples usually results in big data. The Oxford dictionary defines big data as "Extremely large data sets that may be analysed computationally to reveal patterns, trends, and associations, especially relating to human behaviour and interactions" [13].

Arnold investigates the IBM's Watson approach, combines the used techniques with other artificial intelligence methods and develops an interactive concierge service for independent living of elderly people in context easy-to-use interaction models based on natural language processing development [14]. Carvalko describes Medical technology verges on incorporating directly into our anatomy processors with the computational power of the Watson IBM computer and Internet-like communications within the eventual merging of synthetic DNA and artificial intelligence that together will bring new diagnostics, medical treatment, and smart nano-prosthetics well within the horizon of the next generation [15]. The goal of Cervenka is to define various ways to apply cognitive systems for unstructured data analysis and management for further use in marketing analytics with IBM Analytics Tools for analyzing unstructured data found on social media [16–18].

3 Proposed Method for Building Optimized Model of CO_2 Concentration

The Bayes Regulatory Method (BRM) is offered for the optimization training method. BRM is different from the previous two in that it does not work with the verification set. Generally speaking, BRM generalizes rather small or complex data sets containing noise. ANN (BRM) using measured data exhibits naturally expected behaviour. The lowest MSE values as well as the highest correlation coefficients R are given in BRM. The disadvantage for BRM is the relative long duration of ANN.

The proposed application for monitoring technological processes in SHC can be used to obtain information about the current state of measured values from common operating sensors (temperature, rH, CO_2) for other practical applications in the context of operational and technical functions in SHC.

3.1 Materials and Methods

In this part, we present a method for suppressing CO_2 concentration noise based on the Wavelet transformation. In the signal processing, we assume that each signal $y(t)$ is composed from two essential parts, namely they are the signal trend $T(t)$ and a component having a stochastic character $X(t)$ which is perceived as the signal noise and details. For this definition, it is used formulation for signal bellow (1):

$$y(t) = T(t) + X(t), \tag{1}$$

The main problem in signal extraction is noise detection. There are many trend detection applications including CO_2 measurement. To get a smooth signal for further processing it is necessary to remove glitches. The wavelet analysis represents the transformation of $y(t)$ to obtain two types of the coefficients, in particular wave and scale coefficients. These coefficients are completely equivalent to the original CO_2 signal. It is supposed that changes on specific scale refer to wavelet coefficients. In this analysis, we can assume uncorrelated noise, adapting the wavelet estimator in order to works as a kernel estimator.

Advantage of such approach is formulating an estimator based on the sampled data irregularity. In this method, we are using the scaling coefficients as estimators of the signal trend. We suppose that the sampled CO_2 observations are represented by $Y(t_n)$, thus the CO_2 estimator is given by the formulation (2):

$$\widehat{T}(t) = \sum_{n=0}^{N-1} Y(t_n) \int E_J(t,s) ds \tag{2}$$

The integration is as follows, using the interval set $(A_n(s))$ and union forms, you can make a division interval covering all observations t_n, where $t_n \in A_n$. Thus, E_J is defined as:

$$E_J(t,s) = 2^{-J} \sum_{k \in \mathbb{Z}} \theta(2^{-J}t - k)\theta(2^{-J}s - k) \tag{3}$$

In this formula $\theta(t)$ is the scaling function. This function is below:

$$\theta(t) = \sum_{k \in \mathbb{Z}} c_k \theta(2t - k) \tag{4}$$

The wavelet function represents below:

$$\psi(t) = (-1)^k c_{1-k} \theta(2t - k) \tag{5}$$

It is necessary to select a suitable mother's wavelet that would be most suitable for predicted signal filtering. Suppose the Daubechies wavelets can well reflect morphological structure, so this family is suitable for the model in this paper.

Especially, in our approach we are using the Daubechies wavelet (Db6), with the D6 scaling function utilizing the orthogonal Daubechies coefficients.

3.2 Validation Ratings Used

In order to make an objective comparison, the following parameters are considered:

Mean Absolute Error (MAE) is estimating the difference between two continuous variables. The MAE is given by the expression below:

$$MAE = \frac{1}{n} \sum_{i=1}^{n} |y_i - \widehat{y}_i| \tag{6}$$

Mean squared error (MSE) is an estimate that measures the error of squares between two signals. MSE is a risk function that is expected to be a squared or quadratic error loss. The MSE is shown below:

$$MSE(x_1, \widehat{x}_2) = \frac{1}{n} \sum_{i=1}^{n} (x(i) - \widehat{x}(i))^2 \tag{7}$$

Euclidean distance (ED) is an ordinary straight-line distance between two points lying in the Euclidean space. Because of this distance, the Euclidean space becomes a metric space. The lower the Euclidean distance achieved, the more similar signal samples. In our analysis, we consider mean of the ED. ED is described below:

$$d(x_1, \widehat{x}_2) = \sqrt{(x_1 - \widehat{x}_2)^2 + (y_1 - \widehat{y}_2)^2} \tag{8}$$

City Block distance (CB) is a distance between two signals $x_1, \widehat{x}_2$ in the Cartesian coordinate system. This parameter means a sum of the lengths of the projections of the line segments between the points onto the coordinate axes. CB distance is defined as follows:

$$d_{cb}(x_1, \widehat{x}_2) = \|x_1 - \widehat{x}_2\| = \sum_{i=1}^{n} |x_{1i} - \widehat{x}_{2i}| \qquad (9)$$

Correlation coefficient (R) allows measuring of a level of the linear dependency between two signals. Linear dependent can be determined based on the value of the correlation coefficient, the higher the coefficient the more signals are considered linearly dependable. Correlation coefficient is normative parameter in comparison with parameters which were used. Zero correlation means the overall difference between the two signals measured in terms of their linear dependence. Conversely, 1, respectively −1 means full positive, respectively negative correlation.

4   Testing of Proposed Method

Neural network settings were used for the measurement with these amount of neurons 10, 50, 100, 150, 200, 250, 300, 350, 400, 450 and 500 for prediction. In each measurement, 11 expected signals were analyzed. With the reference signal, predicted signals are compared based on the above objective evaluation parameters.

In a term of the Euclidean, City Block distance and MSE lower values indicate a higher agreement between the predicted course CO_2 and reference measurement course CO_2 thus, better result. Conversely, a higher number of correlation coefficients shows better results. In the following part of the analysis we present the results of the comparative analysis. All tests are performed for Wavelet Db6, with 6-level decomposition and Wavelet settings: threshold selection rule - Stein's Unbiased Risk and soft thresholding for selection of the detailed coefficients.

In this part is the description of the experiments, settings of the individual parameters, the calculated and measured results. With this experiment, it is possible to verify the quality of the prediction in spring (8.6.2015–15.6.2015) and winter (8.2.2015–15.2.2015).

Cross validation, the quality of the prediction was experimentally verified from the measured values over 8 days. The periods mentioned in the text in spring and winter were used as experiments for cross validation and testing of trained ANN with BRM on data obtained.

For testing was used samples with number 1152. Training - 70%, 806 samples, which are presented to the network during the training, and the network is adjusted according to its error). Validation - 15%, 173 samples, which were used to measure the network generalization, and to halt the training when the generalization stopped improving. Testing – 15%, 173 samples, these test samples are independent of network performance measurements in training, they must not be influenced by training neural networks. The prediction of CO_2 concentration by ANN with the BRM was performed using the measured values first, of rH (%) indoors, temperature indoors T_{in} (°C), temperature outdoors T_{out} (°C) on the training data from June 8 to June 15, 2015, (Fig. 1), (Table 2). Further, the cross-validation used the training data (rH (%) indoors, temperature indoors T_{in} (°C), temperature outdoors T_{out} (°C)) that was measured from February 8 to February 15, 2015, (Table 3).

In Table 1 is shown the calculated values of R and MSE parameters for the number of neurons (10 to 500) set within the testing of the ANN with the BRM (from June 8 to June 15, 2015) for expected the process of CO_2 using the algorithm ANN with the BRM on the data measured in the winter term from February 8 to February 15, 2015. The lowest value of MSE (MSE = $33.8.*10^{-4}$) and the highest value of R correlation coefficient (R = 94.231%), for expected process of CO_2 are for trained ANN BRM with 100 neurons (Cross Validation).

Table 1. The expected quality of ANN (BRM) in the period from June 8, 2015 to June 15, 2015, with the Cross validation of data after testing in the period from February 2, 2015 to February 15, 2015

Number of neurons	MSE (ppm)	R(-)	d(-)	d_{cb}(-)
10	0.0023	0.819	0.0678	0.0678
50	0.0020	0.839	0.0677	0.0678
100	0.0023	0.818	0.0667	0.0677
150	0.0022	0.822	0.0670	0.0671
200	0.0023	0.827	0.0679	0.0678
250	0.0023	0.819	0.0680	0.0680
300	0.0022	0.818	0.0676	0.0676
350	0.0022	0.823	0.0663	0.0664
400	0.0022	0.826	0.0675	0.0675
450	0.0023	0.816	0.0674	0.0676
500	0.0022	0.826	0.0677	0.0677

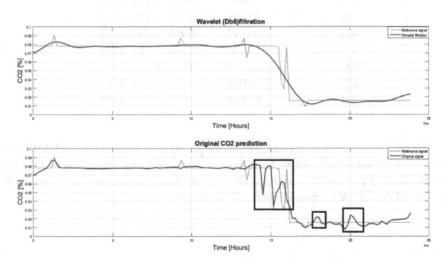

Fig. 1. Daily CO_2 expected signal containing several glitches and peaks labelled with black square, ANN BRM trained with data 8.6.2015, cross validation expected with data 8.2.2015

Table 2. The expected quality of ANN (BRM) in the period from February 8,2015 to February 15, 2015, with the Wavelet noise cancelling of Cross validation of data after testing in the period 8.6.2015 to 15.6.2015

Number of neurons	MSE (ppm)	R (%)	d(-)	d_{cb}(-)
10	0.0021	0.836	0.0663	0.0663
50	0.0019	0.854	0.0664	0.0664
100	0.0021	0.835	0.0653	0.0651
150	0.0021	0.833	0.0659	0.0659
200	0.0020	0.841	0.0666	0.0665
250	0.0021	0.834	0.0668	0.0668
300	0.0021	0.836	0.0661	0.0660
350	0.0021	0.837	0.0650	0.0650
400	0.0021	0.838	0.0660	0.0660
450	0.0021	0.832	0.0661	0.0662
500	0.0020	0.841	0.0663	0.0662

Table 3. The expected quality of ANN (BRM) in the period from February 8,2015 to February 15, 2015, with the Cross validation of data after testing in the period 8.6.2015 to 15.6.2015

Number of neurons	MSE (ppm)	R (%)	d(-)	d_{cb}(-)
10	0.0062	0.887	0.151	0.152
50	0.0049	0.921	0.154	0.154
100	0.0034	0.942	0.152	0.152
150	0.0034	0.941	0.152	0.152
200	0.0040	0.932	0.154	0.153
250	0.0038	0.933	0.153	0.153
300	0.0049	0.918	0.153	0.153
350	0.0176	0.764	0.156	0.156
400	0.0039	0.933	0.152	0.152
450	0.0038	0.934	0.152	0.152
500	0.0048	0.917	0.153	0.152

Figure 2 shows the CO_2 concertation in the period from 8.2.2015 to 15.2.2015 and the predicted CO_2 concentration after using the ANN algorithm with BRM used in the period 8.6.2015 to 15.6.2015 using ANN with BRM at 400 neurons (see Table 3). In graphs red circles are expected values of CO_2 that were incorrect.

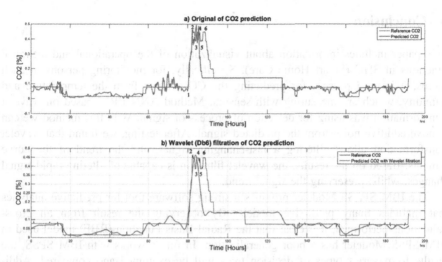

Fig. 2. Measured process of CO_2 concentration in date from 8.2.2015 to 15.2.2015 and the predicted process of CO_2 concentration by the ANN with the BRM learned in date from 8.6.2015 to 15.6.2015, the predicted ANN with the data from 8.2.2015 to 15.2.2015 with the number of neurons - 400, (see Table 3)

5 Discussion

Based on the predicted CO_2 signals, these signals have a lot of glitches and spikes. This means that due to these artefacts, the signal for analysis is worse. These sudden changes can to some extent affect the accuracy of the CO_2. Based on the results in this article, the wavelet transform looks like a good choice for removing artefacts from signals. We used he Daubechies wavelet family from the wavelet transformation, which can reflect morphological structure of the signals. For trend detection, we mainly use Db6. An objective comparison is made in the last part of our analysis. For comparison, CO_2 signals are used with predicted signals after wavelet transform filtration.

For objective comparison of the signals, the MSE (Mean Square Error) parameter was used, where we can objectively evaluate the signals and determine that the signals after the trend detection by the wavelet show better results. In this way, the difference between the gold standard and the filtered signals was minimized. Another parameter chosen was the correlation coefficient, which shows higher values for the predicted CO_2 values.

However, negligible differences were found after this comparison. One possible justification may be that detecting trends largely omits the higher peak. Therefore, the linear dependence after wavelet filtering is smaller than with predicted signals. In conclusion, this type of filter allows more accurate results against predicted signals, signals have much less noise, are smoother, and do not contain steep fluctuations.

Some loss of amplitude can also be assumed. Therefore, it would be worthwhile in the future to investigate the frequency characteristics of CO_2 signals in order to determine frequency modifications in wavelet filtering.

6 Conclusion

This paper includes information about visualization of the operational and technical functions in SHC (Smart Home Care). Specifically, for monitoring persons in each rooms, it is used process for predicting the CO_2 course from the temperature and humidity, which are measuring with sensors. Method ANN BRM based on wavelet transformation was using for detection of process of signal. With this method we can remove additive noise from the predicted signal. After testing, we found that wavelet transformation allows filtering a fast-changing signal, and the trend of the curve remains. Based on the results, the wavelet filtration is capable of filtering rapid signal changes, whilst preserving the signal trend.

The IBM SPSSS Modeler provides a strong software tool for predictive analytics that includes many predictive models. By observing the result from all cross-validations performed, it is clear that the Radial Basis Function (RBF) model used in IBM SPSS Modeler has a poor generalization. In future works with IBM SPSS, the results form varies types of decision trees will be examined and compared. Additionally, different predictive models can be implemented using IBM Watson analytics, which can provide online analytics with possibilities of near real-time data streaming.

Acknowledgment. The work and the contributions were supported by the project SV450994 Biomedicínské inženýrské systémy XV'. This study was also supported by the research project The Czech Science Foundation (GACR) 2017 No. 17-03037S Investment evaluation of medical device development run at the Faculty of Informatics and Management, University of Hradec Kralove, Czech Republic. This study was supported by the research project The Czech Science Foundation (TACR) ETA No. TL01000302 Medical Devices development as an effective investment for public and private entities.

References

1. Basu, D., Moretti, G., Gupta, G.S., Marsland, S.: Wireless sensor network based smart home: Sensor selection, deployment and monitoring. In: 2013 IEEE Sensors Applications Symposium Proceedings, pp. 49–54. IEEE (2013). https://doi.org/10.1109/sas.2013. 6493555. Accessed 07 Nov 2017
2. Fleck, S., Strasser, W.: Smart camera based monitoring system and its application to assisted living. Proc. IEEE **96**(10), 1698–1714 (2008) 2017. https://doi.org/10.1109/jproc.2008. 928765. Accessed 07 Nov 2017
3. Pantazaras, A., Lee, S.E., Santamouris, M., Yang, J.: Predicting the CO2 levels in buildings using deterministic and identified models. Energy Build. **127**, 774–785 (2016)
4. Ríos-Moreno, G.J., Trejo-Perea, M., Castañeda-Miranda, R., Hernández-Guzmán, V.M., Herrera-Ruiz, G.: Modelling temperature in intelligent buildings by means of autoregressive models. Autom. Constr. **16**(5), 713–722 (2007)
5. Aggarwal, M., Madhukar, M.: IBM's Watson analytics for health care: a miracle made true. In: Cloud Computing Systems and Applications in Healthcare, pp. 117–134 (2016)
6. Kaur, A., Jasuja, A.: Health monitoring based on IoT using Raspberry PI. In: 2017 International Conference on Computing, Communication and Automation (ICCCA), pp. 1335–1340 (2017)

7. Petnik, Vanus, J.: Design of smart home implementation within IoT with natural language interface. Ifac Papersonline **51**(6), 174–179 (2018)
8. Xu, B., Zheng, J., Wang, Q.: Analysis and design of real-time micro-environment parameter monitoring system based on Internet of Things. In: 2016 IEEE International Conference on Internet of Things (iThings) and IEEE Green Computing and Communications (GreenCom) and IEEE Cyber, Physical and Social Computing (CPSCom) and IEEE Smart Data (SmartData) (2016)
9. Min, Q., Ding, Y.F., Xiao, T., et al.: Research of visualization monitoring technology based on Internet of Things in discrete manufacturing process. In: 2015 2nd International Symposium on Dependable Computing and Internet of Things (Dcit), pp. 128–133 (2015)
10. Wang, Y., Song, J., Liu, X., et al.: Plantation monitoring system based on Internet of Things. In: 2013 IEEE International Conference on Green Computing and Communications and IEEE Internet of Things and IEEE Cyber, Physical and Social Computing, pp. 366–369 (2013)
11. Windarto, Y.E., Eridani, D.: Door and light control prototype using intel galileo based Internet of Things. In: 2017 4th International Conference on Information Technology, Computer, and Electrical Engineering (Icitacee), pp. 176–180 (2017)
12. Coelho, C., Coelho, D., Wolf, M., et al.: An IoT Smart Home Architecture for Long-Term Care of People with Special Needs. In: 2015 IEEE 2nd World Forum on Internet of Things (Wf-Iot), pp. 626–627 (2015)
13. Oxford dictionaries, Definition of big data in English. https://en.oxforddictionaries.com/definition/big_data. Accessed 25 Nov 2018
14. Arnold, O., Kirsch, L., Schulz, A., IEEE: An interactive concierge for independent living. In: 2014 Ieee 3rd Global Conference on Consumer Electronics (Gcce), Proceedings Paper, pp. 59–62 (2014). (in English)
15. Carvalko, J.R., IEEE: Law and policy in an era of cyborg-assisted-life the implications of interfacing in-the-body technologies to the outer world. In: 2013 IEEE International Symposium on Technology and Society (IEEE International Symposium on Technology and Society, pp. 204–215. IEEE, New York (2013)
16. Cervenka, P., Hlavaty, I., Miklosik, A., Lipianska, J.: Using cognitive systems in marketing analysis. Economic Annals-Xxi, Article **160**(7–8), 56–61 (2016). (in English)
17. Rafl, J., Kulhanek, F., Kudrna, P., Ort, V., Roubik, K.: Response time of indirectly accessed gas exchange depends on measurement method. Biomedizinische Technik **63**(6), 719–727 (2018)
18. Bibbo, D., Conforto, S., Bernabucci, I., Schmid, M., D'Alessio, T.: A wireless integrated system to evaluate efficiency indexes in real time during cycling. In: Van der Sloten, J., Verdonck, P., Nyssen, M., Haueisen, J. (eds.) 4th European Conference of the International Federation for Medical and Biological Engineering, vol. 22, pp. 89–92 (2009)

Integration of Simulation Techniques: System Dynamics and Intelligent Agents Applied to a Case Study

Miroslava Mikusova[1](✉) , Mauro Callejas-Cuervo[2] ,
Helver A. Valero-Bustos[2] , and Andrea C. Alarcón-Aldana[2]

[1] University of Zilina, Zilina, Slovakia
miroslava.mikusova@fpedas.uniza.sk
[2] Universidad Pedagógica y Tecnológica de Colombia, Tunja 150001, Colombia
mauro.callejas@uptc.edu.co

Abstract. Performing macro and microscopic analysis of a complex system, as in the case of measuring variables of quality of service provided by system of public passenger transport, is a problem, even more, if it is about integration of information produced in a minimum period of time that should serve as an input for realization of macroscopic analysis of this information for a longer period of time. The main goal of this paper is describe integration of two paradigms of simulation, one based on intelligent agents for microscopic analysis of the behaviour of selected system of urban public transport in one day of its activity, and another, based on system dynamics, to perform a macroscopic analysis, initially taking into account information from one day of system's operation. Results of pilot study show that data obtained from the simulation with agents are the starting point for realization of wider analysis by allowing simulation of the system in a period of 180 days.

Keywords: Simulation techniques · System dynamics · Intelligent agents · Microscopic and macroscopic analysis · Public passengers transport system

1 Introduction

The models used in planning operation of public passenger transport (PPT) systems in intermediate cities have characteristics that differ from those used in large cities. For analysis and modelling of such systems are used relatively static techniques and methodologies, so the effectiveness of results obtained in the model can be measured only from its implementation, which in practice is costly.

Planning operation of a route or set of routes of PPT system is changing process. It is influenced by factors related to supply and demand, which vary continuously in time and space, meaning that the programming of operation is not exact, it is subject to uncertainties. For this reason, there have to be make continuous adjustments to the process of programming operation of route during the whole time of its implementation. Non proper planning of operation of routes can cause serious decrease of the quality of service, which will be reflected in negative effects, both economic and social.

© Springer Nature Switzerland AG 2019
N. T. Nguyen et al. (Eds.): ICCCI 2019, LNAI 11684, pp. 510–517, 2019.
https://doi.org/10.1007/978-3-030-28374-2_44

Actually there are several studies that present analysis of different aspects of provision of public transport system. In general, they can be divided into two groups: works based on use of agents [1–4] and works based on system dynamics [5–7]. In this context the relevance of this study consists in missing exploration of the integration of simulation techniques to analyse macroscopically and microscopically the measurement of variables that indicate the quality of service provided by PPTS system, such as comfort and speed of service. According to sources [8–11] these two aspects resulted as the most important ones in provision of public transport service, so that's why they are taken into consideration as the main criteria for implementation of this study. Both of variables are part of the operational planning of transport system rather than its analytical planning.

As can be concluded from information described above, objective of this study is to show integration of two models that allow simulate operational behaviour of PPT system in intermediate cities, using intelligent agents and system dynamics. To do this, as a first step analysis of PPT system was effectuated, followed by identification of key agents and rules that are influencing system's behaviour. At second, there were determined feedback loops that arise in the operation of PPT system and correspondent models were designed. Finally, there was carried out analysis of the results obtained from this process.

2 Basic Information About City Selected for Realization of a Case Study

For a case study of this investigation was selected the city of Tunja, which was chosen as a typical city of prototype of the Latin American environment because of its intermediate size and because of available records about PPT travels effectuated since the year 1993.

Tunja, capital of the department of Boyaca, is located in the east-central part of Colombia, 120 km from Bogota and height 2720 m above sea level. It has an area of 270 ha and has a relief with steep slopes and undulations. Its approximate urban area population is 102 000 inhabitants. The population is mostly young: 76% of city inhabitants has age lower that 35 years. The main activities are educational, institutional and commercial. The city is strategically located on important main roads that communicate the city Llanos Orientales, Atlantic Coast and center of the country. The city has an urban road network with length of 90 km, of which 90% is locally type; 12% of these routes is served by PPT system. It was possible to identify the corridor that is used by 78% of PPT system.

PPT service is currently provided by four companies, with a fleet composed mostly of type small buses and microbuses, with capacities between fifteen and thirty-five seats.

The representative sample or analysis unit taken for realization of this study is taken from a route that covers a city road artery. This route has a length of 8.37 km, which are served in 35 min' intervals for a vehicle of urban public transport (result generated from detailed study of routes implemented by majority of companies that provide PPT service in the city of Tunja) (Fig. 1).

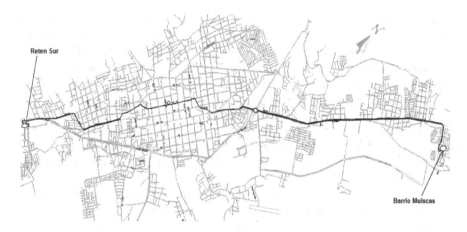

Fig. 1. Map of the Route Retén Sur–Muiscas, city of Tunja

3 Materials and Methods

This part of paper presents definition of system dynamics, then definition of software agents and finally are stated generalities in the construction of both models.

3.1 System Dynamics

The term of dynamics refers to changes that occur in each of the parts of system over time as a result of interactions that occur between them [12]. System dynamics deals with analysing how the internal relations of the system explain its behaviour. Fields of practical application of system dynamics are various, which highlights the construction of computer simulation models, that is a topic of interest of this study.

3.2 Software Agents

Berthet, Demazeau and Boissier [13], define agent as semiautonomous or completely autonomous entity, which acts rationally according to its perceptions from exterior environment and its state of knowledge. According to these authors, the structure of agents can be divided into two parts: first, the knowledge that the agent has about the outside world, the abilities of other agents and its own abilities and topics of interest. The second part is dynamic processing that agent performs from the messages and define its activity of reasoning in front of problems and new information. Communication between agents is essential in order to enable them to interact almost intelligently, managing internal communication to their own components, and set of methods to process these messages. According to Shoham [14], language of agents is a system that allows programming computational systems, hardware or software, in terms developed in some theories or formal models of agents.

3.3   Development of System Dynamics Models and Models Based on Intelligents Agents

To contextualize the stage before construction of the models, it is necessary to describe the operation of system through a case study. The process begins when user has the need to travel, beginning at the starting point of the trip and moving to the stop of origin. Once there, user must select travel route, that means plan the itinerary. Then select vehicle, which serves the journey and ends its trip in the final stop of destination. Finally, it moves to the end point of the trip. This is the whole process that need to be followed by a person who wishes to use PPT system.

Analysis and design for simulation of system described is then given by two models, one based on system dynamics that enables realization of analysis based on the overall system performance (macroscopic), and another, based on agents that reflect behaviour of each of the elements of system (microscopic). Microscopic model allows also show the time spent by each passenger during his/her replacement from the place of origin to the destination, and to analyse what part of this time the passenger perceived suitable comfort. These models are designed to perform an assessment of the quality of service provided by public passenger transport company in terms of comfort and speed.

4   Results

This part describes the models designed for macroscopic and microscopic simulation, presenting results of evaluation of quality of service provided by PPT system.

4.1   Development of Microscopic Model Based on Intelligent Agents

Following are presented steps of development of conceptual model represented by the main characteristics of intelligent agents, involved in the transport system, using Bottom-up technique of modelling. This approach is based on an architecture of reactive agents, which models from particular to general, as it firstly visualizes the system in each one of its parts (unanimated agents); then, rules are assigned to each one of those agents (animated agents); following the union of a society of agents (organization of agents); and finally, there is the analysis of the behavior of said agents or data, a technique that was used as the basis in order to carry out this work.

Steps of development of the model were: A. Contextualization and analysis of the system to be simulated. B. Modelling of the system. C. Creation of the graphic interphase of the user. D. Creation of scenarios to experiment. E. Software simulation of the models. F. Collection of results. G. Analysis of results. More detailed description of the process of development of this model is available in source [15]. In this model, the Unified Modelling Language (UML) was used to create main diagrams that are representing static and dynamic behaviour of the system.

4.2   Development of Macroscopic Model Based on System Dynamics

For the development of macroscopic model based on system dynamics there were used stages of methodologies proposed by Forrester and others [12] as they provide feedback from social systems. The development stages are: A. Definition of the problem. B. Conceptualization of the system. C. Formalization. D. Model of the behaviour. E. Evaluation of the model. F. Exploitation of the model.

In development of the model were used two types of information, information from historical records of system behaviour and information of varied nature in relation to the interactions that are occurring within the system. First type of information will only be of interest at the end of the process, while the second type of information is more relevant in system dynamics.

More detailed description of the development model of system dynamics is available in source [16].

4.3   Interaction Between Macroscopic and Microscopic Model

To start integration of the two paradigms of simulation must be inserted parameters that are allowing application of microscopic model for simulation, which are extracted from a database constructed for this purpose. After feeding initial parameters with the data from database, is executed simulation using model with intelligent agents, obtaining the simulated results for a full day. Configuration of parameters is following: starting time: 6:00 am, ending time: 10:00 pm, number of vehicles: 25 buses, buses despatched daily: 97 despatched per day, daily vehicle capacity: 3100 passengers. Time interval of dispatches is given in different scenarios, which are detailed in Table 1.

Table 1.   Scenarios and time distributions

Scenario	Number of slots	Time in minutes during valley period	Time in minutes during peak period
Real	9	17.5	4
Alternative 1	1	10	10
Alternative 2	9	30	3
Alternative 3	9	13	5.5

The simulator based on agents (microscopic simulation), produces a series of results which are stored in a table called *Results*. These data serve as parameters for macroscopic simulation (simulation with system dynamics).

In Fig. 2 is described the process of storing the results obtained by microscopic simulation in the database (DB) and their subsequent use as "parameters of quality and comfort" at the input (box with dashed lines). In addition, it includes general characteristics of socioeconomic type associated with the city, thus simulating macroscopic model and obtaining a microscopic and macroscopic behaviour.

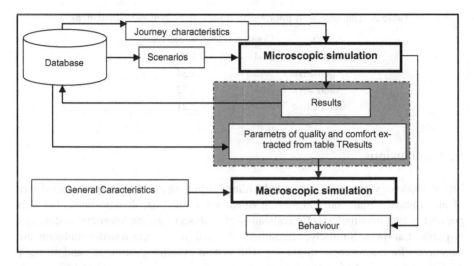

Fig. 2. Scheme of interaction between microscopic and macroscopic models

4.4   Results of Simulations

In Table 2 are provided ratings obtained and stored in the database as a result of simulation with agents. The evaluation is performed on a rating scale from 0 to 5, where 0 indicates the minimum compliance in terms of comfort and speed, and 5 represents an optimum value of compliance.

Table 2. Database with information from agent-based simulations

Schedule	Comfort rating	Speed rating
Real	3.74	2.50
Alternative 1	3.75	2.46
Alternative 2	3.70	2.54
Alternative 3	3.85	2.50

The average results for each of the variables from analysis of model with agents have an average evaluation of comfort on 3.75 points and speed on 2.49 points.

In Table 3 are provided results obtained from simulation of system dynamics for a period of 180 days.

The average results for each of the variables from analysis of model with system dynamics have an average evaluation of comfort on 3.12 points and speed on 2.08 points.

With results obtained from the microscopic model based on agents, macroscopic simulation using system dynamics is performed. These results are contrasted with projections and confirm that the results obtained in different scenarios show stable behaviour. This occurs while there are no radical changes in road infrastructure to raise an optimal scenario for a major evaluation of each complex of variables analysed in this research.

Table 3. Database with information from system dynamics simulations

Schedule	Comfort rating	Speed rating
Real	3.04	1.99
Alternative 1	3.42	2.34
Alternative 2	2.64	1.72
Alternative 3	3.31	2.21

5 Conclusions

The methodology proposed in this study, aimed at finding a way to integrate techniques of agent-based simulation and system dynamics simulation, demonstrated that it is possible to link both methods for realization of analysis of a complex social system like is public transport. Similarly, it resulted obtained with agent-based simulation are parameters for macroscopic simulation with system dynamics, estimating and properly predicting the impact of operational planning on the service for a route of PPT system in intermediated cities. It can be concluded that it is possible to predict the quality of service provided by PPT system using simulation techniques based on system dynamics and agents.

Utility of simulating the problem with microscopic and macroscopic models lies in the degree of abstraction achieved for each of them. Depending on the level of aggregation required by the model, both techniques are useful by allowing better understanding of the problem from microscopic and macroscopic point of view, in terms of space, time and structure. With the use of microscopic simulation can be identified specific problems in the course of daily system operations, enabling propose solutions based on analysis of results and by adjusting operational planning (programming of despatches), for decision –making at management level of the company and at the level of the government administration, achieving migration of users from other transport systems to PPT system. At macroscopic level is possible observe emergent behaviour of the system over a period of time, where the analysis leads to decisions that are not necessarily related to operational planning, but with the analytical planning (infrastructure, vehicle fleet, legislation, e.g.) of PPT system.

Simulation models proposed in this research can be used in other cities with similar characteristics. Successful outcomes will depend on the quality of collected data, sorting and processing of information that is needed to be integrated into the basic data structure required by developed applications.

Construction of similar models and implementation techniques for permanent collection of information in the system will enable constant monitoring and evaluation of behaviour of the system, providing the tools to take proper and adequate decisions related to programming of operation of PPT system. Additionally, the modelling and simulations based on techniques presented, allows first approximations to intelligent transportation systems.

References

1. Saprykin, O., Saprykina, O.: Validation of transport infrastructure changes via microscopic simulation: a case study for the city of Samara, Russia. In: 2017 5th IEEE International Conference on Models and Technologies for Intelligent Transportation Systems, pp. 774–779. Napoles, Italy (2017)
2. Andelfinger, P., et al.: Incremental calibration of seat selection preferences in agent-based simulations of public transport scenarios. In: 2018 Winter Simulation Conference (WSC), pp. 833–844. Gothenburg, Sweden (2018)
3. Golan, B.-D., Eran, B.-E., Itzhak, B.: Assessing the impacts of dedicated bus lanes on urban traffic congestion and modal split with an agent-based model. Procedia Comput. Sci. **130**, 824–829 (2018)
4. Inturri, G., et al.: Multi-agent simulation for planning and designing new shared mobility services. Res. Transp. Econ. **73**, 34–44 (2019)
5. Shuwei, J., Guangle, Y., Aizhong, S., Jun, Z.: A system dynamics model for determining the traffic congestion charges and subsidies. Arab. J. Sci. Eng. **42**(12), 5291–5304 (2017)
6. Sayyadi, R., Awasthi, A.: A system dynamics-based simulation model to evaluate regulatory policies for sustainable transportation planning. Int. J. Model. Simul. **37**(1), 25–35 (2017). https://doi.org/10.1080/02286203.2016.1219806
7. Alsobky, A., Hrkút, P., Mikušová, M.: A smart application for university bus routes optimization. In: Kováčiková, T., Buzna, Ľ., Pourhashem, G., Lugano, G., Cornet, Y., Lugano, N. (eds.) INTSYS 2017. LNICST, vol. 222, pp. 12–20. Springer, Cham (2018). https://doi.org/10.1007/978-3-319-93710-6_2
8. Mikusova, M.: Proposal of benchmarking methodology for the area of public passenger transport. Periodica Polytech. Transp. Eng. **47**(2), 166–170 (2019). https://doi.org/10.3311/PPtr.10271
9. Jankowska, D., Mikusova, M., Wacowska-Ślęzak, J.: Mobility issues in selected regions of poland and slovakia – outcomes of international project SOL (save our lives) survey. Periodica Polytech. Transp. Eng. **43**(2), 67–72 (2015). https://doi.org/10.3311/PPtr.7580
10. Mikusova, M.: Sustainable structure for the quality management scheme to support mobility of people with disabilities. Procedia – Soc. Behav. Sci. **160**, 400–409 (2014). https://doi.org/10.1016/j.sbspro.2014.12.152
11. Mikusova, M., Gnap, J.: Experiences with the implementation of measures and tools for road safety improvement. In: XII Congreso de ingeniería del transporte. 7, 8 y 9 de Junio, Valencia (Spain). Editorial Universitat Politècnica de València, pp. 1632–1638 (2016). https://doi.org/10.4995/cit2016.2015.2555
12. Forrester, J.W.: Industrial Dynamics. Productivity Press, Cambridge (1986)
13. Berthet, S., Demazeau, Y., Boissier, O.: Knowing each other better. In: 11th International Workshop on Distributed Artificial Intelligence. Glen Arbor (1992)
14. Shoham, Y.: Agent-oriented programming. Technical Report STAN-CS-1335-90. Computer Science Department. Stanford University, Stanford. CA (1990)
15. Callejas-Cuervo, M., Valero-Bustos, H.A., Alarcón-Aldana, A.C., Mikušova, M.: Measurement of service quality of a public transport system, through agent-based simulation software. In: Huk, M., Maleszka, M., Szczerbicki, E. (eds.) ACIIDS 2019. SCI, vol. 830, pp. 335–347. Springer, Cham (2020). https://doi.org/10.1007/978-3-030-14132-5_27
16. Callejas-Cuervo, M., Valero-Bustos, H.A., Alarcón-Aldana, A.C.: Simulación basada en dinámica de sistemas y agentes inteligentes, aplicada a un sistema complejo. Edn. UPTC, Tunja, Boyacá, Colombia (2018)

SMART Cities and Applications Used for Communication with Citizens as Part of Sustainable Development: The Czech Local Scene

Libuše Svobodová[1]([⊠]) and Dorota Bednarska-Olejniczak[2]

[1] University of Hradec Kralove, Rokitanskeho 62,
50003 Hradec Kralove, Czech Republic
libuse.svobodova@uhk.cz
[2] Wrocław University of Economics, Komandorska 118-120,
53345 Wrocław, Poland
dorota.olejniczak@ue.wroc.pl

Abstract. Using traditional means of communication such as municipal newspapers or official desk is not enough nowadays for a lot of citizens. Information are more beneficial as they are up-to-date. Direct communication to citizens' email or mobile brings benefits for all stakeholders. Messages with relevant information get immediately to recipient with possibility of feedback. All is measurable and targeting of messages is adapted to citizens. Modern technologies and information on time are one of the issues connected with sustainable development. The paper deals with communication between citizens and city authorities, facilitating collaborative processes and digital participation within the smart city. The issue of mobile applications used by city authorities to inform citizens and companies about actualities and development in the city will be presented in the paper. The purpose of the paper is to present selected mobile applications used by Czech city authorities. Smart infrastructure, informing self-government, active self-government, participative self-government, smart government will be solved in the article. Benefits of use of mobile applications by city authorities will be analyzed.

Keywords: Communication · Mobile application · SMART city ·
Sustainable development

1 Introduction

Smart Cities are a higher level of development [1], in which an already defined smart city uses IT tools to maximize resource efficiency and optimize urban processes, activities and services by linking individual elements and actors into one intelligent organic system [2]. The necessary elements are shown in Fig. 1. Thus, the use of IT tools is not only a tool to increase the efficiency of infrastructure management, but above all to respect environmental and human and social potential aspects [3].

© Springer Nature Switzerland AG 2019
N. T. Nguyen et al. (Eds.): ICCCI 2019, LNAI 11684, pp. 518–529, 2019.
https://doi.org/10.1007/978-3-030-28374-2_45

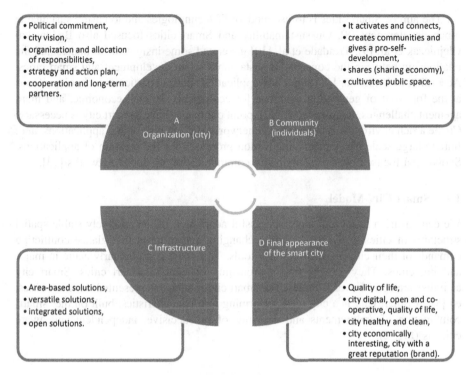

Fig. 1. Concept smart cities [4]

From the perspective of urban development management, Smart Cities can be seen as connection for years of applied strategic planning and expanding IT technology capabilities in city management. Strategic planning is as one of the tools for promoting the principles of sustainable development [5]. According to the Ministry for Regional Development of the Czech Republic Smart City is one of the concepts of applying the principles of sustainable development to the city organization, which is based on the use of modern technologies to improve quality of life and do public administration more effective. The field of energy and transport, which can be addressed more effectively by deploying appropriate information and communication technologies (ICT) are the broadest application of this concept. However, the Smart City concept does not only cover the two areas mentioned above, but it can be also applied to others, such as water management, waste management, e-government or crisis management [4].

For the first time the term Smart City was used in 2007: "The idea of a smart city is to create and connect human capital, social capital and IT infrastructure to ensure sustainable economic development and improve the quality of life of the city's inhabitants" [6]. Another possible definition is: "Smart cities use information and communication technologies to use resources more intelligently and efficiently, resulting in cost, energy, service and quality of life savings and emissions reduction, all supported by innovation and a low carbon economy" [7].

The aim of Smart cities is to use modern IT technologies and to ensure sustainable urban development [8]. On sustainability and Smart cities focused also Bednarska-Olejniczak et al. [9]. Trindade et al. [10] generated some insight for to understand the relationship between the concepts of sustainable urban development and smart cities. According to Yigitcnlar [11] smart city applications place a particular technology focus at the forefront of generating solutions for ecological, societal, economic, and management challenges. Kramers et al. [12], point out that to have a smart city is necessary: Create a rich environment of broadband networks that support digital applications, and; Initiate large-scale participatory innovation processes for the creation of applications. Svobodová focused on the municipality communication on social networks [13].

1.1 Smart City Model

We can ensure a faster and more successful adaptation of the relatively stable spatial structures of cities to the new, rapidly changing and often at first glance conflicting demands of their citizens with the new tools. This issue is particularly acute in major and big cities. They are the first approaching concept of Smart cities. Smart city activities are spread over 6 circles. The smart city model was presented on smart-cities. eu [8]. A Smart City is a city well performing in 6 characteristics, built on the 'smart' combination of endowments and activities of self-decisive, independent and aware citizens (Fig. 2).

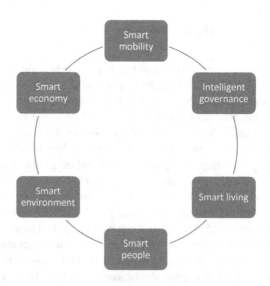

Fig. 2. Smart city model according to [8]

1.2 Bibliographic Coupling – Communication and Smart City

According current research using the Scopus database and search phrase "local AND government AND communication AND smart AND city" in the Article title, Abstract,

Keywords were founded 73 articles. The newest is in May 2019 Ismagilova et al. [23]. This article gained till 27th of May 2019 9 citations on Scopus. Topic is Smart cities: Advances in research-An information systems perspective. The highest number of citations 217 till the same date gain Bakici et al. [24]. Odendaal [25] is the second with number of citations, 115. He focused on Information and communication technology and local governance: Understanding the difference between cities in developed and emerging economies. About being smartness in the smart city 2.0 wrote Trencher [26].

Gil et al. explores the study of digital media platforms [27]. Article shows how e-platforms represent the use of information and communication technologies with the aim of encouraging citizen participation in decision-making processes, improving information and service delivery, reinforcing transparency, accountability, as well as credibility. Musso et al. [21] examines the extent to which innovative applications of Web technology might advance local governance reform. Synthesizing theories from communications, public policy, urban political science, and political philosophy, it develops a theoretical framework for local governance reform that emphasizes two dimensions: entrepreneurial (good management) versus participatory (good democracy). According to results from a structured content analysis of 270 municipal Web sites in California they conclude that most municipal Web sites lack a clear mission and provide few of the features that might effect meaningful improvements to local governance.

1.3 Smart City in the Czech Republic

Brno is one of the first smart cities in the Czech Republic, which approved the Smart City Brno concept in 2015, which represents Brno as a city that uses modern technology and approaches smartly, sensibly and gently.

The Brno city sets out seven principles in the concept:

- openness,
- responsibility,
- modularity,
- consideration,
- efficiency,
- diversity,
- cleverness.

It focuses primarily on improving the quality of life of citizens and increasing the efficiency of public administration in accordance with the approaches in modern metropolises, which is also evident from the areas it perceives as important for achieving the programme's objective:

Smart resources

- Mobility and infrastructure
- Energy and sustainability
- Building and new development

Smart governance (management/operation)

- Innovation, planning and new technologies
- Economy and transparency
- Safety, education and information

Smart living

- Environment and public spaces
- Healthcare and social care
- Leisure time and quality of life [14].

2 Methodology and Goal

The paper deals with communication between citizens and city authorities, facilitating collaborative processes and digital participation within the smart city. The issue of mobile applications used by city authorities to inform citizens and companies about actualities and development in the city will be presented in the paper. The purpose of the paper is to present selected mobile applications used by Czech city authorities. The main part of the article is based on the available resources of the most often used applications in the Czech Republic. It has been downloaded from one representative from all the applications examined and it has been tried what they offer to its citizens. Applications have been downloaded from the play store.

The article was prepared on the basis of print and electronic resources. A lot of articles deal with issue of smart cities can be found. There are not a lot of articles on Web of Science or Scopus that deal with interconnected topic – Smart city and applications for communication with citizens. This topic is still in its infancy. The intention of the article is to stimulate a conversation and proposes ways in which to frame early and future research.

3 Results

3.1 Application Mobile Broadcasting

It was the first smart application for cities in the Czech Republic and it is the most widespread system for communication of municipalities with citizens. The cornerstone of SMART communication is the creation of a unique civic infrastructure, thanks to which municipalities are able to reach citizens instantly, goals physically and measurably, wherever they are. The application (mobile broadcasting), its elements is presented as a modern way of communicating and dividing administrators for citizens and for mayors, see Fig. 3. It covers several hundred towns and villages throughout the Czech Republic. It offers the mayors and administrations an infrastructure for implementing smart communication and enables the use of a wide range of communication channels for direct and two-way communication with real-time evaluation - SMS messages, e-mails or voice mini referends. The system also serves institutions and organizations. It is used, for example, by choirs of free-fire firefighters or crisis management of the capital city of Prague [15].

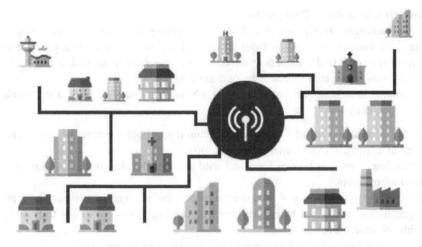

Fig. 3. Mobile broadcasting [15]

In Fig. 4, we can see that more than 450 cities or municipalities have joined in the middle of May 2019 and have already been involved in mobile broadcasting application.

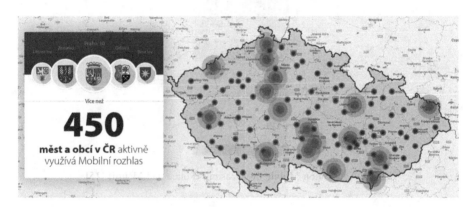

Fig. 4. Cities that use Mobile broadcasting in the Czech Republic [15]

The number of cities involved, the number of messages read, the number of registered citizens, and reported incentives are presented in Fig. 5.

Fig. 5. Mobile broadcasting application informative data [15]

Mobile Broadcasting + Recognition
It is well-arranged application that knows everything about the city or village. It displays the current information from the official authorities, it sends a photo notification (map it) or it finds contacts to the office or its opening hours with a single click. Types of trips in the area that will be find are bonus.

Functions are: Smart information board, photo buzz (map it), info in the municipality, emergency line.

- Smart information board - clarity of the main page about the news of the office, as well as a quick signpost after the application.
- Photo buzz - you can take pictures and send praise to the city, as well as suggestions for improvement.
- Info in the municipality - information about the village/town about their photographs and municipal activities, contacts, opening hours, types for trips and all with information about admission.
- Emergency lines - find all the numbers that you need in one place.

Fig. 6. Application Mobile broadcasting (Police nad Metují) [15]

The application can also send messages, changes in cultural events, crisis situations, the condition is to fill in the application form with your data and interests, see Fig. 6. Sample, you can see in the 10 picture above the text. The application was released on June 21, 2016 and more than 10,000 downloads have been downloaded. It is the predecessor of the Improve Czech Republic application, but now works both.

Improve the Czech Republic + Mobile Broadcasting (Extended Mobile Broadcasting + Map It)
The app is the same as the Mobile broadcasting + Map It, but it is enhanced by the additional features you can see in Fig. 7.

New features are: Lost Animals and Pets, Losses and Findings, Black Landfills and Damaged Property and Search for Lost Persons. The application was created 9th of May 2018. The app has downloaded over 10,000.

Fig. 7. Improve the Czech Republic + Mobile broadcasting [16]

3.2   Czech Town

The main idea of a mobile application is to communicate between the authorities of cities, towns and municipalities with citizens in the simplest, modern, efficient way. In the Fig. 8 you can see the application. The goal is to give municipalities and municipalities the opportunity to communicate through a versatile mobile application without the need for disproportionate investment in its development and maintenance. The application has more 9,000 downloads. Features are: Announcements, News & Board [17].

Fig. 8. Logo of the application the Czech Town [17]

3.3   Informed

The application was released on 18th of June 2017 for the Czech Republic and Slovak Republic. The application only mediates what the cities list on their website and shows it in the app. The user can see clearly the news, events, documents from the official authorities and gallery. The application is a helper for anyone who wants to stay informed about what's going on in his city. The application displays information for more than 300 cities in the Czech Republic. An example of the application is in Fig. 9. The app has over 10,000 downloads.

Fig. 9. Application Informed (Bohuslavice, Solnice) [18]

3.4   Radio Announcements

It contains six communication channels in the one tool. SMS, emails, www pages of municipality, social networks, chat and mobile application. It is the only one provider of mobile application that directly presents the price list of the services. Also their webpages contains a lot of information. They are on the similar level as the most often used application Mobile broadcasting [19].

3.5   My Town

It is not a comprehensive application with information about situation in the city. The main objective of the application is to inform citizens about payment of citizens to municipal budgets. Payment to municipal budget and municipal fees are as easily as in e-shop [20].

3.6   Comparison of Applications

The last part is dedicated to comparison of selected solutions. The most often used applications by municipalities were founded. Data were taken from Google Play. There are no concrete numbers about number of installations. The highest number is 10 000+. Only Mobile broadcasting has on their www pages information about number of read messages, number of registered users, number of complaints and number of involved cities. The best reviews gained Radio Announcements but they have small number of reviews. On the next positions are with the similar values Informed, Mobile broadcasting, My Town and application Czech Town (Table 1).

Table 1. Comparison of mobile applications on Google Play, own elaboration

	Number of installations	Review	Number of reviews
Mobile broadcasting	10 000+	3,6	189
Czech town	10 000+	3,2	92
Informed	10 000+	3,7	59
Radio announcements	1 000+	4,5	8
My town	1 000+	3,4	36

4 Conclusion and Discussion

Mobile applications are one of the components of Smart city. Not only from professional practice, attendance at expert conferences, meetings and discussions, but also from the obtained professional resources, shows that in the area of smart cities and usage of the applications, there is place for innovation and to improve and make more effective communication between the citizens and municipalities. It is necessary to connect all elements mentioned in [8]. For individuals, but also for municipalities it is important to participate in the smart living and well-being. Websites are basically used by Czech cities nowadays. Cities also offer faster and easier access to information to their citizens through the applications. It can be expected that with the growth of smart mobile technologies, this possibility of communication will be one of the most widespread in the future.

The authors of this article agree with Gil et al. [27]. They mentioned that these e-platforms raise implementation challenges for both firms and policy makers, and new research opportunities for scientist to build up new research and to experiment with the aim to make the benefits for citizens wider and the participatory dimension stronger. Freeman [22] explores the e-government goal of the National Digital Economy Strategy, which aims to have four out of five Australians engaging with governments online by 2020 and identifies that local and state governments will drive greater digital engagement. Author suggests that a cohesive e-government policy approach that coordinates knowledge and action through the various tiers of Australian government would facilitate the development of citizen-centric opportunities for e-government engagement.

We are now at a time when citizens are listening to information from the city's radio on the street and a lot of them are starting to use or they already use mobile applications. These technologies support concept Smart Cities. Cities that have already established them are well-arranged and have a positive response from the citizens of their cities and try to promote them more in order to bring them to the public. Most cities contribute to the application alone, with only a few cities having IT workers who are in charge of the applications and distributing the contributions from the city authorities.

A lot of applications are used by Czech municipalities. For citizens they are free of charge, municipalities pay for their use. Five applications, the most often used, were presented in the article. Application My Town is used for payments of citizens to municipalities. Four remaining contain similar functions. All applications have not clearly described what they announce. The best web pages with description and information are from Mobile broadcasting and Radio Announcements. The first three mentioned application have 10 000+ installation. Radio Announcements has only 1 000+. Unfortunately there are no information about development of number of users in time. Not all producers present start of their product. Problem with functioning of the application was the most often problematic area in reviews of products.

New applications are still being developed. Some municipalities use their own applications to communicate with citizens. It is possible to recommend to use functions that enable citizens to gain news and important information in municipality but also for citizens to directly communicate not only about problematic situation (lost animals, losses and findings, black landfills, damaged property, search for lost persons, photo buzz) in the city. It is possible to recommend to use applications not only in the large cities, but in the smaller ones.

Acknowledgement. The paper is supported by the project SPEV 2019 at the Faculty of Informatics and Management of the University of Hradec Kralove, Czech Republic. In addition, the authors thank Anna Borkovcova for her help with the project.

References

1. Hollands, R.G.: Will the real smart city please stand up? City **12**(3), 303–320 (2008)
2. Manville, C., Cochrane, G., et al.: Mapping Smart Cities in the EU (2014). http://www.europarl.europa.eu/RegData/etudes/etudes/join/2014/507480/IPOL-ITRE_ET(2014) 507480_EN.pdf. Accessed 01 Apr 2019
3. Allwinkle, S., Cruickshank, P.: Creating smarter cities: an overview. J. Urban Technol. **18** (2), 1–16 (2011)
4. Concept Smart cities, Ministry of regional development Czech Republic. https://www.mmr. cz/cs/Temp/Smart-Cities/Koncept-Smart-Cities. Accessed 01 Apr 2019
5. Gordon, I.: Integrating cities. In: Buck, N., Gordon, I., Harding, A., Turok, I. (eds.) Changing Cities. Rethinking Urban Competitiveness, Cohesion and Governance. Basingstoke, Palgrave, pp. 78–93 (2005)
6. Giffinger, R., Fertner, C., Kramar, H., Kalasek, R., Pichler-Milanovic, N., Meijers, E.: Smart cities. Ranking of European medium-sized cities (2007). http://www.smart-cities.eu/ download/smart_cities_final_report.pdf. Accessed 01 Apr 2019
7. Cohen, B.: The Top 10 Smart Cities On The Planet, Fast Company Exist (2012). http://www. fastcoexist.com/1679127/the-top-10-smart-cities-on-the-planet. Accessed 01 Apr 2019
8. European smart cities 3.0. http://www.smart-cities.eu/?cid=2&ver=3. Accessed 01 Apr 2019
9. Bednarska-Olejniczak, D., Olejniczak, J., Svobodova, L.: Towards a smart and sustainable city with the involvement of public participation-the case of Wroclaw. Sustainability **11**(2), 332 (2019)
10. Trindade, E.P., Hinning, M.P.F., et. al.: Sustainable development of smart cities: a systematic review of the literature. J. Open Innov.: Technol. Market Complex. **3**(1), 11 (2017)
11. Yigitcanlar, T.: Technology and the City: Systems, Applications and Implications. Routledge, New York (2016)
12. Kramers, A., Höjer, M., Lövehagen, N., Wangel, J.: Smart sustainable cities–exploring ICT solutions for reduced energy use in cities. Environ. Model Softw. **56**, 52–62 (2014)

13. Svobodova, L.: Social networks and web pages used by regional municipalities in the Czech Republic. In: Themistocleous, M., Morabito, V. (eds.) EMCIS 2017. LNBIP, vol. 299, pp. 210–218. Springer, Cham (2017). https://doi.org/10.1007/978-3-319-65930-5_18

14. Smart city Brno. https://www.brno.cz/sprava-mesta/volene-organy-mesta/rada-mesta-brna/komise-rady-mesta-brna/smart-city-brno/. Accessed 01 Apr 2019

15. Mobile broadcasting. www.mobilnirozhlas.cz. Accessed 01 Apr 2019

16. Improve the Czech Republic + Mobile Broadcasting. https://www.mobilmania.cz/clanky/zlepseme-cesko-se-stejnojmennou-mobilni-aplikaci-se-muzete-pridat-i-vy/sc-3-a-1344601/default.aspx. Accessed 01 Apr 2019

17. The Czech Town. http://www.ceskaobec.cz/. Accessed 01 Apr 2019

18. Informed. https://www.igalileo.cz/nase-reseni/produkty-a-sluzby/mobilni-aplikace/. Accessed 01 Apr 2019

19. Radio Announcements. https://hlasenirozhlasu.cz/. Accessed 01 Apr 2019

20. My Town. http://www.mojeobec.cz/. Accessed 01 Apr 2019

21. Musso, J., Weare, C., Hale, M.: Designing web technologies for local governance reform: good management or good democracy? Polit. Commun. **17**(1), 1–19 (2000). https://doi.org/10.1080/105846000198486

22. Freeman, J.: Driving Australia's digital future?: online engagement and the national digital economy strategy. Telecommun. J. Australia **62**(5), 79–81 (2012). https://doi.org/10.7790/tja.v62i5.368

23. Ismagilova, E., Hughes, L., Dwivedi, Y.K., Raman, K.R.: Smart cities: advances in research—an information systems perspective. Int. J. Inf. Manage. **47**, 88–100 (2019)

24. Bakici, T., Almirall, E., Wareham, J.: A smart city initiative: the case of Barcelona. J. Knowl. Econ. **4**(2), 135–148 (2013)

25. Odendaal, N.: Information and communication technology and local governance: understanding the difference between cities in developed and emerging economies. Comput. Environ. Urban Syst. **27**(6), 585–607 (2003)

26. Trencher, G.: Towards the smart city 2.0: empirical evidence of using smartness as a tool for tackling social challenges. Technol. Forecast. Soc. Change **142**, 117–128 (2019)

27. Gil, O., Cortés-Cediel, M.E., Cantador, I.: Citizen participation and the rise of digital media platforms in smart governance and smart cities. Int. J. E-Plann. Res. **8**(1), 19–34 (2019)

New Trends and Challenges in Education: The University 4.0

Ontology-Based Conceptualisation of Text Mining Practice Areas for Education

Martina Husáková[(✉)] [ID]

Faculty of Informatics and Management, University of Hradec Králové,
Rokitanského 62, 500 03 Hradec Králové, Czech Republic
martina.husakova.2@uhk.cz

Abstract. Text mining is highly multi-disciplinary field including various techniques of text analysis. These techniques are used for uncovering hidden information and knowledge in semi-structured and non-structured texts. Text mining concepts are spread among different, but related practice areas. It is often difficult to receive fast insight into this amount of concepts for a non-professional, e.g. for a student. The paper presents the OWL ontology-based prototype which should ease education and learning of facts which are used in the text mining domain. It is mainly aimed to the university students studying text mining at the introductory level. It can also be used as a formal vocabulary of text mining concepts for understanding of methods, techniques, concepts and relations between them by machines.

Keywords: Conceptualisation · Text mining · OWL ontology · Education

1 Introduction

Text Mining (TM) is a multi-disciplinary field which is based on the intersection of related disciplines, especially statistics, data mining, computational linguistics, databases, artificial intelligence and information sciences [1, 2]. TM-related techniques are focused on analysis of semi-structured and non-structured texts for uncovering hidden information and knowledge. Algorithms of TM are basically focused on two types of problems [3]. The first category of algorithms works with collections of documents. These collections are effectively searched, clustered or classified according to their characteristics. The second category analyses the inner structure of these documents (i.e. paragraphs, sentences, words, etc.) and meaning of the parts of these documents. These categories cover a lot of different techniques, methods and concepts. A non-professional can have a problem to receive fast insight into these techniques and to understand possible relationships between them. The paper presents an ontology-based approach which should facilitate learning and education in the second category of analytical methods where topics of Information Extraction (IE), Natural Language Processing (NLP) and Concept Extraction (CE) are included. Selection of these TM practice areas is based on the syllabus of the text mining study subject which is going to be taught at the University of Hradec Králové, Faculty of Informatics and Management.

The paper is structured as follows. Section 2 introduces usage of the formal ontologies in education. Section 3 presents developmental process of the OWL formal

© Springer Nature Switzerland AG 2019
N. T. Nguyen et al. (Eds.): ICCCI 2019, LNAI 11684, pp. 533–542, 2019.
https://doi.org/10.1007/978-3-030-28374-2_46

ontology covering TM practice areas. Section 4 discusses specific aspects of the OWL formal ontology and future directions. Section 5 concludes the paper.

2 Formal Ontologies in Education

Formal ontologies are information and knowledge structures modelling concepts and relations between where hierarchy of these concepts and their possible meaning is represented. Basically, they are used by humans and machines. The ontologies help with understanding of specific concepts and if it is difficult to reach a consensus between humans. Semantics specification improves skills of machines during searching for relevant information where deduction of the new facts can be a part of this process. Ontologies can be applied in various disciplines including education.

Development of the OWL ontology modelling university courses is mentioned in [4]. The main purpose of this ontology is to recommend suitable courses to students with respect to their qualification. The Protégé tool is used in ontology modelling. The formal ontology which represents content of an e-learning course about databases is introduced in [5]. Developmental process is based on a methodology where a new graphical notation, similar to a notation used in drawing the entity-relationship diagrams, is presented. The purpose of the ontology is to help domain experts, especially instructors, to model adequately a domain for which the e-learning course content is created. Entities and procedures which are part of the higher educational curricula and syllabuses are also modelled in the formal ontology [6]. The purpose of the ontology is to receive a knowledge structure which could ease curricula management, e.g. comparison of curricula or syllabuses with different academic institutions, their searching, aligning or matching. Ontological approach is also used in development of a Q/A rule-based system covering facts about Bulgarian history, especially historical, geographical and theoretical information about museums collection and particular exhibits [7]. The authors of the paper [8] introduce development of the ontology for education of the Natural Language Processing (NLP) at the introductory level. This educational ontology facilitates teaching and learning of the NLP-related concepts. Concept mapping [12] is used in preparation stages of the ontology development. The concept map is then converted into the formal ontology which is manually created by authors with assistance of books, online lecture notes and blogs in the Protégé 4. Similar study as [8] is mentioned in [9]. The authors present a formal ontology development for NLP domain understanding. The ontology is manually modelled in the OWL 2 and the Protégé 4. The ontology should be used in the Learning Management System (LMS).

3 Text Mining Ontology Development

3.1 Motivation

The University of Hradec Králové put forward the European Research Found project named *Strategic Development of the University of Hradec Králové* with the administrative support of the Ministry of Education, Youth and Sports of the Czech Republic.

The main aim of the project is to increase educational qualities with respect to the requirements of a labour market of the Czech Republic. Implementation of the new subsequent master study program *Data Science* is one of the main outputs of this project. Data science is a multi-disciplinary field of study where intersection of different application domains including mathematics, statistics, informatics or artificial intelligence is occurred. At present, huge amount of data have to be processed and effectively managed for acquisition useful facts which are used for fast and efficient problem solving and decision making. The above mentioned subsequent master study program is recommended to bachelor students having a strong background of applied informatics. Techniques and methods of data science study program should extend and deepen their knowledge of applied informatics.

Text mining is one of the study subjects which are proposed in the data science study program. TM includes collection of techniques used for mining interesting facts hidden in various types of semi-structured or non-structured documents. It has been already mentioned that TM is highly multi-disciplinary field, similarly as data science. A lot of terms relating with TM are mentioned during teaching. A beginner can be lost quite fast during this study. The main motivation behind development of a formal ontology is to decrease possible chaos in minds of students during study and to ease remembering of the most fundamental facts and knowledge about TM and related subfields. Ontological approach is applied for this purpose because the ontology is a graph-based structure modelling concepts and relations between which can be browsed by a student and where he (she) can easily discover context which exists in this structure. Formal representation of the ontology eases its machine processing where computers can "understand" included concepts and use them for decision making. The ontology can be also shared for support of collective education and used as a vocabulary of "things" for avoiding misunderstanding during communication between humans or machines.

3.2 Analysis and Design

Analysis and design are the first phases in the formal ontology development, because it has to be obvious which concepts and relations between them should be included in the ontological structure. The ontological structure reflects syllabus of seminars in the TM study subject. The concepts of the three practice areas of TM are included in the formal ontology:

- Natural Language Processing (NLP),
- Information Extraction (IE),
- Concept Extraction (CE) including Sentiment Analysis (SA).

Students are going to train TM-based techniques and algorithms with the Python-based Natural Language Toolkit (NLTK) [10]. It is often used platform for managing non-structured textual data and recommended for educational purposes. The TM study subject is not going to teach only the text mining techniques, but Python [11] programming is going to be also trained, because data science program proposal does not consider self-contained subject for programming in Python. This is the reason why the most important Python-related concepts are also included in the formal ontology.

The concepts of above mentioned practice areas have to be concretised for specification a backbone of the formal ontology. The concept map depicts the most fundamental concepts of the ontological structure, see Fig. 1. Inverse relations are not included in the concept map because of the readability of the structure.

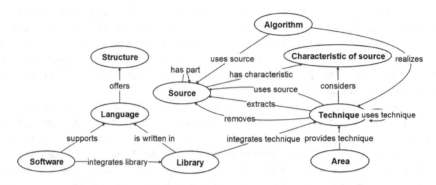

Fig. 1. Backbone of the formal ontology for text mining education

3.3   Ontology Development

Formal ontology for text mining education (TMEO) is manually created and represented in the OWL 2 (Ontology Web Language 2) where scientific books and online sources were used in development. The OWL 2 is the W3C standard which was published in 2009 [13]. This formal language extends the RDF (Resource Description Framework) [14] data model and the RDFS (RDF Schema) [15]. The RDF is mainly used for representation of metadata for sources with simple RDF statements which do not have any structure, i.e. the hierarchies of these RDF statements are not specified. The RDFS extends the RDF where class/property hierarchies can be modelled. Semantics of concepts are represented in the OWL 1 (OWL 2) in more details in comparison to the RDF(S). This is the reason why the OWL is used for the TMEO ontology development.

The ontological structure is modelled in the three phases, see Fig. 2. The first phase is focused on modelling of a backbone of the OWL ontology. Taxonomy of the OWL classes and the OWL properties is developed in this phase. Taxonomies represent concepts of the NLP, the IE and the CE practice areas of TM where general concepts, techniques, algorithms, possible sources for mining and software are mainly taken into account.

The second phase deals with semantics of the OWL classes. The taxonomy of the OWL classes can tell the students which text mining-related concepts are general and more specific. It is also necessary to model semantics of the concepts for their deeper explanation to humans and machines. Semantics is formally represented in the description logic in case of the OWL. Each class has a collection of conditions explaining what a class is. OWL properties, restrictions, logical constructors and related OWL classes are combined together for expression a meaning of a class. As the

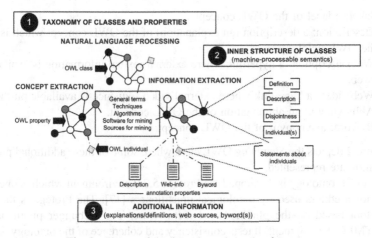

Fig. 2. Phases of the formal ontology development

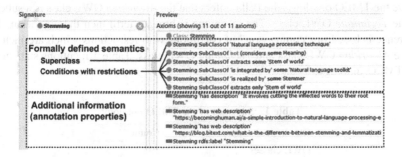

Fig. 3. Stemming OWL class and its semantics

example, Fig. 3 depicts semantics of the *Stemming* OWL class. A student (without any previous knowledge of the ontologies modelling) can deduce that:

- stemming is a technique of the NLP AND
- stemming does not consider meaning of analysed parts of a text AND
- stemming extracts stems of words AND
- stemming is provided by the NLTK library [16] AND
- a stemmer is used for stemming process AND
- stemming extracts only stems of words (and nothing else).

The OWL individuals are also represented, e.g. *Stopwords* or *Brown corpus*.

The third phase is focused on the OWL ontology extension with additional information sources added into the OWL concepts (classes, properties, individuals). These additional pieces of information are represented as values of annotation properties. The following annotation properties are used in the TMEO:

- rdf:label: a label of the OWL concept,
- hasDescription: a description (an explanation) of the OWL concept which is inside of the OWL ontology,
- hasWebDescription: a hyperlink where external textual information is available on the web,
- hasWebVideo: a hyperlink where external video sequence is available on the web,
- hasAbbreviation: an abbreviation of the OWL concept,
- hasByword: a synonym of the OWL concept.

Figure 2 depicts the *Stemming* OWL class where some of these additional pieces of information are represented.

The OWL ontology is developed the Protégé 5.2.0 environment which is one of the most known editors used by ontological practitioners [17]. The Protégé is the open-source tool based on the plugins-based architecture. The Debugger plugin is used during TMEO development. It tests consistency and coherence of the ontology with the Pellet reasoner. The Pellet is a program able to infer the new facts which are not explicitly expressed in the ontology. As the example, if an inference process is run above the TMEO ontology, the Pellet infers that the *Algorithm* OWL class is a subclass of the *Technique* OWL class. The technique is broader term then the algorithm. This inference is based on "comparison" of conditions with restrictions which are included in the *Algorithm* OWL class and *Technique* OWL class. Table 1 mentions statistics of the TMEO ontology.

Table 1. Statistics of the TMEO ontology

Ontological concept	Count
OWL classes	132
OWL object properties	17
OWL inverse object properties	17
OWL annotation properties	5 (+ rdf:label)
OWL individuals	11
SubClassOf axioms	306
Annotation assertion	276

3.4   SPARQL-Based Content Mining

The content of the ontology can be browsed directly in the Protégé with the Classes hierarchy tab. This tab shows the taxonomy of the OWL classes with their semantics and annotations. The OWLViz plugin visualises only taxonomy of the OWL classes where only superclass-subclass relations are visible. The OntoGraf adds a view on the OWL individuals. If the ontology is very complex and a user uses only a visual representation of the ontology, it is difficult to receive fast answer on a specific question. A lot of ontological properties are often crossed. Querying can solve this problem. The Protégé 5.2.0 provides various plugins for ontology querying. The DL Query plugin uses OWL class expressions in querying, but variables cannot be used in a query. The SQWRLTab plugin uses SQWRL (Semantic Query-enhanced Web Rule

Language) [18] extending the SWRL (Semantic Web Rule Language) [19] which is used for integration rules into the ontology. The SQWRL has native support of the OWL, but only individuals can be queried. The above mentioned limitations are eliminated with the SPARQL Query tab. SPARQL (SPARQL Protocol and RDF Query Language) is a standardized language for querying the RDF graphs [20]. It is very similar to the SQL (Structured Query Language) which is used in querying the relational databases. Syntax of the SPARQL is based on the Turtle (Terse RDF Triple Language) - a textual syntax used for formal specification of the RDF-based structures [21]. If a student is familiar with this language, it can receive fast feedback without often time-consuming browsing of complex ontological structure. It has to be said that learning curve is the longest in case of the SPARQL in comparison to the DL Query and SQWRL because of the complexity of the SPARQL. The following examples demonstrate how the SPARQL language can be used in the TMEO ontology querying. The value of the *tmo* prefix represents the ontology IRI.

1. query: *"What is a segmentation?"*
   Solution:

```
SELECT ?description
WHERE
{tmo:Segmentation tmo:hasDescription ?description.}
```

2. query: *"Which corpora we can work in the NLTK with? Order results alphabetically."*
   Solution:

```
SELECT (?corpus AS ?CorpusInNLTK)
WHERE {?corpus rdf:type tmo:CorpusOfNLTKLibrary.}
ORDER BY ?corpus
```

3. query: *"What is a name of an algorithm which extracts stems of words?"*
   Solution:

```
SELECT ?algorithm
WHERE {
?algorithm rdfs:subClassOf* tmo:Algorithm.
?algorithm rdfs:subClassOf ?restriction.
?restriction owl:onProperty tmo:realizes.
?restriction owl:someValuesFrom ?technique.
?technique rdfs:subClassOf* tmo:Technique.
?technique rdfs:subClassOf ?restriction02.
?restriction02 owl:onProperty tmo:extracts.
?restriction02 owl:someValuesFrom tmo:StemOfWord.}
```

4. query: *"How many non-primitive data types are provided by the Python?"*
   Solution:

```
SELECT (COUNT (?dataType) as ?CountOfDataTypes)
WHERE {
tmo:Python rdfs:subClassOf ?restriction.
?restriction owl:onProperty tmo:offers.
?restriction owl:someValuesFrom ?dataType.
?dataType rdfs:subClassOf
tmo:NonPrimitiveDataStructure.}
```

4 Discussion and Future Directions

A student can browse the ontology in an ontological editor supporting OWL (RDF(S)) language. The Protégé tool is used in the seminars of the *Ontologies and Semantic Web* study subject at the University of Hradec Králové. Students learn how to develop the OWL ontologies, how to query or use them in the semantic web context. On the basis of our experience, students are satisfied with this tool, but they can see some imperfections in its use. It takes some time then a student is familiar with this tool. A lot of different tabs/views are visible during ontologies development. If a student is not familiar with this, he (she) can have a problem to orient in this environment. The TMEO ontology should be available also for students which do not have a background in the semantic web. This is the reason why a web application is going to be developed. A content of the TMEO ontology is going to be mined with the SPARQL queries. This extracted content is going to be presented in web pages with the Python-based Owlready2 framework [22] where SPARQL queries are going to be used in querying of the RDFLib graph. Web pages are going to be designed with the Python-based microframework named Flask [23]. NetworkX Python library is going to be used for visualisation of the ontological structure and analysis of its structure [26].

If we consider that a student is not familiar with description logics or ontology-based modelling concepts, it is not so difficult to understand general meaning of concepts in the Protégé. Figure 3 depicts a meaning of the *Stemming* OWL class. The class contains conditions. Their general meaning is clear for the non-experts in the ontological modelling (as our experience in teaching of the OSW subject shows), but it cannot be supposed that a student understand what the OWL restrictions (an existential (some), a universal (only), a cardinality (min, max, equal) or a has value) means. This could be solved with the expression of these conditions in the natural language. Several research papers are focused on this problem, i.e. how to "convert" logical statements expressed in the formal ontology into the natural language, see [24] or [25]. Solution of this problem will be taken into account in the future.

5 Conclusion

Text mining is a complex research and study field. It interconnects facts from various research disciplines. The paper presents a problem where the non-professionals in the text mining, especially students, can have a problem to get oriented in this area. The ontological approach is chosen for provision an educational support for text mining education because the ontology provides formal structure which is machine-processable and useful for understanding the application domain by humans and machines. The ontology can play a role of a vocabulary of "things" where categorisation of these "things" is visible with meaning of these "things". The paper presents development of the prototype using the TMEO ontology which is going to be used in the proposed Text Mining study subject at the University of Hradec Králové. The ontology is not going to be used only at this university, but it will be shared in public. The TMEO ontology is going to be used as a repository of concepts about text mining and in the web application development for more comfortable browsing of the ontology. SPARQL queries will extract specific facts from the TMEO ontology. Owlready2 library [22], Flask micro-framework [23] and NetworkX library [26] are going to be combined for web pages development.

Acknowledgements. The support of the Specific research project at FIM UHK is gratefully acknowledged. The author would like to thank Tomáš Nácházel for figures preparation and Luboš Mercl for administration.

References

1. Miner, G., et al.: Practical Text Mining and Statistical Analysis for Non-Structured Text Data Applications, 1st edn. Academic Press, Orlando (2012)
2. Allahyari, M., et al.: A brief survey of text mining: classification, clustering and extraction techniques. arXiv Repository (2017). https://arxiv.org/abs/1707.02919. Accessed 12 Mar 2019
3. Zhai, Ch., Massung, S.: Text Data Management and Analysis: A Practical Introduction to Information Retrieval and Text Mining. 1st ed. ACM Books (2016)
4. Ameen, A., Khan, K.U.R.: Creation of ontology in education domain. In: The Proceedings of the IEEE Fourth International Conference on Technology for Education, pp. 237–238 (2012). https://doi.org/10.1109/t4e.2012.50
5. Boyce, S., Pahl, C.: Developing domain ontologies for course content. J. Educ. Technol. Soc. **10**(3), 275–288 (2007). https://core.ac.uk/download/pdf/11310019.pdf. Accessed 11 Mar 2019
6. Katis, E., Kondylakis, H., Agathangelos, G., Vassilakis, K.: Developing an ontology for curriculum and syllabus. In: Gangemi, A., et al. (eds.) ESWC 2018. LNCS, vol. 11155, pp. 55–59. Springer, Cham (2018). https://doi.org/10.1007/978-3-319-98192-5_11
7. Baeva, D., Atanasova, D.: Ontology based resource for history education. TEM J. **7**(4), 782–786 (2018). https://doi.org/10.18421/tem74-13
8. Rehman, Z., Kifor, S.: Teaching natural language processing (NLP) using ontology based education design. In: Balkan Region Conference on Engineering and Business Education vol. 1, no. 1. De Gruyter Open (2015). Open-Access Journal. https://doi.org/10.1515/cplbu-2015-0024

9. Alfaries, A.A., Aljably, R.H., Al-Razgan, M.S.: Modeling the NLP research domain using ontologies: an ontology representation of NLP concepts from a research perspective. In: The Proceedings of the Future Technologies Conference (FTC), pp. 1064–1072 (2018). https:// saiconference.com/Downloads/FTC2017/Proceedings/152_Paper_164-Modeling_the_NLP_ Research_Domain.pdf. Accessed 11 Mar 2019

10. NLTK 3.4 documentation. https://www.nltk.org/. Accessed 12 Mar 2019

11. Python Software Foundation. https://www.python.org/. Accessed 10 Feb 2019

12. Novak, J.: Concept maps and Vee diagrams: two metacognitive tools to facilitate meaningful learning. Instr. Sci. **19**, 29–52 (1990)

13. W3C. OWL 2 Web Ontology Language: Document Overview, 2nd edn., W3C Recommendation, 11 December 2012. https://www.w3.org/TR/2012/REC-owl2-overview-20121211/. Accessed 1 Feb 2019

14. W3C: RDF 1.1 Concepts and Abstract Syntax, W3C Recommendation, 25 February 2014. https://www.w3.org/TR/2014/REC-rdf11-concepts-20140225/. Accessed 2 Feb 2019

15. W3C: RDF Schema 1.1, W3C Recommendation, 25 February 2014. https://www.w3.org/ TR/2014/REC-rdf-schema-20140225/. Accessed 2 Feb 2019

16. Bird, S., Klein, E., Loper, E.: Natural Language Processing with Python: Analyzing Text with the Natural Language Toolkit, 1st edn. O'Reilly Media, Sebastopol (2009)

17. Stanford Center for Biomedical Informatics Research. https://protege.stanford.edu/. Accessed 5 Mar 2019

18. O'Connor, M., Das, A.: SQWRL: a query language for OWL. In: The Proceedings of the 6th International Conference on OWL: Experiences and Directions, vol. 529, pp. 208–215 (2009)

19. W3C. SWRL: A Semantic Web Rule Language Combining OWL and RuleML. W3C Member Submission 21 May 2004. https://www.w3.org/Submission/SWRL/. Accessed 4 Mar 2019

20. Harris, S., Garlik, a part of Experian Andy Seaborne, The Apache Software Foundation (eds.) W3C. SPARQL 1.1 Query Language. https://www.w3.org/TR/2013/REC-sparql11-query-20130321/. Accessed 5 Mar 2019

21. W3C. RDF 1.1 Turtle: Terse RDF Triple Language, W3C Recommendation, 2 February 2014. https://www.w3.org/TR/turtle/. Accessed 5 Mar 2019

22. Lamy, J.B.: Owlready: ontology-oriented programming in Python with automatic classification and high level constructs for biomedical ontologies. Artif. Intell. Med. **80**, 11–28 (2017)

23. Ronacher, A.: Flask homepage. http://flask.pocoo.org/. Accessed 4 Mar 2019

24. Androutsopoulos, I., Lampouras, G., Galanis, D.: Generating natural language descriptions from OWL ontologies: the NaturalOWL system. J. Artif. Intell. Res. **48**, 671–715 (2013)

25. Amith, M., et al.: Expressing biomedical ontologies in natural language for expert evaluation. Stud. Health Technol. Inform. **245**, 838–842 (2017). https://doi.org/10.3233/978-1-61499-830-3-838

26. Hagberg, A.A., Schult, D.A., Swart, P.J.: Exploring network structure, dynamics, and function using NetworkX. In: Varoquaux, G., Vaught, T., Millman, J. (eds.) The Proceedings of the 7th Python in Science Conference (SciPy 2008), Pasadena, CA, USA, pp. 11–15 (2008)

Use of Graph Theory for the Representation of Scientific Collaboration

Jared D. T. Guerrero-Sosa[iD], Victor Menendez-Domínguez[✉][iD],
María-Enriqueta Castellanos-Bolaños[iD], and Luis F. Curi-Quintal[iD]

Facultad de Matemáticas, Universidad Autónoma de Yucatán, Mérida, Mexico
jaredgs93@gmail.com, {mdoming,enriqueta.c,cquintal}@correo.uady.mx

Abstract. The objective of this work is to present a proposal for the use of graph theory for the representation of scientific collaboration in a Mexican educational institution based on the retrieval of data available in various repositories of scientific production considering the problem of the inconsistencies in the registry of the name of the authors. In the state of the art, the concepts involved are exposed, such as scientific production, digital repositories, interoperability, the Law of Open Science in Mexico and the theory of graphs. The proposed methodology uses elements for the extraction of knowledge for data mining, involving harvesting, processing and visualization. In the results section, the analysis of the state of scientific collaboration in the Universidad Autónoma de Yucatán is presented through concepts of graph theory, observing that there are 22 scientific collaboration groups and each researcher, on average, collaborates with 6 researchers from the same institution (obtained from the average grade of the graph) and have 18 collaborations in their publications (obtained the average grade of a weighted graph). Finally, conclusions and future work are exposed.

Keywords: Scientific collaboration · Graph theory ·
Digital repositories

1 Introduction

Nowadays, a common activity in scientific production is working in groups (collaborative work). Scientific collaborations involve, among other things, the definition of tasks and the reasons to collaborate, number of constant collaborators and personal factors [10]. On a personal level, researchers collaborate to gain experience, visibility and prestige in the scientific community; to progress scientifically in a more agile way; solve bigger problems; receive incentives by diverse evaluating institutions [2], among other factors. It is established that various institutions grant economic resources and recognition to scientific work in order to motivate their researchers and generate more projects that solve problems in society through science, technology and innovation. And several studies involve more than one area of knowledge, so scientific collaborations become a necessity.

© Springer Nature Switzerland AG 2019
N. T. Nguyen et al. (Eds.): ICCCI 2019, LNAI 11684, pp. 543–554, 2019.
https://doi.org/10.1007/978-3-030-28374-2_47

Several studies have been carried out on the state of scientific collaboration in countries or geographical areas, for example, Latin America [16,24] and in specific institutions such as the Universidad Nacional Autónoma de México [25] and the Universidad Autónoma de Yucatán (UADY) [18], using data visualization tools to present their results. In the present article, a model is proposed for the extraction of the scientific production information from two data sources: Scopus, an abstract and citation database of peer-reviewed literature, considering the problem of the existence of more than one profile of the same researcher; and some open-access repositories (so that, once the information is obtained, it is represented in a graph, for using the theoretical characteristics in order to analyze the status of the scientific collaboration of a institution). For the realization of the present work some previous ones were carried out, such as the analysis of the indicators for the scientific production [12], of the libraries for the metadata harvesting through the interoperability [14] and the proposal of an indicators system for the relevance of scientific production [13].

In this section, the introduction to the proposal of this work was presented. The state of the art section exposes the related topics for the understanding of the concepts used later. The methodology section proposes the use of knowledge extraction techniques for data mining (collection, processing and visualization). The results section explains the graph obtained about scientific collaboration in the UADY (Mexico), and its analysis using statical concepts of graph theory. Finally, the last section explains the conclusions and future work.

2   State of the Art

Scientific publications have been accessible thanks to the existence of repositories of digital resources. A digital repository is a platform that is responsible for storing, preserving and being a tool for disseminating content, and can be classified as follows: as Open Educational Resources (OER), as OER references, as OpenCourseware initiatives and as a system of learning management [21]. A characteristic of repositories is the interoperability, which is the ability to connect with other ones for the exchange and use of their data [9] using specialized protocols, such as OAI-PMH, OpenAIRE and IMS. Among the variety of publications found in the digital repositories are the original articles, the case reports, the technical notes and the pictorial essays [22].

In Mexico, there is the Open Science Law, which establishes that anyone has free access, without making a prior payment, to the publications, products of research works stored in digital repositories of Mexican institutions and made with public resources in order to increase the accessibility of scientific research for all Mexicans through the maximum dissemination of scientific knowledge, technology and innovation [4].

Regarding to publications, they can be indexed, in other words, they can be located in a database that is responsible for collecting citations, even through periodic evaluations. These databases uses quantitative statistical indicators (h-index, impact factor, index i10) to measure scientific productivity and with them determine the quality of publications, generally scientific journals and serialized books. Internationally, the main citation databases are two: Scopus and Web Of Science. However, Google Scholar has been considered as another alternative due to the use of its own indicators for scientific productivity. There are studies that compare characteristics, strengths and weaknesses of citation databases, using as reference Scopus, Web of Science and Google Scholar [1,8,15,17].

Something that characterizes contemporary science (from the mid-twentieth century) is the constant collaboration with scientists of homogeneous and heterogeneous knowledge, being an advantage to complement concepts and conceive new ones. This group of people who collaborate is known as a scientific community, and they do not necessarily have to know each other face to face. Media such as telephone and Internet help the interaction between them, facilitating collaborative work [11].

A useful tool for representing the relation between two elements among a set of several of them is the theory of graphs. In Computer Science, a graph is a mathematical abstraction, represented as

$$G = (V, E) \tag{1}$$

where V is a set of vertices and E is a set of edges. In this way, graphs are useful for modeling relations between elements and allows the resolution of problems associated with their context and requires a less expensive process than even linear programming, and to represent them, there are three options: graphic representation, representation with an adjacent matrix, and the dictionary of the graph [26]. The graphic representation of a graph consists of presenting each vertex as a point or circle, generally. Although they can be represented by other figures, depending on what you want to graph. The relations between the vertices are represented by connecting lines.

There is a wide variety of tools for the construction and visualization of graphs, and among them are NodeXL, Gephi and Google Fusion Tables.

With regard to the representation of scientific collaborations with graph theory, either directly or indirectly, several studies have been carried out considering geographical areas, disciplines, various databases and time windows. Below are some that have obtained relevant results that confirm known facts and also discover specific cases.

In [20] the author studied the relationship between researchers in Biomedicine, Theoretical Physics, High Energy Physics and Computer Science in the period from 1995 to 1999 using MEDLINE databases, Los Alamos e-Print Archive, SPIRES and NCSTRL. This research focuses on the calculation of the distance between authors, but considers important to include the number of collaborators of the scientists, the number of articles they produce, and the probability that two collaborators of a specific researcher have collaborated. This study finds that it is very likely that the formation of scientific communities originates thanks to the existence of a common collaborator between two researchers, except in Biomedicine. In addition, this study reaffirms the high degree of collaboration among Physics researchers and emphasizes that the representation of collaboration is not specific to Computer Science, but began with Mathematics with the concept of Erdös number.

In [5] the authors conducted a study of the analysis of scientific collaboration between the Consejo Superior de Investigaciones Científicas (CSIC) and Latin America focused on various disciplines. They got a dataset from ISI (today ThomsonScientific) and Web of Science considering the publications between 2001 and 2004. In spite of having apparent disadvantages related to the language and the low representation of non-Anglo-Saxon magazines, the authors considered the registers of the names of the researchers. Based on the classification of journals in disciplines and areas, indicators of activity, impact and collaboration were obtained. According to the results obtained, Physics and Chemistry are the areas with the highest degree of collaboration, and the Social Sciences have little research work as a whole.

In [19] authors propose a method for the identification and analysis of the scientific collaboration applicable to universities and research centers in general, considering the need to facilitate the location of the most productive and relevant areas and disciplines for the allocation of economic resources destined to projects. They used the Scopus database. The methodology used is to obtain information from publications, authors and collaborative networks to analyze with elements of graph theory such as the number of nodes, density of the graph, among others.

In [3] the authors studied the interaction and the degree of collaboration between different disciplines through the analysis of social networks from a database provided by the Office of Scientific and Technology Information of the US Department of Energy using statistical techniques based on the graph theory. The study considers the social network as a set of nodes (people, institutions and countries) and edges (relationships between nodes). They created two different networks, one for the publications between 1980 and 2000 and other one for 2000–2012. Among the relevant results are a strong collaboration between nuclear, energy and environmental disciplines, reinforcing the 2013 trend of studies on renewable energies.

3   Methodology

Figure 1 presents the architecture of the system, which proposes a solution for the retrieval of information about the researchers with their corresponding scientific production stored in digital repositories. The architecture has been designed in layers, facilitating the flow of information between them.

Each layer has a specific function. The layer of the user interface presents the information obtained by the services from the obtained data. The service layer consists of modules that work together for representing the results through the user interface and among its functions are the calculation of indicators, location of collaborations between researchers, SPARQL queries and SWRL rules for the ontological model of scientific production. The layer of information storage schemas contains the tools that are responsible for storing the information of the researchers and their production as OWL, an ontological and non-relational

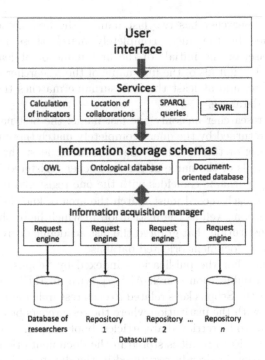

Fig. 1. System architecture

database. The information acquisition manager layer contains request engines that connect directly to different repositories, either through the verbs of the protocol for metadata harvesting OAI-PMH or some API, if the repository requires it. Finally, the datasources are the repositories that contain information about the academic and scientific production of the researchers.

To apply the proposed methodology, it is necessary to have a database of researchers, considering their name, institution that granted his/her last academic degree and the area of knowledge in which they work. Making use of the methodology of data mining, specifically in e-learning applications, we propose one of knowledge extraction, which consists of the following stages [23]:

- Data collection. It is divided into two parts.
  1. Researchers. Once the researchers and their related data are identified, their identifications of authors in Scopus are collected. A query is made to Scopus through its author search API [6], which is an HTTP request, using as parameters the first and the last name of the researcher, and the institution to which he or she belongs or that granted him or her the last academic degree. The result obtained is in XML format by default, or JSON. From all the results obtained, the following are considered as identifications of authors in Scopus of a specific researcher if they meet any of the following conditions:

- If the researcher has two last names: the first name and surnames returned by the query completely match those registered in the database; or the initials of the first name or at least the first one match the initials of the first name of the researcher registered in the database, and at least the first surname matches the one registered in the database.
- If the researcher has only one last name: the first name and the last name returned by the query completely match those registered in the database; or the initials of the name or at least the first one match the initials of the name of the researcher registered in the database, and the surname coincides with the one registered in the database.

In addition, each record must match the area of knowledge registered in the database, as well as the institution in which he or she belongs, or at least the institution that granted the last academic degree. Each result is stored in the document-oriented database.

2. Publications. For the publications indexed by Scopus, a query is made through its publication search API [7], with an HTTP request using as parameters the Scopus keys related to each researcher and the Scopus keys associated with the institution where the researchers belongs. Among the publications to be retrieved are articles, book chapters, books and conference articles. Each result is stored in the document-oriented database. If the publication is already registered in the database, because it belongs to more than one researcher of the institution, the field of authors is updated. For publications not indexed by Scopus and available in open access repositories that use the protocol OAI-PMH, metadata are harvested with the verb *ListRecords*.

- Data processing. To make the graph, it is necessary to represent each researcher by a vertex, and the collaborations with edges. Ordinary combinations of 2 elements are required because the elements of each subset are considered independently of the arrangement. Then, the number of combinations is defined by the following equation

$$C_{n,2} = \frac{n!}{2!(n-2)!} \tag{2}$$

where n is the number of researchers belonging to the institution. Once the groups of combinations are obtained, a query is made to the database for retrieving the number of publications in which the researchers involved have collaborated. The results are generated as a table, where the first and second columns contain the names of the authors of the collaboration and the third column contains the number of publications in common.

- Visualization. With the resulting data from previous stages, the table is imported into some tool for the visualization of graphs and carry out the subsequent analysis of the scientific collaboration in the evaluated institution. The graph fulfills the following characteristics:

- Graph $G(V, E)$
- V is a set of vertices
- E is a set of edges
- G is an undirected graph
- G is a weighted graph, and the weights of the edges are the number of publications in common between the researchers represented by the vertices

4 Results

For the data collection phase of the methodology, we had a database of researchers from the Universidad Autónoma de Yucatán (UADY), located in Mexico, which has the names of researchers, faculty or area of knowledge where they belong, and the institution that granted them the last academic degree. Scopus was consulted to retrieve the identifications of authors in this platform, because a researcher can have multiple profiles in Scopus. In order to collect the information about the indexed publications, the query was made in Scopus using the identifications of authors and the two identifications of institution of UADY as parameters, since only the publications belonging to this institution are considered. For collecting the production not indexed by Scopus, the information was retrieved from various open access repositories that use the protocol for metadata harvesting OAI-PMH. These tasks were executed by Python scripts.

All retrieved data is stored in the MongoDB database. Through another Python script, the data processing phase generates the table of scientific collaborations, which is exported in .xslx format to be later processed by the Google visualization tool, Fusion Tables, which it is useful for clarity in the representation of the graph with a considerable number of vertices. To avoid that the file has unnecessary information, such as the relations between researchers who do not collaborate, these were omitted. Gephi was used to obtain the statistics of the graph.

In this work, 824 teachers were evaluated, of which, 390 have publications in collaboration with other professors of the same institution. Each teacher is represented by a vertex. There are 1181 edges, that represent relations of scientific collaboration. The obtained graph is presented in Fig. 2, where the size of the vertices is determined by the degree (number of collaborators) and degree with weights (number of collaborations). The largest vertex is the Researcher670 with 14 collaborators and 174 collaborations (Fig. 3).

In addition, the obtained graph has 22 subgraphs that show collaborations that have no relation among them, or, collaboration groups, represented in Fig. 2 with numbers in red. Using the Gephi tool, interesting results were obtained about the collaboration, using elements of graph theory, which can be observed in the Table 1.

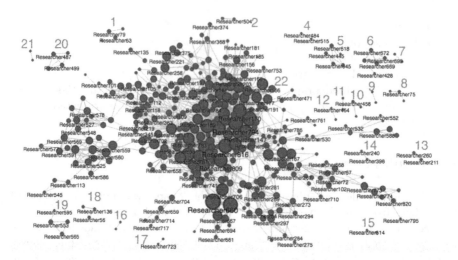

Fig. 2. Graph of representation of the scientific collaboration in the Universidad Autónoma de Yucatán

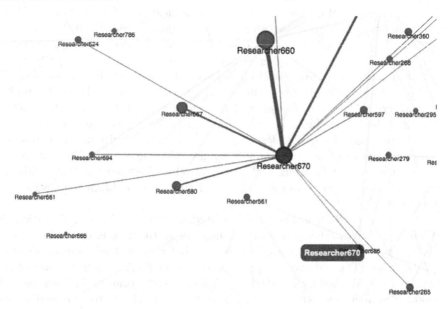

Fig. 3. The researcher with the highest degree of collaboration in UADY

The interesting results of the representation of the collaboration through the graph and its statistics are the following:

– On average, each researcher has collaborated with 6 researchers belonging to the UADY, considering the average degree of the graph.

Table 1. Characteristics and statistics of the obtained graph

Characteristic	Value
Number of vertices	390
Number of edges	1181
Average degree	6.056
Average weighted degree	18.4
Graph density	0.016

- On average, each researcher has 18 collaborations, considering the average weighted degree.
- The graph density is very low, being 0.016 a value very close to 0. If the graph was completely connected, the graph density would be 1. But, considering that the UADY has 390 collaborating researchers, it is very difficult for each researcher to collaborate with each other.
- In the UADY there are 22 collaboration groups.

Additionally, external collaborations with other universities and research centers in Mexico and with other countries were located from the researchers who collaborate internally at UADY. Table 2 shows the Mexican institutions with which UADY has the highest degree of collaboration, and Table 3 shows the countries with which there is greater collaboration. There are 499 Mexican institutions and 89 countries that had collaborated with UADY.

Table 2. Ranking of Mexican institutions with the greatest collaboration with UADY

Rank	Institution	Collaborations
1	Universidad Autónoma de México	375
2	Centro de Investigación Científica de Yucatán	253
3	CINVESTAV Unidad Mérida	226
4	Centro de Investigación y de Estudios Avanzados	208
5	Instituto Politécnico Nacional	175

Table 3. Ranking of countries with the greatest collaboration with UADY

Rank	Country	Collaborations
1	United States	1144
2	Spain	306
3	France	213
4	United Kingdom	206
5	Germany	160

5   Conclusions

The problem presented consists in the retrieval of the production of the researchers from an institution (considering that in the digital repositories, their names are registered in different formats). And from these results, through the theory of graphs, visualize the current state of scientific collaboration. The proposed methodology uses knowledge extraction for data mining considering the system architecture in layers, where each one has a specific function (information acquisition, storage, services and user interface). Results explain the scientific collaboration in the Universidad Autónoma de Yucatán, which consists of 390 researchers, and each one collaborates on average with 6 researchers from the same institution (obtained with the average degree of the graph) and has 18 collaborations in his or her publications (obtained with the average weighted degree of the graph). The results could be used for generating metrics to measure the performance and relevance of scientific productivity and create specific policies for institutional collaboration.

As future work, it is expected to locate the areas of knowledge where there is a constant collaboration in an educational institution, in addition to using the results that can be obtained with the graph theory for making decisions that involve the analysis of scientific production for economic incentive, and locate strong and weak collaborations in the institution.

Acknowledgment. The current work has been developed thanks to the support by Consejo Nacional de Ciencia y Tecnología (CONACYT, Mexico) through the grant: 853088/630948.

References

1. Bakkalbasi, N., Bauer, K., Glover, J., Wang, L.: Three options for citation tracking: Google Scholar, Scopus and Web of Science. Biomed. Digit. Libr. **3**(7) (2006). https://doi.org/10.1186/1742-5581-3-7
2. Beaver, D.D.B.: Reflections on scientific collaboration (and its study): past, present, and future. Scientometrics **52**(3), 365–377 (2001). https://doi.org/10.1023/A:1014254214337
3. Bozdogan, H., Akbilgic, O.: Social network analysis of scientific collaborations across different subject fields. Inf. Serv. Use **33**(3–4), 219–233 (2013). https://doi.org/10.3233/ISU-130715
4. CONACYT: Lineamientos Jurídicos de Ciencia Abierta. http://www.siicyt.gob.mx/index.php/normatividad/conacyt-normatividad/programas-vigentes-normatividad/lineamientos/lineamientos-juridicos-de-ciencia-abierta/3828-lineamientos-juridicos-de-ciencia-abierta/file. Accessed 30 Nov 2017
5. De Filippo, D., Morillo, F., Fernández, M.T.: Indicators of scientific collaboration between CSIC and Latin America through international databases. Revista española de Documentación Científica **31**(1), 66–84 (2008). https://doi.org/10.3989/redc.2008.v31.i1.413, http://redc.revistas.csic.es/index.php/redc/article/view/413/425
6. Elsevier: Author Search API. https://tinyurl.com/yxm7ugcz. Accessed 7 Apr 2019

7. Elsevier: Scopus Search API. https://tinyurl.com/y644xqlc. Accessed 7 Apr 2019
8. Falagas, M.E., Pitsouni, E.I., Malietzis, G.A., Pappas, G.: Comparison of PubMed, Scopus, Web of Science, and Google Scholar: strengths and weaknesses. FASEB J. (2007). https://doi.org/10.1096/fj.07-9492lsf
9. Gómez-Dueñas, L.F.: Interoperabilidad en los Sistemas de Información Documental (SID): la información debe fluir. Códice **3**(1), 23–39 (2007)
10. Gómez-Ferri, J., González-Alcaide, G.: Patrones y estrategias en la colaboración científica: la percepción de los investigadores. Revista española de Documentación Científica **41**(1) (2018). https://doi.org/10.3989/redc.2018.1.1458
11. González-Alcaide, G., Gómez-Ferri, J.: La colaboración científica: principales líneas de investigación y retos de futuro. Revista española de Documentación Científica **37**(4), 1–15 (2014). https://doi.org/10.3989/redc.2014.4.1186
12. Guerrero Sosa, J., Menéndez Domínguez, V.H., Castellanos Bolaños, M.E.: Indicadores de calidad en investigaciones científicas: Antecedentes. Abstraction Appl. **19**, 6–24 (2018). https://intranet.matematicas.uady.mx/journal/descargar.php?id=134
13. Guerrero Sosa, J., Menéndez Domínguez, V.H., Castellanos Bolaños, M.E.: Sistema de índices para valorar la calidad de la producción académica y la investigación, a partir de repositorios digitales y metadatos. In: Prieto-Méndez, M.E., Pech-Campos, S.J., Francesa-Alfaro, A. (eds.) X Conferencia Conjunta Internacional sobre Tecnologías y Aprendizaje, pp. 45–52. CIATA.org-UCLM, Cartago (2018)
14. Guerrero Sosa, J., Sánchez Ferriz, D., Menéndez Domínguez, V.H., Castellanos Bolaños, M.E., Gómez Montalvo, J.: Tools for interoperability between repositories of digital resources. In: Gómez Chova, L., López Martínez, A., Candel Torres, I. (eds.) Proceedings of INTED2019, pp. 6292–6300. IATED, Valencia (2019)
15. Harzing, A.W., Alakangas, S.: Google Scholar, Scopus and the Web of Science: alongitudinal and cross-disciplinary comparison. Scientometrics **106**(2), 787–804 (2016). https://doi.org/10.1007/s11192-015-1798-9
16. Huamaní, C., Mayta-Tristán, P.: Producción científica peruana en medicina y redes de colaboración, análisis del Science Citation Index 2000–2009. Revista Peruana de Medicina Experimental y Salud Pública **27**(3), 315–325 (2010). https://doi.org/10.1590/s1726-46342010000300003
17. Jacso, P.: As we may search - Comparison of major features of the Web of Science, Scopus, and Google Scholar citation-based and citation-enhanced databases. Curr. Sci. **89**(9), 1537–1547 (2005)
18. Luna-Morales, M.E., Luna-Morales, E., Luna-Morales, S.: La UADY en la literatura científica registrada en Web of Science y Scopus: 1900–2016. Educación y Ciencia **7**(50), 17–29 (2018)
19. Montoya, F.G., Alcayde, A., Baños, R., Manzano-Agugliaro, F.: A fast method for identifying worldwide scientific collaborations using the Scopus database. Telematics Inform. **35**(1), 168–185 (2018). https://doi.org/10.1016/j.tele.2017.10.010
20. Newman, M.E.J.: The structure of scientific collaboration networks. Proc. Nat. Acad. Sci. **98**(2), 404–409 (2001). https://doi.org/10.1073/pnas.98.2.404, http://www.pnas.org/cgi/doi/10.1073/pnas.98.2.404
21. Ochoa, X., Duval, E.: Quantitative analysis of learning object repositories. IEEE Trans. Learn. Technol. **2**(3), 226–238 (2009). https://doi.org/10.1109/TLT.2009.28
22. Peh, W.C.G., Ng, K.H.: Basic structure and types of scientific papers. Singapore Med. J. **49**(7), 522–525 (2008)

23. Prieto Méndez, M., Menéndez Domínguez, V.H., Zapata González, A.: Data mining learning objects. In: Romero, C., Ventura, S., Pechenizkly, M. (eds.) Handbook of Educational Data Mining, pp. 315–342. CRC Press Editors (2010)
24. Russell, J.M., Ainsworth, S., Del Río, J.A., Narváez-Berthelemot, N., Cortés, H.D.: Colaboración científica entre países de la región latinoamericana. Revista Española de Documentación Científica **30**(2), 180–198 (2007). https://doi.org/10.3989/redc. 2007.v30.i2.378
25. Russell, J.M., Ainsworth, S., Narváez-Berthelemot, N.: Colaboración científica de la Universidad Nacional Autónoma de México (UNAM) y su política institucional. Revista Española de Documentación Científica **29**(1), 56–73 (2006). https://doi. org/10.3989/redc.2006.v29.i1.287
26. Sallán-Leyes, J.M., Fonollosa-Guardiet, J.B., Fernández-Alarcón, V., Suñé-Torrents, A.: Teoría de grafos. In: Sallán-Leyes, J.M. (ed.) Métodos cuantitativos en organización industrial I, Chap. 7, pp. 137–172. Edicions UPC (2002)

Learning Ecosystem Ontology with Knowledge Management as a Service

Ana Muñoz García[1]([✉]) [iD], Myriam Lamolle[2] [iD],
Rodrigo Martinez-Béjar[3] [iD], and Albert Espinal Santana[4] [iD]

[1] University of Los Andes, Mérida, Venezuela
anamunoz@ula.ve
[2] University of Paris8, Paris, France
m.lamolle@iut.univparis8.fr
[3] University of Murcia, Murcia, Spain
rodrigo@um.es
[4] Espol University, Guayaquil, Ecuador
aespinal@espol.edu.ec

Abstract. The term ecosystem has been used to describe complex interaction between living organisms and the physical world. The principles underlying ecosystems can also apply to human interactions in the digital world. As information and communication technologies increasingly contribute to teaching and learning in higher education, digital ecosystem principles can help to understand how to maximize technology to benefit active learning. The learning ecosystem face several challenges, such as interaction of users with technologies, and also the same interaction in different learning moments. There are proposals for technological integration and learning pedagogy, but we did not find a proposal that integrate and describe the knowledge management processes during learning. This paper proposes the ecosystem learning from the knowledge view as a service supported by ontology.

1 Introduction

An ecosystem is a community of living beings whose vital processes are interrelated and the development is based on environment physical factors. An ecosystem is defined as a technological learning community, with educational, political, rules, applications and team work that allows to coexist in a way that the process are interrelated and its application is based on physical factors of the technologic background [1]. A digital learning ecosystem has an architecture based on software components that combine to work together to allow the gradual evolution of the system through the contribution of ideas and new components by the community.

An intelligent learning background besides allowing students to access digital resources and interact with learning systems any place any time, also provide an active learning guide, suggestions, backup tools and learning necessary suggestions at the right place in the right time and in the right way. At the present time, most authors consider important to support the union of technology and pedagogy in order to create a coherent ecosystem that provides *"Real time evidence and constant changes in*

© Springer Nature Switzerland AG 2019
N. T. Nguyen et al. (Eds.): ICCCI 2019, LNAI 11684, pp. 555–567, 2019.
https://doi.org/10.1007/978-3-030-28374-2_48

knowledge inculcating skills easy to transfer to students while their moving from one context to other" [2].

The objective of an intelligent learning environment is to provide self-motivated and personalized services. Also, it is convenient to contemplate that the intelligent learning environment must provide motivation to a variety of trainees, identifying skills, learning types and interest. Knowledge management transfers knowledge from the place where it is generated to the place where it is going to be used, and implies the development of the necessary skills to share and use it among the members of an organization, as well as to value and assimilate it if it is outside of it. De Freitas [3] considers that *"a knowledge management system comprises everything that contributes to facilitating the processes of creation and transmission of knowledge, as well as its use"*.

Ontologies arise as a management tool more appropriated to support representation, process, storage and knowledge recovery.

"An ontology is a specification of a shared conceptualization of a domain" [4], that is, a definition and formal representation of concepts and its relationships belonging to a particular domain of interest. Once a domain of knowledge or some aspects of it are formally represented using a common and shared language, they become understandable not only by humans but also by automated computer agents [5]. Uschold [6], says that an ontology consists of reaching agreement on what things mean and putting it into a machine-processable form. The formal representation of meaning through ontologies, allows the automatic inference and helps to reduce complexity, improve trustworthiness and increases agility. Ontology clear the meaning and reduce complexity of important elements to achieve interoperability and integration, which in turn is a key element in achieving flexibility. A wide variety of knowledge-based semantic technologies, including machine learning and natural language processing, depend critically on ontologies. Ontologies can be used as a structure to: Integration, decision support, semantic implementation and knowledge management [6]. In addition, ontologies that are available in literature are becoming bigger in terms of number of concepts and relations, so it can be consider Big Data [7–10].

In the computer, in the cloud, there is the promotion for knowledge management. Communities of practice take care of themselves in terms of licensing, agreements and many other things in hardware and software management. These services are: Platform as a service (PaaS, Platform as a Service), Infrastructure as service (IaaS, Infrastructure as a Service), storage as service (DaaS, Storage as a Service) and software as service (SaaS, Software as a Service).

In a computer environment in the cloud, people that are connected obtain knowledge as a service (KaaS, Knowledge as a Service) from a variety of platforms. In the context of the environment of knowledge management systems and cloud computing, each of the knowledge provided by the community of practice is described as a service. Abdullah et al. [11] propose four components: a knowledge platform as a service (K-PaaS), which is a hardware and software combination necessary for the practice community; the framework of knowledge as a service (K-IaaS) its related with infrastructure requirements in knowledge management implementation to support the practice community to share and transfer its benefits to other practice communities; storage knowledge as a service (K-DaaS) related with data storage that allows practice community to storage and be used for developing purposes, test and implementation.

This paper proposes an ontological model that provides intelligence and knowledge capabilities in the creation of a learning ecosystem. The main objective of the model is to generate a learning ecosystem according to the needs and capabilities of the user. An ontological architecture is proposed that represents the knowledge management of the learning ecosystem from the vision of knowledge as a service.

The structure of the article is as follows: Sect. 2 presents papers related to learning ecosystem ontologies. Section 3 describes the methods used to specify the Learning Ecosystem Ontology. Section 4 presents the conceptual model of Ontology. Finally, Sect. 6 presents conclusions and future work.

2 Related Work

The Learning 3.0 is characterized for its collaboration and intelligence where students can have self-organized or personalized learning based on the applications of Web Semantics technologies. There is currently a great deal of research trying to develop intelligent learning systems incorporating ontologies. Some research applies ontologies to the field of education such as creating and describing curricula, organizing learning objects based on ontologies, and retrieving learning content based on ontologies [12]. Studies for the creation of educational ontologies include the creation of curricular ontologies [13] and the creation of theme personalized ontologies [14]. Mizoguchi [15, 16] proposed a solution based on ontology to resolve several problems caused by intelligent instructional systems. There are other works to define the metadata of learning objects and learning paths based on ontological engineering technology [17, 18]. This work focused on managing learning materials and objects and improving the performance of instructional systems.

Hung [22] describe a learning ecosystem that connects: the users of learning, the learning contents, the learning context and the learning technologies. It is an ecosystem centered on individuals, groups and learning networks, and made up of four components: Learning Actor (Subject), Learning content, learning context and learning technology. These four components serve as an integral environment for the teaching and learning process. The learning ecosystem can have other nested ecosystems with interactions and connections, and can be used to create individual, group, or networked learning by learners and instructors of a particular course or learning objective. Some of the elements used for the models that make up our learning ecosystem are those proposed by Hung [22], such as: learning content, learning context and learning technology.

Majd and Marie-Hélène [19], propose a learning ecosystem as an Information Systems System (SoIS, System of Information Systems) developed using a collaborative model with features such as sharing, indexing, annotation and voting for resources. They propose a centralized access point where the student can find, share and index the resources. It uses the Information System approach (SoIS) to implement the central access point as support for the learning ecosystem. Our ecosystem uses this ecosystem vision to make the technological model of the ecosystem.

In Khaled et al. [20], present a learning environment formulated as a social network (iLearn), in order to carry out automatic semantic reasoning that includes interactions between users, as well as their relationships with learning resources. It has a two-engine component: the Inference and the Analyzer. Inference allows reasoning about the knowledge acquired in RDF graphs with rules to deduce conclusions as results. The analyzer extracts and analyzes the results obtained to produce appropriate user behaviors, communities and recommendations. They combine the analysis of social networks with web semantics integrating a semantics of treatment of the knowledge they contain and designed by an ontological formalism. iLearn has two ontologies, one to understand users' emotions about resources and recommendations, and the second to categorize different resources. They present an interactive method of community detection to provide students from the same learning community with the best learning strategies, the most collaborative candidates, and the relevant resources that fit their needs.

In Muñoz et al. [21], developed a knowledge management model for higher education where they describe knowledge management processes, from a vision of the business model and process model for higher education through ontologies. This work shows an evolution of the model seen as a learning ecosystem. In [1] present a system that selects educational objects to support learning. From a graph of data, it suggests the provision of tailor-made educational complements at the right time. The selection of educational complements take into account the way in which the learner is taught and the objectives of his or her training. The system has six ontologies to describe the semantic information to select the educational complements.

Our work proposes an ecosystem of learning from ontologies and supported by knowledge management as a service. This learning ecosystem is an evolution from the Muñoz [21] proposed in 2015. The ecosystem is made up of layers, some of the elements of the models were used. From the work proposed [20], we take a view of the need to store interactions with the user that helped to visualize the layer of systems and knowledge bases. From the work [1] the vision of integrating ontologies into the ecosystem is used and therefore the ontology repository is proposed. The fundamental objective of this work is the development of a model to guide the design and construction of a semantic platform for the creation of learning ecosystems from knowledge as a service. With the development of the model it is expected to structure the elements that intervene in a learning ecosystem and that contemplates the processes of adaptation for learning. The ecosystem offers intelligence and knowledge capabilities in the creation of an intelligent learning environment.

3 Methodology

The learning design is the result of an knowledge engineering process where knowledge, skills, learning design, medias and handing models are built in an integrated frame [24]. To describe elements and interaction of ecosystem learning models its use the engineering learning process MISA [25] that produces specifications for a learning background.

To describe the elements and interaction of learning ecosystems, it uses the learning engineering processes MISA [25] that produces specifications for a learning background. Each MISA phase is subdivided into a number of steps where the parts of a learning system or environment are built. These phases are sequential, but spiral, with frequent returns to modify results from previous tasks:

Phase 1: A description of the learning ecosystem, its context and constraints are constructed. The overall goals that the solution should provide are the most important characteristics of the target population.

Phase 2: The knowledge model for the learning domain is defined. The prerequisites and target competencies are associated with the most important knowledge entities of the model. In this phase a first visual pedagogical model called "the network of learning events" is constructed that groups the main learning modules or units, their sequencing and the necessary resources for the learners and facilitators to produce them.

Phase 3: A detailed learning design is constructed and the necessary infrastructure is specified. Learning scenarios are created for each learning unit defined in phase 2, which describe the learning and facilitate the activities, the actors who carry them out, and the resources needed or produced by these actors. At the same time, a sub-model of the phase 2 knowledge model is associated with each learning unit, thus defining "the content of the learning unit". According to the evolution of the design, the means and delivery principles are refined to prepare the next phase.

Phase 4: Focused on learning resources and model delivery and object properties, in this model different professionals work together, experts, instructional designers and media designers. Another concurrent task is the description of resource properties in the learning scenarios and the association of a sub-model of the knowledge model to provide a specification of the content of the learning resource.

Phase 5: The project manager plans the validation of the learning environment and produces a list of possible revisions and decisions on how to improve the specifications created in previous phases.

Phase 6: Documentation of the learning ecosystem. This produces a synthesized and comprehensive description of the learning environment for maintenance and quality management by various actors.

For the development of the ontology the Methontology methodology [26] is used, and it is developed in three stages:

Stage 1: Determination of ontology requirements. Through the definition of the static and dynamic elements of the Learning Ecosystem. The elements of knowledge are defined, from the questions of requirements of the pedagogical model such as: content, context, technologies, transition and users. For the intelligent behavior of the ecosystem, elements are defined that support the adaptation of the ecosystem to the user, such as: ontological repositories and reasoners to manage ontologies, data integration systems, decision support systems, visualization systems and recommendatory systems.

Stage 2: Development of the ontology. It is used as theoretical support from the point of view of the educational context of [22]. The phases of analysis, conceptualization and implementation of the ontology were carried out following a spiral model, iterative in each phase of each spiral and with feedback at all levels following the Methontology methodology [26] for the development of ontologies.

Stage 3: Validation of the ontology. The logical consistency of the ontology is verified throughout the process. The tools used for the development of the ontology were the OWL 2 language and the Protege 5.0 software version for the construction of the ontology together with the Pellet reasoner that verifies the consistency. It includes aspects of ontology properties such as language conformity (syntax) and consistency (semantics).

The specification of Ontology requirements is described in the conceptual design below.

4   Learning Ecosystem Conceptual Design

An ontology-based model is created to represents the components of the learning ecosystem and their interactions, as shown in Fig. 1, the conceptual design is described as a layered architecture. The first layer is the knowledge portal that represents the interaction of the user with the learning ecosystem, the second layer are the knowledge models that describe the elements that make up the learning ecosystem, the third layer are the adaptive learning processes that together with the knowledge services layer, describe the intelligent behavior of the ecosystem.

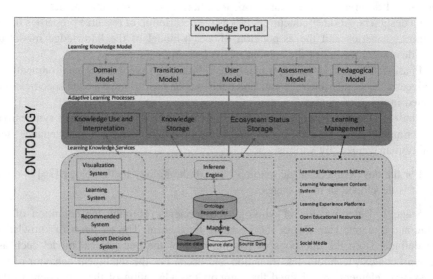

Fig. 1. Learning ecosystem architecture

The **knowledge models layer** contains the domain model, the transition model, the user model, the evaluation model and the pedagogical model. The MISA Learning Engineering process is used to describe the models and their interactions.

Domain Model. It represents the set of knowledge units (UC) required for learning, each UC can be a fragment of knowledge for a domain. Then, by imposing a structure of interdependencies between the Knowledge Units, the Routes of Knowledge are created. In the routes of knowledge, there are interdependencies between the UC that capture the basic relationship of pre-requirements. A prerequisite link represents the fact that one of the related UC must be learned before the other. Additionally, there is the relationship of alternative pre-requirements that express cases where the same state of knowledge can be reached through alternative routes.

Transition Model. The transition model determines the next logical state of knowledge, or what the student is ready to learn from his or her current state. The transition model describes the knowledge attained by the learner at different times of learning. The footprints left by the learner in the transition model allow the profile of the learner to be developed over time. Therefore, it adopts the approach of "superimposing" the model of the apprentice against the model of mastery, which makes it possible to determine the state of knowledge of each apprentice from the correspondence between the state of current knowledge and the desired state.

User Model. The roles of the ecosystem users are the learner, the tutor, and the instructional designer. The representation of the learner within the system includes the definition of his/her learning objectives, his/her favorite learning style, as well as his/her skills and whether the learning is developed individually, in a group or in a network. The tutor describes his or her expertise as a creator of learning content and manages user groups. The instructional designer plans, designs and prepares learning resources and environments.

Evaluation Model. The evaluation model is the one that measures what an apprentice knows. The relationship of a knowledge unit with a learning objective can be considered as one-to-many. Consequently, each unit of knowledge is assigned to a set of learning objectives. A learner has mastered or learned a concept if he has mastered the corresponding set (or some subset) of weighted learning objectives. Generalizing, the evaluation model therefore consists of a mapping from the space of units of knowledge and their corresponding learning objectives over a set of evaluations in the evaluation model.

Pedagogical Model. The pedagogical model configures the organization and execution in the teaching-learning process. Bañados [27] describes the elements that surround the learning situation and has components such as: training goals, learner-tutor relationship, educational experiences and contents, and teaching-learning strategies and techniques. Bañados [27] describes the elements of the pedagogical model as follows: (1) The formative goals are determined by the concept of the human being that is intended to be formed, from there are understood the formative purposes that orient the educational process. (2) Definitions of the educational experiences that are necessary to carry out the educational process and fulfill the proposed goals, including disciplinary contents and curricular design. (4) Definitions of methodology: how the teaching process should be carried out, the specific methods and techniques that enable the educational purposes foreseen in each model to be achieved.

The **Adaptive Learning Processes layer** is made up of the processes of knowledge use and interpretation, knowledge storage processes, storage of the state of the learning ecosystem and learning management processes. Each of these processes is supported by elements found in the learning knowledge services layer as described below.

The **Knowledge Services layer** has three elements, the first element is made up of the Software Services represented through the systems that support learning management processes such as learning management systems, learning content management systems, open educational resources, MOOC (Massive Open Online Course) and Social Networks among others. The second element consists of Storage Services that support the management of knowledge storage through ontologies. And the third element is the Learning Analytics Services supported by visualization systems, decision support, recommenders and learning systems. In this layer are the elements that provide adaptability and intelligence to the ecosystem. This layer supports knowledge management activities as a service.

The creation of a particular learning ecosystem is described from the operational aspects of the ecosystem, such as the recording of experiences of communities of practice, and the creation of new ecosystem elements through the processes of acquisition, storage, dissemination and application of knowledge.

- Knowledge acquisition: where ecosystem communities of practice deposit their new knowledge related to the platform, software, infrastructure and storage of learning elements. The ontology initially describes the elements at its disposal and then the user can provide additional elements that will be validated from the decision systems or by consultation to the different instances of ecosystems.
- Storage of knowledge: Storage of new knowledge for ecosystems through the use of tools for the development of ontologies and marking.
- Dissemination of knowledge: Visualization systems are used to help the community of practice create alerts, inform and remember about the entry of new knowledge.
- Knowledge application: Recording of experiences in community of practice repositories for management purposes, such as records and experience reports.

This allows the obtaining of elements that can provide a frame of reference for innovation in education, provided from knowledge management. From the information contained in the repositories and from the analytical learning services can be obtained innovation indicators such as student training, research results, such as articles, business consulting, etc... Any change that results in a novelty for the ecosystem and produces value for it.

5 Learning Ecosystem Ontological Model

The ontological model describes the elements that make up the learning ecosystem and its relationships, allowing the creation of different ecosystems according to the requirements of the learner and under a knowledge architecture as a service provided by the learning knowledge services layer. Some of the questions answered by the ontology are:

- Elements that conform learning ecosystem
- Knowledge Models of the Learning Ecosystem
- Learning ecosystem adaptive processes
- Learning Ecosystem Repositories

- Learning Ecosystem Knowledge Services
- Learning Ecosystem Users

The axioms describe the rules that define the behavior of the learning ecosystem. The rules of model behavior are described in first-order predicate logic. The Table 1 shows some of the axioms of Ontology.

Table 1. Learning ecosystem axioms

Natural language sentence	First order predicate logic
A Learning Ecosystem has a knowledge portal, has knowledge models, and has adaptive processes	$\forall x\ LearningEcosystem(x) \Rightarrow has\ (x, KnowledgePortal) \wedge has\ (x, KnowledgeModel) \wedge has\ (x, AdaptiveProcesses)$
A knowledge model is a domain model, or it is a transition model or it is a user model or it is an evaluation model or it is a pedagogical model	$\forall x\ KnowledgeModel\ (x) \Rightarrow isA\ (x, DomainModel) \vee isA\ (x, TransitionModel) \vee isA\ (x, UserModel) \vee isA\ (x, EvaluationModel) \vee isA\ (x, PedagogicalModel)$
The domain model has a knowledge domain and has knowledge units and has knowledge routes	$\forall x\ DomainModel\ (x) \Rightarrow has\ (x, KnowledgeDomain) \wedge has\ (x, KnowledgeUnits) \wedge has\ (x, KnowledgeRoutes)$
The Transition model has a knowledge state to reach and current knowledge state	$\forall x\ TransitionModel\ (x) \Rightarrow has\ (x, KnowledgeStatetoReach) \wedge has\ (x, CurrentKnowledgeState)$
The user model has a learner user and has a tutor user and has an instructional designer user	$\forall x\ UserModel\ (x) \Rightarrow has\ (x, LearnerUser) \wedge has\ (x, TutorUser) \wedge has\ (x, InstructionalDesignerUser)$
The type of learning can be individual learning or group learning or network learning	$\forall x\ TypeOfLearning\ (x) \Rightarrow isA\ (x, IndividualLearning) \vee isA\ (x, GroupLearning) \vee isA\ (x, NetworkLearning)$
The Evaluation Model has diagnostic evaluation and has formative evaluation and has final evaluation	$\forall x\ EvaluationModel\ (x) \Rightarrow has\ (x, DisgnosticEvaluation) \wedge has\ (x, FormativeEvaluation) \wedge has\ (x, FinalEvaluation)$
The Pedagogical Model has formative goals, and has apprentice-tutor relationship, has educational experiences, has content and has teaching-learning techniques	$\forall x\ PedagogicalModel\ (x) \Rightarrow has\ (x, FormativeGoals) \wedge has\ (x, ApprenticeTutorRelationship) \wedge has\ (x, EducationalExperiences) \wedge has\ (x, Content) \wedge has\ (x, TeachingLearningTecniques)$
The Knowledge Service has Software Service and has Storage Services and has Learning Analytics Services	$\forall x\ KnowledgeServices\ (x) \Rightarrow has\ (x, SoftwareServices) \wedge has\ (x, StorageServices) \wedge has\ (x, LearningAnalyticsServices)$

Concepts: Learning Ecosystem, Knowledge Models, Knowledge Processes, Knowledge Portal, Knowledge Services, Knowledge Systems and Knowledge Repositories, among others.

Relations: parOf, isA, useRepositories, performStorage, hasFormativeGoal, has LearningScenario, hasContent, hasCurricularDesign, hasFormativeExperience, ...

The definition of the elements and their relationships indicate how the ecosystem works and how the relationships between them allow the ecosystem to indicate the business rules for its operation. Following are the concepts and properties object of the

Fig. 2. Learning ecosystem taxonomy

learning ecosystem in OWL Viz Protégé OWL 5.0. Figure 2 shows the is_a and have relations that indicate the elements that make up the learning ecosystem.

The ontological model guides the construction of the learning ecosystem, where each of the components of the ecosystem is described and also the relationships between them. A first way of verifying this model is from Protégé OWL 5.0, in this tool the ontology was created and verified through the reasoner Pellet the syntactic and semantic consistency.

6 Conclusions

In this paper, the ontological model for a learning ecosystem is proposed as an extension of the knowledge management model proposed in Muñoz [21]. From this point of view, the learning ecosystem can provide a reference framework for innovation in education, from knowledge management.

Through the information contained in the repositories and using learning analytics services can be obtained innovation indicators such as student training, research results, such as articles, etc. Any change that results in a novelty for the ecosystem and produces value for the ecosystem. The architecture shown in Fig. 1 describes the components of the learning ecosystem and describes the ecosystem knowledge models, the adaptive processes that can occur in each of the models, and the knowledge services layer that supports each of the adaptive learning processes. In each of these layers there are static components that define the elements that integrate it and the dynamic components that define the behavior of the elements that make them up depending on the processes to be executed. The ontology represents the concepts that make up the static part, and the axioms that represent the dynamic part. These axioms respond to the inference necessary for decision making when creating an ecosystem.

This architecture can be used to define a learning ecosystem from a teaching unit, through a course, a career, or an entire university. This ontological model is the beginning of the development of a platform for the creation of semantic learning ecosystems under a knowledge as a service architecture.

Knowledge management as a service for learning ecosystems is related to several well-established research areas as shown in the architecture of Fig. 1, which include ontologies, e-learning, decision-making systems, adaptive hypermedia, intelligent tutoring systems, web mining, data mining, etc. The application of knowledge management as a service in learning ecosystems has specific requirements that are found in other domains, mainly the need to consider the pedagogical aspects of the learning ecosystem. We believe that some future researches lines are:

- Standardization of methods and data, through technologies such as Linked Data, it should be available for a common format (RDF), to make either conversion or on-the-fly access to existing databases (relational, XML, HTML, etc.).
- Integration using the Ontologies to organize knowledge.
- Inference of the Semantic web, is one of the tools that allows to improve the quality of data integration in the Web, through the discovery of new relationships, the automatic analysis of the content of the data or the knowledge management in the learning ecosystem.

References

1. Llorens, F., Molina, R., Compañ, P., Satorre, R.: Technological ecosystem for open education. Smart Digit. Futures **262**, 706–715 (2014)
2. Sánchez, A., Regla, I., Ponjuán Dante, G.: Diseño de un modelo de gestión de conocimiento para entornos virtuales de aprendizaje en salud. Revista Cubana de Información en Ciencias de la Salud (ACIMED) **27**(2), 138–153 (2016)
3. DE FREITAS, V., Oltra, G.Y.: Una propuesta de arquitectura para los Sistemas Informáticos de Gestión del Conocimiento en Instituciones de Educación Superior. Revista ESPACIOS **36**(10) (2015)
4. Gruber, T.R.: A translation approach to portable ontology specifications. Knowl. Acquisition **5**(2), 199–220 (1993)
5. Albanese, M., Maresca, P., Picariello, A., Rinaldi, A.M.I.: Towards a Multimedia Ontology System: an Approach Using TAO_XML. *DMS*, 52–57 (2005)
6. Uschold, M.A.: Making the case for ontology. **6**(4), 377–385 (2011)
7. Suchanek, F.M., Kasneci, G., Weikum, G.: YAGO: a large ontology from wikipedia and wordnet. Web Semant. Sci. Serv. Agents WWW **6**(3), 203–217 (2008)
8. Pease, A., Niles, I., Li, J.: The suggested upper merged ontology: a large ontology for the semantic web and its applications. In: Working notes of the AAAI-2002, vol. 28, pp. 7–10, Juky 2002
9. Caldarola, E.G., Picariello, A., Castelluccia, D.: Modern enterprises in the bubble: why big data matters. ACM SIGSOFT Softw. Eng. Notes **40**(1), 1–4 (2015)
10. Caldarola, E.G., Sacco, M., Terkaj, W.: Big data: the current wave front of the tsunami. Appl. Comput. Sci. **10**(4) (2014)
11. Abdullah, R., Eri, Z.D., Talib, A.M.: A model of knowledge management system for facilitating knowledge as a service (KaaS) in cloud computing environment. In: International Conference on IEEE, pp. 1–4. IEEE, November 2011
12. Libbrecht, P.: Cross curriculum search through the GeoSkills Ontology. In: Proceedings of SEAM, vol. 8, pp. 38–50 (2008)
13. Pease, A.N.: The suggested upper merged ontology: a large ontology for the semantic web and its applications. In: Working Notes of the AAAI-2002 Workshop on Ontologies and the Semantic Web, vol. 28, pp. 7–10 (2002)
14. Fok, A.W.P., Ip, H.H.S.: Educational ontologies construction for personalized learning on the web. In: Jain, L.C., Tedman, R.A., Tedman, D.K. (eds.) Evolution of Teaching and Learning Paradigms in Intelligent Environment, vol. 62, pp. 47–82. Springer, Heidelberg (2007). https://doi.org/10.1007/978-3-540-71974-8_4
15. Mizoguchi, R.: Tutorial on ontological engineering Part 2: ontology development, tools and languages. New Gener. Comput. **22**(1), 61–96 (2004)
16. Mizoguchi, R., Bourdeau, J.: Using ontological engineering to overcome ai-ed problems: contribution, impact and perspectives. Int. J. Artif. Intell. Educ. **26**(1), 91–106 (2016)
17. Pease, A., Niles, I., Li, J.: The suggested upper merged ontology: a large ontology for the semantic web and its applications. In: Working Notes of the AAAI-2002 Workshop on Ontologies and the Semantic Web, vol. 28, pp. 7–10 (2002)
18. Nilsson, M., Palmér, M., Brase, J.: The LOM RDF binding: principles and implementation. In: Third Annual ARIADNE Conference, Leuven Belgium (2003)
19. Majd, S., Marie-Hélène, A.: System of information systems as support for learning ecosystem. In: International Symposium on Emerging Technologies for Education, pp. 29–37, September 2017

20. Khaled, A., Ouchani, S., Chohra, C.: Recommendations-based on semantic analysis of social networks in learning environments. Comput. Hum. Behav. (2018)
21. Muñoz, A., Lopez, V., Lagos, K., Vásquez, M., Hidalgo, J., Vera, N.: Knowledge management for virtual education through ontologies. In: Ciuciu, I., et al. (eds.) OTM 2015. LNCS, vol. 9416, pp. 339–348. Springer, Cham (2015). https://doi.org/10.1007/978-3-319-26138-6_37
22. Hung, N.M.: Using ideas from connectivism for designing new learning models in Vietnam. Int. J. Inf. Educ. Technol. 4(1), 76 (2014)
23. Chi, Y.: Developing curriculum sequencing for managing multiple texts in e-learning system. In: Proceedings of International Conference on Engineering Education, pp. 1–8 (2010)
24. Aubin, G.P.C., Crevier, F.: MISA, a knowledge-based method for the engineering of learning systems. J. Courseware Eng. 2, 63–78 (1999)
25. Paquette, G., De La Teja, I., Léonard, M., Lundgren-Cayrol, K., Marino, O.: An instructional engineering method and tool for the design of units of learning. Learn. Des., 161–184 (2005)
26. Fernández-López, M., Gómez-Pérez, A., Juristo, N.: Methontology: from ontological art towards ontological engineering. Am. Asociation Artif. Intell. (1997)
27. Bañados, E.: A blended-learning pedagogical model for teaching and learning EFL successfully through an online interactive multimedia environment. CALICO J. 23(3), 533–550 (2013)

Modeling a Knowledge-Based System for Cyber-physical Systems: Applications in the Context of Learning Analytics

Mamadou Lamine Gueye[✉]

LIUPPA, University of Pau and Pays de l'Adour, Pau, France
mamadou.gueye@etud.univ-pau.fr

Abstract. Knowledge-based systems are major concerns in the field of artificial intelligence for the development of cyber-physical systems capable of self-management and adaptation to their context. The representation and knowledge management of these cyber-physical systems integrating heterogeneous actors must ensure the empowerment and optimization of these systems, as well as their ability to adapt to dynamic and unpredictable changes in their environment. In this document we show how a knowledge-based system based on semantic web technologies and IBM's reference model of Autonomic Computing (AC) can offer intelligent collaboration and coordination between people, data, services, robots and connected objects in the implementation of self-management processes in cyber-physical systems. Our solution consists to design a knowledge base in the field of Learning Analytics (LAs) involving a complex range of knowledge and heterogeneous components. This ontological knowledge base is guided by a functional decomposition approach based on the operating principle of the MAPE-K (Monitor-Analyze-Plan-Execute and Knowledge) autonomous control loop to provide the system with self-management capabilities.

Keywords: Knowledge base · Ontology · Autonomic computing · Learning Analytics

1 Introduction

With the fourth industrial revolution, universities underwent pedagogical transformations (University 4.0) induced by the integration of cyber-physical systems (connected objects, robots etc.) into teaching to improve and optimize the learning environment [5]. Thus, educational institutions are seeking to develop self-managing systems to automate mechanisms for understanding, improving and optimizing learning based on knowledge about learning tracking, traces collected through the use of online tools and services [4, 26]. The representation and knowledge management of these systems integrating both connected objects, data, services, robots, people, etc. must ensure the empowerment and optimization of these systems, as well as their ability to adapt to dynamic and unpredictable changes in their environment.

However, syntax-based methods of representing traditional knowledge offer few opportunities to address the semantic management obstacles that allow the orchestration

© Springer Nature Switzerland AG 2019
N. T. Nguyen et al. (Eds.): ICCCI 2019, LNAI 11684, pp. 568–580, 2019.
https://doi.org/10.1007/978-3-030-28374-2_49

of multiple actors in autonomous systems within the framework of University 4.0. There are also knowledge representation systems that provide empowerment, verification, optimization and adaptation services but are poorly adapted to a functional decomposition approach that allows the levels of maturation of cyber-physical systems to be taken into account (manual, observable, adaptive, self-adaptive, autonomous).

In this article paper, we propose a modeling of a common, scalable, dynamic and adaptive semantic space allowing the generic representation of physical or virtual objects, events, relationships, symptoms, diagnoses and change or action plans for the definition and execution of self-management processes, based on the IBM reference model of the MAPE-K (Monitoring, Analysis, Planning, Execution and Knowledge) control loop for autonomic computing [12].

This document is structured as follows: Sect. 2 provides a state of the art overview of knowledge-based systems and Learning Analytics, which is our case study. The two approaches we have explored for modeling our proposed solution are presented in Sect. 3. Before concluding, in Sect. 4 we will present our case study and the proposed overall solution architecture to show a better appreciation of the contributions of ontologies and Autonomic Computing in industry 4.0, more specifically in the context of University 4.0.

2 State of the Art

In this section, we present a review of the literature on the Knowledge-based systems and Learning Analytics.

2.1 Knowledge-Based Systems

According to Grimm et al. [1], the representation of knowledge and reasoning is a symbolic branch of artificial intelligence that aims to design computer systems that reason around a representation of the world that can be interpreted by the machine, similar to human reasoning. Knowledge-Based Systems (KBS) have a computer model of the real-world domain of interest in which physical or virtual objects, events, relationships, etc. are represented by symbols. KBS reason on this knowledge and use different inputs to help agents (physical or virtual) solve complex problems or make good decisions [24].

In the field of KBS, several works [2, 4–6] have been done in the conceptualization of data, information, knowledge, and intelligence in different forms using different approaches. According to [1] the most widespread knowledge capture and representation formalities are based on:

- semantic networks that can be found in RDF graphs;
- rules in the form of "if-then", for example in business rules or logical programming formalities;
- logic to achieve a precise semantic interpretation of semantic networks and rules.

Several researches have been conducted and many applications developed in the field of KBS [3], as in other areas of IT. In these systems, real-world facts are represented by simple assertions stored in a knowledge base and then manipulated using certain rules defined according to the objective of the system. We will present some research work carried out as part of the design of a knowledge base and reasoning on this knowledge:

Kitchen [2] presents the AM (Lenat) and Teiresias (Davis) projects in the field of expert systems of artificial intelligence. In these projects, the authors have developed knowledge-based systems capable of imitating the process of human intelligence functioning. The first, AM, applied to elementary mathematics, models an aspect of scientific research concerning the creation of new concepts and conjectures about their behaviour. It is based on the definitions of certain theoretical concepts and a large number of general heuristics to decide on useful research axes and generate examples that form the basis for conjectures. The second Teiresias project is a tool that allows an expert to build and maintain a knowledge base in his field of activity. Based on the rules provided by an expert in the field, the system generates models that it uses to organize and control the use of the rules by giving the ability to provide a high-level report on the motivations for its actions. For example, for a programmer when a bug is discovered in the knowledge base, Teiresias is able to explain how it came to the knowledge base and even suggests plausible corrections.

According to Soualah Alila et al. [4], there are constraints of semantic heterogeneity of resources and heterogeneity of use of learning platforms that do not allow learning content to be adapted to the learner's contextual situation. To help solve this problem, the authors developed an m-learning system based on the learner's contextual constraints to recommend training paths without risk of disruption. The system architecture is based on a formal representation of data and business processes in an ontological knowledge base, as well as the use of metaheuristic algorithms to infer knowledge. According to the authors, them m-learning system offers trainers the possibility to model their know-how taking into account environmental and user constraints.

According to Sanin et al. [5], cyber-physical systems and the Internet of Things can lead to the development of increasingly competent and intelligent systems in industry and academia, based on an interesting and attractive scenario. The authors propose Decision DNA, a knowledge-based system that integrates a complete representation of knowledge for the Internet of Things and cyber-physical systems. Decisional DNA collects explicit knowledge based on the experience of formal decision-making events and uses it to assist in the decision-making process. According to the authors, one of the main advantages of its use is to provide predictive capabilities based on knowledge and experience.

Salayandia et al. [6] propose a system of recommendations and advice for researchers, based on Semantic Web technologies, called MetaShare. It represents the researchers' experience, data collection, and management activities in a form that can be exploited by a machine by connecting the associated data. MetaShare is a decision-making support system for researchers on project planning and implementation based on similar project practices and decisions. Its formal representation of knowledge in the form of ontologies and rules allows for the collection, dissemination, and management of data to facilitate tasks related to the use and exchange of scientific data.

According to Marvis [7], current Semantic Web technologies offer the possibility of representing knowledge explicitly, through tools such as ontologies and rules applied to facts rather than implicitly through procedural programming methods. There is a common, evolving, dynamic and adaptive semantic representation of a problem that allows generic modeling of physical or virtual objects, events, relationships, symptoms, diagnoses and change or action plans for the definition and execution of self-management processes. Based on the above work, [4] and [5] can be used as a support for our approach to design the knowledge base of our system.

2.2   Learning Analytics

Through our case study, we will model a knowledge base in the field of Learning Analytics (LAs). LAs are defined at the first international conference on Learning Analytics and Knowledge (LAK) in 2011 as *"measurement, collection, analysis, and communication of data on learners and their contexts, with the aim of understanding and optimizing learning and the environments in which it occurs"*.

Chatti et al. [19] presented a systematic overview of LAs and its key concepts using a reference model based on four dimensions, namely: (1) data, environments and context (what?), (2) stakeholders (who?), (3) objectives (why?) and (4) methods (how?). We will use this reference model as a basis for presenting different research studies in the field of LAs in relation to each dimension.

Arnold et al. [20] have developed an early intervention solution for college faculty called Course Signals at Purdue University in Indiana. In short, Course Signals uses data from the information system, the course management system and the notebook. This data is then manipulated, transformed into compatible forms and entered into an algorithm generating a level of risk with additional information for each student, represented by a green, yellow or red indicator.

The Signals system is intended to help students understand their progress early enough to allow them to seek help and probably get good grades or change their behaviour. The authors propose to use business intelligence to improve student success at the course level, thereby increasing retention and graduation rates. The Signals prediction algorithm is based on the student's performance, effort, academic background, and characteristics.

Agnihotri et al. [21] propose a model for early intervention with students most at risk of attrition, called the Student At-Risk Model (STAR), applied at the New York Institute of Technology (NYIT). The main risk factors include the student's grades, main subject, and certainty of choice of the main subject, as well as financial data such as the cost of tuition fees in relation to the student's means. STAR allows student support staff to screen and intervene early to improve student retention at university using a dashboard. It provides a binary indicator (risk of attrition or not) for each student and identifies the key factors that make a student unlikely to return the following year. STAR in version 2.0 is built from a dataset contained in a data warehouse where they can be created automatically as soon as a new student registers, then the data mining tools are used to form machine learning models to perform the classification task. These models use variables to predict whether or not a student will return the following year, which is then used to signal the risk of new students.

Sclater et al. [22] have developed a sustainable and flexible LAs service for British universities and colleges, called Jisc's learning analytics. The system collects all kinds of data on student activity in various systems such as LMS such as Moodle, library systems, student record systems or other self-reported data through our student application. The objective of the tool is to provide an alert and intervention system to predict student success.

This solution consists of a mix of commercial and open source solutions consisting of collecting and storing data in Learning Records Warehouses (LRW), analyzing these learning traces with the open platform "Apereo Learning Analytics Initiative" in order to present a dashboard for staff and to alert staff and students and allow them to manage the intervention activity through an alert and intervention system.

Admittedly, the list of LAs applications is not exhaustive, but it can be seen that most solutions consist of collecting, manipulating, transforming data in order to make them compatible before analyzing them using predictive algorithms. We note that the architecture of the proposed solutions for LAs is based on a combination of several technical solutions for data encoding, data mining and storage, and data analysis and processing. This presents many obstacles regarding the syntax and semantics required when integrating multiple data sources and also makes the deployment of LAs complex.

3   Proposal of Our Model

We propose a representation of a knowledge base based on an initial ontology-based approach to provide a common, scalable, dynamic, maintainable and adaptive semantic space that provides decision making adapted to the objectives of the system. The second approach to our modeling is based on the Autonomic Computing operating principle (MAPE-K) which consists of breaking down our knowledge base into autonomous components to provide a self-management process adapted to cyber-physical systems. These two approaches to our knowledge base will be detailed in the following sections.

3.1   Ontology Modeling-Based Approach

Our ontology oriented approach [8] has as its main objective to define conceptual equivalences, which are then used to automatically calculate (reason) relationships between classes, properties, and instances.

Ontologies also allow any concept to be represented in a unique way, and adhere to the open world assumption: everything is permitted until it is prohibited. They provide a model of a body of knowledge in a given field, which can be real or imaginary in order to ensure knowledge management and reasoning on this knowledge, with a view to semantic interoperability between human and/or artificial agents [9]. Ontologies can provide cyber-physical systems with the ability to process and understand data, access a set of structured information and inference rules that they can use to achieve autonomous behaviour.

3.2   MAPE-K Oriented Design Approach

For modeling of our KB to ensure self-management capabilities with a functional decomposition approach, we use the IBM reference model [10] to define autonomous managers, modules that provide autonomous behaviour to system components. It also allows us to better structure knowledge about the measures, symptoms, strategies, objectives, plans or requests for change, etc. in our knowledge base. This model is based, as suggested by Horn [11], on a control loop called the autonomous control loop or MAPE-K loop, presented in the figure below (Fig. 1):

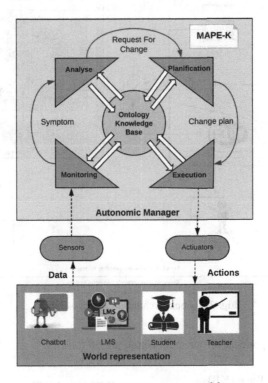

Fig. 1. MAPE-K autonomous control loop

4   Case Study

To illustrate the representation of knowledge guided by an ontologically oriented approach in cyber-physical systems, based on the principle of CA [12], we work on scenarios drawn from Learning Analytics [14]. According to the 2012 report of the US Department of Education [15], with the emergence of LAs, *"e-learning systems have the capacity to capture learners' behaviour to provide feedback to a variety of actors to improve teaching, learning and educational decision-making"*. In these scenarios, we will implement knowledge modeling of learning tracking information, traces collected when using online tools and services. This formalization of knowledge in a form that can be interpreted by humans and machines will be used to automate and empower the understanding, improvement, and optimization of learning.

Such a use case is relevant for illustrating the modeling of a KB for cyber-physical systems, as learning systems consist of a variety of interacting physical and/or virtual components (LMS, student, robots, teacher, etc.) and overflowing with a mass of information from different sources (Fig. 2).

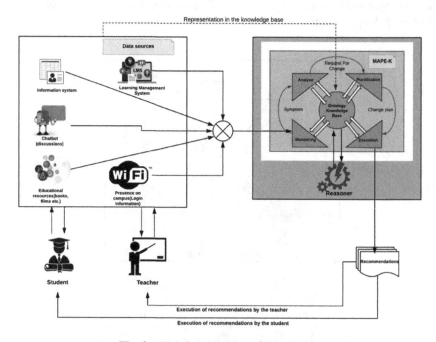

Fig. 2. Global architecture of the solution

The main components of our architecture are as follows:

4.1 Knowledge Base (KB)

The knowledge base is the central core element of the MAPE-K loop, it contains all the knowledge relevant to the management of the system. The knowledge represented in our knowledge base concerns the learning management system (LMS), students, teachers, information system, pedagogical resources (books, films, computers, etc.) and chatbot, as well as the concepts, ensuring the functionalities of the MAPE-K autonomous control loop modules providing the system with autonomous behaviour.

We propose a knowledge base with an ontology oriented approach to ensure the heterogeneity constraints of data from different physical and/or virtual components (LMS, student, robots, teacher, etc.) of a learning environment.

This formal representation of knowledge offers us the opportunity to better manage the automation and empowerment of educational decision-making processes for the understanding, improvement, and optimization of learning. We used Protege [23] as an ontology editor to create the ontology of our case study and reason on knowledge using integrated inference engines.

4.2 Reasoner

The reasoner is the trigger for the automatic and autonomous execution of our MAPE-K loop. This inference engine is an important component of the KB, without this software, it would be impossible to reason about knowledge. It applies logical rules of correspondence, selection, and execution [16, 17] to data captured by agents of the learning system and knowledge stored in the knowledge base in order to generate symptoms leading to diagnoses in order to make recommendations to the learner and/or teacher (Figs. 3 and 4).

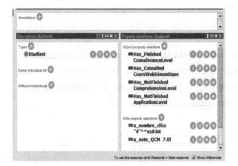 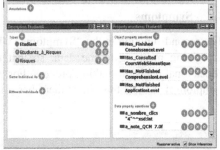

Fig. 3. Representation of a student's traces on the learning environment

Fig. 4. Classification of the student by the reasoner as being at risk

To ensure the different functions of the system, we defined each function by a set of rules [16, 17] applied to the data captured by the agents of the learning system and the knowledge stored in the knowledge base in order to make recommendations to the learner and/or the teacher.

4.3 Monitoring

The basic function of our system is "Monitoring" which recovers the data captured by the different components of the learning system, presented in the form of facts, figures, etc.; for example (Fig. 5):

- *The learner consulted the course on the Semantic Web for 10 min*
- *The learner had a score of 7/20 on the Semantic Web exam.*

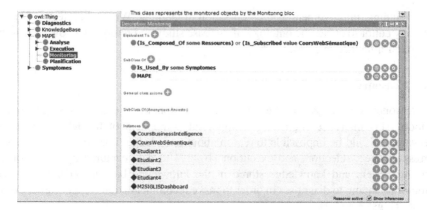

Fig. 5. Monitored components of the system

4.4 Symptoms

The second function is the "Symptoms" which consists in determining the symptoms, i.e. giving meaning to the data, so that they become relevant information for our educational decision-making process. For example, it may generate a "student at risk" symptom if it finds that the student has a score below 7/10 (Fig. 6).

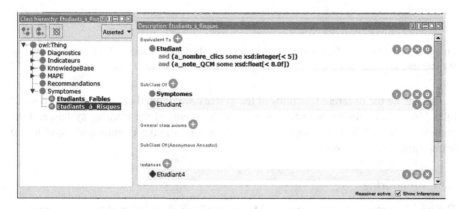

Fig. 6. Symptom of an at-risk student

4.5 Analysis

Analysis, the third function is the subjective interpretation of information in order to determine the causes and the way to act in the process of achieving the objectives of Learning Analytics (Fig. 7).

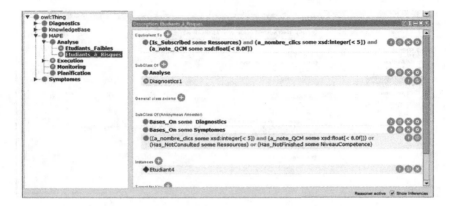

Fig. 7. System analysis results

4.6 Diagnostics

The fourth function is the "Diagnostics", it is based on the symptoms, the results of the "Analysis" function, as well as the knowledge and rules defined in the system leading to the establishment of the diagnosis in a particular way to associate an objective with its diagnosis. This is what generates recommendations (educational decisions) for "Planning" to improve learning. For example, the diagnosis shows that the student has not completed all levels of knowledge acquisition (Fig. 8).

Fig. 8. System diagnostic results

4.7 Planning

The fifth function is "Planification", based on each diagnosis and the reasoning behind each diagnosis, it provides the "Execution" function with a sequential list of possible action plans leading to the implementation of recommendations (Fig. 9).

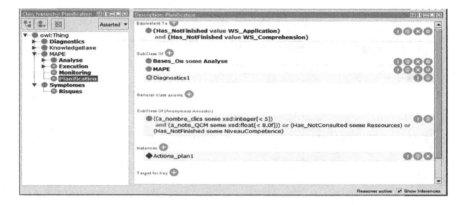

Fig. 9. System planification results

4.8 Execution

Finally, execution generates actions in the form of recommendations to the learner or teacher to improve learning. The latter will be responsible for carrying out these actions in order to implement the necessary changes (Fig. 10).

Fig. 10. System execution results

5 Conclusion

In this work, we proposed modeling of an ontology-based knowledge base with a functional decomposition approach, as well as self-management capabilities provided by the CA. In this article, let us implement the continuous improvement of automated decision making and the resolution of problems related to the self-management constraints of cyber-physical systems.

This scalable, dynamic and adaptive system allows the generic representation of physical objects, events, relationships, symptoms, diagnoses and action plans for the definition and execution of self-management processes. It can be further improved to provide better diagnostics for a variety of purposes and results to make its applications more intelligent and efficient.

So, we note that in the LAs, two methods are preferred (xAPI and Caliper) [18] for encoding information on learning follow-up, traces collected when using online tools and services in the form of RDF triplets with the form "subject-predicate-object" + context. The statements are then stored in a Learning Record Store (LRS). We find that ontologies are native with an encoding of information in the form of RDF triplets with the form "subject-predict-object" + context, they also offer a controlled syntax and semantics to ensure interoperability. The knowledge base can be used in data mining and data warehousing.

In terms of perspectives, we intend to improve the work by working on in-depth documentation of the systematic diversification of scenarios and hypotheses in the knowledge base to arrive at a solution that makes it possible to assess the real contributions of a combination of ontologies and knowledge-based systems in LAs.

References

1. Grimm, S., Abecker, A.: Knowledge representation and ontologies logic, ontologies and semantic web languages (2007)
2. Kitchen, A.: Knowledge based systems in artificial intelligence. Proc. IEEE **73**(1), 171–172 (1985)
3. Akerkar, R., Sajja, P.: Knowledge-Based Systems. Jones & Bartlett Publishers, Burlington (2010)
4. Soualah-Alila, F., Nicolle, C., Mendes, F.: Archive ouverte HAL - context-aware adaptive system For M- learning personalization (2015). https://hal.archives-ouvertes.fr/hal-01238330. Accessed 24 May 2019
5. Sanin, C., Haoxi, Z., Shafiq, I., et al.: Experience based knowledge representation for internet of things and cyber physical systems with case studies. Future Gener. Comput. Syst. **92**, 604–616 (2019)
6. Salayandia, L., Pennington, D., Gates, A.Q., et al.: MetaShare: from data management plans to knowledge-based systems. In: 2013 AAAI Fall Symposium Series (2013)
7. Marvis, U., Shade, K., Atisi, F., Olayiwola, B.: Overview of knowledge-based system. Int. J. Comput. Commun. Eng. Res. **2**(3), 125–129 (2014)
8. Wikipedia: Ontologie (informatique) (2019). https://fr.wikipedia.org/w/index.php?title=Ontologie_(informatique)&oldid=156460030. Accessed 15 Mar 2019
9. Fürst, F., Trichet, F.: Raisonner sur des ontologies lourdes à l'aide de Graphes Conceptuels, p. 17 (2006)
10. Kephart, J.O., Chess, D.M.: The vision of autonomic computing. Computer **36**(1), 41–50 (2003)
11. Horn, P.: Autonomic computing : IBM's perspective on the state of information technology. Technical report. IBM (2001)
12. Aaron Computing: An architectural blueprint for autonomic computing. Technical report. IBM (2006)
13. Makhfi, P.: Introduction to knowledge modeling. http://www.makhfi.com/KCM_intro.htm. Accessed 27 Mar 2019

14. Numérique, France Université: Learning Analytics, une tendance émergente dans l'éducation - sup-numerique.gouv.fr (2017). http://www.sup-numerique.gouv.fr/cid113065/learning-analytics-une-tendance-emergente-dans-l-education.html. Accessed 14 Mar 2019
15. U.S. Department of Education: Enhancing learning and training through educational data mining and Learning Analytics (2012). https://tech.ed.gov/wp-content/uploads/2014/03/edm-la-brief.pdf. Accessed 14 Mar 2019
16. Gong, Y., Janssen, M.: An interoperable architecture and principles for implementing strategy and policy in operational processes. Comput. Ind. **64**(8), 912–924 (2013)
17. Umar, M.M., Mehmood, A., Song, H.: A survey on state-of-the-art knowledge-based system development and issues (2015). https://www.researchgate.net/publication/290481752_A_Survey_on_State-of-the-Art_Knowledge-based_System_Development_and_Issues. Accessed 1 Apr 2019
18. WIKIPEDIA: Analyse de l'apprentissage (2018). https://fr.wikipedia.org/w/index.php?title=Analyse_de_l%E2%80%99apprentissage&oldid=153731273. Accessed 2 Apr 2019
19. Chatti, M.A., Dyckhoff, A.L., Schroeder, U., Thüs, H.: A reference model for learning analytics. Int. J. Technol. Enhanc. Learn. **4**(5/6), 318–331 (2012)
20. Arnold, K.E., Pistilli, M.D.: Course signals at purdue: using learning analytics to increase student success. In Proceedings of the 2nd International Conference on Learning Analytics and Knowledge (LAK 2012), pp. 267–270 (2012)
21. Agnihotri, L., Ott, A.: Building a student at-risk model: an end-to-end perspective. In: Proceedings of the Intenational Conference on Educational Data Mining Conference (EDM), pp. 209–212 (2014)
22. Sclater, N., Peasgood, A., Mullan, J.: Learning analytics in higher education. A review of UK and international practice full report (2016)
23. Musen, M.A.: The Protégé project: a look back and a look forward. AI Matters. **1**(4), 4 (2015). https://doi.org/10.1145/2557001.25757003. Association of Computing Machinery Specific Interest Group in Artificial Intelligence
24. Zaraté, P., Liu, S.: A new trend for knowledge-based decision support systems design. Int. J. Inform. Decis. Sci. **8**(3), 305–324 (2016)
25. Duron, T., Gallon, L., Aniorte, P.: Modelling learner's perseverance in education software. In: Information Systems Education Conference (ISECON 2019), 4–6 Apr 2019, Galveston, TX, USA (2019)

Internet of Everything and Educational Cyber Physical Systems for University 4.0

Samia Bachir[✉] and Angel Abenia[✉]

University of Pau and Pays Adour, Pau, France
{samia.bachir,angel.abenia}@univ-pau.fr

Abstract. The Internet of Things (IoT) is overwhelming education due to the expansion of smart connected devices. This offers an open gate for knowledge access and ubiquitous learning. However, many challenges remain with regard to educational system policies, at university in particular. A consistent and harmonious platform, that could bring together the different aspects of learning/teaching with the smartness of things, to offer a better learning/educational experience, has not yet been reached. The aim of this paper is to illustrate the different components of the Internet of Everything (IoE) educational ecosystem that should be taken into consideration before generating the learning/teaching processes. We propose the concept of Educational Cyber Physical System as a key element for monitoring the educational environment. We also give some examples illustrating the implementation of such processes.

Keywords: Internet of Everything · Educational ecosystem ·
Educational Cyber Physical System · University 4.0

1 Introduction

The evolution of information technology has revolutionised the way people and objects behave in everyday lives. This is due to the emergence of Internet of Things (IoT) and to the Internet of Everything (IoE), especially in the last decade. This fourth wave, as described in [1], was preceded by three others. The first was categorized by the arrival of computers in the late 1960s where one computer was allocated to several people. Then, a second wave raised after a decade to refer one personal computer to one person. After the appearance of embedded and ubiquitous computing, a third wave occurred to designate many computers to one person.

Different revolutions have taken place in other fields to raise a fourth generation thanks to the Internet of Everything. Industry 4.0 is one of the concerned fields where different research works have started to bring standardisation efforts to create mature contributions in the field. Key elements of Industry 4.0, such as Cyber Physical Systems (CPS), coupled with the Autonomic Computing (AC) principles have lead us to rethink the educational ecosystem of education and thus proposing a fourth generation of University, correspondingly.

© Springer Nature Switzerland AG 2019
N. T. Nguyen et al. (Eds.): ICCCI 2019, LNAI 11684, pp. 581–591, 2019.
https://doi.org/10.1007/978-3-030-28374-2_50

In this paper, we address the following research question: *How could a teaching/learning context affect the different interactions between and within the different components of the Internet of Everything educational ecosystem that are managed by the bias of Educational Cyber Physical Systems?*. In order to answer this inquiry, we refine the educational ecosystem based on the Internet of Everything paradigm and define its main components, as well as its implementations according to different levels of use throughout the whole educational journey. The remainder of this paper is organized as follow: Sect. 2 presents the related works covering different elements. Section 3 focuses on a refined educational ecosystem based on the Internet of Everything. A definition of Educational Cyber Physical System is then proposed in Sect. 4. In order to illustrate this concept, proposed scenarios are also explored. Conclusion and future works will resume the paper.

2   Related Works

University 4.0 has started to gain attention from the educational community. It is still in its infancy and at an earlier stage as an explored research field. For the time being, there are barely any research papers which could be cited or relied on. For this purpose, we build upon ideas from Autonomic Computing (AC) perspective and Industry 4.0 principles to propose a reference framework for the fourth revolution of such educational environment.

AC is considered as a holistic vision of self-managing capabilities in a system [13]. The latters cover different aspects of self-management that implement control loops (monitor, analyse, plan and execute) which collect details from the system and act accordingly, as stated in [6]. Control loops are executed by autonomic managers to bring forward significant information to another level of treatment ensured by orchestrating autonomic managers which execute control loops in order to make decisions in a top level of management and orchestrate the different autonomic managers.

Industry 4.0 was first raised among the German industrial community in 2011. It is a complex initiative that embraces several overlapping areas [10]. It was defined by Herman et al. [9] as the integration of complex physical machinery and devices with networked sensors and software, used to predict, control and plan for better business and societal outcomes. In such manufacturing environment, smart machines, installations, workpieces and other components exchange data and information in real time which represents a shift from rigid, centralised factory control systems to decentralised intelligence. This revolution is founded on a set of technologies which together promote the fourth revolution, happening currently in our world. Internet of things, Cyber Physical Systems, Cloud Computing, etc. are the basis of Industry 4.0.

On the other hand, IoT has effected the education business model. Several value propositions [2] are empowering, directly or not, students' achievement. One of these value propositions concerns the real-time personalization of learning experiences. This could engage more students [2]. A recent review was published in [16] about exploring IoT in education. Interesting efforts have been conducted to improve the educational ecosystem based on the Internet of Things.

We classify them according to the way IoT are used. We opt for the following classification to show precisely the contributions of IoT to improving learning and teaching processes.

- Learning/Teaching **of** Internet of Things: This classification concerns the teaching and leaning of Internet of Things as a learning subject. The aim is to teach/learn the different core knowledge of the subject. [3,5,15,17] are examples of such research works. Education 4.0 could be classified in this type of IoT exploitation. It focuses on teaching/learning IoT to prepare future professionals who will have the required competences and skills of the subject and then will be able to work on an IoT equipped environment like Industry 4.0.
- Learning/Teaching **by** Internet of Things: This classification concerns the use of Internet of Things as an artifact to acquire other knowledge. [12,20] are examples of research works which focused on such aspect. Experiment based Learning is one of the conducted pedagogies that could be viewed as a way to serve knowledge through the bias of smart objects manipulation.
- Learning/Teaching **based on** Internet of Things: This classification is not really explored in improving teaching and learning processes. However, it is addressed in some research works to monitor students' healthcare or in classroom access control, like in [14,19].
- Another category could be drawn according to further uses of IoT in the educational context, which are not directly linked to learning and teaching. These applications focus on energy management, enhancing safety, reducing cost, improving comfort, etc. [2].

According to this classification, we consider research efforts are not explored enough to directly improve educational processes based on IoE. However, they are in an advanced level for the other categories. We thus adopt the positioning of our work on the third categorisation of IoE application (Learning/teaching **based on** IoT). This does not exclude the possibility of a further association between the other purposes of IoE applications. Our aim is to improve learning and teaching occuring in a connected environment. The collected data from different learning resources or others are monitored, collected and then analysed for a decision-making process to better manage the educational process.

3   Internet of Everything Ecosystem in Education

Many definitions have been proposed for Internet of Things within the existant literature. A review about different propositions is provided in [16]. As it was considered, in [12], as an ecosystem that is able to scale and exploit the existing infrastructure of embedded and connected devices, this definition fits well with the expansion that then has occurred with the Internet of Everything (IoE). Silva and Braga [7] argue that IoE is the next evolutionary step of Internet of Things where not only *embedded devices* are making up the network but also *people*, *processes* and *data* have to be taken into account. Few works have been explored in the scientific area of this new paradigm [7].

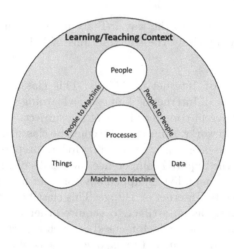

Fig. 1. Main components of the Educational Internet of Everything Ecosystem (revised from [7])

As depicted in Fig. 1, in the educational ecosystem:

– *"People"* refers to the students, teachers, administrators or other stakeholders who are involved in the learning/teaching processes.
– *"Objects"* refers not only to physical devices that can establish connection with the Internet and utilize sensors to capture environment information (as it is presented in [7]), actuators to act on the environment, but also to smart learning resources that can establish connection with the internet for a, directed or in-directed, knowledge access (e.g computer, telepresence-robot).
– *"Processes"* refers to how people and objects must interact to generate data that can be transformed into usable knowledge. These processes allow information to be addressed to the right people, at the right time and properly [7]. Examples will be provided later in the next section.
– *"Data"* refers to all the different data flows coming from historical information about people, objects, processes and the interactions between the different elements. Cloud computing and learning analytics are examples of technologies for data management.
– **Learning/teaching context**: We propose to add the concept of learning/teaching context to illustrate a key element of the educational ecosystem. We believe that the general context, where the learning and teaching occur, affects all the different types of interactions between and within the elements listed above. In the literature [18], the context was almost relied basically on the knowledge-to-be-taught and the psychology of learners. However, it is not the case with the arrival of the Internet of Everything and the different designs of physical and virtual spaces. Little details about the context would alter all the predefined processes. We will see later how these elements of context (e.g. Physical space (Auditorium, classroom, e-education), the number and nature

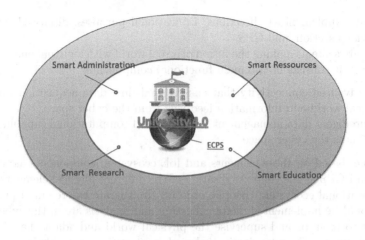

Fig. 2. University 4.0

of objects, number of people (present, tele-present), long/medium/short term learning/teaching planning, etc.) are important for Educational Cyber Physical System in generating the required learning/teaching processes.

Putting the different elements of the ecosystem together offers a rich educational experience. At the same time, various nested challenges could be encountered. The interoperability of different computer systems, the establishment of an accurate collaboration scheme between such systems, environments with intelligent software agents to better support the teaching learning process are among the challenges listed in [7]. In the following section, we will explore how such parameters from the learning/teaching context element could affect the scenarisations as well as the interactions between the different elements (people to people, machine to machine, people to machine).

4   Educational Cyber Physical System for University 4.0 - Proposed Scenarios

As shown in Fig. 2, there are various aspects within the university as an institutional entity: educational, administrative, research, etc. In our research, we focus on educational aspects and more precisely on improving directly learning and teaching based on a connected environment with everything (people, data, processes, objects, learning/teaching context). However, we present a key concept that could be defined in different levels of use. It is Educational Cyber Physical System (ECPS). To the best of our knowledge, very few studies have focused on the establishment of a definition of ECPS where teaching and learning could occur in both virtual and physical spaces. An attempt was presented in [4] in which explicit representation of the different structural components and their correspondent relations or behaviors were not given. Actually, ECPS stands from two complementary directions: Educational purposes, discussed above in the previous section, and CPS.

CPS are systems making the fusion of a real world with a virtual one. According to [11], it consists of two main functional components:

- The advanced connectivity that ensures real-time data acquisition from the physical world and information feedback from the cyber space.
- An intelligent data management, analytics and computational capability that constructs the cyber space.

Hence, based on these elements and IoE ecosystem components as well, we define an ECPS as the contextualisation of the different physical elements of the IoE educational ecosystem (people, objects) to generate the required processes that should be implemented. Data collection and analysis are in the cyber level in order to monitor and supervise the physical world and adapt the processes when it is needed. This monitoring is based on executing control loops (monitor, analyse, plan and execute), induced from the Autonomic Computing perspective.

We consider that the different parameters of the learning/teaching context affect the processes configuration, and so the interactions between and within the different educational elements. We believe that there are three main types of processes which refer to the learning outcomes throughout the whole learning journey (knowledge, competence, expertise [8]):

- **Classroom processes**: refer to a combination of a set of activities occurring in a physical/virtual classroom. The learning outcomes of such process are knowledge. As presented in [8], knowledge management must address its acquisition, creation, storage, redistribution and application. Learners and teachers are the main actors of this management which highly depends to the choice of pedagogy.
- **Course processes**: cover the strategy of learning/teaching which highly depends on the knowledge-to-be-taught. Competences are the learning outcomes of this kind of process. They imply the ability to demonstrate a consistent level of performances.
- **Curriculum processes**: cover the strategy of learning/teaching which highly depends on the learners background/performances/needs. This will lead to expertise acquisition which comprises related value judgements, knowledge and skill sets, lived experiences, and problem solving abilities.

For instance, the definition of temporal parameters (short/medium/long term) and the educational staff roles (teacher/course manager/studies director) allows us to determine the process type we are dealing with (classroom/course/curriculum), respectively. A context parameter can intervene in one or more types of processes. Table 1 shows some examples of context parameters and their interventions in different types of processes. The latters are provided in the following subsections.

The followings are examples of sub-processes (a part of complete processes respectively) we propose, that can be generated by different ECPS according to some context parameters that may be required at a given time.

Table 1. The intervention of context parameters in different types of processes

	Classroom process	Course process	Curriculum process
Process administrator	Teacher	Course manager	Studies director
Process duration	Short (hours)	Medium (weeks)	Long (semester/year)
Learner's prerequisites	-	-	X
Pedagogy	X	X	-
Knowledge-to-be-taught	-	X	-
Course typologic structure	X	X	-
(Tele-)Presence	X	-	-
Things	X	-	-

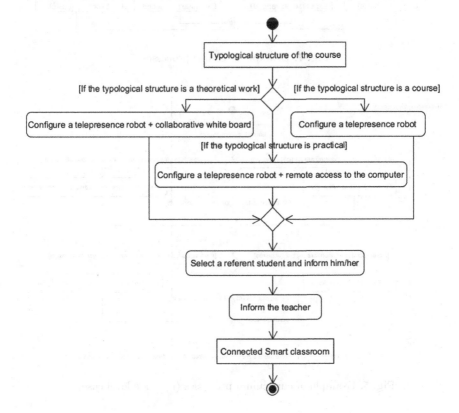

Fig. 3. Example of a classroom process

- Classroom process (Fig. 3): <u>Aim:</u> Configure the smart objects for a telepresent student according to the typological structure of the course. This also affects indirectly the interactions between people (students, teachers, etc.). If we need to connect telepresent-students, according to the typological structure of the course, the correspondant ECPS will propose the right activity

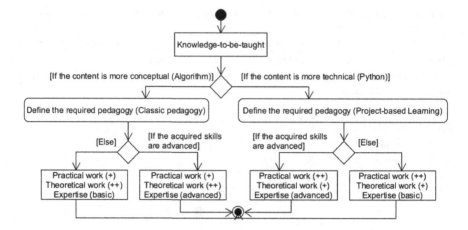

Fig. 4. Example of course processes

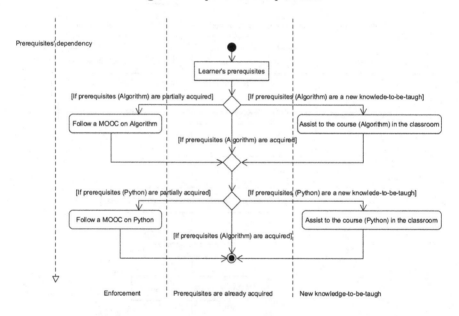

Fig. 5. Example of curriculum processes (upgrade level case)

to do in order to configure the required objects for configuring the connection. Other sub-activities related to the selected action will also be defined consequently, like the designation of a referent student who will be in charge of the communication with the remote student. The teacher will be notified once the designation is done. This translates the kind of interactions between people that the ECPS reports according to the components of IoE.

– Course process (Fig. 4): <u>Aim:</u> Based on the knowledge-to-be-taught, the strategy of the course plan and learning objectives could change. In our example, if the knowledge-to-be-taught is more conceptual, we will design the course focusing more on theoretical aspects, elsewise, the focus will be on the practical works. The design of the knowledge-to-be-taugh will depend on the nature of the subject itself. In addition, according to the students' acquired skills, the design of the learning will differ for each student in order to personalise the required learning processes. For example, if a student has already acquired the basic skills, we can propose for him/her (or choose for him/her) to follow an advanced course instead.

- Curriculum process (Fig. 5): <u>Aim:</u> Upgrade students' level: the adaptation of the curriculum according to collected data about student background. In the given example, if the learners' prerequisites are not acquired, we could propose them to follow a MOOC (Massive Open Online Course) or to assist to the course in the classroom if it is about a new subject to learn. They could have the possibility to not follow the course if it is proven that they have the required competences. Prerequisite dependency is a key parameter in every curriculum design, Algorithm before Python in this case. Hence, for the upgrade of students' level, one may find activities when it comes to enforcement, other activities for learning new knowledge and others when prerequisites are acquired.

Each type of process is continuously implemented, monitored and supervised by a specific ECPS which mobilizes different managed ressources according to an ongoing process. The given examples are not about complete processes but rather some samples of a set of activities that ECPS generate according to a given situation. The situation includes the different elements of the IoE (people, things, data, processes, learning/teaching context). In fact, the ECPS in charge of the curriculum processes will manage a set of ECPS running in a set of course processes, correspondingly. Similarly, the ECPS in charge of the course process will manage a set of ECPS running in a set of classroom processes. Finally, a classroom process run out by an ECPS could be specific for each student or a group of students to monitor and adapt the educational processes.

5   Conclusion and Future Works

Dealing with the Internet of Everything in the educational ecosystem is different from other domains. Various challenges about setting up a connected environment, coupled with optimising the educational experience as a whole package, drive us to rethink the different elements of IoE. The context factor is very interesting to study as it leads the way processes could get defined or adapted, something we have started doing in this paper. In this research work, we proposed a revised version of the Internet of Everything elements of the educational ecosystem and a key concept for University 4.0: ECPS. We are currently working on refining a generic reference architecture for university 4.0 through the bias of ECPS. This generic architecture will define the main global elements of such system and their interactions supported by bidirectional data flows (from physical to cyber and vice-versa). Then, we will define a model driven method to propose an Architecture Description for Educational Cyber Physical System. Different views will be provided by the bias of Domain Specific Language (DSL) to depict the different elements of an ECPS covering the IoE components.

References

1. Educause (2016). https://er.educause.edu/articles/2016/6/the-internet-of-things-riding-the-wave-in-higher-education. Accessed 27 May 2019
2. Bagheri, M., Movahed, S.H.: The effect of the internet of things (IoT) on education business model. In: 2016 12th International Conference on Signal-Image Technology & Internet-Based Systems (SITIS), pp. 435–441. IEEE (2016)
3. Burd, B., et al.: Courses, content, and tools for internet of things in computer science education. In: Proceedings of the 2017 ITiCSE Conference on Working Group Reports, pp. 125–139. ACM (2018)
4. Cecil, J., Chandler, D.: Cyber physical systems and technologies for next generation e-learning activities. Cyber Phys. Syst. Technol. Next Gener. e-Learn. Activities **10**, 1–11 (2014)
5. Ciolacu, M., Svasta, P.M., Berg, W., Popp, H.: Education 4.0 for tall thin engineer in a data driven society. In: 2017 IEEE 23rd International Symposium for Design and Technology in Electronic Packaging (SIITME), pp. 432–437. IEEE (2017)
6. Autonomic Computing. An architectural blueprint for autonomic computing. IBM White Paper **31**, 1–6 (2006)
7. de Amorim Silva, R., Braga, R.T.V.: An acknowledged system of systems for educational internet of everything ecosystems. In Proceedings of the 12th European Conference on Software Architecture: Companion Proceedings, p. 25. ACM (2018)
8. Herling, R.W., Provo, J.: Knowledge, competence, and expertise in organizations. Adv. Dev. Hum. Resour. **2**(1), 1–7 (2000)
9. Hermann, M., Pentek, T., Otto, B.: Design principles for industrie 4.0 scenarios. In: 2016 49th Hawaii International Conference on System Sciences (HICSS), pp. 3928–3937. IEEE (2016)
10. Kagermann, H., Wahlster, W., Helbig, J.: Final report of the industrie 4.0 working group. Federal Ministry of Education and Research, p. 82 (2013)
11. Lee, J., Bagheri, B., Kao, H.-A.: A cyber-physical systems architecture for industry 4.0-based manufacturing systems. Manufact. Lett. **3**, 18–23 (2015)
12. Moreira, F.T., Magalhães, A., Ramos, F., Vairinhos, M.: The power of the internet of things in education: an overview of current status and potential. In: Mealha, Ó., Divitini, M., Rehm, M. (eds.) SLERD 2017. SIST, vol. 80, pp. 51–63. Springer, Cham (2018). https://doi.org/10.1007/978-3-319-61322-2_6
13. Nami, M.R., Bertels, K.: A survey of autonomic computing systems. In: Third International Conference on Autonomic and Autonomous Systems, 2007, ICAS07, p. 26. IEEE (2007)
14. Palma, D., Agudo, J., Sánchez, H., Macías, M.: An internet of things example: classrooms access control over near field communication. Sensors **14**(4), 6998–7012 (2014)
15. Puncreobutr, V.: Education 4.0: new challenge of learning. St. Theresa J. Humanit. Soc. Sci. **2**(2) (2016)

16. Ramlowat, D.D., Pattanayak, B.K.: Exploring the Internet of Things (IoT) in education: a review. In: Satapathy, S.C., Bhateja, V., Somanah, R., Yang, X.-S., Senkerik, R. (eds.) Information Systems Design and Intelligent Applications. AISC, vol. 863, pp. 245–255. Springer, Singapore (2019). https://doi.org/10.1007/978-981-13-3338-5_23

17. Sackey, S.M., Bester, A., Adams, D.: Industry 4.0 learning factory didactic design parameters for industrial engineering education in South Africa. S. Afr. J. Ind. Eng. **28**(1), 114–124 (2017)

18. Sharma, D.S.: Accounting students' learning conceptions, approaches to learning, and the influence of the learning-teaching context on approaches to learning. Acc. Educ. **6**(2), 125–146 (1997)

19. Takpor, T., Atayero, A.A.: Integrating internet of things and ehealth solutions for students' healthcare. In: Proceedings of the World Congress on Engineering, World Congress on Engineering, London, UK, vol. 1 (2015)

20. Yuqiao, Y., Kanhua, Y.: Construction of distance education classroom in architecture specialty based on internet of things technology. Int. J. Emerg. Technol. Learn. (iJET) **11**(05), 56–61 (2016)

Design of a Web System of Learning Evaluation of Students with Visual Disability by Voice Recognition

Carmen Cerón$^{(\boxtimes)}$ (ID), Etelvina Archundia$^{(\boxtimes)}$ (ID),
Jorge Fernández$^{(\boxtimes)}$ (ID), and Carlos Flores$^{(\boxtimes)}$

Benemérita Universidad Autónoma de Puebla,
4 Sur no. 104, Puebla, Puebla, Mexico
{mceron, etelvina}@cs.buap.mx, jafp58@prodigy.net.mx,
carma.camacho@gmail.com

Abstract. In the actuality, exists a variety of applications of the information and communication technologies for the educational ambit. Nevertheless, is required to attend students with special educative necessities. The objective is to present the design, development and implementation of a web system as an inclusive tool for people with visual disability to support the learning evaluation in courses of high education, achieving a digital transformation of the educative processes and services for in the education 4.0. The methodology utilized was the inclusive design centered in the user and the implementation uses PHP, MySQL, JavaScript, voice libraries. The tests of functionality and usability were realized in a focal group of students with visual disability.

Keywords: Inclusive education · Accessibility · Evaluation · Interfaces

1 Introduction

The education in Mexico requires attending the students with different capabilities, which entails to generate inclusive educative systems. The current programs must be inclusive guaranteeing that the students can have access to the obligated and superior education. The inclusive education should incorporate the students with different disabilities in the ordinary classrooms, which implies a permanent effort and the development of digital abilities in the use of new tools of the trend of the learning 4.0.

According to the results of the Census of Population and Housing realized by the National Institute of Statistic and Geography [1] Mexico has a population of 129,9 millions of people, of which 35.2 million are registered as students in basic schooled education, which represents 73.4% of the enrollment of educative system. In middle high education, is offered an educative service to 4.4 millions of young, and in high education are 3.3 millions of students, which means 29.2% of coverage, distributed in seven thousand schools in the whole country [1]. In agreement to the statistics published, the students in age to enter to middle high education, who obtain a place is 15% and for people with disability is reduced even more in 2%. Since despite the technological advances and the opening to the education continues existing the lack of

© Springer Nature Switzerland AG 2019
N. T. Nguyen et al. (Eds.): ICCCI 2019, LNAI 11684, pp. 592–602, 2019.
https://doi.org/10.1007/978-3-030-28374-2_51

inclusion to the people with disability without having the materials, technologies or instillations to support the admission exam to obtain a place in the schools.

According to UNESCO [2], in Mexico, the students with disability its access to the education is limited for diverse factors: the educative services are not relevant, due to its environment, which does not make easier the access, like is the transport or by factors of discrimination.

Since 2008, the inclusive education has formed part of the World Declaration of "Education for Everyone", as an alternative to transform the educative systems. In agreement with inclusive UNESCO [3], the inclusive education can be understand as: *The inclusive education can be conceived as a process that allows approaching and respond to the diversity of the necessities of all the learners through greater participation in the learning, the cultural and community activities and reduce the exclusion within and out of the educative system.*

In the 2014, the National Program for the Development and the Inclusion of the People with Disability 2014–2018 [4] one of its objective is to attend the necessity of "Strengthen the participation of the people with disability in the inclusive and especial education", *and search to "Impulse inclusive educative politics to favor the access, permanence and egress of the people with disability in all the type, modalities and educative levels".*

For the students with disabilities, the use of digital technologies means principally two advantages: a major possibility of access to the information and the use of didactic resources to be able to support their learning [5]. Which implies, be able to generate materials, platforms, learning resources, strategies, educative process that can improve their academic life of the students.

The voice recognition is a technology that refers to the capacity to listen (input audio), is being incorporated like the ideal interface for the communication between people and the computer due to the naturalness of the communication that present the current systems of voice recognition. This voice recognition includes the steps: voice recordings, detection of word limit, extraction characteristics and recognition of knowledge models, like the acoustic model, language models, interpreter model, that help the recognition system and currently can support to people with some visual disability low or total and combine different technologies as are screen readers, platforms and browsers to ease the interaction and access to the information.

The purpose of this work is to present the design of a prototype to support the learning evaluation for students with visual disability using natural interfaces of voice recognition and the processing of natural language to ease the evaluation. The software EV@-INCLU allows to the user to interact through the voice commands in every section of the evaluation, realizing exercises and simulating diverse proves of evaluation, the system stores the results of the evaluation and generates an file of results in pdf format, which can be consulted later by the user and evaluator.

This paper is organized in the following form: in the Sect. 2 is presented the revision of work related to our research work. In the Sect. 3 is defined the methodology, the analysis and design of the prototype. In the Sect. 4 are showed the results of the pilot prove and the evaluation for the students with disabilities in the focal group through a qualitative methodological approach and the inspection and exploration technic. Finally, the results of the research, conclusions and future work are presented.

2 State of the Art

In this section, are presented the revision of some works that are found related with voice processing and natural interfaces of voice used to support people with disability in their daily life.

A system text-to-speech converts the language of normal text in speech; other systems recreate the linguistic symbolic representations as phonetic transcriptions in speech. The synthesis of text-to-speech (TTS) is the automatic conversion of a text to a native language. The TTS is a technology that allows use an algorithm that analyses, processes and synthesizes the text, generating sound data in an audio format as output. The quality of a voice synthesizer is judged by its similarity with the human voice and by its capacity of being understandable. An intelligible program of text to voice allows people with visual or reading disability to listen documents and be able to interact.

There are several available platforms that work in the voice recognition like Google, Facebook, Microsoft, being the tool HTK the most managed and effective to implement systems of voice recognition, based on the technic of hide models of Markov, developed in the University of Cambridge, UK [6] achieving the conversion of speech to text. Being this tool used in platforms UNIX, LINUX and Windows.

In [7] the investigation was focused in determine the effectiveness of the software to covert "speech-text". With the objective of realize the diagnosis and determine if the cognitive load for its training would decrease for the participants that were classified in three categorical disabilities that affect the reading and written expressions areas. For which was analyzed writing samples of the students with and without support of the software, verifying that the participants improve in relation to the ones who used the software. The software that was used were applications in platforms of iOS and Windows.

In [8] the presented work is focused to the use of TTS software to improve the reading abilities for students with difficulties of academic performance. The TTS software used for this studio was the Kurzweil 3000, which was designed as a countervailing tool for people with disabilities, included learning disabilities (LD), attention-deficit/hyperactivity (ADHD), reading difficulties and some physical disabilities, like the tetraplegia. The TTS software provides a synchronized visual and auditory presentation of text. Reproduce text through spoken words of electronic documents. Finally, the results demonstrated that the participants that used the TTS software had improved in the reading, the vocabulary and comprehension.

In the realized investigation in [9], designed a software for the conversion of text to voice for people with visual disabilities. The development of the synthesizer of text to voice in form of a simple application, converts the joined text in synthesized voice and later is read to the user, which can be kept as a mp3 file. Achieving to obtain a motor for the English idiom and later for the Nigerian.

Regarding the Natural User Interfaces (NUI), the researchers focuses in the creation and evaluation of gestures and natural actions realized for a multitouch interaction. In [9] affirm that the NUI, are considered new methods for the Human Computer Interaction (HCI) and the design of informative applications based on interfaces with which the interactions are realized from the natural actions of the human beings, that is to say, that allow reconsider the existent abilities of the user. Whereby, are considered quite adaptable and accessible for the people with some disability. On the other hand, affirm that the characteristics of the NUI are centered in the user (necessities, wishes and limitations), multichannel (sensorial and motor abilities), extended, of great bandwidth, and of interaction based on voice (voice and communication processing), based on image (integrate images for the communication of the user), based on behavior (recognition of the human behavior and of the expressions) achieving to support the users in their necessities.

The Automatic Speech Recognition (ASR) [10] is the process of converting a signal of voice to a sequence of words by an algorithm, implemented as a computer program. The voice interfaces are mechanisms designed to allow the control of device or application by the verbal interaction. The voice recognition must comply these three tasks:

1. Processing: Convert the input of voice into a form that the recognizer can process, that is to say, convert the analog signal into a digital one.
2. Recognition: Identify what was said, realizing the translation.
3. Communication: Sends the recognition to the software of application.

Traditionally, the three main areas of work in the voice-processing field since the processing of the signals are codification, synthesis and recognition.

Which in [11] and [12] show that the synthesis of text to voice is computational technology of fast increase and perform a roll every time more important in the form that the users interact with the system and the interfaces achieve to integrate to a variety of platforms and adapt to the user necessities. The interactions of voice are a trend in the natural interfaces as are considered apt to improve the lives of the peoples with disabilities achieving to join text to documents, reading of books and realize activities of self-study [13].

3   Methodology

The methodology that was used was a qualitative approach, using the Centered Design in the Inclusive User (DCUI) and the model of prototypes, which is described in the analysis and design of the system.

3.1   Analysis and Design of the Prototype

The DCU inclusive use the usability criteria of heuristics [14] and in the lines of the Accessibility guide to the content in the Web. For which was applied the criteria of use of color, independence of the device, the navigation by voice and keyboard commands. In the same way, was realized a series of interviews and surveys with the focal group, achieving to identify the interaction necessities [15]. For the analysis and the design of the system were determined the cases of use and of sequence, such as is showed in Fig. 1. The system allows identifying two users for the access and manipulation of the system:

- Teacher User: Can realize general consults of the evaluation of the theme, generate exercises for the evaluation and review the exam.

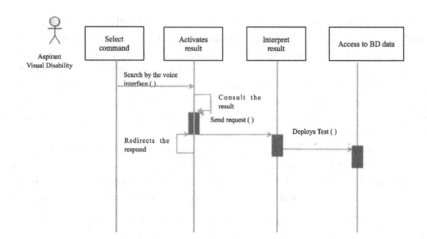

Fig. 1. Diagram of user interaction user with the software.

- Student User with low vision/blindness: choose time of evaluation for knowledge area and can realize series of exercises of a guide before applicate evaluation and finally it shows the summary of evaluation.

3.2 Architecture and Development of Prototype

The voice recognition, for prototype, is handled an extractor of characteristics and classifiers. When is received the signal of voice for the microphone, pass through a recognizer that gives as a result the word. After a processing of natural language, is realized a semantic representation and finally one action, been the process as is shown in the Fig. 2.

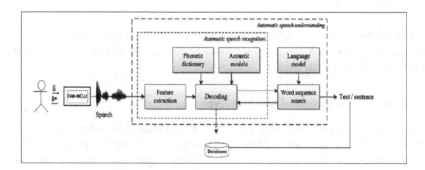

Fig. 2. Design speech recognition of system.

The interface through the device is in charge to send the user voice (the input) and later is in charge to process the voice and execute the corresponding function (voice processing) by one lambda function to interpret the voice commands of the user and convert them in actions that the API through the JavaScript libraries Artyom.js and

Annyang.js, both ease the use in HTML5 for the voice recognition, allowing that the user control and navigate in the web application through the instruction by voice in JavaScript.

The integration of speech technology into web system pages a client-server based architecture is applied. This allows implementing into web page with libraries of JavaScript that provides the speech services such as speech recognition, speaker verification and speech synthesis. Using these services voice control and speech output can be easily incorporated into existing web pages, the requirement on the client side is a JavaScript enabled browser and Java-Plugin, view in Fig. 3.

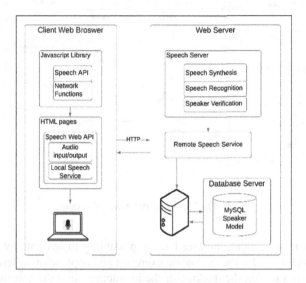

Fig. 3. Architecture of system.

The libraries implemented in the JavaScript language for the recognition and synthesis of voice Artyom.js and Annyang.js that is based in the "web-kit-speech-recognition". The first library has English and Spanish support and the other in various languages so that the voice recognition and use of the platform can realize in both languages.

For the implementation was used HTML5, CSS and JavaScript, acceding directly to the API of voice recognition with the libraries Artyom.js and Annayang.js. In the same way, is used the recognition of keyboard commands, so that the user can use some combinations of keys to access to the platform.

3.3 Design of the Database

The Fig. 4 shows the design of the database implemented in MYSQL to stock the information regarding the web system for the tracking of the evaluation, is of rational type and accomplish with the rules of normalization. The DBMS stocks the disability level and register the results of the evaluation of every proof that is applied, as well as the relation that has with every topic and block that allows giving an academic tracking to the student.

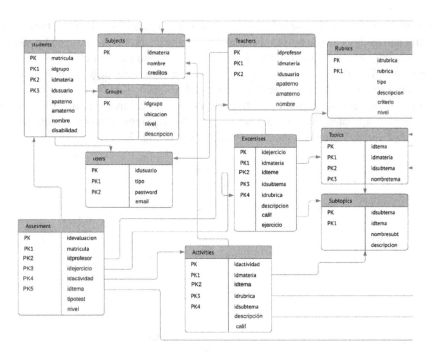

Fig. 4. Design of the database of system.

After the screen of login, the user has the possibility to navigate by the platform, either between sections for the evaluation exercises and application of test. The system realize by a screen reader, the tracking of the instructions in order that the student can interact with the evaluations and answer the questions with voice or keyboard selecting the correct answer as is observed in the Fig. 5.

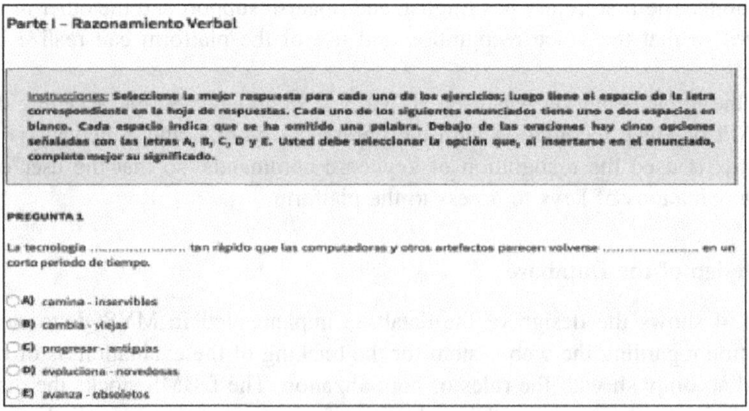

Fig. 5. Interaction with screen reader and user voice.

So too, for the tracking of the learning, is proportionated the results, are stocked and is generated a file in the pdf format, that afterwards the student or evaluator can consult, see Fig. 6.

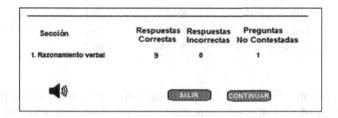

Fig. 6. Results send to a pdf file.

4   Results

The web system of evaluation of the learning to support the students with visual disability, was realized a pilot test that was made with a focal group conformed by two students with visual disability, and one blind student, which have worked with screen readers, realized the exercises and the evaluation of verbal and mathematical reasoning learnings.

The size of the selected sample is small because the admission processes and conditions of the institution for students with visual impairment are very limited and exclusive. For this purpose, the technique of inspection and exploration was applied under three possible stages that are described below:

- Situation 1: To the user was given a brief explanation of the use of the system and was accompanied in the system in the navigation and execution of the evaluation.
- Situation 2: To the user was explained the use of the system and only was accompanied in the beginning of the evaluation.
- Situation 3: To the user was explained the use of the system and was not accompanied either the navigation or execution of activities.

The users should comply certain tasks to check the system functionality:

- Task 1: Access to the system registering the key and password, selecting the voice control and commands through the keyboard.
- Task 2: In the navigation menu, select the exercise or test options made up of the reading, writing, mathematics and English sections.
- Task 3: Travel the systems through the selected interaction of voice, commands and use of keys.
- Task 4: Consult the results of exercises and tests to generate the evaluation in a pdf file.

The obtained results of the inspection prove are presented in the Table 1. Which reflects that the users with a brief explication of the Situation 1 their development was of an 87.5% of the accomplishment of the tasks meanwhile that the users of the Situation 2 was 82.5% and for the Situation 3 achieved the tasks only in an 80.75%.

Table 1. Inspection tests of the development of users

Task	Situatión No. 1	Situatión No. 2	Situatión No. 3
Task 1	90%	85%	80%
Task 2	90%	80%	85%
Task 3	85%	85%	80%
Task 4	85%	80%	78%
Average	87.5%	82.5%	80.75%

This implies that the inclusive software supports the exercise for the preparation and simulation of evaluations as was the admission exam in a way that the voice interfaces ease the interaction with the software to the people with visual disability.

Wherefore, can be affirmed that the applicability of technology device is measured by its actual usage, ease in accessibility by its users and in their satisfaction in interaction with their environment. The users must participate directly in the design and development having present the following.

1. According to the necessities of the user and environment, achieving be helpful in different situations.
2. Accessible and easy to obtain cost-benefit to support students with visual disability.
3. Integrate the technologies to support a transformative education to generate the digital abilities in the students achieving an inclusive education.

Finally, was applied a survey of satisfaction, to value the software [16], which evaluates seven criteria: Navigation, Interactivity, Immersion, Usability, Creativity, Effectiveness and Quality, with a scale of 1 to 5.

Whose obtained average was of 4.6 (92%), what indicates that the satisfaction of the student was high to be able to develop their competences and a significant learning, due to the use of interfaces with voice as is showed in the following Fig. 7.

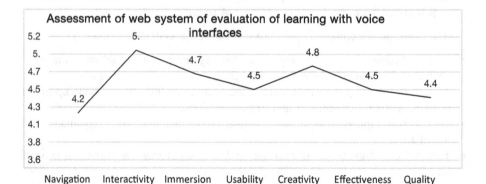

Fig. 7. Results of assessment of satisfaction of the software

This implies that the use of the voice interfaces should be considered for the design of the software for people with visual disabilities and to support the inclusive education and offer major accessibility to the people that have special necessities. The evaluation process of learning requires support of informative tools that achieve easily an evaluation according to the student and teacher profile can recommend actions and strategies to improve the level of performance of the student achieving an inclusive education.

5 Conclusion and Future Work

One of the principle contributions is the input of a software to support the preparation and realization of evaluations to students with visual disabilities achieving to integrate the technologies of voice processing and natural language processing to support the interaction with the student and the academic environment.

This research work, whose objective was to offer a tool to support the assessment of learning to motivate the students with visual disability to continue their studies and promote an evaluation according profile and disabilities of to the student.

Giving guideline to a new panorama in the inclusive education supported by the technologies of voice recognition, which offer assistance and interaction with the people with disability and allow reducing the digital gap.

As perspective of this work, is generate more reactives for the database that support to distinct evaluations for the middle high and high education. In such a way that can be constructed as an alternative to support the periodic and admission evaluations in the middle high and high education.

As well, as apply the usability tests and be able to extend the sample to other academic units and institutions.

References

1. Instituto Nacional de Estadística y Geografía (INEGI): Censo de Población y Vivienda (2015). http://www.beta.inegi.org.mx/temas/estructura/
2. UNESCO: Superar la exclusión mediante planteamientos integradores en la educación. París (2003)
3. UNESCO: Directrices sobre políticas de inclusión en la educación. http://unesdoc.unesco.org/images/0017/001778/177849s.pdf
4. Programa Nacional para el Desarrollo y la Inclusión de las Personas con Discapacidad 2014–2018. http://www.gob.mx/conadis/documentos/programa-nacional-para-el-desarrollo-y-la-inclusion-de-las-personas-con-discapacidad-2014-2018
5. Carrillo, R.: Diseño y manipulación de modelos ocultos de Markov, utilizando herramientas HTK. Una tutoría. Ingeniare. Revista Chilena de Ingeniería 15(1), 18–26. (2007). https://www.redalyc.org/articulo.oa?id=77215103
6. Fernández, J.: Necesidades educativas especiales en el contexto universitario español. Mag. Educ. Super. 33, 149–162 (2004)

7. McCollum, D., Nation, S., Gunn, S.: The effects of a speech-to-text software application on written expression for students with various disabilities. Natl. Forum Spec. Educ. J. **25**, 1–13 (2014)
8. Stoddena, R., Robertsa, K., Takahashia, K., Parka, H., Stoddena, J.: Use of text-to-speech software to improve reading skills of high school struggling readers. Procedia Comput. Sci. **14**, 359–362 (2012)
9. Isewon, I., Oyelade, J., Olufunke, O.: Design and implementation of text to speech conversion for visually impaired people. Int. J. Appl. Inf. Syst. **7**(2), 25–30 (2014).
10. Lozada, R., Rivera, L., Molina, F.: Interfaces de Usuario Natural (2012). https://www.researchgate.net/publication/285927377_Interfaces_de_Usuario_Natural
11. Zheng, H., Hu, H., Liu, S., Meng, H.: The study and implementation of text-to-speech system for agricultural information. In: Li, D., Zhao, C. (eds.) CCTA 2009. IAICT, vol. 317, pp. 291–296. Springer, Heidelberg (2010). https://doi.org/10.1007/978-3-642-12220-0_42
12. Sung, J., Kyun, D., Shin, Y.: Design and implementation of a voice based navigation for visually impaired persons. Int. J. Bio-Sci. Bio-Technol. **5**(3), 61–68 (2013)
13. Lleida, E.: Reconocimiento automático del habla. Centro Politécnico Superior Universidad de Zaragoza. http://www.gtc.cps.unizar.es/ ~ eduardo
14. Nielsen, J.: Ten Usability Heuristics. http://www.useit.com/papers/heuristic/heuristic_list.html
15. Newell, A., Gregor, P.: User sensitive inclusive design: in search of a new paradigm. In: CUU First ACM Conference on Universal Usability (2000)
16. Acuña, A., Romo, M.: Diseño Instruccional Multimedia. Pearson Education, Mexico (2011)

Education + Industry 4.0: Developing a Web Platform for the Management and Inference of Information Based on Machine Learning for a Hydrogen Production Biorefinery

Luis A. Rodríguez[1]([✉]), Christian J. Vadillo[1]([✉]), Jorge R. Gómez[1]([✉]), and Ixbalank Torres[2]([✉])

[1] Universidad Autónoma de Yucatán, Yucatán, Mexico
filirodriguez94@hotmail.com, christianvadillo@hotmail.com,
gomez.jorge@gmail.com
[2] Universidad de Guanajuato, Guanajuato, Mexico
ixbalank@gmail.com

Abstract. Nowadays, humans depend on the operation of different complex systems. For example, transportation systems (trains, ships and planes), public services (water, gas and electricity), manufacturing plants, hospitals and banks, to name a few. In recent years, given the improvement of sensors it is normal to have a large amount of data of a complex system. This creates a major challenge for analysis, visualization, and decision making about this data. In these days, it is not enough a statistical analysis of the data, but a machine learning needs to be applied for better inferential information. In this paper, as part of our formation in masters in computer science, we propose a new architecture for a web platform for the management and inference of information based on Machine Learning. It can receive, clean, pre-process and transform the data for the statistical analysis and application of machine learning algorithms. The proposed architecture is validated with experimental tests obtained from a simulator of a hydrogen production biorefinery, but can be abstracted and applied in different complex systems.

Keywords: Big Data · Biorefinery · Machine Learning · Data mining

1 Introduction

Industry 4.0, a German strategic initiative, is aimed at creating intelligent factories where manufacturing technologies are upgraded and transformed by cyberphysical systems (CPSs), the Internet of Things (IoT), and cloud computing [1]. In the Industry 4.0 era, manufacturing systems are able to monitor physical processes, create a so-called "digital twin" of the physical world, and make smart decisions through real-time communication and cooperation with humans,

© Springer Nature Switzerland AG 2019
N. T. Nguyen et al. (Eds.): ICCCI 2019, LNAI 11684, pp. 603–613, 2019.
https://doi.org/10.1007/978-3-030-28374-2_52

machines, sensors and so forth [2]. Industry 4.0 combines embedded production system technologies with intelligent production processes to pave the way for a new technological age that will fundamentally transform industry value chains, production value chains, and business models [3].

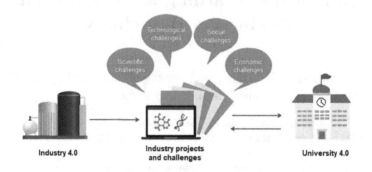

Fig. 1. Industry 4.0 linked to University 4.0

Industry 4.0 involves many aspects (CPSs, IoT and cloud computing), and faces many types of difficulties and challenges, including scientific, technological, economic and social challenges (see Fig. 1). These challenges of the industry are a great opportunity for the development of universities towards University 4.0, since they offer not only issues to solve, but also provide Industry 4.0 real world scenarios in which universities can apply new University 4.0's concepts. Some of the challenges of industry 4.0 are the development of smart devices, the construction of the network environment, big data analysis and processing, and digital production [4].

The large amount of data, which is generated every day, is growing at an unprecedented rate as a result of the evolution of web technologies, social networks and mobile devices [5]. Big Data is a term for massive data sets that have a large, varied and complex structure, with the difficulties of storage, analysis and visualization for future processes or results [6]. Due to the large amount of information, the databases and repositories are also growing exponentially. In fact, it has been suggested that data grow at the same speed as computational resources, which, according to Moore's law, double every 18 months [7]. One of the biggest challenges in computer science, in general, is the generation of systems that are capable of processing growing datasets [7].

The computational science of extracting useful information from large volumes of data or databases is known as data mining. It is a discipline, found at the intersection of statistics, machine learning, data management and databases, pattern recognition, artificial intelligence and other areas [8]. Thus, the objective of data mining is to discover new and useful information in databases, and repositories, using various data mining algorithms, such as Support Vector Machines (SVM), Classification and Regression Trees (CART), A priori, among others, to find patterns of information for a clearer analysis in large volumes of data [9].

Like data mining, Machine Learning plays an important role as a fundamental component of data analysis, and is one of the main drivers of the Big Data revolution [10].

Today, various areas of knowledge (e.g., biology, artificial intelligence, biochemistry, etc.) have generated and stored enormous volumes of data, which describe their operations, products and processes. Such amount of data complicates the inference of information and knowledge, since the different areas of knowledge do not have the necessary data mining algorithms (e.g., SVM, CART, A priori, etc.) and automatic learning (e.g., Supervised Learning (SL), Unsupervised Learning (UL) and Reinforcement Learning (RL)) necessary to process all information. The field of data mining and automatic learning, addresses the issue of extracting interesting patterns, associations, rules, changes and anomalies of data to improve the decision-making process in the various areas of knowledge [11].

As part of our formation in masters in computer science, at the Autonomous University of Yucatan (UADY), in this project we propose a web platform that uses methods and algorithms of automatic learning and data mining to receive, store, process and analyze large amounts of data that generates a biorefinery that produces hydrogen from wastewater. This, in order to be able to explore all the processes of a biorefinery and learn more about its operation through the aforementioned statistical analyzes.

2 State of the Art

"Large" as an adjective fails to describe the size of the data sets that are now analyzed and manipulated [12]. The databases have existed for decades. What is new is the growth of scale, sophistication and ubiquity of data processing to identify new patterns of information and inference [13]. Researchers can now extract potentially useful patterns that would otherwise remain hidden in petabytes of data (10^{15} bytes) [14]. Big Data presents a paradigm shift in the way we use and think about the data [15]. For example, the data may come from internal and/or external data sources. More importantly, the data can come in various formats, such as transaction data and records of various applications, structured data such as database table, semi-structured data such as XML data, unstructured data such as text, images, video sequences, audio statements and more.

Techniques such as data mining and Machine Learning improve the quality of decision making [16]. The business sector, government administration, scientific research and many other sectors can be improved by analyzing the data with these techniques [17]. Particularly people with great experience in statistics and Machine Learning, stand out in the use of Big Data information [13]. Data mining (also known as knowledge discovery from data) can be defined as the process of discovering patterns and knowledge from large amounts of data [18]. Data sources can include databases, the Web or other information or data repositories that are transmitted dynamically [18].

In current years, data mining has become important when working with Big Data. For example, in [19] a method of data analysis on the execution of work flows based on data mining is presented. The main idea is to recover data from a data warehouse and adopt online analytical processing technology. The objective is to help clients to select different measurements and see the corresponding data in different dimensions and different levels of summary, which is important for decision making. The results of these studies provide information on techniques to improve the pedagogical process, evaluate the performance of students, compare the accuracy of data extraction algorithms and demonstrate the maturity of open source tools. The authors of [21] propose a flight safety monitoring platform that uses Big Data technology. The structure of the functions module consists of five layers: data acquisition, data extraction, data mining, data analysis and data visualization.

On the other hand, Machine Learning is a type of artificial intelligence (AI) technique that makes the system obtain knowledge automatically without the explicit intervention of the human being [22]. The goal of Machine Learning is to build computer systems that can adapt and learn from their experience [23]. Usually refers to changes in systems that perform tasks associated with artificial intelligence (AI). Such tasks involve recognition, diagnosis, planning, robot control, prediction, etc. [24]. A major advantage of Machine Learning algorithms is to discover formerly unknown knowledge and to identify relationships in datasets. Depending on the characteristics of the algorithm, the requirements toward the available data may vary. In [25] they talk about the application of Machine Learning techniques to a set of data collected to improve the method of progression, prediction, self-control and clinical intervention of a sick patient.

3   Context and Problematic

Figure 2 shows the proposed biorefinery to treat agroindustrial waste. First, an anaerobic digester is proposed to treat agroindustrial waste and generate mainly volatile fatty acids (VFAs). Additionally, anaerobic digestion will generate carbon dioxide (CO_2) as a by-product. The effluent to be treated will be vinasses from the tequila industry, known to have a high organic load (40–50 COD/l), and high generation of VFAs in the acid phase when treated by anaerobic digestion (AD). Volatile fatty acids generated by anaerobic digestion will be used as a substrate in microbial electrochemical cells, which will produce hydrogen. On the other hand, the CO_2 generated as a by-product will be injected into the production PBR of microalgae to produce revaluable biomass.

In the same Fig. 2 we can observe the anaerobic acid phase that is responsible for treating agroindustrial waste and generate, mainly, Volatile Fatty Acids (VFAs). The anaerobic acid phase uses the following inputs: Dilution rate (Dil), Chemical Oxygen Demand (COD) and Volatile Fatty Acids (VFAs). In the same way, the anaerobic acid phase has as variables of the state of interest the following: biomass, COD, VFAs and CO_2.

The VFAs generated by the anaerobic acid phase are used as entry data in the microbial electrochemical cells, which have as variables of interest the hydrogen, biomass of anodophilic bacteria, biomass of methanogenic bacteria, biomass

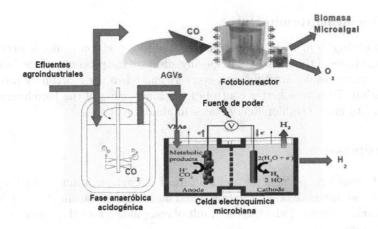

Fig. 2. Proposed hydrogen production biorefinery.

of hydrogenotropic bacteria, mediator of oxidation, current (in amperes), flow of hydrogen (QH_2) and VFAs. On the other hand, the CO_2 generated by the anaerobic acid phase is injected, as input, into the photoreactor of microalgae production. The variables of interest status of the photobioreactor are the biomass, the nutrient, the nutrient quota and the inorganic carbon.

This project occurs in the context of this biorefinery, which uses sensors for the measurement and/or estimation of state variables of the anaerobic acid phase, the photobioreactor and the microbial electrochemical cell.

3.1   Reception and Storage of Data

The biorefinery generates approximately 550 data every 10 min, and captures them in a format established by it. The inference of knowledge from these data turns out to be complicated, since there is no format or data standard established by the biorefinery and, without the necessary computational calculations (e.g, Data mining, Machine Learning, etc.), the end user can not make the knowledge inference properly. In this project it is proposed to specify a format for the data generated by the biorefinery, which will be stored, by a storage module, in a database.

3.2   Decision Making

In the decision-making process, biotechnologists perform basic statistical calculations using the information generated by the biorefinery to verify that the biorefinery is functioning correctly or not. A problem is when there is information with capture errors, this causes that erroneous decisions are made and changes are made in the processes of the biorefinery that can cause errors in its operation.

3.3 Displaying Results

When a change is made in the biorefinery due to a decision made, biotechnologists hope to see if those changes made any effect on the processes of the biorefinery, but, those results are only seen every 10 min when the biorefinery produces information. To have a better control of the functioning of the biorefinery, it is necessary to know the biorefinery states in almost real time.

4 Proposal

Figure 3 shows a proposal of the architecture of the web environment for the management and inference of information based on Machine Learning for a hydrogen production biorefinery, which is the result of compliance with the aforementioned methodology.

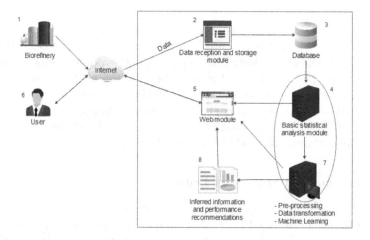

Fig. 3. Reception and data processing platform

Next, points 1 to 8 of Fig. 3 are explained:

- **Point 1: Biorefinery.** The biorefinery has approximately 30 sensors, which take home samples 10 s. Samples are sent, through the internet, every 10 min to the data reception and storage module.
- **Point 2: Data reception and storage module.** Receive the data sent by the biorefinery and, subsequently, process them so that they have a valid format for storage.
- **Point 3: Database.** Module where all the acquired information of the biorefinery will be stored.
- **Point 4: Basic statistical analysis module.** With the information stored in the database, this module is responsible for applying basic statistical analysis to these data (average, variance, covariance, standard deviation).

- **Point 5: Web module.** The web module performs various functions. One of them is to grant the necessary tools to the user to make queries of the information stored in the database, another function is to graph the results of the statistical analysis, to graph the data in specific days, among others.
- **Point 6: User.** The user can access the web module through any device (computer, smartphone, etc.) through the internet service, and can make queries of the information of the biorefinery that is stored.
- **Point 7: Preprocessing module.** It is in charge of carrying out the preprocessing and transformation of the data to subsequently perform calculations with Machine Learning algorithms.
- **Point 8: Inferred information.** It is the information generated by the machine learning algorithms of point 7.

The reception and data processing platform allows the student to know more in detail the performance and results of a biorefinery in almost real time. In the same way, the student can make graphs with the results obtained by the statistical analysis mentioned in point 4, and make inference of the information in more detail.

4.1 Methodology

The proposed methodology to achieve the objectives of this project is:

- Investigate specifications of data formats to store information in a database.
- Perform analysis on the functioning of relational and non-relational databases, in order to verify which of these allows a better management of the information generated by the biorefinery.
- Develop a module of reception and storage of information that is in charge of receiving all the information generated by the biorefinery and that, in turn, stores it using a format established in a database system (relational or non-relational).
- Develop a web module that allows biotechnologists to make a selection of specific data among all the information stored in the database and visualize the statistical results of information processing.
- Develop a module that is responsible for the preprocessing of the information previously selected. The preprocessing of the data consists of three steps: **Formatting, Cleaning** and **Sampling** [26].
- Develop a system that is responsible for the transformation of data, consisting of three steps: **Scalability, Decompose** and **Aggregate** [26].
- Develop a third process that is responsible for statistical inference applying corresponding Machine Learning algorithms to determine if the biorefinery will continue to function correctly or a possible failure is detected.

4.2 Experimental Tests

While the hydrogen production biorefinery is under construction, the University of Guanajuato created a biorefinery simulator using Matlab. The simulator provides the input and output values of the three biorefinery processes (anaerobic digester, microbial electrolysis cell and photobioreactor). To achieve the objectives mentioned in the methodology, a large amount of data generated by the biorefinery is necessary, therefore, the biorefinery simulator was used to generate 10 years of production data to continue with the development of the aforementioned modules. To start processing the data generated by the biorefinery simulator, the web platform was created using a web framework called Django and the programming language Python. The web platform has the following modules already developed: reception and storage, database, basic statistical analysis and preprocessing. The reception and storage module allows the user to upload a file of CSV (Comma Separated Values) format to save them in the database. For the database module, the database called MongoDB was implemented, which stores the information in the form of documents, which is appropriate for the proper management of the information and facilitates queries. The statistical analysis module allows the user to select what kind of statistical analysis to apply to the data stored in the database, for example, average, standard deviation, variance, covariance, anova and fisher test. Likewise, the basic statistical analysis module allows the user to generate graphs of the results obtained by the aforementioned analyzes. Graphs can be created with correlation between multiple variables as shown in Fig. 4.

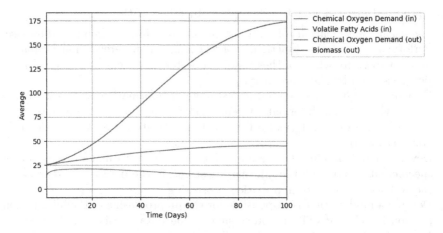

Fig. 4. Graph of the average of 4 different variables

Figure 4 shows a graph generated within the web platform, which has a correlation between four variables of the biorefinery (chemical demand for oxygen (input and output), volatile fatty acids and biomass). Like this graph, the web platform allows the user to create various combinations of graphs with different correlations between variables. This in order to help the user with making decisions for future changes that can be applied to biorefinery.

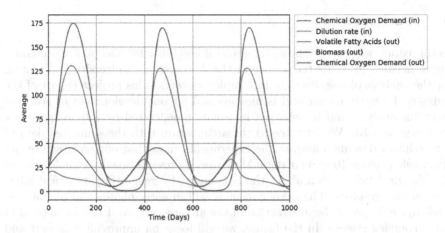

Fig. 5. Correlation of input and output variables of the anaerobic digester.

Figure 5 is another example of correlations that can be created with the web platform. In this case, a correlation was made of the input variables (chemical demand for oxygen and dilution rate) and the output variables (volatile fatty acids, biomass and chemical oxygen demand) of the anaerobic digester.

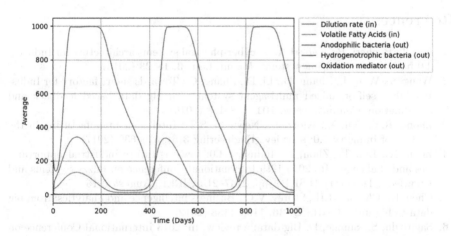

Fig. 6. Correlation of input and output variables of the microbial electrolysis cell

Figure 6 shows the correlation of the input variables (dilution rate and volatile fatty acids) and the output variables (anodophilic bacteria, hydrogenotrophic bacteria and oxidation mediator) of the microbial electrolysis cell.

5   Conclusion

In this paper, we propose the architecture of a web platform as part of our training in masters in computer science at the Autonomous University of Yucatan, for the analysis of massive data in complex systems. This project is part of the industry 4.0 environment and is fundamental for our development as students since the analysis and inference of information generated by a biorefinery is a challenge to solve. We have tested the architecture with the simulated data of a biorefinery described above. The experiments show that our architecture can effectively manage 10 years of data. Moreover, it provides an easy visualization of the historical information about the biorefinery, by generating statistical information and graphics. The development is still in early phases and our biggest challenge is improve the abstraction of the architecture, so it can be applied in other complex system. In the future, we will focus on improving this part and test it in more complex systems. We will also attempt to extend our work by the integration of a monitoring and fault detection module, in order to provide crucial information about the variables interacting in a fault. Perhaps, the integration of the monitoring and fault detection module, can be assigned to future students of the masters in computer science, both for their academic formation in the university and to know about the manipulation and development of applications for the management of large amounts of data.

References

1. Lee, J., Bagheri, B., Kao, H.A.: A cyber-physical systems architecture for Industry 4.0-based manufacturing systems. Manuf. Lett. **3**, 18–23 (2015)
2. Wang, S., Wan, J., Zhang, D., Li, D., Zhang, C.: Towards smart factory for Industry 4.0: a self-organized multi-agent system with big data based feedback and coordination. Comput. Netw. **101**, 158–168 (2016)
3. Zhong, R.Y., Xu, X., Klotz, E., Newman, S.T.: Intelligent manufacturing in the context of Industry 4.0: a review. Engineering **3**(5), 616–630 (2017)
4. Zhou, K., Liu, T., Zhou, L.: Industry 4.0: towards future industrial opportunities and challenges. In: 2015 12th International Conference on Fuzzy Systems and Knowledge Discovery (FSKD), pp. 2147–2152. IEEE, August 2015
5. Chen, H., Chiang, R.H., Storey, V.C.: Business intelligence and analytics: from big data to big impact. MIS Q. **36**, 1165–1188 (2012)
6. Sagiroglu, S., Sinanc, D. Big data: a review. In: 2013 International Conference on Collaboration Technologies and Systems (CTS), pp. 42–47 (2013)
7. Bell, G., Gray, J.N.: The revolution yet to happen. In: Denning, P.J., Metcalfe, R.M. (eds.) Beyond Calculation, pp. 5–32. Springer, New York (1997). https://doi.org/10.1007/978-1-4612-0685-9_1
8. Hand, D.J.: Principles of data mining. Drug Saf. **30**(7), 621–622 (2007)
9. Wu, X., et al.: Top 10 algorithms in data mining. Knowl. Inf. Syst. **14**(1), 1–37 (2008)
10. James, M., Michael, C., Brad, B., Jacques, B.: Big Data: The Next Frontier for Innovation, Competition, and Productivity. McKinsey Global Institute, New York (2011)

11. Mitchell, T.M.: Machine learning and data mining. Commun. ACM **42**(11), 30–36 (1999)
12. Barnes, T.J.: Big data, little history. Dialogues Hum. Geogr. **3**(3), 297–302 (2013). https://doi.org/10.1177/2043820613514323
13. Manyika, J., Chui, M., Bughin, J., Dobbs, R., Roxburgh, C., Hung Byers, A.: Big Data: The Next Frontier for Innovation, Competition and Productivity. McKinsey Global Institute, San Francisco (2011)
14. Bollier, D.: The Promise and Peril of Big Data. The Aspen Institute (2010). https://doi.org/10.2307/j.ctv3znx58
15. Wang, J., Crawl, D., Purawat, S., Nguyen, M., Altintas, I.: Big Data provenance: challenges, state of the art and opportunities. In: Proceedings of the 2015 IEEE International Conference on Big Data, IEEE Big Data 2015, pp. 2509–2516 (2015). https://doi.org/10.1109/BigData.2015.7364047
16. Wang, J., Tao, Q.: Machine learning: the state of the art. IEEE Intell. Syst. **23**(6), 49–55 (2009). https://doi.org/10.1109/mis.2008.107
17. Yin, J., Zhao, D.: Data confidentiality challenges in big data applications. In: Proceedings of the 2015 IEEE International Conference on Big Data, IEEE Big Data 2015, pp. 2886–2888, August 2015. https://doi.org/10.1109/BigData.2015.7364111
18. Han, J., Kamber, M., Pei, J.: Data Mining: Concepts and Techniques. Morgan Kaufmann, San Francisco (2001)
19. Feng, L., Chen, H.: Analysis methods of workflow execution data based on data mining. In: Proceedings of the 2009 2nd International Workshop on Knowledge Discovery and Data Mining, WKKD 2009, pp. 116–118 (2009). https://doi.org/10.1109/WKDD.2009.181
20. Anoopkumar, M., Md Zubair Rahman, A.M.J.: A review on data mining techniques and factors used in educational data mining to predict student amelioration. In: Proceedings of 2016 International Conference on Data Mining and Advanced Computing, SAPIENCE 2016, pp. 122–133 (2016). https://doi.org/10.1109/SAPIENCE.2016.7684113
21. Li, B., Ming, X., Li, G.: Big data analytics platform for flight safety monitoring. In: 2017 IEEE 2nd International Conference on Big Data Analysis, ICBDA 2017, pp. 350–353 (2017). https://doi.org/10.1109/ICBDA.2017.8078837
22. Mannila, H.: Data mining: machine learning, statistics, and databases. In: Proceedings of the 8th International Conference on Scientific and Statistical Data Base Management, SSDBM 1996, pp. 2–8 (1996). https://doi.org/10.1109/SSDM.1996.505910
23. Bakiri, G., Dietterich, T.G.: Achieving high-accuracy text-to-speech with machine learning. In: Data Mining in Speech Synthesis, vol. 10 (1999)
24. Selman, B., Brooks, R.A., Dean, T., Horvitz, E., Mitchell, T.M., Nilsson, N.J.: Challenge problems for artificial intelligence. In: Proceedings of the National Conference on Artificial Intelligence, pp. 1340–1345, August 1996
25. Ahamed, F., Farid, F.: Applying Internet of Things and machine-learning for personalized healthcare: issues and challenges. In: Proceedings of the International Conference on Machine Learning and Data Engineering, ICMLDE 2018, pp. 22–29 (2018). https://doi.org/10.1109/iCMLDE.2018.00014
26. Brownlee, J.: Supervised and unsupervised machine learning algorithms (2016). https://machinelearningmastery.com/supervised-and-unsupervised-machine-learning-algorithms/

Intelligent Processing of Multimedia in Web Systems

Application of an Intelligent Request Distribution Broker in Two-Layer Cloud-Based Web System

Krzysztof Zatwarnicki[(✉)] and Anna Zatwarnicka

Opole University of Technology, 76 Proszkowska Street, 45-758 Opole, Poland
k.zatwarnicki@gmail.com, anna.zatwarnicka@gmail.com

Abstract. Nowadays, a significant part of human activity is supported by information systems, especially Web systems, hosted in the Web clouds. In the article, we attempt to answer the question whether the cooperation of the non-intelligent and intelligent HTTP request distribution strategies eliminates the shortcomings of these strategies and increases the quality of request servicing in a Web cloud. We present the strategies used, a test bed and the results of the conducted experiments. At the end of the article we discuss results and present final conclusions.

Keywords: Fuzzy-neural network · Adaptive distribution system ·
Web systems modelling · Web cloud computing · HTTP request distribution

1 Introduction

For many decades intelligent IT systems have been supporting and complementing human capabilities in the area of human professional work, in public space as well as in facilitating everyday life and providing entertainment. Neural Networks, due to their learning and adaptive abilities, perfectly improve the quality of decision making by computer systems, especially when there are numerous and changing operating conditions of these systems.

Changing conditions of IT systems are particularly problematic when inputs of the systems are characterized by a large range of values. Fuzzy logic can cope with this problem. The mechanisms of fuzzy logic in combination with the possibilities offered by artificial neural networks allow very accurate adaptation of IT systems to significantly changing working conditions of these systems.

One of the most complex systems is the Internet network – especially World Wide Web services, which are the combination of extremely numerous resources, Web content, access devices and a large number of users. Over the last decade the number of active Internet users has increased to 4.30 billion. Almost 88% of WWW users use mobile devices as well as mobile phone network and this percentage will increase [18].

To ensure efficient and fast access to Web content, many companies use cloud computing solutions instead of keeping IT infrastructure at their headquarters. Cloud computing is a growing trend and forecasts indicate that in 2019 the worldwide Public

N. T. Nguyen et al. (Eds.): ICCCI 2019, LNAI 11684, pp. 617–628, 2019.
https://doi.org/10.1007/978-3-030-28374-2_53

Cloud Services Market is projected to grow by 17.3% to a total of 206.2 billion USD [6]. We can distinguish three main types of cloud computing solutions [3]:

- Software as a Service (SaaS), dedicated to consumers who have the need to manage their applications running on a cloud, but not to manage software or cloud infrastructure,
- Platform as a Service (PaaS), in this approach consumers control only applications running in the cloud environment,
- Infrastructure as a Service (IaaS), targeted at those consumers who want to supervise and control applications, operating systems as well as hardware infrastructure with the storage.

An extremely important issue in Web clouds is to provide efficient distribution of incoming HTTP requests, which can be carried out by specialized brokers implementing various types of distribution strategies. Among those strategies we can distinguish non-intelligent and intelligent ones.

Cloud systems contain server rooms named regions divided into availability zones in which the load is distributed by brokers working on region and zone levels [3]. Due to the specific two-layer architecture of the cloud infrastructure, appropriate mechanisms are implemented in the brokers at each level.

We have been bothered by the question if the cooperation of intelligent and non-intelligent strategies in brokers at different levels eliminates the disadvantages of specific mechanisms. And are they able to achieve a synergy effect in cooperation? This article is an attempt to answer these questions.

We have examined the work of two-layer cloud-based Web systems containing intelligent and non-intelligent Web brokers. Experiments have been conducted for different combinations of request distribution algorithms. As an example of an intelligent request distribution approach a Fuzzy-Neural Request Distribution strategy (FN) has been used [21]. The FN strategy has been designed by the authors of the article and achieves very good results in minimalizing HTTP request response times in one-layer cloud-based Web systems.

The article is structured as follows: Sect. 2 contains a presentation of related work, in Sect. 3 there is a description of the examined strategies and methods. Section 4 presents a description of the test bed and the results of the experiments carried out. Section 5 concludes the paper.

2 Related Work

For several decades various techniques of artificial intelligence have been used in computer systems for solving everyday problems and supporting human work. Web services available through the Internet are important elements in the present times and deserve special attention due to the need to ensure fast and efficient delivery of Web content to end users in a finite and preferably the shortest time. According to the research conducted, an average user is willing to wait about 2 s for the content of a Web page [15].

Artificial intelligence mechanisms, especially Artificial Neural Networks (ANN), are often used in issues related to Web and Web Cloud services. For years they have been used in the classification of Web content [9], issues related to Web Mining [14] and cloud computing resource allocation [1]. ANN and adaptive learning mechanisms are used in the prediction of the load of Web servers [20] and in the cloud computing infrastructures [7] as well as for predicting the workload of e-business services [17].

However, ANN and ANN with Fuzzy Logic are not widely used for HTTP request distribution in the Web cloud environment. There are approaches containing Artificial Intelligence mechanisms like Neuro-Fuzzy Inference System (ANFIS) [8] or Particle Swarm Optimization (PSO) based on a heuristic method [13].

Distribution of HTTP requests in a Web cloud is connected with an effective redirection of the flow of incoming requests to subordinated elements of the infrastructure to deliver the content to the end users. We have observed only a few approaches that use two-layer approaches: typically those methods use DNS systems to distribute HTTP requests [16] without using intelligent mechanisms in two-layer strategies.

Based on literature and our knowledge, we can say that smart and intelligent approaches are not commonly used in combination with non-intelligent ones. Additionally, only a few HTTP request distribution strategies are focused on delivering the content to the end user in the shortest possible time. In this article we try to answer if intelligent methods are able to cooperate and overcome the shortcomings of non-intelligent methods in the situation of the high load of the Web cloud.

As the reference non-intelligent HTTP request distribution strategies we chose strategies used by Amazon Web Service (AWS) – the largest player on the Cloud computing market – namely Round-Robin (RR), Last-Loaded (LL) and modified Path-based routing (P) [5]. In our opinion, the interaction and cooperation between the request distribution strategies in the Web cloud brokers is interesting and strategic to ensuring the high quality of Web services provided through the Web cloud.

3   Two-Layer Strategies of Web Cloud Systems

As mentioned previously, Web cloud systems are built of regions located in different parts of the world [3]. Each of the regions is divided into smaller parts named availability zones consisting of Web servers and other elements of infrastructure like database servers, storages etc.

HTTP requests sent from the user's Web browser are delivered through the Internet to the Web cloud, and more precisely – to the region broker. The region broker redistributes requests among zones according to a distribution strategy. A Web cloud architecture with two brokers, where one distributes requests among zones in the region and the other distributes requests among servers inside the zone, is called the two-layer architecture (Fig. 1).

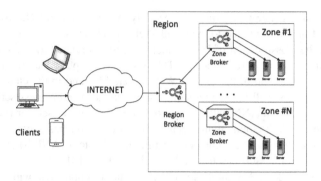

Fig. 1. Two-layer architecture of Web cloud systems.

3.1 Request Distribution Strategies in a Web Cloud Environment

Most of the HTTP request distribution strategies used in Web systems are simple and unsophisticated. The Round-Robin approach is based on a carousel mechanism: it redirects successive upcoming HTTP requests cyclically. The Last-Loaded mechanism works in accordance with another rule: it forwards the upcoming HTTP request to the Web server that currently has the lowest number of serviced requests. The Path-based Routing method redistributes incoming HTTP requests based on their URI (Uniform Resource Identifiers) according to the table where a given pattern of URI is assigned to one of the Web servers.

There are also many approaches and strategies constructed on the basis of the aforementioned strategies and their mutations [5]. Because indicated approaches may not satisfy the end users, we have developed a more complex approach that distributes requests well, minimizing response time to HTTP requests.

3.2 Fuzzy-Neural Request Distribution Strategy

The main task of the fuzzy-neural broker is to redirect incoming HTTP requests r_i, $i = 1, \ldots, I$ to those of the zones or servers in the zone (called 'an executor') that are able to service the request in the shortest time according to:

$$z_i = \min_w \{\hat{s}_i^w : w \in \{1, 2, \ldots, W\}\}, \tag{1}$$

where z_i is the executor chosen out of W executors, $\hat{s}_i^w$ means an estimated response time to upcoming request r_i for the w th server, and i symbolizes the index of the request. Each broker consists of following modules: executor models, a decision module, a redirection module and a measurement module (Fig. 2).

The executor model estimates the request response time $\hat{s}_i^w$ taking into account the load of the executor $M_i^w = [e_i^w, f_i^w]$, where e_i^w is the number of all requests being serviced by the executor at the same time concurrently and f_i^w is the number of a dynamic request. The executor model is able to adapt to the changing Web cloud and the network environment on the basis of the current response time $\tilde{s}_i^w$. There are W

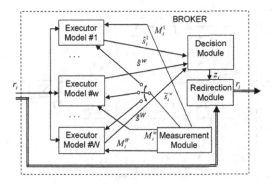

Fig. 2. Broker design.

executor modules in the broker, each corresponds to one executor. The decision module selects the proper executor according to formula 1. Finally, the redirection module forwards the request r_i to the chosen executor. The measurement module constantly collects information M_i^w and $\tilde{s}_i^w$.

The executor module is complex and it is built of two modules: classification and neuro-fuzzy (Fig. 3). The classification module classifies incoming requests to class k_i, where $k_i \in \{1, \ldots, K\}$. Every requested HTTP objects belonging to the same class have similar response times. Static objects (files) are classified by their sizes, but all dynamic objects (created during processing on the server) get a separate class.

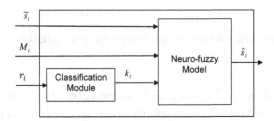

Fig. 3. Executor model.

For each class k_i the neuro-fuzzy model stores separately appropriate parameters $Z_i = [Z_{1i}, \ldots, Z_{ki}, \ldots, Z_{Ki}]$, where $Z_{ki} = [C_{ki}, D_{ki}, S_{ki}]$ represents parameters of input $C_{ki} = [c_{1\,ki}, \ldots, c_{l\,ki}, \ldots, c_{(L-1)\,ki}]$, $D_{ki} = [d_{1\,ki}, \ldots, d_{m\,ki}, \ldots, d_{(M-1)\,ki}]$ and output $S_{ki} = [s_{1\,ki}, \ldots, s_{j\,ki}, \ldots, s_{J\,ki}]$ fuzzy set functions (Fig. 4a). There are K separated neuro-fuzzy networks in each neuro-fuzzy module, one per each class. Fuzzy set functions for inputs $\mu_{F_{el}}(e_i)$, $\mu_{F_{fm}}(f_i)$, $l = 1, \ldots, L$, are triangular (Fig. 4b). However, fuzzy sets functions for outputs $\mu_{S_j}(s)$ are singletons (Fig. 4c).

We have conducted preliminary experiments to determine the adequate and optimal number of input fuzzy sets $L = M = 10$. The number of output fuzzy sets is equal to $J = L \cdot M$. The request response time is calculated in the defuzzification phase

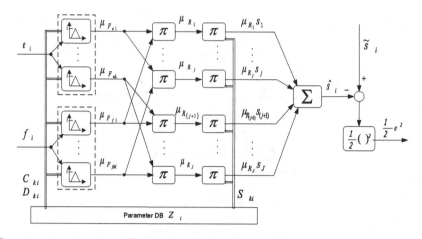

a)

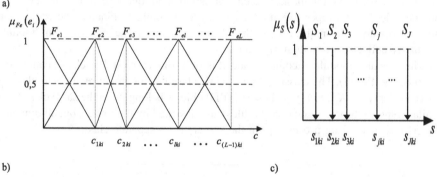

b)   c)

Fig. 4. Server model: (a) neuro-fuzzy model, (b) input fuzzy sets functions, (c) output fuzzy sets functions.

according to formula $\hat{s}_i = \sum_{j=1}^{J} s_{jki}\mu_{R_j}(e_i,f_i)$, where $\mu_{R_j}(e_i,f_i) = \mu_{F_{el}}(e_i) \cdot \mu_{F_{fm}}(f_i)$. After finishing the service of the HTTP request, the broker receives the real response time $\tilde{s}_i^w$ and can adapt to the changing environment by the modification of fuzzy sets parameters with the use of the Back Propagation Method:

$s_{jk(i+1)} = s_{jki} + \eta_s \cdot (\tilde{s}_i - \hat{s}_i) \cdot \mu_{R_j}(e_i,f_i)$,

$c_{\phi k(i+1)} = c_{\phi ki} + \eta_c(\tilde{s}_i - \hat{s}_i) \sum_{m=1}^{M} \left(\mu_{F_{fm}}(f_i) \sum_{l=1}^{L} \left(s_{((m-1)\cdot L + l)ki}\partial\mu_{F_{el}}(e_i)/\partial c_{\phi ki} \right) \right)$,

$d_{\gamma k(i+1)} = d_{\gamma ki} + \eta_d(\tilde{s}_i - \hat{s}_i) \sum_{l=1}^{L} \left(\mu_{F_{el}}(e_i) \sum_{m=1}^{M} \left(s_{((l-1)\cdot M + m)ki}\partial\mu_{F_{fm}}(f_i)/\partial d_{\gamma ki} \right) \right)$,

where η_s, η_c, η_d are adaptation ratios, $\phi = 1,\ldots,L-1$, $\gamma = 1,\ldots,M-1$ [21].

4   Test Bed and Results of Experiments

In this article we wanted to examine if the intelligent, neuro-fuzzy broker can cooperate with the standard non-intelligent brokers, and which combination of cooperating brokers can give the satisfying results in two-layer cloud-based Web systems.

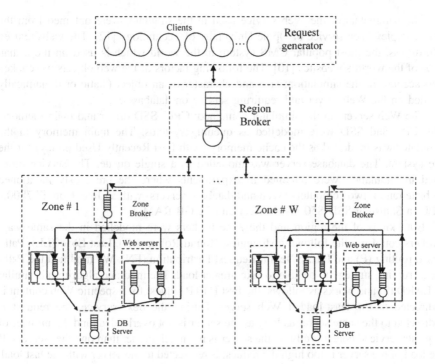

Fig. 5. Simulation model.

To conduct the experiments we used OMNET++ [11] discreet event simulation library. The simulation program imitated the behavior of many elements of the real cloud Web system, including: clients who sent HTTP requests, Web brokers, Web servers and database servers. The model of the simulator is presented on Fig. 5.

The construction of Web clients that imitate the behavior of Web browsers was very complex as the HTTP request flow had to be compatible with the flow observed in the Internet, which is characterized by a high variety, burst and self-similarity [4, 19]. Each of the clients, likewise the Web browsers, was able to open up to 6 concurrent TCP connections to download objects (pictures, js scripts, cs files e.t.c.) belonging to the Web page. The first object downloaded for a given Web page was always the HTML file that was the base of the page. Requests were send by means of the HTTP 1.1 protocol (pipelining was not used).

Within each page and TCP connection, the client sent HTTP requests after receiving a response to the previous request. The time to open a next Web page was modelled on the Pareto distribution ($\alpha = 1.4, k = 1$) while the number of Web pages downloaded by one user during one session was modelled on the Inverse Gaussian distribution ($\mu = 3.86, \lambda = 9.46$) [4]. After finishing the session the old client was deleted and new one was invoked. The probability of opening a given page in the service depended on the distance (number of links) from the main page, where the probability of opening the main page of the service was the highest.

The parameters of the Web service used in the simulator were obtained from the real, complex Web service of Opole University of Technology [12]. The website used WordPress, the most popular CMS system in the world which is used on more than 25% of the world's websites [10]. The following factors of the web objects were taken into account in the simulation: size and character of an object (static or dynamically created on the Web server and requiring service on database).

The Web servers in the simulator contained: CPU, SSD driver and main memory. The CPU and SSD were modelled as queuing systems. The main memory in the simulator was modelled as the cache memory (with Last Recently Used policy) for the file system. The database server was modelled as a single queue. The service times used in simulation were obtained in experiments where the previously mentioned website ran on two computers (Web and database servers) with an Intel Core i7 7800X CPU, a Samsung SSD 850 EVO driver and 32 GB RAM.

Both kinds of the region and the zone brokers were modelled in the same way. Brokers could run the following strategies: Round-Robin (RR), Last Load (LL), Path-based routing (P) and Fuzzy-Neural Request Distribution (FN). We modified the Path-based routing strategy to be able to take greater load. The modified algorithm is similar to LARD [2] and works as follows: the first HTTP request for a specific Web content is redirected to the least-loaded Web server. During the next service, the request is redirected to the same server as long as the server is not overloaded, and the number of requests serviced concurrently by the server is not much higher than on other servers. If the load of the server is too high the request is redirected to the server with the last load.

In the simulator each broker contained a single queue modelling the time to make distribution decision and servicing the requests. The service times obtained for Intel Xeon E5-2640 v3 processor for different distribution strategies were as follows: FN 0.2061 μs, LL 0.0103 μs, RR 0.00625 μs, P 0.0101 μs.

Experiments were conducted for different combinations of region and zone brokers: the region broker with the FN strategy and the zone brokers with the FN strategy (marked as FNFN) as the reference, the region broker with FN and the zone brokers with LL (FNLL), the region broker LL and the zone brokers FN (LLFN), the region broker LL and the zone brokers LL (LLLL), the region broker FN and the zone brokers RR (FNRR), the region broker RR and the zone brokers FN (RRFN), the region broker RR and the zone brokers RR (RRRR), the region broker FN and the zone brokers P (FNP), the region broker P and the zone brokers FN (PFN), and the region broker P and the zone brokers P (PP).

In the experiments two different configurations of zones were used. In the first configuration there were 3 zones and 4 Web servers in each zone (marked as 3 × 4). The second configuration consisted of 4 zones, each containing 3 Web servers (4 × 3).

Results of the experiments for the configuration 3 × 4 are presented on the Fig. 6, while for the configuration 4 × 3 on the Fig. 7. Bests results from diagrams a, b and c are presented on diagrams d. The plots present 95 percentile of HTTP request response time in load function, where the load is measured as the number of clients working concurrently. Each point on the plots is a result of simulation conducted for 40 million of HTTP requests, of which 10 million were sent to warm up the model.

As it can be noticed, in many cases, results obtained for two non-intelligent strategies, presented here as the reference, are the worst. The best results were obtained

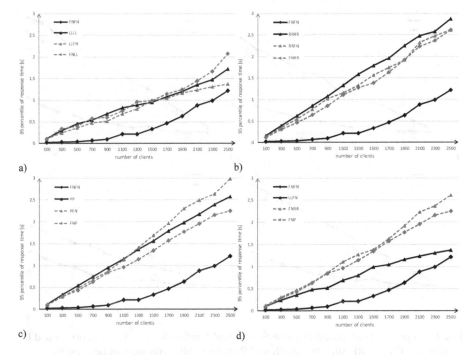

Fig. 6. 95 percentile of request response time in load function for 3 × 4 region, (a) FN and LL strategy, (b) FN and RR strategy, (c) FN and P strategy, (d) comparison of best results.

for the combination of two intelligent neuro-fuzzy brokers. The good results with the participation of LL strategy were obtained for the LLFN combination of brokers. In case of the 3 × 4 region configuration results for FNLL were the worst.

For other strategies (RR and P) the configurations where the intelligent FN broker was working in the region were better than the configurations with the FN broker working in the zones. The fact that the LL broker works better in the region layer, contrary to RR and P brokers that behave better in the zone layer, is puzzling and requires further research to explain it.

Before conducting the experiments we had expected that an intelligent broker would cooperate much better with non-intelligent brokers. The results obtained are not quite bad. However, they are not very good either. The best result of intelligent and non-intelligent cooperating brokers was obtained for the LLFN combination for both configurations of the regions 3 × 4 and 4 × 3.

The results obtained for the FNFN configuration of two cooperating intelligent brokers are surprisingly good. The 95 percentile of response time in many cases is several times lower than for the other configurations. The low 95 percentile also reveals that the variance is low, which is especially important for the HTTP request service. Brokers working in zone and region layers do not know of each other, however, in some way they cooperate yielding very good results. This confirms the thesis indicated in the [8] that a fast changing, burst Web environment needs application of intelligent solutions that can adapt to changes.

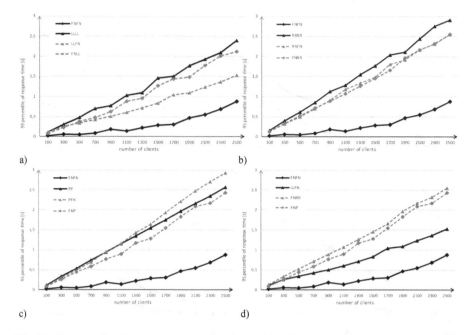

a)   b)   c)   d)

Fig. 7. 95 percentile of request response time in load function for 4 × 3 region, (a) FN and LL strategy, (b) FN and RR strategy, (c) FN and P strategy, (d) comparison of best results.

5 Summary

The main aim of the article was to examine if the intelligent, neuro-fuzzy broker can cooperate with the standard non-intelligent brokers. We wanted to examine which combination of cooperating brokers can get good results in two-layer cloud-based Web systems.

To achieve the aim we chose the most popular request distribution strategies applied in Web cloud brokers, namely: Round Robin, Last Load and Path-based routing. In the experiments the neuro-fuzzy Web broker designed by the authors cooperated with non-intelligent brokers.

The results of experiments show that a neuro-fuzzy broker can cooperate well with other brokers achieving in most cases good results, better than non-intelligent strategies in two-layer architecture. Good results in this case were obtained for the region broker running the Last Load strategy and the zone broker running the neuro-fuzzy strategy. However, the experiments show that the best results (in many cases, several times lower 95 percentile of response time) were gained for two cooperating neuro-fuzzy Web brokers.

The application of intelligent strategies in devices controlling Web clouds can, in the future, significantly increase the efficiency and reduce delays. Nevertheless, before introducing these solutions to industrial devices, additional thorough studies in real conditions should be carried out.

References

1. Aaron, K., et al.: Workload adaptive cloud computing resource allocation. Patent: US8793381B2 (2014)
2. Aron, M., Druschel, P., Zwaenepoel, Z.: Efficient support for P-HTTP in cluster-based Web servers. In: Proceedings of the 1999 USENIX Annual Technical Conference, Monterey, CA, June, pp. 185–198. USENIX Assoc., Berkeley (1999)
3. AWS documentation, How Elastic Load Balancing Works. https://docs.aws.amazon.com/elasticloadbalancing/latest/userguide/how-elastic-load-balancing-works.html. Accessed 23 Feb 2019
4. Cao, J., Cleveland, W.S., Gao, Y., Jeffay, K., Smith, F., Weigle, M.: Stochastic models for generating synthetic HTTP source traffic. In: Proceedings of Twenty-Third Annual Joint Conference of the IEEE Computer and Communications Societies, INFOCOM 2004, Hong-Kong, pp. 1547–1558 (2004)
5. Cardellini, V., Casalicchio, E., Colajanni, M., Yu, P.S.: The state of the art in locally distributed web-server systems. ACM Comput. Surv. **34**(2), 263–311 (2002)
6. Columbus, L: Roundup of Cloud Computing Forecasts and Market Estimates, 23 September 2018. https://www.forbes.com/sites/louiscolumbus/2018/09/23/roundup-of-cloud-computing-forecasts-and-market-estimates-2018/. Accessed 23 Feb 2019
7. Kumar, J., Singh, A.K.: Workload prediction in cloud using artificial neural network and adaptive differential evolution. In: Future Generation Computer Systems, vol. 81, Issue C, pp. 41–52. Elsevier Science Publishers, B. V. Amsterdam (2018)
8. Lee, S.-P., Nahm, E.-S.: Development of an optimal load balancing algorithm based on ANFIS modeling for the clustering web-server. In: Lee, G., Howard, D., Ślęzak, D., Hong, Y.S. (eds.) ICHIT 2012. CCIS, vol. 310, pp. 783–790. Springer, Heidelberg (2012). https://doi.org/10.1007/978-3-642-32692-9_100
9. Li, Y., Cao, Y., Zhu, Q., Zhu, Z.: A novel framework for web page classification using two-stage neural network. In: Li, X., Wang, S., Dong, Z.Y. (eds.) ADMA 2005. LNCS (LNAI), vol. 3584, pp. 499–506. Springer, Heidelberg (2005). https://doi.org/10.1007/11527503_60
10. Munford, M.: How WordPress ate the internet in 2016… and the world in 2017. https://www.forbes.com/sites/montymunford/2016/12/22/how-wordpress-ate-the-internet-in-2016-and-the-world-in-2017/. Accessed 2 Feb 2019
11. Omnet++. https://omnetpp.org/. Accessed 18 Feb 2019
12. Opole University of Technology website. https://www.po.opole.pl/. Accessed 2 June 2018
13. Pandey, S., Linlin, W.L., Guru, S.M., Buyya, R.: A particle swarm optimization-based heuristic for scheduling workflow applications in cloud computing environments. In: 2010 24th IEEE International Conference on Advanced Information Networking and Applications, Perth, WA, Australia, pp. 20–23 (2010)
14. Chou, P.-H., Li, P.-H., Chen, K.-K., Wu, M.-J.: Integrating web mining and neural network for personalized e-commerce automatic service. J. Expert Syst. Appl. Int. J. **37**(4), 2898–2910 (2010)
15. Prakash, A.: Acceptable Website Load Times for Best User Experience. https://sprout24.com/acceptable-website-load-times-best-user-experience/. Accessed 21 Nov 2016
16. Ramana, K., Ponnavaikko, M., Subramanyam, A.: A global dispatcher load balancing (GLDB) approach for a web server cluster. In: Kumar, A., Mozar, S. (eds.) ICCCE 2018. LNEE, vol. 500, pp. 341–357. Springer, Singapore (2019). https://doi.org/10.1007/978-981-13-0212-1_36

17. Sahi, S., Dhaka, V.S.: Study on predicting for workload of cloud services using Artificial Neural Network. In: Proceeding of 2nd International Conference on Computing for Sustainable Global Development (INDIACom), New Delhi, India, pp. 331–335 (2015)
18. Global digital population as of January 2019 (in millions). https://www.statista.com/statistics/617136/digital-population-worldwide/. Accessed 18 Feb 2019
19. Suchacka, G., Wotzka, D.: Modeling a session-based bots' arrival process at a web server. In: Paprika, Z.Z., Horák, P., Váradi, K., Zwierczyk, P.T., Vidovics-Dancs, A. (eds.) Proceedings of the 31st European Conference on Modelling and Simulation (ECMS 2017), Budapest, Hungary, pp. 605–612 (2017)
20. Van Giang, T., Debusschere, V., Seddik, B.: Neural networks for web server workload forecasting. In: 2013 IEEE International Conference on Industrial Technology (ICIT), Cape Town, South Africa, 25–28 February 2013. https://doi.org/10.1109/icit.2013.6505835
21. Zatwarnicki, K.: Adaptive control of cluster-based web systems using neuro-fuzzy models. Int. J. Appl. Math. Comput. Sci. (AMCS) 22(2), 365–377 (2012)

Real Time Region of Interest Determination and Implementation with Integral Image

Frédéric Amiel[1($\boxtimes$)], Barry Boubacar[1], Anand Krishnamoorthy[1],
Maria Trocan[1($\boxtimes$)], and Marc Swynghedauw[2]

[1] Institut Supérieur d'Electronique de Paris, 28, rue NdC, 75006 Paris, France
{frederic.amiel,boubacar.barry,maria.trocan}@isep.fr
[2] CTO Suricog, 130, rue de Lourmel, 75015 Paris, France
ms@suricog.com

Abstract. In this paper we propose a real time (100 frames/sec) Region of Interest (ROI) detection algorithm based on the Integral Image calculation and its implementation on FPGA, while considering algorithm's optimization and power consumption. This system is designed for an embedded system connected to a CCD sensor inserted on glasses for precise eye tracking purposes. The ROI detection permits to select the useful data for a precise eye tracker algorithm. Compared with the state-of-the-art methods, this architecture proves its efficiency considering the processing speed and the power consumption for data flow operations in real time. We also explore the possibility to handle the computation load by embedded processors in order to show that FPGAs are ten time more efficient when considering power dissipation.

Keywords: Integral image · Power optimization · Processing speed · FPGA · Embedded processors

1 Introduction

The gaze data are the fastest and the most human responsive signal [1]. Detecting precisely the location of pupil is part of such a system. Combined with head precise orientation, it allows detecting the direction of the gaze. This information can be used to control devices in a digital environment but also to analyze eyes parallelism or movement for medical diagnosis.

SuriCog 2 is a start-up on the market of precise eye tracking systems. They have developed algorithms that identify gaze direction by using the combination of the analysis of two systems: one camera mounted on glasses close to one of the eyes, which determines pupil localization, and an external smart sensor [2] which localizes head position. The combination of these two sources gives the gaze direction. In this paper, we consider the real time detection of candidate ROIs. This part of the image is then passed to some further algorithms which will precisely determine pupil contour in order to identify gaze direction [3].

The sensor will provide black and white images at 100 frames per second with a resolution of 640 pixels by 480 pixels. This provides a data rate of more than 38 Mbytes per second, flow difficult to handle in real time by a microcontroller. On our

© Springer Nature Switzerland AG 2019
N. T. Nguyen et al. (Eds.): ICCCI 2019, LNAI 11684, pp. 629–638, 2019.
https://doi.org/10.1007/978-3-030-28374-2_54

architecture, this information is processed by a System on Programmable Chip (SoPC) which associates a microprocessor (ARM) with an FPGA. The FPGA operates the Region of Interest detection which permits to reduce the amount of data. The ROI is further compressed [3] by the embedded processor or the FPGA [4] and transmitted to an external system (p-Box) via a Bluetooth link. This p-Box models the pupil as an ellipse and combines this information with head direction to project gaze direction.

The full algorithm used to localize pupil with a high precision uses floating point calculation and it is protected by SuriCog Company. The camera is integrated on glasses connected to WEETSY system by a cable. The WEETSY system is wearable; it handles the SoC system and the Bluetooth transmitter (Fig. 1).

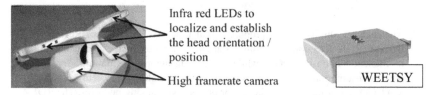

Fig. 1. Glasses used for eye image acquisition and its receiving box.

In this paper we use the ROI detection to compare the implementation on processor and on FPGA with respect to their speed performances and their power consumption.

The chosen algorithm to find the ROI uses summed-area table proposed by Crow [6] also denominate Integral Image followed by an analyzer which uses this data to determine the ROI [5].

In the sequel, we introduce the algorithm and its design in Sect. 2; Sect. 3 describes the implementation on the mixed processors-FPGA system. Section 4 summarizes the measures of speed and power of FPGA solution versus a processor- based one, and finally, conclusions are drawn in Sect. 5.

2   Algorithm Description

The ROI detection permits to reduce the amount of data to further processing (identifying and modeling the pupils as an ellipse). As the images are quite simple (Fig. 2) the further described algorithm has proved its efficiency.

The size of the pupil may vary depending on the lighting conditions (Fig. 2) and the ROI must include its size (i.e., pupil's size). The pupil is black when the outer parts are clearer (depending on the iris color the contrast is more or less important). We define a box (Candidate ROI) which should contain the pupil and an outside bigger box around it. The principle is to count the summation of the pixel luminance in each box and compute the ratio between them (Eq. 1) (Fig. 3) shows two different examples with two different sizes of the pupil due to different light conditions. In the equation $P(x, y)$ refers to the pixels in the corresponding area.

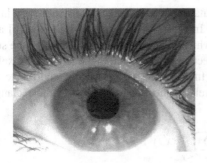

Fig. 2. Eye images as recorded by the sensors.

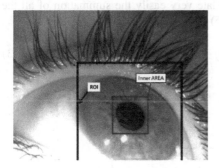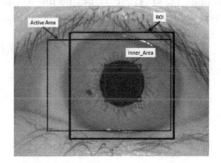

Fig. 3. Examples of ROI candidates.

$$R = \frac{\sum_{ROI} P(x,y)}{\sum_{InnerAREA} P(x',y')} \qquad (1)$$

In some cases the ROI contains pixels outside the original image. In this case, we complete the image by mirroring the used border.

We test different positions for the ROI, when the inner box contains the pupil and the outside box contains the iris, and quantify them to a maximum ratio. Figure 4 shows two different propositions with their ratios.

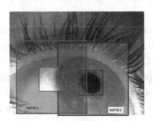

Fig. 4. Ratio1 = 8,40 (in red) Ratio2 = 19,38 (in blue). (Color figure online)

Determining the ROI implies the computation of luminance pixels sum for a huge number of possible positions. The Integral Image ii(x, y) proposed by Crow [6] and defined in Eq. 2 is a two dimensions table which contains for each of its value the sum of all the pixels of the image located in the rectangle above and to the left of the pixel in x, y. As example, the value of the Integral Image table in Fig. 5 in A (coordinate Ax and Ay) correspond to the sum of the pixels in the image enclose in the rectangle defined by (0, Ax, A, Ay).

$$ii(x, y) = \sum_{x' < x, y' < y} i(x', y') \qquad (2)$$

The integral image sums thus all the pixels above and to the left of a given pixel position (x, y). These values permit to calculate very easily the summation of all the pixel values inside a rectangular area (Fig. 5) (Eq. 3) [6].

$$\sum_{\substack{x0 < x \leq x1 \\ y0 < y \leq y1}} i(x', y') = ii(D) + ii(A) - ii(B) - ii(C) \qquad (3)$$

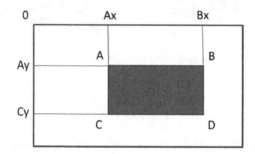

Fig. 5. Location of reference points in (3).

3 Implementation Framework

The used sensor provides an image of 640 * 480 pixels (VGA resolution) of 10 bits each with a frame rate of 100 images par second. This provides a stream of 38 Mega Bytes per second.

According to algorithm parameterization, we define an active area of 400 × 288 pixels where the pupil is still located indifferent of the gaze direction.

After its detection, the ROI will be processed by a further algorithm which will model the contour as an ellipse. The ROI will be searched with a step of 16 pixels inside the active zone. Then 450 ROI candidates have to be estimated.

We use an internal area of 112 * 112 pixels when the ROI has a size of 336 * 336 pixels.

The process is then the following for each image:

- Compute the Integral Image and store only 4 * 450 = 1800 results.
- Compute the 450 ratio and keep the best result.

According to these parameters, the ratio uses a divide operator which needs at least a precision of 25 bits divided by 22 bits.

The classical algorithm to compute the Integral Image is given in Eq. 4:

$$s(x,y) = s(x, y-1) + i(x,y)$$
$$ii(x,y) = ii(x-1), y) + s(x,y)$$

(4)

However, this implies to store the result of the ii array for all the pixels with a resolution of 28 bits. As an addition step of 16 pixels is suitable for our Integral Image results, we use a counter to store the summation of pixel values from the beginning of the line to the current position (Fig. 6).

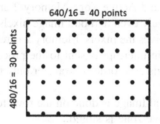

Fig. 6. One point/16 pixels to store the Integral Image values.

The Integral Image table contains 1200 values of 28 bits each at the maximum. As the pupil can be at the border of the active zone, some pixels used to compute the Integral Image are outside the border. In this case we mirror the inner part of image to the outer part.

Integral Image calculation is a data flow algorithm, this kind of process is quite easy to implement in FPGA. Also FPGA is mandatory to handle the image acquisition sensor. In this section we will describe the realized architecture.

The FPGA is connected to an external 32 bits wide static memory which is used to store the image and provide it to the processor on charge to send the selected part of the image (ROI) to the communication device.

The sensor provides a stream with the pixels luminance. The pixels are grouped by four. Each pixel inside the active zone is stored into a memory and a line buffer memorize 640/16 = 40 sums of 16 pixels (Fig. 6).

The following processing line uses the information of the previous line summation (stored in the line buffer) to calculate the integral image value (Fig. 7) [7].

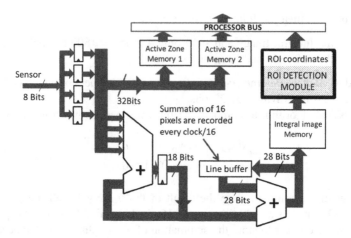

Fig. 7. Integral Image calculator.

Active Zone Memory 1 and Active Zone Memory 2 are dual port memory (inside FPGA). They store respectively even and odd image pixels (only the part in the active zone). When Memory 1 receives the pixels, Memory 2 is readable by the processor and vice versa. At each frame, an interrupt is sent to the processor which reads the coordinate of the ROI from a register in order to transfer only the interesting part (ROI) to the communication link.

The calculation of Integral Image is done on the row, for the full 640 * 480 pixels, but only the part on the active zone is stored.

The internal memory of the FPGA is used and configured as dual port which permits to store the image on one of the bus when the processor can read by the other one.

The pixel clock is set at 50 MHz and the internal FPGA clock is set at 100 MHz maximum in order to optimize power consumption. Two clocks periods are available to manage each pixel. Using 32 bits wide busses permit to handle 4 pixels on a row during 8 clock periods.

For each ROI, the sum of pixel values of Inner Area and ROI (Fig. 3) must be calculated.

Fig. 8. Integral image truncation in ROI image determination.

As the Inner Area is 112 pixels, the maximum sum of all pixels fit on 23 bits when the summation of al pixels in the ROI needs 25 bits at maximum to be represented.

The ratio to quote the ROI requires a division of a 25 bits number by a 23 bits number. But the simulation proves it is possible to round the number of bits as shown in Fig. 8.

A comparator on the quotient permits to keep the greatest ratio. If the quotients are equals the rest permits to determine the best choice. In this case, the coordinates of the ROI are stored in a register to be read by the processor.

The calculation of the 450 ROI ratios starts as soon as the results are recorded in the Integral Image Table. The determination of the best ROI is completely accomplished after each frame.

The architecture of the best ROI detection module is represented in Fig. 9.

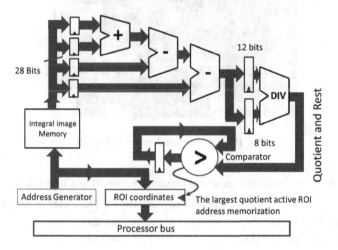

Fig. 9. Best ROI detection module.

The processor bus is clocked at 60 MHz on one side; at the other side (and due to dual access memory configuration) two clock periods are used at each access. The FPGA uses a 200 MHz clock to sequence the memory.

4 Measurements and Experimental Comparison

The previously described hardware architecture permits to handle 100 frames per second and we have implemented this scheme on two different boards.

(1) A custom board (Fig. 10) with an INTEL 10 Cyclone III [8] (65 nm technology) associated with a RENESAS RZ processor [9] (ARM core A9 clocked at 400 MHz).

(2) A custom board with an INTEL Cyclone V [8] (28 nm technology FPGA) with an ARM processor core A8 integrated in a microcontroller from Renesas company [9].

On these platforms, a 32 bits wide external static memory is used for other processes (as compression and part of pupil position modeling). Table 1 shows the results concerning the maximum speed reachable by these FPGAs.

Fig. 10. Custom board with Cyclone III

Table 1. Performance comparison between Cyclone III and V FPGA boards.

	FPGA working freq max	Time	Frames/sec at freq max
FPGA Cyclone III	203	4,9 ms	203
FPGA Cyclone V	434	2,3 ms	434

We also have programed the algorithm on the embedded processor and Table 2 describes the results.

Table 2. Performance comparison between ARM Cortex A8 and A9 processors.

	Time	Nb frames/sec
ARM Cortex A8 1 GHz	9 ms	111
ARM Cortex A9 400 MHz	18	55

Another important point is the power consumption; Table 3 gives the results for those platforms.

As it can be seen in Table 3 embedded processors can reach a high speed but dissipates ten times more power than FPGAs.

Table 3. Performance in terms of power consumption.

	Power	Nb frame/sec	mW/Frame
FPGA C III 100 MHz	193 mW	100	1,93
FPGA C III 203 MHz	280 mW	203	1,38
FPGA C V 100 MHz	107 mW	100	1,07
FPGA C V 434 MHz	249 mW	434	0,57
RENESAS 400 MHz	624 mW	55	11,34
Core A8 1 GHz	1560 mW	111	14,05

Table 4 summarizes some comparison results with respect to the state of the art in integral image implementations. In general, the authors focus on processing speed to handle images with various resolutions. In order to increase the speed they use some large memory bus to access to the source image. This approach is not useable in our case where we have an 8 bits sensor providing the stream of pixels.

Table 4. Performance of the proposed implementation with respect to existing algorithms.

	Processing time for a frame	Power/frame
Ouyang [10] –Large BW-	0,2 ms	9 mW
Velenzuela [11] - 4 pixels-	0,78 ms	–
Bilgic [12] –GPU-	0,7 ms	210 mW
Our Work Cyclone III	5 ms	1,38 mW
Our Work Cyclone V	2 ms	0,57 mW

Ouyang [10] uses a parallel approach in order to increase the speed when using a large bus to access to the memory. Velenzuela [11] uses a Xilinx Zync-7000 device and operate at 100 MHz, but take 4 pixels on a row which is not possible with one sensor at VGA resolution. Bilgic [12] demonstrate the performances reachable with GPU we select the same resolution for comparison purpose. In his description Bilgic [12] uses a NVIDIA Geoforce GTC 295 which is not designed for embedded systems. Its power consumption is around 300 W and is far more than those of FPGAs or embedded CPU-based implementations. NVIDIA propose some GPU modules more specifically designed for embedded application which are not tested here.

Concerning application purpose, this architecture will be used to handle one or two sensors. In this latter case, it is possible to choose between using an operating frequency at 200 MHz instead of 100 MHz, which implies to increase the complexity of the sequencer or to double the area of the component.

5 Conclusion

In this paper, we have proposed a ROI detector based on real time Integral Image calculation for VGA resolution images. Compared with the state-on-the-art methods the proposed architecture achieves the needed computation speed with less power than existing implementations. We demonstrate in this use-case that FPGAs and moreover new FPGA families are more suitable to implement data flow algorithms for embedded systems, than solutions based on CPUs. This solution can be used for applications which need real time processing but are not competitive to act as an external Integral Image IP.

References

1. Dodge, R., Cline, T.S.: The angle velocity of eye movements. Psychol. Rev. **8**(2), 145–157 (1901)
2. www.suricog.fr
3. Morozkin, P., Swynghedauw, M., Trocan, M.: An image compression for embedded eye-tracking applications. In: International Symposium on Innovations in Intelligent Systems and Applications (INISTA) (2016)
4. Amiel, F., Barry, B., Trocan, M., Swynghedauw, M.: Real time image compression for eye tracking applications. In: Latin American Symposium on Circuits and Systems (LASCAS) (2015)
5. Morozkin, P., Swynghedauw, M., Trocan, M.: Neural network based eye tracking. In: Nguyen, N.T., Papadopoulos, G.A., Jędrzejowicz, P., Trawiński, B., Vossen, G. (eds.) ICCCI 2017. LNCS (LNAI), vol. 10449, pp. 600–609. Springer, Cham (2017). https://doi.org/10.1007/978-3-319-67077-5_58
6. Crow, F.: Summed-area tables for texture mapping. In: Proceedings of SIGGRAPH, vol. 18, no. 3, pp. 207–212 (1984)
7. Ehsan, S., Clark, A.F., McDonald-Maier, K.D.: Novel hardware algorithms for row-parallel integral image calculation. In: Digital Image Computing: Techniques and Applications (2009)
8. www.intel.com
9. www.renesas.com
10. Ouyang, P., Yin, S., Zhang, Y., Liu, L., Wei, S.: A fast integral image computing hardware architecture with high power and area efficiency. IEEE Trans. Circ. Syst.—ii: Express Briefs **62**(1), 75–79 (2015)
11. Valenzuela-López, O.G., Tecpanecatl-Xihuitl, J.L., Aguilar-Ponce, R.M.: A novel low latency integral image architecture. In: IEEE Autumn Meeting on Power, Electronics and Computing (ROPEC) (2017)
12. Bilgic, B., Horn, B.K.P., Masaki, I.: Efficient integral image computation on the GPU. In: 2010 IEEE Intelligent Vehicles Symposium University of California, San Diego, CA, USA (2010)

Automatic Detection of Play and Break Segments in Basketball Videos Based on the Analysis of the Slope of the Basketball Court Boundary

Kazimierz Choroś(✉) and Kamil Paruszkiewicz

Faculty of Computer Science and Management, Wrocław University of Science and Technology, Wyb. Wyspiańskiego 27, 50-370 Wrocław, Poland
kazimierz.choros@pwr.edu.pl

Abstract. Content-based video analysis is still a very intensively developed area of research in computer science. One of the most frequent purpose of content-based analysis is a video summarization. A basketball game coverage usually lasts for around two hours whereas the game itself is less than one hour. The basketball video can be modeled as a sequence of plays being defined as the segments when an important action occurs interleaved with breaks which can be ignored in video summarizing or highlight detection automatic processes. The paper proposes a method a basketball game segmentation into plays and breaks. The proposed method is based on the analysis of the slope of the basketball top court boundary. The tests performed in the AVI Indexer showed that the analysis of the slope of the playing field leads to the correct detection of more than 85% of play and break segments.

Keywords: Content-based video analysis · Automatic video summarization · Highlight detection · Basketball video segmentation · Slope of the court boundary · Play and break segments · AVI Indexer

1 Introduction

Videos are usually very long sequences of recorded events. In many sports disciplines a game, a match, a cycling or car race, a duel of two or more players, and other sports competitions may last up even several hours. After recording such a game it is desirable to summarize this game and edit short video only with the most interesting highlights such as goals scored, free kicks or penalties, corners, fouls, volleyball spikes, basketball shot or slam dunk, tennis winner balls, cycling race finishes, very nice ski jumping, etc. The main purpose of content-based analysis is to automatically detect these highlights in recorded sports videos.

In many sports disciplines a game is composed of play sequences but also of different types of breaks, that is idle time when the ball is not in play, e.g. pre-game performance and ceremonies, performance of cheerleader groups, change of players, commercials, time-outs, etc. In some sports the play sequences which contain the most important moments of intense action are the main part of a game although they may

© Springer Nature Switzerland AG 2019
N. T. Nguyen et al. (Eds.): ICCCI 2019, LNAI 11684, pp. 639–648, 2019.
https://doi.org/10.1007/978-3-030-28374-2_55

occur sparsely during the game. It happens in basketball, hokey, tennis, and others sports. Whereas the remaining time that is break (non-play) parts are usually less important. Therefore, we can model the video as a sequence of plays being defined as the segments when an important action occurs interleaved with breaks which can be ignored when video summarizing or automatic highlight detection.

A basketball game usually lasts for around two hours although the game itself is less than an hour. The detection of play and break shots enables us to skip fouls, free throws, and time-out events.

In this paper a method a basketball game segmentation into plays and breaks is proposed. The presented new method is based on the analysis of the slope of the basketball top court boundary. The paper is structured as follows. The next section describes related work on the basketball video analysis and the detection of plays and breaks scenes in sports videos. The experiment to verify the new method is presented in the third and forth sections. The fifth section presents the results of the tests. The final conclusions and remarks are presented in the last section.

2   Related Work

Basketball videos have been used in many experiments on content-based video indexing. The first works were based on event detection by selecting significant shots. In [1] nine major events were detected such as team offense at left court, team offense at right court, fast break to left, fast break to right, score in left court, score in right court, dunk in left court, dunk in right court, and close-ups for audience or players (nongame shots). A supervised rule-based video classification system was developed and classification accuracies from 70% to 82% and the recall rate from 76% to 89% were obtained in the experiments.

Ekin and Tekalp [2] proposed a general framework for sports video summarization where a method of shot type classification distinguishing play and break shots in football, tennis, basketball, and soccer was proposed. The proposed algorithm uses only shot type and shot length.

Whereas a method proposed in [3] is based on tracking score changes of the game by reading the numbers on the score board. The authors noticed that it leads to the selection of semantically important and interesting scenes. They performed the experiments to show that the proposed method can summarize basketball video with reasonable accuracy.

Then in [4] it has been shown that segments can be automatically detected in a basketball video on the basis of the analysis a GOP-based scene. The length of a shot and the number of dominant color pixels of each frame were used to classify shots into close-up view, medium view, and full court view. The goal of this approach was to gather the information about the most possible shooting positions of a player, which can be useful for opponents to adopt appropriate defense tactics.

The authors of [5] aimed to correctly detect interested events, long shots, and close-up shots suitable for user preferences. To get it for the basketball video a shot ontology inferred by such shot manipulations as: shot detection, shot type classification, score board detection, and motion statistics was developed.

In [6] the court-based camera calibration technique was ameliorated to be applicable to broadcast basketball videos. Player trajectories are extracted from the video by one of the tracking methods and then mapped to the real-world court coordinates according to the calibrated results.

Also in [7] a technique of calibrating camera motions in basketball videos was proposed. This method transformed player positions to standard basketball court coordinates and in consequence facilitated the analysis of basketball team tactics.

A new feature-representation method was proposed in [8] for recognizing actions in broadcast videos, which focuses on the relationship between human actions and camera motions. The key point trajectories were extracted as motion features in spatio-temporal sub-regions. The basketball players are frequently and quickly moving and changing the position in broadcast sports videos. The co-occurrence between player actions and camera motion actions was observed and therefore it can be useful to separate the player motion from the background motion. The experiments confirmed that the proposed method can significantly detect specific human actions in broadcast basketball videos.

In order to detect players on the basketball court in basketball videos including their body parts it has been proposed in [9] to use a model based on mixture of non-oriented pictorial structures and information on locations. Unfortunately, the player detection process also resulted in detecting people from the audience and the referees as players. Some solutions based on the detection of court boundaries and the area below the basket were also proposed to remove fans or referees and to identify only the positions of players. However, the recognition of postures and gestures of referees for example holding the penalty card above the head and looking towards the player that has committed a serious offense can be very useful in highlights extraction process [10]. These special gestures and postures of referees can be recognized mainly in close-up and medium close view shots.

The method of the movement prediction of basketball referees has been proposed in [11] using a multilayered perceptron neural network. Such a network is working on the basis of a ball movement during a play action.

The paper [12] verified the effectiveness of leveraging contextual cues derived from the environment in selecting the most amazing throws into the basket and the most exciting highlights in a basketball game.

In a very recently published paper [13] an interesting observation is noticed that in broadcast basketball videos specific camera motions are used to present specific events. And therefore, an ontology-based global and collective motion pattern algorithm for basketball event classification was proposed. The experimental results demonstrated that the proposed scheme improved the average precision of the event classification process.

One of the interesting challenges in sports video analysis is the detection of plays and breaks segments. It is especially important in basketball but also in such sports disciplines as volleyball, tennis, ski jumping, ice hockey, and to different extent in many others. A basketball game usually lasts for around two hours whereas the game itself is less than one hour. Therefore, the basketball video can be modeled as a sequence of plays being defined as the segments when an important action occurs interleaved with breaks which can be ignored in video summarizing or highlight detection automatic processes.

In [14] shot length and shot type features were used to determine play and break segments. It was there noticed that a long shot usually indicates a play. Basketball rules allow a team to play 24 s to prepare the throw into the basket. The most plays last less than 24 s and more than 10 s. But if during a play or immediately after an interesting action on the field, medium shots or player close-ups are detected, they should be also classified as play. Generally, if the shot between two play shots lasts less than a threshold value defined as the maximum allowable time between two long shot play events, it should be labeled as play.

The play event in the racket sports, which has a unique structure characteristic, was referred in [15] to as rally. In this research a racket sports video was segmented into rally and break events and then ranked according to their degrees of excitement. Thus, this approach combined the structure event detection with the highlight ranking.

According to the ratio of the number of dominant-color pixels to that of the whole frame, shots can be classified into court view or non-court view. The authors of the paper [16] simply stated that in tennis matches court view and non-court view shots respectively represent plays and breaks.

The paper [17] presents a two-stage hierarchical method for play and break detection in non-edited sports videos. In the first stage, bag-of-words event detectors are trained to recognize key events. These key events are line changes, face-offs, and preliminary play-breaks. Whereas in the second stage, a context descriptor is created to classify the output of the detectors along with a novel feature based on spatio-temporal interest points. The accuracy achieved in the experiments with ice hockey games was very satisfactory comparing to the results of other methods.

Finally, we can distinguish different meanings of plays and break video segments. Sport videos such as sports news are edited videos and then they are structured [18]. Sometimes they are continuous when the whole game is recorded by the only one camera. The play part is composed of the sequence of shots in which the ball is inside the field and the game is going on. These can also be shots when a player is running, jumping, swimming, etc. While the break part represents shots when the ball is outside the playing field or for example the audience is shown. This differentiation is not obvious in the case of surveillance videos. The surveillance video is usually a continuous video, so, we can distinguish the parts with some recorded activities and without any activity. Then, the TV streams have different characteristics. TV video content should be first of all segmented into individual programs by detecting the start and end of all the programs and breaks in the stream and later trying to annotate automatically each program by some metadata that summarizes its content or identifies its type. Most of the breaks are simply commercials which we usually want to skip. In [19] TvToC – TV stream table of content is defined that adds a new level in the hierarchical traditional video decomposition.

3 Basketball Video Used in the Tests

Segmentation of a video is a fundamental process leading to the identification of the standard basic video units, and then to annotate the content of these parts. The basketball video used in the experiment performed in the AVI Indexer [20] was the basketball match recorded during the XXXI Olympic Games in Rio de Janeiro. The Table 1 presents the characteristics of the part of the game used in the experiments. The detailed results will be presented and analyzed for this part of the video (Fig. 1).

Table 1. Events in the analyzed part of the basketball video.

Event symbol	Time	Description
Z1	04:32.00	Break, close-up view of the player
B1	04:34.45	Camera change, view on the right side of the playing field, referee with a ball
Z2	04:41.40	Close-up view of the player
B2	04:44.15	Long view of the playing field, game start from the right basket, offence at the left side
S1	04:45.46	Centre of the playing field, camera is moving to the left
A1	04:54.46	Ball throw into the basket
Z3	04:57.11	Play, close-up view of the player running to the right
B3	05:00.17	View on the playing field, team running to the right
S2	05:01.42	Centre of the playing field, camera is moving to the right
A2	05:12.08	Taking over the ball near right basket
S3	05:14.11	Centre of the playing field, camera is moving to the left
A3	05:18.09	Taking over the ball near left basket
S4	05:20.44	Centre of the playing field, camera is moving to the right
B4	05:30.06	Break, referee whistled foul, view on the playing field
Z4	05:34.05	Cut, close-up view of the player

(a) Event Z1   (b) Event B1   (c) Event Z2   (d) Event B2   (e) Event S1

(f) Event A1   (g) Event Z3   (h) Event B3   (i) Event S2   (j) Event A2

(k) Event S3   (l) Event A3   (m) Event S4   (n) Event B4   (o) Event Z4

Fig. 1. Key-frames of the events in the analyzed part of the basketball video.

4   Slope of the Basketball Top Court Boundary

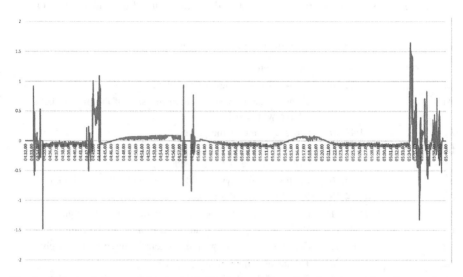

Fig. 2. Values of slope of the basketball top court boundary for the analyzed part of the basketball game.

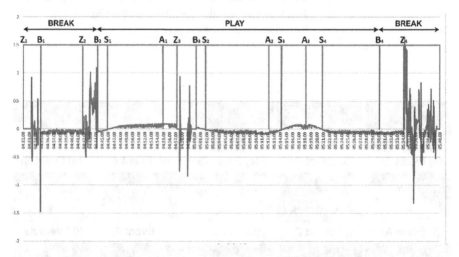

Fig. 3. Comparison of events occurring in the analyzed part of the basketball video with the slope of the basketball top court boundary.

The changes in a basketball game can be analyzed by examining the plot of the values of slope of the basketball top court boundary (Fig. 2). The positive value in the plot signals that the game is played on the left part of the basketball court, whereas the negative value – on the right part of the court. The curve passes the horizontal axis when the camera is directed exactly to the centre of the court. It results from the fact that during the basketball game the main camera is usually placed just in front of the center of the basketball court.

Figure 3 presents the events occurring in the analyzed part of the basketball video in comparison to the slope of the basketball top court boundary. Whereas Fig. 4 shows the differences between consecutive values of the slope of the basketball top court boundary.

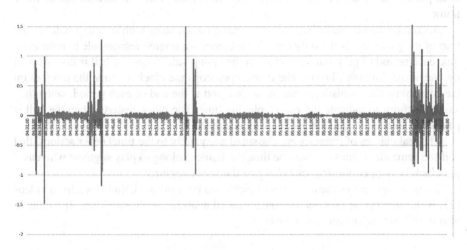

Fig. 4. Differences between consecutive values of the slope of the basketball top court boundary for the analyzed part of the basketball video.

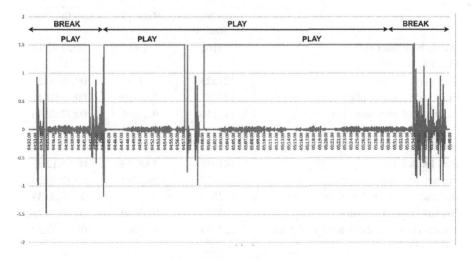

Fig. 5. Results of classification of frames into play frames and break frames in comparison with disturbances in slope shape (differences of consecutive values of the slope). On the top of the graph real types of game (plays or breaks) are marked.

The last figure (Fig. 5) justifies the assumption that the changes and the distur-bances in slope shape can be a criterion for play and break classification.

5   Analysis of the Classification Results

To verify the usefulness of the observations of changes in the slope of the basketball top court boundary the classification of all frames of the tested basketball video have been performed. Then the results have been compared with real annotations of these frames.

According to the basketball rules the game commences with a "jump ball" at the start of the game this is the only time. Timekeeper – a referee responsible to accurately time each period of play starts the clock at the "jump ball" when the ball is first touched by one of the jumping players. The timekeeper stops the clock anytime the referees on the court blow their whistle, violation or foul, and at the end of each period, when they sound the horn to indicate the end of playing time. The clock restarts when the ball is passed on to the court and is touched by a player.

The real classes of frames were classified adequately to the timekeeper actions, that is if the game clock counts down the time the frames belong to play segment whereas if the clock is stopped the frames belong to the break segment.

In some approaches the detection of clock and the reading digital clock from videos [21] is the supporting process for content-based analysis of digital videos. It would be also useful for basketball video analysis.

Table 2. Results obtained in the classification process based on the analysis of the differences of the values of slope of the basketball top court boundary.

	Number of frames	Ratio [%]	Length of time
Whole basketball video	263161	100	01:27:43.11
PLAYS			
Real plays	121523	46.1782	00:40:30.23
Frames detected as plays	141241	53.6709	00:47:04.41
Accuracy of play detection	112146	92.2838	00:37:22.46
Positive predictive value	112146	79.4005	00:37:22.46
BREAKS			
Real breaks	141638	53.8218	00:47:12.38
Frames detected as breaks	121920	46.3291	00:40:38.20
Accuracy of break detection	112543	79.4582	00:37:30.43
Negative predictive value	112543	92.3089	00:37:30.43
Total accuracy of the detection of plays and breaks	224689	85.3808	01:14:53.39

The results obtained in the classification process based on the analysis of the differences of the values of slope of the basketball top court boundary are very promising (Table 2). The accuracy of play detections on the level of 92% is very satisfactory. The accuracy of break detections is slightly lower (almost 80%) than for play detections. In average the accuracy of this process was over 85%.

6 Conclusions

Sports videos are considered to be the most popular videos in the Internet. Many attempts have been undertaken to automatically retrieve sports highlights such as soccer goals, penalty kicks, very nice ski jumping, race finishes, and other amazing and great sports moments in player behaviors or actions, etc.

One of the most frequent purpose of content-based sports video analysis is a video summarization. Because a basketball game usually lasts even more than two hours whereas the game itself is less than one hour, it is desirable to be able to automatically select play segments and to ignore break segments. A method a basketball game segmentation into plays and breaks based on the analysis of the slope of the basketball top court boundary was proposed.

The results obtained in the classification process based on the analysis of the differences of the values of slope of the basketball top court boundary confirm that the tracking of the court boundaries can be applied in the process of highlight detection, mainly in the detection of play and break segments.

References

1. Zhou, W., Vellaikal, A., Kuo, C.C.: Rule-based video classification system for basketball video indexing. In: Proceedings of the 2000 ACM Workshops on Multimedia, pp. 213–216. ACM (2000)
2. Ekin, A., Tekalp, A.M.: Generic play-break event detection for summarization and hierarchical sports video analysis. In: Proceedings of the International Conference on Multimedia and Expo, ICME 2003, Vol. 1, pp. 169–172. IEEE (2003)
3. Kim, E.-J., Lee, G.-G., Jung, C., Kim, S.-K., Kim, J.-Y., Kim, W.-Y.: A video summarization method for basketball game. In: Ho, Y.-S., Kim, H.J. (eds.) PCM 2005. LNCS, vol. 3767, pp. 765–775. Springer, Heidelberg (2005). https://doi.org/10.1007/11581772_67
4. Tien, M.C., Chen, H.T., Chen, Y.W., Hsiao, M.H., Lee, S.Y.: Shot classification of basketball videos and its application in shooting position extraction. In: IEEE International Conference on Acoustics, Speech and Signal Processing, ICASSP 2007, vol. 1, pp. 1085–1088. IEEE (2007)
5. Chen, Y.H., Deng, L.Y.: Event mining and indexing in basketball video. In: Fifth International Conference on Genetic and Evolutionary Computing, pp. 247–251. IEEE (2011)
6. Hu, M.C., Chang, M.H., Wu, J.L., Chi, L.: Robust camera calibration and player tracking in broadcast basketball video. IEEE Trans. Multimed. 13(2), 266–279 (2011)

7. Wen, P.C., Cheng, W.C., Wang, Y.S., Chu, H.K., Tang, N.C., Liao, H.Y.M.: Court reconstruction for camera calibration in broadcast basketball videos. IEEE Trans. Visual Comput. Graph. **22**(5), 1517–1526 (2016)

8. Takahashi, M., Naemura, M., Fujii, M., Little, J.J.: Recognition of action in broadcast basketball videos on the basis of global and local pairwise representation. In: IEEE International Symposium on Multimedia, pp. 147–154. IEEE (2013)

9. Ivankovic, Z., Rackovic, M., Ivkovic, M.: Automatic player position detection in basketball games. Multimed. Tools Appl. **72**(3), 2741–2767 (2014)

10. Choroś, K.: Highlights extraction in sports videos based on automatic posture and gesture recognition. In: Nguyen, N.T., Tojo, S., Nguyen, L.M., Trawiński, B. (eds.) ACIIDS 2017. LNCS (LNAI), vol. 10191, pp. 619–628. Springer, Cham (2017). https://doi.org/10.1007/978-3-319-54472-4_58

11. Pecev, P., Racković, M., Ivković, M.: A system for deductive prediction and analysis of movement of basketball referees. Multimed. Tools Appl. **75**(23), 16389–16416 (2016)

12. Bettadapura, V., Pantofaru, C., Essa, I.: Leveraging contextual cues for generating basketball highlights. In: Proceedings of the 24th ACM International Conference on Multimedia, pp. 908–917. ACM (2016)

13. Wu, L., et al.: Ontology based global and collective motion patterns for event classification in basketball videos. Preprint arXiv:1903.06879 (2019)

14. Ekin, A., Tekalp, A.M.: Shot type classification by dominant color for sports video segmentation and summarization. In: Proceedings of the International Conference on Acoustics, Speech, and Signal Processing, ICASSP 2003, vol. 3, pp. 173–176. IEEE (2003)

15. Liu, C., Huang, Q., Jiang, S., Xing, L., Ye, Q., Gao, W.: A framework for flexible summarization of racquet sports video using multiple modalities. Comput. Vis. Image Underst. **113**(3), 415–424 (2009)

16. Chu, W.T., Tsai, W.H.: Modeling spatiotemporal relationships between moving objects for event tactics analysis in tennis videos. Multimed. Tools Appl. **50**(1), 149–171 (2010)

17. Carbonneau, M.A., Raymond, A.J., Granger, E., Gagnon, G.: Real-time visual play-break detection in sport events using a context descriptor. In: Proceedings of the International Symposium on Circuits and Systems, ISCAS, pp. 2808–2811. IEEE (2015)

18. Choroś, K.: Video structure analysis for content-based indexing and categorisation of TV sports news. Int. J. Intell. Inf. Database Syst. **6**(5), 451–465 (2012)

19. Ibrahim, Z.A.A.: TV Stream table of content: a new level in the hierarchical video representation. J. Comput. Sci. Appl. **7**(1), 1–9 (2019)

20. Choroś, K.: Video structure analysis and content-based indexing in the automatic video indexer AVI. In: Nguyen, N.T., Zgrzywa, A., Czyżewski, A. (eds.) Advances in Multimedia and Network Information System Technologies. Advances in Intelligent and Soft Computing, vol. 80, pp. 79–90. Springer, Heidelberg (2010). https://doi.org/10.1007/978-3-642-14989-4_8

21. Yu, X., Ding, W., Zeng, Z., Leong, H.W.: Reading digital video clocks. Int. J. Pattern Recogn. Artif. Intell. **29**(04), 1555006-1-21 (2015)

Public Cloud Kubernetes Storage Performance Analysis

Lubos Mercl[✉] and Jakub Pavlik

Faculty of Informatics and Management, University of Hradec Kralove,
Rokitanskeho 62, 50003 Hradec Kralove, Czech Republic
{lubos.mercl,jakub.pavlik.7}@uhk.cz

Abstract. Public cloud solutions offer a lot of possibilities for application configuration. The well-chosen architecture and configuration are
important for the correct and efficient application run and affect performance and also user friendliness. If application runs on top of Kubernetes cluster on public cloud solutions (e.g. Amazon Elastic Container
Service for Kubernetes, Google Kubernetes Engine, Azure Kubernetes
Service) you have to, among other things, also decide what data storage to use and this decision should be based on the workload type and
requirements for other application and storage parameters. It is needed
to consider whether your application needs to store data and, in case of
failure, data are still needed (stateful application) or data are not needed
in the future with a new container (stateless application). The storage is
connected to containers via volumes and there are a lot of types of Volumes which can be mounted to containers. There can be used volumes for
block storage through dynamic provisioning but only a few technologies
for public cloud solutions, which can be used. However, it is not easy to
say which technology is the best or to use some simple test to get this
result or a similar one. The main analysis and tests have been done on
Microsoft's Azure Kubernetes Service where have been tested these storage back-ends: AKS native storage class, AWS cloud volume mapped into
the instance (via Azure hostPath with attached Azure managed disk),
OpenEBS, Portworx, Gluster with Heketi and Ceph with Rook.

Keywords: Public cloud · Kubernetes · Storage performance ·
Container virtualization · Performance measurement

1 Introduction

In past years, the application became to be more opened and cloud native. The
cloud native applications are oriented to run on some cloud computing solutions
and they are built to run on more platforms and are opened for movement
between several cloud computing solutions. The cloud native application should
also use the benefit of cloud solutions [5, 6, 33].

© Springer Nature Switzerland AG 2019
N. T. Nguyen et al. (Eds.): ICCCI 2019, LNAI 11684, pp. 649–660, 2019.
https://doi.org/10.1007/978-3-030-28374-2_56

One of cloud computing solutions, which can be used on public or private clouds, is Kubernetes [20]. Kubernetes is a platform for building cloud cluster using the container virtualization. But Kubernetes is not running computing solution, Kubernetes is a system for orchestrating and a management container application which is running on some container virtualization solution (e.g. Docker, rkt, containerd, LXD) [14,20].

Kubernetes clusters can run in private cloud solution but there are also public cloud solutions from a few companies where is provided hosted Kubernetes cluster solution in their public cloud. Between these companies belong mainly Amazon with Amazon Elastic Container Service for Kubernetes (Amazon EKS) [1,18], Microsoft with Azure Kubernetes Service (AKS) [25], and also Google with Google Kubernetes Engine (GKE) [15]. In addition, there are some small global and local providers who are providing Kubernetes cluster solution.

2   Problem Definition

One of the main goals of application development is its usage and great performance. There are several impacts which are affecting performance, from the great architecture to the well-functioning individual components. The storage is also a part of the application and a well-chosen and good working storage impact the well-working application and its performance [33,35].

2.1   Cloud Native Applications

The term Cloud Native Application includes the way how the application can be developed [9,20].

The main indicator of cloud native application is that it is working on container-based environments [7,36]. The application written for working in containers usually includes one or rather more containers where application parts are running [17]. These parts are also called microservices and their functions together make services - application. For Cloud Native Application is also important well-working elastic infrastructure, DevOps approach, Continuous Integration and Continuous Delivery (CI/CD) [24,37].

2.2   Kubernetes Architecture and Storage

The Kubernetes architecture from the application perspective is mainly based on the containers [20,34]. The applications are not created there like simple containers but they are clustered into larger objects - pods, deployments and others. The pod is the smallest object in Kubernetes which represents some application and can contain one or more containers. The deployment represents also some application and consists of pods which can be in more replicas for providing high availability feature and features for scaling and application life cycle [5–7].

From a storage perspective, storage objects in Kubernetes are persistent volumes and persistent volumes claims [20]. The persistent volume (PV) is basically placed on some storage solution which can be used for deploying services on the cluster. Storage is mounted to pods via persistent volume claim (PVC) which is a request for the storage from the cluster and these PVC requests are bounded to predefined PVs.

Another important object is a storage class which is object used for mapping quality-of-service levels and backup policies to persistent volumes.

2.3 Kubernetes Storage on Azure Kubernetes Service

This work is primarily dedicated to the testing and verification on Azure Kubernetes Service and there are several technologies, which can be used [20,25].

Native Azure Storage Class. On Azure, there is offered default storage class which is dynamically created and provided to the pods and mounted like the volume [25]. Because this is a native solution, there is not need to configure or create some additional features in your tenant on AKS cloud. This solution has 2 variants by default: default class, using normal disks for the volumes, and managed-premium class, using SSD-based high-performance and low-latency disks for the volumes.

The benefits of using this solution are mainly native support, no additional configuration, and the mounting to your configuration is simple. On the other hand, there are some disadvantages such as a very slow fail-over scenario belongs.

For the test scenarios, they were used 2 alternatives [20]:

- Azure via pvc, which is attaching a volume to the pod via Persistent Volume Claim from Persistent Volume,
- Azure via hostpath, which is attaching a volume to the pod via hostPath feature (directly from the host node's file system into the pod).

OpenEBS. OpenEBS is fully open-sourced project of containerized block storage and it is based on the new Container Attached Storage (CAS) concept where there are a single microservice-based storage controller and multiple microservice-based storage replicas [28]. OpenEBS currently provides 2 possible back-ends – Jiva and cStor.

OpenEBS's advantages are that it is an open-source project so there is community support behind it and in CAS concept support. Since it is open-source, there is a disadvantage that this solution has low maturity for production deployment, yet this should be reached soon. There is also required to install additional software (for iSCSI) on Kubernetes nodes.

Portworx. Portworx is also container-native storage designed for Kubernetes that focuses on highly distributed environments [31]. Portworx is host-addressable storage where volumes are directly mapped and attached to the nodes. This is a commercial production-ready solution but without an open code and owned by Portworx company. This product is easy to deploy and configure on Kubernetes side. Portworx solution advantage is in the possibility of tuning of performance I/O configuration.

GlusterFS with Heketi. GlusterFS is an open-source project for a storage solution which is one of the traditional open-source storage back-ends by Red Hat [13,16]. Heketi provides RESTful volume management interface for GlusterFS which provides a way for strong dynamic GlusterFS volume deployment tool.

GlusterFS with Heketi solution is proven and simple for deployment storage solution but Heketi is not well-designed for public Kubernetes clusters and also not for structured data (e.g. SQL databases).

Ceph with Rook. Ceph is a proven storage solution, too which is more complex then GlusterFS solution and provides advanced architecture and more features that can be used [10]. In a combination with Rook, which is orchestration tool, it provides a possibility of delivery of Ceph storage solution for Kubernetes on only three nodes and mainly an easy way of deployment and orchestration [32].

The advantage of this solution is the provision of a robust storage tool for large production environment and that Rook also provides a very handy orchestration tool which makes usage simpler. On the other hand, the solution is so robust that much more experience and knowledge is needed for the correct usage.

2.4   Performance Attributes

The main attributes that are needed to be analyzed are performance metrics [3,27,30]. Between these metrics belong:

- Read and write bandwidth which indicates the amount of data, that are possible to handle in a given time period (e.g. megabyte per second),
- Read and write input/output operations per second (IOPS) which indicates the number of operations per second,
- Read and write latency which indicates the response of storage when some small request is sent there.

There is also a difference between writing large data blocks and the small ones. Writing of large blocks should be faster (concerning the amount of saved data per time) because data are written sequentially. The same situation is in the read operations.

3   Related Works

Most of the research in this area is aimed at optimizing and improving the performance of existing technologies.

Arumugam [2] developed a solution for cloud storage and file systems based on cache usage and increased performance in his solution. Bhimani [4] dealt with Docker scheduler for an application running on SSD drives.

Callaghan [7] scaled workflow-based application and because of that, developed a framework to help with these applications and in addition, Calzarossa [8] researched workflow optimization for cloud computing. Zhang [41] developed an architecture for tiered cloud storage.

Liu [23] developed a software-defined file system (SDFS) for cloud storage solution where is used multi-tenancy.

Nathuji [27] developed Q-Clouds framework for dealing with performance and QoS-aware clouds.

Tarasov [34] deals with Docker container storage and its optimization of configuration.

Another area of the optimization of cloud computing solutions and cloud computing storage is security. Kavin [19] proposed a solution for secure storage on the cloud and for the Internet of Things solutions as well, and Xu [38] deals with storage platform for IoT in connection with data analysis. Modak's research [26] also deals with security and compares simple Docker Swarm and Kubernetes orchestration tool.

Juve [18] did an analysis of costs and performance on Amazon EC2 in relation to scientific operations and workflows. This analysis gets a good view of the usage of Amazon's cloud computing solution.

A few types of research focused on the optimization of resource allocation. Between these works belong Bharadwaj [3], Calzarossa [9], Javaid [17], Kumar [22], Wu [37] and Zhan [40]. Between interesting researches belongs Kumar [22] with his usage of neural network for workflow prediction in usage and allocations.

There are a lot of researches focused on the management tools and architecture for cloud computing solutions.

Masip-Bruin [24] analyzed the requirements of cloud computing solutions and proposed some rules and drafts. Padala [29] analyzed and developed a tool for the management of virtual resources, inclusive of storage resources.

Xu [39] used blockchain for decentralized image store of Docker images.

4 Methodology

The whole test procedure includes a few steps for being able to evaluate results and draw the right conclusions.

Before testing, it was needed to prepare the Azure Kubernetes Services infrastructure. There was provisioned simple Azure AKS cluster with 3 virtual machines with 1 TB of an empty disk in each instance (VM) prepared for tests.

Each technology implementation and test procedure basically consist:

1. Configuration of external third-party storage services (if any),
2. Configuration of storage back-end on Kubernetes cluster side (creating storage class, persistent volume and/or persistent volume claims),

3. Deployment of test pod for testing and mounting volume to this pod,
4. Automatic test procedure.

There are several ways to perform tests for the comparison of performance on the storage layer [21]. It can be used some existing commercial or open-source solution or write a new one. As the tool for load tests has been used project DBENCH [11] and its additional project for implementation on Kubernetes clusters [12]. By default, DBENCH tool is a tool for generating I/O workloads to either a file system or to a networked CIFS or NFS server [11]. And additional project from LogDNA company [12] is the Kubernetes deployment manifest of the pod where runs the Flexible I/O Tester with 8 test cases. Tests are specified in the Docker entrypoint.

The test procedure consists of a few tests which were performed during the performance tests and then evaluated:

- Random read and write bandwidth,
- Random read and write IOPS,
- Read and write latency,
- Sequential read and write,
- Mixed read and write IOPS.

5   Results and Discussion

After carrying out a few runs of the test, the whole data runs were analyzed, compared between each run and after validation, the average values were written into tables where can be analyzed and used for comparison of solutions.

5.1   Random Read and Write Bandwidth

This test tested the bandwidth during read and write operations. The results are shown in Table 1 and Fig. 1.

The best results for reading are shown for Portworx and GlusterFS solution. Ceph also shows great result against the native Azure solutions. The main reason is the usage of read caching. The writing shows similar results.

Table 1. Random Read and Write bandwidth.

Storage type	Read bandwidth	Write bandwidth
Azure pvc	29.9 MiB/s	28.5 MiB/s
Azure hostPath	30.4 MiB/s	28.1 MiB/s
OpenEBS	23.1 MiB/s	2.6 MiB/s
Portworx	749.0 MiB/s	21.6 MiB/s
GlusterFS	235.0 MiB/s	28.7 MiB/s
Ceph	118.0 MiB/s	13.1 MiB/s

5.2   Random Read and Write IOPS

This test tested the input and output operations per second. The results are shown in Table 2 and Fig. 2. In this case, Portworx also shows the best results for reading, thanks to read cache, and in writing tests shows almost the same result as the best solution in this area - Azure PVC.

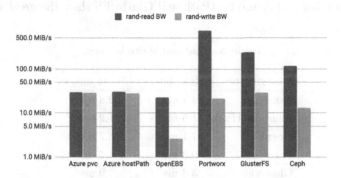

Fig. 1. Random Read and Write bandwidth.

Table 2. Random Read and Write IOPS.

Storage type	Read IOPS	Write IOPS
Azure pvc	2857	2759
Azure hostPath	3146	1080
OpenEBS	1351	715
Portworx	35200	2637
GlusterFS	2124	827
Ceph	10900	1324

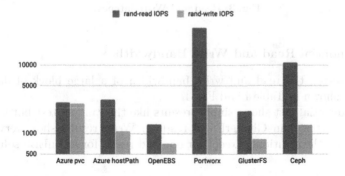

Fig. 2. Random Read and Write IOPS.

5.3   Read and Write Latency

This test tested the read and write latency, results are shown at Table 3 and Fig. 3.

The latency test shows surprising results because Azure pvc shows almost the slowest solution that the rest of them. The best results show Portworx and Ceph for reading and Azure hostPath and GlusterFS show the great result for writing.

Table 3. Read and Write latency.

Storage type	Read latency	Write latency
Azure pvc	4.4 ms	32.8 ms
Azure hostPath	1.5 ms	1.2 ms
OpenEBS	37.1 ms	466.7 ms
Portworx	0.3 ms	4.5 ms
GlusterFS	3.4 ms	2.0 ms
Ceph	0.8 ms	20.0 ms

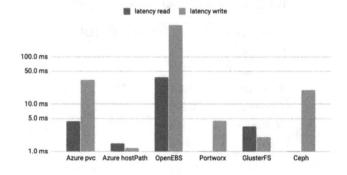

Fig. 3. Read and Write latency.

5.4   Sequential Read and Write Bandwidth

This test tested the read and write bandwidth of a large block of data. The results are shown in Table 4 and Fig. 4.

The sequential test shows similar results like the random test but Ceph was two times better than GlusterFS in reading. Write results show very similar results for all the solutions, except for one bad result for OpenEBS solution.

Table 4. Sequential Read and Write bandwidth.

Storage type	Read bandwidth	Write bandwidth
Azure pvc	31.5 MiB/s	32.2 MiB/s
Azure hostPath	31.4 MiB/s	22.8 MiB/s
OpenEBS	7.8 MiB/s	5.4 MiB/s
Portworx	824.0 MiB/s	23.6 MiB/s
GlusterFS	35.9 MiB/s	17.7 MiB/s
Ceph	81.4 MiB/s	20.8 MiB/s

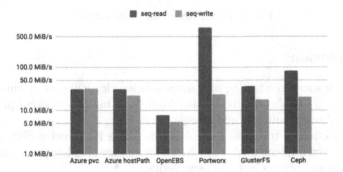

Fig. 4. Sequential Read and Write bandwidth.

5.5 Mixed Read and Write IOPS

This test tested the input and output operations per second. The results are shown in Table 5 and Fig. 5. In this test, Portworx and Ceph show better IOPS than native Azure pvc and even better write operations.

Table 5. Mixed Read and Write IOPS.

Storage type	Read IOPS	Write IOPS
Azure pvc	2144	712
Azure hostPath	1690	573
OpenEBS	185	64
Portworx	2901	971
GlusterFS	1283	422
Ceph	2612	882

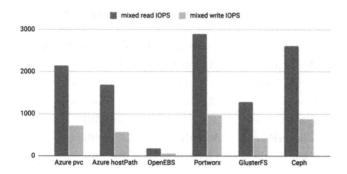

Fig. 5. Mixed Read and Write IOPS.

6   Conclusion

This research shows the testing of storage solutions for Kubernetes clusters with usage mainly on public clouds solution from three big public cloud providers – Microsoft's Azure, Amazon, and Google.

The collection of tests has been done on Azure Kubernetes Service (AKS) where have been implemented technologies for storage cloud-native solutions and the performance metrics test has been verified.

The native Azure solution is great for a simple and fast deployment without any additional features and with solid performance values. From the test results can be claimed that Portworx solution is the fastest container storage for Azure Kubernetes Service. The OpenEBS has a great concept but it needs some extra back-end optimizations from the upstream developers before this solution will be production-ready storage solution. The Ceph solution is the best storage solution for hardware clusters but it is not really for the usage of public cloud solution run because it is a complex solution.

In the end, it is needed to take into account that there are more inputs for choosing the great storage solution for specific usage and it is not only about measurable values (e.g. performance results, price) but also about non- measurable parameters of individual solutions (e.g. production ready status).

Acknowledgment. The research has been partially supported by the Faculty of Informatics and Management UHK Specific Research Project 2107 Computer Networks for Cloud, Distributed Computing, and Internet of Things II.

References

1. Amazon Web Services offers reliable, scalable, and inexpensive cloud computing services. https://aws.amazon.com/. Accessed 13 Apr 2019
2. Arumugam, R.V., Xu, Q., Shi, H., Cai, Q., Wen, Y.: Virt cache: managing virtual disk performance variation in distributed file systems for the cloud. In: IEEE 6th International Conference on Cloud Computing Technology and Science (Cloud-Com), pp. 210–217 (2014)

3. Bharadwaj, A.S.: A resource-based perspective on information technology capability and firm performance: an empirical investigation. MIS Q. Manag. Inf. Syst. **24**, 169–193 (2000)
4. Bhimani, J., et al.: Docker container scheduler for I/O intensive applications running on NVMe SSDs. IEEE Trans. Multi-Scale Comput. Syst. **4**(3), 313–326 (2018)
5. Buyya, R., Yeo, C.S., Venugopal, S., Broberg, J., Brandic, I.: Cloud computing and emerging IT platforms: vision, hype, and reality for delivering computing as the 5th utility. Future Gener. Comput. Syst. **25**(6), 599–616 (2009)
6. Buyya, R., Vecchiola, C., Selvi, S.T.: Mastering Cloud Computing, 3rd edn. McGraw Hill, New York (2013)
7. Callaghan, S., et al.: Scaling up workflow-based applications. J. Comput. Syst. Sci. **76**(6), 428–446 (2010)
8. Calzarossa, M.C., Della Vedova, M.L., Massari, L., Petcu, D., Tabash, M.I.M., Tessera, D.: Workloads in the clouds. In: Fiondella, L., Puliafito, A. (eds.) Principles of Performance and Reliability Modeling and Evaluation. SSRE, pp. 525–550. Springer, Cham (2016). https://doi.org/10.1007/978-3-319-30599-8_20
9. Calzarossa, M.C., Della Vedova, M.L., Tessera, D.: A methodological framework for cloud resource provisioning and scheduling of data parallel applications under uncertainty. Future Gener. Comput. Syst. **93**, 212–223 (2019)
10. Ceph Documentation. https://docs.ceph.com/. Accessed 13 Apr 2019
11. DBENCH website. https://dbench.samba.org/. Accessed 13 Apr 2019
12. logdna/dbench: Benchmark Kubernetes persistent disk volumes with fio: Read/write IOPS, bandwidth MB/s and latency. https://github.com/logdna/dbench. Accessed 13 Apr 2019
13. Gluster Docs. https://docs.gluster.org/. Accessed 13 Apr 2019
14. Docker - Build, Ship, and Run Any App, Anywhere. https://www.docker.com/. Accessed 13 Apr 2019
15. Google Cloud Engine. https://cloud.google.com/compute/. Accessed 13 Apr 2019
16. heketi/heketi: RESTful based volume management framework for GlusterFS. https://github.com/heketi/heketi. Accessed 13 Apr 2019
17. Javaid, S., Javaid, N., Saba, T., Wadud, Z., Rehman, A., Haseeb, A.: Intelligent resource allocation in residential buildings using consumer to fog to cloud based framework. Energies **12**(5), 818 (2019)
18. Juve, G., Deelman, E., Berriman, G.B., Berman, B.P., Maechling, P.: An evaluation of the cost and performance of scientific workflows on Amazon EC2. J. Grid Comput. **10**(1), 5–21 (2012)
19. Kavin, B.P., Ganapathy, S.: A secured storage and privacy-preserving model using CRT for providing security on cloud and IoT-based applications. Comput. Netw. **151**, 181–190 (2019)
20. Kubernetes - Production-Grade Container Orchestration. https://www.kubernetes.io/. Accessed 13 Apr 2019
21. kubernetes/perf-tests - Performance test and benchmarks. https://github.com/kubernetes/perf-tests. Accessed 13 Apr 2019
22. Kumar, J., Singh, A.K.: Workload prediction in cloud using artificial neural network and adaptive differential evolution. Future Gener. Comput. Syst. **81**, 41–52 (2018)
23. Liu, J.H., Wang, F., Zeng, L.F., Feng, D., Zhu, T.W.: SDFS: a software-defined file system for multitenant cloud storage. Softw. Pract. Exp. **49**(3), 339–558 (2019)
24. Masip-Bruin, X., Marin-Tordera, E., Tashakor, G., Jukan, A., Ren, G.J.: Foggy clouds and cloudy fogs: a real need for coordinated management of fog-to-cloud computing systems. IEEE Wirel. Commun. **23**(5), 120–128 (2016)

25. Microsoft Azure. https://azure.microsoft.com/. Accessed 13 Apr 2019
26. Modak, A., Chaudhary, S.D., Paygude, P.S., Idate, S.R.: Techniques to secure data on cloud: Docker Swarm or Kubernetes? In: 2018 Second International Conference on Inventive Communication and Computational Technologies (ICICCT) (2018)
27. Nathuji, R., Kansal, A., Ghaffarkhah, A.: Q-clouds: managing performance interference effects for QoS-aware clouds. Association for Computing Machinery, Inc. (2010)
28. OpenEBS - Container Attached Storage. https://openebs.io/. Accessed 13 Apr 2019
29. Padala, P., et al.: Automated control of multiple virtualized resources. In: Proceedings of the 4th ACM European Conference on Computer Systems, EuroSys 2009, pp. 13–26 (2009)
30. Pavlik, J., Sobeslav, V., Komarek, A.: Measurement of cloud computing services availability. In: Vinh, P.C., Vassev, E., Hinchey, M. (eds.) ICTCC 2014. LNICST, vol. 144, pp. 191–201. Springer, Cham (2015). https://doi.org/10.1007/978-3-319-15392-6_19
31. Portworx. https://portworx.com/. Accessed 13 Apr 2019
32. Rook.io. https://rook.io/. Accessed 13 Apr 2019
33. Scheepers, M.J.: Virtualization and containerization of application infrastructure: a comparison. In: 21st Twente Student Conference on IT, pp. 1–7 (2014)
34. Tarasov, V., et al.: In search of the ideal storage configuration for Docker containers. In: 2017 IEEE 2nd International Workshops on Foundations and Applications of Self* Systems (FAS*W), pp. 199–206 (2017)
35. Tchernykh, A., Schwiegelsohn, U., Talbi, E., Babenko, M.: Towards understanding uncertainty in cloud computing with risks of confidentiality, integrity, and availability. J. Comput. Sci. (2016)
36. Vecchiola, C., Pandey, S., Buyya, R.: High-performance cloud computing: a view of scientific applications. In: 2009 10th International Symposium on Pervasive Systems, Algorithms, and Networks (2009)
37. Wu, F., Wu, Q., Tan, Y.: Workflow scheduling in cloud: a survey. J. Supercomput. **71**(9), 3373–3418 (2015)
38. Xu, Q., Aung, K.M.M., Zhu, Y., Yong, K.L.: Building a large-scale object-based active storage platform for data analytics in the Internet of Things. J. Supercomput. **72**(7), 2796–2814 (2016)
39. Xu, Q., Jin, C., Rasid, M.F.B., Veeravalli, B., Aung, K.M.M.: Blockchain-based decentralized content trust for Docker images. Multimed. Tools Appl. **77**(14), 18223–18248 (2018)
40. Zhan, Z.H., Liu, X.F., Gong, Y.J., Zhang, J., Chung, H.S.H., Li, Y.: Cloud computing resource scheduling and a survey of its evolutionary approaches. ACM Comput. Surv. **47**(4) (2015)
41. Zhang, Y., Ghosh, A., Aggarwal, V., Lan, T.: Tiered cloud storage via two-stage, latency-aware bidding. IEEE Trans. Netw. Serv. Manag. **16**(1), 176–191 (2019)

Big Data Streaming, Applications and Security

Exploring Non-Human Traffic in Online Digital Advertisements: Analysis and Prediction

Sawsan Almahmoud[1], Bassam Hammo[2], and Bashar Al-Shboul[3（✉）]

[1] Department of Computer Science, King Abdullah II School for Information Technology, The University of Jordan, Amman 11942, Jordan
[2] Department of Computer Information Systems, King Abdullah II School for Information Technology, The University of Jordan, Amman 11942, Jordan
[3] Department of Information Technology, King Abdullah II School for Information Technology, The University of Jordan, Amman 11942, Jordan
bashar.shboul@gmail.com

Abstract. An advertisement (ad) click fraud occurs when a user or a bot clicks on an ad with a malicious intent where advertisers need to pay for those fake clicks. Click-fraud is a serious problem for the online advertising industry. Our study demonstrates a hybrid approach using a two-level fingerprint to detect the illegitimate bots targeting ad click fraud. The approach consists of two detection phases: (1) a rule-based phase and (2) a machine learning-based phase. The first level of the fingerprint is used for rule-based detection phase. It is generated using immutable information about the user and traversing a website's page. The second level of the fingerprint is generated using ad click behavioral patterns. It is used for machine learning-based detection phase. Different traditional classification algorithms were evaluated to be applied in the machine learning-based detection phase. To test our approach, we used a real commercial website for ads called Waseet where the access log of the website server was utilized as a dataset for our experiments. The results of our experiments show that our proposed hybrid approach entails promising results.

Keywords: Non-Human Traffic · Illegitimate bots · Legitimate bots · Click fraud

1 Introduction

Websites are usually visited by human and non-human users. Non-Human users (i.e. bots) are computer programs mimicking human keystrokes, clicking patterns, or web browsing behaviors [1]. Non-Human Traffic (NHT) has two subclasses: legitimate and illegitimate. On one hand, legitimate bots usually help websites in crawling and indexing, while illegitimate bots are software applications generated to act like humans and engage themselves into fraud [2]. It was reported that NHT represents 51.8% of the web traffic, with the illegitimate part represents 28.9% of the web traffic [3].

Examples on illegitimate NHT include Denial-of-Service (DoS) attack, spammers, ads click fraud and impersonators [1]. Ad click fraud is a program induced to imitate a

© Springer Nature Switzerland AG 2019
N. T. Nguyen et al. (Eds.): ICCCI 2019, LNAI 11684, pp. 663–675, 2019.
https://doi.org/10.1007/978-3-030-28374-2_57

legitimate user of a website by clicking on an ad without having an actual interest in the target of the ad's link. Therefore, ad click fraud is considered to be a serious problem in the online advertising market. Based on the studies that discussed in Sect. 2, we can divide the bots that target ad click fraud into three types:

1. Naive bots, which have empty or invalid HTTP user agent, where the HTTP user agent is the web browser identification string for the user
2. Primitive bots, which targeting ad click fraud and the interval time between every two clicks is fixed
3. Advanced bots, which targeting ad click fraud and the interval time between every two clicks is variable

In this study, we demonstrate a hybrid approach for ad click fraud detection. It consists of two phases: rule-based, and Machine Learning (ML)-based. The rule-based detection phase is for detecting naive illegitimate bots while the ML-based detection phase is for detecting advanced illegitimate bots; therefore, several traditional ML classification algorithms were empirically evaluated where one of which was adopted for the ML-based detection phase. In this work, also, the hybrid approach uses two different fingerprints, one for each detection phase.

In this work, a commercial advertisement website i.e. Waseet was used to test and experiment with our approach [4]. The server access logs of the website were used as dataset for the rule-based detection phase. For the ML-based detection phase, we generated ad click behavior patterns based on some observations from experiments conducted on actual users of Waseet website. The evaluation results show that the hybrid approach is promising.

The rest of this paper is organized as follows. Section 2 shows the related works. In Sect. 3, the proposed hybrid detection approach with its fingerprints is presented. The evaluation results of the proposed hybrid approach are discussed in Sect. 4. Finally, we conclude in Sect. 5.

2   Related Works

Different studies have attempted to detect the ad click fraud problem. Few researchers focused on raising the awareness of NHT and the threat in the online campaigns. Some others provided analysis for a hacked campaign account based on real-world data of online campaigns of 28 companies [5]. They provided suggestions and recommendations for damage prevention, detection, and limitation. While other researchers highlighted the increasing sophistication of ad fraud schemes as in [6]. An economic model of the effect of ad fraud for the online advertising market was suggested in [7] showing that ad networks have an incentive to aggressively combat fraud. In [8], a report about fraud and identity theft with the use of e-commerce was revealed suggesting steps that employees and customers may take to avoid identity theft [8].

In [9], the authors presented the Anodot anomaly detection system. The results of the system performed on a large set of metrics collected from multiple companies were presented. The system required advanced algorithms to learn normal behavior, an abnormal behavior probabilistic model, and scalable methods for discovering relationships between time series for the purpose of anomaly grouping. Others focused on real-time bidding in the mobile advertising industry [10] where a system for click fraud detection using server side solution was proposed. The system scanned the ads before passing them over to the end mobile device. Additionally, an extra layer was added on the backend to pass the ad payload through a headless browser and check for auto redirection via Javascript or HTML headers. The fraud detection logic then checked to see whether after the payload was loaded, there was no auto re-direction to another domain that was different from the initial domain from where all the ad assets were requested. In [11], the authors proposed a scheme to detect whether a web service is hosted by a fast-flux botnet in real time. This scheme relied on certain characteristics of fast-flux botnets. The evaluation results showed that the proposed scheme was able to detect fast-flux bots in a few seconds with more than 96% accuracy, while the false positive/negative rates were both lower than 5%. In [12], a social honeypot-based approach for social spam detection was presented. By focusing on MySpace and Twitter, the authors have seen how the general principles of social honeypot deployment, robust spam profile generation, and adaptive and ongoing spam detection could effectively harvest spam profiles and support the automatic generation of spam signatures for detecting new and unknown spam.

In [13], the authors proposed a game-theoretic model to study the behavior and interactions of the ISPs and ad networks. Cooperation between the ad networks and the ISP helped in reducing the level of online crime and improved Web security in general. In [14], the SBotMiner system was presented, i.e. a system for detecting search bot traffic from query logs at a large scale. The system identified 700K bot groups from sampled query logs collected over two different months. The percentage of bot traffic was 3.8% of total traffic stressing on the importance of computing accurate statistics from query logs. In [15], a method for botnet detection was proposed. The authors found that the technique successfully recognized Command & Control (C&C) servers with multiple domain names, while at the same time generating few or no false positives. In [16], the Dendritic Cell Algorithm (DCA) was applied to detect the ad click fraud bot showing capability of discriminating between bots and normal processes on a host machine. Using the appropriate weights for this application appeared to be useful in the reduction of potential false positives without generating false negative errors. In [17], BotSniffer was presented i.e. a network-based anomaly detection to identify botnet C&C channels in a local area network without any prior knowledge of signatures or C&C server addresses. It was able to capture spatial-temporal correlation in network traffic and utilized statistical algorithms to detect botnets with theoretical bounds on the false positive and false negative rates, showing high accuracy and a very low false positive rate. In [18], the authors evaluated two approaches for identifying botnet C&C servers based on anomalous DDNS traffic by looking for domain names whose query rates were abnormally high or temporally concentrated, and then looking for abnormally recurring DDNS replies indicating that the query was for an inexistent name. In [19], a technique was presented to detect bot-infected machines using the communication channel between bot and the C&C server. It used n-gram analysis and a scoring system to detect bots that used uncommon communication channels.

Other researchers used machine learning approaches to detect ad click fraud. A machine learning approach is proposed to identify the spam bots from normal ones on Twitter [20]. Based on the spam policy on Twitter, graph-based features and content-based features were extracted from the user's social graph and most recent tweets collected from Twitter public available information. Several popular classification algorithms were applied showing that the Bayesian classifier has the best overall performance. In [21], the authors proposed the FraudDroid approach. It was a hybrid approach to detect ad frauds in mobile Android apps by analyzing apps dynamically to build UI state transition graphs and collect their associated runtime network traffics, which are, then, leveraged to check against a set of heuristic-based rules for identifying ad fraudulent behaviors. It was reported that FraudDroid detected ad frauds with high precision and recall. In [22], a ML-based technique to Fight Click-Fraud, FCFraud, was presented showing effectiveness exceeding 99% in classifying ad requests from all user processes and it was 100% successful in finding the fraudulent processes.

Many approaches focused on raising the awareness of NHT and ad fraud [5–8] while others focused on running server scripts to detect NHT based on some static rules [9–19]. Others applied a ML approach to detect spam in social networks [20–22]. Although state-of-the-art works reported high effectiveness for detecting spams, we aim at detecting NHT for online digital ads using a hybrid detection approach based on two-level fingerprint generation, then show that our proposed approach will entail high effectiveness, as well.

3   The Hybrid Detection Approach for Illegitimate NHT

In this section, our hybrid approach for ad click fraud detection is proposed. It includes two phases: a rule-based detection phase, and a ML-based detection phase. Figure 1 depicts the framework of the suggested approach. In our approach, each user will have two fingerprints. The first fingerprint is used for the rule-based detection phase. It is generated using immutable features (i.e. information about the user and the web page request), while the second fingerprint is used for the ML-based detection phase, and it is generated using behavioral features. As shown in Fig. 1, when a user requests a web page, the rule-based detection phase starts by generating the immutable fingerprint and then applying rules to check whether the user is a human or not.

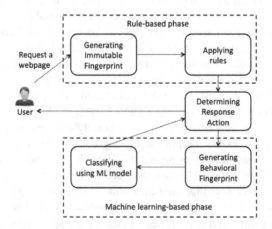

Fig. 1. The framework of the suggested hybrid approach.

Based on the results of the rule-based detection phase, a response action should be taken. The response action can be denying access or granting access to the user on the website. If the user passes the rule-based detection phase, and one click on an ad of the website is received, the ML-based detection phase initiated by generating the behavioral fingerprint and then classifying it into a human or not. The results of the ML-base phase will entail a response action to be taken.

3.1 The Rule-Based Detection Phase

In this phase, the detection method of naive bots using straightforward rules is discussed. This phase starts by generating the first fingerprint for the user. A website request has information about the user and the request itself [23]. This information is immutable. In other words, it is not changing for a certain user at a certain time. This information may include the following:

- Remote address is the remote host (i.e. the client IP address).
- Remote user is the identity of the user.
- Local time is the time the request was received.
- Request the URL of the requested web page.
- Status of request is the status code sent from the server to the client.
- HTTP referrer is the URL of the web page from which this request was initiated, (if any).
- HTTP user agent is the browser identification string.

A legitimate bot identifies itself in its HTTP user agent string [24]. This information allows the website to determine whether the bot is legitimate; hence, allowing it to access the website. An illegitimate bot identifies itself using a fake HTTP user agent string. Therefore, it deems necessary to detect those illegitimate bots by analyzing their information and behavior by generating a fingerprint then checking it. Figure 2 shows the structure of the fingerprint.

Fig. 2. The immutable fingerprint.

As shown in Fig. 2, the fingerprint carries the: User ID (i.e. a combination of the remote address and remote user values), Session ID (i.e. a unique identifier for the session), User agent (i.e. is the browser identification string for the user), and CSS sub-request (i.e. the child request of the original request as we will explain next).

After the fingerprint is generated, the rules are applied to check whether this user is a human or not. First, we check if the HTTP user agent is empty or invalid. If the user passed these rules and the access to the website is granted, we then check if the CSS sub-request corresponding to the original request is requested or not. For instance, if user X requested home.php, home.php should auto request home.css. In some cases, non-human bots need only the HTML elements in home.php because they are running using CURL command [25], which is a tool used to transfer data from/to a server and is designed to work without user interaction. On the other hand, if not requested, then the user is classified as illegitimate NHT.

The previous steps are for detecting naive bots of NHT that may target ad click fraud, DOS attacks, viewability busters, etc. At the end of this stage, we were able to detect naive bots, but we are not sure whether they intend to commit ad click fraud or not. Finally, when the user passes the rule-based detection phase and receive the web page with online ads rendered in it, the ML-based detection phase of our hybrid approach is triggered.

3.2   The Machine Learning-Based Detection Phase

Primitive and advanced bots can fake the user agent value surpassing detection techniques towards the online digital ads to commit click frauds. In this phase, we aim at detecting bots using a ML classifier. Detection starts by generating the second fingerprint (i.e. behavioral fingerprint) upon the user click on the ad. If a matching fingerprint of one of the known illegitimate bots' patterns learned by the classifier, the user will be classified illegitimate.

3.3   Data Preparation

A commercial advertisement website i.e. Waseet is used to experiment and test our approach. Waseet is popular in the Middle East, covering 9 countries in the Arab world, and providing classified ads for autos, real estate, jobs, and employment opportunities, as well as, general classifieds and items.

3.3.1   Data Preparation for Rule-Based Detection Phase

For the rule-based detection phase, we used anonymized server access logs of Waseet. The access logs of 2,002,985 users during 10 h on September 17th, 2018 were obtained. Figure 3 shows a sample record of the dataset.

```
$remote_addr: 37.186.104.216
$remote_user: 37.186.104.216
$time_local: [19/Nov/2017:06:56:55 +0000]
$request: "GET /site-images/sites/default/files/prod/Abu-Dhabi/car/4928733/%D9%86%D9%8A%D8%B3%D8%A7%D9%86-
%D8%A8%D8%A7%D8%AA%D8%B1%D9%88%D9%84-
%D8%A8%D9%84%D8%A7%D8%AA%D9%8A%D9%86%D9%8A%D9%88%D9%85-Platinum-LE-
%D9%85%D9%88%D8%AF%D9%8A%D9%84-2018-%D8%AC%D8%AF%D9%8A%D8%AF-
%D9%84%D9%84%D8%A8%D9%8A%D8%B9-4928733-2-1508936533.JPG?preset=detail_slid_img_watermark HTTP/1.1"
$status: 200
$body_bytes_sent: 91239
$http_referer: "https://www.google.am/"
$http_user_agent: "Mozilla/5.0 (Windows NT 6.1) AppleWebKit/537.36 (KHTML, like Gecko) Chrome/62.0.3202.94 Safari/
537.36"
```

Fig. 3. Sample record of Waseet dataset.

The access logs' contents were first analyzed to group human users, legitimate bots, and illegitimate bots based on the user agent value. Next, user agents matching a known HTTP structure were identified. Finally, distinct user agents were manually classified into valid/invalid agents. The evaluation results on the training datasets of the rule-based detection phase are reported in Table 1.

Table 1. Evaluation results of the training dataset of the rule-based phase.

Measurement metrics	Training results (%)
Accuracy	99.97
Recall	98.94
Precision	91.72

After validating the training dataset manually, it was found that the total number of the naive bots is 24,515, representing 1.22% of the users. For testing, three different datasets will be used. These datasets were collected from the Waseet's access log over different dates. The details of the datasets are shown in Table 2.

Table 2. Details of the obtained datasets.

Dataset name	Total instances	Date
Dataset 1	8952322	April 28th, 2018
Dataset 2	12038869	May 5th, 2018
Dataset 3	9565821	September 18th, 2018

3.3.2   Data Preparation for ML-Based Detection Phase

Given that a percentage of 98.78% of the users passed the rule-based detection phase, the dataset used in this phase is a set of ad-click patterns generated automatically based on observations from the experiments conducted on actual users. To generate ad click patterns while preserving the privacy of user sessions, an experiment with the help of 10 real users was conducted to observe their behaviors; thus, creating rules for generating ad click patterns. According to Google analytics, the average session time on Waseet website was approximately 4 min, and the approximate number of pages visited per session was slightly less than five; therefore, users were asked to explore the website for 4 min while getting their browsing behaviors recorded. Three major types of behaviors were observed: users didn't click any ad at all, users clicking on an ad of interest from 1 to 4 times during one session, users clicking ads with various time intervals. Therefore, some conclusions can be drawn as follows:

1. Because the maximum number of ad clicks in one session in the recorded behaviors was 4, each pattern should consist of at least 5 clicks to determine whether it is illegitimate or not, at the fifth click; therefore, the fifth click represents non-human user behavior; hence, it should be blocked immediately.

2. Between each two clicks there is an interval of time. We split the time slots based on our observations into three categories: less than 1 s, from 1 s to 1 min, and over 1 min. Based on the observations, all possible legitimate human behaviors were examined, while other behaviors were assumed as illegitimate non-human behaviors. The observations are summarized in Table 3 where columns from C1 to C5 represent the first click to the fifth click with a value of zero (i.e. no-click) or one (i.e. click). The table also shows the time interval between each two clicks denoted as S (i.e. small time span < 1 s), I (i.e. intermediate time span < 1 min), and/or L (i.e. large time span > 1 min). The class appears at the last column having one of two values: the "N" value denotes (No) and represents a legitimate bot, while the "Y" value denotes (Yes) and represents an illegitimate bot.

Table 3. The rules for generating ad clicks patterns.

C1	C2 time	C2	C3 time	C3	C4 time	C4	C5 time	C5	Class
C1 & C2 rules									
1	S | I | L	1	0	0	0	0	0	0	N
C3 Rules									
1	S	1	S	1	0	0	0	0	Y
1	I | L	1	I | L	1	0	0	0	0	N
1	L	1	S | I	1	0	0	0	0	N
1	S | I	1	L	1	0	0	0	0	N
C4 rules									
1	S | I	1	S | I	1	S | I	1	0	0	Y
1	S | I	1	S | I	1	L	1	0	0	N
1	L	1	L	1	L	1	0	0	Y
1	L	1	L	1	S | I	1	0	0	N
1	L	1	S | I	1	L	1	0	0	N
1	S | I	1	L	1	S | I	1	0	0	N
1	S | I	1	L	1	L	1	0	0	N
1	L	1	S | I	1	S | I	1	0	0	Y
C5 rules									
1	S | I | L	1	S | I | L	1	S | I | L	1	S | I | L	1	Y

3. The patterns summarized in Table 3 were input as the training dataset for the ML classifier.

The dataset used for training was automatically generated with 500 instances of ad-click patterns, covering the following scenarios:

1. All the human user cases with various time between clicks value combinations
2. Primitive bots cases with fixed interval time between clicks
3. Advanced bots cases with random interval time between clicks

Effectiveness of various classifiers was measured through precision, recall, true positive (TP), and false positive (FP) scores. As shown in Table 4, Support Vector Machine (SVM), K-Nearest Neighbor (KNN), AdaBoost, Decision Tree (DT), and Bagging were evaluated after empirically tuning their parameters. From Table 4, various conclusions can be drawn as follows:

Table 4. Evaluation of the different ML classifiers.

Classifier	Parameters	Values	TP rate	FP rate	Precision	Recall
SVM	Kernel (values)	Poly	0.865	0.338	0.864	0.865
	C = 1	normalized ploy	**0.882**	**0.286**	**0.881**	**0.882**
	Gamma = auto	RPF	0.747	0.747	?	0.747
	C (values)	1	0.882	0.286	0.881	0.882
	Kernel = Normalized Poly	5	**0.929**	**0.147**	**0.928**	**0.929**
	Gamma = default	50	0.935	0.145	0.935	0.935
		100	0.941	0.128	0.941	0.941
K-NN	N (values)	1	**0.988**	**0.004**	**0.989**	**0.988**
		3	0.976	0.023	0.977	0.976
		5	0.953	0.124	0.954	0.953
		7	0.935	0.160	0.936	0.935
AdaBoost	Base-estimator (values)	DT	0.988	0.035	0.988	0.988
	n-estimators = 50	Random Forest	0.976	0.023	0.977	0.976
	Algorithm = SAMME	K-NN(1)	**0.988**	**0.004**	**0.989**	**0.988**
		K-NN(3)	0.976	0.023	0.977	0.976
		SVM	0.865	0.338	0.864	0.865
DT	Pruning (values)	With	0.947	0.095	0.947	0.947
		Without	**0.976**	**0.039**	**0.976**	**0.976**
Bagging	Classifier (values)	DT	0.965	0.043	0.966	0.965
		Random Forest	**0.971**	**0.025**	**0.972**	**0.971**
		Naïve Bayes	0.741	0.088	0.872	0.741
		SVM	0.853	0.373	0.852	0.853

1. The SVM classifier: The performance of the SVM classifier is based on its parameters: gamma, kernel, and C, which controls the cost of misclassification on the training data. Table 4 shows that SVM's best performance was when gamma is set to auto, kernel is set to normalized-poly and C is set to 1. As a result, we decided to fix the values of the kernel and gamma, then started to empirically test for the best value of the C parameter. Table 1 shows that different values of the C parameter didn't show any significant improvements when C was larger than 5. Therefore, we picked the value of C to be 5

2. The K-NN classifier: The classifier's effectiveness is primarily based on the value of its N-neighbors' parameter. The value of "N" controls the number of neighbors. Table 4 shows the results provided by K-NN for different setups of the N value. As one can see from Table 4, the best performance of K-NN was when N = 1

3. The AdaBoost classifier: The performance of the AdaBoost classifier is primarily based on the setup of its parameters. The main parameters of AdaBoost are: base-estimator, n-estimators, and algorithm. In this experiment, we fixed the value of the n-estimators to be 50 as it suited the specification of the computer machine where we intend to conduct the testing experiments. For the algorithm parameter, the value was fixed to be "SAMME" as it suited the classifiers we are evaluating. The other possible value was ("SAMME.R"); however, it suits the linear classifiers, which does not suite our experiment. Finally, we varied the value of the base-estimator parameter to be one of four different classifiers: DT, Random-Forest, K-NN for N = 1 and N = 3, and the SVM classifier. Table 4 reveals that when the base-estimator was set to KNN with N = 1, AdaBoost showed the highest performance

4. The DT classifier: The DT classifier setup depends on the value of its pruning parameter: with pruning or without pruning. Table 4 shows that the best performance of DT was when the value of pruning was set to be "without pruning"

5. The Bagging classifier: The Bagging classifier mainly depend on the value of its classifier parameter. To test this classifier, we set the classifier value to be: DT, Random-Forest, Naive-Bayes, and SVM. Table 4 shows that Random-Forest returned the best results with low efficiency, making it not suitable to run a web server; therefore, our next best choice was the DT classifier

Given the experiment results of the ML classifiers aforementioned, the best results intrinsically are summarized in Table 5.

Table 5. The setup values of the classifiers selected for the testing phase.

Classifier	Parameters values
SVM	Kernel = "Normalized-Poly", gamma = "default", C = "5"
K-NN	N = "1"
AdaBoost	Base-estimator = "K-NN", N = "1", n-estimators = "50", algorithm = "SAMME"
DT	Pruning = "without"
Bagging	Classifier = "DT"

4   Evaluation Results

4.1   The Evaluation of the Rule-Based Detection Phase

Table 6 shows the evaluation results of the testing datasets of the rule-based detection phase. Applying the rules on Dataset 1, Dataset 2, and Dataset 3 provides high accuracy, recall, and precision. In Dataset 3 the precision is 100% as the rules correctly marked all naive illegitimate bots.

Table 6. Evaluation results of the testing datasets of rule-based phase.

Measurement metrics	Dataset 1	Dataset 2	Dataset 3
Accuracy	99.99%	99.98%	99.99%
Recall	99.23%	98.66%	98.81%
Precision	94.74%	90.57%	100% => FP = 0

4.2   The Evaluation of the ML-Based Detection Phase

Table 7 shows the results obtained after evaluating the classifiers. As depicted in Table 7, the classifiers were validated on two folds: a percentage split of 66%, and a 10 folds cross-validation.

The results show that KNN provides the lowest FP and it also provides the highest TP rate, precision and recall. Accordingly, KNN was selected to be used in the ML-based phase of our suggested hybrid detection approach.

Table 7. Comparative results of various ML classifiers using both: percentage split of 66% and 10 folds cross-validation.

Classifier	TP rate		FP rate		Precision		Recall	
	66%	10 folds	66%	10 folds	66%	10 folds	66%	10 folds
zeroR	0.747	0.747	0.747	0.747	0.558	0.559	0.747	0.747
SVM	0.865	0.886	0.338	0.286	0.864	0.886	0.865	0.886
K-NN (1)	**0.986**	**0.976**	**0.026**	**0.034**	**0.986**	**0.976**	**0.986**	**0.976**
AdaBoost	0.829	0.828	0.442	0.332	0.828	0.821	0.829	0.828
Bagging	0.935	0.958	0.114	0.062	0.935	0.958	0.935	0.958
Decision tree	0.976	0.940	0.039	0.089	0.976	0.941	0.976	0.940

After experimenting with the ML-classifiers, we sampled 10 instances among the different cases of legitimate and illegitimate users for applying KNN. The prediction effectiveness of KNN classified all sampled instances correctly.

4.3   Discussions

In a real environment, our model consists of two parts: an offline model generation, and an online user visit classification. Given that we implemented our proposed approach on a PC, it is important to report that the time taken to build the model of the generated 500 instances is 0.01 s, while the time taken to classify a single instance whether legitimate or illegitimate is 0.05 s. It is also important to report that the average number of concurrent users who visited Waseet is 168. The reported numbers show that our approach is scalable for the studied case considering the classifier efficiency and the number of concurrently connected users.

5   Conclusions

In recent years, ad click fraud has been marked as a serious problem for the online advertising industry because advertisers pay for fake clicks. In this paper, we suggested a hybrid approach using a two-level fingerprint to detect the illegitimate bots that targeting ad clicks fraud. The approach has two detection phases; rule-based detection phase and ML-based detection phase. The first level of the fingerprint is generated using immutable features of the user and the web page request. This fingerprint is used for the rule-based detection phase. The second level of the fingerprint is used for the ML-based detection phase. It is generated using ad clicks behavioral patterns of real users of Waseet website. The website's access logs and the ad clicks patterns of its users are used as datasets to train and test our approach.

Different ML classifiers have been evaluated to select the best one of them for the ML-based detection phase. The selection was based on FP and TP rates, recall, and precision measurements factors. The hybrid approach shows promising evaluation results. The average testing results of the rule-based detection phase show an accuracy of 99.9%, recall of 98.9%, and precision of 95.1%. For the ML-based detection phase, we tested it using a sample set of ad clicks patterns of legitimate and illegitimate cases. The selected ML method predicted all instances of the sample set correctly.

References

1. In: incapsula.com. https://www.incapsula.com/blog/bot-traffic-report-2016.html. Accessed 26 May 2019
2. Truth #2: Illegitimate Traffic Sourcing is the Main Cause of Fraud. In: Alliance For Audited Media, Knowledge Base. https://knowledge.auditedmedia.com/blog/illegitimate-traffic-sourcing-is-the-main-cause-of-fraud. Accessed 26 May 2019
3. Zeifman, I.: Imperva Incapsula, January 2017. https://www.incapsula.com/blog/bot-traffic-report-2016.html
4. Waseet website, classifieds ads. http://waseet.net. Accessed 4 Nov 2018
5. Mladenow, A., Novak, N.M., Strauss, C.: Online ad-fraud in search engine advertising campaigns. In: Khalil, I., Neuhold, E., Tjoa, A.M., Da Xu, L., You, I. (eds.) CONFENIS/ICT-EurAsia -2015. LNCS, vol. 9357, pp. 109–118. Springer, Cham (2015). https://doi.org/10.1007/978-3-319-24315-3_11
6. Alrwais, S.A., Gerber, A., Dunn, C.W., Spatscheck, O., Gupta, M., Osterweil, E.: Dissecting ghost clicks: ad fraud via misdirected human clicks. In: Proceedings of the 28th Annual Computer Security Applications Conference, pp. 21–30. ACM, December 2012
7. Mungamuru, B., Weis, S.: Competition and fraud in online advertising markets. In: Tsudik, G. (ed.) FC 2008. LNCS, vol. 5143, pp. 187–191. Springer, Heidelberg (2008). https://doi.org/10.1007/978-3-540-85230-8_16
8. Smith, A.D., Lias, A.R.: Identity theft and e-fraud as critical CRM concerns. Int. J. Enterp. Inf. Syst, (IJEIS) 1(2), 17–36 (2005)
9. Toledano, M., Cohen, I., Ben-Simhon, Y., Tadeski, I.: Real-time anomaly detection system for time series at scale. In: KDD 2017 Workshop on Anomaly Detection in Finance, pp. 56–65, January 2018

10. Badhe, A.: Click fraud detection in mobile ads served in programmatic inventory. Neural Netw. Mach. Learn. 1(1), 1 (2017)
11. Hsu, C.-H., Huang, C.-Y., Chen, K.-T.: Fast-flux bot detection in real time. In: Jha, S., Sommer, R., Kreibich, C. (eds.) RAID 2010. LNCS, vol. 6307, pp. 464–483. Springer, Heidelberg (2010). https://doi.org/10.1007/978-3-642-15512-3_24
12. Lee, K., Caverlee, J., Webb, S.: Uncovering social spammers: social honeypots + machine learning. In: Proceedings of the 33rd International ACM SIGIR Conference on Research and Development in Information Retrieval, pp. 435–442. ACM, July 2010
13. Vratonjic, N., Manshaei, M.H., Raya, M., Hubaux, J.-P.: ISPs and ad networks against botnet ad fraud. In: Alpcan, T., Buttyán, L., Baras, John S. (eds.) GameSec 2010. LNCS, vol. 6442, pp. 149–167. Springer, Heidelberg (2010). https://doi.org/10.1007/978-3-642-17197-0_10
14. Yu, F., Xie, Y., Ke, Q.: Sbotminer: large scale search bot detection. In: Proceedings of the Third ACM International Conference on Web Search and Data Mining, pp. 421–430. ACM, February 2010
15. Villamarín-Salomón, R., Brustoloni, J.C.: Bayesian bot detection based on DNS traffic similarity. In: Proceedings of the 2009 ACM symposium on Applied Computing, pp. 2035–2041. ACM, March 2009
16. Al-Hammadi, Y., Aickelin, U., Greensmith, J.: DCA for bot detection. In: IEEE Congress on Evolutionary Computation, 2008. CEC 2008 (IEEE World Congress on Computational Intelligence), pp. 1807–1816. IEEE, June 2008
17. Gu, G., Zhang, J., Lee, W.: BotSniffer: detecting botnet command and control channels in network traffic (2008)
18. Villamarín-Salomón, R., Brustoloni, J.C.: Identifying botnets using anomaly detection techniques applied to DNS traffic. In: 5th IEEE Consumer Communications and Networking Conference, 2008, CCNC 2008, pp. 476–481. IEEE, January 2008
19. Goebel, J., Holz, T.: Rishi: identify bot contaminated hosts by IRC nickname evaluation. HotBots 7, 8 (2007)
20. Wang, A.H.: Detecting spam bots in online social networking sites: a machine learning approach. In: Foresti, S., Jajodia, S. (eds.) DBSec 2010. LNCS, vol. 6166, pp. 335–342. Springer, Heidelberg (2010). https://doi.org/10.1007/978-3-642-13739-6_25
21. Dong, F., et al.: FraudDroid: automated ad fraud detection for android apps. In: The 26th ACM Joint European Software Engineering Conference and Symposium on the Foundations of Software Engineering (ESEC/FSE 2018) (2018)
22. Iqbal, M.S., Zulkernine, M., Jaafar, F., Gu, Y.: Fcfraud: fighting click-fraud from the user side. In: 2016 IEEE 17th International Symposium on High Assurance Systems Engineering (HASE), 7 January 2016, pp. 157–164. IEEE (2016)
23. HTTP headers. In: MDN Web Docs. https://developer.mozilla.org/en-US/docs/Web/HTTP/Headers. Accessed 26 May 2019
24. MDN web docs. User-Agent. https://developer.mozilla.org/en-US/docs/Web/HTTP/Headers/User-Agent. Accessed 4 Nov 2018
25. Curl command line tool and library. https://curl.haxx.se/. Accessed 4 Nov 2018

Applying Supervised Machine Learning to Predict Virtual Machine Runtime for a Non-hyperscale Cloud Provider

Loïc Perennou[1,2]($\boxtimes$) and Raja Chiky[2]($\boxtimes$)

[1] OUTSCALE, Saint-Cloud, France
loic.perennou@outscale.com
[2] ISEP - LISITE, Paris, France
raja.chiky@isep.fr

Abstract. Cloud computing offers an online, on-demand and pay-as-you-go access to computing resources. The cloud enables users to adjust their consumption to their needs. Users deploy their application code, libraries and operating systems on the provider's hardware. The resources can be allocated under the form of virtual machines (VMs). Predicting the runtime of VMs can be useful to optimize the resource allocation. We propose a formulation of this objective as a multi-class classification problem by using as much features as available when launching a VM. Experimentation carried out on real traces from the public cloud provider Outscale show that the inclusion of features extracted from *tags*, which are freely-typed pieces of text used to describe VMs for human operators, improve the model performance.

Keywords: Virtual machine runtime · Machine learning · Cloud computing · Classification

1 Introduction

Cloud computing was invented to enable easy and affordable access to computing resources. It is used, for instance, to develop autonomous vehicles [1] or medical treatments [13], which have in common the need to find meaningful information in large datasets. Since the amount of data collected, stored, and processed worldwide nearly doubles every two years [3], it is primordial to optimize the affordability of computing resources.

Cloud computing does so by making resources accessible online and on-demand [14]. The main advantage is *elasticity*: users are able to provision and de-provision resources autonomously to adapt to their needs [9], and they are billed exactly for their usage. Hence, they are financially incentivized to release the resources they no longer need for the benefit of other users.

There are three cloud computing models [14]:

- In *Software as a Service* (SaaS), users share an application that is maintained by the provider.

© Springer Nature Switzerland AG 2019
N. T. Nguyen et al. (Eds.): ICCCI 2019, LNAI 11684, pp. 676–687, 2019.
https://doi.org/10.1007/978-3-030-28374-2_58

- In *Platform as a Service* (PaaS), users deploy their application code in an execution environment that includes the necessary software libraries.
- In *Infrastructure as a Service* (IaaS), users deploy their application code, libraries and operating systems on the provider's hardware. The hardware is made of fundamental computing resources such as servers that embed RAM and CPU.

We base our study on a IaaS Cloud provider that relies on *virtualization*: CPU and RAM of servers are allocated under the form of virtual machines (VMs), which provide an isolated execution environment for an OS and an application [19]. We are specifically interested by a non hyperscale cloud providers as we demonstrated in a previous work that their usage is different from the well known hyperscale platforms [16].

Cloud computing's main feature, elasticity, enable users to run VMs for short periods of time. A workload made of short-running VMs is incompatible with the resource allocation algorithms that require to profile the long-term behavior of VMs and consolidate the complementary ones with migrations. This brings a main questions: Can the behavior of a VM be predicted from information available when it is started?

Finding the best server when a VM starts is an online problem. The decision must be made before the algorithm receives all the problem's inputs. For instance, nor the amount of resources the VM will consume, nor its runtime, nor the arrival time of future VMs is known. In this paper, we use supervised machine learning to mitigate this uncertainty. Supervised machine learning aims at making predictions based on historical data. In this use case, we predict the runtime of a VM, at startup, based on the associated resource request, its context, and the runtime of previous VMs. Our contribution is to present a feature engineering and modeling pipeline whose performance is competitive with a state-of-the art but closed-source model from the literature [4]. Our experimental study has been carried out on real data traces from a non hyperscale cloud provider called Outscale.

Section 2 presents supervised machine learning approaches used in the context of VM prediction. The data extraction from Outscale's cloud is explained in Sect. 3. Our implementations are given in Sect. 4, and results are in Sect. 5. Finally, Sect. 6 concludes the paper by giving some ongoing and future work.

2   State of the Art

The resource utilization of virtual machines is dynamic. Machine learning is used to anticipate changes in utilization, and optimize resource allocation pro-actively. We divide the existing approaches into three categories: *Individual* model, *Collective* model, and *Startup* model.

2.1   Individual Model

In the *individual* model, the resource utilization of each VM is modeled independently. Many solutions have been proposed to predict the resource usage of a

VM based on its past utilization. A survey of time series forecasting techniques is given in [8]. The paper also presents a decision tree allowing to choose the best technique based on the problem context, and feedback over prediction quality. Both *Press* [7] and *Agile* [15] make short term CPU usage predictions using signal processing. The former uses Fast Fourier Transform and the latter uses wavelets transform. In [2], the time series of CPU usage is decomposed into a periodic components and a residual. The residual is modeled as an Auto Regressive process: its predicted value at t is a linear combination of the previous values. In [20], the CPU utilization of a VM is modeled with a bag of neural network. The period of the time series, measured with the auto-correlation, is used as a feature. Bagging, which is the process of training several learners with random splits of data (from the same VM) and combining their predictions, is used to reduce overfitting. Server utilization is modeled with a Bayesian classifier in [5]. As seen, any of these methods are used for predicting VM runtime at startup.

2.2   Collective Model

In [10], a single Hidden Markov Model is trained for a group of VMs. This choice is motivated by the observation that individual VMs have a noisy resource usage. This noise can be filtered out by taking advantage of load correlations that exist between VMs, which arise because VMs are collaborating to support complex services. The same argument is used in [17], and a deep neural network is used to predict the CPU load of all VMs. In [11], a method called "tracking the best expert" is used to predict traffic demand. Traffic demand between all pairs of VMs is represented as a matrix. The future matrix is estimated with a linear combination of past measurements. The weights are adjusted online every hour. In this category, the approaches are not meant for VM runtime prediction at startup.

2.3   Startup Model

Predictive systems presented so far can only help to optimize resource allocation after the start of the VM, because they require the observation of its past resource usage. Other systems have been designed to serve predictions when the VM starts, in order to optimize the initial resource allocation.

In [4], the CPU usage, running time, deployment size and workload class of VMs is predicted with a Random Forest and Extreme Gradient Boosting Tree. A deployment is a cluster of collaborating VMs. Yadwadkar et al. use support vector machines to predict the likelihood of a task to be a straggler [21]. Straggler tasks are the ones that finish late due to contention for shared resources, and they cause the slowdown of data mining jobs. A differentiated resource allocation that depends on job runtime is proposed in [12]. Short batch jobs are consolidated aggressively whereas long-running and interactive ones have dedicated resources. A prediction of job runtime is made at startup, and the model uses support vector machines too. The features correspond to the job's resource request.

On high performance computing and grid platforms, one objective of the scheduler is to minimize the total execution time of the job waiting queue. Historically, users provided a maximum allowed job run time to help scheduling. But, since their estimation is often too cautious, this is not optimal. Linear regression is used in [6] to predict the exact job run time. Interestingly, many features are related to the previous jobs of the same user, e.g. their running time, submission time, initial resource request and user submission rate. We find this work very interesting and close to our context. hence, we adapt the approach to the Outscale data characteristics.

3 Outscale Data Trace

Outscale is specialized in Infrastructure as a Service (IaaS), where *hardware resources* – servers, networks and storage – are *virtualized* into virtual machines (VMs). Virtualization allows users to securely share the same hardware. IaaS providers are responsible for the allocation of hardware resources to the VMs. They must take advantage of the complementarity of individual workloads to maximize the number of VMs that can be served while providing them an acceptable Quality of Service (QoS).

Contrary to on premise deployments, Outscale's platform is used by diverse industries, from software vendors to banks. Yet, with 100k VMs/month, Outscale's workload is at least an order of magnitude smaller than that of the biggest providers, such as Azure. Hence, we refer to Outscale as a *non-hyperscale* provider [16].

To perform the experiments, we collected a workload trace of the execution of 400k VMs on Outscale's European region, from August to October 2017 (3 months). The orchestrator logs all requests received from users, and the VM management operations that were performed on behalf of users. Management operations requests include the start or stop of VMs. VM start requests contain a variety of parameters, such as the amount of resources (CPU and RAM) requested for a new VM; or tags, which are freely-typed text strings used to distinguish VMs. In the next section, we will present the machine learning pipelines used to predict VM runtime, as well as the exact features extracted from the raw trace.

4 Implemented Approaches

We present in this section the tho approaches that we implemented based on the literature study. We adapt these existing methods to Outscale's context.

4.1 Regression Based Method

In [6], the runtime of jobs submitted to a grid is predicted with a linear regression. Each job is represented by four categories of features:

- resource request (e.g, CPU request)
- request timing
- history of previous jobs (e.g, the runtime of the last finished job of the same user)
- user account's current state (e.g, number of running jobs of that user).

The motivation for using historical information comes from [18], where it was shown that the performance of a backfilling scheduler improved if the runtime of a new job was estimated from the average runtime of last two completed jobs of the same user.

We adapt the proposed technique to the context of IaaS. We use the same features as in [6] (listed in Table 1), except for the upper bound on job runtime, which we do not have in IaaS cloud architecture. The prediction targets the log of runtime. We use scikit learn's[1] implementation of Ridge Regression, which uses gradient descent.

Table 1. Features describing VM_j, started by user u at time t in experiment 1

Feature name	Description
f1	runtime of the last VM of user u
f2	runtime of the second-to-last VM of user u
f3	runtime of the third-to-last VM of user u
f4	average runtime of the two last VMs of user u
f5	average runtime of the three last VMs of user u
f6	average runtime of all VMs of user u
f7	amount of CPU requested by VM_j
f8	average amount of CPU requested by VMs of user u
f9	normalized CPU request of VM_j (f7/f8)
f10	number of VMs of user u running at time t
f11	longest runtime (so far) among running VMs of user u
f12	sum of the runtimes (so far) of running VMs of user u
f13	sum of CPU requested by VMs of user u
f14	time elapsed between time t and the last VM stop time
f15	cosine of the hour of the day at time t
f16	sine of the hour of the day at time t
f17	cosine of the day of week at time t
f18	sine of the day of week at time t

---

[1] https://scikit-learn.org.

4.2   Classification Based Method

In this third approach, we propose to formulate the VM runtime prediction as a classification problem as proposed in [4]. VM runtime and mean CPU utilization are originally two continuous variables. We segment their values into classes according to thresholds given in Table 2, the same thresholds were used in [4].

Table 2. Metric segmentation

Metric	Class S	Class M	Class L	Class XL
runtime	<15 min	>=15 min & <60 min	>=1 h & <24 h	>=24 h

In this approach, the features used are uniquely related to the VM whose runtime is being predicted. So, there is no feature related to how many VMs the user is already running, or what resources were requested for previous VMs (i.e. historical requests like in the previous method). In order to study the importance of the different features (given in Table 3), we divided them into three sets. A *minimal* set of features contains the time-stamped resource request. The *noText* includes additional information, such as the VM's operating system, placement affinity or number of network security groups. The *all* feature set contains all previous features and tags. Tags are freely-typed text given by the user after the VM is started. This information can be collected from the Outscale traces. They are used by administrators to keep a record of their VMs' roles. Textual tags were transformed into binary features with *dictionary vectorization*. It is a four-step process: Firstly, the tags related to the same VM are merged in a document. Secondly, documents are pre-processed (we removed non-alphabetical characters and kept words of at least three letters). Then, a dictionary (i.e., a list of existing words) is built from the corpus. We included the 2000 most frequent words in the dictionary. The last step is to transform word documents into binary vectors, where the vector's component is 1 if the document contains the corresponding word, and 0 otherwise.

5   Results

5.1   Regression Results

For the model evaluation, we use the coefficient of determination R^2, defined as the proportion of the variance in the dependent variable that is predictable from the independent variables (Eq. 3). Its maximum value, 1, is reached when the residuals sum of square SS_{res} is 0. A naive model that constantly predicts the average value of y would achieve the minimum R^2 score, 0.

$$SS_{tot} = \sum_i (y_i - \bar{y})^2 \tag{1}$$

Table 3. Composition of the Feature Sets. Most features are available in the VM request, others such as DISK type/performance and text tags are given through subsequent API calls.

Feature category	Feature set name		
	minimal	noText	all
CPU/RAM requested	yes	yes	yes
VM type/family/generation	yes	yes	yes
start time	yes	yes	yes
OS	no	yes	yes
DISK type/performance	no	yes	yes
shutdown behavior	no	yes	yes
placement affinity	no	yes	yes
security groups	no	yes	yes
count	no	yes	yes
text tags	no	no	yes

$$SS_{res} = \sum_i (y_i - \hat{y}_i)^2 \tag{2}$$

$$R^2 = 1 - \frac{SS_{res}}{SS_{tot}} \tag{3}$$

The model has an $R^2 = 0.12$, which is better than a naive model.

5.2   Classification Results

In this section, we report the results of classification based method, where runtime prediction was formulated as a classification problem. We performed a grid search over a range of models and parameters. The evaluation metric is the macro-averaged F1 score i.e., the unweighted average of the F1 score for each class. As shown in Eq. 4, the F1 score combines precision P and recall R. This makes it ideal for classification problems involving unbalanced classes. The optimal value of the F1 score is 1, and the worst is 0.

$$F1 = 2\frac{P * R}{P + R} \tag{4}$$

Choice of Model and Feature Set. Figure 1 compares the performance of all combinations of models (Boosted naive Bayes BNB, Gaussian Naive Bayes GNB, Adaboost and Decision tree) and feature set (Minimal, notext and All described in Table 3). With a macro-averaged F1 score of 0.72, Adaboost trained with the most complete set of features is the best-performer, followed by random forests. Tree-based ensemble models constantly outperform Bayesian models. On the minimum subset of features, the performance of tree-based models (F1 = 0.47) is better than a random classifier that would follow the class probabilities. Performance slightly increases (+0.07) if we add additional non-text features, such as disk request or affinity tags. The utilization of text features brings a major improvement (+0.18).

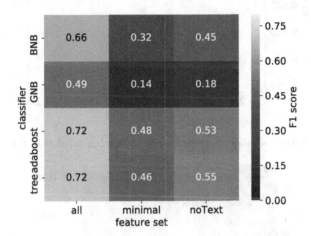

Fig. 1. Model performance on various feature sets

Model Complexity. There are at least two possible reasons why one would limit the number of features (mainly textual ones). First, the computational cost of text feature extraction increases with their number. Secondly, keeping non-informative features does not ease the learning task. Figure 2 shows how the performance of the model evolves with the number of available text features. The performance quickly increases from 0 to 100 features, and then reaches a plateau. Hence, based on our data the optimal number of text features is 100.

Our tree ensemble models have two hyperparameters that must be carefully chosen to obtain optimal performance. The first one is the depth of each decision tree, and the second is the number of trees combined in the ensemble. We performed a grid search to find the best combination of hyperparameters for extreme randomized trees and boosted trees. The results for boosted trees are reported in Fig. 3. The best results are obtained with an ensemble of 5 decision trees of depth 25.

Comparison with Azure. Figure 4 compares the performance of Outscale's best model against Azure's. The macro-averaged F1 scores of both providers are similar (0.75 for Azure and 0.72 for Outscale). But the per-class results differ. Azure's F1 score is in a tighter range than Outscale's ([0.74; 0.79] vs [0.60, 0.72]). We observed that at Outscale, the F1 score is positively correlated with the class frequency. Consequently, the class that has the worst score (XL) is the one with

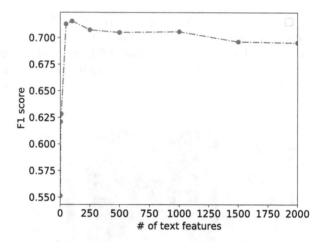

Fig. 2. Evolution of model performance with varying number of text features

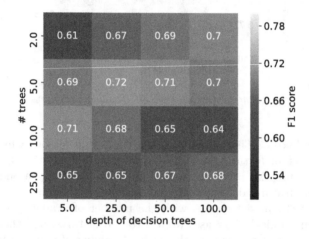

Fig. 3. Grid search over Adaboost model (F1 score, brighter is better)

lowest frequency. Correlation does not imply causation, but it is well known that class imbalance challenges machine learning. We trained models on new datasets containing relatively fewer occurrences of the S and L classes. But we did not observed improved results.

Our main result, is that machine learning models can predict the runtime of VMs at Outscale with a performance comparable to Azure's models, whose features were not disclosed [4]. We have observed that features derived from freely-typed text tags were bringing valuable information to our models. Currently, our API does not allow one to tag a VM in the same call than the VM request. Allowing this would be a first step towards optimizing VM placement.

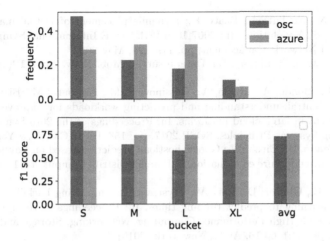

Fig. 4. Class frequency (top) and prediction score (bottom) for Outscale (osc) and Azure

6   Conclusion

The cloud infrastructures are very greedy in material resources and energy since they centralize the requests of thousands of customers (and even more). It is therefore important to optimize the allocation of physical machines to reduce consumption while preserving the overall performance of the system. The cloud provider Outscale allows users to use virtual machines to deploy applications, perform computation, and so on. At the startup of each VM, the user is asked several parameters such as the desired amount of CPU and RAM. These settings allow placement of VMs on the servers. In order to optimize the allocation of physical resources, it can be useful to predict the VM runtime at the startup. We proposed in this paper to implement two approaches (regression based model and classification based model) from the state of the art that we adapted to the context of the non hyperscale cloud Outscale. Thanks to the novel utilization of text tags, the experimental study shows very promising results, competitive with closed-source models.

In a future work, we will test whether models can be improved by adding features related to the users' historic usage. We also plan to test other machine learning methods such as LSTM (Long Short-Term Memory) network that introduce units in the cell that are dedicated to storing past information and are suitable for time series forecasting.

References

1. Bernstein, D., Vidovic, N., Modi, S.: A cloud PaaS for high scale, function, and velocity mobile applications - with reference application as the fully connected car. In: 2010 Fifth International Conference on Systems and Networks Communications, pp. 117–123, August 2010

2. Bobroff, N., Kochut, A., Beaty, K.: Dynamic placement of virtual machines for managing SLA violations. In: 2007 10th IFIP/IEEE International Symposium on Integrated Network Management, pp. 119–128, May 2007
3. Chen, M., Mao, S., Liu, Y.: Big Data: a survey. Mob. Netw. Appl. 19(2), 171–209 (2014)
4. Cortez, E., Bonde, A., Muzio, A., Russinovich, M., Fontoura, M., Bianchini, R.: Resource central: understanding and predicting workloads for improved resource management in large cloud platforms. In: Proceedings of the 26th Symposium on Operating Systems Principles, SOSP 2017, pp. 153–167. ACM, New York (2017)
5. Di, S., Kondo, D., Cirne, W.: Google hostload prediction based on Bayesian model with optimized feature combination. J. Parallel Distrib. Comput. 74(1), 1820–1832 (2014)
6. Gaussier, E., Glesser, D., Reis, V., Trystram, D.: Improving backfilling by using machine learning to predict running times. In: Proceedings of the International Conference for High Performance Computing, Networking, Storage and Analysis, SC 2015, pp. 64:1–64:10. ACM, New York (2015)
7. Gong, Z., Gu, X., Wilkes, J.: Press: predictive elastic resource scaling for cloud systems. In: 2010 International Conference on Network and Service Management, pp. 9–16, October 2010
8. Herbst, N.R., Huber, N., Kounev, S., Amrehn, E.: Self-adaptive workload classification and forecasting for proactive resource provisioning. In: Proceedings of the 4th ACM/SPEC International Conference on Performance Engineering, ICPE 2013, pp. 187–198. ACM, New York (2013)
9. Herbst, N.R., Kounev, S., Reussner, R.: Elasticity in cloud computing: what it is, and what it is not. In: Proceedings of the 10th International Conference on Autonomic Computing (ICAC 2013), San Jose, CA, pp. 23–27. USENIX (2013)
10. Khan, A., Yan, X., Tao, S., Anerousis, N.: Workload characterization and prediction in the cloud: a multiple time series approach. In: 2012 IEEE Network Operations and Management Symposium, pp. 1287–1294, April 2012
11. LaCurts, K., Mogul, J.C., Balakrishnan, H., Turner, Y.: Cicada: introducing predictive guarantees for cloud networks. In: 6th USENIX Workshop on Hot Topics in Cloud Computing (HotCloud 2014), Philadelphia, PA. USENIX Association (2014)
12. Liu, J., Shen, H., Narman, H.S.: CCRP: customized cooperative resource provisioning for high resource utilization in clouds. In: 2016 IEEE International Conference on Big Data (Big Data), pp. 243–252, December 2016
13. Marx, V.: The big challenges of Big Data. Nature 498, 255–260 (2013)
14. Mell, P., Grance, T., et al.: The NIST definition of cloud computing (2011)
15. Nguyen, H., Shen, Z., Gu, X., Subbiah, S., Wilkes, J.: AGILE: elastic distributed resource scaling for Infrastructure-as-a-Service. In: Proceedings of the 10th International Conference on Autonomic Computing (ICAC 2013), San Jose, CA, pp. 69–82. USENIX (2013)
16. Perennou, L., Callau-Zori, M., Lefebvre, S.: Understanding scheduler workload on non-hyperscale cloud platform. In: Proceedings of the 19th International Middleware Conference (Posters), Middleware 2018, pp. 23–24. ACM, New York (2018)
17. Qiu, F., Zhang, B., Guo, J.: A deep learning approach for VM workload prediction in the cloud. In: 2016 17th IEEE/ACIS International Conference on Software Engineering, Artificial Intelligence, Networking and Parallel/Distributed Computing (SNPD), pp. 319–324, May 2016
18. Tsafrir, D., Etsion, Y., Feitelson, D.G.: Backfilling using system-generated predictions rather than user runtime estimates. IEEE Trans. Parallel Distrib. Syst. 18(6), 789–803 (2007)

19. Vogels, W.: Beyond server consolidation. Queue **6**(1), 20–26 (2008)
20. Xue, J., Yan, F., Birke, R., Chen, L.Y., Scherer, T., Smirni, E.: PRACTISE: robust prediction of data center time series. In: 2015 11th International Conference on Network and Service Management (CNSM), pp. 126–134, November 2015
21. Yadwadkar, N.J., Ananthanarayanan, G., Katz, R.: Wrangler: predictable and faster jobs using fewer resources. In: Proceedings of the ACM Symposium on Cloud Computing, SOCC 2014, pp. 26:1–26:14. ACM, New York (2014)

A Distributed Pollution Monitoring System: The Application of Blockchain to Air Quality Monitoring

Cameron Thouati de Tazoult[1(✉)], Raja Chiky[2], and Valentin Foltescu[3]

[1] Stanford University, Stanford, USA
cameron8@stanford.edu
[2] ISEP - LISITE, Paris, France
raja.chiky@isep.fr
[3] UNEP, Paris, France
valentin.foltescu@un.org

Abstract. Global increases in anthropogenic emissions of pollutants have resulted in sometimes hazardous fluctuations in air quality worldwide. This has led to a need for a publicly available, scalable, and tamper-proof pollution monitoring system for use by authorities, private citizens and researchers alike. In this paper, we investigate the applications of blockchain in such a system and propose a prototype that attempts to meet all of the above criteria. The use of blockchain technology ensures a public and permanent, tamper-proof record of all air quality data. Our prototype demonstrates that, despite the cost of storage and transactions on the blockchain, a cost-effective blockchain-based solution for a pollution monitoring system is possible, and such a solution could solve problems of data reliability that persist in pollution monitoring.

1 Introduction

The World Health Organization estimates that nine out of ten people breathe air containing high levels of pollutants and attributes about 7 million deaths annually to causes induced by air pollution[1]. Air pollution is a widespread phenomenon that demonstrably causes serious health risks such as acute lower respiratory, chronic obstructive pulmonary disease, stroke, ischemic heart disease, and lung cancer. A 2012 World Health Organization report attributed one out of every nine deaths that year to these air pollution-related conditions [1].

Air quality monitoring can reveal long term trends that help inform researchers and influence policy makers. Air quality can also be monitored at industrial plants and factories to ensure corporations are complying with emissions regulations. More immediately, air quality can vary from day to day due to emission patterns and weather, and monitoring these fluctuations is important for staying informed about potential health risks in daily life. For example,

---

[1] https://www.who.int/airpollution/en/.

© Springer Nature Switzerland AG 2019
N. T. Nguyen et al. (Eds.): ICCCI 2019, LNAI 11684, pp. 688–697, 2019.
https://doi.org/10.1007/978-3-030-28374-2_59

certain air quality ranges may indicate that those with asthma or sensitive respiratory systems should stay indoors[2]. Pollution monitoring systems often collect data on mass particulate concentrations in the air as well the levels of various other pollutants such as sulfur dioxide and carbon monoxide. These readings can be output as a single numerical quantity which corresponds to a qualitative category from "Good" to "Hazardous" that is easily interpreted for safety purposes.

To maximize impact, an air quality system should be able to accept data from as many sources as possible while also validating the data and making it publicly accessible. The data should be secure and robust to prevent tampering. Researchers can then use the data with confidence when analyzing trends. Private citizens benefit from such a system as well as they receive access to up to date information about the quality of air in their location. The air quality information on any given day could inform lifestyle decisions to minimize health risks.

However, the majority of current air quality monitoring systems fail to meet the above criteria. This paper investigates the possible role of blockchain technology bringing a solution to these problems. The remainder of this paper will be structured as follows. Section 2 will present an overview of current air quality monitoring systems and their drawbacks. Section 3 will present a model of a blockchain-based air quality monitoring system that aims to solve the problems discussed in the previous section. Section 4 will present a proof of concept prototype that incorporates the discussed solutions. Finally, Sect. 5 will discuss possible next steps and room for improvement in the prototype.

2   Overview and Limitations of Current Air Quality Monitoring Systems

2.1   The Current Model

Growing awareness of the health and environmental risks posed by air pollution have led to widespread increases in air quality monitoring investment that are expected to continue to rise[3]. This market growth has led to a shift from monitoring via sparsely deployed, expensive government-run sensing infrastructure to widely deployed low-cost sensors [6]. Modern commercially-available, low-cost air quality sensors can capture information regarding the concentration of specific pollutant gases as well as general concentrations of different sizes of particulates (i.e. the concentration of particulate matter $10 \mu m$ or less in diameter).

As higher quality low-cost sensors are developed and more data is collected to use in validating sensor readings, the use of cheaper, portable sensors is growing drastically, however, currently much of the data collected from these sensors may not be unreliable [4]. The current model generally involves a government

---

[2] https://terra.nasa.gov/citizen-science/air-quality.
[3] https://www.psmarketresearch.com/market-analysis/air-quality-monitoring-devices-market.

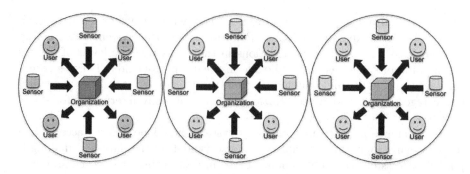

Fig. 1. Model of current air quality monitoring systems with multiple centralized entities controlling data collection and distribution. Users must go through the central organization to get access to the sensor data, requiring a high level of trust. Arrows represent the flow of air quality data.

agency, non-profit, or corporation deploying a web of low cost sensors that can forward air quality data to a central database maintained by the organization as shown in the Fig. 1. Aside from the variable quality of data collected by the sensors, security analyses of these systems have shown that they can be exploited through unencrypted message communications, poor authentication mechanisms, and other vulnerabilities [5]. Some air quality APIs are for profit and only provide paying members with data[4,5]. Those that are public still have the problem of centralization, meaning that all transactions must go through a single entity who has full control over the database.

2.2   Limitations of Current Model

Based on the model above, we can summarize the shortcomings of current air quality monitoring systems as follows:

- data integrity
- transparency
- centralization

What this means qualitatively is that data is spread out heterogeneously across many separate entities. Some of this data is publicly available, some is not. It is difficult to gauge the validity of much of this data as the origins of the data and all sensor metadata are managed centrally. This centralized model requires a great deal of trust between users and the entity in control of the data; trust that the sensing was accurate, trust that the data was not tampered with, and trust that the data will persist. Additionally, with data spread out heterogeneously across many separate databases, querying across this data becomes nearly impossible due to compatibility issues across different database interfaces (APIs).

---

[4] https://www.airvisual.com/air-pollution-data-api.
[5] https://breezometer.com/products/air-quality-api.

3   Overview of a Blockchain-Based Model for Air Quality Monitoring Systems

3.1   Why Blockchain?

The ideas behind blockchain technology were pioneered by the anonymous creator of Bitcoin, the original cryptocurrency [7]. Bitcoin was ground-breaking because it provided a framework for truly secure online peer-to-peer transactions without the need for a third party. This is made possible by the blockchain. The blockchain is a distributed ledger with records of every transaction ever made on the platform. The key here is that no single entity hosts the servers, or nodes, that store the blockchain. Nodes are hosted by volunteers, who do so because this allows them to engage in "mining," where they use their computers' CPUs to solve computationally complex equations in order to verify transactions and create new blocks in the blockchain. Miners are rewarded with Bitcoin for verifying transactions. Using CPU power to verify transactions ensures that the longest blockchain, or transaction history, represents the largest pool of CPU power. As such, the only way to alter the data is to control a majority of CPU power on the platform, redo the work for all blocks up to the block being targeted, and then outpace all the honest nodes adding blocks to the chain until the altered chain is the longest. This feat is practically impossible and becomes more difficult with each added block, rendering the blockchain effectively tamper-proof. Additionally, each block has the hash of a transaction as well as the hash of the previous block. Anyone can verify the integrity of the entire blockchain by following the block hashes. Thus, the blockchain offers complete transparency, security, and no requirement of implicit trust thanks to distribution.

3.2   A Blockchain-Based Model

We now propose a model for a blockchain-based air quality monitoring system that overcomes the limitations of current models. Blockchain technology requires some kind of monetary incentive for miners to verify transactions otherwise nobody would ever maintain servers to host the blockchain and no transactions would get made. This incentive usually comes in the form of built-in coin that can be used to make transactions. For this reason, it makes sense that cryptocurrency would be the earliest and most natural use case for blockchain technology. However, as technologies such as Bitcoin have become more widespread, other non-currency use cases for blockchain have emerged, taking advantage of the benefits of a secure, decentralized platform that requires no third party to operate. Applications range from secure voting systems[6] to online notaries[7]. Related work in using blockchain for air quality monitoring is sparse but does exist. Research on using long-range communications protocols to transmit sensor data to a decentralized database has used the Ethereum Blockchain to store air

---

[6] https://followmyvote.com/.
[7] https://www.proofofexistence.com/.

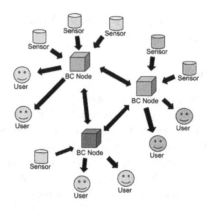

Fig. 2. Model of a blockchain-based decentralized air quality monitoring system.

quality data [8,9]. However, this research has been hardware oriented and little information is available about the software components.

Our model proposes that live sensor data be sent directly to the Ethereum Blockchain where it will be stored in a distributed manner. Basic data validity checks, such as verifying sensor calibration, should be put in place before the data is inserted into the blockchain. The benefit of using the Ethereum Blockchain to store live air quality sensor data is that it public, so everyone has access to the blockchain and anyone can read the data or verify the integrity of the entire blockchain via block hashes. The data is protected from actors who may have an interest in altering the data as the blockchain is effectively tamper proof. This model provides a public and completely transparent, permanent, and secure record of all air quality sensor data. Since the blockchain is decentralized, anybody can host an Ethereum node to acquire a full copy of the entire history of the blockchain and all the data on it. Figure 2 visualizes this model where "BC Node" is an Ethereum Blockchain node. Sensor data that is uploaded to one node is shared between all nodes and all data is available to everybody. Arrows represent the flow of sensor data.

3.3   The Problem of Scalability

The cost of storing data directly on the Ethereum Blockchain can be extremely high. The following calculation gives the cost of storing 1 GB of data on the Ethereum Blockchain given current prices of ETH and gas. ETH is the cryptocurrency on which Ethereum transactions run and gas/gwei refer to separate variables used to calculate the cost of Ethereum transactions.

According to Ethereum's yellow paper [9], it costs approximately 20,000 gas to store 8 bytes of data. This calculation is based on the March 19, 2019 gas price of 3 gwei per gas[8]. As of March 19, 2019, 1 ETH equals 136.79 USD. Thus, 1,000,000,000 gwei equal 1 ETH.

---

[8] https://ethgasstation.info/index.php.

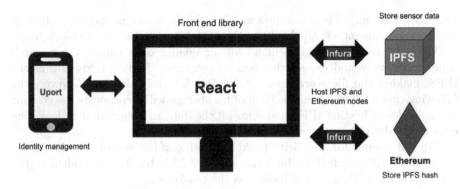

Fig. 3. Model of the main components of our blockchain-based air quality monitoring system prototype.

$20,000 \ gas/8bytes \ * \ 3 \ gwei/gas \ = \ 60,000 \ gwei/8bytes$
$60,000 \ gwei/8bytes \ * \ 1,000 \ bytes/8 \ = \ 7,500,000 \ gwei/kB =$
$.0075 \ ETH/kB$
$.0075 \ ETH/kB \ * \ 1000 \ kB \ = \ 7.5 \ ETHtostore1MB$

$7.5 \ ETH/MB \ * \ 136.79 \ USD/ETH \ = \ 1,025.925 \ USD/MB$

$1025.925 \ USD/MB \ * \ 1000 \ MB/GB \ = \ 1,025,925 \ USD/GB$

As of the writing of this paper, it would cost over 1 million USD to store a single GB of data on the Ethereum Blockchain. In a network that could scale to receive data from hundreds or thousands of sensors, 1 million USD/GB is not sustainable. As such, there is a need for an inexpensive method of data storage that does not compromise the transparency, security, or decentralized nature of blockchain storage.

To solve this problem, we propose the use of a distributed file system for file storage. In this model, we use the InterPlanetary File System (IPFS) [3]. Like blockchain, this distributed file system is not managed by any central authority. Rather, distributed volunteer entities host the file system's servers to gain access to the data. A user's data remains in the IPFS as long as they run a node, or as long as at least one other entity is hosting the data. When data is uploaded, the file system returns a hash based on the data. Anyone with the hash can access the data. We propose to replace uploading data directly to the blockchain by uploading it to a distributed file system and only storing the hash of the data on the blockchain. This model remains effectively tamper-proof. Any attempt at altering data would necessarily alter the hash (the hash is computed from the content of the data). The original hash would then have to be replaced in the blockchain with the hash of the altered data, which, as previously discussed, is nearly impossible, since any tampering entity would need to control over 50% of the computational power in the network (effectively impossible on a network as large as Ethereum). Thus, the data is still publicly available and the history of the data remains intact, all thanks to the hash being stored on the blockchain.

With the relatively high demand for air quality data among the research community, we would expect the data to propagate fairly quickly within the IPFS, making the file storage essentially free for the uploader. However, the following cost analysis of this method of file storage will incorporate the cost for the uploader of hosting IPFS nodes for all the data to ensure that at least one copy of the data always remains on the IPFS.

We will assume for simplicity's sake that a file of live sensor data has a size of about 1.5 MB. Each IPFS hash has a size of 32 bytes. We will calculate the cost of storing a GB worth of hashes on the blockchain.

$$1000\,MB/GB/1.5\,MB/file \;=\; 666.67\,files/GB$$

$$666.67\,files/GB \;*\; 32\,bytes/filehash \;=\; 21.33\,KB/GB$$

By only storing the file hashes, we can store a GB worth of data for the price of storing 21.33 kB on the blockchain. This price in USD is:

$$21.33\,kB \;*\; .0075\,ETH/kB \;=\; 0.159975\,ETH$$

$$0.159975\,ETH \;*\; 136.79\,USD/ETH \;=\; 21.88\,USD$$

Thus, we can store the hashes for a GB worth of files on the Ethereum Blockchain for $21.88. We now add the cost of hosting the servers for 1GB of data on IPFS. IPFS data hosting service Pinata offers to store data at $0.2–$0.3/GB depending on the number of GBs stored, charged monthly[9]. Assuming use of the most expensive tier for 12 months, we add $3.6 to our total: $21.88 + $3.6 = $25.48. The use of a distributed file system cheapens the price of storage by a factor of about 40,000 while maintaining the integrity of blockchain storage. Additionally, there is no upper limit to the size of data that can be stored on the IPFS under a single hash, so the cost of hash storage could be lessened significantly by simply aggregating sensor data and uploading it to the IPFS in larger batches. The cost of server hosting could be greatly decreased by using enterprise level server farms such as Amazon Web Services[10] to host IPFS nodes. The example used of Pinata is a fully integrated IPFS host that likely represents a worst case scenario for the cost of server hosting.

4   Prototype

Following model outlined above, we implemented a prototype air quality monitoring system using IPFS to store data and storing the IPFS hashes of the

---

[9] https://medium.com/pinata/whats-the-real-cost-of-ipfs-3623f274cfaa.
[10] https://aws.amazon.com/.

data on the Ethereum Blockchain. Figure 3 shows the main components of the prototype. The components details are outlined as follows:

- *Ethereum Blockchain.* The Ethereum Blockchain [9] is an open source blockchain platform. We chose to work with Ethereum because it is the second most used blockchain platform by market cap[11] and it is permissionless, meaning anyone can host a node and join the network. This was important to meet the goal of creating a public and transparent air quality monitoring system. Equally important was the fact that Ethereum functions more as a decentralized software platform than a cryptocurrency, with excellent support for smart contracts and decentralized applications. Once the IPFS hashes are added to the blockchain, they remain a part of the ledger permanently and are distributed across Ethereum nodes where they can be accessed by anyone. The storage and retrieval of the IPFS hashes occurs through the use of smart contracts.
- *Smart Contracts.* Smart contracts are pieces of code written in the Solidity coding language that run autonomously on Ethereum nodes. These pieces of code can be triggered by transactions sent by user accounts. All transactions incur a certain cost (this is the price of storage on the Blockchain from our cost analysis). Our smart contract stores and retrieves IPFS hashes.
- *InterPlanetary File System (IPFS).* As discussed in the model overview, IPFS is a distributed file storage system [3]. Our prototype uploads air quality data to the IPFS, which returns a hash based on the content of the data. This hash can be used to retrieve the IPFS data for as long as it persists in the network. You cannot delete data from IPFS if another node chooses to rehost it, and since the hash is based on the data, any data uploaded to IPFS is tamper-proof.
- *uPort.* uPort is an identity management system that allows users to control what data to disclose to other parties and to digitally sign blockchain transactions [2]. We use uPort to login to the application and sign transactions (submitting IPFS hashes to the blockchain). The user must have the uPort application on their mobile device and must use it to read a QR code on the web application to login. Upon submission of air quality data, the user must then sign the transaction on their mobile device on the uPort application before the transaction can be completed.
- *Infura.* Infura[12] is a free blockchain infrastructure service that facilitates access to Ethereum for distributed applications. We use Infura to host Ethereum and IPFS nodes that we can connect to without the need for complicated and computationally expensive infrastructure. Essentially, Infura allows decentralized applications to interact with the Ethereum network without running a full node. There are no major comparable services.
- *Front-end.* The front-end of the application uses React.js, a JavaScript library made for creating user interfaces. The user must login with uPort before

---

[11] https://coinmarketcap.com/.

[12] https://infura.io/.

proceeding. Then the user may query for air quality data. We use an API from openaq[13] for querying to simulate the injection of live sensor data. The data is immediately uploaded to IPFS and the hash is stored on the blockchain. The react-vis[14] graphics library can then be used to perform data visualization.

To summarize, the user logs in to the application by reading a QR code with the uPort application on their mobile device. The user can then query openaq's API for air quality data, which is immediately uploaded to the IPFS. The hash returned by IPFS is stored on the Ethereum blockchain via a transaction that must be signed with the uPort mobile application. The data is then retrieved and may be visualized with the react-vis graphics library.

5   Conclusions

5.1   Evaluation of the Proposed Application

We believe that the model and prototype presented in this paper make meaningful contributions towards the development of public pollution monitoring systems and provides a template for the application of blockchain to air quality monitoring. Our solution demonstrates the possibility of completely transparent, public, robust, and secure air quality monitoring systems without the need for a central authority. The use of a distributed file system in conjunction with blockchain technology also adds to the greater discourse on problems of scalability and data storage that persist among distributed applications.

Specifically, all available air quality monitoring data, from any validated source, can be shared on a single repository available to all without restrictions, political or otherwise. The cost of storage is practical to the application and can be lowered further through compression, usage of server farms, and batch uploading of sensor data. The data itself is for all practical purposes tamper-proof, even by government entities: it requires hacking the blockchain itself. Because the present system provides fully transparent and accessible data to all, it allows crowdsourcing analysis to any air-pollution related applications or problems. The widespread use of such a system could enable the birth of quantities of startups exploiting its data for the direct benefits of local citizens. Finally, because what can be measured can be controlled, we might hope that the high availability of such data could make air quality control easier to enforce, for instance allowing for a quick pinpointing of the source of newly detected air pollutants.

5.2   Future Work

While this prototype provides a good starting point for blockchain-based air quality monitoring systems, there are several areas that leave room for improvement in future work. Data validation is one such area. The current prototype

---

[13] https://docs.openaq.org/.
[14] https://github.com/uber/react-vis.

does not do basic data quality checks before uploading the data to the IPFS. Performing these checks before uploading the data could prevent obviously incorrect data (due to miscalibrated sensors for example) from being uploaded. Given the nature of a distributed file system, it is often impossible to remove uploaded data, so inaccurate data would remain in the file system permanently. User verification is another area that could be built upon. The current application allows anybody with a uPort account to login. uPort can also be used to issue users credentials, thus allowing only verified users to upload data. Beyond issues of data and user verification, we recommend that in future work the system be tested with higher throughput and with live sensor data to demonstrate its real-world validity.

Acknowledgment. This paper was part of a joint effort between ISEP Engineering School and the UN Environment Programme (UNEP) to investigate the possible role of blockchain technology in assisting sustainability initiatives.

References

1. Ambient air pollution: a global assessment of exposure and burden of disease (2016). https://www.who.int/phe/publications/air-pollution-global-assessment/en/. Accessed 22 Mar 2019
2. Lundkvist, C., Heck, R., Torstensson, J., Mitton, Z., Sena, M.: uPort: a platform for self-sovereign identity, 21 February 2017. http://static.benet.ai/t/ipfs.pdf. Accessed 22 Mar 2019
3. Benet, J.: IPFS - content addressed, versioned, p2p file system (2014). http://static.benet.ai/t/ipfs.pdf. Accessed 22 Mar 2019
4. Snyder, E., et al.: The changing paradigm of air pollution monitoring. Environ. Sci. Technol. **47**, 11369–11377 (2013)
5. Luo, L., Zhang, Y., Pearson, B., Ling, Z., Yu, H., Fu, X.: On the security and data integrity of low-cost sensor networks for air quality monitoring. Sensors (2018)
6. Maag, B., Zhou, Z., Thiele, L.: A survey on sensor calibration in air pollution monitoring deployments. IEEE Internet of Things J. **5**(6), 4857–4870 (2018)
7. Nakamoto, S.: Bitcoin: a peer-to-peer electronic cash system (2008). http://bitcoin.org/bitcoin.pdf
8. Niya, S.R., Jha, S.S., Bocek, T., Stiller, B.: Design and implementation of an automated and decentralized pollution monitoring system with blockchains, smart contracts, and LoRaWAN. In: 2018 IEEE/IFIP Network Operations and Management Symposium, NOMS 2018, Taipei, Taiwan, 23–27 April 2018, pp. 1–4 (2018)
9. Wood, G.: Ethereum: a secure decentralised generalised transaction ledger. Ethereum Project Yellow Pap. **151**, 1–32 (2014)

Author Index